Handbook of
Aggressive and Destructive Behavior in Psychiatric Patients

3- 16
288-304 -322
509-20

Handbook of
Aggressive and Destructive Behavior in Psychiatric Patients

EDITED BY

MICHEL HERSEN
Nova Southeastern University
Fort Lauderdale, Florida

AND

ROBERT T. AMMERMAN AND LORI A. SISSON
Western Pennsylvania School for Blind Children
Pittsburgh, Pennsylvania

Plenum Press • New York and London

Library of Congress Cataloging-in-Publication Data

Handbook of aggressive and destructive behavior in psychiatric
  patients / edited by Michel Hersen and Robert T. Ammerman and Lori
  A. Sisson.
       p.   cm.
     Includes bibliographical references and index.
     ISBN 0-306-44549-2
     1. Aggressiveness (Psychology) 2. Violence--Psychological
  aspects. 3. Self-destructiveness.   I. Hersen, Michel.
  II. Ammerman, Robert T.   III. Sisson, Lori A.
     [DNLM: 1. Mental Disorders--psychology. 2. Aggression.   WM 600
  H236 1993]
  RC569.5.A34H36   1993
  616.85'82--dc20
  DNLM/DLC
  for Library of Congress   93-36072
                                                               CIP

ISBN 0-306-44549-2

© 1994 Plenum Press, New York
A Division of Plenum Publishing Corporation
233 Spring Street, New York, N.Y. 10013

Printed in the United States of America

To Vicki, Jonathan, and Nathaniel—M.H.

To Betty and Ken Haughin—R.T.A.

To Jay—L.A.S.

Contributors

Donna Ames, Department of Psychiatry and Biobehavioral Sciences, UCLA School of Medicine, and West Los Angeles Veterans Affairs Medical Center, Los Angeles, California 90073.

Paul F. Brain, School of Biological Sciences, University of Wales, Swansea, SA2 8PP, United Kingdom.

Oscar G. Bukstein, Department of Psychiatry, Western Psychiatric Institute and Clinic, Pittsburgh, Pennsylvania 15213.

Allen G. Burgess, College of Business Administration, Northeastern University, Boston, Massachusetts 02115.

Ann W. Burgess, University of Pennsylvania School of Nursing, Philadelphia, Pennsylvania 19104.

John E. Douglas, Investigative Support Unit, Federal Bureau of Investigation Academy, Quantico, Virginia 22135.

Joshua Ehrlich, Department of Psychiatry, University of Michigan, Ann Arbor, Michigan 48104.

John W. Fantuzzo, Graduate School of Education, University of Pennsylvania, Philadelphia, Pennsylvania 19104.

Barry Fisher, Comprehensive Alcohol and Drug Abuse Program, Western Psychiatric Institute and Clinic, University of Pittsburgh School of Medicine, Pittsburgh, Pennsylvania 15213.

Willard B. Frick, Professor of Psychology, Albion College, Albion, Michigan 49224.

David M. Garner, Department of Psychiatry, Michigan State University, East Lansing, Michigan 48824.

Russell G. Geen, Department of Psychology, University of Missouri, Columbia, Missouri 65211.

Gerald Goldstein, Department of Veterans Affairs, VA Medical Center, Pittsburgh, Pennsylvania 15206.

D. M. Gorman, Center of Alcohol Studies, Rutgers University, The State University of New Jersey, Piscataway, New Jersey 08855.

Grant T. Harris, Mental Health Centre, Penetanguishene, Ontario, Canada.

Lori A. Head, Department of Psychiatry, Medical University of South Carolina, Charleston, South Carolina 29425.

Tara Hicks-Gray, Department of Psychiatry and Biobehavioral Sciences, UCLA School of Medicine, and West Los Angeles Veterans Affairs Medical Center, Los Angeles, California 90073.

J. Dee Higley, Laboratory of Clinical Studies, Division of Intramural Clinical and Biological Research, National Institute of Alcohol Abuse and Alcoholism, Poolesville, Maryland 20837.

Dale J. Hindmarsh, Division of Child and Adolescent Psychiatry, Department of Psychiatry, Allegheny Neuropsychiatric Institute, Medical College of Pennsylvania, Oakdale, Pennsylvania 15071.

Stephen P. Hinshaw, Department of Psychology, University of California at Berkeley, Berkeley, California 94720.

Honore M. Hughes, Department of Psychology, St. Louis University, St. Louis, Missouri 63103.

Berne Jacobs, Professor of Psychology, Kalamazoo College, Kalamazoo, Michigan 49007.

Richard P. Kluft, The Institute of Pennsylvania Hospital, Philadelphia, Pennsylvania 19139, and Department of Psychiatry, Temple University School of Medicine, Philadelphia, Pennsylvania 19140.

David J. Kolko, Western Psychiatric Institute and Clinic, University of Pittsburgh School of Medicine, Pittsburgh, Pennsylvania 15213.

Howard D. Lerner, Department of Psychiatry, University of Michigan, Ann Arbor, Michigan 48104.

Miriam S. Lerner, Department of Child and Adolescent Psychiatry, Medical College of Pennsylvania, Allegheny General Hospital, Wexford, Pennsylvania 15090.

Markku Linnoila, Laboratory of Clinical Studies, Division of Intramural Clinical and Biological Research, National Institute of Alcohol Abuse and Alcoholism, Poolesville, Maryland 20837.

Marco Marchetti, Department of Forensic Psychopathology, University of Rome Tor Vergata, Rome, Italy.

Stephen R. Marder, Department of Psychiatry and Biobehavioral Sciences, UCLA School of Medicine, and West Los Angeles Veterans Affairs Medical Center, Los Angeles, California 90073.

Nathaniel McConaghy, The Prince of Wales Hospital, Randwick, N.S.W. Australia.

Howard B. Moss, Comprehensive Alcohol and Drug Abuse Program, Western Psychiatric Institute and Clinic, University of Pittsburgh School of Medicine, Pittsburgh, Pennsylvania 15213.

Robert A. Prentky, Joseph J. Peters Institute, Philadelphia, Pennsylvania 19101.

Vernon L. Quinsey, Queen's University, Kingston, Ontario, Canada.

Robert K. Ressler, Forensic Behavioral Services, Spotsylvania, Virginia 22553.

Marnie E. Rice, Mental Health Centre, Penetanguishene, Ontario, Canada.

Lionel W. Rosen, Department of Psychiatry, Michigan State University, East Lansing, Michigan 48824.

Alan Rosenbaum, Department of Psychiatry, University of Massachusetts Medical Center, Worcester, Massachusetts 01655.

Alec Roy, Department of Psychiatry, University of Medicine and Dentistry, New Jersey Medical School, Newark, New Jersey 07103-2770.

Floyd R. Sallee, Department of Psychiatry, Medical University of South Carolina, Charleston, South Carolina 29425.

Ihsan M. Salloum, Comprehensive Alcohol and Drug Abuse Program, Western Psychiatric Institute and Clinic, University of Pittsburgh School of Medicine, Pittsburgh, Pennsylvania 15213.

Cassandra Simmel, Department of Psychology, University of California at Berkeley, Berkeley, California 94720.

Lori A. Sisson, Western Pennsylvania School for Blind Children, Pittsburgh, Pennsylvania 15213.

Shirley A. Smoyak, Institute for Health, Health Care Policy and Aging Research, Rutgers University, The State University of New Jersey, New Brunswick, New Jersey 08903.

Robert M. Stowe, Neurobehavioral Unit Program, Department of Veterans Affairs, VA Medical Center, and University of Pittsburgh School of Medicine, Pittsburgh, Pennsylvania 15206.

Stephen J. Suomi, Laboratory of Comparative Ethology, National Institute of Child Health and Human Development, Poolesville, Maryland 20837.

Alfonso Troisi, Department of Psychiatry, University of Rome Tor Vergata, Rome, Italy.

Jennifer Waltz, Department of Psychology, University of Montana, Missoula, Montana, 59812-1075.

William J. Warnken, Department of Psychiatry, University of Massachusetts Medical Center, Worcester, Massachusetts 01655.

Robert M. Wettstein, Western Psychiatric Institute and Clinic, Department of Psychiatry, University of Pittsburgh School of Medicine, Pittsburgh, Pennsylvania 15213.

William C. Wirshing, Department of Psychiatry and Biobehavioral Sciences, UCLA School of Medicine, and West Los Angeles Veterans Affairs Medical Center, Los Angeles, California 90073.

Preface

Scarcely a day passes without the media detailing some form of human aggression, whether it be on its grandest scale in the form of war, random bombings and shootings in the streets, torture in a prison camp, murder by gangs, wife abuse resulting in the murder of the husband, or the physical abuse of children, sometimes resulting in their death. Frequently perpetrators of human aggression, when arrested and tried in court, resort to a psychiatric defense. But are all such aggressors indeed appropriately psychiatric patients? And if so, what are their particular diagnoses and how do these relate to aggression? Also of concern is aggression directed against self, as evidenced in the rising incidence of suicide among young people or the self-mutilation of patients suffering from certain personality disorders. Both violence directed outward and aggression toward oneself pose considerable challenges to clinical management, whether in the therapist's office or in the inpatient unit.

Although we have not been able to find successful deterrents to aggression, a sizeable body of evidence does exist, certainly of a descriptive nature. Such data for psychiatric patients are scattered, however, and can be found in literatures as diverse as the biological, ethological, epidemiological, legal, philosophical, psychological, psychiatric, and criminological. Therefore, given the increased frequency with which mental health professionals encounter cases of violence in their day-to-day work, we believed it important that existing data be adduced in one comprehensive volume.

The book is divided into five parts, together comprising 28 chapters. Part I focuses on the theoretical perspectives and includes the following points of view: biological–physiological, ethological, sociological, social psychological, psychoanalytic, and humanistic. In Part II, we consider in detail such general issues as epidemiology, legal and ethical questions, and the problems of aggression control in both adult and child psychiatric settings. The chapters in Parts III and IV, make up the bulk of the book and review how, and if, aggression is manifested in the various diagnostic groups of adult, juvenile, and adolescent patients. The modified diagnostic criteria for DSM-IV are considered in these chapters. To ensure cross-chapter readability and comparisons, each of the contributions follows a standard format: Description of the Disorder, Epidemiology (concerning aggressive and destructive behavior), Etiology (concerning aggressive and destructive behavior), Aggression toward Self, Aggression toward Others, Clinical Management (aggression and destructive behavior), Longitudinal Perspectives, Case Illustration, and Summary.

Finally, in Part V, family violence with adults, family violence with children, and serial murder are considered.

Many individuals have contributed to this volume, and we wish to acknowledge their special efforts. First, we thank our eminent contributors for sharing with us their thoughts about the issues. Second, we thank our respective assistants, Burt G. Bolton and Ann Huber, for their technical contributions. Finally, we thank our editor at Plenum, Eliot Werner, who was willing to tolerate the inevitable delays and who understands the crucial nature of the material that follows.

MICHEL HERSEN
ROBERT T. AMMERMAN
LORI A. SISSON

Contents

I. THEORETICAL PERSPECTIVES

II. GENERAL ISSUES

V. SPECIAL ISSUES

PART I

THEORETICAL PERSPECTIVES

CHAPTER 1

Biological–Physiological

Paul F. Brain

INTRODUCTION

It is an apparent paradox that while aggression is a biological phenomenon, biology and physiology cannot be simply linked to behaviors that receive the aggressive or destructive label. To provide a critical evaluation of developments within the area of hostility research, it is essential initially to clarify some terminologies. Brain (1990a), as well as others (Archer, 1988; Browne & Archer, 1989; Buss, 1971; Goldstein, 1986; Huntingford & Turner, 1987; Klama, 1988; Kutash et al., 1978), has recently reexamined the nature of aggression for a general audience. In both animal and human sciences, terms like *aggression* and *violence* are used with enormous flexibility, making it difficult to confirm definite associations with biological factors. It is generally agreed that such activities must have the potential for harm or damage. One should note, however, that predation (which certainly has this characteristic) is usually eliminated from definitions (on the basis of its lacking obvious arousal). Further, both competitive (offensive) and defensive responses have the potential for harm. There is also debate concerning whether both physical and psychological damage can be included in these considerations.

Many authorities also rule that the actions of the aggressor have to be intentional rather than accidental, although others suggest that the victim merely has to perceive them as such. Some biologists maintain that aggression has to involve arousal. *Arousal* is a psychological term applied to evidence of internal changes including alterations in heart rate, respiration, and the distribution of blood in the tissues. It is well known, however, that psychopaths show few signs of arousal. Finally, a basic problem with the clinical use of the term *aggression* is that people often act as if they are discussing an entity ("thing") rather than a concept.

Humans deal with a complex world where a vast array of so-called independent variables (potential causes) have to be related to a large collection of dependent variables (potential consequences). They attempt to make sense of the world by creating intervening

PAUL F. BRAIN • School of Biological Sciences, University of Wales, Swansea, SA2 8PP, United Kingdom.

Handbook of Aggressive and Destructive Behavior in Psychiatric Patients, edited by Michel Hersen, Robert T. Ammerman, and Lori A. Sisson. Plenum Press, New York, 1994.

variables that link together groups of independent and dependent variables. The concept of aggression is one of these intervening constructs. The trouble with concepts is that they are theoretically infinitely definable—one does not assess a concept by its accuracy but by its usefulness in explanation. It is clear both that applying the terms *aggressive* and *destructive* involves making value judgments and that activities may be perceived in different ways by the participants (the patient, peers, the ward orderly, the relative, and the psychiatrist). This fact accounts for the difficulty of specifying *biological markers* for such activities. In spite of this difficulty, Madden and Lion (1978) claim that "the goal of therapy with the aggressive patient is to help him effectively control his own aggression to the point where he can be personally and socially, a useful member of society" (p. 412).

The Heterogeneous Nature of Human Aggression and Violence

Aggressive behavior is certainly a heterogeneous phenomenon in our own species. Buss' (1971) classification, based on three dichotomies, provides a clear indication of the diversity of human aggression as viewed through the eyes of a social psychologist. According to Buss, aggression may be physical or verbal, active or passive, and direct or indirect. Activities receiving this epithet range from punching, stabbing, and shooting (physical/active/direct aggression), to "failing to carry out a necessary task" (physical/passive/indirect aggression) or "refusing consent" (verbal/passive/indirect aggression). Obviously, the social psychologist includes a much wider range of activities under the heading "aggression" than most biologists.

Such diversity of human aggression has led to an enormous range of methods for assessing the attribute in our species. Obviously, the types of behavior of relevance to psychiatrists are seen in a variety of criminals and noncriminals (i.e., the categories are created largely on the basis of past events). Distinctions are often made between impulsive and premeditated actions. One should understand that producing the "same" crime does not necessarily mean that one is dealing with the same motivation. For example, rape is said by several authorities (e.g., Groth, 1979) to have various etiologies and to be generated by a plethora of influences. Similar critiques can be advanced for homicide, assault, and the like. The term *violence* is used almost interchangeably with *aggression* in most reviews, but the former term is often applied to aggressive actions that attract a greater than normal social disapproval. In this respect, the term clearly fulfills the role of labeling behavior that transgresses normative values. Obviously, as judgments of sections of society may be involved in determining which behaviors receive the labels "aggression" and "violence," relating biological factors to such human activities is not easy. I personally doubt whether one can always differentiate adaptive forms of aggression from maladaptive violent and aggressive acts, since this implies a very accurate knowledge of the motivations of all participants at all times.

BIOLOGY AND BEHAVIOR

What we call aggression is (like any other behavioral concept) influenced by diverse factors that are difficult (impossible?) to disentangle. These include:

1. Biological factors (i.e., genes, neural systems, neurotransmitters and hormones).
2. Situational determinants (i.e., environmental or social contexts).
3. Accumulated individual experiences.

In interindividual forms of aggression, one is really dealing with some quite complex interactions between biology and experience. Some of these effects are mediated by changes in aggressive motivation, some by influencing other behaviors that compete for expression with the aggression, and others by changing the social signals that people direct toward each other. Still others actually involve how individuals perceive those social signals. There are also temporal changes and the impacts of particular environments to consider. One has to add to this complex mix the fact that whether one chooses to call a behavior aggression or not is based on one's value judgment. It is consequently highly improbable that one will find simple relationships between any biological factor and expressed behavior.

Although Brain (1984) has already suggested that the roles of biological factors in aggressive and destructive behaviors *cannot* be easily compartmentalized (e.g., genes influence hormonal production and hormones can have an impact on neurotransmitters), it is probably most useful to organize the available information in terms of the well-accepted specialties.

Genes and Human Aggression

Animal studies have confirmed that genes do not directly cause behavior, rather providing (after gene–environment interactions) an anatomy and physiology that can change predispositions for behaving in particular ways. Although there has at times been considerable enthusiasm for linking genes to human behavioral traits, the situation is no less complex in our own species.

Christïansen (1978) decided (on the basis of a Danish twin study) that the "combined influence of heredity and environment is greater for crimes of violence than property crimes" (p. 115). As one would expect, monozygotic twins showed more concordance than dizygotic counterparts, but (less predictably) females were more similar than were males. Mednick and Handel (1988) studied 173 violent recidivist offenders from Danish health records and found that the early commission of violent crimes predicted later commissions (see also Farrington, 1989). By contrast, biological parent–child relationships in adoptive studies predicted property rather than violence convictions. Unlike Christïansen (1978), Mednick and Handel concluded that the commission of violent acts is more dependent on environmental than on genetic factors.

Razavi (1975) has reviewed the impact of abnormalities of the X and Y ("sex") chromosomes on hostility and noted that some subjects showed polyendocrine disorders that could "provide a mechanism connecting cytogenetic abnormality, focal somatic variation and social failure" (p. 251). Brain's (1984) review of the available data on the claimed link between the XYY syndrome and hostility provides a cautionary tale. Initial interest was stimulated by the finding (Jacobs et al., 1965) that this chromosomal abnormality was much more common among individuals imprisoned for violent crimes than in the population at large. Forty-seven XYY subjects appeared to be characterized by excessive height, often a slight mental retardation, and occasional, unpredictable outbursts of extreme violence. Interestingly, they showed lower than normal plasma concentrations and production rates of testosterone (Sharma et al., 1975). A mythology rapidly developed suggesting that the possession of the extra Y chromosome created "aggressive supermales genetically programmed for violence" (Baron, 1977). Indeed, the phenomenon was also said to provide a mechanism accounting for sexual dimorphism in violent/destructive behaviors. The more destructive male has a Y chromosome, whereas the more peaceful female lacks this genetic material. The truth actually seems less exciting. Baron (1977) concluded that the majority of the 47 XYY subjects were "relatively dull and mild-mannered persons who are no more likely than others to engage in criminal behavior, but who are likely, when they do, to be apprehended" (p. 217). One can also suggest that legal and prison attitudes are likely to direct large and "aggressive" individuals to maximum security establishments (accounting for the Jacobs et al. [1965] distribution).

It is obviously true that genetic endowment can influence an individual's predisposition to show particular mood changes and alter the efficiency of the processing mechanism facilitating social interactions, but there is *no* evidence (in humans or animals) of specific genes for aggressive and destructive behavior.

Neurobiology and Human Aggression

The impact of dysfunctions and manipulations of the central nervous system on violence and aggression is excellently reviewed by Siegel and Mirsky (1990). These workers examine the recently revealed complexities of studies on the neural substrates of animal models of aggression, concluding that the neural sites where predatory attack and affective defense can be elicited or modulated (in, for example, the cat) are well established. Further, the basic anatomical pathways utilized for the expression or modulation of attack responses, as well as the basic response systems, have been identified. Siegel and Mirsky (1990) are less impressed by the current state of knowledge concerning the roles of putative neurotransmitters in aggressive and destructive behavior. Indeed, they conclude that "certainly, a thorough understanding of the neuropharmacology of aggressive behavior and the substrates where transmitters act along the limbic–midbrain axis will be required before any attempts at intervention strategies for the control of human aggression can be considered" (p. 39).

Siegel and Mirsky (1990) note the distinction between adaptive (part of the normal survival mechanisms of a species) and maladaptive violence and aggression (where it is a clear disorder) but suggest that "it seems reasonable to hypothesize that humans who are engaging in maladaptive, violent behavior have some brain abnormality that somehow either temporarily (and possibly repeatedly) short circuits the aggression/violence pathways leading to truly violent behavior" (p. 40).

We are largely concerned with violence in persons with neuropsychiatric disorders (an area reviewed by Siegel and Mirsky, 1990). The popular view that there is a concurrence between schizophrenia and violent behavior is not well supported by available studies. Although some reports (e.g., Karson & Bigelow, 1987; Krakowski et al., 1986; Tardiff & Sweillam, 1980) do suggest that patients diagnosed as schizophrenic (rather than given other diagnoses) show increased aggressiveness or assaultiveness, the violence seems most easily attributed to gender (male), low socioeconomic status, the fact that other severe psychiatric illnesses often preclude individuals from carrying out assaults, age, drug exposure (both legal and illegal), and/or prior histories of violence. As in the case of the 47 XYY syndrome, schizophrenic men are often socially incompetent, resulting in easy detection when they carry out a criminal act and their simple apprehension.

Brain (1990b) has reviewed the popular association between alcoholism and violence, concluding that the claimed link is, at least partially, a consequence of the impact of this drug on neural functioning (it produces profound anatomical deficits, reduces bioavailability of thiamin, generates electrophysiological changes, and modifies levels of neurotransmitters). It is suggested that, rather than acting on aggression circuits, alcohol produces at least some of its behavioral actions by changing an individual's ability to compute appropriate responses in a social situation. The drug produces residual impairment of cognitive-perceptual functioning and reduces the ability to abstract and conceptualize, as well as destroying visual-spatial and simple sensory-motor performance. It is interesting to note that alcohol's negative impact on memory test performance is greater in females than in males. Other drugs may produce some of their associated changes in behavior in a similar fashion.

Siegel and Mirsky (1990) have also reviewed the available data on violence and epilepsy, carefully distinguishing between acts occurring as part of the seizure (ictal manifestations) and behavior occurring between seizures (interictal events). The evidence suggests that aggressive behavior or angry feelings are extremely rare in ictal manifestations. Epileptics much more commonly reported a feeling of fear accompanying the seizure whose characteristics (although involving thrashing about and apparent striking out) are incompatible with directed attack upon another person. There is considerable debate concerning interictal violence, with one school maintaining that the violence represents a hidden (occult) seizure (e.g., Mark & Ervin, 1970) and another school insisting that it is a trait associated with this type of cerebral disorder. Siegel and Mirsky (1990) suggest that many of the studies in this area have sampling biases that make it difficult to draw unambiguous conclusions (e.g., persons engaged in assaultive behavior during their lives are more likely to have suffered from head injuries leading to seizure disorders than "controls"). Some authorities conclude that there is an association between the occurrence of seizure disorders and the likelihood of violent or aggressive behavior (Weiger & Bear, 1988); others suggest that the association is spurious and related to other factors (e.g., Virkkunen, 1983); a third group concludes that there is no relation between epilepsy and violence that cannot be accounted for by the socioeconomic class of the patients (Tardiff & Sweillam, 1980).

If violence is used as the independent variable and one attempts to assess whether there is a brain disorder in such patients, a complex picture emerges (Siegel & Mirsky, 1990). Perhaps it is best to separate violent sexual offenders from individuals involved in nonsex crime. Siegel and Mirsky (1990) found seven studies in literature reviews on the latter category in the period 1974–1989. Six of these varied papers, including two on episodically violent patients (Bach-Y-Rita et al., 1971; Volkow & Tancredi, 1987), concluded that there was an association between aggressive/violent behavior and brain abnormalities. The seventh, a study by Mungas (1983) that compared subgroups of patients differing in the degree of intensity of violence, suggested that there was no association between violence and brain dysfunction.

The six recent (1971–1987) studies or reviews of violent sex offenders identified by Siegel and Mirsky (1990) include five papers from the same group (Langevin and colleagues). The results are described as "provocative," but there are no uniform findings implicating specific brain regions in the pathophysiology of the violent sexual offender. It has been suggested that the brain abnormalities are subtle, requiring sensitive measurement techniques. It was also claimed that there may be specific abnormalities associated with different types of sex offenders (e.g., pedophiles and sadists).

Miczek et al. (1990) have ably reviewed the neurochemistry and pharmacotherapeutic management of violence. They also emphasized the diversity of the topics that receive the label of aggression and the complexity of neurochemistry. These workers suggest that brain norepinephrine undergoes large changes before, during, and following different kinds of aggressive and defensive behavior and that these changes are localized in specific brain regions that appear to work in opposition. They suggest that brain dopamine is particularly significant in rewarding aspects of violence and in the neural mechanisms initiating, executing, and terminating aggressive behavior patterns. More directly, Miczek et al. (1990) review the evidence that serotonin metabolism can be implicated in human aggression. The authors suggest that "anatomically discrete serotonin systems importantly contribute to brain mechanisms subserving a range of violent behaviors in humans" (p. 15). Miczek et al. maintain, however, that it is highly problematical to extrapolate from single peripheral measures such as blood or cerebrospinal fluid 5-HIAA (5-hydroxyindoleacetic acid—a major metabolite of serotonin) to the complexities of serotonin activity in violent or aggressive individuals. These authors suggest that gamma-aminobutyric acid (GABA) and benzodiazepine receptors are implicated (in a complex manner) with violent and aggressive behavior.

Hormones and Human Aggression

Brain (1990c) has reviewed the impact of endocrine secretions on human aggressive and destructive behaviors. The enormous body of available data reveals diverse approaches and methodologies, making extracting generalities exceedingly difficult. These earlier reviews confirm that the topic of hormones and aggression in vertebrates can be effectively subdivided into the following subtopics:

1. Studies on the effects of early hormonal "programming" of adult aggressiveness.
2. Direct motivational effects (presumedly via the CNS) of endocrine changes on fighting and threat.
3. Indirect effects (presumedly via changed social signals etc.) of endocrine manipulations on fighting and threat.
4. Influences of fighting or threat on endocrine function.

Early Programming Effects of Hormones in Humans

Meyer-Bahlburg (1980) and Meyer-Bahlburg and Ehrhardt (1982) comprehensively reviewed studies on the lasting impact of variations in early hormone exposure on human aggressiveness. Some data involve endocrine syndromes (partial androgen insensitivity and congenital adrenal hyperplasia) and other data involve treatment with hormones (generally to reduce the probability of miscarriage). There are few reliable data on the incidence of those syndromes in particular populations (which are anyhow variable in their degree of severity). Their importance is not as potential causes of problems in society but as indicators of the normal biological mechanisms that influence behavioral differences between the sexes.

Although the data are characterized by small sample sizes, Meyer-Bahlburg (1980) suggests that exogenous sex hormones that slightly increase aggressiveness in females produce some degree of genital masculinization. The data from girls and boys, resulting from treating toxemic pregnancies with progesterone, appear inconsistent. There was, however, some evidence of decreased aggressiveness in boys from diabetic pregnancies exposed to progestogen–estrogen combinations and from boys and girls whose mothers were treated with medroxyprogesterone acetate (MPA). It is, of course, uncertain precisely how such behavioral effects are generated, because features such as parental rearing styles, degree of exercise, and changes in the musculoskeletal system are involved in such phenomena and are likely to be influenced (directly or indirectly) by early hormonal factors.

Early exposure to androgens is said to increase an individual's "impetuosity." Olweus (1984) has suggested that this factor has a weak direct action on the aggression potential of boys and may actually have a stronger indirect action on this potential by increasing the mother's permissiveness for aggression (via exhaustion?).

Hormones and Puberty

Predictors of adolescent, teenage, and adult violence in humans are complex (Farrington, 1989), the best appearing to be measures of economic deprivation, family criminality, poor child rearing, school failure, and hyperactive (impulsive), attention deficient, and antisocial child behavior. Although Hamburg (1971) failed to find a clear relationship between testosterone levels and aggressive behavior in postpubertal boys, Benson and Migeon (1975) reviewed the physiological and psychological changes occurring around adolescence/puberty in human males. They noted marked changes in serum levels of luteinizing hormone (LH) and follicle-stimulating hormone (FSH), as well as sex steroids from the testes and adrenal cortices, and tentatively implicated these in the development of a "rebellious attitude" around this time. Hays (1978) provides a review of strategies for studying psychoendocrine aspects of puberty, speculating that changes in hypothalamic luteinizing hormone releasing factor (LHRF), which occur around puberty, may (by altering mood) induce sexuality and hostility in our species. She felt that the involvement of androgens in behavioral changes could be studied by comparing pubertal status of highly aggressive and nonaggressive boys of the same ages. Hays (1978) noted that developmental changes are evident with respect to thyroid-releasing factor, thyroid-stimulating hormone, prolactin, and somatotrophic hormone and that one or a combination of these factors may alter mood and hence aggression. She pointed out four important conclusions from the (then) available data:

1. Mood changes induced by hormones may be consequences of the instigation of drives that have no socially acceptable outlet in young people.
2. Development may involve changes in behavioral sensitivity to hormones as well as changes in the hormones per se.
3. All studies should consider the effects of circadian rhythms on hormonal secretion.
4. Interactions between hormones may prove more important than titers of single hormone.

These points are equally valid today.

Archer (1991) reviewed recent developments in this area, noting that the only studies that measure hormonal levels and aggressiveness at or soon after puberty in human males are those of Olweus et al. (1980), Mattsson et al. (1980), Olweus (1986), and Susman et al. (1987). Olweus (1986) noted that the items involving responses to provocation from his physical and verbal scales correlated particularly well with plasm testosterone. In contrast, Eccles et al. (1988) studied hormones and affect in early adolescence and recorded that increased levels of androgens were not correlated with increased levels of anger–impatience of aggression.

There has been great interest in the claim that pseudohermaphroditism with changed gender identity and role at puberty is a consequence of a deficit in 5 α-reductase activity (an enzyme that converts testosterone to dihydrotestosterone). There are conflicting claims about the relevance of these data to the debate about the biological versus environmental determination of gender in our species (Aron et al., 1990; Gotz et al., 1990; Money, 1990).

In a Swedish study of 82 boys at 13 years of age, Magnusson (1987) found negative correlations between aggressiveness/restlessness and urinary secretion of adrenomedullary epinephrine under both active and passive conditions. This supported the more general finding of a positive correlation between good social and personal adjustments and elevated epinephrine excretion. Even more intriguingly, there is a strong inverse relationship between epinephrine excretion by those 13-year-olds and their adult delinquency at 18 to 26. More detailed statistical analysis showed, however, that the changes in epinephrine levels were more closely related to motor restlessness than to aggression. Highly aggressive individuals who are not highly restless have about the same epinephrine levels as subjects who are neither restless or aggressive. Magnusson (1988) reviewed these data, warning that the traditional mechanistic model viewing the epinephrine excretion as the cause of both behavior in a current perspective and adult delinquency in a longitudinal perspective is probably inadequate. He suggests considering individual subsystems (e.g., cognitions, emotions, physiological factors and conduct) that are in constant reciprocal interaction and influence each other in current processes with developmental consequences. Simultaneous appearance of low epinephrine level, elevated aggressiveness, and substantial motor restlessness at an early age in subjects later involved in crimes does not necessarily show that these factors are causative or that they have a common etiology. Similar considerations apply to many of the other hormone–behavior associations mentioned here.

Levander et al. (1987) studied 40 recidivists in a Swedish state institution for delinquent males, comparing these individuals with 59 "normal" school boys. In spite of the stressful backgrounds of the recidivists, they showed patterns of stress hormone production suggestive of very low psychophysiological arousal. In this group, the common deviant psychoendocrine pattern consisted of low epinephrine, norepinephrine, and cortisol with high thyroid hormone levels. Different behavioral subtypes showed different hormonal profiles. Half the subjects had a history of hyperactivity associated with low epinephrine. Levander speculates that elevated thyroid levels represent a compensatory mechanism attempting to correct the deviance in norepinephrine and, to some extent, epinephrine turnover.

Influences of Sex Hormones on Adult Aggressive Motivation

Brain (1984) has critically reviewed the use of endocrine manipulations in controlling human aggression. Castration has been applied to curb sexual aggression in Scandinavian and American populations. In spite of the considerable ethical problems associated with its use and the fact that it changes many aspects of physiology and behavior, castration has been claimed to produce impressively low rates of recidivism (one should, of course, examine the impacts of aging and self-image).

Therapies with hormones or antihormones are generally more ethically acceptable than castration since they seem (in theory at least) reversible. Estrogens have been used in attempts to control aggressive tendencies in intact men. The synthetic estrogen stilbestrol has been given orally to treat hyperirritable aggression and "excessive libido," but it has many unfortunate side effects, including gynecomastia (development of breasts), fluid retention, and phlebothrombosis (production of blood clots), making its use problematical (Dunn, 1941). Chatz (1972) and Field and Williams (1970) advocated intramuscular or subcutaneous injections of long-acting estradiol BPC or estradiol valerate to facilitate the release of otherwise highly dangerous individuals. Both aggressive and sexual drive were essentially eliminated by such treatment.

Antiandrogens (e.g., cyproterone acetate) largely replaced castration and estrogen therapies in the treatment of European (aggressive?) sexual offenders. Berner et al. (1983) described the treatment of 21 prison inmates in Vienna with a combination of cyproterone acetate (100 mg per day orally for 1 to 10 years) and supportive psychotherapy. Taking the drug had no effect on release from prison, and the rearrest rate for sexual offenses was 28% in individuals that were followed up. There was no comparison with inmates treated with psychotherapy only.

Progesterone derivatives (e.g., A-norprogesterone and MPA) have also been used (especially in the USA) in clinical therapy of human hostility. These compounds all reduce endogenous testosterone production/action and are said to produce variable improvements in behavior. They certainly have rather complex actions, are not without associated problems, and seem currently used with less enthusiasm for a variety of technical, legal, and ethical reasons.

Antihormones can have quite wide repercussions on the endocrine system. Further, categories of antihormones are not homogeneous. For example, antiandrogens may be subdivided into pure antiandrogens, antiandrogens with antigonadotrophic effects, and progestins. Administration of a pure antiandrogen (e.g., Flutamide) to an intact male increases LH production and consequently augments plasma testosterone. Cyproterone acetate, an antiandrogen with antigonadotrophic effects, acts directly on the testes and results in a decline in plasma testosterone. Progestins alter liver steroid metabolism, augmenting the metabolic clearance rate of testosterone (Albin et al., 1973). Some progestins are without apparent actions on testosterone uptake and binding in target tissues, whereas others (e.g., MPA) produce minor inhibition (Suffrin & Coffey, 1973).

Although there are strong indications that neural androgen receptors are implicated in some forms of aggressive behavior, not all forms of violence depend on their activation. Certainly, it is uncertain which neural androgen receptor populations are implicated in which aspects of behavior, and relatively little is known about the enzyme changes and transformations involved in androgen-mediated violent behavior. Sheard (1987) maintains that treatment with MPA is "the most common approach [to the treatment of aggression] in the USA." For example, O'Connor and Baker (1973) used MPA as an adjuvant in the treatment of three males (22 to 40 years of age) diagnosed as having chronic schizophrenia. In a double-blind study involving staff evaluations of behavior with the Brief Psychiatric Rating Scale, two of the patients who were assaultive showed significant dose-related drug improvements.

Many of the early attempts to correlate levels of testosterone with aggression in hostile and nonhostile prisoners (reviewed in Brain, 1984) have proved difficult to replicate. The behavioral measures (e.g., rating by courts or the individuals per se) were often vague and carried out at a time remote from the endocrine measurements (generally a single plasma determination of testosterone—a hormone which is secreted in a highly fluctuating manner—using samples that were taken in a "stressful" fashion, thus potentially reducing hormone secretion). Rather obvious complications, such as the incidence of homosexual activity in the populations and alcohol consumption, were generally uncontrolled for.

Archer (1991) performed a limited meta-analysis on the five available studies and attempted to associate aggression as measured on the Buss–Durkee Hostility Inventory (Buss & Durkee, 1957) with plasma testosterone. The analysis suggested a very low but positive relationship between testosterone levels and overall Buss–Durkee inventory score for the 230 males tested over the five studies. Social environment was more highly correlated with testosterone level than this score, and there was a closer association between aggression and the hormone when external assessments of the subject's behavior (rather than self-assessments) were made. One should note that the Buss–Durkee scale is intended to measure aggressive feelings rather than aggressive actions. Indeed, Buss–Durkee factor II (the item correlated with testosterone in the above studies) is a composite of several measures, and there is little evidence of its relevance to violent or dominant behavior.

Langevin et al. (1985) performed studies on predictive factors of sexual aggression in which hormones were examined as one factor (total testosterone, LH, follicle-stimulating hormone [FSH], estradiol, dehydroepiandrosterone sulfate [DHAS], androsterone, cortisol, and prolactin). Adrenal production of sex hormones (notably DHAS) seemed important in sexually aggressive males. Sex hormones other than testosterone may prove of relevance to sexual aggression. It may be possible to distinguish sadists (abnormal LH and FSH) from rapists (elevated DHAS, cortisol, and prolactin). Bain et al. (1987) failed to find significant hormonal differences between murderers, assaulters, and controls but did suggest that further study of the complex interactions of these factors is necessary. There were indications that changes in LH and LHRF might be implicated in some forms of violent behavior. Bain et al. (1988) studied baseline values of eight hormones in sexually aggressive males and found no significant group differences. In an ACTH stimulation test, however, sexually aggressives had lower baseline values of DHAS than controls. These results appear more clear cut than most, probably because they focus on sexual aggression, distinguish subcategories of this behavior, and seem prepared to measure a range of hormonal factors. One would still like to establish whether these approaches extrapolate to other populations and situations.

McEwen and Pfaff (1985) have emphasized that the effects of hormones on hypothalamic neurons can involve neurotransmitter effects and neuromodulator actions, including LHRF and prolactin. They speculate that such interactions can be involved in processes such as the regulation of aggression. It has been suggested that LHRF is involved in behavioral change in young children after testosterone treatment (Tiwary, 1974). Such studies are contentious, since there is considerable debate concerning the ethics of giving a synthetic analog of LHRF (Gorerelin, Zoladex, ICI) to a pedophile in England (Brahams, 1988). The treatment was said to suppress sexual urges in a manner superior to cyproterone acetate or MPA.

Archer (1991) has emphasized the essentially correlational nature of the existing evidence for an association between androgenic hormones and measures of aggression in humans. He suggests that future research might involve more extensive longitudinal studies (as in Olweus et al., 1988) or the manipulation of hormone levels, as in investigations of human sexual behavior (e.g., Sherwin et al., 1985). Archer (1991) also suggests that the current methods of measuring aggression are confused and inadequate and often based on rating scales that measure traits rather than states. He advocates (where appropriate) using direct assessments of aggression. Ratings by peers, teachers, and staff may be useful in some cases, but one could also employ direct responses to provocation, diary accounts of anger, anger inventories, or the Conflict Tactics Scale, which involves asking subjects to rate how often they use particular strategies to solve conflicts. A broad approach should be taken before attempting to standardize techniques.

Androgens do not have a simple causal effect on human aggression and violence, but the patterns of production of sex steroids do appear to alter several factors (e.g., aggressive feelings, self-image, and social signaling) predisposing individuals to carry out actions that can receive this label. As environmental and experimental factors can profoundly influence androgen production in a wide range of organisms (including human), the impact of such variables on the incidence of violence should be assessed.

Adrenomedullary Function and Human Aggression

In line with the studies on boys by Magnusson (1987, 1988), Woodman (1983) reviewed the utility of predicting dangerousness by examining the ratio of norepinephrine to epinephrine in response to a period of anticipation in a variety of incarcerated males (18 to 45 years old, with no evidence of brain damage, renal dysfunction, or sensory defects and a verbal I.Q. greater than 80 [Wechsler Adult Intelligence Scale]). It was found that subjects with convictions for violent crimes had a higher ratio of these adrenomedullary hormones than either subjects with a mixed violence and property crime background or with convictions for sexual offenses. Woodman (1983) suggested that this finding supported the view that increased norepinephrine production (relative to epinephrine) "is found in more aggressive personalities."

As mentioned earlier, hormones can also alter behavior by changing the production of social cues and their perception. Such phenomena have been much described in animals, and there is no reason to suppose that they are not present in our own species. One should also remember that the experiences generated when performing aggressive and destructive behaviors can have powerful effects on the endocrine system.

SUMMARY

There is a considerable range of good and bad material in the literature investigating the biology of human aggression. Some authors appear to have overly simplistic views of this complex concept and apply uniformly negative attributes to behaviors receiving this label (this is not a view held by all biologists). These authors also appear selective in finding support from animal studies for their therapies. One should certainly recognize that aggression is an extremely diverse phenomenon and that various models may have differing relevances to particular human conditions (e.g., the features of psychopaths actually seem to show more commonality with predatory behavior than with territorial behavior). One may also comment that although associations have been found between aggression and genetic endowment, neuroanatomical treatments, drugs, and hormones, there are considerable problems associated with most current treatments derived from such studies. The problems are partially technical and partially ethical. It is urged that more attention be paid to multifactorial approaches to aggression research, in which biological factors are one aspect. It seems unlikely (even if these problems are solved) that therapies based on biology alone will be appropriate in more than a small minority of cases. This is not to deny the importance of biology but to reiterate that treatments derived from such approaches should not be regarded as the only or, indeed, necessarily the most appropriate means of curbing aggressive and destructive behaviors. One should perhaps add that (if sensitively handled) biological factors may play a role as predictors of potential violence.

REFERENCES

Albin, J., Vitteck, J., Gordon, G. G., Altman, K., Olivo, J., & Southren, A. L. (1973). On the mechanism of the anti-androgenic effect of medroxyprogesterone acetate. *Endocrinology, 93,* 417.

Archer, J. (1988). *The behavioural biology of aggression.* Cambridge, England: Cambridge University Press.

Archer, J. (1991). The influence of androgens on human aggression. *British Journal of Psychology, 82,* 1–28.

Aron, C., Chateau, D., Schaeffer, C., & Roos, J. (1990). Heterotypic sexual behaviour in male mammals: The rat as an experimental model. In M. Haug, P. F. Brain, & C. Aron (Eds.), *Heterotypical behaviour in man and animals* (pp. 98–126). London, England: Chapman and Hall.

Bach-Y-Rita, G., Lion, J. R., Climent, C. E., & Ervin, F. R. (1971). Episodic dyscontrol: A study of 130 violent patients. *American Journal of Psychiatry*, *127*, 49–54.

Bain, J., Langevin, R., Dickey, R., & Ben-Aron, M. (1987). Sex hormones in murderers and assaulters. *Behavioral Science and the Law*, *5*, 95–101.

Bain, J., Langevin, R., Dickey, R., Hucker, S., & Wright, P. (1988). Hormones in sexually aggressive men I. Baseline values for eight hormones II. The ACTH test. *Annals of Sex Research*, *1*, 63–78.

Baron, R. A. (1977). *Human aggression: Perspectives in social psychology*. New York: Plenum.

Benson, R. M., & Migeon, C. J. (1975). Physiological and pathological puberty and human behavior. In B. E. Eleftheriou & R. L. Sprott (Eds.), *Hormonal correlates of behavior* (pp. 155–184). New York: Plenum.

Berner, W., Brownstone, G., & Sluga, W. (1983). The cyproteroneacetate treatment of sexual offenders. *Neuroscience and Biobehavioral Reviews*, *7*, 441–443.

Brahams, D. (1988). Voluntary chemical castration of mental patient. *Lancet*, 1291–1292.

Brain, P. F. (1984). Biological explanations of human aggression and the resulting therapies offered by such approaches: A critical evaluation. In R. J. Blanchard & D. C. Blanchard (Eds.), *Advances in the study of aggression: Volume 1* (pp. 63–102). New York: Academic Press.

Brain, P. F. (1990a). *Mindless violence? The nature and biology of aggression*. Swansea, Wales: University College of Swansea Press.

Brain, P. F. (1990b, December). *Bewitched, bothered or bewildered: The physiology of alcohol and aggression*. Paper presented at a conference on drinking and public disorder, Oxford, England.

Brain, P. F. (1990c, April). Hormonal aspects of aggression and violence. *Symposium on the Understanding and Control of Violent Behavior*. Destin, FL.

Browne, K. D. & Archer, J. (1989). *Human aggression: Naturalistic approaches*. London, England: Routledge.

Buss, A. H. (1971). Aggression pays. In J. L. Singer (Ed.), *The control of aggression and violence: Cognitive and physiological factors* (pp. 7–18). New York: Academic Press.

Buss, A. H. & Durkee, A. (1957). An inventory for assessing different types of hostility. *Journal of Consulting Psychology*, *21*, 343–349.

Chatz, T. L. (1972). Recognizing and treating dangerous sex offenders. *International Journal of Offenders and Therapy*, *2*, 109–115.

Christïansen, K. O. (1978). The genesis of aggressive criminality: Implications of a study of crime in a Danish twin study. In W. W. Hartup & J. de Wit (Eds.), *Origins of aggression* (pp. 99–120). The Hague: Mouton.

Dunn, C. W. (1941). Stilbestrol-induced testicular degeneration in hypersexual males. *Journal of Clinical Endocrinology and Metabolism*, *1*, 643–648.

Eccles, J. S., Miller, C., Tucker, M. L., Becker, J., Schramm, W., Midgley, R., Holmes, W., Pasch, L., & Miller, M. (1988). *Hormones and affect at early adolescence*. Paper presented at the biannual meeting of the Society for Research on Adolescence, Alexandra, VA.

Farrington, D. P. (1989). Early predictors of adolescent aggression and adult violence. *Violence and Victims*, *4*, 79–100.

Field, L. H. & Williams, M. (1970). The hormonal treatment of sexual offenders. *Medicine, Science, and the Law*, *10*, 27–34.

Goldstein, J. H. (1986). *Aggression and crimes of violence*. New York: Oxford University Press.

Gotz, F., Rohde, W., & Dorner, C. (1990). Neuroendocrine differentiation of sex-specific gonadotrophin secretion, sexual orientation and gender role behavior. In M. Haug, P. F. Brain, & C. Aron (Eds.), *Heterotypical behaviour in man and animals* (pp. 169–194). London, England: Chapman and Hall.

Groth, A. N. (1979). *Men who rape: The psychology of the offender*. New York: Plenum.

Hamburg, D. A. (1971). Recent research on hormonal factors relevant to human aggressiveness. *International Social Science Journal*, *23*, 36–47.

Hays, S. E. (1978). Strategies for psychoendocrine studies of puberty. *Psychoneuroendocrinology*, *3*, 1–15.

Huntingford, F. & Turner, A. (1987). *Animal conflict*. London, England: Chapman and Hall.

Jacobs, P. A., Brunton, M., & Melville, M. M. (1965). Aggressive behaviour, mental subnormality and the XYY males. *Nature (London)*, *208*, 1351–1352.

Karson, C. & Bigelow, L. B. (1987). Violent behavior in schizophrenic inpatients. *The Journal of Nervous and Mental Disease*, *175*, 161–164.

Klama, J. (1988). *Aggression: Conflict in animals and humans reconsidered*. Burnt Mill, Harlow, England: Longman Group.

Krakowski, M., Volavka, J., & Brizer, B. (1986). Psychopathology and violence: A review of literature. *Comprehensive Psychiatry*, *27*, 131–148.

Kutash, I. L., Kutash, S. B., Schlesinger, L. B., & Associates (Eds.). (1978). *Violence: Perspectives on murder and aggression*. San Francisco, CA: Jossey-Bass.

Langevin, R., Bain, J., Ben-Aron, M., Coulhard, R., Day, D., Handy, L., Heasman, G., Hucker, S., Purins, J., Roper, V. Russan, A., Webster, C., & Wortzman, G. (1985). Sexual aggression: Constructing a predictive equation. In R. Langevin (Ed.), *Erotic preference, gender identity and aggression in men* (pp. 50–93). Hillsdale, NJ: Lawrence Erlbaum Associates.

Levander, S., Mattsson, A., Schalling, D., & Dalteg, A. (1987). Psychoendocrine patterns with a group of male juvenile delinquents as related to early psychosocial stress, diagnostic classification, and follow-up data. In D. Magnusson & A. Ohman (Eds.), *Psychopathology: An international perspective* (pp. 235–252). Orlando, FL: Academic Press.

Madden, D. J. & Lion, J. (1978). Treating the violent offender. In I. L. Kutash, S. B. Kutash, L. B. Schlesinger and Associates (Eds.), *Violence: Perspectives on murder and aggression* (pp. 404–412). San Francisco: Jossey-Bass.

Magnusson, D. (1987). Adult delinquency in the light of conduct and physiology at an early age: A longitudinal study. In D. Magnusson & A. Ohman (Eds.), *Psychopathology: An international perspective* (pp. 221–234). Orlando, FL: Academic Press.

Magnusson, D. (1988). *Individual development from an interactional perspective: A longitudinal study*. Hillsdale, NJ: Lawrence Erlbaum Associates.

Mark, V. H. & Ervin, F. H. (1970). *Violence and the brain*. New York: Harper and Row.

Mattsson, A., Schalling, D., Olweus, D., Low, H., & Svensson, J. (1980). Plasma testosterone, aggressive behavior and personality dimensions in young male delinquents. *Journal of the American Academy of Child Psychiatry, 19*, 476–490.

McEwen, B. S. & Pfaff, D. W. (1985). Hormone effects on hypothalamic neurons: Analysing gene expression and neuromodulator action. *Trends in Neuroscience, 8*, 105–110.

Mednick, S. A. & Handel, E. S. (1988). Congenital determinants of violence. *Bulletin of the American Academy of Psychiatry and Law, 16*, 101–109.

Meyer-Bahlburg, H. F. L. (1980). Androgens and human aggression. In P. F. Brain & D. Benton (Eds.), *The biology of aggression* (pp. 263–290). Alphen aan den Rijn, Holland: Sijthoff and Noordhoff.

Meyer-Bahlburg, H. F. L. & Ehrhardt, A. A. (1982). Prenatal sex hormone and human aggression: A review and new data on progestogen effect. *Aggressive Behavior, 8*, 39–62.

Miczek, K. A., DeBold, J. F., Haney, M., Tidey, J., Vivan, J., & Weerts, E. M. (1990, April). Neurochemistry and pharmacotherapeutic management of violence. *Symposium on the Understanding and the Control of Violent Behavior*, Destin, FL.

Money, J. (1990). The development of sexuality and eroticism in human kind. In M. Haug, P. F. Brain, & C. Aron (Eds.), *Heterotypical behaviors in man and animals* (pp. 127–166). London, England: Chapman and Hall.

Mungas, D. (1983). An empirical analysis of specific syndromes of violent behavior. *The Journal of Nervous and Mental Disease, 171*, 354–361.

O'Connor, M. & Baker, H. W. G. (1983). Depo-medroxy progesterone acetate as an adjunctive treatment in three aggressive schizophrenic patients. *Acta Psychiatrica Scandinavica, 67*, 399–402.

Olweus, D. (1984). Development of stable aggressive reaction patterns in males. In R. J. Blanchard & D. C. Blanchard (Eds.), *Advances in the study of aggression: Volume 1* (pp. 103–137). Orlando, FL: Academic Press.

Olweus, D. (1986). Aggression and hormones: Behavioral relationship with testosterone and adrenaline. In D. Olweus, J. Block, & M. Radke-Yarrow (Eds.), *Development of antisocial and prosocial behavior: Research, theories and issues* (pp. 51–72). New York: Academic Press.

Olweus, D., Mattsson, M., Schalling, D., & Low, H. (1980). Testosterone, aggression, physical and personality dimensions in normal adolescent males. *Psychosomatic Medicine, 42*, 253–269.

Olweus, D., Mattsson, A., Schalling, D., & Low, H. (1988). Circulating testosterone levels and aggression in adolescent males. *Psychosomatic Medicine, 50*, 261–272.

Razavi, L. (1975). Cytogenetic and somatic variation in the neurobiology of violence: Epidemiological, clinical and morphological considerations. In W. S. Fields & W. H. Sweet (Eds.), *Neural bases of violence and aggression* (pp. 205–272). St. Louis: Warren H. Green.

Sharma, M., Meyer-Bahlburg, H. L. F., Boon, D. A., Slaunwhite, W. R., Jr., & Edwards, J. A. (1975). Testosterone production by XYY subjects. *Steroids, 26*, 175–180.

Sheard, M. H. (1987). Psychopharmacology of aggression in humans. In B. Olivier, J. Mos, & P. F. Brain (Eds.), *Ethopharmacology of agonistic behaviour in animals and humans* (pp. 257–266). Dordrecht, Holland: Martinus Nijhoff Publishers.

Sherwin, B. B. Gelfand, M. M., & Brender, B. (1985). Androgen enhances sexual motivation in females: A prospective crossover study of sex steroid administration in the surgical menopause. *Psychosomatic Medicine, 47*, 339–351.

Siegel, A. & Mirsky, A. F. (1990, April). The neurobiology of violence and aggression. *Symposium on the Understanding and Control of Violent Behavior*, Destin, FL.

Sosowsky, L. (1980). Explaining the increased arrest rate among mental patients: A cautionary note. *American Journal of Psychiatry*, *137*, 1602–1605.

Suffrin, G. & Coffey, D. S. (1973). A new model for studying the effect of drugs on prostatic growth I. Antiandrogens and DNA synthesis. *Investigative Urology II*, 45–54.

Susman, E. J., Inoff-Germain, G., Nottlemann, E. D., Loriaux, D. L., Cutler, G. B., & Chrousos, G. P. (1987). Hormones, emotional dispositions and aggressive attributes in young adolescents. *Child Development*, *58*, 1114–1134.

Tardiff, K. & Sweillam, A. (1980). Assault, suicide and mental illness. *Archives of General Psychiatry*, *37*, 164–169.

Tiwary, C. M. (1974). Testosterone, LHRF and behaviour. *Lancet*, p. 993.

Virkkunen, M. (1983). Psychomotor epilepsy and violence. *American Journal of Psychiatry*, *140*, 646–647.

Volkow, N. D. & Tancredi, L. (1987). Neural substrates of violent behavior: A preliminary study with positron emission tomography. *British Journal of Psychiatry*, *151*, 668–673.

Weiger, W. A. & Bear, D. M. (1988). An approach to the neurology of aggression. *Journal of Psychiatric Research*, *22*, 85–98.

Woodman, W. D. (1983). Biological perspectives of 'dangerousness.' In J. W. Hinton (Ed.), *Dangerousness: Problems of assessment and prediction* (pp. 103–113). London, England: George Allen and Unwin.

CHAPTER 2

Ethological Contributions

J. DEE HIGLEY, MARKKU LINNOILA, AND STEPHEN J. SUOMI

INTRODUCTION AND RATIONALE FOR USING NONHUMAN PRIMATES TO UNDERSTAND PSYCHIATRIC DISORDERS

Developing the capacity to inhibit and express aggression in a socially acceptable fashion is crucial for normative social functioning and the acquisition of social competence. It is clear that individuals differ vastly in their capacity to exhibit and inhibit aggression, yet little is known concerning both the underlying etiology of inappropriate aggressiveness and the long-term outcomes of individuals who inappropriately express aggression early in life. Evidence is now emerging that shows excessive aggressiveness in human children to be a risk factor for increased aggressivity in adulthood (Eron, 1987; Huesmann, Eron, Lefkowitz, & Walder, 1984). Such longitudinal studies in humans are crucial to our understanding of etiological mechanisms producing abnormalities in the regulation of aggressive impulses and competent use of aggression. Longitudinal studies of human children, however, take decades to complete, and studies that control for both genetic backgrounds and exposure to environmental stimuli are extremely difficult if not impossible to conduct.

One time-honored method that has been used to test and model behavioral and psychiatric disorders is the use of animal models. Nonhuman primates have been widely used to investigate the development and etiology of behavioral abnormalities and psychiatric disorders. This is in large part due to the genetic heritage that other primates share with humans. For example, it is estimated that one frequently studied species, the rhesus monkey, shares approximately 90–94% of its genetic material with humans (Sarich, 1985; Sibley & Ahlquist, 1987; Sibley, Comstock, & Ahlquist, 1990). Such homologies in genetic makeup produce numerous similarities between the development of nonhuman primates and man, including morphological, physiological, and behavioral parallels (Ciochon & Fleagle,

J. DEE HIGLEY and MARKKU LINNOILA • Laboratory of Clinical Studies, Division of Intramural Clinical and Biological Research, National Institute of Alcohol Abuse and Alcoholism, Poolesville, Maryland 20837. STEPHEN J. SUOMI • Laboratory of Comparative Ethology, National Institute of Child Health and Human Development, Poolesville, Maryland 20837.

Handbook of Aggressive and Destructive Behavior in Psychiatric Patients, edited by Michel Hersen, Robert T. Ammerman, and Lori A. Sisson. Plenum Press, New York, 1994.

1985; Fleagle, 1988; King, Yarbrough, Anderson, Gordon, & Gould, 1988). One of the major reasons for using nonhuman primates to study complex social behaviors such as aggression is the high degree of similarity to humans in central nervous system development and structure. Like humans, other primates have highly developed central nervous systems, requiring relatively long periods to mature. This protracted period of development allows increased behavioral flexibility and adjustment to a wide number of environments. Also, like human children, most nonhuman primate juveniles grow up in highly complex social networks, involving multiple social relationships and a nexus of interrelated social interchanges. A high degree of sophistication is required to function adequately in these elaborate societies. Thus, a major task for a developing monkey is to acquire and rehearse the behaviors and skills that will be needed to initiate and maintain social relationships.

DEVELOPING SOCIAL COMPETENCE AND THE APPROPRIATE EXPRESSION OF AGGRESSION

The acquisition of social competence is an interactive process between genetic and environmental influences. From the moment of birth, the infant's first reflexive behaviors are based on maintaining social contact and interactive interchanges (e.g., see Harlow & Harlow, 1965). There are also genetic contributions to the acquisition of social competence. For example, monkeys raised in total isolation show greater interest in pictures of individuals from their own species than in pictures of humans, landscapes, building interiors, or geometric patterns (Sackett, 1973). Furthermore, after 80 days of age, they are more likely to show fear to pictures of monkeys with aggressive postures and facial expressions than to pictures of monkeys showing other behaviors or expressions (Sackett, 1973). While genetic mechanisms contribute to the emergence of social behaviors, studies of nonhuman primates have made a major contribution to our understanding of the importance of experience in the acquisition of social competence. Unlike rodents and many other mammalian species, primate social behaviors do not emerge in full sophistication without social experience. To acquire the capacity to competently express social behaviors, primates require frequent social experiences, especially early in life (Mitchell, 1970; Suomi, 1982). Social skills must be practiced and perfected to have utility in primate societies.

Primate societies are explicitly structured to assure that the infant primate acquires and practices its social skills in a relatively safe, protected environment. Among most old-world monkey societies, neonate monkeys initially develop their social skills under the watchful tutelage of their biological mother. Mothers are especially important social agents through which infant and juvenile monkeys develop the capacity to properly inhibit and express emotions, including aggression (Bernstein & Ehardt, 1986a; Harlow, 1969; Harlow & Harlow, 1965; Higley & Suomi, 1986; Higley & Suomi, 1989). Infants and young monkeys deprived of opportunities to interact with their mothers are likely as adolescents and adults to show diminished affiliative social behaviors necessary for maintaining social bonds and relationships (Coelho & Bramblett, 1984), and in initial interactions with peers, they show less frequent and less skilled aggression to maintain social dominance (Coelho & Bramblett, 1981). Later in development, as young monkeys' motor and cognitive capacities mature, peers become central in developing and practicing social skills. Through social play, peer interactions wield a crucial role in the process of acquiring knowledge regarding the proper settings and intensity for exhibiting aggression. Monkeys deprived of adult role models and opportunities to practice social behaviors with peers are likely to express aggression in inappropriate settings or toward inappropriate targets, and demonstrate deviant social responses and social relationships (Capitanio, 1986; Mitchell, 1970; Suomi, 1982). It is no accident that evolution has favored primate societies that provide training in the appropriate expression of aggression. Under normal conditions, such evolutionarily designed social structures provide infants with exposure to partners and situations in which complex social skills and strategies can be practiced while under the vigilant eye and protection of adults. This strategy also has its cost, since it results in protracted periods of immaturity and parental dependence. These costs, however, are born by society; when social structures deviate too far from evolutionary norms and fail to provide for the infant's needs and opportunities to practice the appropriate expression of aggression, inappropriate aggression is probable, and the cost to society is great.

Developing the capacity to use aggression appropriately is crucial for primates to acquire social competence. Excessive behavioral withdrawal from social challenges and inappropriate aggression hinder the capacity to acquire social competence. Developmental studies have shown that traits characterizing behavioral withdrawal and aggression are present early in life, with behavioral withdrawal showing interindividual stability in infancy and aggression showing interindividual stability by late childhood (Eron, 1987; Huesmann et al., 1984; Kagan, Reznick, & Snidman, 1988). Emerging evidence concerning the underlying etiology of these traits indicates that both are linked to biological substrates, especially the monoaminergic neurotransmitter systems (Ballenger et al., 1983; Banki & Arato, 1983a, 1983b; Cloninger, 1986; Higley, Hasert, Suomi, & Linnoila, 1991; Higley & Suomi, 1989; Higley, Suomi, & Linnoila, 1990a, 1990b; Kagan et al., 1988; Miczek & Donat, 1990; Redmond, 1987; Schalling, Asberg, Edman, & Oreland, 1987; Soubrie, 1986; von Knorring, Monakhov, & Perris, 1978). Because of their serious and enduring nature, and their links to other forms of psychopathology such as anxiety, affective, and impulse control disorders (Banki & Arato, 1983a; Banki, Molnar, & Fekete, 1981; Brown & Linnoila, 1990; Cloninger, 1986; Linnoila, 1988; Siever, 1987), it is crucial that these traits are prospectively studied beginning early in life to assess etiological mechanisms, identify potential preventive measures, and develop treatments to reduce inappropriate aggressiveness. Given the underlying distress to those involved and these traits' potential biological underpinnings, studies of children are especially difficult to perform. Animal models based on appropriate developmental theory can provide important information and insights in the study of the role of aggression and fearfulness in the development and maintenance of social competence.

A large component in the acquisition of social competence for developing nonhuman primates is learning to express and inhibit aggression appropriately across different situations and to develop skills for recruiting support from other individuals in times of social challenge (Altmann, 1980; Bernstein & Ehardt, 1985b). Aggression is a basic part of most primate societies, and when appropriately expressed, it plays an important role in the socialization process and in maintaining social cohesion and order (Bernstein, 1981; Bernstein & Ehardt, 1985b; Bernstein & Ehardt, 1986a, 1986b; Bernstein & Gordon, 1974). The expression of aggression, however, must be controlled and expressed in proper settings and toward appropriate targets. One of the primary deficits found in monkeys reared in isolation (where they cannot practice social skills) is inappropriate aggression (Bernstein, Gordon, & Rose, 1974; Kraemer & Clarke, 1990; Mitchell, 1970). These monkeys also frequently exhibit self-directed injurious behaviors (Capitanio, 1986). It is not unusual for a juvenile monkey raised in isolation to attack a full-grown male rhesus monkey (Suomi, 1982). Monkeys raised in isolation, showing inappropriate aggression, make poor social companions. As a result, when placed into social settings, they are not preferred as social partners (Sackett, 1970) and are generally shunned by the other monkeys (Capitanio, 1986; Sackett, 1970). Similarly, monkeys with orbital frontal damage exhibit inappropriate aggression, less social competence, and as a result are ostracized by other group members (Raleigh & Steklis, 1981).

THE USE OF SOCIAL SKILLS BY ADOLESCENT MONKEYS

By the time they reach puberty, young monkeys are no longer able to practice under the watchful tutelage of the mother and protection of other adults. The social challenges that these individuals face at this point have important consequences for future social success. Social competence is reflected through successful participation in day-to-day functions of the troop, the use of social skills to form and maintain sociosexual bonds, and the transmission of social competence to offspring. For females, a major social challenge occurs when they are confronted with infant-care responsibilities as new parents. While the majority of young adult females cope with this challenge by showing appropriate care-giving behavior, a significant proportion of females do not exhibit adequate care-giving to their infants (Altmann, 1980; Drickamer, 1974; Hrdy, 1976). This is especially true for younger first-time mothers, mothers with disadvantaged rearing experiences (Drickamer, 1974; Fairbanks, 1990; Hrdy, 1976; Lancaster, 1971; Mitchell, 1970; Ruppenthal, Arling, Harlow, Sackett, & Suomi, 1976; Suomi, 1982; Suomi & Ripp, 1983), mothers with low social rank, and mothers who are subjected to social stress (Altmann, 1980; Capitanio, 1986; Drickamer, 1974).

While there are some new-world monkey species in which the male makes a contribution to infant care, in most advanced nonhuman primates, particularly old-world monkeys, males are typically not the major caregivers (Higley & Suomi, 1986). Instead, they play important roles in group leadership and defense. Most males, however, do not function in leadership roles until early to middle adulthood. This usually occurs after they have left their natal monkey troop, immigrated into a new troop, and built numerous social relationships within their new troop.

Most old-world male monkeys, either voluntarily or involuntarily, leave their natal social group during early or late adolescence and eventually join a new group (Berard, 1989; Colvin, 1986). Migration from one's natal troop is a major stressor for adolescent male monkeys. Even before leaving their social group, relative to other aged males and females, they are the targets of increased aggression, prolonged group attacks, and aggressive chases by other members of the troop (Bernstein & Ehardt, 1985a). After leaving their troop, they face further stress as a consequence of losing their network of social support, and they subsequently face frequent aggressive challenges from adult males and females from other troops of monkeys (Cheney, 1983; Packer, 1979; Packer & Pusey, 1979). Indeed, migrating monkeys have significantly more wounds and trauma from fights than monkeys who remain in their troop of origin (Crockett & Pope, 1988). Social competence is especially crucial during this period because males must establish new social relationships to garner the social support needed to gain access to new social groups. Among most old-world adolescent and adult male monkeys, predators play only a minimal role in producing injuries and mortality. Instead, the greatest danger to adolescents and adults is aggression from other monkeys (Crockett & Pope, 1988). In feral environments, aggressive encounters with other monkeys are relatively frequent. These encounters often result in injuries and trauma (Berard, 1989;

Colvin, 1986; Crockett & Pope, 1988). Indeed, a dependent measure used to assess individual differences in aggressivity among adolescent male rhesus monkeys involves counting the recent wounds and scars on a monkey's head, torso, and limbs (Higley, Mehlman, et al., 1991). During the migratory period, these aggressive encounters place the migrating male at considerable risk for injury, and in the unprotected feral environment, death is not uncommon (Berard, 1989; Colvin, 1986; Crockett & Pope, 1988; Drickamer, 1974).

After leaving the natal troop, some males spend a period of time in all-male gangs. Others make multiple attempts to gain acceptance into another troop. Preliminary analyses of mortality rates among adolescent males migrating to new troops indicate that males who bully or use aggression as a strategy to gain acceptance into a new troop are clearly at increased risk for injury and mortality (K. L. R. Rasmussen, personal communication, 1992). To gain access to a new troop, the migrating adolescent male's charge is to build social bonds with members of the new troop. On occasion, peers, siblings, or other male kin who have migrated previously may already be members of the troop that the adolescent male attempts to join (Boelkins & Wilson, 1972; Cheney & Seyfarth, 1977; Packer, 1979). Males who safely and successfully migrate to new troops seem able to use both the social relationships they previously formed and new social relationships to gain acceptance into the new troop (Boelkins & Wilson, 1972; Cheney & Seyfarth, 1977; Packer, 1979; Pusey, 1980; Smuts, 1987).

One measure of social competence in nonhuman primates is social dominance ranking. Social dominance in nonhuman primates is generally measured by observing who has primary access to prized or limited resources. As male monkeys' tenure in their new troop is prolonged, competence in forming and maintaining social relationships increases their social dominance rank. Because size and weight play little role in acquiring social dominance (McGuire & Raleigh, 1985; Smuts, 1987), it is clear that physical prowess alone is not sufficient to gain success in social competition. Indeed, rarely is the highest ranking male of a troop the most aggressive (Raleigh & Steklis, 1981; Smuts, 1987). Instead, monkeys acquire and maintain social dominance through the formation of affiliative bonds with other troop members who then support them in hostile and challenging social encounters (Packer & Pusey, 1979; Raleigh & Steklis, 1981; Smuts, 1987; Walters & Seyfarth, 1987). There is a strong association between the length of a male's tenure in a troop, the number of relationships he is able to form and maintain—especially with adult females of the troop—and the social dominance ranking he attains (Drickamer & Vessey, 1973).

There is evidence that early experiences that produce increased behavioral withdrawal may place subjects at risk for expressing inappropriate aggression. Monkeys reared in isolation from other social companions are likely to withdraw from most challenges and when the challenge is continued, they are likely to respond with aggression (Capitanio, 1986; Mitchell, 1970). Isolate-reared females are likely to be aggressive toward and even abuse their infants (Mitchell, 1970; Ruppenthal et al., 1976; Suomi, 1982). There is evidence, however, that exposure to peers greatly ameliorates the risk for offspring abuse that early social isolation brings (Novak & Harlow, 1975; Suomi, 1972). Nevertheless, experience with peers does not completely eliminate the incidence of infant abuse and neglect (Suomi & Ripp, 1983). Practice with the first infant appears also to ameliorate the risk for subsequent infant abuse in isolate-reared mothers (Ruppenthal et al., 1976).

Other rearing conditions producing behavioral withdrawal also appear to diminish social competence and increase aggressivity. Through a series of studies of monkeys reared with responsive or unresponsive surrogate mothers, Mason and his co-workers demonstrated that contingent feedback was crucial for developing social and emotional competence (Mason & Berkson, 1975; Mason & Capitanio, 1988). Monkeys reared with surrogate mothers were more likely to exhibit increased behavioral withdrawal and engage in inappropriate and excessive aggression relative to mother-reared monkeys. Nevertheless, monkeys reared with surrogates that provided contingent feedback were less likely to show behavioral withdrawal and to engage in inappropriate aggression, and they were more likely to exhibit competent social interchanges (Capitanio, 1984, 1985).

A rearing condition that has been widely studied in monkeys is peer-rearing. Even in the absence of threatening stimuli, juvenile-age peer-reared monkeys are highly fearful, and in the face of a prolonged stressor such as social separation, they are more likely to exhibit behaviors characteristic of despair (Higley & Suomi, 1989). There is evidence that these differences persist into early adulthood. In a recent study, 22 young adult rhesus monkeys (8 peer-reared and 14 mother-reared, 60 months of age), were tested prior to and after being removed four times from their social group, with each separation lasting four days. During these periods, the peer-reared monkeys were more likely to show regressive, infantlike behaviors such as self-orality and self-clasping. In addition, they had higher blood plasma concentrations of adrenocorticotrophin (ACTH) and cortisol (Higley et al., 1991). It is noteworthy that the peer-reared monkeys were also more likely to abuse alcohol than the mother-reared monkeys (Higley et al., 1991), inasmuch as excessive alcohol consumption is a risk factor for excessive and inappropriate aggression in both animals and humans (Berry & Smoothy, 1986; Coid, 1986; Evans, 1986). When 12 of these subjects were each placed alone in a novel room with an infant, all of the mother-reared monkeys demonstrated high levels of care-giving to the infant. The peer-reared monkeys, on the other hand, were more likely to threaten and show aggression toward the infant (see Figure 1).

There are indications that differences in aggression between peer- and mother-reared monkeys persist beyond adolescence. During a colonywide assessment of inappropriate maternal behavior, adult female monkeys who were peer-reared were more likely than adult female mother-reared monkeys to neglect and abuse their own infants (Suomi & Ripp, 1983). In addition, we have recently acquired new evidence regarding long-term effects of early peer rearing. Over the past 2 years we have identified those adult males and females who participated in aggressive episodes that produced injuries requiring medical treatment or necessitated transfer to a new social group. In the first part of the assessment, the background of adult males participating in our selective breeding program was investigated. In this breeding program each adult male is paired alone with an adult female for one week. Although in our colony adult mother-reared monkeys outnumber peer-reared monkeys by 3 to 1, over a 2-year period, of 12 adult males producing injuries to a female requiring veterinary treatment, 10 were peer-reared (statistically significant at $p < .05$ using a chi-square test). Of the 7 females who had to be removed from stable social groups because of fight wounds or self-aggression requiring veterinary treatment, 6 were peer-reared (statistically significant at $p < .05$ using a chi-square test).

While it is clear that early experience can play a major role in developing social competence, recent evidence indicates that genetic factors also contribute to differences in social competence. While within-species genetic differences in aggression have received little attention, when different species within the same genus are compared, there are clear species differences in the frequency of behavioral withdrawal, aggression, and social competence (Bernstein, 1970; Bernstein, Williams, & Ramsay, 1983; Clarke, Mason, & Moberg, 1988a, 1988b; Crockett & Pope, 1988; Rosenblum, 1973; Thierry, 1986). There is

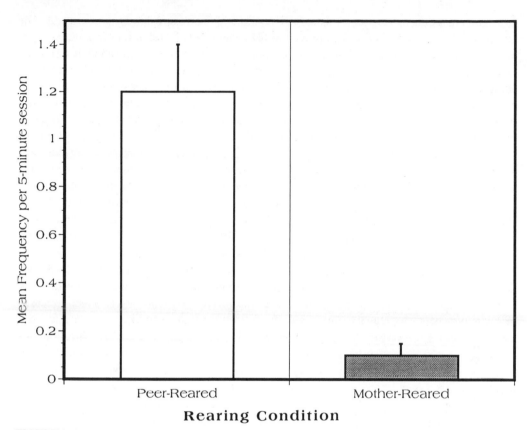

FIGURE 1. Mean frequency of aggression directed toward an infant per 5-min session by peer-reared and mother-reared monkeys.

also evidence for within-species genetic contributions to aggressivity and social competence. Within homogeneous rearing conditions, such as peer-reared groups, there are notable individual differences in social competence. Although peer-reared monkeys are never exposed to their biological fathers in our colony, Scanlan (1988) found that some fathers in this colony consistently produced infants who developed high social dominance rankings; still other fathers consistently produced offspring that were relegated to low social dominance rankings (Higley, 1989). Traditional heritability analyses of these data indicated that social dominance was highly heritable, with paternal genetic contributions accounting for a high percentage of the variance in dominance rankings.

INDIVIDUAL DIFFERENCES IN AGGRESSION AND BEHAVIORAL WITHDRAWAL

While the expression of aggression and behavioral withdrawal are context dependent, the predisposition to express aggression or withdraw from challenging social settings is clearly traitlike, with some individuals consistently more or less likely to exhibit aggression or behavioral withdrawal within the same setting (Higley, 1985; Higley, Mehlman, et al., 1992; Higley et al., 1990a). Studies of both human and nonhuman primates have shown that individual differences in aggression and behavioral withdrawal are two of the most stable of all traits (Higley, 1985; Higley & Suomi, 1989; Huesmann et al., 1984; Huesmann, Eron, & Yarmel, 1987; Kagan et al., 1988). For behavioral withdrawal, stable individual differences emerge in infancy, show modest stability across childhood, and are highly correlated from adolescence into adulthood (Higley, 1985). While individual differences in aggression have been less widely studied in nonhuman primates, the evidence available to date shows that stable individual differences emerge later than behavioral withdrawal, first showing stability in early childhood and continuing into adolescence and adulthood (Higley, 1985).

We have suggested that both environmental and genetic influences play important roles in the development and maintenance of aggressivity and social competence. Evidence is now emerging that illustrates how genetic and environmental influences interact and impact on each other, and it is clear that these two influences are not independent. While peer-rearing has a profound influence on the developing monkey, even within this relatively homogeneous treatment group large individual differences remain. Conversely, while monkey siblings reared apart from each other show behavioral similarities, the differences between a sibling reared by its mother and one reared in a peer-reared group is substantial. By making use of both such genetic and rearing background information, valid predictions can be made concerning which individuals are most likely to exhibit excessive aggression or to develop effective social competence. To illustrate, a male may inherit a low threshold for exhibiting aggression. However, when he is reared by his mother, the threshold for exhibiting aggression may be increased by her rearing practices and constraints on her offspring's aggressive predisposition. The same monkey, however, if raised in an environment containing only peers, would not experience the same environmental constraints. His threshold for exhibiting aggression would therefore be lower. Indeed, the environmental influence of peer-rearing might even exaggerate the diminished threshold that the genetic influences have produced. Models such as this can be especially useful when considering genetic and environmental influences on the developing central nervous system.

THE RELATIONSHIP BETWEEN MEASURES OF CNS FUNCTIONING AND THE ACQUISITION AND EXPRESSION OF BEHAVIORAL WITHDRAWAL AND AGGRESSION

There is increasing evidence that individual differences in the predisposition to exhibit excessive behavioral withdrawal or inappropriate aggression are related to differences in central nervous system functioning. Of the numerous neurotransmitter systems studied to date, the noradrenergic and serotonergic systems show the clearest links with behavioral withdrawal and aggression. It is worth noting, however, that other systems (e.g., the dopaminergic, GABAergic, and cholinergic systems) are also undoubtedly involved in controlling and expressing both behavioral withdrawal and aggression. There appears to be a positive link between norepinephrine activity and behavioral withdrawal, with high concentrations of the norepinephrine metabolite 3-methoxy-4-hydroxyphenylgycol (MHPG) found in individuals who are more likely to exhibit high levels of behavioral withdrawal (Higley, Hasert, et al., 1991; Higley, Mehlman, et al., 1992; Higley et al., 1990a; Higley, Suomi, & Linnoila, 1991, 1992; Kagan et al., 1987, 1988; Kraemer & McKinney, 1979; Rosenbaum et al., 1988). Similarly, excessive serotonin activity has been shown to be related to increased latencies to approach challenging or uncertain situations (Soubrie, 1986).

Redmond and colleagues (Redmond, 1987) found that stimulating the major noradrenergic cell bodies in the locus coeruleus of stumptailed macaques resulted in behaviors characteristic of fear and behavior withdrawal. Other studies by his group demonstrated that pharmacologically increasing or decreasing norepinephrine resulted in parallel increased or decreased displays of behavioral withdrawal (Redmond, 1987).

The clearest links between a specific neurotransmitter system and aggression are found with serotonin. Both the human and animal literature show a link between diminished serotonin and increased or inappropriate aggression (Linnoila, 1988; Linnoila, Virkkunen, & Roy, 1986; Olivier, Mos, Tulp, Schipper, den Daas, & van Oortmerssen, 1990; Raleigh, 1987). This appears to be especially true for impulsive aggression (Linnoila, 1990; Moss, 1987; Olivier & Mos, 1990; Olivier et al., 1990; Soubrie, 1986). Studies of both rodent and primate species show that pharmacologically depleting or augmenting serotonin acts to increase or decrease aggression, respectively (Olivier & Mos, 1990; Olivier et al., 1990; Raleigh, 1987; Raleigh, Brammer, Ritvo, Geller, McGuire, & Yuwiler, 1986).

In a classic study, Brown and his colleagues (Brown, Goodwin, Ballenger, Goyer, & Major, 1979) showed that men who were discharged from the marines due to excessive violence had diminished cerebrospinal fluid (CSF) concentrations of the serotonin metabolite CSF 5-hydroxyindoleacetic acid (5-HIAA). In addition, these individuals were not favored as companions by other marines and largely described themselves as loners. Since this initial finding, a number of human studies have linked diminished CSF 5-HIAA concentrations with excessive aggression (Brown, Linnoila, & Goodwin, 1990; Brown & Linnoila, 1990; Linnoila, DeJong, & Virkkunen, 1989a, 1989b; Linnoila et al., 1986; Linnoila, Virkkunen, Scheinin, Nuutila, Rimon, & Goodwin, 1983). Recent findings in monkeys also show an inverse relationship between CSF 5-HIAA and aggression. A recently completed study of free-ranging rhesus monkey adolescent males found that diminished CSF 5-HIAA was associated with increased physical wounds and ratings for aggressivity (Higley, Mehlman, et al., 1992).

As with Brown's original findings, there is also evidence that diminished serotonin is associated with diminished social competence. Raleigh and his colleague have demonstrated that vervet monkeys with diminished whole blood serotonin levels exhibit less competence in social behavior, with low social dominance ranking correlating positively with whole blood serotonin levels (Raleigh, Brammer, & McGuire, 1983; Raleigh, McGuire, Brammer, & Yuwiler, 1984), and monkeys with diminished whole blood serotonin, or who have their CNS serotonin pharmacologically depleted, more likely to be avoided and ostracized as social companions (Raleigh & Steklis, 1981). There is evidence that within an optimal range, higher concentrations of 5-HIAA are related to increased social competence. When we measured concentrations of the serotonin metabolite 5-HIAA in the CSF of rhesus monkeys, there was a significant positive correlation between time in close social proximity to other monkeys and CSF 5-HIAA concentrations ($r = .57$, $p < .005$). Moreover, low-ranking monkeys tended to have lower concentrations of CSF 5-HIAA (see Figure 2). When Raleigh and colleagues rated personality traits in vervet monkeys, individuals who were rated high in social deviance also had low concentrations of CSF 5-HIAA (Raleigh, McGuire, & Brammer, 1989). Consistent with these findings, 12 of 60 free-ranging male monkeys from which we have obtained CSF have been expelled from their social groups. Their average CSF 5-HIAA concentrations were significantly lower than those of monkeys who remained behind in their natal troops.

Preliminary evidence also suggests that excessively high CSF 5-HIAA concentrations may be linked to inappropriate aggressivity. Socially deprived monkeys not only show

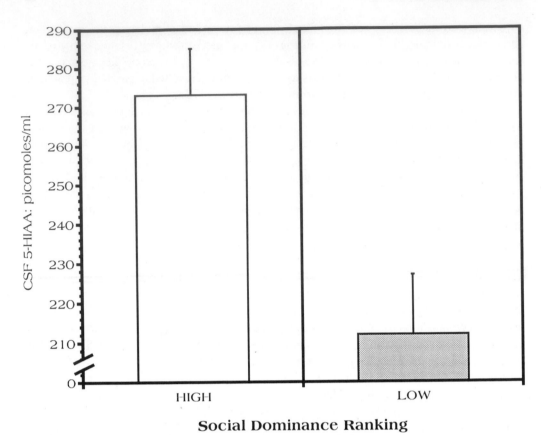

FIGURE 2. Mean CSF concentrations of 5-hydroxyindoleacetic acid (5-HIAA) for high- and low-ranking monkeys. Social dominance was measured by direction of physical displacements between each pair of 22 monkeys.

inappropriate and excessive aggressivity, they also possess increased concentrations of CSF 5-HIAA, with many individuals well above the normal range for monkeys (Higley et al., 1990a; Kraemer et al., 1989). Indeed, the highest concentrations of CSF 5-HIAA we have seen in adult animals are in a male monkey raised in social isolation who exhibited self-aggression. When he was treated with a serotonin synthesis inhibitor, self-aggression stopped (Lilly, Nix, Mehlman, Higley, Ward, Taub, & Brown, 1992).

These findings are especially interesting because they allow one to link the effects of early experience both to aggression and to central nervous system functioning with a high degree of explanatory power. We have noted how both early experiences and genetic background appear to affect both aggression and behavioral withdrawal. Consistent with our earlier discussion concerning stability of individual differences in aggression and behavioral withdrawal, individual differences in the CSF monoamine metabolites are highly correlated across time (Higley, Suomi, & Linnoila, 1992; Kraemer, Ebert, Schmidt, & McKinney, 1989). In a parallel fashion, early experiences modify the future activity of both the serotonergic and noradrenergic systems (Higley et al., 1990a; Kraemer et al., 1989). For example, by late infancy and continuing into adulthood, peer-reared monkeys not only display increased behavioral withdrawal but also show increased CSF concentrations of MHPG (Higley, Suomi, & Linnoila, 1992) and norepinephrine (Kraemer et al., 1989). There is also evidence that the serotonin system may be dysregulated in socially deprived monkeys. While for mother-reared monkeys CSF 5-HIAA correlates with the dopamine metabolite homovanillic acid (HVA) and MHPG, socially deprived monkeys do not show such close linkage across the noradrenergic, dopaminergic, and serotonergic systems (Kraemer et al., 1989), and, as previously discussed, varying degrees of social deprivation appear to increase CSF 5-HIAA (Higley et al., 1990a; Kraemer et al., 1989).

There is also evidence for paternal and maternal genetic influences on the monoamine systems that parallel the development of aggression and social competence in monkeys. In a recently completed study, we sampled CSF from 50 infants who were sired by 1 of 10 fathers. When the results were statistically pooled according to the biological sire, CSF concentrations of 5-HIAA and HVA were highly heritable for both sons and daughters, whereas MHPG showed paternal genetic effects only for sons (Higley, Thompson, Champoux, Goldman, Hasert, Kraemer, Scanlan, Suomi, & Linnoila, 1993). In addition, there were substantial maternal genetic influences on the young monkeys' CSF levels of MHPG and 5-HIAA concentrations. Infants were removed from their mothers at birth and fostered to an unrelated lactating female. Analyses indicated a maternal genetic contribution without a maternal environmental contribution for CSF 5-HIAA, in that the infants' CSF 5-HIAA concentrations were correlated with their biological but not their adopted mothers' monoamine concentrations. However, for the norepinephrine metabolite MHPG, there was evidence for both genetic and environmental maternal influences (Higley et al., 1993). Such findings suggest that behaviors that are mediated via norepinephrine are more likely to be modified by both maternal genetic and environmental influences than behaviors that are mediated via the serotonergic system, which are influenced mainly by maternal genetic influences.

SUMMARY

From a theoretical perspective, findings from the nonhuman primates indicate that acquiring the competence to use aggression appropriately requires the functional interaction of genetic background and early experiences. While it is commonly believed that genetic influences produce somewhat immutable traits, the nonhuman primate data indicate that at least during development the expression of aggression is modifiable. An important implication of these findings is an indication that aggressivity is not just a function of genetic or environmental influences, but an ongoing interplay of both influences. One cannot fully understand the underlying etiology of an aggressive impulse control disorder by studying only genetic or environmental backgrounds; the two must be considered as interacting. A second implication of the findings from research with nonhuman primates is that differences in aggressivity may be rooted in differences in the central nervous system. These CNS factors leading to differences in aggression are a function of genetic coding and experiential modification of the chemistry and physiology of the brain. This also suggests that when treatments for aggressive disorders are attempted, the modification, whether behavioral or pharmacological, should be oriented at modifying the differences in the nervous system that produce the behavior. It is acknowledged, however, that this proposed approach is currently more theoretical than practical in its application, inasmuch as directly relating behavioral traits to specific CNS functions is difficult using present technology. Finally, a certain amount of aggression is not only appropriate but indeed necessary in functional primate societies, including those of humans. From an evolutionary perspective, it is crucial to structure society in a manner that provides for the acquisition and proper control of aggression, while infants and children are under adult supervision and discipline, with access to other age-mates to practice proper sociocultural aggression. In the absence of such structure, the appearance of excessive and inappropriate aggression will be inevitable.

REFERENCES

Altmann, J. (1980). *Baboon mothers and infants*. Cambridge, MA: Harvard University Press.

Ballenger, J., Post, R. M., Jimerson, D. C., Lake, C. R., Murphy, D. L., Zuckerman, M., & Cronin, C. (1983). Biochemical correlates of personality traits in normals: An exploratory study. *Personality and Individual Differences*, *4*, 615–625.

Banki, C. M., & Arato, M. (1983a). Amine metabolites, neuroendocrine findings, and personality dimensions as correlates of suicidal behavior. *Psychiatry Research*, *10*, 253–261.

Banki, C. M., & Arato, M. (1983b). Relationship between cerebrospinal fluid amine metabolites, neuroendocrine findings and personality dimensions (Marke-Nyman scale factors) in psychiatric patients. *Acta Psychiatrica Scandinavica*, *67*, 272–280.

Banki, C. M., Molnar, G., & Fekete, I. (1981). Correlation of individual symptoms and other clinical variables with cerebrospinal fluid amine metabolites and tryptophan in depression. *Archiv fuer Psychiatrie und Nervenkrankheiten*, *229*, 345–353.

Berard, J. D. (1989). Life histories of male Cayo Santiago macaques. *Puerto Rico Health Science Journal*, *8*, 61–64.

Bernstein, I. S. (1970). Primate status hierarchies. In R. A. Rosenblum (Ed.), *Primate behavior: Developments in field and laboratory research* (pp. 71–109). New York: Academic Press.

Bernstein, I. S. (1981). Dominance: The baby and the bathwater. *The Behavioral and Brain Sciences*, *4*, 419–457.

Bernstein, I. S., & Ehardt, C. L. (1985a). Age-sex differences in the expression of agonistic behavior in rhesus monkey (*Macaca mulatta*) groups. *Journal of Comparative Psychology*, *99*, 115–132.

Bernstein, I., & Ehardt, C. L. (1985b). Agonistic aiding: Kinship, rank, age, and sex influences. *American Journal of Primatology*, *8*, 37–52.

Bernstein, I. S., & Ehardt, C. (1986a). The influence of kinship and socialization on aggressive behavior in rhesus monkeys (*Macaca mulatta*). *Animal Behaviour*, *34*, 739–747.

Bernstein, I. S., & Ehardt, C. L. (1986b). Selective interference in rhesus monkey (*Macaca mulatta*) intragroup agonistic episodes by age-sex class. *Journal of Comparative Psychology*, *100*, 380–384.

Bernstein, I. S., & Gordon, T. P. (1974). The function of aggression in primate societies. *American Scientist*, *62*, 304–311.

Bernstein, I.S., Gordon, T.P., & Rose, R. M. (1974). Aggression and social controls in rhesus monkey (*Macaca mulatta*) groups revealed in group formation studies. *Folia Primatologica*, *21*, 81–107.

Bernstein, I.S., Williams, L., & Ramsay, M. (1983). The expression of aggression in Old World monkeys. *International Journal of Primatology*, *4*, 113–125.

Berry, M.S., & Smoothy, R. (1986). A critical evaluation of claimed relationships between alcohol intake and aggression in infra-human animals. In P. F. Brain (Ed.), *Alcohol and aggression* (pp. 84–137). London: Croom Helm.

Boelkins, R. C., & Wilson, A. P. (1972). Intergroup social dynamics of the Cayo Santiago rhesus with special reference to changes in group membership by males. *Primates*, *13*, 125–140.

Brown, G. L., & Linnoila, M.I. (1990). CSF serotonin metabolite (5-HIAA) studies in depression, impulsivity, and violence. *Journal of Clinical Psychiatry*, *51* (Suppl.), 31–41.

Brown, G. L., Goodwin, F. K., Ballenger, J. C., Goyer, P. F., & Major, L. F. (1979). Aggression in humans correlates with cerebrospinal fluid amine metabolites. *Psychiatry Research*, *1*, 131–139.

Brown, G. L., Linnoila, M., & Goodwin, F. K. (1990). Clinical assessment of human aggression and impulsivity in relationship to biochemical measures. In H. M. van Praag, R. Plutchik, & A. Apter (Eds.), *Violence and suicidality: Perspectives in clinical and psychobiological research* (pp. 184–217). New York: Brunner/Mazel.

Capitanio, J.P. (1984). Early experience and social processes in rhesus macaques (*Macaca mulatta*): I. Dyadic social interaction. *Journal of Comparative Psychology*, *98*, 35–44.

Capitanio, J.P. (1985). Early experience and social processes in rhesus macaques (*Macaca mulatta*): II. Complex social interaction. *Journal of Comparative Psychology*, *99*, 133–144.

Capitanio, J.P. (1986). Behavioral pathology. In G. Mitchell & J. Erwin (Eds.), *Comparative primate biology: Behavior, conservation and ecology* (pp. 411–454). New York: Alan R. Liss.

Cheney, D. L. (1983). Proximate and ultimate factors related to the distribution of male migration. In R. A. Hinde (Ed.), *Primate social relationships: An integrated approach* (pp. 241–249). Oxford, England: Blackwell.

Cheney, D. L., & Seyfarth, R. M. (1977). Recognition of individuals within and between free-ranging groups of vervet monkeys. *American Zoologist*, *22*, 519–529.

Ciochon, R. L., & Fleagle, J. G. (1985). *Primate evolution and human origins*. Menlo Park, CA: Benjamin/Cummings.

Clarke, A. S., Mason, W. A., & Moberg, G. P. (1988a). Differential behavioral and adrenocortical response to stress among three macaque species. *American Journal of Primatology*, *14*, 37–52.

Clarke, A. S., Mason, W. A., & Moberg, G. P. (1988b). Interspecific contrasts in responses of macaques to transport cage training. *Laboratory Animal Science*, *38*, 305–309.

Cloninger, C. R. (1986). A unified biosocial theory of personality and its role in the development of anxiety states. *Psychiatric Developments*, *3*, 167–226.

Coelho, A. M. J., & Bramblett, C. A. (1981). Effects of rearing on aggression and subordination in Papio monkeys. *American Journal of Primatology*, *1*, 401–412.

Coelho, A. M., & Bramblett, C. A. (1984). Early rearing experiences and the performance of affinitive and approach behavior in infant and juvenile baboons. *Primates*, *25*, 218–224.

Coid, J. M. (1986). Alcohol, rape and sexual assault. In P. F. Brain (Ed.), *Alcohol and aggression* (pp. 161–183). London: Croom Helm.

Colvin, J. D. (1986). Proximate causes of male emigration at puberty in rhesus monkeys. In R. G. Rawlins & J. J. Kessler (Eds.), *The Cayo Santiago macaques* (pp. 131—157). Albany: State University New York Press.

Crockett, C. M., & Pope, T. (1988). Inferring patterns of aggression from red howler monkey injuries. *American Journal of Primatology*, *15*, 289–308.

Drickamer, L. C. (1974). A ten-year summary of reproductive data for free-ranging *Macaca mulatta*. *Folia Primatologica*, *21*, 61–80.

Drickamer, L. C., & Vessey, S. H. (1973). Group changing in free-ranging male rhesus monkeys. *Primates*, *14*, 249–254.

Eron, L. D. (1987). The development of aggressive behavior from the perspective of a developing behaviorism. *American Psychologist*, *42*, 435–442.

Evans, C. M. (1986). Alcohol and violence: Problems relating to methodology, statistics and causation. In P. F. Brain (Ed.), *Alcohol and aggression* (pp. 138–160). London: Croom Helm.

Fairbanks, L. A. (1990). Reciprocal benefits of allomothering for female vervet monkeys. *Animal Behaviour*, *40*, 553–562.

Fleagle, J. G. (1988). *Primate adaptation & evolution*. New York: Academic Press.

Harlow, H. F. (1969). Age-mate or peer affectional system. *Advances in the Study of Behavior*, *2*, 333–383.

Harlow, H. F., & Harlow, M. K. (1965). The affectional systems. In A. M. Schrier, H. F. Harlow, & F. Stollnitz (Eds.), *Behavior of nonhuman primates* (pp. 287–334). New York: Academic Press.

Higley, J. D. (1985). *Continuity of social separation behaviors in rhesus monkeys from infancy to adolescence*. Unpublished doctoral dissertation, University of Wisconsin, Madison.

Higley, J. D., & Suomi, S. J. (1986). Parental behavior in non-human primates. In W. Sluckin & M. Herbert (Eds.), *Parental behavior in animals and humans* (pp. 152–207). Oxford, England: Blackwell.

Higley, J. D., & Suomi, S. J. (1989). Temperamental reactivity in non-human primates. In G. A. Kohnstamm, J. E. Bates, & M. K. Rothbart (Eds.), *Temperament in childhood* (pp. 153–167). New York: Wiley.

Higley, J. D., Hasert, M. F., Suomi, S. J., & Linnoila, M. (1991). Nonhuman primate model of alcohol abuse: Effects of early experience, personality, and stress on alcohol consumption. *Proceedings of the National Academy of Science USA*, *88*, 7261–7265.

Higley, J. D., Linnoila, M., & Suomi, S. J. (1989). Genetic and experiential influences on CSF monoamine metabolites in a primate model of temperament and psychopathology. *Biological Psychiatry*, *25*, 146–147A.

Higley, J. D., Mehlman, P., Taub, D., Higley, S. B., Champoux, M., Suomi, S. J., Vickers, J. H., & Linnoila, M. (1992). CSF monoamine metabolite and adrenal correlates of aggression in free-ranging rhesus monkeys. *Archives of General Psychiatry*, *49*, 436–441.

Higley, J. D., Suomi, S. J., & Linnoila, M. (1990a). Parallels in aggression and serotonin: Consideration of development, rearing history, and sex differences. In H. M. van Praag, R. Plutchik, & A. Apter (Eds.), *Violence and suicidality: Perspectives in clinical and psychobiological research* (pp. 245–256). New York: Brunner/Mazel.

Higley, J. D., Suomi, S. J., & Linnoila, M. (1990b). Developmental influences on the serotonin system and timidity in the nonhuman primate. In E. F. Coccaro & D. L. Murphy (Eds.), *Serotonin in major psychiatric disorders* (pp. 29–46). Washington, DC: American Psychiatric Press.

Higley, J. D., Suomi, S. J., & Linnoila, M. (1991). CSF monoamine metabolite concentrations vary according to age, rearing, and sex, and are influenced by the stressor of social separation in rhesus monkeys. *Psychopharmacology, 103*, 551–556.

Higley, J. D., Suomi, S. J., & Linnoila, M. (1992). A longitudinal study of CSF monoamine metabolite and plasma cortisol concentrations in young rhesus monkeys: Effects of early experience, age, sex and stress on continuity of interindividual differences. *Biological Psychiatry, 32*, 127–145.

Higley, J. D., Thompson, W. W., Champoux, M., Goldman, D., Hasert, M. F., Kraemer, G. W., Scanlan, J. M., Suomi, S. J., & Linnoila, M. (1993). Paternal and maternal genetic and environmental contributions to cerebrospinal fluid monoamine metabolites in rhesus monkeys (*Macaca mulatta*). *Archives of General Psychiatry, 50*, 615–623.

Hrdy, S. B. (1976). Care and exploitation of non-human primate infants by conspecifics other than the mother. *Advances in the Study of Behavior, 6*, 101–158.

Huesmann, L. R., Eron, L. D., Lefkowitz, M. M., & Walder, L. O. (1984). Stability of aggression over time and generations. *Developmental Psychology, 20*, 1120–1134.

Huesmann, L. R., Eron, L. D., & Yarmel, P. W. (1987). Intellectual functioning and aggression. *Journal of Personality and Social Psychology, 52*, 232–240.

Kagan, J., Reznick, J. S., & Snidman, N. (1987). The physiology and psychology of behavioral inhibition in children. *Child Development, 58*, 1459–1473.

Kagan, J., Reznick, J. S., & Snidman, N. (1988). Biological bases of childhood shyness. *Science, 240*, 167–171.

King, F. A., Yarbrough, C. J., Anderson, D. C., Gordon, T. P., & Gould, K. G. (1988). Primates. *Science, 240*, 1475–1482.

Kraemer, G. W., & Clarke, A. S. (1990). The behavioral neurobiology of self-injurious behavior in rhesus monkeys. *Progress in Neuro-Psycho-Pharmacology and Biological Psychiatry, 14*, S141–S168.

Kraemer, G. W., & McKinney, W. T. (1979). Interactions of pharmacological agents which alter biogenic amine metabolism and depression—an analysis of contributing factors within a primate model of depression. *Journal of Affective Disorders, 1*, 33–54.

Kraemer, G. W., Ebert, M. H., Schmidt, D. E., & McKinney, W. T. (1989). A longitudinal study of the effect of different social rearing conditions on cerebrospinal fluid norepinephrine and biogenic amine metabolites in rhesus monkeys. *Neuropsychopharmacology, 2*, 175–189.

Lancaster, J. B. (1971). Play-mothering: The relations between juvenile females and young infants among free ranging vervet monkeys. *Folia Primatologica, 15*, 161–182.

Lilly, A., Nix, P., Mehlman, P. T., Higley, J. D., Ward, G., Taub, D. M., Brown, G. L. (1992). Effect of PCPA in a male rhesus monkey with an extremely deviant CNS serotonin metabolism disorder. *American Journal of Primatology, 27*, 44.

Linnoila, M. (1988). Monoamines and impulse control. In J. A. Winkels & W. Blijleven (Eds.), *Depression, anxiety, and aggression* (pp. 167–172). Houten: Medidact.

Linnoila, M. (1990). Monoamines, glucose metabolism and impulse control. In H. M. van Praag, R. Plutchik, & A. Apter (Eds.), *Violence and suicidality: Perspectives in clinical and psychobiological research* (pp. 218–244). New York: Brunner/Mazel.

Linnoila, M., DeJong, J., & Virkkunen, M. (1989a). Monoamines, glucose metabolism, and impulse control. *Psychopharmacology Bulletin, 25*, 404–406.

Linnoila, M., DeJong, J., & Virkkunen, M. (1989b). Family history of alcoholism in violent offenders and impulsive fire setters. *Archives of General Psychiatry, 46*, 613–616.

Linnoila, M., Virkkunen, M., & Roy, A. (1986). Biochemical aspects of aggression in man. *Clinical Neuropharmacology, 9* (Suppl.), 377–379.

Linnoila, M., Virkkunen, M., Scheinin, M., Nuutila, A., Rimon, R., & Goodwin, F. K. (1983). Low cerebrospinal fluid 5-hydroxyindoleacetic acid concentration differentiates impulsive from nonimpulsive violent behavior. *Life Sciences, 33*, 2609–2614.

Mason, W. A., & Berkson, G. (1975). Effects of maternal mobility on the development of rocking and other behaviors in rhesus monkeys: A study with artificial mothers. *Developmental Psychobiology, 8*, 197–211.

Mason, W. A., & Capitanio, J. P. (1988). Formation and expression of filial attachment in rhesus monkeys raised with living and inanimate mother substitutes. *Developmental Psychobiology, 21*, 401–430.

McGuire, M. T., & Raleigh, M. J. (1985). Serotonin-behavior interactions in vervet monkeys. *Psychopharmacology Bulletin, 21*, 458–463.

Miczek, K. A., & Donat, P. (1990). Brain 5-HT system and inhibition of aggressive behavior. In T. Archer, P. Bevan, & A. Cools (Eds.), *Behavioral pharmacology of 5-HT* (pp. 117–144). Hillsdale, NJ: Lawrence Erlbaum Associates.

Mitchell, G. (1970). Abnormal behavior in primates. In R. A. Rosenblum (Eds.), *Primate behavior: Developments in field and laboratory research* (pp. 195–249). New York: Academic Press.

Moss, H. B. (1987). Serotonergic activity and disinhibitory psychopathy in alcoholism. *Medical Hypotheses, 23*, 353–361.

Novak, M. A., & Harlow, H. F. (1975). Social recovery of monkeys isolated for the first year of life: 1. Rehabilitation and therapy. *Developmental Psychology, 11*, 453–465.

Olivier, B., & Mos, J. (1990). Serenics, serotonin and aggression. *Progress in Clinical and Biological Research, 361*, 203–230.

Olivier, B., Mos, J., Tulp, M., Schipper, J., den Daas, J., & van Oortmerssen, G. (1990). Serotonin involvement in aggressive behavior in animals. In H. M. van Praag, R. Plutchik, & A. Apter (Eds.), *Violence and suicidality: Perspectives in clinical and psychobiological research* (pp. 79–137). New York: Brunner/Mazel.

Packer, C. (1979). Inter-group transfer and inbreeding avoidance in *Papio anubis. Animal Behaviour, 27*, 1–36.

Packer, C., & Pusey, A. E. (1979). Female aggression and male membership in troops of Japanese macaques and olive baboons. *Folia Primatologica, 31*, 212–218.

Pusey, A. E. (1980). Inbreeding avoidance in chimpanzees. *Animal Behaviour, 28*, 543–552.

Raleigh, M. J. (1987). Differential behavioral effects of tryptophan and 5-hydroxytryptophan in vervet monkeys: Influence of catecholaminergic systems. *Psychopharmacology, 93*, 44–50.

Raleigh, M. J., & Steklis, H. D. (1981). Effect of orbitofrontal and temporal neocortical lesion on the affiliative behavior of vervet monkeys (*Cercopithecus aethiops sabaeus*). *Experimental Neurology, 73*, 378–379

Raleigh, M. J., Brammer, G. L., & McGuire, M. T. (1983). Male dominance, serotonergic systems, and the behavioral and physiological effects of drugs in vervet monkeys (*Cercopithecus aethiops sabaeus*). *Progress in Clinical and Biological Research, 131*, 185–197.

Raleigh, M. J., Brammer, G. L., Ritvo, E. R., Geller, E., McGuire, M. T., & Yuwiler, A. (1986). Effects of chronic fenfluramine on blood serotonin, cerebrospinal fluid metabolites, and behavior in monkeys. *Psychopharmacology, 90*, 503–508.

Raleigh, M. J., McGuire, M. T., & Brammer, G. L. (1989). Subjective assessment of behavioral style: Links to overt behavior and physiology in vervet monkeys. *American Journal of Primatology, 18*, 161–162.

Raleigh, M. J., McGuire, M. T., Brammer, G. L., & Yuwiler, A. (1984). Social and environmental influences on blood serotonin concentrations in monkeys. *Archives of General Psychiatry, 41*, 405–410.

Redmond, D. E. (1987). Studies of the nucleus locus coeruleus in monkeys and hypotheses for neuropsychopharmacology. In H. Y. Meltzer (Ed.), *Psychopharmacology: The third generation of progress* (pp. 967–975). New York: Raven Press.

Rosenbaum, J. F., Biederman, J., Gersten, M., Hirshfeld, D. R., Meminger, S. R., Herman, J. B., Kagan, J., Reznick, J. S., & Snidman, N. (1988). Behavioral inhibition in children of parents with panic disorder and agoraphobia. A controlled study. *Archives of General Psychiatry, 45*, 463–470.

Rosenblum, L. A. (1973). Maternal regulation of infant social interactions. In C. R. Carpenter (Ed.), *Behavioral regulators of behavior in primates* (pp. 195–217). Lewisburg, PA: Bucknell University Press.

Ruppenthal, G. C., Arling, G. L., Harlow, H. F., Sackett, G. P., & Suomi, S. J. (1976). A 10-year perspective of motherless-mother monkey behavior. *Journal of Abnormal Psychology, 85*, 341–349.

Sackett, G. P. (1970). Unlearned responses, differential rearing experiences, and the development of social attachments by rhesus monkeys. In R. A. Rosenblum (Ed.), *Primate behavior: Developments in field and laboratory research* (pp. 111–140). New York: Academic Press.

Sackett, G. P. (1973). Innate mechanisms in behavior. In C. R. Carpenter (Ed.), *Behavioral regulators of behavior in primates* (pp. 56–67). Lewisburg, PA: Bucknell University Press.

Sarich, V. (1985). A molecular approach to the question of human origins. In R. L. Ciochon & J. G. Fleagle (Eds.), *Primate evolution and human origins* (pp. 314–322). Menlo Park, CA: Benjamin/Cummings.

Scanlan, J. M. (1988). *Continuity of stress responsivity in infant rhesus monkeys (Macaca mulatta): State, hormonal, dominance, and genetic influences.* Unpublished doctoral dissertation, University of Wisconsin, Madison.

Schalling, D., Asberg, M., Edman, G., & Oreland, L. (1987). Markers for vulnerability to psychopathology: Temperament traits associated with platelet MAO activity. *Acta Psychiatrica Scandinavica, 76*, 172–182.

Sibley, C. G., & Ahlquist, J. E. (1987). DNA hybridization evidence of hominoid phylogeny: Results from an expanded data set. *Journal of Molecular Evolution, 26*, 99–121.

Sibley, C. G., Comstock, J. A., & Ahlquist, J. E. (1990). DNA hybridization evidence of hominoid phylogeny: A reanalysis of the data. *Journal of Molecular Evolution, 30*, 202–236.

Siever, L. J. (1987). Role of noradrenergic mechanisms in the etiology of the affective disorders. In H. Y. Meltzer (Ed.), *Psychopharmacology: The third generation of progress* (pp. 493–504). New York: Raven Press.

Smuts, B. B. (1987). Gender, aggression and influence. In B. B. Smuts, D. L. Cheney, R. M. Seyfarth, R. W. Wrangham, & T. T. Struhsaker (Eds.), *Primate societies* (pp. 400–412). Chicago: University of Chicago Press.

Soubrie, P. (1986). Reconciling the role of central serotonin neurons in human and animal behavior. *Behavioral and Brain Sciences*, *9*, 319–364.

Suomi, S. J. (1972). Social rehabilitation of isolate-reared monkeys. *Developmental Psychology*, *6*, 487–496.

Suomi, S. J. (1982). Abnormal behavior and primate models of psychopathology. In J. L. Fobes & J. E. King (Eds.), *Primate behavior* (pp. 171–215). New York: Academic Press.

Suomi, S. J., & Ripp, C. (1983). A history of mother-less mother monkey mothering at the University of Wisconsin Primate Laboratory. In M. Reite & N. Caine (Eds.), *Child abuse: The nonhuman primate data* (pp. 50–78). New York: Alan R. Liss.

Thierry, B. (1986). A comparative study of aggression and response to aggression in three species of macaque. In J. G. Else & P. C. Lee (Eds.), *Primate ontogeny, cognition, and social behaviour* (pp. 307–318). New York: Cambridge University Press.

von Knorring, L., Monakhov, K., & Perris, C. (1978). Augmenting/reducing: An adaptive switch mechanism to cope with incoming signals in healthy subjects and psychiatric patients. *Neuropsychobiology*, *4*, 150–179.

Walters, J. R., & Seyfarth, R. M. (1987). Conflict and cooperation. In B. B. Smuts, D. L. Cheney, R. M. Seyfarth, R. W. Wrangham, & T. T. Struhsaker (Eds.), *Primate societies* (pp. 306–317). Chicago: University of Chicago Press.

CHAPTER 3

Sociological

SHIRLEY A. SMOYAK AND D. M. GORMAN

INTRODUCTION

The view that there is a definite association between aggressive and/or destructive behavior and mental instability is widespread within the United States, not only in private beliefs, but in such cultural products as jokes, cartoons, and television programs (Link, 1987; Scheff, 1966). Indeed, in recent years, we have seen our politicians attribute acts of aggression and hostility committed by other nations to the mental instability of their leaders, and argue that the need to remove such persons from power (or at least contain their activities to within their own borders) represents sufficient justification for military intervention. In light of such pervasive presentations of what a "mentally ill" person might do or be, it is not surprising that for many people the term conjures up images of an unpredictable, volatile, and potentially dangerous person (Link & Cullen, 1986; Link, Cullen, Frank & Wozniak, 1987).

In this chapter we review the contribution of sociology to our understanding of the relationship between aggressive and destructive behaviors and psychiatric illness. The review is selective, given space limitations, with the emphasis being on broad theoretical perspectives within sociology. We begin by briefly addressing two issues of definition: (1) What are aggressive and destructive behaviors and what is psychiatric illness? and (2) What is sociology?

WHAT ARE AGGRESSIVE AND DESTRUCTIVE BEHAVIORS AND WHAT IS PSYCHIATRIC ILLNESS?

While it is not our intention to dwell on issues of definition, some discussion of what sociologists may mean by the terms *aggressive and destructive behavior* and *psychiatric*

SHIRLEY A. SMOYAK • Institute for Health, Health Care Policy and Aging Research, Rutgers University, The State University of New Jersey, New Brunswick, New Jersey 08903.   D. M. GORMAN • Center of Alcohol Studies, Rutgers University, The State University of New Jersey, Piscataway, New Jersey 08855.

Handbook of Aggressive and Destructive Behavior in Psychiatric Patients, edited by Michel Hersen, Robert T. Ammerman, and Lori A. Sisson. Plenum Press, New York, 1994.

illness is required in order that the ideas to be explored in this chapter are more easily grasped. As will be discussed later, some sociologists argue that the answer to the question "What is psychiatric illness?" is that "Psychiatric illness is behavior that society so defines" (the same type of answer would be given to the question "What is destructive and aggressive behavior?"). While such a relativistic stance might be viewed as sidestepping any real effort to be definitive, it is important to acknowledge that both conceptually and operationally many types of destructive and aggressive behaviors and many types of psychiatric illnesses are difficult to differentiate (Swanson, Holzer, Ganju, & Jono, 1990). This issue can be briefly illustrated by the example of alcohol dependence, which is included in both the American Psychiatric Association (1987) and World Health Organization (1990) nomenclature describing psychiatric disorders.

Historically, excessive consumption of alcohol was not considered a form of illness in the USA. In colonial times, for example, heavy drinking was widespread throughout the adult population and generally not considered problematic; drunkards—those who were financially unable to support their drinking—were grouped with the poor and criminals (Levine, 1978). By the nineteenth century the harmful consequences of drinking were beginning to be recognized, but the explanation of these was not one that focused on individual pathology (i.e., illness) but on the inherently addictive and dangerous properties of alcohol (Levine, 1984). As a result of such views, expressed most vociferously in the USA by the Temperance Movement, prohibition of distilling and sale of alcohol was introduced in 1919. It was only with the repeal of prohibition in 1933 that the "disease model" of alcoholism became dominant (Fingarette, 1989). Thus, what is now considered by many to be a psychiatric illness was, until fairly recently, considered a form of problem behavior, the solution to which was to be found at the level of social policy rather than medical intervention. Moreover, in contemporary times, many highly plausible alternatives to the disease model of alcoholism have been elaborated, each of which carries with it a certain set of assumptions about etiology, course, treatment, and prevention (see Miller & Hester, 1989). A number of these alternative models consider alcohol dependence (along with other substance abuse disorders) to be a form of self-destructive behavior, the causes of which reside not within the individual but within the societal and cultural norms and values that govern such behavior (Fingarette, 1989; Peele, 1987).

The argument that alcohol dependence is more appropriately considered a form of deviant or nonnormative behavior rather than an illness is understandable when one considers the various diagnostic criteria proposed over the years by the American Psychiatric Association. The earliest of these—*Diagnostic and Statistical Manual of Mental Disorders* (DSM) (American Psychiatric Association, 1952) and DSM-II (American Psychiatric Association, 1968)—grouped alcoholism with three other forms of *sociopathic personality disturbance*: drug addiction, antisocial behavior, and sexual deviations. As Nathan (1991) observes, the implication of this grouping was that "persons who exhibited any of the four constituted a threat to societal order different from—perhaps more serious than—that posed by victims of other mental or emotional disorders" (p. 356). DSM-III (American Psychiatric Association, 1980) assigned substance abuse disorders their own category and emphasized the importance of tolerance and withdrawal in the diagnostic criteria for dependence. DSM-III-R (American Psychiatric Association, 1987) increased the diagnostic criteria for dependence to nine items. The majority of these were descriptions of behaviors indicating impaired control over the use of a psychoactive substance (e.g., important social, occupational, or recreational activities given up or reduced because of substance use). Only two criteria (marked tolerance and withdrawal symptoms) described phenomena that are clearly indicators of some underlying biological disturbance. Thus, the relative importance of the behavioral indicators to the physiological indicators has changed within the USA in the space of 10 years, with DSM-III-R emphasizing the former and DSM-III emphasizing the latter. This tension appears to have been played out in deciding the criteria for DSM-IV, with early reports indicating a shift back to the DSM-III emphasis on physiological indicators (Nathan, 1991), but the more recent draft criteria of the proposed changes remaining essentially the same as those of DSM-III-R (American Psychiatric Association, 1993). The focus on nonphysical symptoms in the definition of substance abuse disorders has some distinct advantages, such as enabling clearer delineation of onset and course (Gorman, 1987, 1992). However, this focus has also led to the idea that other potentially destructive forms of behavior, such as gambling and hypersexuality, should be integrated "into the conceptual network of scientific psychiatry and psychology" thereby providing "the basis for a more comprehensive and effective approach to the understanding and treatment of people experiencing these disorders" (Goodman, 1990, p. 1407).

For many sociologists, the inclusion of such behaviors in psychiatric diagnostic nomenclature is a clear indicator of the dual trend toward the medicalization of deviant behavior and the increased use of medicine as an agent of social control in industrial societies (e.g., Conrad, 1981). However, even if one does not entirely accept the medicalization thesis, careful consideration of the way in which we define and classify such behaviors remains important, because the ways in which problems are defined have clear implications for how society responds to such problems (e.g., treatment or punishment) and chooses to allocate its resources in overcoming them. In addition, the way in which a problem is defined (as an illness, as a deviant behavior, as a normal behavior) will also influence the level of analysis at which we search for causal factors. As Wing (1978) observes, the greater the social component in the definition of a problem, the less useful a disease theory is likely to be in explaining it. Put simply, we tend to explain illness in terms of biological phenomena, and deviant behavior in terms of social phenomena. As the above discussion of alcohol dependence makes clear, a particular phenomenon can variously be described in either social/behavioral or disease/biological terminology. The more the definition emphasizes the former, the more likely we are to see sociological theories offered as explanation.

WHAT IS SOCIOLOGY?

In a recent discussion of the state of present-day sociology in Great Britain, Bulmer (1989) made two observations that are useful in framing the present discussion of the role of sociology in understanding aggressive and destructive behaviors in psychiatric settings. First, in an attempt to explain the relationship between various subspecialties, he likened the discipline to a fish, observing that each specialized area represents a scale that slightly overlaps those adjacent to it (e.g., industrial sociology, sociology of organizations, sociology of professions) but is distant from those scales located on other parts of the fish (e.g., sociology of emotions or sociology of knowledge). Second, he observed that since the trend within sociology is toward ever greater specialization, each subspecialty has tended to become more inward looking and less informed by developments within general sociological theory. Moreover, there is no one unifying "sociological theory" or "sociological method" by which to integrate and unify the subspecialties.

Taking each of these observations in turn, it can first be said that the study of aggressive and destructive behavior and the study of psychiatric disorder can be seen within sociology as two distinct subdisciplines with, to date, only minimal overlap. The former is essentially the domain of criminology or deviance research, and the latter the domain of medical sociology (or, more recently, psychiatric sociology). Thus, to use Bulmer's metaphor, we have two scales located on different parts of the fish. Second, within both of these subspecialties there exist sociologists who work with very different theoretical models and who use diverse methodologies. These aspects of the discipline of sociology make the task of the reviewer somewhat difficult, there being no comprehensive body of literature to review and no one dominant theoretical perspective to discuss. This being so, however, it should be noted that two approaches have dominated the sociological study of both deviancy and psychiatric illness over the past three decades. One approach attempts to explain phenomena, including violent behavior and psychopathology, in terms of factors such as social disorganization, which can be studied at either macro or micro levels of analysis. The latter includes a number of studies conducted by sociologists in clinical settings. The other approach attempts to explain such phenomena in terms of societal norms and sanctions which regulate individual and group behavior. These approaches correspond to what Dawe (1970) termed the "two sociologies"—the former concerned with analysis of the influence of the social system on social action and the latter with an analysis of the construction of meaning through social action.

THE SOCIOSTRUCTURAL PERSPECTIVE

In his discussion of the origins of sociology, Fletcher (1972) observes that the distinctive subject matter of the discipline is that of "social systems," these being the organizational and associational elements of social life beyond physical, biological, and psychological processes. Thus, a concern with the influence of sociostructural factors has been central to the discipline of sociology from its inception, and there now exists a considerable body of work concerned with the influence of such factors on deviant behavior and on psychiatric disorder. The starting point for such research is the observation that these phenomena are not simply randomly distributed within a society, but vary according to such factors as gender, age, ethnicity, geographic region, and social class. For example, in the United States both the perpetrators and victims of violence are disproportionately male, young, black, urban dwellers of low socioeconomic status (Messner, 1988; Sampson, 1987). This suggests that there might be something about the conditions under which specific groups of individuals live, such as economic deprivation and family disruption, that is important in the development of social problems such as violence.

It should be noted that this broad body of research within sociology varies considerably, both in terms of the types of theoretical concepts that are described (e.g., social deprivation, alienation, overcrowding, anomie) and in the type of data used to test theories (e.g., secondary analysis of official data sets [Hakim, 1982] or social surveys [Marsh, 1982]). There is obviously not the space here to discuss all of these theories. Also, many would be of only minimal relevance to the study of aggressive and destructive behavior in psychiatric patients. However, this approach can be examined for current purposes through one work, namely Durkheim's (1897/1951) study of suicide. Durkheim is one of a handful of individuals who established sociology as an academic discipline (Tiryakian, 1979), and his analysis of suicide addresses both the issue of destructive behavior and mental illness.

Durkheim and the Sociological Study of Suicide

One of the main concerns of Durkheim was to establish sociology as a scientific discipline. For this to be so, it must have a subject matter distinct from that of other disciplines such as psychology. For Durkheim (1897/1951), the distinctive subject matter of sociology as a scientific discipline was that of "social facts," which, he maintained, "must be studied as things, that is, as realities external to the individual" (pp. 37–38). These external realities operated so as to exercise control over the behavior of individuals and, according to Durkheim, could only be explained in terms of other social facts. As Lukes (1973) observes, the study of suicide was well suited to Durkheim's task of establishing sociology as a discipline, because to explain such a seemingly individual and personal act in terms of purely social factors would represent something of a triumph.

The question arises as to why a phenomenon such as suicide should be considered a social (as opposed to individual) fact, and hence a subject appropriate to sociological analysis. Durkheim contended that the existence of suicide as a social phenomenon was evident from an examination of the rates of suicide displayed by contemporary European countries, since these tended to remain stable within each country but to show consistent variation across countries (Jones, 1986). For Durkheim (1897/1951), this stability in the rates of specific societies indicated that one was dealing with "a new fact *sui generis*, with its own unity, individuality, and . . . nature" (p. 46), since clearly the individuals who contributed to the suicide rate from one year to the next were not the same. Something other than individual impulses or drives must explain this stability. Thus, the suicide rate of a given society constituted a collective total—that is, a social fact—beyond the mere sum of the independent deaths of which it was comprised. Durkheim set about developing a purely sociological explanation of this social fact—that is, one focused purely on social forces and influences.

Like most of the founders of sociology, Durkheim was concerned with the issue of social dissolution and, in particular, with the forms of moral obligation through which individuals were bound to society (Lukes, 1973). Given this interest, Durkheim was especially concerned with the roles of regulation and integration in determining the suicide rate. More specifically, he argued that either excessive or insufficient regulation or excessive or insufficient integration led to a high rate of suicide (Lukes, 1973; Hynes, 1975).

Under conditions where individuals were insufficiently integrated into society, there resulted a state of "excessive individualism" that Durkheim termed "egoism." He also argued that the rate of suicide varied inversely with the degree of integration into religious, domestic, and political groupings, and he called the specific type of suicide resulting from such excessive individualism *egoistic suicide*. In contrast, *altruistic suicide* results "when social integration is too strong" (1897/1951, p. 217). Durkheim argued that this form of self-destructive behavior was most frequent in primitive societies (e.g., wives killing themselves upon the death of their husbands), although he also explained the high rate of suicides in the military in contemporary European societies in terms of altruism. In such cases, it is the individual's duty or obligation to sacrifice himself or herself for the perceived good of society.

In addition to its integrative functions, Durkheim (1897/1951) considered society to be "a power controlling [individuals]" and argued that there was "a relation between the way this regulative action is performed and the social suicide rate" (p. 241). As Hynes (1975) observes, Durkheim considered humankind to have biological desires and needs that were potentially insatiable since there was nothing about his organic or psychological constitution that would limit these. Upon this biological base social humankind was superimposed, and it was this social dimension that kept the biological in check. If no such external constraints exist, such insatiable needs become a source of torment. In discussing the regulatory functions of society, Durkheim was principally concerned with conditions in which these were insufficient, such as during economic crises. He argued that during such times the suicide rate was high, and called this specific form of self-destruction *anomic suicide*. In contrast, where societal regulation was excessive (for Durkheim, a situation rare in the societies he studied), individuals would feel their "futures pitilessly blocked and passions violently choked by oppressive discipline" (p. 276), and this would result in *fatalistic suicide*.

In attempting to provide a uniquely sociological explanation of suicide, Durkheim was at pains to eliminate all individualistic explanations. This led him to reject the idea that suicide was related to psychiatric disorder or to alcoholism. The methods whereby he did this—namely the selective presentation of competing hypotheses, argument by elimination, and comparison of the geographic distribution of the conditions—have been subject to much criticism both from sociologists (Jones, 1986; Lukes, 1973) and from those working within other disciplines (Berrios & Mohanna, 1990). In addition, such a narrowly focused approach is unnecessary, for, as Mechanic (1978) points out, the sociostructural interpretation is not at odds with the observation that psychiatric disorder and suicide are related, since factors such as lack of integration, cohesion, and social constraints are probably conducive to both types of problems. Mechanic goes on to note that such macrolevel variables are, however, influential only through their effects on microlevel variables such as interpersonal relationships and personal affect. Ultimately, an explanation focused exclusively on sociostructural variables begs some psychological theory (Jones, 1986; Lukes, 1973), the focus of which is why some individuals are more vulnerable to their effects than others. This vulnerability may be sociopsychological—such as the effects of childhood loss and lack of care on depression (Harris, Brown, & Bifulco, 1990) and suicide (Bron, Strack, & Rudolph, 1991), or psychobiological—such as the dysfunctions in arousal processes hypothesized to be important in the etiology of schizophrenia (Bebbington & Kuipers, 1988) and substance abuse disorders (Gorman & Brown, 1992). These are the types of factors that have been studied by sociologists in clinical settings.

SOCIOLOGICAL THEORY AND CLINICAL RESEARCH

An excellent example of such sociological research is that of George Brown and his colleagues. They studied the role of social factors on the course of schizophrenia, beginning in the late 1950s in Great Britain. This work led to the development of the concept of expressed emotion (Brown, 1985). Here the sociological variables studied do not pertain to broad macro-level concepts, such as regulation and integration, but to family relationships. To be sure, Durkheim was also concerned with such factors; for example, he noted that suicide rates were higher among divorced males than their married counterparts. However, the interpretation of such relationships was always in terms of some higher level "social fact" such as anomie, which could provide a complete explanation of suicide (i.e., one without recourse to individual variables). In contrast, the importance of family relationships in schizophrenia is seen as a result of the stress that these engender for individuals who are vulnerable at a psychobiological level to such emotional arousal (Bebbington & Kuipers, 1988; Vaughn, 1989).

The first of this series of studies showed that male schizophrenic patients were more likely to relapse within one year of discharge if they returned to live with their parents or spouses than if they went to live in lodgings or with siblings (Brown, 1959; Brown, Carstairs, & Topping, 1958). In addition, those who returned to different households were less likely to relapse than those who returned to households in which they had been living prior to hospitalization. Of particular interest to the present discussion was the finding that a smaller proportion of those who had been violent before admission but changed their living group relapsed, compared with those who had been violent but returned to the same domestic situation (4/19 versus 21/44, $p < .05$). Outbursts of temper and violence occurred more often among those living with parents and wives, whereas the incidence of symptoms such as delusions was comparable in all living groups. As Brown (1985) observes, such findings were suggestive of influences emanating from relationships within the home, particularly that patients might be reacting adversely to close relationships. Alternatively, it could simply be that the more disturbed patients were returning to live with spouses and parents, and hence the relationship between living group and relapse was simply spurious.

Subsequent studies designed to address this issue demonstrated that the relationship between family living group and relapse was not simply the result of differences in severity of disorder at the time of discharge (Brown, Birley & Wing, 1972; Brown, Monck, Carstairs, & Wing, 1962). In addition, through the use of in-depth interviews (Brown & Rutter, 1966; Rutter & Brown, 1966), the research specified which aspects of family life were important, demonstrating that the level of "expressed emotion" (as measured by an index comprised of critical comments, hostility, and emotional overinvolvement) was a powerful predictor of relapse. The severity of behavioral disturbance (defined in terms of aggressive or delinquent acts) before admission was also predictive of relapse. Brown et al. (1972) noted that although it was not possible to unequivocally specify the direction of cause and effect from their data, "the fact that a decrease in expressed emotion at follow-up accompanies an improvement in the patient's behavior strongly suggests that there is a two-way relationship, each depending on the other" (p. 255).

While the basic findings concerning the predictive power of expressed emotion in schizophrenic relapse have been replicated in a number of cross-cultural studies (Bebbington & Kuipers, 1988), the role of the patient's level and type of behavioral disturbance in mediating this relationship has not been extensively studied (Glynn, Randolph, Eth, Paz, Leong, Shaner, & Strachan, 1990). In particular, the extent to which aggressive and violent behaviors in former psychiatric patients elicit marked expression of emotion from relatives or are themselves a response to family environment remains unclear. Most likely some reciprocal process of the type suggested by Brown et al. (1972) is involved, with factors such as the age, gender, and diagnostic profile of the patient (Hogarty, 1985) influencing the exact nature of the relationship.

In a related longitudinal study of three psychiatric hospitals, Brown and his colleagues examined the role of social factors on the course of institutionalized schizophrenics (Brown, Bone, Dalison & Wing, 1966; Wing & Brown, 1970). Here the variables of interest were not those pertaining to family relations and dynamics, but rather to the therapeutic conditions and organizational structure prevailing on the ward. The conclusion drawn from this research was "that a substantial proportion, though by no means all, of the morbidity shown by long-stay schizophrenic patients in mental hospitals is a product of their environment" (Wing & Brown, 1970, p. 177). More specifically, it was found that "environmental poverty" (e.g., being engaged in few activities and having few personal possessions) was highly correlated with a syndrome of "clinical poverty" or negative symptoms (e.g., flatness of affect and poverty of speech) as well with a set of "secondary" impairments (e.g., disappearance of previous social identities and roles and indifference or fear at the prospect of discharge). Florid or positive symptoms such as delusions and socially embarrassing behavior were not associated with the level of environmental poverty found on the hospital wards. Subsequent increases in the level of activity on specific wards (particularly through work and occupational therapy) and reduction in ward restrictiveness were found to be related to clinical improvements, while increases in contacts outside of the hospital and in the number of personal possessions reduced secondary impairments (Wing & Brown, 1970).

Thus, specific aspects of the social milieu of the hospitals, which could be broadly characterized as understimulating, were found to be related to a specific clinical profile of negative symptoms and specific secondary social impairments. In contrast, the over-stimulation of living in a family which was high in terms of expressed emotion was usually found to be related to an exacerbation of positive symptoms (Wing, 1989). Since the exact manifestations of violence, at least among schizophrenics, appear to vary according to such differences in symptomatology (Volavka & Krakowski, 1989), this raises the question as to whether certain types of ward structure and organization might be conducive to the manifestation of specific forms of aggressive and destructive behaviors by patients.

A recent study by Palmstierna, Huitfeldt, and Wistedt (1991) in Sweden suggests that the level of restrictiveness of the ward (in terms of not granting patients' requests) and increased crowding might be two such factors influencing the level of aggressive behavior in psychiatric settings. Other ward and staff variables that may be important include level and adequacy of training, staff-to-patient ratios, the type of therapeutic regime that is in operation, and staff attitudes and morale—although in each of these areas the evidence is inconclusive (Shah, Fineberg, & James, 1991).

A sociological perspective suggests that understanding any event requires stepping back and seeing it in a broader or systems context. For instance, Straus (1973) suggests that escalation of violence is best understood within a model that emphasizes institutionalized rules of order and expectations for both expanding and diminishing behaviors. Although Straus's model was originally designed to analyze violence within families, it has been used by clinicians in their efforts to change hospital ward environments typified by increasing rates of violent episodes.

When the composition of patients in psychiatric hospital units began to change because of deinstitutionalization, staff were confronted with increasing numbers of difficult-to-manage patients (Mechanic, 1989). The patients were younger, stronger, and more severely disturbed than previously, and the staff, who had become accustomed to more chronic conditions, were fearful and at a loss regarding how to cope with this changing situation. Public sector psychiatric hospital staff are faced with more challenges because they are more likely to have proportionately more violent/dangerous patients on their units than staff in the private sector (Smoyak, 1991).

In the late 1970s and early 1980s, staff education programs provided information and strategies for managing the problematic behaviors of individual patients. The assumption was that the focus should be on the patients themselves, rather than the staff. Content of these education programs included early recognition of escalating behavior, steps in defusing potentially violent situations, and factors associated with the increased likeli-hood of violence. Clinical strategies included methods to contain or prevent violent episodes, such as verbal persuasion. Seclusion, restraints, and the use of medication were seen as necessary only if the verbal tactics failed.

The tide of interest has shifted now to training clinicians to be aware of interaction effects, rather than to focus on the patient in isolation from other factors. Both staff attitudes and behaviors, and environmental conditions such as crowding, room temperature, cigarette smoke, and availability of recreational resources, are included in education and procedural manuals. As noted above, research into such interactive effects is still at an early stage, and there remains much controversy as to how these might operate. For example, Palmstierna et al. (1991) suggest that staff restrictiveness and increased instances of violent episodes are positively correlated, whereas Rosenbaum (1990) has suggested that increased violence of psychiatric units can be understood as a consequence of "dismantling hierarchal structures and instituting democratic principles in the formulation of ward policies and decision making" (p. 721). He advocates reinstituting the medical model and returning the psychiatrist to a position of leadership. Future research, as well as attempting to identify clinical and demographic characteristics of patients that predict aggressive and destructive behavior, should also examine how these interact with features of the settings and environments (e.g., hospital, community, family) in which those with psychiatric disorders receive treatment and care.

THE SOCIETAL REACTION (LABELING) PERSPECTIVE

The societal reaction or labeling approaches emerged within sociology in the 1960s as a reaction against both the sociostructural explanations of deviant behaviors and sociological research that took clinical descriptions, such as schizophrenia, as a "given" rather than as a socially constructed phenomenon. In the 1970s a number of critiques of the perspective were published, and its influence within the discipline subsequently declined. Recently, societal reaction theorists have endeavored to specify more precisely the mechanisms and processes through which labeling occurs, and in this respect the public's perceptions of how "dangerous" the mentally ill are have been shown to be important. Each of these areas (early societal reaction theory, critiques, and recent developments) will be discussed in turn.

Early Societal Reaction Theories

Societal reaction or labeling theory emerged within sociology in large part as a critique of sociostructural explanations of deviant behavior. Like sociostructural theories, however, acts of criminality and delinquency (such as violence toward others and destructive behaviors) and psychiatric disorders were dealt with separately by labeling theorists. The former is generally the domain of criminologists, and, given the nature of the societal reaction perspective, there is a rejection of the idea that any pathology, such as psychiatric illness, accounts for the manifestation of such behaviors. The latter has been most thoroughly discussed by Scheff (1966), who considers the violations of social norms that invoke the label of mental illness to represent a residual category of rule-breaking for which modern industrial society has no other name. In other cultures, such "residual rule-breaking" is labeled witchcraft or spiritual possession.

The central tenet of the labeling approach, and the way in which this differs from the sociostructural approach, was perhaps most clearly stated by Howard Becker in 1963. Becker began by observing that many sociologists

> look at society, or some part of society, and ask whether there are processes going on in it that tend to reduce its stability, thus lessening its chance of survival. They label such processes deviant or identify them as symptoms of social disorganization. They discriminate between those features of society which promote stability (and thus are "functional") and those which disrupt stability (and thus are "dysfunctional"). (Becker, 1963, p. 7)

He goes on to state that the societal reaction perspective also starts with the premise that deviance "is created by society." But, Becker also says that this statement is not meant

> in the way it is ordinarily understood, in which the causes of deviance are located in the social situations of the deviant or in "social factors" which prompt his action. I mean, rather, that *social groups create deviance by making the rules whose infraction constitutes deviance*, and by applying those rules to particular people and labeling them as outsiders. From this point of view, deviance is *not* a quality of the act the person commits, but rather a consequence of the application by others of rules and sanctions to an "offender." The deviant is one to whom that label has successfully been applied; deviant behavior is behavior that people so label. (p. 9, emphases in original)

It is not difficult to find examples that lend support to the general contention stated by Becker that "social groups create deviance by making the rules whose infraction constitutes deviance." To take one example, Segal (1989) has observed how countries differ in their standards of civil commitment, which vary principally along two dimensions—the need for treatment and the degree of dangerousness. Depending upon which of these dimensions is emphasized in the legal statutes, a different subgroup of the mentally ill population is institutionalized (and hence, from the societal reaction perspective, formally labeled). In England and Wales the emphasis upon need for treatment leads to more older females being committed, whereas in the USA the emphasis on dangerousness leads to more young males being committed. Thus, each country gets the deviants that its laws define.

In addition to such national differences, a single society can show marked variations in definitions of deviance even over relatively short periods of time. For example, use of opiates was commonplace and not illegal in the United States prior to the Harrison Act of 1914 (Hoffman, 1990). Once sanctions prohibiting the use of these substances were introduced, a new form of deviance named "opiate addiction" was created. Such a new class of deviant is socially constructed through a number of processes, such as the development of a nomenclature to describe the behavior and "symptoms" associated with use of opiates (e.g., the diagnostic criteria described by the American Psychiatric Association, 1987) and the establishment of institutions that enforce legal sanctions (e.g., Bureau of Narcotics and Drug Enforcement Agency) and that serve to punish (e.g., imprisonment, seizure of assets) or treat (e.g., detoxification, methadone maintenance) the deviant.

Both of the above examples indicate the manner in which social norms and sanctions can create a particular *deviant category*. The question arises, however, as to the extent that such processes create the *individual deviant*. Put another way, while the use of heroin would not be a deviant act (in the legal sense) were it not for the Harrison legislation of 1914, would the absence of such legislation mean that opiate addiction would no longer manifest itself as a clinical syndrome (in the sense that prolonged use increases most individuals' psychological and physiological tolerance for the drug and leads to the onset of a withdrawal syndrome should they abruptly abstain)?

The early labeling theorists were, in fact, primarily concerned with explaining how societal rules and sanctions have an impact on the individual (that is, explaining the consequences of medical and legal practice), rather than in exploring the ways in which the concepts and categories of scientific knowledge are socially constructed such that defini-tions of deviance change over time.[1] In doing so, their emphasis was not on the processes that influenced the etiology of a behavior but rather on those processes that served to maintain it. Thus, much research focused upon the mechanisms whereby agencies of social control such as courts and psychiatric hospitals set about ascribing individuals the status of "criminal" or "mental patient." According to such studies, the formal ascription of such labels was largely perfunctory and once affixed it became difficult for individuals to resume their "unspoilt" identities (Goffman, 1961; Rosehan, 1973; Scheff, 1964).

The separation of etiology and course in societal reaction theory was first formally expressed by Lemert (1967) in his distinction between "primary deviance" and "secondary deviance." The former refers to the behaviors and actions that initially invoke a societal reaction, and the latter to the behaviors, actions, and role adaptation that develop in response to the societal reaction. Wing (1978) has observed that the idea of secondary deviance can be expressed in two forms, one "moderate" and one "radical." The moderate form states that certain behaviors, which are initially caused by biological and/or psychosocial factors, will evoke negative public attention, which in the long term may lead to individuals being defined exclusively by a single characteristic and eventually changing their self-concept in line with this stereotype. Wing cites his study with Brown (discussed above) on the effects of institutionalism on schizophrenia as an example of the moderate approach (Wing & Brown, 1970). In its radical form, the idea of secondary deviance negates the study of primary deviation and, in particular, the factors that influenced its etiology, and instead focuses exclusively on the effects of societal reaction. From this perspective, the behaviors that first draw public attention are not intrinsically deviant; rather, they become deviant because a particular society at a particular point in time defines them as such.

As Wing (1978) observes, the radical perspective within societal reaction theory is stated most clearly in the writings of Scheff (1966, 1974). As noted above, Scheff argues that the violations of social norms that become labeled mental illness represent a residual category of rule-breaking for which modern industrial society has no other name. Scheff is largely unconcerned with the etiology of this type of behavior, and focuses instead upon the factors that serve to maintain it once it has manifested itself. Regarding this issue, Scheff (1966) maintains that "among residual rule breakers, labeling is the single most important cause of careers of residual deviance" (pp. 92–93). Viewed in terms of the present discussion, this statement means that once individuals are diagnosed as suffering from a psychiatric disorder and as prone to violence, the key determinant of their future behavior and actions (i.e., future manifestations of symptoms and violent behavior) is the attaching of a diagnostic label by others to the initial behavior.

Criticisms of the Societal Reaction Perspective

It is this latter aspect of labeling theory that provoked the most criticism in the mid-1970s, both from psychiatrists working from within a traditional disease framework

---

[1]More recently, some sociologists have taken the very concepts and diagnostic categories of psychiatry as their primary object of study, arguing that these are best considered as social constructs rather than as representing advancements over previous "nonscientific" models (e.g., Room, 1985). This work is heavily influenced by the philosopher Michel Foucault, whose writings attempt to trace the "genealogy" of various forms of scientific discourse, such as clinical medicine (Foucault, 1963/1973) and penology (Foucault, 1975/1977), that emerged during the latter part of the eighteenth century. For a discussion of the influence of social constructivism on medical sociology, see Bury (1986).

and from sociologists working from a more traditional social causation perspective. According to these critics, recurrence of the behaviors and actions that initially led to a diagnosis of psychiatric disorder and violence is explained principally in terms of the natural history of the pathology from which the individual is suffering or through the continued influence of the factors that first precipitated the disorder (e.g., continued stress or social disorganization). Also, these critics of the societal reaction perspective maintain that the reaction of others to disturbed individuals can be explained primarily in terms of their behavior, rather than others' responses being the cause of continued manifestation of symptoms.

As Horwitz (1979) notes, the debate between the proponents and critics of labeling theory has taken the form of a series of rebuttal and counterrebuttals centered principally on the question of whether the central hypothesis of labeling theory (namely, that labeling is the most important cause of the subsequent behavior of ex-psychiatric patients) is supported by empirical evidence (e.g., Gove, 1970; Scheff, 1974). This empirical evidence will not be reviewed here; suffice to say that a detailed review of the literature has shown that the weight of evidence from experimental and quasi-experimental studies supports the view that it is the behavior and symptoms manifested by psychiatrically ill persons that activate societal reaction, rather than vice versa (Link et al., 1987). The general consensus that existed concerning the societal reaction perspective (at least in its radical form) by the late 1980s has been summarized by Mechanic (1989):

> Although the societal reaction approach is provocative and obviously identifies processes that occur to some extent in the definition and care of mental patients, the relative importance of such processes were very much exaggerated. No one would deny that social labels can have powerful effects on individuals, but little evidence supports the idea that such labeling processes are sufficiently powerful to be major influences in producing chronic mental illness. (pp. 77–78)

Recent Developments in Societal Reaction Theory

Thus, in its most extreme form (i.e., that labeling is the most important factor influencing the course of psychiatric disorder), the societal reaction perspective was simply unsupported by empirical evidence.[1] However, as the quote from Mechanic makes clear, this is not to say that labeling has no influence on the lives of individuals suffering from psychiatric disorders (and certainly the accounts of many former patients attest to the fact that stereotyping by others does affect their lives—see Link et al., 1987). However, as Mechanic further notes, one of the main problems with the early societal reaction approach was that it was extremely vague in specifying the conditions and processes under which labeling will have an effect and precisely what this effect might be. In short, the theory was poorly specified and therefore difficult to test empirically.

More recently, an attempt has been made to address such issues in a series of studies conducted by Link and his colleagues (Link, 1982; Link & Cullen, 1986; Link et al., 1987). This research has introduced a greater level of refinement and sophistication to the societal reaction perspective, and it is of especial interest because a number of the studies deal directly with the issue of dangerousness. Before discussing these, it is worth considering the research reported by Link (1982), in that this illustrates the potential value of the societal

[1] More recently, Scheff has acknowledged the original labeling theory he presented was insufficiently detailed (Scheff & Retzinger, 1991). The revised labeling theory he proposes emphasizes the role of "unacknowledged shame" in the development and course of psychiatric illness and in the societal reaction to it.

reaction perspective in understanding psychiatric disorders. Link observes that the consequences of applying a label to an individual might be any of the following: first, to create a deviant behavior (i.e., to affect it etiologically); second, to stabilize a deviant behavior (i.e., to affect its course); and third, to influence other areas of the person's life such as employment and social life. As noted above, it is in the first and second of these domains that the early societal reaction perspective was found wanting. The focus of Link's (1982) study is the third of these domains, and more specifically the influence of labeling on level of income and employment status. Link observes that to examine this relationship it is necessary to control for the possible effects of residual illness on income and employment. The study, therefore, compared a group of treated cases (i.e., persons with a psychiatric disorder who had received treatment and therefore had been formally labeled) with a group of untreated cases (i.e., persons with a psychiatric disorder who had not received treatment and had not been formally labeled). Three different sets of analyses were presented, all of which demonstrated a lower income among the treated cases than untreated cases, even when psychiatric condition was held constant. Thus, labeling does appear to affect important areas of ex-patient's lives, even if, as critics such as Gove (1970) would argue, it does not directly affect the course of the disorder. Link argues that labeling may in fact indirectly influence the course of a psychiatric disorder, in that a negative label is likely to increase environmental stresses such as job losses and financial hardships, which may undermine individuals' coping strategies and hence make them vulnerable to relapse. In this manner, he sees the societal reaction perspective as complementing, and not challenging, the type of clinical research discussed above.

In a later study, Link et al. (1987) set out to examine the issue on which most previous tests of the societal reaction perspective had focused, namely, the relative importance of labeling and behavior as determinants of responses to the mentally ill. However, they went beyond previous research in attempting to understand the meaning that the label "mental patient" has to the general public and, in particular, the extent to which beliefs about the dangerousness of such persons influenced social distancing. Data were collected using vignettes. These took one of six forms, according to which of three types of behavior were described (*no objectionable behavior*, *mildly objectionable behavior*, or *severely objectionable behavior*) and which of two levels of labeling were applied to the vignette (*hospitalized for a psychiatric problem* or *hospitalized for a back problem*). Subjects ($n = 152$) were randomly assigned one of the six vignettes and asked to rate the individual depicted on seven social distance questions. In addition, subjects completed an eight-item questionnaire concerned with perceived dangerousness of the mentally ill in general. At one level, the results of the study were consistent with the research reported by critics of the labeling perspective (e.g., Gove, 1970) in that while an increase in the severity of behavior depicted in the vignette led to greater social distancing, the presence or absence of the label "hospitalized for a psychiatric problem" did not. However, there was a strong interaction effect between labeling and the perceived dangerousness of psychiatric patients (i.e., with the unlabeled vignettes the perceived level of dangerousness had no effect on social distancing, whereas with the labeled vignettes the extent to which subjects felt that psychiatric patients were dangerous influenced the amount of social distancing they expressed).

This research suggests that what is important about the label "psychiatric patient" is the meaning that it has, in this case that such a person is potentially dangerous. When the meaning of the label is specified in this manner it becomes apparent that for a large number of persons it is not simply the behavior of the mentally ill that will influence their response to them. Rather, the beliefs about mental illness that they bring with them to the interaction will influence their response, and this might explain why many former patients feel that they are unfairly stigmatized. Link et al. (1987) estimate that 39% of subjects in their study consider psychiatric patients to be dangerous to such a degree that they will endeavor to distance themselves from persons so labeled.

One question that arises from this research is the manner in which such interaction with former patients influences such beliefs. Link and Cullen (1986) examined the effects of two types of contact with the mentally ill (contact that persons choose versus contact that is beyond their control) on perceptions of dangerousness. In line with previous work (e.g., Brockman & D'Arcy, 1978) it was found that the more contact persons had with the mentally ill, the less dangerous they considered the mentally ill to be. This relationship held for both males and females, and across groups of varying age and levels of education. In addition, the association between degree of contact and perceptions of dangerousness held for both types of contact (i.e., contact that was chosen and contact where choice was limited). The latter result helps clarify the direction of the relationship between contact and views of dangerousness, suggesting that increased contact with the mentally ill results in more favorable attitudes rather than already existing favorable attitudes leading to the initiation of more contact.

The above research focused specifically upon the societal reaction hypothesis. In contrast to this research, the most recent study carried out by Link and his colleagues took as its starting point the observation that ex-psychiatric patients appear to be more violent than the general population (Link et al., 1990). This association between status as a former psychiatric patient and violence has been established primarily on the basis of official statistics of arrest rates (e.g., Steadman, 1981) and is, as Link and his colleagues observe, subject to a number of interpretations other than that which posits a simple causal relationship. Two of these competing interpretations are of special relevance to the present discussion—one because it explains the association between arrest rates and psychiatric status from a broadly societal reaction perspective, and the other because it does so in terms of sociostructural factors, such as socioeconomic status. In the first of these interpretations, higher arrest rates simply reflect differential reactions on the part of law enforcement officers to the psychiatrically ill; that is, they are more likely to be arrested than "normal" individuals even when the type of offense is the same (the so-called criminalization hypothesis). In the second interpretation, it is proposed that the high arrest rates of ex-psychiatric patients simply reflect the social environment in which they live, rather than their propensity to violence. In arrest rate studies, chronically ill ex-patients, who typically reside in disadvantaged areas, tend to be compared with the "general population," which in socioeconomic terms is extremely heterogeneous. Thus, in terms of the type of broad sociostructural factors that influence violent behavior and arrest rate, such studies are not comparing like with like.

In testing these (and other) explanations, Link and his colleagues (1990) used data collected from 232 psychiatric patients (both inpatient and outpatient) attending a large New York hospital and 521 community residents recruited in a household survey conducted in the neighborhoods in which the patients lived. What is especially noteworthy about this study is that data from a number of diverse sources were used in testing the competing hypotheses. First, in order to overcome the problems inherent in arrest rate data (i.e., bias introduced by possible differential responses of police officers to the psychiatrically ill) both official arrest statistics and self-reports of arrests and violent behavior were used. Second, in order to assess the influence of sociostructural factors on the association between psychiatric illness and violence, macrolevel data pertaining to socioeconomic status, ethnic heterogeneity, family disruption, residential mobility, and homicide rates were used to assess the "crime potential" of the communities in which subjects resided. Third, data were collected concerning psychiatric symptoms, to allow more detailed specification of the relationship (assuming any was found) between mental health and violent behavior.

The results of the study showed that ex-patients displayed higher rates of violent behavior than community residents who had never received psychiatric treatment, *whether assessed by official arrest statistics or by self-reports obtained during the interviews*. Thus, the correlation between violence and psychiatric status reported in previous research does not appear to be simply an artifact of the type of data used (as suggested by the criminalization hypothesis), since the association holds even when assessed in terms of self-reports of violent acts that involved no arrest and that are therefore uncontaminated by the types of bias found in official statistics. In addition, although the sociostructural variables were found to be significantly related to arrest rates and reports of violent behavior, they did not account for the elevated rate of these variables among patients.

Thus, the association between psychiatric status and violence could not be explained in terms of either the criminalization hypothesis or the sociostructural hypothesis. This finding suggests that the frequently observed association between psychiatric disorder and violent behavior is real rather than an artifact created by inadequate measures or explicable in terms of some third variable. However, the analysis presented by Link and his colleagues also indicates that the risk of violence by ex-psychiatric patients is extremely limited in both scope and magnitude. First, when compared with variables such as age, gender, and level of education, the magnitude of effect associated with status as a former psychiatric patient was modest. The authors note that were one to use the higher rate of arrests and violent behavior as a rationale for avoiding former psychiatric patients, then one might also set about avoiding males in preference to females and high school graduates in preference to college graduates. Second, the association between violent behavior and psychiatric disorder was limited to those patients exhibiting current psychotic symptoms, and such symptoms were relatively rare. The risk among all other ex-patients (the vast majority) was no greater than that for the comparison group of nonpatients. In addition, the authors point out that even among currently psychotic individuals one cannot assume a simple causal relationship between symptoms and expressions of violence, since the association may well be mediated by the fearful and/or coercive reactions to such symptoms of those within the patient's social milieu. As noted above, a similar interactive model has been proposed by researchers in the field of expressed emotions.

SUMMARY

Understanding aggressive and destructive behavior in psychiatric patients, from a sociological perspective, requires a willingness to use lenses in an uncommon way. Far more has been written, in both scholarly and popular literature, from perspectives that are intrapsychic, behavioral, or simply demographic. Belief systems, rather than science, permeate what is published. What we have done is to suggest how sociological theory can be applied to lend an understanding of this important topic, and then to present what is known from the standpoint of two broadly defined perspectives.

While most sociologists look at variables and concepts at levels beyond human systems, what they choose to hold as operating premises for their theory development and design of studies produce significantly different outcomes. Some approach the phenomena associated with psychiatric patients as if they were objective data, withstanding the demands for stability across time and culture; these sociologists accept as "given" the diagnoses and treatment language and assumptions found in clinical areas. Others see, instead, that reality is what one makes it and view diagnosis and treatment as just as variable as social class or categories of deviance.

The societal reaction perspective was initially developed as a critique of sociostructural explanations of social problems. In addition, it was hostile to those sociologists who accepted as given the psychiatric diagnostic categories. They argued that behaviors such as those associated with schizophrenia were entirely understandable as products of a social, negotiated order, rather than as caused by any psychobiological vulnerability, which might react to social factors such as family stress. However, the work of Link and colleagues, as well as that of Brown and associates, suggest that these approaches need not be seen as necessarily contradictory, but instead are parts of a much more complex interactive model. First, sociostructural factors, such as social deprivation and anomie, will influence the overall levels of violence in a society. In addition, individuals will be vulnerable to the differential effects of such structural factors, at both a psychobiological and a sociopsychological level. Finally, once an individual is suffering from a psychiatric disorder, social factors such as the response of family and treatment personnel will influence its course and outcome both directly in terms of risk of relapse and indirectly in terms of secondary impairments.

REFERENCES

American Psychiatric Association (1952). *Diagnostic and statistical manual of mental disorders*. Washington, DC: Author.

American Psychiatric Association (1968). *Diagnostic and statistical manual of mental disorders*, 2nd Edition, Washington, DC: Author.

American Psychiatric Association (1980). *Diagnostic and statistical manual of mental disorders*, 3rd Edition, Washington, DC: Author.

American Psychiatric Association (1987). *Diagnostic and statistical manual of mental disorders*, 3rd Edition, Revised. Washington, DC: Author.

American Psychiatric Association (1993). *DSM-IV draft criteria*. Washington, DC: Author.

Bebbington, P., & Kuipers, L. (1988). Social influences on schizophrenia. In P. Bebbington & P. McGuffin (Eds.), *Schizophrenia: The major issues* (pp. 201–225). Oxford: Heinemann.

Becker, H. S. (1963). *Outsiders: Studies in the sociology of deviance*. New York: Free Press.

Berrios, G. E., & Mohanna, M. (1990). Durkheim and French psychiatric views on suicide during the 19th century: A conceptual history. *British Journal of Psychiatry, 156*, 1–9.

Brockman, J., & D'Arcy, C. (1978). Correlates of attitudinal social distance toward the mentally ill: A review and re-survey. *Social Psychiatry, 13*, 69–77.

Bron, B., Strack, M., & Rudolph, G. (1991). Childhood experiences of loss and suicide: Significance in depressive states of major depressed and dysthymic or adjustment disordered patients. *Journal of Affective Disorders, 23*, 165–172.

Brown, G. W. (1959). Experiences of discharged chronic schizophrenic patients in various types of living groups. *Milbank Memorial Fund Quarterly, 37*, 105–131.

Brown, G. W. (1985). The discovery of expressed emotion: Induction or deduction? In J. Leff & C. Vaughn (Eds.), *Expressed emotions in families: Its significance for mental illness* (pp. 7–25). New York: Guilford Press.

Brown, G. W., & Rutler, M. (1966). The measurement of family activities and relationships: A methodological study. *Human Relations, 19*, 241–263.

Brown, G. W., Birley, J. L. T., & Wing, K. K. (1972). Influence of family life on the course of schizophrenia disorder: A replication. *British Journal of Psychiatry, 121*, 241–258.

Brown, G. W., Bone, M., Dalison, B., & Wing, J. K. (1966). *Schizophrenia and social care: A comparative follow-up study of 339 schizophrenic patients*. Maudsley Monograph Number 17. New York: Oxford University Press.

Brown, G. W., Carstairs, G. M., & Topping, G. (1958). Post-hospital adjustment of chronic mental patients. *Lancet, ii*, 685–689.

Brown, G. W., Monck, E. M., Carstairs, G. M., & Wing, J. K. (1962). Influence of family life on the course of schizophrenic illness. *British Journal of Preventive and Social Medicine, 16*, 55–68.

Bulmer, M. (1989). Theory and method in recent British sociology: Whither the empirical impulse? *British Journal of Sociology, 40*, 393–417.

Bury, M. R. (1986). Social constructivism and the development of medical sociology. *Sociology of Health and Illness, 8*, 137–169.

Conrad, P. (1981). On the medicalization of deviance and social control. In D. Ingleby (Ed.), *Critical psychiatry: The politics of mental health* (pp. 103–119). New York: Penguin.

Dawe, A. (1970). The two sociologies. *British Journal of Sociology, 21*, 207–218.

Durkheim, E. (1952). *Suicide: A study in sociology* (J. A. Spaulding & G. Simpon, Trans.). London: Routledge & Keegan Paul. (Original work published 1897).

Fingarette, H. (1989). *Heavy drinking: The myth of alcoholism as a disease.* Berkeley, CA: University of California Press.

Fletcher, R. (1972). *The making of sociology: A study of sociological theory. Volume 1: Beginnings and foundations.* London: Nelson's University Paperbacks.

Foucault, M. (1973). *The birth of the clinic: An archaeology of medical perception* (A. S. Sheridan, Trans.). New York: Pantheon. (Original work published 1963).

Foucault, M. (1977). *Discipline and punish: The birth of the prison* (A. S. Sheridan, Trans.). New York: Pantheon. (Original work published 1975).

Glynn, S. M., Randolph, E. T., Eth, S., Paz, G. G., Leong, G. B., Shaner, A. L., & Strachan, A. (1990). Patient psychopathology and expressed emotion in schizophrenia. *British Journal of Psychiatry, 157*, 877–880.

Goffman, E. (1961). *Asylums: Essays on the social situation of mental patients and other inmates.* Garden City, NY: Doubleday (Anchor).

Goodman, A. (1990). Addiction: Definition and implications. *British Journal of Addiction, 85*, 1403–1408.

Gorman, D. M. (1987). Measuring onset of 'caseness' in studies of stressful life events and alcohol abuse. *British Journal of Addiction, 82*, 1017–1020.

Gorman, D. M. (1992). Distinguishing primary and secondary disorders in studies of alcohol dependence and depression. *Drug and Alcohol Review, 11*, 23–29.

Gorman, D. M., & Brown, G. W. (1992). Recent developments in life event research and their relevance for the study of addictions. *British Journal of Addiction, 87*, 837–849.

Gove, W. (1970). Societal reaction as an explanation of mental illness: An evaluation. *American Sociological Review, 35*, 873–884.

Hakim, C. (1982). *Secondary analysis in social research: A guide to data sources and methods with examples.* Boston: George Allen & Unwin.

Harris, T. O., Brown, G. W., & Bifulco, A. T. (1990). Depression and situational helplessness/mastery in a sample selected to study childhood parental loss. *Journal of Affective Disorders, 20*, 27–41.

Hoffman, J. P. (1990). The historical shift in the perception of opiates: From medicine to social menace. *Journal of Psychoactive Drugs, 22*, 53–62.

Hogarty, G. E. (1985). Expressed emotion and schizophrenic relapse: Implications from the Pittsburgh study. In M. Alpert (Ed.), *Controversies in schizophrenia: Changes and constancies* (pp. 354–365). New York: Guilford Press.

Horwitz, A. V. (1979). Model, muddles, and mental illness labeling. *Journal of Health and Social Behavior, 20*, 296–300.

Hynes, E. (1975). Suicide and *homo duplex*: An interpretation of Durkheim's typology of suicide. *Sociological Quarterly, 16*, 87–104.

Jones, R. A. (1986). *Emile Durkheim: An introduction to four major works.* Beverly Hills, CA: Sage.

Lemert, E. M. (1967). *Human deviance, social problems and social control.* New York: Prentice-Hall.

Levine, H. G. (1978). The discovery of addiction: Changing conceptions of habitual drunkenness in America. *Journal of Studies on Alcohol, 39*, 143–174.

Levine, H. G. (1984). The alcohol problem in America: From temperance to alcoholism. *British Journal of Addiction, 79*, 109–119.

Link, B. G. (1982). Mental patient status, work, and income: An examination of the effects of a psychiatric label. *American Sociological Review, 47*, 202–215.

Link, B. G., & Cullen, F. T. (1986). Contact with the mentally ill and perceptions of how dangerous they are. *Journal of Health and Social Behavior, 27*, 289–303.

Link, B. G., Andrews, H., & Cullen, F. T. (1990, August). *Reconsidering the dangerousness of mental patients: Violent and illegal behavior of current and former patients compared to controls*. Paper presented at the Society for the Study of Social Problems Conference, Washington, DC.

Link, B. G., Cullen, F. T., Frank, J., & Wozniak, J. F. (1987). The social rejection of former mental patients: Understanding why labels matter. *American Journal of Sociology, 92*, 1461–1500.

Lukes, S. (1973). *Emile Durkheim: His life and work: A historical and critical study*. New York: Harper & Row.

Marsh, C. (1982). *The survey method: The contribution of surveys to sociological explanation*. Boston: George Allen & Unwin.

Mechanic, D. (1978). *Medical sociology* (2nd ed.). New York: Free Press.

Mechanic, D. (1989). *Mental health and social policy* (3rd ed.). Englewood Cliffs, NJ: Prentice-Hall.

Messner, S. F. (1988). Research on cultural and socioeconomic factors in criminal violence. *Psychiatric Clinics of North America, 11*, 511–525.

Miller, W. R., & Hester, R. K. (1989). Treating alcohol problems: Toward an informed eclecticism. In R. K. Hester & W. R. Miller (Eds.), *Handbook of alcoholism treatment approaches: Effective alternatives* (pp. 3–13). New York: Pergamon Press.

Nathan, P. (1991). Substance use disorders in the *DSM-IV*. *Journal of Abnormal Psychology, 100*, 356–361.

Palmstierna, T., Hiutfeldt, B., & Wistedt, B. (1991). The relationship of crowding and aggressive behavior on a psychiatric intensive care unit. *Hospital and Community Psychiatry, 42*, 1237–1240.

Peele, S. (1987). A moral vision of addiction: How people's values determine whether they become and remain addicts. *Journal of Drug Issues, 17*, 187–215.

Room, R. (1985). Dependence and society. *British Journal of Addiction, 80*, 133–139.

Rosehan, D. L. (1973). On being sane in insane places. *Science, 179*, 250–258.

Rosenbaum, M., (1990). Violence and the unstructured patient milieu. *Hospital and Community Psychiatry, 41*, 721.

Rutter, M., & Brown, G. W. (1966). The reliability and validity of measures of family life and relationships in families containing a psychiatric patient. *Social Psychiatry, 1*, 38–53.

Sampson, R. J. (1987). Urban black violence: The effect of male joblessness and family disruption. *American Journal of Sociology, 93*, 348–382.

Scheff, T. J. (1964). The societal reaction to deviance: Ascriptive elements in the psychiatric screening of mental patients in a midwestern state. *Social Problems, 11*, 401–413.

Scheff, T. J. (1966). *Being mentally ill: A sociological theory*. Chicago: Aldine.

Scheff, T. J. (1974). The labelling theory of mental illness. *American Sociological Review, 39*, 444–452.

Scheff, T. J., & Retzinger, S. M. (1991). *Emotions and violence: Shame and rage in destructive conflicts*. Lexington, MA: Lexington Books.

Segal, S. P. (1989). Civil commitment standards and patient mix in England/Wales, Italy, and the United States. *American Journal of Psychiatry, 146*, 187–193.

Shah, A. K., Fineberg, N. A., & James, D. V. (1991). Violence among psychiatric inpatients. *Acta Psychiatrica Scandinavica, 84*, 305–309.

Smoyak, S. A. (1991). Psychosocial nursing in public vs. private sectors: An introduction. *Journal of Psychosocial Nursing and Mental Health Services, 29*, 6–12.

Steadman, H. J. (1981). Critically reassessing the accuracy of public perceptions of the dangerousness of the mentally ill. *Journal of Health and Social Behavior, 22*, 310–316.

Straus, M. A. (1973). A general systems theory approach to a theory of violence between family members. *Social Science Information, 12*, 105–125.

Swanson, J. W., Holzer, C. E., Ganju, V. K., & Jono, R. T. (1990). Violence and psychiatric disorder in the community: Evidence from the Epidemiologic Catchment Area Surveys. *Hospital and Community Psychiatry, 41*, 761–770.

Tiryakian, E. A. (1979). Emile Durkheim. In T. Bottomore & R. Nisbet (Eds.), *A history of sociological analysis* (pp. 187–236). London: Heinemann.

Vaughn, C. E. (1989). Annotation: Expressed emotion in family relationships. *Journal of Child Psychology and Psychiatry, 30*, 13–22.

Volavka, J., & Krakowski, M. (1989). Schizophrenia and violence (editorial). *Psychological Medicine, 19*, 559–562.

Wing, J. K. (1978). *Reasoning about madness*. New York: Oxford University Press.

Wing, J. K. (1989). The concept of negative symptoms. *British Journal of Psychiatry, 155* (Suppl. 7), 10–14.

Wing, J. K., & Brown, G. W. (1970). *Institutionalism and schizophrenia: A comparative study of three mental hospitals, 1960–1968*. Cambridge: Cambridge University Press.

World Health Organization. (1990). *International classification of diseases and related health problems* (10th ed.). Geneva: Author.

CHAPTER 4

Social Psychological

Russell G. Geen

Social psychological approaches to aggression begin with the assumption that aggression is a reaction to situations. These situations involve the provocation of one person by another, followed by some act of retaliation. Other antecedents of aggression, whether genetic, temperamental, social or cultural in origin, are usually considered to act as moderators of situational effects but not to motivate aggression in and of themselves (Geen, 1990). This review is focused on several contemporary lines of theory and research on aggression as a response to provocations in interpersonal settings. Each proposes a set of intervening variables that mediate the connection between provocation and aggression, and several describe processes whereby aggressive behaviors are acquired and maintained. Of the latter, the most widely studied have been social learning theories.

SOCIAL LEARNING THEORIES OF AGGRESSION

Cognitive Social Learning Theory

The analysis of aggression in terms of social learning processes received its major impetus from work begun by Bandura in the early 1960s. The viewpoint that guided this research, which was based on constructs of learning and memory dominant at that time, came to be known as cognitive social learning theory (Bandura, 1973). Essentially, the theory described (1) processes by which aggressive behaviors are initially acquired, (2) the performance of aggressive acts after acquisition, and (3) the maintenance of learned aggression over time. In a well-known series of experiments, Bandura and his students (e.g., Bandura et al., 1963) showed that novel aggressive behaviors were acquired by children through simple observation of an adult model. Whether aggression acquired in this way was later enacted by the observer was found to depend on other conditions, such as incentives for aggressing (Bandura, 1965), the approval of supervising adults (Eisenberg,

RUSSELL G. GEEN • Department of Psychology, University of Missouri, Columbia, Missouri 65211.

Handbook of Aggressive and Destructive Behavior in Psychiatric Patients, edited by Michel Hersen, Robert T. Ammerman, and Lori A. Sisson. Plenum Press, New York, 1994.

1980), and social support from other children observing the aggressive model (Leyens, Herman, & Dunand, 1982).

According to cognitive social learning theory, aggression is maintained by reinforcement, which is a joint function of the expectancy of future outcomes and the value of those outcomes for the person. A person with a long history of attaining valuable ends through aggressing in certain situations comes to believe that continued aggression in the same settings will deliver worthwhile rewards. As a result, aggression will have a high degree of utility and will likely be repeated when appropriate situational cues are present (Kornadt, 1984). In addition, aggression, like any learned behavior, may generalize to other situations along a gradient of similarity.

The expectancy-value analysis of aggression has received some empirical support. Perry, Perry, and Rasmussen (1986) asked children to express their level of confidence that various types of outcomes would follow aggressive behavior. Children classified on the basis of peer ratings as highly aggressive were more confident than their less aggressive counterparts that aggression would produce tangible rewards and would also cause other people to stop behaving in aversive ways. High expectancies of desired outcomes following aggression were therefore shown to be related to levels of general aggressiveness.

In a subsequent study, Boldizar, Perry, and Perry (1989) found that peer-rated aggressiveness also predicted the values that children associated with the outcomes of aggression. Children rated as high in aggressiveness attached greater positive value than did less aggressive children to "control of the victim" resulting from aggression against the latter. In addition, highly aggressive children placed less negative value on such outcomes as the victim's suffering, threat of retaliation, rejection by peers, and negative feelings about themselves. In short, children who were highly aggressive saw more good outcomes arising from aggression, and fewer bad ones, than less aggressive children. Boldizar et al. (1989) also showed that girls differed from boys in the values they placed on the outcomes of aggression, being less likely than boys to value positive outcomes and more likely to reject negative outcomes.

Cognitive Scripting Theory

An alternative version of the social learning approach to aggression has been proposed by Huesmann (1988). This version incorporates concepts from contemporary theorizing on the encoding, storage, and retrieval of material in long-term memory. Huesmann (1988) attempts to answer a question raised by studies reviewed above; that is, how do children acquire and maintain high levels of aggressive behavior? His answer is that persistent aggressive behavior is to be understood in terms of the internal cognitive representations, or *schemata*, that people form of their environments. The person who, as a child, uses aggression as a means of settling interpersonal conflicts exposes himself or herself, by virtue of this behavior, to a large number of aggressive events, called *scenarios*. These scenarios are the units from which more complicated behavioral *scripts* are constructed. Scripts become encoded in memory, maintained through rehearsal, and retrieved as guides for behavior. In addition, subsequent aggressive experiences may lead the child to elaborate on available scripts and, as a result, develop more abstract and generalized aggressive strategies for dealing with conflicts. The outcome is a high probability that the child will retrieve an aggressive script when future conflicts arise and that aggressive behavior will be the consequence. The recall of an aggressive script is especially likely in situations that resemble the ones in which the scripted scenarios were acquired. Aggression, in turn, adds new aggressive scenarios to memory. In this way, aggression can become self-perpetuating in ongoing and ever-mounting cycles.

Huesmann's theoretical viewpoint is derived in large part from the conclusions of a 22-year longitudinal study. More than 800 children, whose modal age was 8 years at the time, comprised the original sample (Eron, Walder, & Lefkowitz, 1971). Follow-up studies were done with more than 400 of the original subjects after both 10 and 22 years. In each period of the study, the aggressiveness of each child was assessed through ratings by peers, parent and teacher interviews, and self-reports. Additional data concerning any criminal activity by the subjects in later years were obtained from the appropriate authorities. The findings of the entire project showed a statistically reliable general aggressiveness factor over the 22-year period. For both men and women, aggressiveness at age 8 was found to predict several antisocial and criminal behaviors at age 30 (Huesmann, Eron, Lefkowitz, & Walder, 1984).

Huesmann and his associates also found an interesting correlation between early aggressiveness and subsequent cognitive processing. Included in the data from the 22-year study were measures of I.Q. and intellectual functioning. An analysis of the relationships between these measures and those of aggressiveness showed that aggressiveness at age 8 was a better predictor of adult intellectual functioning than intellectual functioning at age 8 was a predictor of adult aggression (Huesmann, Eron, & Yarmel, 1987). In fact, early I.Q., while being related to aggressiveness at age 8, was not a reliable correlate of aggression at later ages. As a result of these findings, Huesmann (1988) formulated a dual-process model of aggressiveness and intellectual activity.

The first of the two processes operates early in the life of the child and explains the positive relationship between aggressiveness and intellectual functioning at age 8. Poor intellectual processing may produce aggression by causing frustration in normal problem-solving settings such as those encountered by children at school. Several consequences may follow. The child may react to the frustration with aggression. Because of his or her intellectual deficit, the child is relatively unable to understand the inappropriateness of aggression or to formulate alternative reactions. At the same time, the child's aggressive behavior brings about a low rate of reinforcement for nonaggressive responses. The child therefore encodes mainly aggressive strategies for frustrating situations.

Matters do not end there. Once an aggressive strategy has been encoded, it tends to persist and to exert a reciprocating effect on intellectual processes. By hindering good relationships between the child and both teachers and peers, aggressive behavior interferes with the child's chances for intellectual opportunities and advancement. The child therefore continues to do poorly in school, the low level of intellectual functioning is maintained, and the cycle is repeated. Whereas poor intellectual functioning led originally to aggression, aggression now becomes the source of continued intellectual deficits. This explains the correlation between aggressiveness at age 8 and intellectual functioning later in life.

Huesmann also predicts a relationship between aggressive fantasy behavior and overt aggression. In the cognitive approach to behavior, fantasizing is regarded as a type of script rehearsal. Every time an idea is mulled over in fantasy, it is rehearsed and possibly elaborated. Because rehearsal maintains the strength of a script in memory, children who fantasize about violence a great deal should be more likely to retrieve aggressive scripts than those who fantasize less about violence. They should, therefore, be more likely to show general aggressiveness than infrequent fantasizers. In a 3-year longitudinal study of primary school children, Huesmann and Eron (1984) found, as expected, that children who frequently fantasized about aggression were rated by their peers as being more aggressive than children who fantasized less. Aggressive fantasizing also has been shown to be correlated with the extent to which children identify with aggressive heroic television figures (Fenigstein, 1979; Huesmann & Eron, 1986). One reason that television violence is often associated with aggressive behavior (Geen & Thomas, 1986) may be that fantasy behavior and identification with aggressive characters elicited by television cause the rehearsal and strengthening of aggressive scripts in memory. Thus strengthened, they become more likely to be retrieved and to guide behavior.

Cognitive Neo-Associationism

Negative Affect and Aggression

Another theory of cognitive mediation in aggression is Berkowitz's (1988) theory of cognitive neo-associationism. The underlying basis for this theory is found in the concept of associative networks in memory. The starting point in the theory is that a person's immediate response to provocation is the experience of negative affect (Berkowitz, 1989). Following the suggestion of certain cognitive theorists (e.g., Bower, 1981), Berkowitz considers negative affective states to be encoded in hypothetical nodes in memory. Linked to affect in these nodes are related thoughts, emotions, and expressive motor patterns. Activation of an affective condition in turn activates these other processes along directional pathways. The immediate reaction to aversive stimulation is therefore a complex of emotions and thoughts related to aggression along with what may appear to be reflexive aggressive behaviors.

The theory predicts that any stimulus can elicit aggression if it generates enough negative affect. In an experiment illustrating this point, Berkowitz, Cochran, and Embree (1981) found that immersion of a subject's hand in ice water was followed by increased aggression toward a bystander who was in no way responsible for the subject's discomfort. If negative affect is the immediate antecedent to reactive aggression, then this may explain the reported links between aggression and certain conditions of the environment such as noise (Geen, 1978), air pollution (Zillmann, Baron, & Tamborini, 1981), and high temperatures (Anderson, 1989). Another matter to consider is that the cognitive neo-associationist theory does not make aggression absolutely dependent on higher cognitive functioning. Activities such as appraisals of the situation, attributions of cause, and judgments of the appropriateness of aggression to the situation have all been shown to play important roles in aggressive behavior (Ferguson & Rule, 1983). While accepting this as true, Berkowitz argues that cognitive processes may come into play only after the initial affect-driven reaction. In the immediate aftermath of an aversive stimulus, aggression is not mediated by cognition (Berkowitz & Heimer, 1989).

The theory of cognitive neo-associationism also separates the emotion of anger from any necessary connection with aggression. Anger is an emotion elicited by negative affect in the same way, and presumably at the same time, as expressive motor behavior. It is, therefore, not an intervening variable that mediates the relationship of provocation to aggression but instead a parallel process going on at the same time as aggression. By defining anger in this way, Berkowitz has broken with the long tradition of neo-Hullian theory, in which emotions were defined as intervening variables in behavior. One example of this thinking is found in the original frustration–aggression hypothesis (Dollard, Doob, Miller, Mowrer, & Sears, 1939).

Cognitive Priming

Consistent with the theories of semantic memory from which it was derived, the concept of cognitive priming (Collins & Loftus, 1975) is also included in Berkowitz's approach to aggression. Aggressive thoughts may be elicited by stimuli that are not themselves causes of negative affect. Such thoughts may *prime* a network of association; that is, they may increase its accessibility to retrieval, so that when an aversive event is subsequently experienced, the activation of negative affect and aggressive behavior patterns is facilitated. Berkowitz (1984) has proposed that stimuli associated with violence, such as those commonly observed in movies and on television, have such a priming function. In an experiment designed to test this possibility, Bushman and Geen (1990) found that subjects who had been shown brief videotapes of violent action from motion pictures later listed a greater number of aggressive themes among their thoughts than subjects who had been shown a nonviolent scene.

A priming process may also influence the judgments of hostility that people make of one another. For example, Srull and Wyer (1979) found that when subjects had to rate the hostility in another person's ambiguous behavior, the ratings were higher if they were made after the subjects performed a sentence completion task in which hostile material had been made salient. Presumably, the hostile material in the task primed thoughts of hostility in subsequent judgments. An even more subtle illustration of this effect is found in a study by Wann and Branscombe (1990). These authors showed that judgments of a target person's hostility were higher following a task in which the names of violent sporting activities (e.g., boxing, hockey) were prominent than after a task containing the names of nonviolent sports (e.g., billiards, golf).

Evidence from an experiment by Rule, Taylor, and Dobbs (1987) indicates that a cognitive priming effect may also be involved in the relationship between aversive environmental conditions and aggression. Rule and her associates found that high temperature increases the probability that subjects will have aggressive thoughts when aggression-related stimuli are presented. Subjects provided endings for story stems while working in either hot (33° C) or cool (21° C) surroundings. Some of the story stems had the potential for aggressive endings, whereas others did not. When aggression-related stems were given, a higher proportion of subjects' endings were aggressive under hot conditions than under cool conditions. No effects of temperature on story endings were found when neutral stems were used. Rule and her colleagues interpreted these findings as meaning that heat primes aggressive thoughts by producing negative affect. They also proposed that a person who is primed to think aggressively may be more likely to aggress when provoked than one who has not been so primed. This prediction is consistent with the theory proposed by Berkowitz.

Interpretation of the Situation

In both theories discussed in the previous sections, cognition plays an important role in aggression through such processes as schema formation, script retrieval, and associative priming. Another line of social psychological research also places cognition in a central position by exploring the judgmental and attributional processes that precede the experience of anger and retaliatory motivation. In the two major approaches of this type, which are reviewed below, the major emphasis is on how people interpret attacks and provocations, and whether these interpretations generate anger.

Cognition and Arousal

One of the two approaches is that of Zillmann and his colleagues (Zillmann, 1979). In broad outline, this approach to aggression begins with the assumption that aggression is motivated by anger. It then goes on to describe ways in which states of anger are generated from an underlying physiological arousal. Central to Zillmann's reasoning is the principle that the immediate stimulus for aggression is recognition of endangerment (Zillmann, 1988). Perceived danger elicits both increased autonomic activation and behavioral tendencies to flee or to fight. Zillmann (1988) agrees with Berkowitz (1989) that endangering stimuli, such as attacks, can elicit aggression as an immediate and reflexlike response. Zillmann's major emphasis, however, is on those cognitive elaborations which Berkowitz considers to come after the initial reaction.

As has already been noted, for Zillmann, these cognitive elaborations consist mainly of processes involved in the generation of anger. If the victim of an attack thinks that the assault was animated by malice, anger is more likely than if a more benign appraisal is made. Given the motivating effect of anger on aggression, retaliation is likewise more probable after an attribution of malicious intent than in the absence of such an attribution. Cognitive judgments can also attenuate the magnitude of arousal in response to an attack. Zillmann and Cantor (1976) found that when information that mitigated the seriousness of an insult was given to the target person before an insult, arousal was less than when no mitigating information was given. In addition, subjects who received the mitigating information after an insult showed a decrease in arousal, but were nevertheless more aroused than those who had been given the information beforehand.

Zillmann's research on the joint functioning of cognition and arousal also has shown that anger can be exacerbated through the mislabeling of arousal arising from some irrelevant source. This process, called *excitation transfer*, occurs when some event arouses the person in close proximity to a provocation. Under certain conditions, some part of the arousal elicited by the irrelevant event becomes labeled as anger through a misattribution process. In advancing this argument, Zillmann assumes that emotion is a joint product of physiological arousal and an available cognition by which the arousal is labeled and understood. It should be noted that certain precise conditions must prevail before excitation transfer will occur (Geen, 1990; Reisenzein, 1983).

The overriding purpose of Zillmann's work has been to determine how cognition and arousal relate to each other in the generation of aggressive behavior. It is clear from what has been reviewed here that cognitive processes (1) influence the intensity of arousal following provocation, and (2) shape the emotional consequences of that arousal. In addition, arousal may have a reciprocating effect on cognition. Zillmann (1979) has proposed that the sort of attributional processing discussed here takes place only when the person is moderately aroused. Basing his argument on the Yerkes–Dodson Law (the principle that performance is related to activation by an inverted-U function), Zillmann concludes that high levels of excitation interfere with the cognitive control of behavior. Thus, when the person is highly aroused, the provision of mitigating information about a provocation is less likely to be attended to and/or processed than when the person is moderately aroused. As a result, it will also be less likely to reduce hostility and the desire to retaliate (Zillmann, Bryant, Cantor, & Day, 1975).

Cognitive Attribution

A detailed analysis of the processes that underlie anger and retaliatory motives has been made by Ferguson and Rule (1983), who base their attributional approach on the answers to three questions that a person asks after having been harmed by someone:

1. *What was the act of harmdoing?* The answer to this question involves examination of the intent of the actor and whether the actor could foresee the harmful consequences of the act.

2. *What ought to have been done in this situation?* The answer to this question is based on consideration of what is normative in the situation and what values are held by persons, including the victim of the harm, who observe the act.

3. *Does any discrepancy exist between what was done and what ought to have been done?* In other words, was the act of harmdoing contrary to accepted normative behavior?

Depending on one's answers to these questions the victim of harm will either hold the actor culpable or absolve that person of blame. Anger will be experienced to the extent that the other person is held responsible for harm that has been done. Aggression is assumed to be a direct outgrowth of anger.

The first judgment that the victim of aggression makes is whether the other person acted intentionally and whether the harm was anticipated. If the harm is judged to have been intentional, it is further classified as either malevolent or not malevolent in purpose. If the act of harm is judged to be unintentional, a further determination is made as to whether the harmdoer could foresee the consequences of the act. Thus, the act of harmdoing may be one of four types: (1) intentional and malevolent, (2) intentional but not malevolent, (3) not intended but foreseeable, and (4) unintentional and unforeseeable. The last of the four types is truly accidental. Three separate attributions must therefore be made before an act of harmdoing can be located within a meaningful space: intent, motive, and foreseeability.

Intent. Judgments of intentionality are made along two general lines. One has to do with the nature of the situation and the other with the character of the harmdoer. In the first case, a judgment is made as to whether the harmdoing was the only act possible, whether any reasons for it (other than the infliction of harm) could be imagined, and whether the consequences of the act for the actor were mainly detrimental or beneficial. In addition, intent may be inferred from judgments about whether the actor enjoyed the harmdoing or not (Nelson, 1980) and from the amount of effort expended by the transgressor in carrying out the act (Joseph, Kane, Gaes, & Tedeschi, 1976). Planning the harmdoing carefully represents a significant expenditure of effort, a principle seen in the consideration by the legal system of premeditation as a criterion for first-degree murder. The second type of appraisal that leads to a judgment of intentionality has to do with characteristics of the harmdoer. If this person is known to have done harm in the past, any subsequent harmful acts should more likely be judged intentional than if the person has no such reputation. In addition, stereotypes based on race, class, sex, and physical attractiveness also enter into judgments of the intent behind harmdoing (Duncan, 1976).

Motive. Once a judgment of intentionality has been made, the victim must decide whether the intent was malicious. Harmful behavior that is regarded as instrumental to the attainment of other ends is generally regarded as less malevolent than harmdoing for its own sake (Rule, 1978). If the harmdoing serves some prosocial purpose, it also tends to be regarded as nonmalevolent. Finally, harmdoing that is seen as retaliation for a prior provocation tends to be judged as less malevolent than harm inflicted without any apparent desire for retribution (Harvey & Rule, 1978).

Foreseeability. An act of harmdoing need not be intentional to be regarded as blameworthy. Ferguson and Rule (1983) point out that sometimes the failure to avoid doing unintended harm that can be foreseen is a cause for assigning moral culpability to the actor.

Foreseeability can be of two types. One is negligence on the actor's part. If the actor knows that something he or she is about to do to another person will cause unintended harm but is either too lazy or too indifferent to seek an alternative course of action, negligent foreseeability is attributed to that person. The other type of foreseeability is the result of ruthlessness on the part of the actor who makes no attempt to prevent unintended harm from coming to the victim because some other selfish purpose is served by the action.

DEINDIVIDUATION AND AGGRESSION

One of social psychology's oldest problems is that of collective violence. It is usually framed as a question: Why do people often behave more aggressively when they are in a crowd than they normally would as individuals? Psychologists have tended to give reductionist answers to this question by attempting to account for collective violence in terms of changes in the dynamics of individual members of the crowd. In recent years this approach to the problem has produced the concept of *deindividuation*, a process by which individuals lose their sense of self-awareness in group settings.

Deindividuation has been associated with aggressive behavior in two ways. In his pioneering work on the concept, Zimbardo (1969) proposed that aggression may be a result of loss of individual identity. According to Zimbardo, such an identity loss releases inhibitions against expressing behavior that would otherwise be suppressed because of fear of social disapproval. The immediate effects of deindividuation are twofold: the person experiences a reduction in self-evaluation (i.e., he or she becomes less introspective and critical of the self), and a reduced sense of concern over being evaluated by others. From these two immediate effects comes a weakening of behavioral inhibition through such normal controls as fear, guilt, shame, and anxiety. Once these normal inhibitory controls have been weakened, the individual is more prone to express any behavior that has hitherto been suppressed because of those controls.

An alternative to Zimbardo's theory of deindividuation stresses the influences of social settings on the person's sense of self-awareness. Diener (1980) placed less emphasis on anonymity as an antecedent of aggression than Zimbardo. Instead, Diener proposed that group settings draw the person's attention away from the self and toward external stimuli. This shift in attention is accompanied by a lowering in importance of internalized personal and social standards as guides for behavior, and the person becomes controlled by cues in the immediate situation. If the situation provides cues for aggressive behavior, the deindividuated person will react to them more than to internal standards of right and wrong.

A similar approach has been taken by Prentice-Dunn and Rogers (1983), who stipulate that any conditions that promote reduced self-awareness are by definition causes of deindividuation. These authors also realize that self-awareness has both a public and a private aspect and that each aspect is elicited by specific situations. Public self-awareness is consciousness of oneself as an object of the attention of others. The person who is in this state is sensitive to social evaluation and personal accountability. In any situation in which personal accountability is seen as weak, a person will feel less publicly self-aware.

Private self-awareness is associated with a consciousness of one's own inner values, standards, thoughts, and feelings. Any turning of attention away from the self is followed by reduced private self-awareness. Conditions for deindividuation cause this type of change in attentional focus and hence lead to behavior that is controlled less by internal standards than by salient stimuli in the environment. The person who becomes deindividuated is therefore less likely to restrain aggressive behavior on the basis of personal or social values.

The approaches to deindividuation and aggression taken by Zimbardo and by Prentice-Dunn and Rogers differ from each other in their explanations of the locus of origin of the aggressive act. Zimbardo assumes that aggression is motivated by causes outside the immediate situation, and that deindividuation merely releases these behaviors. Prentice-Dunn and Rogers propose that aggression originates in situational stimuli. These stimuli gain control over behavior to the extent that public and private self-awareness have been weakened. None of the research carried out to date permits a comparison of the two theories. However, it should be noted that the theory linking deindividuation to lack of self-awareness is consistent with a body of literature showing that conditions that *enhance* self-awareness bring about an increased conformity of aggressive behavior to personal and social standards, which can be thought of as the opposite of deindividuation (e.g., Carver, 1975; Scheier, Fenigstein, & Buss, 1974).

SOCIAL INSTRUMENTAL THEORIES OF AGGRESSION

The theories and research that have been reviewed so far have addressed the ways in which situational conditions lead to affective and retaliatory aggression. In addition, aggression is assumed in most of this work to be a pathological behavior occurring in response to strong situational provocations (e.g., Huesmann, 1988). Moreover, even though aggression is behavior carried out in an interpersonal setting, the emphasis of most social psychologists is on the acts of individuals.

Another social psychological approach to aggression is characterized by a different set of assumptions. The first assumption is that aggression is not pathological, but a normal element in human interaction. The second is that aggression is instrumental behavior that is always carried out for some purpose. The third is that aggression is a reaction to the violation of norms or expectancies that people share and by which they define the terms of social interaction. The fourth is that aggression is not only the act of one person toward another, but also a condition for the response of the latter to the former. Aggression is, in other words, a normal product of dyadic interaction.

Aggression as Instrumental Behavior

Coercive Social Power

A radical alternative to most contemporary psychological theories of aggression has been proposed by Tedeschi, Smith, and Brown (1974), who define aggressive behavior not as harmdoing but as an attempt at social influence. The reason that people attack or threaten to attack others is to establish a basis for exerting coercive power. Tedeschi and his colleagues advocate abolishing the word *aggression* from the language of psychology on the grounds that it is value-judgmental and does not adequately explain behavior. By defining acts usually called aggressive as assertions of social power, they make these acts a part of normal interaction and "the mere extension of other means of gaining compliance" (Tedeschi et al., 1974, p. 550). According to this theory, coercive power is used under certain conditions, such as when there is severe interpersonal conflict and one person clearly has greater power than the other, when other means are not likely to succeed, and when intense time pressures to reach a goal are present.

Impression Management

The term *impression management* refers to behavior carried out by a person to establish a desired identity in the eyes of others. Felson (1984) has applied the concept to retaliatory aggression by proposing that when a person is attacked or insulted, he or she takes on a negative identity, or, in more common terminology, is made to look bad. To restore a good self-impression, the attacked person may retaliate and thereby look like a strong counterattacker rather than a weak victim. Thus, loss of a negative identity and creation of a positive one constitute the instrumental basis for aggression. The need to create an impression through aggressing should be strongest when third parties are witnesses to the interaction because these parties constitute an audience on whom an impression is made. In support of this idea, Felson (1982) has reported that retaliatory aggression among insulted persons is intensified by the presence of a third party.

Restoration of Self-Esteem

A position similar to Felson's has been taken by DaGloria (1984), who regards aggression as one of many responses that a person may make to loss of self-esteem. The specific response that a person makes depends on the nature of the situation:

> Social actors react to events which imply a reduction in their sense of worth by performing acts which, under the conditions at hand, will restore their self-evaluation. This proposition applies to aggressive behavior, as far as this appears to the individual as a mean of asserting his worth. (DaGloria, 1984, p. 132)

If, for example, a person is frustrated in pursuit of a goal by the deliberate blocking actions of another, aggression against the frustrator may be the best means of restoring lost self-esteem. If frustration is accidental, however, some other action may be more likely to raise self-esteem, such as renewed effort to reach the goal. No necessary connection exists between frustration, or any other provocation, and aggression. Whether aggression occurs depends upon its functional utility in the situation.

Aggression and Violation of Norms

Earlier it was noted that people make complex attributional judgments in deciding whether a provocation is maliciously intended. Such judgments presuppose an ideal standard to which one can compare the actions of the provocateur. What is the source of this ideal? To answer this question one must remember that interpersonal aggression takes place in an interactive setting involving two people. Aggression is not an isolated act in most cases. It arises in the context of an ongoing relationship. Each party to the relationship has a perspective on the situation, including a set of expectancies regarding the proper behavior of the two people involved. A set of shared norms exists for behavior in that setting. Concepts like "attack," "malice," and "aggression" must be defined with reference to those norms.

This approach to aggression has been elaborated by DaGloria and DeRidder (1977, 1979), who discuss aggression as one possible outcome in a situation in which both parties strive for a goal that each attempts to prevent the other from reaching. In the course of this process, each party must deliver some level of aversive stimulation to the other. The norm that is implicit in such a setting is that participants will deliver such stimulation only in the amount necessary to attain their goals. Should a participant exceed that normative level, his or her behavior will be judged by the other to be excessive and motivated by an intent to hurt. It will, in other words, be regarded as a malicious attack.

In two studies, DaGloria and DeRidder (1977, 1979) found evidence supporting this line of reasoning. In each study, two subjects responded alternately to a series of signals with a motor response. Each subject tried to disrupt the other's commission of the response by giving an electric shock precisely at the time the other person responded. The shock could be delivered at one of three levels of intensity. Both subjects were told that shocks at either the highest or the intermediate level would be sufficient to disrupt the other person's reactions 100% of the time. The experimenter then manipulated the proceedings so that the subject received shocks at either the intermediate or the maximum level. When given a chance to retaliate, subjects gave stronger shocks after having received maximum shocks than after receiving shocks of intermediate intensity. Recognizing that shocks at the maximum level were unnecessary, the subjects interpreted these as indicators of malice worthy of retaliation. Along these same lines, DeRidder (1985) has shown that people who observe others engaged in interpersonal attacks take the normative nature of the attacks into account when judging their malevolency. DeRidder found that harmful attacks are labeled as being more aggressive and malicious than nonharmful ones only when the attack is regarded as a violation of what is normative for that situation.

A study by Ohbuchi (1982) also may be taken as evidence that normative judgments enter into perceptions of malice in others. Ohbuchi found that when one subject attacked another with electric shocks of widely varying intensity, retaliation by the victim was greater than it was when the range of shock intensities was narrow, even though the average intensity level was the same in the two conditions. Giving shocks of widely variable intensity may remind the victim that some of the shocks seem excessive in contrast with others.

To summarize the main findings reported in this section, malicious intent is attributed to an attacker by the victim when the level of aversiveness of the attack is considered excessive, given the norms governing behavior in that situation. This judgment justifies retaliation. There is also some evidence that the victim of an attack considers the attack more inappropriate to the situation than the attacker. Mummendey, Linneweber, and Loschper (1984) showed not only that the attacker is less likely than the victim to regard his or her acts as aggressive and inappropriate, but that the two persons reverse their perspectives when, at a later time, the roles are reversed and the former victim is given a chance to retaliate. The authors concluded that "irrespective of the position in an aggressive interaction sequence, one's own behaviour is evaluated as more appropriate and less aggressive than [another's] behaviour" (Mummendey et al, 1984, p. 307). Such an egocentric judgment by the attacker may reinforce aggressive tendencies in any situation that allows bilateral opportunities for attack. People can always conclude that norms have been violated when they are attacked, but that the same behavior is justified when they are the ones committing it.

SUMMARY

The social psychological theories reviewed in this chapter assume that aggression is a reaction to situational provocations. In part, it may be an immediate reflexlike response elicited by thoughts, emotions, and expressive motor patterns associated with negative affect and primed by related stimuli, but subsequently, aggression also involves higher cognitive activity. At this later stage, aggression is guided by cognitive scripts stored in memory as a result of past experiences with aggression and/or the observation of violence. Considerable processing of information about the situation, whereby the person interprets and understands the nature of the provocation, goes into the activation of aggressive scripts. In part this consists of judgments that social norms have been violated by the provocateur. This same processing simultaneously influences the arousal level of the person following provocation, and by this means plays a role in the generation of anger. The entire process is also probably enhanced by conditions that increase the person's sense of self-awareness. When the person is not self-aware, behavior may be more under the control of situational demands than of personal standards. Aggression may also serve an instrumental function as a normal part of human interaction, by furthering the ends of coercive social power and the restitution of status and self-esteem threatened by the provocation.

REFERENCES

Anderson, C. A. (1989). Temperature and aggression: The ubiquitous effects of heat on the occurrence of human violence. *Psychological Bulletin, 106,* 74–96.

Bandura, A. (1965). Influence of models' reinforcement contingencies on the acquisition of imitative responses. *Journal of Personality and Social Psychology, 1,* 589–595.

Bandura, A. (1973). *Aggression: A social learning analysis.* Englewood Cliffs, NJ: Prentice-Hall.

Bandura, A., Ross, D., & Ross, S. A. (1963). Imitation of film-mediated aggressive models. *Journal of Abnormal and Social Psychology, 66,* 3–11.

Berkowitz, L. (1984). Some effects of thoughts on anti- and prosocial influences of media events: A cognitive neoassociationist analysis. *Psychological Bulletin, 95,* 410–427.

Berkowitz, L. (1988). Frustrations, appraisals, and aversively stimulated aggression. *Aggressive Behavior, 14,* 3–11.

Berkowitz, L. (1989). The frustration–aggression hypothesis: An examination and reformulation. *Psychological Bulletin, 106,* 59–73.

Berkowitz, L., & Heimer, K. (1989). On the construction of the anger experience: Aversive events and negative priming in the formation of feelings. In L. Berkowitz (Ed.), *Advances in experimental social psychology,* Vol. 22, pp. 1–37). New York: Academic Press.

Berkowitz, L., Cochran, S., & Embree, M. (1981). Physical pain and the goal of aversively stimulated aggression. *Journal of Personality and Social Psychology, 40,* 687–700.

Boldizar, J. P., Perry, D. G., & Perry, L. C. (1989). Outcome values and aggression. *Child Development, 60,* 571–579.

Bower, G. (1981). Mood and memory. *American Psychologist, 36,* 129–148.

Bushman, B. J., & Green, R. G. (1990). Role of cognitive-emotional mediators and individual differences in the effects of media violence on aggression. *Journal of Personality and Social Psychology, 40,* 687–700.

Carver, C. S. (1975). Physical aggression as a function of objective self-awareness and attitudes toward punishment. *Journal of Experimental Social Psychology, 11,* 510–519.

Collins, A., & Loftus, E. (1975). A spreading-activation theory of semantic memory. *Psychological Review, 82,* 407–428.

DaGloria, J. (1984). Frustration, aggression, and the sense of justice. In A. Mummendey (Ed.), *Social psychology of aggression: From individual behavior to social interaction* (pp. 127–141). New York: Springer-Verlag.

DaGloria, J., & DeRidder, R. (1977). Aggression in dyadic interaction. *European Journal of Social Psychology, 7,* 189–219.

DaGloria, J., & DeRidder, R. (1979). Sex differences in aggression: Are current notions misleading? *European Journal of Social Psychology, 9,* 49–66.

DeRidder, R. (1985). Normative considerations in the labelling of harmful behavior as aggressive. *Journal of Social Psychology, 125,* 659–666.

Diener, E. (1980). Deindividuation: The absence of self-awareness and self-regulation in group members. In P. Paulus (Ed.), *The psychology of group influence* (pp. 209–242). Hillsdale, NJ: Erlbaum.

Dollard, J., Doob, L. W., Miller, N. E., Mowrer, O. H., & Sears, R. R. (1939). *Frustration and aggression.* New Haven: Yale University Press.

Duncan, B. L. (1976). Differential social perception and attribution of intergroup violence: Testing the lower limits of stereotyping in blacks. *Journal of Personality and Social Psychology, 34,* 590–598.

Eisenberg, G. J. (1980). Children and aggression after observed film aggression with sanctioning adults. *Annals of the New York Academy of Science, 347,* 304–318.

Eron, L D., Walder, L. O., & Lefkowitz, M. M. (1971). *Learning of aggression in children.* Boston: Little, Brown.

Felson, R. B. (1982). Impression management and the escalation of aggression and violence. *Social Psychology Quarterly, 45,* 245–254.

Felson, R. B. (1984). Patterns of aggressive social interaction. In A. Mummendey (Ed.), *Social psychology of aggression: From individual behavior to social interaction* (pp. 107–126). New York: Springer-Verlag.

Fenigstein, A. (1979). Does aggression cause a preference for viewing media violence? *Journal of Personality and Social Psychology, 37,* 2307–2317.

Ferguson, T. J., & Rule, B. G. (1983). An attributional perspective on anger and aggression. In R. G. Geen & E. Donnerstein (Eds.), *Aggression: Theoretical and empirical reviews* (Vol. 1: *Theoretical and methodological issues,* pp. 41–74). New York: Academic Press.

Geen, R. G. (1978). Effects of attack and uncontrollable noise on aggression. *Journal of Research in Personality, 12,* 15–29.

Geen, R. G. (1990). *Human aggression.* Pacific Grove, CA: Brooks-Cole.

Geen, R. G., & Thomas, S. L. (1986). The immediate effects of media violence on behavior. *Journal of Social Issues, 42,* 7–27.

Harvey, M. D., & Rule, B. G. (1978). Moral evaluations and judgments of responsibility. *Personality and Social Psychology Bulletin, 4,* 583–588.

Huesmann, L. R. (1988). An information processing model for the development of aggression. *Aggressive Behavior, 14,* 13–24.

Huesmann, L. R., & Eron, L. D. (1984). Cognitive processes and the persistence of aggressive behavior. *Aggressive Behavior, 10,* 243–251.

Huesmann, L. R., & Eron, L. D. (Eds.). (1986). *Television and the aggressive child: A cross-national comparison.* Hillsdale, NJ: Erlbaum.

Huesmann, L. R., Eron, L. D., Lefkowitz, M. M., & Walder, L. O. (1984). Stability of aggression over time and generations. *Developmental Psychology, 20,* 1120–1134.

Huesmann, L. R., Eron, L. D., & Yarmel, P. W. (1987). Intellectual functioning and aggression. *Journal of Personality and Social Psychology, 52,* 232–240.

Joseph, J. M., Kane, T. R., Gaes, G. G., & Tedeschi, J. T. (1976). Effects of effort on attributed intent and perceived aggressiveness. *Perceptual and Motor Skills, 42,* 706.

Kornadt, H. J. (1984). Development of aggressiveness: A motivation theory perspective. In R. M. Kaplan, V. J. Konecni, & R. W. Novaco (Eds.), *Aggression in children and youth* (pp. 73–87). The Hague: Nijhoff.

Leyens, J. P., Herman, G., & Dunand, M. (1982). The influence of an audience upon the reactions to filmed violence. *European Journal of Social Psychology, 12,* 131–142.

Mummendey, A., Linneweber, V., & Loschper, G. (1984) Actor or victim of aggression: Divergent perspectives— divergent evaluations. *European Journal of Social Psychology, 14,* 297–311.

Nelson, S. A. (1980). Factors influencing young children's use of motives and outcomes as moral criteria. *Child Development, 51,* 823–829.

Ohbuchi, K. (1982). On the cognitive integration mediating reactions to attack patterns. *Social Psychology Quarterly, 45,* 213–218.

Perry, D. G., Perry, L. C., & Rasmussen, P. (1986). Cognitive social learning mediators of aggression. *Child Development, 57,* 700–711.

Prentice-Dunn, S., & Rogers, R. W. (1983). Deindividuation in aggression. In R. G. Geen & E. Donnerstein (Eds.), *Aggression: Theoretical and empirical reviews* (Vol. 2: *Issues in research,* pp. 155–171). New York: Academic Press.

Reisenzein, R. (1983). The Schachter theory of emotion: Two decades later. *Psychological Bulletin, 94,* 239–264.

Rule, B. G. (1978). The hostile and instrumental functions of human aggression. In W. W. Hartup & J. DeWit (Eds.), *Origins of aggression* (pp. 121–141). The Hague: Mouton.

Rule, B. G., Taylor, B. R., & Dobbs, A. R. (1987). Priming effects of heat on aggressive thoughts. *Social Cognition, 5,* 131–143.

Scheier, M. F., Fenigstein, A., & Buss, A. H. (1974). Self-awareness and physical aggression. *Journal of Experimental Social Psychology, 10,* 264–273.

Srull, T. K., & Wyer, R. S. (1979). The role of category accessibility in the interpretation of information about persons: Some determinants and implications. *Journal of Personality and Social Psychology, 37,* 1660–1672.

Tedeschi, J. T., Smith, R. B., & Brown, R. C. (1974). A reinterpretation of research on aggression. *Psychological Bulletin, 81,* 540–562.

Wann, D. L., & Branscombe, N. R. (1990). Person perception when aggressive or nonaggressive sports are primed. *Aggressive Behavior, 16,* 27–32.

Zillmann, D. (1979). *Hostility and aggression.* Hillsdale, NJ: Erlbaum.

Zillmann, D. (1988). Cognition-excitation interdependencies in aggressive behavior. *Aggressive Behavior, 14,* 51–64.

Zillmann, D., & Cantor, J. R. (1976). Effect of timing of information about mitigating circumstances on emotional responses to provocation and retaliatory behavior. *Journal of Experimental Social Psychology, 12,* 38–55.

Zillmann, D., Baron, R. A., & Tamborini, R. (1981). Social costs of smoking: Effects of tobacco smoke on hostile behavior. *Journal of Applied Social Psychology, 11,* 548–561.

Zillmann, D., Bryant, J., Cantor, J. R., & Day, K. D. (1975). Irrelevance of mitigating circumstances in retaliatory behavior at high levels of excitation. *Journal of Research in Personality, 9,* 282–293.

Zimbardo, P. G. (1969). The human choice: Individuation, reason, and order versus deindividuation, impulse and chaos. In W. J. Arnold & D. Levine (Eds.), *Nebraska symposium on motivation* (pp. 237–307). Lincoln, NE: University of Nebraska Press.

CHAPTER 5

Psychoanalytic

HOWARD D. LERNER AND JOSHUA EHRLICH

INTRODUCTION

In approaching the topic of aggression in psychiatric patients from the perspective of psychoanalysis, it is important to recognize that contemporary psychoanalysis is not a unified theory. As the original Freudian theory has been modified and expanded, it has gradually developed into several distinctive approaches within psychoanalysis. Though overlapping, each provides coherent and distinct approaches to human development, psychopathology, and treatment. Most prominent among these are modern structural theory (most closely connected with Freud's drive theory), self psychology (associated with the theories of Heinz Kohut), and object relations theory.

In regard to aggression, a basic disagreement exists, for instance, between structural theorists, who tend to see aggression as an innate drive, and self psychologists, who tend to view aggression as secondary to narcissistic injury. Despite such differences, psychoanalytic theorists share certain basic agreements: aggression plays a crucial role in the infant–parent and child–parent dyads, the successful modulation of aggression is critical to healthy development, and managing aggression successfully is critical to the therapeutic endeavor. In addition, psychoanalytic theorists concur in their understanding that difficulties in modulating or integrating aggression are critical to psychopathology—on a continuum from its milder to its more severe forms.

In this chapter, we offer a brief review of Freud's approach to aggression and detail some of its problems and recent modifications. We then explore aggression using Kernberg's notion of personality organization. A prominent contemporary theorist who has addressed severe psychopathology at length, Kernberg uses a conceptual framework that integrates both drive theory and object relations theory. Thus, in our opinion, he offers the most representative, coherent approach to aggression and its role in psychopathology within contemporary psychoanalysis. We hope that by offering both a rich conceptual

HOWARD D. LERNER and JOSHUA EHRLICH • Department of Psychiatry, University of Michigan, Ann Arbor, Michigan 48104.

Handbook of Aggressive and Destructive Behavior in Psychiatric Patients, edited by Michel Hersen, Robert T. Ammerman, and Lori A. Sisson. Plenum Press, New York, 1994.

framework and extensive case material we can capture the unique perspective on aggression that psychoanalysis offers. We conclude with a brief overview of psychoanalytic approaches to treatment.

THE CONCEPT OF AGGRESSION IN FREUD'S WORK

At a time when prevailing cultural and scientific opinion held that childhood was free of any evidence of sexuality, Freud proclaimed the opposite. He proposed the libido theory, which stressed the influence of sexuality on mental life. His vast clinical experience, including his self-analysis and the analysis of his patient's fantasies, associations, and memories from childhood, led him to conclude that sexual urges provided a prime motivation for psychic functioning. He postulated that a force or psychic energy propelled sexual behavior, and he termed this energy *libido*. He was convinced that psychopathological disturbances in adulthood were based on vicissitudes of early childhood sexual development.

As more clinical data accumulated, Freud (1920) expanded his instinctual drive, or libido, theory to include an aggressive or destructive component. His clinical observations and experience led him to the compelling conclusion that feelings of anger and hostility result in conflict and unconscious guilt in the same manner that sexual wishes do, and that these affects initiate defensive activity. Further, he observed that many impulses contain both sexual and aggressive components, and that many clinical manifestations, including sadism, masochism, and ambivalence, can be explained in terms of varying degrees of conflict between these drives or their fusion. Freud also believed that nondestructive dimensions of aggression provide motivation for activity and mastery, just as libido does. In essence, he postulated that the libidinal and aggressive drives are fundamental aspects of human nature.

Though compelling, Freud's formulations of aggression were also problematic. Just as he had proposed a biological basis for libido, he felt it necessary to provide one for aggression. In contrast to libido, however, he did not view aggressive impulses as related to specific body zones. He therefore viewed aggressive impulses as being in close association to sexual ones. In his first model of the mind, Freud (1905) thought of aggression as a component of the sexual drive: "The history of civilization shows beyond any doubt that there is an innate connection between cruelty and the sexual instinct" (p. 159). The observation that aggressive impulses frequently appear to be a reaction to external stimuli led Freud (1915) to describe aggression as an attitude in the service of "self-preservation."

In a more philosophical context, completely divorced from the clinical, Freud (1920) hypothesized the existence of a fundamental and lifelong conflict between a death instinct (Thanatos) and a life instinct (Eros). He viewed the aggressive drive as originating from an organically based death instinct. The principle by which the death instinct operated was that the organism strived to discharge excitation and reach an ultimate state of Nirvana, or the total absence of excitation. This revision in theory has provided fuel for theoretical controversy for many years.

Presently, the followers of Melanie Klein are the primary proponents of the death instinct, unlike others (Parens, 1979) who find it problematic and unnecessary. However, a dual-drive theory of libidinal and aggressive drives has persisted in psychoanalysis and has almost universal clinical application. Sexuality and aggression are postulated to be intimately entwined with the developmental phases of infantile sexuality. Both drives are seen as a source of conflict, and defenses are employed against the awareness or expression of each. In early childhood, problems in the expression of aggression may manifest themselves in feeding disturbances (e.g., food is unconsciously equated with mother, so that rejecting food means hurting mother), unstable emotional attachments, inhibition of intellectual activity, and other difficulties. At the extreme, one may find exaggerated aggressive and destructive manifestations ranging from overemphasized assertiveness to unmanageable, sadistic destructiveness. According to the dual-drive theory, if the aggressive impulses are not combined with or adequately "bound" or fused with love (sexuality in the general sense), then increased aggression and destructiveness can be expected. Deprivation, object loss, or child abuse are all traumas that can interfere with attachment and the normative fusion of love and aggression.

Presently, the instinctual drives are seen by some as subsumed under the *id*, which is understood as a system of motivation encompassing processes that have a preemptory quality and that function to impel the mind toward activity in search of gratification. According to Loewald (1960), instinctual drives are organized within object relations and also organize object relations and reality. Here instincts are regarded as mental representations of organismic stimuli that can be described as a unit of motivation.

In a corrective vein, Klein (1976) emphasized that Freud's drive theory encompassed two theories. One emerged from clinical experience, while the other, more abstract theory involved a quasi-physiological model of energic forces seeking discharge. Most psychoanalytic theorists, clinicians, and researchers argue that the clinically based theory remains useful because it is amenable to continued empirical testing and growth. The more abstract energic model, however, is thought to be less useful because it is out of date and emerged more from a need for theoretical consistency with other disciplines than from the data of human experience. Instinctual drives, such as sexuality and aggression, can be conceptualized as ideas, affects, impulses, or wishes that have motivational impact to impel the mind to activity. According to Tyson and Tyson (1991), viewing drives in such a multidimensional way enhances clinical discrimination between various kinds of impulses and their sources, fosters a deeper understanding of the personal meaning of the urges, feelings, and defenses of varying intensity, and places the individual's conflicts and symptoms into a coherent developmental context.

AGGRESSION AND LEVELS OF PERSONALITY ORGANIZATION

Aggression conceptualized as an instinctual drive has its own developmental line (A. Freud, 1965). In normative child development, the experience and expression of aggression progresses from a less differentiated, more intense form to a more complex, modulated form (e.g., the ability to control feelings of impatience until relief arrives rather than immediately screaming and crying in rage). While psychoanalysts have conceptualized a normative developmental pathway for the integration and modulation of the aggressive drive, they believe that, in actuality, the intensity of aggression varies from individual to individual. This variation depends upon a wide range of factors that influence development: the inherent strength of the drive, the relative ability of the ego to deal with the drive, the degree of frustration within relationships with early caregivers (which can intensify the drive), early trauma, or other factors. The consequences for adults of excessive aggression include difficulties in tolerating frustration without becoming enraged, deficits in the capacity to self-soothe, difficulty in modulating the intensity of affective reactions, and difficulty in using evocative memory for self-comforting. In examining aggression in a clinical population, one finds that the intensity of the aggressive drive varies along a broad continuum—from a raw, primitive, unmodulated expression of the drive to a more adaptive, modulated manifestation of aggression in the form of assertiveness.

In a seminal theoretical contribution, Kernberg (1975) formulated a classification of personality organizations, which provides a useful framework for examining the spectrum of meanings and expressions of aggression in psychiatric patients. Kernberg described three types of personality structures: normal-neurotic, borderline, and psychotic personality organizations. These hierarchical levels of personality organization are determined by developmental, constitutional, psychosocial, genetic, and intrafamilial factors. Kernberg's classification of personality organizations involves a systematic appraisal of levels of instinctual development, manifestations of ego strength, level of defensive organization, quality of internalized object relations, level of superego or moral development, and attainment of ego identity. The degree of differentiation, articulation, and integration of these, both individually and as a gestalt, determines the level of personality organization and, in turn, determines the intensity and personal meaning as well as the expression of aggressive behavior. According to Kernberg, the personality organization, once formed, functions as the underlying matrix out of which behavioral symptoms develop, and it serves to stabilize psychological functioning. Kernberg's schema suggests that the quality, intensity, and meaning of aggression for an individual with a psychotic personality organization will differ significantly from the aggression of the borderline individual, which, in turn, will differ from the quality of aggression in an individual with a neurotic personality organization.

Personality organization serves as a key prognostic indicator of specific treatment needs and treatment response. Kernberg's classification schema has received wide currency in the literature related to psychopathology, and the structural variables he has identified and described have proven especially useful in empirical investigations of more severe psychopathology (Kwawer, Lerner, Lerner, & Sugarman, 1980; Lerner & Lerner, 1988; P. Lerner, 1991).

In what follows, we examine more closely these three levels of personality organization—normal-neurotic, borderline, and psychotic—to illuminate specific characteristics of each and how these determine the experience and expression of aggression. We will explore each in terms of seven structural variables of personality functioning that distinguish them and contribute to differences in aggression: object relations, ego identity, defensive organization, reality testing, ego strength, superego formation, and genetic-dynamic considerations. First, we briefly define these seven structural variables.

In psychoanalytic theory the term "object" can refer to interpersonal relationships, but it generally is taken to refer to an individual's *internal* relationships with others. As Greenberg and Mitchell (1983) suggest, in summarizing a vast psychoanalytic (and more recently, cognitive) literature, people carry "internal images" of self and others that, to a great extent, determine the individual's experience of the world. They write:

> What is generally agreed upon about the internal images is that they constitute a residue within the mind of relationships with significant others. In some way crucial exchanges with others leave their mark; they are "internalized" and so come to shape subsequent attitudes, reactions, perceptions, and so on. (p. 11)

From the perspective of psychoanalysis, insight into an individual's internalized object relations is crucial to an understanding of that individual's developmental experience, level of personality organization, and experience of the world.

Ego identity, according to Kernberg (1976), "is the highest level of organization of the world of object relations in the broader sense" (p. 32). Ego identity is developed, according to Kernberg, through the gradual internalization of object relations at progressively higher, more differentiated levels. In its more integrated form, ego identity offers a sense of continuity with the self, a sense of consistency in one's interpersonal interactions, and confirmation by the environment of one's stable characteristics.

Defense, according to Brenner (1982), is an aspect of mental functioning that reduces anxiety or depressive affect. Psychoanalysts have delineated a wide spectrum of defenses that can be arranged hierarchically—from "upper level" defenses (such as repression and sublimation) found in individuals with a neurotic personality organization to the more "primitive" defenses (such as splitting and projective identification) found in individuals with borderline and psychotic personality organizations. According to Kernberg, different levels of personality organization show different constellations of defenses, or defensive organizations, which reflect the individual's level of ego functioning and are employed to contend with the particular sorts of conflicts and dilemmas faced by individuals with that particular personality organization.

Frosch (1964) distinguishes three types of involvement with reality: the relation to reality (adaptive social behavior), the feeling of reality (absence of depersonalization and derealization), and the capacity to test reality. The capacity to test reality can be conceptualized on a continuum including, first, the ability to distinguish self from others; second, the ability to distinguish between internal ideas, images, and affects (intrapsychic stimuli) and perceptions (external stimuli); and third, the ability to assess accurately one's own actions, impulses, and thoughts within the context of the culture in which one lives.

Ego strength refers to the capacity to tolerate anxiety (to modulate increased levels of stress without developing symptoms or regressing), the capacity for impulse control (to experience intense affects, fantasies, and experiences without acting on them against one's best interest), and the capacity for sublimation (to develop creative outlets for gratification and self-interest). Difficulty in these three domains represents a failure of both ego and superego integration. Ego and superego integration allows individuals to sublimate both aggressive and sexual impulses in a variety of adaptive activities rather than immediately discharging them in the pursuit of instant gratification.

Superego integration refers to the degree to which an individual is able to regulate his or her functioning according to ethical principles—that is, to abstain from exploitation, manipulation, or mistreatment of others and to maintain honesty and moral integrity in the absence of external control. Brenner (1982) cites five superego functions: the approval or disapproval of actions and wishes on the grounds of moral considerations, a critical self-observation capacity, self-punishment, the demand for reparation or repentance of wrong-doing, and self-praise or self-love as a reward for virtuous behavior and thoughts. Extremes of any of these functions is thought to be pathological. The internalization of object relations constitutes the major organizing factor for superego development.

Within psychoanalytic theory, "genetic" describes how conflicts develop from multiple origins in childhood. The term "dynamic" refers to competing, conflicting forces that prevent an idea or feeling from becoming conscious or allow it to enter consciousness only in disguised form. While genetic-dynamic issues vary from individual to individual, certain themes predominate at different levels of personality organization, according to Kernberg.

Normal-Neurotic Personality Organization

At the normal-neurotic level of personality organization, a firm and cohesive ego identity includes a stable self-concept and a stable representational world. Values tend to be consistent, goals tend to be realistic, and the sense of reality provides an organizing function by guiding and directing behavior. In terms of superego functioning, neurotic individuals tend to be guided by ethical values in their daily lives and respond to difficult choices with modulated, goal-directed responses. The relatively direct or fantasized expression of aggression or destructiveness, then, is likely to be accompanied by guilt, which, among other things, provides a protective, self-regulating function. Neurotic individuals are prone to experience excessive guilt or depression around specific internal, conflictual areas, aggression being prominent among them.

Genetically, oedipal-level conflicts around sexuality and aggression predominate. These conflicts revolve around competition in the child–mother–father triad. In normative development, the oedipal triangle takes place when the daughter is attached to the father (an attachment that includes aggressive, competitive wishes directed toward the mother and sexual feelings directed toward the father) and fears that the mother will punish her for this attachment. The opposite situation occurs for the boy through his attachment to the mother and his fear of his father's retaliation. In adulthood, then, competitive, aggressive, and sexual strivings often catalyze unconscious, childlike feelings of guilt and fears of reprisal.

Individuals with a normal-neurotic level of personality organization employ higher-level (more adaptive) defenses than individuals with a borderline or psychotic personality organization. These function to restrict anxiety-provoking thoughts and feelings from consciousness. Such defensive maneuvers as repression, intellectualization, reaction formation, and rationalization are typical. These defenses often lead to inhibitions of sexuality or aggression. Generally, however, they do not compromise reality testing and contribute to chaotic interpersonal relations, as do defenses found in the borderline or psychotic personality organization, discussed below. For individuals with neurotic personality organization, reality testing tends to be intact; these individuals only experience difficulty in assessing their own actions, emotions, and thoughts, secondary to internal conflict and in circumscribed areas of their lives. In contrast to the often chaotic and destructive expression of aggression in individuals with borderline and psychotic personality organizations, the neurotic's greater ego strength and more mature defenses, along with his or her more mature superego functioning, contribute to his or her ability to integrate, modulate, and use aggression in more adaptive ways.

While generally adaptive in terms of maintaining a degree of interpersonal stability and compliance with societal expectations, the excessive bottling up of aggression in the form of rigid defenses and inhibitions in individuals with neurotic personality organizations often contributes to unsatisfying interpersonal relationships and, frequently, fear of success in the workplace and other domains. Often, this is what leads neurotic individuals to seek treatment. In psychotherapy, in contrast to the more chaotic presentation of more disturbed patients, neurotic patients are able to explain their problems and conflicts in an integrated fashion, they can empathize with others with whom they are in conflict, and frequently experience excessive guilt. Their internal world is well integrated but in conflict.

The case of a 32-year-old single man, illustrates well many of the features of individuals with a neurotic personality organization and, as is our focus, how such an individual expresses and experiences aggressive wishes.

M., a graduate student at a major university, struggled intensely with worries about his competence in many domains: in work, in athletics, and, especially, in terms of his sexual functioning. Although he had achieved success as a student, managed his day-to-day life with relative ease, and had engaged in two close, positive long-term relationships with women, he still worried about his competence and adequacy.

In reflecting on his intimate relationships, M. noted a longstanding fear that "something bad" might happen in his relationships. He tied this to fiercely critical, aggressive thoughts that welled up inside him as he engaged in close relationships—thoughts that he worked hard to suppress but was unable to do. A gentle man, who, in fact, was not violent at all, M.'s harsh superego led him to feel extremely guilty and self-denigrating for having aggressive wishes. He tended to view himself as a "jerk" and "insensitive."

Afraid that he might hurt others' feelings, M. tended to assume a passive stance in his relationships. He let women take the lead, both sexually and in other contexts, and worked almost desperately to inhibit any overt expression of anger. In school and on the ballfield, he functioned adequately, but he tended to inhibit himself because of worries about self-assertion (which he tied to aggression), and thus he failed to come close to performing to his potential.

Genetically, M.'s neurotic difficulties appeared bound up to a great extent in his trouble negotiating the triadic relationship with his mother and father. As a boy, M. had aligned himself closely with his mother, whom he had experienced as "confidante." His father, who had been prone to angry outbursts when M. was a child, had frightened him and angered M.'s mother. While M. had admired his father's outgoing style and competitive drive, he had feared aligning himself with his father for fear of losing his alliance with his mother. M. described how furious he had been at his father for demanding so much attention and also for denigrating him. Afraid of how angry he felt, however, he tended to retreat from confrontation with his father and seek a safe haven in his mother's arms.

As an adult, in an unconscious defensive manner, M. shifted back and forth between these two primary identifications. At moments, he identified with his father's competitive, self-assertive strivings. Then, anxious about his emerging aggressive wishes and fears of alienating the woman, he shifted to an identification with what he experienced as the woman's "softer features." From this position, he suffered less anxiety about his aggressive wishes, but also found himself unable to assert himself, sexually and otherwise, in an outgoing manner. He felt inhibited and, as he described, out of touch with his masculinity.

Borderline Personality Organization

Most major psychoanalytic theorists agree that lack of an integrated self-concept, or identity diffusion, is a core conflict for those individuals with a borderline level of personality organization. The lack of a stable, integrated self-concept involves two dimensions: split self-images resulting in contradictory attitudes, feelings, and behaviors directed toward the self and life choices, and splits in the image of significant others, with subsequent turmoil in interpersonal relationships. Kernberg (1980) reports that borderline individuals are unable to maintain any long-term integration of the concept of self or others. In essence, they rely on others for what is missing in the self—the ability to evaluate oneself and others realistically over time and across situations. Consequently, borderline individuals' perceptions and interpersonal relationships become increasingly chaotic and distorted over time because of their inability to evaluate others realistically. Despite what often appears to be a stable, well-integrated veneer, these individuals often are "stable in their instability" (Schmideberg, 1959, p. 398), because over time and with increased interpersonal closeness they rely on primitive cognitive and affective states to relate to others in increasingly conflicted, manipulative, and infantile ways.

Glenn Close's portrayal of Alex in the movie *Fatal Attraction* offers an excellent example and caricature of the borderline individual. Unlike more neurotic people, she is unable to maintain relationships with others by expressing warmth, concern, and dedication. It is extremely difficult for these individuals to maintain empathy and understanding in a relationship once conflicts arise. Yet, paradoxically, they are unable to separate or take perspective. This is one reason why the relationships of borderline individuals are often chaotic and embellished with either idealization or aggression. As with Alex, manipulation often replaces empathy as a way of relating to others. Deficits in reality testing also contribute to these presentations. Borderline individuals experience difficulty in distinguishing between external perceptions and their own intense affective reactions to those perceptions. This contributes to the borderline's tendency to overreact to external stimuli, often aggressively and self-destructively.

According to Kernberg (1975, 1976, 1980), individuals with borderline and psychotic personality structures rely on more primitive defenses, such as splitting, idealization, devaluation, denial, projective identification, and omnipotence. As noted by Kernberg (1977), these defenses "protect the ego from conflicts by means of dissociating or actively keeping apart contradictory experiences of the self and significant others" (p. 107). A reliance on such defenses is thought to weaken the person's overall level of functioning as well as capacity for adaptation.

Kernberg's formulation of primitive defenses encompasses several areas. Common to these defensive operations are contradictory ego states, which are actively kept separate from one another. These states are activated alternatively as a way of either reducing or eliminating painful affects, such as anxiety or depression. On the borderline level, individuals can cognitively acknowledge the different ego states, but either emotionally deny or are emotionally indifferent to this contradictory state of affairs. For the borderline patient, this state of indifference can protect them from potential psychosis.

Splitting, particularly on the borderline level, is a central defense that supports and maintains other primitive defense mechanisms. The most common clinical expression of splitting is the division of self and others into "all good" or "all bad" representations. These splits are often accompanied by rapid shifts from an all-good to an all-bad array of affective reactions. Clinical implications of splitting frequently involve an inability to experience ambivalence, leading to a rapid devaluation and idealization of others (or rapid shifts in allegiances and chaotic relationships); impaired decision-making capacity; rapid oscillation of self-esteem; ego-syntonic impulsive behavior, such as shoplifting, promiscuity, substance abuse or destructiveness, with little guilt; and an intensification of affect such that positive feelings are often experienced euphorically, while bad feelings are overwhelming, frequently rageful and murderous and/or suicidal in their intensity.

Primitive idealization, a typical defensive maneuver in borderline individuals, refers to the tendency to experience some objects as all good in order to feel protected from other objects that are experienced as all bad, or to protect good objects from one's own aggression. Envy and aggression are thought to underlie idealization. *Devaluation*, another defensive maneuver, refers to the tendency to depreciate, tarnish, and lessen the importance of one's inner and outer objects. The devaluation of others is often accompanied by a haughty and grandiose self-presentation.

Projective identification, another defensive maneuver typical among borderlines, has important interpersonal implications. Kernberg (1975) defines *projective identification* as a "group of fantasies and accompanying object relations having to do with the ridding of the self of unwanted aspects of the self, the depositing of these unwanted 'parts' into another person; and, finally, with the 'recovery' of a modified version of what was extruded" (p. 357). Attribution theory and empirical studies on the induction of affects help to explain projective identification. Borderline individuals are exquisitely sensitive and often have their antennae out, looking for others who accept their projections—that is, people who unconsciously resonate with them. For example, most people have conflicts in the area of self-esteem as well as the desire to help other people. Therefore, when borderline individuals project either rage or victimization with the fantasy of being rescued, the projections will resonate with the internal conflicts of others, who will be willing to accept them. Another example involves patients who may accuse therapists of being seductive when they are actually trying to induce seductiveness by ingratiation, coyness, or by exhibiting parts of their body.

The presentation of a contradictory, misleading, and vexing clinical picture (e.g., Glenn Close in *Fatal Attraction*) has become the sine qua non of the borderline patient. There is compelling clinical and research evidence indicating that more disturbed, (i.e., hospitalized) borderline patients, unlike more floridly psychotic patients, are unable to escape the experience of interpersonal distortions, malevolence, and destruction into an idyllic fantasy world of benevolence, stability, and order (Lerner & St. Peter, 1984). Interpersonal distortions, angry affect storms, and the turbulent enactment of subjective experience swiftly become available in treatment relationships and often lead to impulsive acting out.

Kernberg (1976) points to heightened constitutional aggression as the major cause and underlying etiological precondition for borderline conditions. Excessive aggression results in splitting, which prevents integration and object constancy, that is, the capacity to integrate loving and hating feelings toward the same individual. Lack of integration leaves the patients vulnerable to impulsive action because they are unable to modulate aggression. In fact, it is the relative degree to which aggression infiltrates superego development and object relations that serves as the major prognostic indicator for these patients.

The following are case vignettes that illustrate both the wide spectrum of borderline conditions as well as the vicissitudes of aggression, ranging from mild to self-destructive to more antisocial forms.

> B., a 21-year-old single white male, was the youngest of three children in a wealthy, intact suburban family. He was unemployed after having attended one year of college. Although behavioral and interpersonal difficulties were apparent as early as age 9, severe difficulties, including self-mutilation, polymorphous perverse sexual activities, drug abuse, and several arrests for forging checks, began only after his unsuccessful attempt to leave home and attend college. B. presented an effeminate, exceptionally well-dressed and well-groomed appearance, with a gold earring in his left ear. He stated that his major problems were: "I keep trying to succeed, and I just don't," "I hate hard work," "I have a terrible fear of the unknown," and "I don't know where I live emotionally." Behind exhibitionistic displays of bravado about his bisexuality and ability to please a woman, B. reported feelings of low self-esteem, bodily defectiveness, an inability to tolerate discomfort, a fear of rejection, strong dependence on and rage at his father, and an inability to feel emotions. "The trouble is, my emotions are not connected. I go through life physically and intellectually, but without feeling." He stated that he learned how to act angry, for example, by watching others, but that until recently

he rarely experienced anger. He reported an awareness of a disjunction between how angry he acts and how angry he feels. He asserts that he presents himself to the world "in images and facades."

Interestingly, his mother described B. as ". . . a delight from the very beginning . . . the child mothers dream of . . . he would go to sleep happy and wake up happy." According to the mother, B. "loved people . . . was flirtatious, and even at a very early age, women were charmed by him." B., however, never developed peer relationships and complained about being bullied and taken advantage of. He was characterized as a loner and effeminate. During early adolescence, B. became involved with neighborhood boys whom he recalls stripping him, trying him to a tree, and then striking him with branches. Although repulsed by his "friends," he smiled as he spoke about his suffering, and seemed to enjoy describing it. He was introduced to alcohol by these friends and several times they abandoned him drunk in the street. He said that his parents did not interfere because they knew he "needed friends."

There was little constructive interaction between B. and his parents, who continue to view him as a child, fearful of eliciting "temper tantrums." B. viewed his father as the ideal business tycoon, "a stingy cocksucker who denies me the essentials." He described his sisters in polarized fashion, the older as "bad" and the younger as "good."

P., a 30-year-old married woman and mother of an 8-year-old son, was a home-maker and part-time student. Her husband, C., was a successful corporate executive. P. was recommended for treatment because of suicidal thoughts: "I've been having thoughts of killing myself and others; I am afraid of losing control over my destructive-ness." She reported suffering from lifelong feelings of inadequacy, depression, empti-ness, loneliness, fears of losing control of her anger, and destructive fantasies—all of which intensified after the birth of her son. She found the task of being a mother "insurmountable." As rage toward her husband and son reached unmanageable, chaotic proportions, she began having thoughts of chopping off her hands or killing herself. She was hospitalized during a stressful period when she was experiencing insomnia, weight loss, and profound feelings of hopelessness and despair.

Information concerning P.'s early family history described many uprootings, sudden unexpected losses, and frequent traumatic events. Her father died after a long illness when P. was six. There were several moves, and when P. was 11, her mother married a deeply troubled man who committed suicide when P. was 14. Throughout high school, P. reported severe anxiety, compared herself unfavorably with older siblings, and experienced acute attacks of feeling inadequate and anxious. Amidst lectures on sexual morality by her mother, on the one hand, and feeling unattractive, on the other, P. initiated several destructive relationships and began to engage in promiscuous sexual behavior. She felt unable to attract men in any other way. P. attended college sporadically, traveled frequently, and continued to have sexual relationships without any feelings of intimacy. One of these relationships resulted in a pregnancy and an abortion. What attracted P. to her husband was his "strength" and the fact that his financial success would give her leisure time to pursue her own career goals in music. Her marriage was an attempt to structure and revitalize her life. Soon after the wedding, however, she bitterly complained of her husband's domination, intrusiveness, and chauvinism, al-though she encouraged him to take responsibility for most areas of her life. P. steadfastly asserted that her relationship with her husband, their sexual life, and parenthood never gave her any pleasure. They were a relatively isolated couple, with few friends.

P. presented herself as a pained, tearful woman, intensely shamed by seeking treatment. Although exhibiting no signs of thought disorder or impaired memory or concentration, she strenuously avoided eye contact. Her affect was that of profound depression and intense rage directed at her husband and mother. She described intense suicidal ideation, as well as homicidal thoughts, and a profound sense that she had failed to adequately plan and manage her life.

In discussing clinical aspects of superego psychopathology, Kernberg (1984) offers several examples of the antisocial or psychopathic personality, which is considered a variant of borderline personality organization. One patient entered treatment under pressure from his parents and to avoid going to prison because of his involvement in several break-ins. He talked openly in his therapy sessions about a planned robbery. He made it crystal clear through "subtle but unmistakable threats" that he would know how to protect himself in case the therapist reported him to legal authorities. Kernberg describes this patient as conveying an "overpowering sense of superiority and security." His relaxed smile conveyed a depreciation of the therapist and within the countertransference the therapist experienced difficulty thinking constructively and intervening. The treatment was interrupted after the therapist reached the conclusion that the combination of legal problems and therapeutic issues was beyond his capacity.

Kernberg (1984) describes a young woman, V., who one evening told a man that she loved him and that he was the only man in her life. As an intense sexual relationship was developing between the two, she simultaneously was developing a similar relationship with another man. The next evening, she told the second man that indeed she loved him and that he was the only man in her life. Ms. V. talked about this openly in her sessions. When the therapist raised the question of whether this behavior was a source of conflict for her, she reassured him that it was not, because the two men did not know each other. She felt completely sincere in making these statements to both men and that her feelings had changed completely from one night to the next. Within this, she felt that each man could be certain of her being honest with him. She never made any secret of the fact that her feelings could change and that, therefore, she could not guarantee anybody "eternal love." In fact, one of her major complaints was of the lack of appreciation of her honesty and the contradictory behavior of men with whom she had been involved. This woman suffered from severe pathology of object relations, an inability to commit herself in depth to anyone or to permit herself to depend fully on anyone. Through the course of therapy, she learned that a radical abandonment of all hope for love defended her against deep fears of disappointment and rage.

Psychotic Personality Organization

Like the patient with a borderline personality organization, the patient with a psychotic personality organization is unable to maintain a stable integration of the concept of self or others. This inability undermines the capacity to realistically assess oneself and others over time and across situations. Like the borderline patient, patients with a psychotic-level personality organization employ a range of primitive defenses—such as splitting and projective identification—which further undermine their ego functioning. The reasons for the employment of such defensive operations, however, are different in borderline and psychotic patients, according to Kernberg (1975). In the borderline patient, as noted, splitting and other defenses protect the patient from intolerable feelings of ambivalence and the overwhelming rage that infiltrates all significant relationships. In contrast, the psychotic patient employs these defenses in an effort to avoid the experience of disintegration or merger. Merger refers to the intrapsychic fusion of self- and object representations. The regressive experience of merger manifests in a total and frightening loss of reality testing—in delusions, hallucinations, and confusion between self and other.

As in the borderline patient, primitive defenses in the psychotic patient often lead to chaotic, contradictory forms of behavior. For instance, a patient who has just attacked a worker on an inpatient unit might insist that he or she was feeling absolutely calm and content at the time of the attack. In contrast to borderline patients, who often are able to acknowledge such contradictions and begin to work to sort them out, psychotic patients usually decompensate when these contradictions are pointed out: they become overwhelmed by disorganizing affects and chaotic fantasies, which often prompt behavioral regressions. Often, especially under stress, psychotic patients experience a frightening blurring of interpersonal boundaries, which they attempt to deal with through aggressive behavior.

R., a 19-year-old, single, white male, was referred for long-term, intensive inpatient treatment after several brief hospitalizations. He had progressively decompensated beginning at age 15, shortly after his first lengthy separation from his mother in order to attend prep school. R., a tall, slender, gangly adolescent, was bodily and interpersonally awkward, stiff, constricted, mechanical, vague, and indefinite. He presented a startlingly painful sense of reality and history of thought disorder, auditory hallucinations, poor school performance, and seriously impaired social skills.

R. was raised in an extended family in which there were two divorces, and he had an overly enmeshed, symbioticlike relationship with his infantilizing mother. The mother was strikingly attractive, overly seductive, overstimulating, and intrusive. She used her relationship with R. to gain some relief from her own intense depression and loneliness. Her intrusiveness often left R. feeling passive, withdrawn, and unable to differentiate or express his own autonomous strivings. He seemed paralyzed by intense feelings of anxiety, rage, helplessness, and despair. His room at school was described as a "virtual altar" to his mother, with her pictures and letters arranged throughout the room in almost religious fashion. He felt "lost," isolated, listless, distant from others, and unable to concentrate. As his disjointed speech, hallucinations, and withdrawal gradually increased at school, he began to behave in an increasingly bizarre fashion, which culminated with him attacking his mother with a knife.

J., a 17-year-old, white, single, female high school student, had an attractive appearance, with long blond hair strewn over her eyes. Initially, she appeared frightened, inappropriately giddy, and quite disorganized. Her verbalizations had a pressured, cliché-ridden quality, with comments about LSD trips, cosmic experiences, and quests for boundariless bliss. The content of her speech was highly sexualized, replete with reference to her body, kissing, petting, intercourse, and abortions. She cried profusely about separations from her boyfriend—"I feel like a nobody without a boyfriend." She was referred for hospitalization after she had been found at a rock concert wandering around in a confused state.

J. came from a close-knit, well-educated, liberal upper middle-class family where both parents were successful professionals. The family was characterized as overly enmeshed, with diffuse generational boundaries and strong evidence of an inappropriate mother who was intrusive, needy, and infantilizing, and a passive, withdrawn, depressed father. J. was described by her parents as always having been "a perfect baby," and in adolescence as having "more boyfriends than she knew what to do with." J. was sexually precocious beginning around the age of 8, when she performed oral sex on a cousin. She had intercourse beginning at age 13. While interactions between J. and her parents were overinfantilizing and inappropriately erotic, with frequent stroking and kissing, the parents seemed unaware of their daughter's sexual precociousness as well as her desperate need for closeness, her sensitivity to rejection, and her proneness to depression and disorganization. Her parents stated that 10 months prior to her admission, following a legal abortion of an unwanted pregnancy, they noticed a steady decline in J.'s personal hygiene and social judgment. One month after her abortion, J. met her present boyfriend, with whom she felt deeply in love. J.'s school performance declined, she quit her part-time job, and she spent increasing periods of time with her boyfriend, smoking pot and staying out all night. Her relationship with peers, which were always superficial, declined rapidly as she became increasingly absorbed with her boyfriend.

Upon admission, J. seemed to crave social contact in a compliant manner, eager to avoid any sign of discomfort in others. Easily overwhelmed by strong affect and prone to panic and flight, she maintained an apologetic, self-derogatory posture. She reported her earliest memory of running home after school in the third grade, where she was picked on by other children. Clinging to her mother and sobbing, she recalls her mother yelling at her for "not hitting back" and putting her in a closet as punishment. Shortly after reporting this, in an affect-laden moment, J. described the meaning of love for her: ". . . it means having someone to look after you who really cares, when they offer to do things for you, to walk you home from school, buy presents, pay attention to you . . . to be taken care of."

PSYCHOANALYTIC TREATMENT

There is a wide range and spectrum of psychoanalytically oriented psychotherapies based on the structural features previously mentioned. Each has its own techniques and treatment goals that are considered optimal for neurotic, borderline,, and psychotic personality organizations. In brief, *psychoanalysis* refers to a treatment modality that makes use of an analytic couch to facilitate access to fantasy; utilizes free association and specific guidelines that govern the analyst's behavior in terms of technical neutrality (maintaining an equidistant listening perspective between the id, superego, and external reality, and offering no advice or moral judgment); and employs the interpretation of the transference with a view toward resolving the "transference neurosis." Psychoanalysis is both intensive and extensive, with meetings often on a five-times a week basis over several years. This form of treatment is best suited for individuals with neurotic level personality organizations. *Intensive* or *expressive* psychotherapy utilizes psychoanalytic theory to understand the patient but does not use the analytic couch. This approach has guidelines for the therapist's behavior, which include parameters or modification of psychoanalytic technique with a view to achieve the goal of structural change. Specific techniques, such as clarification of confusing communications, the confrontation of primitive defenses, and the interpretation of the transference in the "here and now," make this treatment modality well suited for individuals with higher-level borderline personality organizations that can be treated on an outpatient basis. Therapist and patient usually meet between two to four times per week, and the treatment lasts a number of years. *Supportive* psychotherapy utilizes psychoanalytic theory to understand the individual, but less with a view toward implementing psychoanalytic interpretive techniques than with the goal of increasing the patient's ability to cope. While psychanalysis and individual psychotherapy remain the cornerstone of psychoanalytically oriented treatments, many patients with borderline and psychotic structures can benefit from concurrent treatment in other psychoanalytically informed modalities.

TRANSFERENCE AND COUNTERTRANSFERENCE CONSIDERATIONS

Clinical work within the therapeutic relationship, termed the *transference*, is considered the basis of psychoanalytic treatment modalities. Within psychoanalysis, transference is (1) broadly defined as an inherent human tendency to impose the organizing of prior perception of experience upon the present (Freud, 1925; McLaughlin, 1991; Stern, 1977); (2) regarded as fundamental to shaping internal reality, interpersonal perception and experience; and (3) viewed as the major vehicle for mutative change, not through education or manipulation, but through analysis. In essence, transference is an unconscious tendency to shift emotional interest and investment toward significant others in the present with the hope of either reexperiencing earlier relationships or succeeding where one has formerly failed. It is maladaptive to the extent that new experiences and individuals are perceived according to earlier formed experiences and relationships, which are repeated. The transference is potentially adaptive to the extent that it reflects an urge to master the past and provides repeated opportunities to do so.

Transference is ubiquitous in all relationships. This is to say that a certain "double relationship" is established in all relationships between self and other: a realistic, socially appropriate one of self and other, and an underlying, more or less subtle one reflecting the self's predominant fantasies, schemata, or self–other representations and expectancies. Psychoanalysis and psychoanalytic treatments are designed to safely foster the emergence of this second relationship with a view toward fully experiencing, coming to understand, and resolving the conflictual interference of previous relationships and experiences upon the present. In this sense, the role of transference can be conceptualized in terms of self and object representations. Formulations about therapeutic action in psychoanalysis and psychoanalytic psychotherapy have emphasized the therapeutic matrix as a significant interpersonal relationship in which the therapeutic relationship is mediator for the patient's development of increasing levels of organization (Blatt & Erlich, 1982; Loewald, 1960). In that the internalization of object relations—that is, significant, formative interactions with parental figures—results in the formation of psychic structures, including self and object representations during development, the internalization of significant interactions between the patient and the therapist can be seen to play an important role in the therapeutic process. In this way, the therapist becomes available as a new object in terms of eliminating, step by step, the transference distortions that interfere with the establishment of new relationships (Loewald, 1960). It is the internalization of new and relatively undistorted relations with the therapist that leads to therapeutic change. Psychoanalytic treatment can also be conceived of as an experimental setting within which the patient can display his or her predominant constellation of disturbed internalized self and object representations, which can be safely diagnosed and therapeutically modified within the context of psychotherapeutic interactions.

It is well known that the therapist and patient react to each other in ways that profoundly influence the quality and outcome of treatment. In its most narrow meaning, *countertransference* refers to the therapist's conscious or unconscious reaction to the patient's transference. In its broadest meaning, it refers to all the therapist's conscious or unconscious reactions to the patient. Because patients with borderline and psychotic personality organizations comprise a broad spectrum, the scope and intensity of these patients' transference and the therapists' countertransference reactions vary accordingly. Reactions extend from mild and subtle to highly intense, with a wide range of manifestations. With lower-level borderline patients, the transference–countertransference is typically intense and vivid, often involving the graphic repetition of early traumas, terrifying affects and confusion between self and other. Therapists attempt to use their reactive feelings to assess the internalized object representations that patients are reliving with them and attempt to respond in a fashion that does not repeat the traumas of the patient's early environment or development. Most clinical work with borderline patients involves the activation of idealizing, devaluing, and psychotic transference. Within these transferences, certain interactional paradigms emerge that frequently involve rescuing, depleting, victimizing, and "walking on eggshells" interactions.

PROGNOSTIC INDICATORS

According to Kernberg (1984), basic issues regarding the probability of therapeutic resolution with patients who exhibit excessive aggressive and destructive behavior span all types of psychoanalytically oriented treatment and include (1) the patient's capacity to maintain a dependent relationship to the therapist, (2) the patient's capacity to tolerate maintaining a psychotherapeutic relationship when strong negative transference feelings predominate, and (3) the availability of treatment arrangements that realistically protect the patient from severely destructive or self-destructive acting out that might threaten not only the continuation of treatment but the very life of the therapist or patient. For example, patients who need to control their immediate environment by repetitive physical threats must be able to renounce this behavior before its meaning can be therapeutically understood and worked through. Issues of chronic lying need to be a treatment priority in terms of being clarified, confronted, and resolved analytically if possible or by means of external social control. The patient's capacity or incapacity to depend on the therapist is a significant prognostic indicator. The most significant characteristic of the activation of malignant aggression in treatment is the need to destroy the therapist psychologically in terms of his or her interpretations, creativity, values, autonomy, and possessions. The unconscious motivation for these destructive needs includes sadism and envy, specifically, envy of the therapist for not being a victim of the same disturbance as the patient. The awareness that the therapist is able to function as a nurturant person and enjoy life becomes intolerable to patients imprisoned by a grandiose, sadistic self.

SUMMARY

In the course of this chapter, we have attempted to provide an overview of how the psychoanalytic theorist might approach the issue of aggression in psychiatric patients. Our brief discussion of Freud's approaches to aggression, some of its limitations, and contemporary modifications of Freud's approach should suggest the complexity of the topic from the perspective of psychoanalysis and also its continuing evolution.

As noted at the outset, contemporary psychoanalysis is not a unified theory, and thus different psychoanalytic theorists offer various approaches to crucial conceptual and treatment issues, which include divergences in approaches to aggression. Kernberg's theory of hierarchical levels of personality organization, the central conceptual framework in this chapter, offers a coherent, integrative psychoanalytic approach to the meaning and experience of aggression at different levels of psychopathology. Kernberg's theory suggests that the factors that determine the meaning and expression of aggression in psychiatric patients are varied and complex. They include level of superego development, level of object relations, ego strength, and genetic factors. Understanding each of these structural variables—both individually and as a gestalt—is critical to understanding the patient's level of personality organization, the role of aggression in a particular patient and to formulating an appropriate therapeutic approach.

REFERENCES

Blatt, S. J., & Erlich, H. S. (1982). Levels of resistance in the psychotherapeutic process. In P. L. Wachtel (Ed.), *Resistance: Psychodynamic and behavioral approaches* (pp. 69–91). New York: Plenum.

Brenner, C. (1982). *The mind in conflict*. New York: International Universities Press.

Freud, A. (1965). *Normality and pathology in childhood. Assessment of developments* (Vol. VI). New York: International Universities Press.

Freud, S. (1905). *Three essays on the theory of sexuality (Standard Edition)*. London: Hogarth Press.

Freud, S. (1915). *Instincts and their vicissitudes (Standard Edition*, Vol. XIV). London: Hogarth Press.

Freud, S. (1920). *Beyond the pleasure principle (Standard Edition*, Vol. XVIIII). London: Hogarth Press.

Freud, S. (1925). *Some psychical consequences of the anatomical distinction between the sexes (Standard Edition*, Vol. XIX). London: Hogarth Press.

Frasch, J. (1964). The psychotic character: Clinical psychiatric consideration. *Psychiatric Quarterly, 38*, 81–96.

Greenberg, J., & Mitchell, S. (1983). *Object relation in psychoanalytic theory*. Cambridge, MA: Harvard University Press.

Kernberg, O. (1975). *Borderline conditions and pathological narcissism*. New York: Jason Aronson.

Kernberg, O. (1976). *Object relations theory and clinical psychoanalysis*. New York: Jason Aronson.

Kernberg, O. (1977). Normal psychology of the aging process revisited—II. *Journal of Geriatric Psychiatry, 10*, 27–45.

Kernberg, O. (1980). *Internal world and external reality*. New York: Jason Aronson.

Kernberg, O. (1984). *Severe personality disorders*. New Haven: Yale University Press.

Klein, G. (1976). *Psychoanalytic Theory*. New York: International Universities Press.

Kwawer, J., Lerner, H., Lerner, P., & Sugarman, A. (1980). *Borderline phenomena and the rorschach test*. New York: International Universities Press.

Lerner, H. (1986). Research perspectives on psychotherapy with borderline patients. *Psychotherapy, 23*, 57–69.

Lerner, H., & Lerner, P. (1988). *Primitive mental states and the rorschach*. Madison, CT: International Universities Press.

Lerner, H., & St. Peter, S. (1984). Patterns of object relations in neurotic, borderline, and schizophrenic patients. *Psychiatry, 47*, 77–92.

Lerner, P. (1991). *Psychoanalytic theory and the rorschach*. Hillsdale, NJ: The Analytic Press.

Loewald, H. (1960). On the therapeutic action of psychoanalysis. *International Journal of Psychoanalysis, 41*, 16–33.

McLaughlin, J. (1991). Clinical and theoretical aspects of enactment. *Journal of the American Psychoanalytic Association, 39*, 595–614.

Parens, H. (1979). *The development of aggression in early childhood*. New York: Jason Aronson.

Schmideberg, M. (1959). The borderline patient. In S. Arieti (Ed.), *American handbook of psychiatry: Vol I.* (pp. 398–416). New York: Basic Books.

Stern, D. (1977). *The first relationship: Infant and mother*. Cambridge, MA: Harvard University Press.

Tyson, P., & Tyson, R. (1991). *Psychoanalytic theories of development*. New Haven: Yale University Press.

CHAPTER 6

Humanistic

WILLARD B. FRICK AND BERNE JACOBS

A BRIEF INTRODUCTION TO HUMANISTIC PSYCHOLOGY

In the relatively short span of 30 years, the humanistic "third-force" movement has had an enormous impact on the theoretical and philosophical outlook in psychology, including a reassessment of the very nature of scientific inquiry itself (Giorgi, 1985; Moustakas, 1990). More specifically, humanistic psychology hastened the demise of classic behaviorism, altered and enriched the entrenched psychoanalytic position by stimulating the growth of self-theory, contributed to the recognition of important cognitive variables in personality development, and pioneered theoretical development and research on healthy personality, self-actualization, and optimum human functioning. Moreover, the humanistic thrust to create a more human (and humane) science has had a significant impact on all psychological disciplines. There are few psychology texts today that do not give some attention to the humanistic perspective. Much more important than this pervasive influence on the profession, however, is the fact that humanistic theory is making a positive impact on the way people feel and think about themselves and how they conceptualize their development, their experience, and their potentials.

The story of the emergence of the humanistic revolution in psychology began in the 1950s, when a small group of psychologists, disenchanted with the prevailing psychoanalytic and behaviorist models of the person, began to establish an informal network of communication, organized and set in motion by the vigorous leadership of Abraham Maslow, and with strong backing by Gordon Allport. The institutionalization of humanistic psychology followed with the founding meeting of the American Association of Humanistic Psychology (eventually to become the Association for Humanistic Psychology) in Philadelphia in the summer of 1963 (DeCarvalho, 1990). The first issue of the *Journal of Humanistic Psychology* had already appeared in the spring of 1961.

In the early years, the humanistic movement was a radical and reactionary one, a

WILLARD B. FRICK • Department of Psychology, Albion College, Albion, Michigan 49224.   **BERNE JACOBS** • Department of Psychology, Kalamazoo College, Kalamazoo, Michigan 49007.

Handbook of Aggressive and Destructive Behavior in Psychiatric Patients, edited by Michel Hersen, Robert T. Ammerman, and Lori A. Sisson. Plenum Press, New York, 1994.

passionate and rebellious protest against the deterministic and reductionistic models of humans espoused by psychoanalysis and behaviorism. These early years of the movement paralleled the heady but chaotic years of the Vietnam protests, the civil rights struggle, and the counterculture rebellion, and, at times, it seemed difficult to distinguish humanistic psychology from the goals and purposes of these movements. Free-wheeling experimentation became the norm as more and more psychologists, identifying with the humanistic movement, began to explore new territory and redefine the boundaries of psychology. Under the aegis of the human potential "craze," everything from intimate nude groups and sensory awareness encounters to marathon encounter groups became legitimate areas for exploration. At that time, then, under the banner of the human potential movement, these were some of the more radical ways psychologists sought to express their discontent with the rigid, mechanistic establishment of psychology within a data-bound, technological society. In spite of its immaturities and excesses, these initial developments were sincere attempts to free psychology from its rigidities and outdated views. Gradually, the chaos and excess of the revolution subsided, and with the calmer and wiser voices of humanistic leaders such as Rollo May, Carl Rogers, and Abraham Maslow, humanistic psychology moved toward a more serious and sustained effort to explore and establish its unique role and identity within psychology and society as a whole. Without rejecting the valid contributions of psychoanalysis and behaviorism, humanistic psychology gradually began to expand and enrich the answer to the fundamental question, what does it mean to be fully human? Humanistic psychology, since its inception, has considered the answers to this question to be its central mission. It has sought to establish a truly human science that will help shape a new, empirically based image of human nature and its possibilities.

The centrality of certain values to humanistic psychology suggests that a brief explication of these values will identify significant attributes of this third-force psychology. The position taken here is that eight fundamental, or core values represent much of what is held in common by the diverse set of theoreticians and practioners who call themselves humanistic psychologists. These core values also help distinguish the philosophical position of humanistic psychology from the orientations of behaviorism and psychoanalysis, and serve as organizing principles or themes in humanistic psychology.

While all humanistic psychologists agree, in principle, with all of the core values presented here, each individual tends to emphasize one or more over the rest. Also, applications of humanistic psychology to everyday affairs can be characterized according to which core value or values are emphasized. It is the plan of this chapter to present the eight core values as (1) important identifying features of humanistic psychology, (2) an organizing scheme to structure the later presentation of selected theorists, and (3) a way of linking the views of humanistic psychology to a humanistic perspective on violence and aggression.

The Core Values of Humanistic Psychology

Experience Is Central

There is a focus on inner experience and the importance of drawing upon this subjective reservoir as a prelude to decision making and the creation of meaning. The self as experience and the experience of the self are both viewed as valid. Subjective experience, therefore, is seen by humanistic psychologists as a creative inner resource leading to the discovery of meaning and value. Research in humanistic psychology frequently focuses on these phenomenological correlates of behavior rather than on the behaviors themselves.

Human Potential

From the very beginning, humanistic psychology has been identified with a concern for human potential and its development. Guided by the self-actualization theories of Maslow (1968) and Rogers (1963), and Allport's (1960) emphasis on the personality as an open system, the third-force school of psychology has stressed the human need for growth, change, becoming, and self-actualization. These theoretical developments and subsequent research led to the important concept of *healthy personality*, one of the significant contributions of humanistic psychology.

Holism

Holistic theory is a guiding principle in humanistic psychology and is reflected in its emphases on an integration of all aspects of the person. Humanistic psychology seeks to discover the unity and pattern, the "gestalt," in human development, and to discover the complex mechanisms and resources for integration within the personality. Reductionistic analysis, research on isolated part-functions, and serious attention to conflict theories are viewed as relatively meaningless in efforts to understand the person and answer the question, what does it mean to be fully human? Thus, humanistic psychology seeks to identify the holistic principles that operate to create complex unities both within the person and in person–world interaction.

Uniqueness

Humanistic psychology has a great respect for the uniqueness of each and every person. There is a valuing of the idiosyncratic, the unusual, the unpredictable, the irregular and eccentric features as important expressions of being human. The dynamic components and their interactions within the personality system are uniquely fashioned, integrated, and expressed by each person. For humanistic psychologists these unique features supersede the "common" or nomothetic elements and dimensions of personality. Basic to this value of uniqueness is the underlying assumption that, given its uniqueness and complexity, the human personality can never be fully understood, predicted, and controlled.

Consciousness

Every human being has the capacity for awareness on many levels. This awareness may extend from a simple reflexive sensitivity to the profound awareness that is awakened in various altered states of consciousness. For humanistic psychologists, the "hidden" nature of humans lies not in the unconscious, but in the neglected powers of consciousness. Our desire and potential for awareness, for higher consciousness, is far greater than our inclination to live life in the shadows of some relatively unconscious or unaware state. It is this capacity for higher levels of awareness that allows the person to make informed choices and decisions. Wheelis (1973) has defined freedom as the awareness of alternatives and the ability to choose, and this, of course, is contingent upon consciousness. "Alternatives without awareness yield no leeway" (1973, p. 14).

It is for these reasons that humanistic psychologists place such importance on the human capacity for conscious living and strive to increase this "awareness of awareness" as an important part of its agenda, particularly in psychotherapy and education.

Meaning and Values

Humanistic psychology sees values and meaning as central to its concern for the integration and integrity of the person. Without values and significant meanings in life there would be no integration and stability in the personality. Indeed, Frankl (1970, 1984) emphasizes that the sovereign motivation of the human being is not to pursue self-actualization, but to discover meaning. Any measure of human happiness and fulfillment, therefore, depends on a strong sense of meaning in life. It is around these central meanings and values that all other dynamics of the personality revolve.

Freedom and Responsibility

This value is, perhaps, central to all other values espoused by humanistic psychologists. Its importance rests on the fact that one's freedom constitutes the existential ground for choice, decision making, autonomous developments, self-direction, and self-control. Freedom always exists, however, in a dialectical tension with responsibility for the consequences of ones choices. Freedom for humanistic psychologists is not an illusion, as behaviorists have contended, but, rather, a fundamental reality within the existential parameters of our lives. We are free. This is the one existential truth that honors the human claim for dignity and integrity. The alternative is to view human beings as objects acted upon by internal and external forces over which they have no control.

People develop as creative agents, as subjects rather than objects, as choosers and decision makers only to the extent that they become both conceptually and experientially aware of this freedom.

The Person-Centered Focus

Humanistic psychology places human beings and the health and quality of human life as the focus of concern. All efforts of humanistic psychology, both theoretical and methodological, are founded on a sensitivity to human needs and healthy human development. There is an effort, in this respect, to put the person back in touch with the validity of his or her own being and subjective experience and to extend this principle to a wider human context, the development of healthy and productive interpersonal relationships.

THE HUMANISTIC PERSPECTIVE ON VIOLENCE AND AGGRESSION

It is not surprising that, in general, those of the humanistic persuasion reject all theories of violence that are based on a genetic determinism. Such views would include the psychoanalytic tenets of Freud's aggressive drive and "death instinct," and the instinct theories of naturalists Ardrey (1966) and Lorenz (1963).

While we obviously have the emotional and biological equipment to act violently and aggressively, humanistic psychology rejects the presence of some genetically coded mandate to explain these behaviors. In the following section we explore alternative views. It should be made clear that humanistic psychology does not reject these theories merely because they do not correspond to the humanistic values. Genetic and instinct theories of human violence and aggression are rejected because there is little or no empirical evidence to support them.

In his book *The Brighter Side of Human Nature*, Kohn (1990) reviews the evidence on the nature of human aggression and concludes that such behaviors are a reaction to perceived threat but that, in terms of aggression's innateness, "it is not any more real or integral a response than reacting to the same threat by fleeing, embracing, laughing, weeping, or writing" (p. 45). Kohn strongly supports Baron's assessment and conclusion, based on Baron's review of over 300 studies on the issue, that

> contrary to the views espoused by Freud, Lorenz, Ardrey and others, aggression is *not* essentially innate. Rather, it seems to be a learned form of social behavior, acquired in the same manner as other types of activity and influenced by many of the same social, situational, and environmental factors. (Baron, 1977, p. 26)

While we must agree with the essence of Baron's conclusion, his primary emphasis on social learning in the formation of aggression contains a serious omission neglecting perhaps the most crucial variable in the development of human aggression and violence; that variable is the *self*. We believe that it is in the area of *self-theory in relation to values* that humanistic psychology has made a unique and distinct contribution to understanding the genesis and dynamics of human destructiveness. In the following section we explore certain aspects of self-theory as it relates to these issues.

For humanistic psychology, the issue of the nature of violence and aggression in human behavior was first joined, in a formal sense, in 1957. In the spring of that year, Carl Rogers and Martin Buber held an open dialogue at the University of Michigan, moderated by the philosopher Maurice Friedman.

During this dialogue, Rogers spoke to the issue of "basic human nature":

> I think that one of the things I have come to believe and feel and experience is that what I think of as human nature or basic human nature . . . is something that is really to be trusted. . . . It's been my experience in therapy that one does not need to supply motivation toward the positive or toward the constructive. That exists in the individual. In other words, if we can release what is most basic in the individual, it will be constructive. (Buber, 1965, p. 179–180)

Buber's response to Rogers, emphasizing the polarity of good and evil, frames the issue that was to be the focus in another important exchange some 25 years later between Carl Rogers and Rollo May. Buber replied:

> And my experience is . . . if I come near to the reality of this person, I experience it as a *polar* reality. . . . I would say now when I see him, when I grasp him more broadly and more deeply than before, I see his whole polarity and then I see how the worst in him and the best in him are dependent on one another, attached to one another. (Buber, 1965, p. 180)

Rollo May expressed a similar view to that of Buber, a view that emphasized both our constructive and destructive impulses, driven by what May calls the "daimonic urge." Rogers took issue with May's position in a manner consistent with his earlier views expressed during the Rogers–Buber dialogue. In response to May, Rogers stated:

> I do not find that this evil is inherent in human nature. In a psychological climate, which is nurturant of growth and choice, I have never known an individual to choose the cruel or destructive path. Choice always seems to be in the direction of greater socialization. . . . so I see members of the human species, as essentially constructive in their fundamental nature but damaged by experience. (Rogers, 1982a, p. 8)

In an open letter to Rogers, May (1982) responded to Rogers's criticism and point of view. May accused humanistic psychology of a narcissistic denial of the evil potential within human nature and a reluctance to confront this issue, and he reiterated his concept of the daimonic in human nature, a fundamental life force that contains the propensity for both good and evil. May's daimonic is a passionate energy that may express itself in constructive motivations and creative activity or take the destructive form of aggression, hostility, and cruelty. Within the daimonic, it is the same energy and passion that empowers both the good and evil expressions of the personality. (Occasionally, we also use the term *evil* as synonymous with violence and destructive aggression. This raises the question: Should all such behaviors be considered evil? This question, of course, suggests certain moral, ethical, and philosophical issues that are beyond the scope of this chapter.) What, exactly, determines the direction and expression of this daimonic energy? What variables operate to tip the scales toward good or evil, toward constructive or destructive behaviors?

May (1969) has stated that the daimonic is not evil in itself, and, further, he states that "violence is the daimonic gone awry" (p. 130). Now, we must ask, what makes the daimonic go awry? In his book *Love and Will*, May (1969) strongly suggests that it is a sense of powerlessness rooted in anonymity, in aloneness transformed into loneliness:

> For his self-doubts—I don't really exist since I can't affect anyone—eat away at his innards; he lives and breathes and walks in a loneliness which is subtle and insidious. It is not surprising that he gets a gun and trains it on some passerby—also anonymous to him. (p. 162)

In his book *Power and Innocence*, May (1972) interprets his patients' disturbances and tendencies to violence as resulting from feelings of powerlessness and from an inability to establish an effective bridge to significant others in their lives. This bridge, May suggests, is the power to reach out to affect and be affected by others. It is the power to assert oneself in forming relationships that opens one up to self-affirmation. May emphasizes the importance of dialogue, the interpersonal experience, in restoring power to the individual and in releasing the growth forces within the daimonic. Dialogue thus becomes the one crucial experience that opens one to an awareness of the positive potentials of the daimonic, erases the faceless anonymity of being, and restores a constructive and creative power to the person. The major purpose of psychotherapy, therefore, is to restore consciousness through dialogue.

May also observes that the daimonic is more likely to take a violent expression and be projected onto others when one's propensity to violence and evil behavior is denied. This would result in the perception of the world as hostile and threatening and lead the person to aggression in response. It is essential to May, therefore, that we remain in touch with the propensity for evil within the daimonic.

When we examine May's construct of the diamonic with its polarities of good and evil, it appears to be a prime illustration of Angyal's holistic theory of the "ambiguous Gestalt." Angyal (1965) proposes that there are two primary and autonomous organizations within the personality—one characterized as healthy and the other as neurotic. Because each organization represents an inclusive Gestalt formation, each incorporates all of the elements, materials, and subsystems of the individual's personality. Thus, each and every dynamic force and characteristic within the personality has a position and value in both organizations. Angyal (1965) states this arrangement as follows: "In an ambiguous Gestalt, the parts do not belong independently to one pattern or another. All parts belong to both patterns and have their function assigned to them by the currently dominant system principle" (p. 104).

From this theoretical perspective, May's powerful life force energy, the daimonic, maintains a functional position and potential for expression within both the dynamic organizations of health and pathology. From its position within the healthy Gestalt, the diamonic will be creative and constructive. Expressed as a dynamic within the neurotic organization, however, the diamonic will express itself in destructive ways.

Following the prevailing system principle, one organization will be dominant over the other, the relative strength or weakness of the pattern depending on whether the individual has developed primarily within a healthy or neurotic environment. Angyal (1965) also postulates that only one organization is in control at any given time. Although there can be shifts between the two organizations, he states that "at any given moment the person is either healthy or neurotic, depending on which system is dominant" (p. 103). That is, if the healthy organization is strong and dominant, the person will not engage in or be attracted to violence and destructive behavior. However, as Angyal points out, the recessed and weaker organization always exists as potential.

Angyal's theory of the ambiguous Gestalt lends theoretical support to May's concept of the daimonic, and also clarifies the ambiguity in Buber's "polar reality" when he states that "I see his whole polarity and then I see how the worst of him and the best of him are dependent on one another, attached to one another" (Buber, 1965, p. 180). Angyal (1965) also asserts, from his holistic perspective, that "health is present potentially in its full power in the most destructive, most baneful, most shameful behavior" (p. 104).

Critical to our interpretation is May's view of violence as "the daimonic gone awry." This strongly suggests that the destructive expression of the daimonic is not a natural tendency, but a perversion, an epiphenomenon, the inevitable result of feelings of power-lessness, loneliness, and anonymity. Rogers's view of violence and evil as a consequence of social conditioning and damaging self-experiences appears to be very much in agreement with May's statements. To push our interpretation to its limit, could we infer from May's statement "violence is the daimonic gone awry" that he is also in support of Rogers's position that, given the proper nutrients for human growth, the daimonic would express itself in positive, creative, self-actualizing ways? We believe so. Thus, when we examine carefully the views of both Rogers and May toward violence and evil, and clear away the rhetoric contained in their exchange, we must agree with Rogers (1982b) when he comments that "we agree in so many ways it is difficult to be exactly certain where we differ" (p. 86).

In any case, the debate between Rogers and May that suggested an irreconcilable division within the ranks of humanistic psychology, upon more careful study, does not lead to this conclusion. We suggest that for both May and Rogers, notwithstanding May's concept of the diamonic, human violence and evil behavior are natural, even predictable, consequences of destructive social forces and personal experiences. Such behavior, both Rogers and May seem to be saying, is an expression of an enraged impotence, a desperate effort to assert the self, to experience personal power, and to be recognized. Greening (1971), in a detailed study of assassins focusing on Sirhan Sirhan, seems to confirm this view. He notes that many assassins have been emotionally deprived "loners" and that assassination represents a "last-ditch attempt to establish a connection with society and save themselves from total alienation" (p. 24). Violence and aggression, therefore, are viewed by both theorists as secondary or derived phenomena rather than as innate tendencies.

A similar position has been taken by humanistic scholars from a variety of disciplines. The most powerful and articulate view that affirms a major humanistic perspective on violence and aggression, a view that emphasizes damage to the structure of the self, comes from Gruen's *The Betrayal of the Self* (1988). In this book, Gruen gives major attention to the psychic and social origins of hatred, aggression, and evil destructiveness.

For Gruen, the source of all evil in human affairs can be traced to self-alienation and to a fragmented self that inhibits and distorts healthy autonomous development in the personality. Gruen (1988) stresses the social forces that contribute to this widespread condition:

> The source of aggression and destructiveness lies in our culture, not in the individual. And everything that reinforces the fragmentation of our personality and closes off access to our inner world contributes to the creation and growth or our destructive drive. (p. 14)
>
> When adjustment to social reality demands a splitting in the psyche and makes this a guiding principle of development, people become evil. (p. 114)

It is our sense of helplessness, Gruen believes, that leads us to seek strength, confirmation, and power by victimizing others. Thus, he states, "a distorted development of autonomy is the root cause of the pathological and, ultimately, evil element in human beings" (p. xv).

Gruen (1988) boldly concludes his analysis by stating that "A self that is firmly grounded in autonomy cannot live with destructiveness. Destructiveness is something that develops in people, it is not innate but requires a complex process of growth marked by the failure to attain autonomy" (p. 114). Gruen's position clearly parallels May's view of the dangerous impact of anonymity, feelings of impotence, and powerlessness in releasing the destructive potential of the daimonic within the self. For both Gruen and May, violence becomes the ultimate expression of impotence, and they both suggest that in a desperate effort to exercise our power we may turn to violence.

The healthy assertion of power for Gruen lies in the achievement of wholeness and autonomy within the personality. Self-affirmation leads to affirmation of others and to the constructive and creative development of the personality.

Two other views are relevant to the position taken here. Fromm (1981), in reviewing Schecter's (1959) "Infant Development," concludes that "all data indicate that heteronomous interference with the child's and the later person's growth process is the deepest root of mental pathology, especially of destructiveness" (pp. 67–68).

Hall (1977), an anthropologist, also lends support to the positions of May, Rogers, Gruen, and Fromm when he states that "powerlessness and lack of self-affirmation lead to aggression, as repeatedly asserted by psychologists and psychiatrists" (p. 6). "It is our powerlessness in the face of culture and the cultural limitations placed on the development of the self that result in aggression" (p. 7).

We agree with Kohn that violence and aggression are responses to perceived threat. Yet, it is not just any threat that provokes such extreme responses. We believe that the catalyst for such behavior lies in threats to the most central values of the person and, in light of our foregoing discussion, that *the prototype of all human values is maintaining the structure and integrity of the self*.

As a prototype, this sovereign value is not culturally derived but is deeply rooted in the biopsychic structure and need system of the organism. It is the most primal element in Goldstein's (1963) theory of self-actualization, and in what Rogers (1963) has identified as the actualizing tendency. Threats to this organismic value, maintaining the structure and integrity of the self, is perceived as the most fundamental threat to our existence.

These assaults on the construction of one's identity usually begin in childhood and create a basic disruption in the continuity and integration of the self. Such attacks may take the form of overt cruelty, but there are many other expressions and subtle refinements of abuse that undermine the child's construction of truth and reality, which, in another context, Frick (1989) has termed the intimidation of experience.

> Many parent-child relations are based on this formula of intimidation until children become so estranged from their own inner processes and from the validity of their own experiences that they either go "crazy" in hate and self-denial or rebel in defiance against such violations to these most intimate aspects of selfhood. (p. 5)

The intimidation of experience goes on at all levels of human interaction: between parent and child, husband and wife, and teacher and student. The intimidation of the child's experience, however, is particularly pernicious because it undermines the psychic foundations for all later developments of the self.

To underscore the profound impact upon the child of abuse and intimidation, Shengold (1989) has referred to the phenomenon as "soul murder." Shengold documents, in excruciatingly painful detail, the great variety of forms such victimization can take.

Laing (1971) also addresses this issue. He describes a 17-year-old schizophrenic girl, Jane, who was lost in the delusion of a perpetual game of tennis. "Mixed doubles. Center Court, Wimbledon. The crowds, the court, the net, the players, and the ball, back and forth, back and forth, back and forth. She was all of these elements, especially the ball" (p. 15). Jane's reverie included the ball as it metamorphosed into a grenade, an atom bomb, a time bomb. To emphasize the accuracy of the metaphor, Jane was almost literally a ball in a family game. She served as a major conduit for most communications within the family. Father and mother and grandparents under one roof were aligned against each other and for weeks at a time they would refuse to speak except through Jane, who served as their only line of communication.

A consideration of the central role of values in violent and destructive behavior must also include more culturally derived values. Violence and aggressive behaviors are frequently linked to the protection, expression, or fulfillment of a culturally coded value, meaning, or belief. Such behavior serves as a means to a value-centered end that is central to the identity of an individual or group. In this sense, all culturally derived values are connected to the prototype value of protecting and preserving the structure and integrity of the self. Wars fought to protect "our way of life," the civil rights struggle, the bombing of abortion clinics, and the terrorist violence of the IRA in the struggle to "free" Northern Ireland serve as examples. In all of these cases, the eruption of violence and destruction serves to uphold, defend, or perpetuate a system of cherished values and beliefs.

In such shared values, the expression of violence often becomes a group phenomenon. Bakan (1982) views this group phenomenon within a larger and more insidious context. He sees the essence of evil as an institutional or collective phenomenon. In a response to the Rogers–May exchange, Bakan (1982) observes that

> the real evil in the modern world arises out of actions of major institutions such as those of governments and corporations. These system-problems may hardly be moved by motives of sex, aggression, and avarice in the way we might see these in individuals. Often they are motivated by a kind of Dr. Strangelove rationality, characterized by exaggerated rationality in connection with means and a dwarfed rationality in connection with values. (p. 91)

In outlining a value theory of violence and aggression, we have identified three primary levels of value organization in relation to the self:

1. *Individual, organismic values*. These involve protecting and enhancing the developing structure and integrity of the self. Interference with this project is likely to lead to the development of primal anger and aggression.

2. *Group values*. These involve protecting and promoting shared beliefs and meanings central to both the individual's and group's identity. These group values evolve
   from and constitute an expression of the prototype organismic value. If this latter
   value is nurtured, honored, and respected, the individual will identify himself or
   herself with life-positive, socially constructive group values. Anger, resentment,
   and hostility arising from early deprivation and damage to the growth process,
   however, will transfer to appropriate group values that support and express these
   hostile feelings.

3. *Institutional values*. These involve protecting and promoting values that have
   become rigidly embedded in our institutions. Where institutionalized values are
   antithetical to the healthy growth of the self, fostering a denigration of human needs
   and human dignity, it is the value itself that becomes destructive and evil. As Bakan
   (1982) suggests, such values may be particularly pernicious and damaging since
   they are so firmly entrenched and pervasive in our society and determine many
   governmental priorities and corporate policies. A recent research report (Stone,
   1991) concluded, for example, that over one-fourth of all children in the United
   States under the age of 12 are hungry or at risk of hunger. The U.S. infant mortality
   rate is now higher than those of 23 countries, while the appropriation to fight infant
   mortality is only one-sixth ($25 million) the amount authorized to purchase rockets
   for the U.S. Army ($152 million). Priorities reveal values and, whether it is a
   household budget or a government budget, nothing is quite as revealing as what
   we are willing to spend our money for.

The health, productivity, and creativity of a social system depends on a firm
commitment to the health, education, and welfare of children, and we cannot consider the
psychic health of children apart from government priorities and social policy. The psychic
health of children, therefore, depends upon social values that nurture the family, that
provide for proper housing, education, and health care. These supports create an environment that fosters the growth forces within the child. The more we can support and actualize
those values that enhance the growth of the self, the more we prevent the conditions that
contribute to violent, antisocial, and destructive behaviors.

While there is no simplistic solution to the problem of values or to the resolution of
value conflicts, the view we present provides us with a guidance system for discriminating
between false (pathological) and healthy values. Does the value in question provide a
nurturing environment for the growth of the self?

In a dissertation designed to explore the humanistic psychological interpretation of
violence, Posey (1972) provides strong support for a values theory of violence and
aggression. Although he deals with many other complex issues, he concludes his study by
offering the following hypotheses:

1. The single most reliable predictor of habitual responses of violence to frustration,
   instrumentation, and modeling is the individual's valuing process.
2. The more a person is predisposed to the realization of his unique meaning in life,
   the more he is committed to an internalized process of valuing and the less likely
   his habitual behavior will be characterized by violence.
3. The more social inhibitions to the actualization of the individual's unique set of
   meanings the greater chance of reactive and instrumental violence.
4. The more a person experiences support in his unique personal growth, the more he
   will provide support to the unique growth of others, and the general level of
   violence will diminish (Posey, 1972, p. 307).

PSYCHIATRIC PATIENTS IN RELATION
TO VIOLENCE AND AGGRESSION

We believe that the humanistic model outlined in this chapter serves as a sound theoretical approach in comprehending and addressing the destructive aggression of psychiatric patients. In these men and women we see the raw and violent forces that erupt from conditions of self-alienation, social isolation, and feelings of anonymity.

Psychiatric patients not only suffer from a fractured self-image and diminished sense of worth, but they are placed in institutions that, by their very nature, dehumanize and reinforce their feelings of helplessness. Hall (1977) captures the essence of this tragic situation. He observes that

> the ultimate in human degradation and the subservience of human needs to institutional forms is shown in Ken Kesey's novel *One Flew over the Cuckoo's Nest*. Big Nurse in Kesey's book epitomizes all the anti-humanism and destructiveness, all the distortions of the communication process, all the violations of cultural norms that one finds in the bureaucracies that we have created. The book is an exquisitely apt metaphorical statement of the powerlessness and lack of self-affirmation so common in our times. (p. 6)

We believe that such patients (even this medical label encourages a sense of helplessness), most of whom have been incarcerated involuntarily, resort to the only means available to them to express their pain and anger. In a desperate effort to assert the self and establish control, they often become violent, striking out in a rage born of despair.

SUMMARY

In this chapter, we have presented a humanistic view of violence and aggression. Rollo May was correct in saying that, for whatever reasons, humanistic psychology has been reluctant to deal with the issues of violence and evil in human behavior. In developing our interpretation of the humanistic position, therefore, we have had little to guide us in the form of previous scholarship in the area. With the exception of the Rogers–May exchanges, there have been only one or two articles that have appeared in the *Journal of Humanistic Psychology* that approach the subject at all. In this chapter we not only have presented our interpretation of the humanistic position, but have also taken the liberty of supplementing this interpretation by weaving within it our own humanistic theory of violence and aggression. This effort is seen, primarily, in our attempt to relate self-theory to human values.

We believe that the humanistic position developed here is consistent with, and complementary to, the core humanistic values outlined earlier in the chapter. We know, of course, that we do not, indeed cannot, speak for all humanistic psychologists. We are hopeful, however, that our presentation will accommodate most of them and prove fruitful in stimulating further thought and research on this most crucial, yet complex, issue. We also realize that the problems of violence and destruction in our society are sufficiently complex to transcend any one theoretical approach in our attempt to understand the meanings of such behavior and develop appropriate preventative and treatment strategies.

REFERENCES

Allport, G. (1960). The open system in personality theory. *Journal of Abnormal and Social Psychology*, *61*, 301–310.
Angyal, A. (1965). *Neurosis and treatment: A holistic theory*. New York: Wiley.

Ardrey, R. (1966). *The territorial imperative*. New York: Kingsport Press.

Bakan, D. (1982). On evil as a collective phenomenon. *Journal of Humanistic Psychology*, *22*, 91–92.

Baron, R. A. (1977). *Human aggression*. New York: Plenum.

Buber, M. (1965). *The knowledge of man*. New York: Harper and Row.

DeCarvalho, R. J. (1990). A history of the "third force" in psychology. *Journal of Humanistic Psychology*, *30*, 22–44.

Frankl, V. (1970). *The will to meaning*. New York. New American Library.

Frankl, V. (1984). *Man's search for meaning* (rev. ed.). New York: Washington Square Press.

Frick, W. (1989). *Humanistic psychology: Conversations with Abraham Maslow, Gardner Murphy, and Carl Rogers*. Bristol, IN: Wyndham Hall Press.

Fromm, E. (1981). *To have or to be*. New York: Bantam.

Giorgi, A. (Ed.). (1985). *Phenomenology and psychological research*. Pittsburgh: Duquesne University Press.

Goldstein, K. (1963). *The organism*. Boston: Beacon Press.

Greening, T. C. (1971). The psychological study of assassins. In W. J. Crotty (Ed.), *Assassins and the political order*. New York: Harper & Row.

Gruen, A. (1988). *The betrayal of the self*. New York: Grove Press.

Hall, E. T. (1977). *Beyond culture*. Garden City: Anchor Book.

Kohn, A. (1990). *The brighter side of human nature*. New York: Basic Books.

Laing, R. (1971). *The politics of the family*. New York: Vintage Books.

Lorenz, K. (1963). *On aggression*. New York: Harcourt, Brace, & World.

Maslow, A. (1968). *Toward a psychology of being* (2nd. ed.). Princeton: Van Nostrand.

May, R. (1969). *Love and will*. New York: Norton.

May, R. (1972). *Power and innocence: A search for the sources of violence*. New York: Norton.

May, R. (1982). The problem of evil: An open letter to Carl Rogers. *Journal of Humanistic Psychology*, *22*, 10–21.

Moustakas, C. (1990). *Heuristic research: Design, methodology, and applications*. Newbury Park, CA: Sage.

Posey, J. R. (1972). *Humanistic psychological interpretation of violence*. University Microfilms International Dissertation Information Service, Ann Arbor.

Rogers, C. R. (1963). The actualizing tendency in relation to "motives" and to consciousness. In M. Jones (Ed.), *Nebraska Symposium on Motivation* (pp. 1–24). Lincoln: University of Nebraska Press.

Rogers, C. R. (1982a). Notes on Rollo May. *Journal of Humanistic Psychology*, *22*, 8–9.

Rogers, C. R. (1982b). Reply to Rollo May's letter to Carl Rogers. *Journal of Humanistic Psychology*, *22*, 85–89.

Schecter, D. E. (1959). Infant development. In S. Arieti (Ed.), *American handbook of psychiatry (Vol. 2)*. New York: Basic Books.

Shengold, L. (1989). *Soul murder: The effects of childhood abuse and deprivation*. New Haven, CT: Yale University Press.

Stone, C. (1991, April). Fighting to save American babies. *Newspaper Enterprise Association*, *Albion* (Mich.) *Evening Recorder*, April 12, 1991, p. 4.

Wheelis, A. (1973). *How people change*. New York: Harper Torch Books.

PART II

GENERAL ISSUES

CHAPTER 7

Epidemiology

Alfonso Troisi and Marco Marchetti

INTRODUCTION

Psychiatric epidemiology is the quantitative study of the distribution and causes of mental disorders in human populations. Epidemiological studies involve three sequential levels of investigation: description, analysis, and experimentation (Regier & Burke 1989). Epidemiological method has the potential to make substantial contributions to the study of the relationship between aggressive behavior and mental disorders. At the descriptive level, epidemiological studies should produce basic estimates of the rate of aggression in psychiatric patients and compare the rate with that of the general population. At the analytical level, epidemiological studies should analyze the basis of variations in aggression rates between different diagnostic groups to identify risk factors that may contribute to the occurrence of violence. At the experimental level, epidemiological studies should test the presumed association between risk factors and aggressive behavior and seek to reduce the occurrence of aggression by controlling for risk factors.

Considering the amplitude of the three levels of investigation delineated above, an ideal epidemiological data base should be able to answer a variety of questions: Do psychiatric patients as a group commit violent acts more frequently than people who do not have psychiatric diagnoses? Are there differences in the factors that control aggression in normal subjects and psychiatric patients? What are the clinical and social features that make a patient more likely to engage in violent behavior? Among psychiatric patients, which are the diagnostic groups more likely to show such behavior?

Unfortunately, current knowledge on violence in the mentally ill does not provide conclusive answers to any of these questions. In part, this can be explained by considering that violent behavior is very complexly determined by a wide variety of biological, psychological, and sociological factors. Also, the vast majority of studies examining the

ALFONSO TROISI • Department of Psychiatry, University of Rome Tor Vergata, Rome, Italy.   MARCO MARCHETTI • Department of Forensic Psychopathology, University of Rome Tor Vergata, Rome, Italy.
Handbook of Aggressive and Destructive Behavior in Psychiatric Patients, edited by Michel Hersen, Robert T. Ammerman, and Lori A. Sisson. Plenum Press, New York, 1994.

nature, correlates, and predictors of aggression in psychiatric patients suffer from methodological problems that limit the validity of their findings.

The aim of this chapter is twofold: (1) to review the findings that have emerged from studies of behavior in psychiatric patients from an epidemiological perspective and (2) to critically examine the data reported in the literature. Data on two different forms of violent behavior—aggression toward others and suicide—will be reviewed separately. Before reviewing the epidemiological data concerning the distribution and correlates of aggression and suicide among patients with psychiatric disorders, we will delineate the methodological problems that complicate the interpretation of findings in these two areas of research. Finally, we will discuss some conceptual aspects that are likely to inspire future research on violence and psychiatric disorders.

AGGRESSION

Methodological Issues

The epidemiological study of the relationship between aggressive behavior and psychiatric disorders is complicated by a number of factors (see also Haller & Deluty, 1988). One factor is the difficulty in defining and measuring aggression. Until recently, the lack of suitable instruments for depicting the nature and severity of aggression has undoubtedly handicapped research on its prevalence, covariates, and predictors. In the psychiatric literature, operational definitions of aggressive behavior are often either vague or absent. For example, several studies either did not distinguish between physical and verbal aggression in their inferential statistical analyses or did not address the issue at all. A recent study by Kay, Wolkenfeld, and Murrill (1988a) shows the relevance of such a distinction: these authors identified different predictors for verbal and physical aggression, despite their exceptionally strong covariation.

In recent years a number of instruments have become available for measuring aggression. For example, Yudofsky, Silver, Jackson, Endicott, and Williams (1986) have developed a rating scale (Overt Aggression Scale [OAS]) for measuring overt aggression in psychiatric inpatients. On this scale, violent behavior is divided into four categories: verbal aggression, physical aggression against objects, physical aggression against self, and physical aggression against other people. A psychometrically improved version of this scale (MOAS) has been constructed by Kay et al. (1988a). Although the adoption of these instruments in epidemiological studies holds the promise of improving case definition, it is worth noting that these rating methods for aggression require detailed knowledge of patients and observation of their behavior. For this reason, they are most useful in inpatient settings (Plutchik & van Praag, 1990).

Another complicating factor is the difficulty of separating the *direct* effects of a mental disorder, such as psychological or physiological changes altering the probability of engaging in violent behavior, from the *indirect* effects resulting from disorder-associated changes, such as social ostracism, commitment status, and drug treatment, all of which may affect the threshold for aggressive response. In this regard, it is important to distinguish between violent acts committed by persons with mental disorders outside the hospital setting and those committed by psychiatric patients during hospital stay. On the one hand, the very fact that a patient is hospitalized may cause frustrations inherent in closed situations that lower the patient's threshold for aggressive response. On the other hand, in institutions, ward staff take a number of actions (e.g., seclusion and/or administration of increased medication) to prevent violent behavior. As a result, less violence may occur, and patient characteristics that might predict violence in the absence of intervention may appear to bear no relationship with violent behavior in the hospital environment (Tanke & Yesavage, 1985).

Another problem that complicates the interpretation of the findings is the procedure of data collection. Studies that focus on violent crime by psychiatric patients generally use arrest records as the source data. The results of these studies are hard to interpret. On the one hand, arrest rates of psychiatric patients may reflect their reduced capacity to avoid prosecution rather than their increased propensity to engage in violent behavior (Temple & Ladouceur, 1985). On the other hand, arrest rates may underestimate the frequency of violence among mentally ill people because of the police officers' unwillingness to subject a disturbed individual to the criminal process (Krakowski, Volavka, & Brizer, 1986).

Finally, the procedure of data analysis can affect the results. By the multivariate approach, several factors that would reach significance if analyzed one by one do not reach significance (Palmstierna & Wistedt, 1989). Considering the multidetermined causation of aggressive behavior, this statistical aspect is particularly relevant in evaluating data from epidemiological studies of violence.

Demographic Factors

There is controversy about the importance of demographic factors as opposed to mental status changes in predicting potential violence by psychiatric patients. At one extreme are those investigators who say that the role of mental illness is unimportant. They state that factors associated with violence in the mentally ill population are the same as those associated with violence in the general population (e.g., age, gender, social class, educational level; Monahan & Steadman, 1983). At the other extreme are those investigators who say that demographic variables are not very useful in either understanding or predicting violence among the mentally ill. They say that violent behavior in psychiatric patients is related to the type and degree of patients' psychopathology (e.g., Craig, 1982; Rossi, Jacobs, Monteleone, Olsen, Surber, Winkler, & Wommack, 1986). Advocating the latter position, Rossi et al. (1986) have concluded that "the accumulated results in the literature to date present inconsistent findings on just about every demographic variable that has been studied" (p. 158).

Age

Although some studies (Rossi et al., 1986; Tanke & Yesavage, 1985) found no significant association between age and assaultive or fear-inducing behavior in psychiatric patients, most researchers concur that assaultive patients tend to be relatively young, usually under age 40 (e.g., Fottrell, 1980; Tardiff & Koenigsberg, 1985; Tardiff & Sweillam, 1980). The reason for the association between young age and aggressive behavior is not clear. Tardiff and Sweillam (1979) suggested that differences in the incidence of disorders between age groups may be an important factor, with schizophrenia, personality disorder, and drug abuse being more common in the young. However, the finding that younger patients (aged 25 years or less) are more likely to be violent than older patients has been recently confirmed by a study controlling for the psychiatric diagnosis (James,

Fineberg, Shah, & Priest, 1990). Two independent sources of evidence suggest that the association between young age and aggressive behavior is not a spurious one. First, violent crime, including homicide, is more common among young people in the general population as well (Lewis, 1989). Second, patients with psychiatric disorders in which aggressive behavior is an essential feature (e.g., antisocial personality disorder) improve as they get older (Perry & Vaillant, 1989).

Gender

Studies on the relationship between gender and violence in psychiatric patients have yielded conflicting results. Several investigators have found that men are more likely to be violent than women (e.g., Pearson, Wilmot, & Padi, 1986; Rossi et al., 1986; Tardiff & Koenigsberg, 1985); others have found that women are more likely to be violent than men (e.g., Fottrell, 1980); still others have found that men and women are almost equally likely to be violent (e.g., Craig, 1982; Kay et al., 1988a; Tardiff & Sweillam, 1982).

The relationship between gender and assaultiveness is complex, with moderator variables such as age likely playing an important role. Tardiff and Sweillam (1979) noted that 65% of their assaultive sample was male; however, when stratified by age, they found that the majority of assaultive patients under 25 years old were female, that the majority of those between 25 and 64 were male, and that there were no gender differences for the assaultive patients over 65. Binder and McNiel (1990) have recently demonstrated that the relationship between gender and violence varies depending on the context. During the period shortly before hospitalization, men are more physically assaultive and also display more fear-inducing behavior (i.e., verbal attacks, threats to attack, or attacks on objects) than women. During the initial phase of hospitalization, a different pattern emerges: men show more fear-inducing behavior and women are more physically assaultive. To explain their results, the authors have suggested the possibility that, in the hospital environment, staff members may react differently to male and female patients: staff may be fearful of male patients and take more precautions (e.g., use of medications and seclusion to prevent violence).

Socioeconomic Factors

Like the relationship between age and gender and patient assaultiveness, the relationship between socioeconomic factors and patient assaultiveness is uncertain and requires further study. Investigating the relationship between socioeconomic status and violence in the general population, Messner and Tardiff (1986) found that economic inequality and race were not related to homicide, but rather the prime determinants were absolute poverty and marital disruption. It is likely that these factors play a role in precipitating violence among psychiatric patients as well.

In fact, Edwards, Jones, Reid, and Chu (1988) reported that there were significantly more patients from lower socioeconomic classes in the assaultive group than in the control group of psychiatric inpatients of their study. Tardiff and Sweillam (1980) found that patients with lower educational levels were more likely than others to have had problems with assaultive behavior before hospital admission. This finding has not been confirmed by Rossi et al. (1986), who found no significant association between educational levels and either fear-inducing or assaultive behavior.

Studies focusing on the relationship between socioeconomic status and violence in psychiatric patients should control for the diagnosis because some disorders (e.g., schizo-phrenia) are more common in lower socioeconomic classes. Unfortunately, the vast majority of the studies have not given appropriate consideration to this methodological aspect.

Situational Factors

A full understanding of violent behavior must take into account both the characteristics of the potentially violent person and situational factors. Most of the available information concerns the contextual variables associated with the hospital setting. There is some evidence in the literature to suggest that inpatients behave aggressively when they are bored and not involved in therapeutic activities (Fottrell, 1980; Pearson et al., 1986). Pearson et al. (1986) reported that, within three acute wards, the commonest events precipitating violence were patients being detained on the ward or given medication against their will. James et al. (1990) found an association between a decrease in permanent staffing and an increase in violence in a psychiatric ward. As a possible explanation for their results, these authors referred to the studies indicating that disturbed patients are in need of stability and continuity around them (e.g., Armond 1982). Confirming this, there is also evidence that intrahospital relocation may be a risk factor for precipitating aggression in psychiatric patients. Reviewing the patient records of 201 individuals who had been admitted to a state hospital and subsequently transferred to another ward in the same hospital, Thomas, Ekland, Griffin, Hagerott, Leichman, Murphy, and Osborne (1990) found that the highest mean aggression for a single day was the day following transfer.

The time of the day and the period of the year have also been shown to play a role in affecting the psychiatric patients' likelihood of being violent. Fottrell (1980) reported data on the timing of violent incidents in the hospital setting: 30% of all incidents occurred between 7 a.m. and 9 a.m. In keeping with this finding, Edwards et al. (1988) found that most of the assaults in a psychiatric unit took place during the mornings. Roitman, Orev, and Schreiber (1990) found a distinct difference in monthly patterns of violent behavior (as measured by the need for physical restraint) throughout the year between affective and nonaffective groups of hospitalized psychiatric patients. While the number of restrained nonaffective patients was constant throughout the year, the number of restrained affective patients showed a circannual rhythm, with nadirs in May and November and peaks in June and December.

The interaction between situational variables and type of psychopathology in influenc-ing aggressive behavior is demonstrated by a recent study (Binder & McNiel, 1988) showing that the risk of violence by different diagnostic groups varies according to context. These authors found that, in the community during the period before hospitalization, both schizophrenic and manic patients had a higher risk of assaultive behavior than patients with other diagnoses. During acute hospitalization, however, manic patients were more likely to be assaultive than schizophrenic patients and patients with other diagnoses.

Psychiatric Patients as a Whole

Epidemiological studies of the incidence of aggressive behavior among the generality of patients with psychiatric disorders have yielded conflicting results (see Table 1).

According to Fottrell (1980), there is no substantial body of evidence to prove that psychiatric patients as a group are more violent than the general population. In fact, a

TABLE 1.   **Prevalence Rates of Aggression among Psychiatric Patients in the Community and Hospital Setting**

Study	Number of patients	Percentage of violent patients and type of aggressive behavior	Context
Tardiff & Sweillam (1980)	$N = 9,365$ (inpatients)	10%; type of behavior not specified	Community
Craig (1982)	$N = 876$ (inpatients)	11%; type of behavior not specified	Community
Tardiff & Koenisberg (1985)	$N = 2,916$ (outpatients)	3%; type of behavior not specified	Community
Pearson et al. (1986)	$N = 1,220$ (inpatients)	11.8%; type of behavior not specified	Hospital
Binder & McNeil (1988)	$N = 253$ (inpatients)	20.9%; attacks on persons 25.3%; fear-inducing behavior	Community
Binder & McNeil (1988)	$N = 253$ (inpatients)	13%; attacks on persons 32%; fear-inducing behavior	Hospital
Kay et al. (1988a)	$N = 114$ (inpatients)	7%; physical aggression	Hospital
Palmistierna & Wistedt (1989)	$N = 105$ (inpatients)	27.6%; type of behavior not specified	Hospital

number of studies (Fottrell, 1980; Tardiff & Sweillam, 1979, 1982) have indicated that the vast majority of psychiatric patients are not assaultive. There appears to be a small core of patients, typically 7–10% of the total population, who display assaultive behavior. Craig (1982) reported that assaultive behavior occurred among 11% of a total sample ($N = 876$) of public hospital psychiatric inpatients before admission to the hospital. Surveys of New York area psychiatric hospitals indicate the rate of reported assault to be in the range of 7% to 10% of patients, as based on a 1- to 3-month period of observation (Bureau of Evaluation and Research, 1984). Among outpatients, the rate of assaultive behavior seems to be much lower: Tardiff and Koenigsberg (1985) found that, of 2,916 patients who came for evaluation in two outpatient clinics, 3% had manifested recent assaultive behavior toward other persons.

In contrast with the above data, several studies have reported substantially higher rates of aggression among psychiatric patients. Rabkin (1979) reviewed a number of studies and concluded that arrests and conviction rates for violent crimes are greater for psychiatric patients than for the general population. In a three-unit sample of 114 inpatients, mostly with a diagnosis of schizophrenia, Kay et al. (1988a) reported that some form of aggression was measured in about one-fourth of patients during only a 5-day observation period. The prevalence was lowest among chronic patients (15%) but more than double that rate for new admissions. On the secure care unit—a unit providing for more dangerous patients—almost half exhibited aggressive behavior in the span of 5 days. Examining preadmission (within 2 weeks of hospitalization) and in-hospital (during the first 24 hours) violence in a sample of 253 patients admitted to a short-term psychiatric unit, Binder and McNeil (1988) found that 46% of the patients had either engaged in fear-inducing behavior or had attacked a person before admission, and 45% had done so during the first 24 hours of hospitalization.

These conflicting data suggest that psychiatric patients should not be regarded as a homogeneous group and, therefore, no statements with regard to mental patients in general appear justified. It is likely that mental illness in and of itself contributes little to the prediction of the predisposition to act aggressively. Psychiatric populations may contain subgroups with unusually violent predispositions balanced by larger groups with less than average propensities to aggression.

PSYCHIATRIC DIAGNOSIS

To test the hypothesis that within the generality of mentally abnormal individuals there are definable groups or classes with an increased risk of violent behavior, many studies have searched for relationships between specific psychiatric diagnoses and increased rates of aggression. A major problem with most of these studies is that primary diagnoses of the nonassaultive patients in each sample were not assessed or reported (Haller & Deluty, 1988). Following the lead of Tardiff (1988), we summarize the main results on diagnosis and violence by categorizing psychiatric disorders into three groups: organic mental disorders, psychotic disorders, and nonorganic, nonpsychotic disorders.

Organic Mental Disorders

Several studies report a high prevalence of assaultiveness (ranging between 20% and 23%) in patients with organic mental syndrome (Craig, 1982; Rossi et al., 1986; Tardiff & Sweillam, 1980). Reviewing the medical records of 195 geriatric patients admitted to a psychiatric hospital over a 9-year period, Kalunian, Binder, and McNiel (1990) found that, during the 2 weeks before admission, 20% of the patients had physically assaulted others and 20% had engaged in fear-inducing behavior. Several studies indicate that psychosis is the important factor producing aggressive behavior among geriatric patients rather than organic mental syndrome per se. Kalunian et al. (1990) found that patients with senile organic psychotic conditions were significantly more likely to attack others than were patients with other diagnoses. In a sample of 208 psychiatric inpatients, Kay, Wolkenfeld, and Murrill (1988b) found that the diagnosis of organic brain syndrome with psychosis was overrepresented among patients showing aggressive behavior. Reviewing the medical records of 222 patients admitted to a geriatric psychiatry unit, Petrie, Lawson, and Hollender (1982) reported that organic illness accounted for a minority of acts of violence, the majority having been perpetrated by patients with functional diagnoses of late paraphrenia, schizophrenia, or mania. In dementia, violence is seen in advanced forms of the illness and is but one feature in the global deterioration of personality. Unlike geriatric patients who experience paranoid delusions in a clear sensorium, patients suffering from dementia pose a much less serious threat to others (Petrie et al., 1982).

One of the most extensively investigated brain syndromes that has been associated with violence is complex-partial seizures. There seems to be an increased frequency of epilepsy in prison inmates: Gunn and Bonn (1971) found a prevalence of epilepsy in prisons of 7.1 per thousand men (normal population 4.2 per thousand). However, in this study, epileptic prisoners were no more violent than nonepileptic prisoners. In a review of EEGs carried out on 333 men convicted of violent crimes, Williams (1969) found that 57% of those with a history of habitual aggression or explosive rage showed EEG abnormalities as opposed to 12% of those who had committed an isolated act of aggression.

A high proportion of patients with temporal lobe epilepsy appear to show explosive aggressive tendencies, not only in relation to attacks but as an enduring trait of their personalities. Outbursts are described as typically sudden, extreme, inexplicable, and without remorse. Even though there is a good deal of presumptive evidence for a relationship between temporal lobe epilepsy and aggression, it is possible that such a relationship depends on factors such as poor parenting, neglect, and impaired general health, which are not always readily apparent (Lishman, 1987). In addition, it is worth noting that some studies (Mungas, 1983; Rodin, 1973) failed to demonstrate a relationship between violence and epilepsy in general or temporal lobe epilepsy in particular.

The nosological status of other organic mental disorders related to violent behavior seems doubtful, and epidemiological data on their prevalence are lacking. The term *syndrome of episodic dyscontrol* is used for patients characterized by uncontrollable storms of aggression, sometimes on minimal or no provocation and sometimes associated with phenomena of a quasi-epileptic nature. Maletzky (1973) suggests that these patients suffer from abnormalities of the limbic regions that set the threshold for episodes of uncontrollable anger at an unusually low level.

Violent acts have frequently been associated with the acute ingestion of exogenous substances including alcohol, amphetamines, LSD, and cocaine (reviewed in Burrowes, Hales, & Arrington, 1988). Few drugs (phencyclidine and amphetamines), in and of themselves, are known to cause violence (Ellinwood, 1971; McCardle & Fishbein, 1989). The term *pathological intoxication* refers to irrational combative behavior leading to seriously destructive actions and occurring abruptly during the course of alcohol intoxication. As typically described, the behavior is out of character for the individual concerned, the duration is short, and there is subsequently amnesia for the entire episode (Coid, 1979). The relative contribution of alcohol to the development of violent behavior, versus the role of an underlying psychiatric disorder, is unclear.

Psychotic Disorders

Schizophrenia

Comparing the crime rate of schizophrenics with that of the general population, Lindqvist and Allebeck (1990) reported that the rate of violent offenses was four times higher among schizophrenics, even though the violence recorded was almost exclusively of minor severity. Several studies have found that schizophrenic patients are more likely than other patients to be violent in the period preceding hospitalization (Craig, 1982; Krakowski et al., 1986; Rossi et al., 1986; Tardiff & Sweillam, 1980) and to be assaultive in the hospital (Fottrell, 1980; Krakowski et al., 1986; Yesavage, Werner, & Becker, 1981). Tardiff (1984) has argued that the relative risk of violence by schizophrenic patients varies depending on whether the patients are in the hospital or not: during hospitalization, schizophrenic patients are less likely to be violent than other patients. A recent study (Binder & McNiel, 1988) has confirmed that the frequency of violence by schizophrenic patients decreases after admission. Whereas before admission schizophrenic and manic patients were almost equally likely to attack persons, during the early phase of hospitalization manic patients were more likely than schizophrenics to attack persons.

Several studies have analyzed the occurrence of violence in schizophrenic patients with various clinical symptomatology. Assessing the prevalence of agitation, anger, and assaultiveness in all patients admitted during one year from a single catchment area to public mental hospitals, Craig (1982) found that, in schizophrenic patients, the prevalence rate for attacks on people was almost 20%. Assaultive patients with schizophrenia were significantly more likely to be agitated and angry than nonassaultive schizophrenic patients. The author concluded that assaultiveness is specifically linked with emotional distress among patients with schizophrenia and that schizophrenic patients without overt agitation and anger are less likely to be assaultive.

The majority of studies (reviewed in Krakowski et al., 1986) indicate that paranoid schizophrenics are more dangerous than nonparanoid ones and that their violent behavior is usually well planned, directed at a specific person, and associated with high levels of hostility and resentment. However, Tardiff and Sweillam (1982) found higher rates of aggression in nonparanoid schizophrenics. Neurological impairment associated with schizophrenia may also play a role in altering the likelihood of engaging in acts of violence. Krakowski, Convit, Jaeger, Lin, and Volavka (1989) classified schizophrenic inpatients into high-, low-, or no-violence groups. Neurological and neuropsychological abnormalities differentiated the groups, with the high-violence group evidencing more abnormalities than the other two groups in the area of integrative sensory and motor functions.

Mania

The issue of dangerousness of acute manic patients remains an open question. Krakowski et al. (1986) state that, in mania, violence occurs in the context of marked irritability and agitation, but while these features are prominent in the disorder, serious violence itself is rare. Two studies that did examine the preadmission behavior of manic patients reported that mania was associated with high levels of agitation, anger, and fear-inducing behavior but not actual assaultiveness (Craig, 1982; Rossi et al., 1986). To explain these findings, Craig (1982) hypothesized that manic patients, while suffering emotional distress similar to that of schizophrenic and organic brain syndrome patients, may retain a degree of impulse control that is absent in the two former groups.

Contrary to the findings reported above, Binder and McNeil (1988) found that, in their sample ($N = 46$) of manic patients, 30% attacked persons and 26% engaged in fear-inducing behavior during the 2-week period before hospitalization. Such figures were similar to those of schizophrenic patients and significantly higher than those of patients with other diagnoses. The authors' conclusion was that a decompensating patient with poor impulse control may be at risk for violence in the community regardless of the diagnostic type of functional psychosis (i.e., schizophrenia or mania). Another finding of Binder and McNeil's (1988) study concerns the violence potential of manic patients in the hospital. Manic patients were the most likely diagnostic group to be assaultive during the initial phase of hospitalization. In a previous study, Yesavage (1983) had already shown that manic patients may be liable to commit assaults in the hospital.

Depression

When compared with patients with other psychiatric diagnoses, especially schizophrenia and mania, patients with a diagnosis of depression, with or without active psychotic phenomena, are significantly less likely to be violent (e.g., James et al., 1990). Based on 10-year incidence data collected in Germany, Böker and Häfner (1973, quoted in Harrer & Kofler-Westergren, 1986) reported that the violent crime rate in affective psychosis amounted to 0.006% compared with a rate of 0.05% in schizophrenic patients. However, this numerical depiction of violence by depressed patients is misleading. The extended suicide is regarded as the most typical act of violence associated with depression. Often this concerns severely depressed young mothers of 30 to 40 years of age, who in a delusional frame of mind include their children in their suicide, to prevent them from a presumably unavoidable disaster (Harrer & Kofler-Westergren, 1986). In addition to depressed mothers of young children, the phenomenon of homicide-linked depression also involves other types of "domestic murderers" (those with no previous criminal record who kill family members and intimates, in contrast to "criminal murderers" who kill while carrying out a crime) and instigators of a suicide pact (Rosenbaum & Bennett, 1986).

Rosenbaum and Bennett (1986), reviewing the literature on homicide and depression, suggested that depressed patients at risk for homicide (or murder-suicide) are those in whom there is a personality disorder, a history of child abuse, alcohol or drug abuse, or suicidal behavior, and for whom the precipitating factor of the depression is sexual infidelity, real or fantasized. These authors have called attention to a characteristic of depressed patients that can explain the tendency to overlook the relationship between depression and outward aggression in the psychiatric literature: many depressed patients usually give no hint of violent behavior when in the doctor's office, where they tend to appear compliant and inactive, which may be in stark contrast to their behavior at home, where they may be argumentative and explosive.

Nonorganic, Nonpsychotic Disorders

There is a general agreement that neurotic disorders are generally associated with a relatively low rate of aggressive behavior (Noble & Rodger, 1989; Pearson et al., 1986; Tardiff & Sweillam, 1980). The relationship of personality disorder to violent behavior is more complicated. Fottrell (1980) has argued that, in determining whether violence is exhibited, the underlying personality of the individual is far more important than psychiatric illness from which the individual suffers. Several studies conducted in the hospital setting confirm that personality disorder is an overrepresented diagnosis among violent patients (Craig, 1982; Tardiff & Sweillam, 1980, 1982). Also among psychiatric outpatients, there is an association between assaultive behavior and personality disorder (Tardiff & Koenisberg, 1985). Criminological studies report even higher rates: Gunn (1977) diagnosed abnormal personality in 20% of prisoners, and Guze (1976) described 70% of prisoners discharged from American prisons as "sociopathic."

In evaluating the relationship between personality disorder and violence, two considerations are important. First, according to current nosography, patients with personality disorders are a heterogeneous group that includes subgroups with unusually violent predispositions (antisocial personality disorder, borderline personality disorder) and subgroups with less than average propensities to aggression (e.g., avoidant personality disorder). Second, in examining a person with repeatedly antisocial or aggressive behavior, clinicians may tend to diagnose antisocial personality disorder even if independent evidence of psychiatric disorder is absent (Lewis, 1989). Therefore, further studies based on accurate diagnostic assessment are necessary before concluding that personality disorder is a risk factor for violent behavior.

The relationship of alcohol or drug abuse to violent behavior is complex, and epidemiological data are conflicting. Studies of inpatients have reported a relatively infrequent occurrence of assaultive behavior among alcohol and drug abusers (Craig, 1982; Tardiff & Sweillam, 1979, 1980). Noble and Rodger (1989) found very few violent patients with a primary diagnosis of drug addiction or alcoholism, in spite of the fact that the hospital in their study had special inpatient units dealing with these conditions. In contrast with these results, Kay et al. (1988b) found aggressive behavior to be associated with diagnosis of alcoholism and substance abuse disorder, and Palmstierna and Wistedt (1989) reported that drug abuse correlated significantly with violent behavior during acute involuntary admission.

Alcohol has been found to have a biphasic relationship with aggressive behavior. Using data collected from 1,149 convicted male felons, Collins and Schlenger (1988) contrasted the acute (drinking just before the violent event) and chronic (a psychiatric diagnosis of alcohol abuse or dependence) effects of alcohol use on violence. They found that acute, but not chronic, effects of alcohol were significantly associated with incarceration for a violent offense. Similarly, the stage of the substance abuse disorder is likely to influence the probability of aggressive responses. In their sample of 132 narcotic addicts with multiple periods of addiction, Hanlon, Nurco, Kinlock, and Duszynsky (1990) found a much higher frequency of violent crimes during the first phase of addiction and a progressive decrease during subsequent periods. There is a general agreement in the literature that the contribution of drugs to violent crime occurs most prominently when addicts in search of funds to support their habits become involved in robberies and burglaries in which victims resist (Watters, Reinarman, & Fagan, 1985).

SUICIDE

People who commit suicide (completed suicide) and those who survive after taking an overdose or harming themselves (deliberate self-harm) differ in many respects. Because such differences are largely reflected in the epidemiology of these two forms of self-aggression, epidemiological data concerning suicide and deliberate self-harm should be analyzed separately. The data reported below are limited to the epidemiology of suicide, even though it is worth noting that, from the clinical perspective, the two forms of behavior are not distinctly separate. Indeed, in a third to a half of completed suicides there is a history of previous deliberate self-harm (Gelder, Gath, & Mayou, 1989).

Methodological Issues

Methodological strategies used in suicide research include ecological analyses across total populations, retrospective studies, and prospective studies. Ecological studies compare suicide rates between nations or, within a nation, between sex and age groups. Trend analyses are used to examine the patterns of suicide mortality in various populations over time. The problem with these studies is that accurate statistics about suicide are difficult to obtain. Occasionally it is uncertain whether a death is caused by suicide or murder. Much more often it is difficult to decide whether death was by suicide or accident. Among people whose deaths are recorded as accidental, many have recently been depressed or dependent on drugs or alcohol, thus resembling people who commit suicide (Gelder et al., 1989). For these reasons, it is not surprising that official statistics appear to underestimate the true rates of suicide.

Lacking the opportunity to interview the proband, retrospective studies of patients who died from suicide cannot describe the psychopathology as completely as a prospetive study can, even when an accurate "psychological autopsy" is made. Conducting a psychological autopsy allows one to make a retrospective diagnosis based on a variety of sources of information, such as relatives, medical records, suicide notes, and coroner's reconstructions of the events surrounding the suicide itself (Robins & Kulbock, 1986). Another disadvantage of retrospective studies is that they cannot generate a true control group to distinguish between those features associated with suicide and those associated with the presence of an affective disorder. Prospective studies allow personal interviews with the individuals, and thus provide more and better quality information than those obtainable after death. However, prospective investigations yield fewer data about circumstances immediately antecedent to the suicide act, because it is unlikely that the suicide will follow closely upon an interview. In addition, the ethical requirement to attempt to prevent a suicide (if there is a clear and imminent danger) compromises the scientific objectivity of prospective studies (Robins & Kulbock, 1986).

Demographic Factors

Age

In both men and women, suicide rates increase with age. Suicide rates in the elderly have decreased recently but are still much higher than in younger people. Recently, there has been a sharp increase in the 15- to 25-year age group (Robins & Kulbock, 1986). As a population grouping, adolescents are the second most at risk for completion of suicide. There are significant differences between the young and the old for both psychiatric diagnoses and antecedent stressors (Roy, 1989). Diagnoses of drug use disorders and antisocial personality disorder are more frequent among suicide victims under 30 years of age, while diagnoses of mood and organic disorders are found more often among suicide victims aged 30 and over. The most common stressors associated with suicide in those under 30 are separation, rejection, unemployment, and legal troubles; illness stressors are more common among suicide victims over 30.

Gender

Many studies have shown that men commit suicide three times as often as women. Such a difference in the suicide rate between men and women is complexly determined as shown by a recent study (Rich, Ricketts, Fowler, & Young, 1988) of 204 consecutive suicides indicating that: (a) men used more violent, immediately lethal methods of suicide; (b) men were almost three times more likely to be substance abusers; and (c) men were more likely to have economic problems as stressors.

Socioeconomic Factors

Because of cultural and social differences, national suicide rates vary considerably. The highest suicide rates have been reported in Hungary (about 40 per 100,00 per year). Among the lowest rates are those of Spain (about 4 per 100,000) and Greece (about 3 per 100,000). Rates are generally lower in Roman Catholic countries. Countries vary greately not only in their rates in a particular year but also in the stability of their rates. The rate for the United States (12 per 100,000) has been quite stable over the last two decades, while in Europe the rates for some countries have fallen and those for other countries have risen (Robins & Kulbock, 1986).

Social isolation is a prominent risk factor for suicide. Compared with the general population, people who have committed suicide are more likely to have been divorced, unemployed, or were living alone. Suicide rates are lowest among the married and increase progressively through those classified as never married, widowers and widows, and divorced. Rates are higher in social class V (unskilled workers) and social class I (professional) than in the remaining social classes (Gelder et al., 1989). Immigrants, who are likely to feel alienated, have higher rates than natives of either their adopted countries or their countries of origin. Suicide rates are higher in urban than rural areas, although this situation is reversing in the United States because of the availability of guns in rural areas (Roy, 1989).

Situational Factors

Suicide rates vary with the seasons. In the northern hemisphere, spring and early summer are the seasons of higher incidence. Also, the weekly distribution has been reported to show significant variations with the highest incidence of suicide on Monday. As for contextual variables, there is evidence that, among psychiatric patients, suicide is much more common after discharge from a hospitalization than while in the hospital (see below).

Nonpsychiatric Populations

The overwhelming majority (94% according to Barraclough, Bunch, Nelson, & Sainsbury, 1974) of suicide victims suffer a psychiatric illness at the time of the suicide act. It is debated whether, occasionally, suicide may be the rational act of a mentally healthy person. For example, in some cases, suicide may be seen to result from a rational exercise of personal rights, that is, a clear choice of death over pain (Stevenson, 1988). Also, descriptions of mass suicides suggest that the suicidal act is not necessarily associated with psychiatric illness because it is unlikely that the victims were all suffering from mental disorder (Gelder et al., 1989).

Physical illness is an important contributing factor in a relevant percentage of suicides. Chronic painful illnesses (e.g., cancer, Cushing's disease, porphyria, kidney diseases requiring dialysis, epilepsy, Huntington's chorea, and dementia) are particularly prominent among the medical diagnoses associated with a high risk of suicide. It is difficult to determine the specific contribution of these medical diagnoses to suicide risk because all are diseases in which an associated mood disorder is known to occur (Roy, 1989). In the last few years, AIDS has emerged as a risk factor for suicide: the suicide rate in patients with AIDS is 66 times higher than the general population rate (Marzuk, Tierney, Tardiff, Gross, Morgan, Hsu, & Mann, 1988). Suicide generally occurs in the early stages of disease (i.e., the first six months following diagnosis). It is unclear whether the emotional stress or the neurological damage associated with the disease process is the most important factor in increasing suicide risk among patients with AIDS.

Psychiatric Diagnosis

Two specific psychiatric disorders are associated with more than two-thirds of all completed suicides. Affective illness, usually major depression, was identified in 40% to 80% of the victims in a consecutive series of suicides (Barraclough et al., 1974), and alcoholism was found in 20% to 30% (Grinspoon, 1986).

The lifetime incidence of suicide among depressed patients is 15%, a rate about four times higher than that of other psychiatric diagnostic groups and 22 to 36 times higher than that of the general population (Pokorny, 1964). Suicide among depressed patients occurs infrequently in the early stages of affective complaints. As among other psychiatric patients, the months after discharge from a hospitalization are a time of high risk. Specific symptoms seem to be associated with a higher suicide risk. In a prospective study of 954 patients with major affective disorder followed for an average of four years, Fawcett, Scheftner, Clark, Hedeker, Gibbons, and Coryell (1987) found that hopelessness, anhedonia, and mood cycling during the index episode differentiated the suicide group. Within the various diagnostic categories of affective illness, patients with psychotic depression are more likely to commit suicide compared to those in the larger category of nondelusional depressive illnesses. Also, patients with a diagnosis of bipolar disorder are at exceptionally high risk for committing suicide, constituting (with unipolar depressed patients) the single highest risk group for suicide. In these patients, 10% to 30% of all deaths are due to suicides. Studies that have divided bipolar patients into diagnostic subgroups suggest that those patients with histories of hypomania but no mania (Bipolar II) have higher rates of suicide (Jamison, 1986). The most critical phases of the illness are the depressive state and the mixed state (i.e., combination of depressive symptoms and tense, restless behavior). It is worth noting that, although the majority of the studies have reported that psychotic depression and bipolar disorder are associated with a higher suicide risk, some reports do not support this finding. Robins (1986), analyzing psychological autopsy data on 134 subjects who had committed suicide, found that over 80% of the patients were not psychotic at the time of suicide. Black, Winokur, and Nasrallah (1988) have found no significant difference in the suicide rates for psychotic and nonpsychotic patients with major depression or bipolar disorder, and a lower suicide risk for bipolar patients. A possible explanation for these conflicting findings is that the psychopharmacological advances of the last decades (e.g., lithium prophylaxis) have changed the relative risk of suicide among the various subgroups of patients with mood disorders (Roy, 1989).

The lifetime risk of suicide in the schizophrenic patient is 15% (Bleuler, 1978). Unlike a patient with a psychotic depression, who may have a higher risk for suicide than the nonpsychotic depressive patient, the actively hallucinating schizophrenic patient has a lower incidence of death by suicide than the schizophrenic patient who is in the depressive, recovery phase of an exacerbation of the schizophrenic illness (Roy, 1989). The highest suicide rate in the schizophrenia population is among young men who are in the earliest stages of their illnesses, principally the first four years. These patients tend to experience severe functional deterioration, yet retain a basically nondelusional awareness of the chronicity of their illness. In sum, the risk factors for suicide among schizophrenics are young age, male sex, single marital status, a previous suicide attempt, a vulnerability to develop depressive symptoms, and recent discharge from hospitalization (Roy, 1989).

Several studies suggest that patients with personality disorders represent a significant proportion of completed suicides. A methodological problem involved in this type of research is that most studies have tended to lump all personality disorder diagnoses together, so that data on suicidality in any particular personality disorder are scarce. However, there is evidence that antisocial personality disorder and borderline personality disorder constitute a relevant risk factor for suicide (Frances, Fyer, & Clarkin, 1986). Among patients with antisocial personality disorder, a 5% rate of completed suicide has been reported. A similar suicide rate has been estimated for patients with borderline personality disorder. There is evidence that, in both of these personality disorders, suicide completers are likely to have a concurrent diagnosis, especially depression or substance abuse. These epidemiological data suggest that, even though suicide attempts in personality disorders are in most cases repetitive and without lethal intent, clinicians should be especially concerned about those patients who present with comorbid diagnoses, for example, a combination of borderline personality disorder with major affective disorder.

The relationship between substance abuse, and more specifically alcoholism, and suicide is well documented. Alcoholism is the second most frequent psychiatric disorder among those who die from suicide. Among alcoholics, the lifetime risk of suicide is commonly estimated to be about 15% (Frances, Franklin, & Flavin, 1986). However, Murphy and Wetzel (1990) have recently argued that current estimates of a 10% to 15% lifetime risk in suicide in alcoholism are statistically untenable. They maintain that the lifetime risk is closer to 2% to 3.4%. Even at this rate, the likelihood of suicide is conservatively diagnosed alcoholism is between 60 and 120 times that of the non-psychiatrically ill. Comorbidity, particularly the supervention of a depressive disorder, is relevant to risk in the individual alcoholic, as are psychosocial changes such as inter-personal losses and social isolation. Suicide generally occurs after years of alcoholism.

The age-adjusted rate of suicide for opiate addicts is estimated to be 5 to 20 times that of the general population (Murphy, Rounsaville, Eyre, & Kleber, 1983). In a sample of 533 treated opiate addicts, Rounsaville, Weissman, Kleber, and Wilber (1982) reported a 17% lifetime prevalence of suicide attempts. Substance abuse is a risk factor for suicide especially among young people: 70% of teen suicides are associated in some way with substance abuse. Like alcoholics, drug addicts are more likely to commit suicide after many years of substance abuse.

SUMMARY AND FUTURE DIRECTIONS FOR RESEARCH

The full potential of the epidemiological study of the relationship between violence and mental illness has yet to be realized. We have noted that some aspects of the epidemiological data on aggressive behavior appear to be quite inadequate, and there are major gaps in suicide research. Thus, the accumulated results in the literature to date present inconsistent findings, and even prevailing opinions (e.g., that young, male patients with psychotic symptoms and concomitant personality disorder constitute a group at high risk for aggressive behavior) have been occasionally disconfirmed. Epidemiological re-search designed to avoid the methodological problems mentioned earlier is more likely to reveal consistent relationships between specific predictor variables and measures of aggres-sive behavior. However, not only methodological improvements but also conceptual changes seem to be necessary to reach a better understanding of the normal and patholog-ical aspects of violence.

A concept that should receive more consideration is that aggression is not necessarily a negative attribute nor a sure sign of psychopathology. Many aspects of aggression are biologically valuable in humans as in other animals, and, from an evolutionary perspec-tive, aggressive behavior is viewed as a capacity serving different adaptive functions. Therefore, attempts to understand aggression in its own right should precede efforts to understand aggression in terms of specific psychiatric disorders (McGuire & Troisi, 1989). An implication for epidemiological research is that, in each instance of aggression, the researcher must ask: "Is this aggressive patient acting as most normal people would or as a consequence of his or her psychiatric disorder?" The answer to this question requires data about the context of aggression more detailed than those reported in most epidemiological studies.

Another conceptual change that is likely to inspire future research is a stronger emphasis on individual characteristics beyond nosology. In earlier years, the focus in the literature was often on the propensity for aggression in various diagnostic categories. In contrast, recent studies have aimed at developing a biobehavioral (as opposed to strictly diagnostic) profile of individuals most likely to be assaultive. Two variables that have attracted much interest are biological markers and type and severity of family violence. A number of laboratory and clinical studies have indicated that lowered serotonergic function correlates with both outward directed aggression (i.e., assaultive behavior) and inward directed aggression (i.e., suicidal behavior) (Burrowes et al., 1988). Another consistent finding in the histories of violent recidivists is previous physical abuse (Lewis, 1989). Neither of these personal features is strictly associated with a specific psychiatric diagnosis. In our opinion, the inclusion of these conceptual contributions originating from a multidisciplinary view of aggression is likely to improve our understanding of the impact of psychiatric disorder on an individual's propensity for violence.

ACKNOWLEDGMENTS.   We thank Michael McGuire, M.D., for his helpful comments on an earlier version of this chapter.

REFERENCES

Armond, A. D. (1982). Violence in the semi-secure ward of a psychiatric hospital. *Medicine, Science and the Law*, *22*, 203–209.

Barraclough, B. M., Bunch, J., Nelson, B., & Sainsbury, P. (1974). A hundred cases of suicide: Clinical aspects. *British Journal of Psychiatry*, *125*, 355–373.

Binder, R. L., & McNiel, D. E. (1988). Effect of diagnosis and context on dangerousness. *American Journal of Psychiatry*, *145*, 728–732.

Binder, R. L., & McNiel, D. E. (1990). The relationship of gender to violent behavior in acutely disturbed psychiatric patients. *Journal of Clinical Psychiatry*, *51*, 110–114.

Black, D. W., Winokur, G., & Nasrallah, A. (1988). Effect of psychosis on suicide risk in 1,593 patients with unipolar and bipolar affective disorders. *American Journal of Psychiatry*, *145*, 849–852.

Bleuler, M. (1978). *The schizophrenic disorders*. New Haven, CT: Yale University Press.

Bureau of Evaluation and Research (1984). *Level of care study: 1982*. New York: New York State Office of Mental Health.

Burrowes, K. L., Hales, R. E., & Arrington, E. (1988). Research on the biologic aspects of violence. *Psychiatric Clinics of North America*, *11*, 499–509.

Coid, J. (1979). Mania à potu: A critical review of pathological intoxication. *Psychological Medicine*, *9*, 709–719.

Collins, J. J., & Schlenger, W. E. (1988). Acute and chronic effects of alcohol on violence. *Journal of Studies of Alcoholism*, *49*, 516–521.

Craig, T. J. (1982). An epidemiological study of problems associated with violence among psychiatric inpatients. *American Journal of Psychiatry*, *139*, 1262–1266.

Edwards, J. G., Jones, D., Reid, W. H., & Chu, C. C. (1988). Physical assaults in a psychiatric unit of a general hospital. *American Journal of Psychiatry*, *145*, 1568–1571.

Ellinwood, E. H. (1971). Assault and homicide associated with amphetamine abuse. *American Journal of Psychiatry*, *127*, 1170–1175.

Fawcett, J., Scheftner, W., Clark, D., Hedeker, D., Gibbons, R., & Coryell, W. (1987). Clinical predictors of suicide in patients with major affective disorders: A controlled prospective study. *American Journal of Psychiatry*, *144*, 35–40.

Fottrell, E. (1980). A study of violent behaviour among patients in psychiatric hospitals. *British Journal of Psychiatry*, *136*, 216–221.

Frances, A., Franklin, J., & Flavin, D. K. (1986). Suicide and alcoholism. *Annals of the New York Academy of Sciences*, *487*, 316–325.

Frances, A., Fyer, M., & Clarkin, J. (1986). Personality and suicide. *Annals of the New York Academy of Sciences*, *487*, 281–293.

Gelder, M., Gath, D., & Mayou, R. (1989). *Oxford textbook of psychiatry*, (2nd ed.). Oxford: Oxford University Press.

Grinspoon, L. (Ed.) (1986). Suicide—Part I. *The Harvard Medical School Mental Health Newsletter*, *2*, 8.

Gunn, J. (1977). Criminal behaviour and mental disorder. *British Journal of Psychiatry*, *130*, 317–329.

Gunn, J., & Bonn, J. (1971). Criminality and violence in epileptic prisoners. *British Journal of Psychiatry, 118,* 337–343.

Guze, S. B. (1976). *Criminality and psychiatric disorders.* New York: Oxford University Press.

Haller, R. M., & Deluty, R. H. (1988). Assaults on staff by psychiatric in-patients. A critical review. *British Journal of Psychiatry, 152,* 174–179.

Hanlon, T. E., Nurco, D. N., Kinlock, T. W., & Duszynsky, K. R. (1990). Trends in criminal activity and drug use over an addiction career. *American Journal of Drug and Alcohol Abuse, 16,* 223–238.

Harrer, G., & Kofler-Westergren, B. (1986). Depression and criminality. *Psychopathology, 19,* 215–219.

James, D. V., Fineberg, N. A., Shah, A. K., & Priest, R. G. (1990). An increase in violence on an acute psychiatric ward. A study of associated factors. *British Journal of Psychiatry, 156,* 846–852.

Jamison, K. R. (1986). Suicide and bipolar disorders. *Annals of the New York Academy of Sciences, 487,* 301–315.

Kalunian, D. A., Binder, R. L., & McNiel, D. E. (1990). Violence by geriatric patients who need psychiatric hospitalization. *Journal of Clinical Psychiatry, 51,* 340–343.

Kay, S. R., Wolkenfeld, F., & Murrill, L. M. (1988a). Profiles of aggression among psychiatric patients. I. Nature and prevalence. *Journal of Nervous and Mental Disease, 176,* 539–546.

Kay, S. R., Wolkenfeld, F., & Murrill, L. M. (1988b). Profiles of aggression among psychiatric patients. II. Covariates and predictors. *Journal of Nervous and Mental Disease, 176,* 547–557.

Krakowski, M., Volavka, J., & Brizer, D. (1986). Psychopathology and violence: A review of literature. *Comprehensive Psychiatry, 27,* 131–148.

Krakowski, M., Convit, A., Jaeger, J., Lin, S., & Volavka, J. (1989). Neurological impairment in violent schizophrenic inpatients. *American Journal of Psychiatry, 146,* 849–853.

Lewis, D. O. (1989). Adult antisocial behavior and criminality. In H. I. Kaplan & B. J. Sadock (Eds.), *Comprehensive textbook of psychiatry* (5th ed). (pp. 1400–1405). Baltimore: Williams & Wilkins.

Lindqvist, P., & Allebeck, P. (1990). Schizophrenia and crime: A longitudinal follow-up of 644 schizophrenics in Stockholm. *British Journal of Psychiatry, 157,* 345–350.

Lishman, W. A. (1987). *Organic psychiatry* (2nd ed). Oxford: Blackwell Scientific Publications.

Maletzky, B. M. (1973). The episodic dyscontrol syndrome. *Diseases of the Nervous Systems, 34,* 178–185.

Marzuk, P. M., Tierney, H., Tardiff, K., Gross, E. M., Morgan, E. B., Hsu, M. S., & Mann, J. J. (1988). Increased risk of suicide in persons with AIDS. *Journal of the American Medical Association, 259,* 1333–1337.

McCardle, L., & Fishbein, D. H. (1989). The self-reported effects of PCP on human aggression. *Addictive Behavior, 14,* 465–472.

McGuire, M. T., & Troisi, A. (1989). Aggression. In H. I. Kaplan & B. J. Sadock (Eds.), *Comprehensive textbook of psychiatry* (5th ed). (pp. 271–282). Baltimore: Williams & Wilkins.

Messner, S., & Tardiff, K. (1986). Economic inequality and levels of homicide: An analysis of urban neighborhoods. *Criminology, 24,* 297–317.

Monahan, J., & Steadman, H. J. (1983). Crime and mental disorder: An epidemiological approach. In M. Torny & N. Morris (Eds.), *Crime and justice: An annual review of research* (pp. 145–189). Chicago: University of Chicago Press.

Mungas, D. (1983). An empirical analysis of specific syndromes of violent behavior. *Journal of Nervous and Mental Disease, 171,* 354–361.

Murphy, G. E., & Wetzel, R. D. (1990). The lifetime risk of suicide in alcoholism. *Archives of General Psychiatry, 47,* 383–392.

Murphy, S. L., Rounsaville, B. J., Eyre, S., & Kleber, H. D. (1983). Suicide attempts in treated opiate addicts. *Comprehensive Psychiatry, 241,* 79–88.

Noble, P., & Rodger, S. (1989). Violence by psychiatric in-patients. *British Journal of Psychiatry, 155,* 384–390.

Palmstierna, T., & Wistedt, B. (1989). Risk factors for aggressive behaviour are of limited value in predicting the violent behaviour of acute involuntarily admitted patients. *Acta Psychiatrica Scandinavica, 81,* 152–155.

Pearson, M., Wilmot, E., & Padi, M. (1986). A study of violent behaviour among in-patients in a psychiatric hospital. *British Journal of Psychiatry, 149,* 232–235.

Perry, J. C., & Vaillant, G. E. (1989). Personality disorders. In H. I. Kaplan & B. J. Sadock (Eds.), *Comprehensive textbook of psychiatry* (5th ed). (pp. 1352–1387). Baltimore: Williams & Wilkins.

Petrie, W. M., Lawson, E. C., & Hollender, M. H. (1982). Violence in geriatric patients. *Journal of the American Medical Association, 248,* 443–444.

Plutchik, R., & van Praag, H. M. (1990). A self-report measure of violence risk, II. *Comprehensive Psychiatry, 31,* 450–456.

Pokorny, A. (1964). Suicide rates in various psychiatric disorders. *Journal of Nervous and Mental Disease, 139,* 499–506.

Rabkin, J. G. (1979). Criminal behavior of discharged mental patients: A critical review of the research. *Psychological Bulletin, 86*, 1–27.

Regier, D. A., & Burke, J. D. (1989). Epidemiology. In H. I. Kaplan & B. J. Sadock (Eds.), *Comprehensive textbook of psychiatry* (5th ed). (pp. 308–326). Baltimore: Williams & Wilkins.

Rich, C. L., Ricketts, J. E., Fowler, R. C., & Young, D. (1988). Some differences between men and women who commit suicide. *American Journal of Psychiatry, 145*, 718–722.

Robins, E. (1986). Psychosis and suicide. *Biological Psychiatry, 21*, 655–672.

Robins, L. N., & Kulbock, P. A. (1986). Methodological strategies in suicide. *Annals of the New York Society of Sciences, 487*, 1–15.

Rodin, E. A. (1973). Psychomotor epilepsy and aggressive behavior. *Archives of General Psychiatry, 28*, 210–213.

Roitman, G., Orev, E., & Schreiber, G. (1990). Annual rhythms of violence in hospitalized affective patients: Correlation with changes in the duration of the daily photoperiod. *Acta Psychiatrica Scandinavica, 82*, 73–76.

Rosenbaum, M., & Bennett, B. (1986). Homicide and depression. *American Journal of Psychiatry, 143*, 367–370.

Rossi, A. M., Jacobs, M., Monteleone, M., Olsen, R., Surber, R. W., Winkler, E. L., & Wommack, A. (1986). Characteristics of psychiatric patients who engage in assaultive or other fear-inducing behaviors. *Journal of Nervous and Mental Disease, 174*, 154–160.

Rounsaville, B. J., Weissman, M. M., Kleber, H., & Wilber, C. (1982). Heterogeneity of psychiatric diagnosis in treated opiate addicts. *Archives of General Psychiatry, 39*, 161–166.

Roy, A. (1989). Suicide. In H. I. Kaplan & B. J. Sadock (Eds.), *Comprehensive textbook of psychiatry* (5th ed). (pp. 1415–1427). Baltimore: Williams & Wilkins.

Stevenson, J. M. (1988). Suicide. In J. A. Talbott, R. E. Hales, & S. C. Yudofsky (Eds.), *The American Psychiatric Press textbook of psychiatry* (pp. 1021–1035). Washington, DC: American Psychiatric Press.

Tanke, E. D., & Yesavage, J. A. (1985). Characteristics of assaultive patients who do and do not provide visible cues of potential violence. *American Journal of Psychiatry, 142*, 1409–1413.

Tardiff, K. (1984). Research on violence. In J. A. Talbott (Ed.), *The chronic mental patient five years later*. San Francisco: Grune & Stratton.

Tardiff, K. (1988). Violence. In J. A. Talbott, R. E. Hales, & S. C. Yudofsky (Eds.), *The American Psychiatric Press textbook of psychiatry* (pp. 1037–1057). Washington, DC: American Psychiatric Press.

Tardiff, K., & Koenigsberg, H. W. (1985). Assaultive behavior among psychiatric outpatients. *American Journal of Psychiatry, 142*, 960–963.

Tardiff, K., & Sweillam, A. (1979). Age and assaultive behavior in mental patients. *Hospital and Community Psychiatry, 30*, 709–711.

Tardiff, K., & Sweillam, A. (1980). Assault, suicide, and mental illness. *Archives of General Psychiatry, 37*, 164–169.

Tardiff, K., & Sweillam, A. (1982). Assaultive behavior among chronic patients. *American Journal of Psychiatry, 139*, 212–215.

Temple, M., & Ladouceur, P. (1985). The alcohol-crime relationship as an age-specific phenomenon: A longitudinal study. *Contemporary Drug Problems, 15*, 351–373.

Thomas, M. D., Ekland, E. S., Griffin, M., Hagerott, R. J., Leichman, S. S., Murphy, H., & Osborne, O. H. (1990). Intrahospital relocation of psychiatric patients and effects on aggression. *Archives of Psychiatric Nursing, 4*, 154–160.

Watters, J. K., Reinarman, C., & Fagan, J. (1985). Causality, context and contingency: Relationships between drug use and delinquency. *Contemporary Drug Problems, 15*, 351–373.

Williams, D. (1969). Neural factors related to habitual aggression: Consideration of the differences between those habitual aggressives and others who have committed crimes of violence. *Brain, 92*, 503–520.

Yesavage, J. A. (1983). Bipolar illness: Correlates of dangerous inpatient behavior. *British Journal of Psychiatry, 143*, 554–557.

Yesavage, J. A., Werner, P. D., & Becker, J. (1981). Inpatient evaluation of aggression in psychiatric patients. *Journal of Nervous and Mental Disease, 169*, 299–302.

Yudofsky, S. C., Silver, J. M., Jackson, W., Endicott, J., & Williams, D. (1986). The Overt Aggression Scale for the objective rating of verbal and physical aggression. *American Journal of Psychiatry, 143*, 35–39.

CHAPTER 8

Legal and Ethical Issues

Robert M. Wettstein

Legal issues permeate a clinician's contact with every patient, whether the clinician directly attends to the patient or not. Legal matters are of particular concern when clinicians evaluate and treat aggressive and destructive patients.

This chapter considers several of the many legal issues involved in the diagnosis and management of aggressive and self-destructive behavior in mental health settings. Given the limitations of space, only some of the many relevant issues can be covered. The chapter initially reviews some general principles in professional liability, followed by discussion with case illustrations of particular areas of liability with regard to aggressive or destructive patients. It also discusses some of the legal regulation of psychiatric practice in civil commitment, outpatient commitment, and the right to refuse treatment.

Throughout, the reader will note a fundamental dilemma faced by clinicians in this area of clinical work: society must attempt a balancing of interests between the patient, the clinician, and the nonpatient public. Achieving this equilibrium is difficult, and there is likely to be error or overreaching of one sort or another along the way.

PROFESSIONAL LIABILITY

General Principles

Mental health clinicians risk professional liability in a wide variety of situations, some more frequent, and costly, than others. These typically obtain in the tort or civil law system rather than in the criminal justice system. While legal rules, standards, and procedures technically vary from state to state, the effect upon the clinician is often similar.

Plaintiffs (i.e., the injured party or the party's legal representative) can bring litigation against mental health professionals under several legal theories or causes of action,

ROBERT M. WETTSTEIN • Western Psychiatric Institute and Clinic, Department of Psychiatry, University of Pittsburgh School of Medicine, Pittsburgh, Pennsylvania 15213.

Handbook of Aggressive and Destructive Behavior in Psychiatric Patients, edited by Michel Hersen, Robert T. Ammerman, and Lori A. Sisson. Plenum Press, New York, 1994.

including negligence (unintentional torts), breach of contract, civil rights, and intentional torts. Clinicians are also subject to criminal liability from state or federal agencies and sanction from professional societies of which they are members and state and federal licensing agencies.

For the plaintiff to prevail in tort litigation, he or she must prove, with clear and convincing evidence, the following elements to the judge or jury deciding the case:

1. There was a legally recognized clinician–patient relationship, and a standard of professional care or practice in the case at bar.
2. The clinician deviated from that professional standard in the case, whether by commission or omission.
3. The patient suffered injury or damage (emotional, somatic, or both).
4. The patient's injury or damage proximately resulted form the clinician's negligence.

Professional liability for mental health clinicians currently occurs under a "fault-based" system rather than the "no-fault" system, which is prevalent, for example, under workers' compensation programs. Clinicians are not the insurers of the patient's outcome and are not responsible for all iatrogenic injuries. Rather, they are only responsible for a patient's injuries that result from clinical practices falling outside of clinical standards. Research data indicate that, in fact, while there is a substantial amount of substandard health care, few negligently injured patients file a legal claim, and few of these succeed (Brennan, et al., 1991; Localio, Lewthers, Brennan, Laird, Hebert, Peterson, Newhouse, Weiler, and Hiatt, 1991). Psychiatric patients as a group bring fewer malpractice claims against their treating clinicians than do medical patients because (1) psychiatric diagnosis is ostensibly problematic, (2) the etiology of mental disorders is difficult to discern, (3) clinical standards in mental health care are sometimes vague, (4) emotional damages are not as highly valued by contemporary society as somatic damages, and (5) patients are reluctant to publicize their mental disorders or sue a therapist to whom they have become attached (Fishalow, 1975).

The clinician's legal duty to the patient is typically described as that reasonable degree of knowledge, skill, and care ordinarily exercised by members of that particular specialty under similar circumstances. The standard of care is established in the litigation by expert witness testimony, a professional organization's recommended policies and guidelines, clinical practice parameters, professional literature, relevant law (statutes, regulations, and case law), and hospital or facility policies. Clinical standards are articulated from a national rather than local perspective, given the wide dispersal of professional literature and conferences (*Pederson v. Dumouchel*, 1967). Clinician-defendants who employed an atypical/nonstandard treatment modality for a patient may defend themselves successfully so long as the treatment for that disorder is still practiced by a "respected minority" of practitioners.

Patient-litigants bring professional liability claims against their clinicians for a variety of reasons. Many litigants have suffered economic losses such as need for additional health care or loss of job-related income. Others sue to relieve emotional pain and suffering, deter future negligence by the clinician, publicize the incident or problems, or punish the clinician (Imershein & Brents, 1992). With regard to the last motivation, punitive damages are available to plaintiffs when the defendant's conduct is considered outrageous, malevolent, or fraudulent (*Adams v. Murakami*, 1990).

Patient-litigants must initiate legal proceedings against the clinician within a statutory time limit referred to as the "statute of limitations." Failure to do so is grounds for dismissal of the suit regardless of its merits. The statute of limitations is variously defined; relevant considerations include the time since the clinician last treated the patient (when the negligence occurred), when the patient discovered his injury, and when the patient discovered the cause of his injury. The statute of limitations is often 2 or 3 years, but does not begin to run for minors until they reach 18 years of age.

Psychopharmacology Litigation

Psychotropic medications are among the most common treatment modalities for aggressive and destructive patients, whether in facilities or in the community. Psychiatrists incur liability for negligence in several general areas when they prescribe, or fail to prescribe, psychotropic medication (Wettstein, 1983, 1988). These areas include:

1. Failure to take an adequate history.
2. Failure to obtain an adequate physical examination.
3. Failure to obtain an adequate laboratory examination.
4. Lack of indication for a prescription.
5. Contraindication for a prescription.
6. Prescription of an improper dosage.
7. Prescription for an improper duration.
8. Failure to recognize, monitor, and treat side effects.
9. Failure to abate drug reactions and interactions.
10. Failure to consult with other physicians.
11. Failure to diagnose and treat a disorder.

The following cases illustrate some of the problems especially encountered by clinicians in managing aggressive and destructive patients with psychotropic medication. These problems range from failing to adequately treat a patient's disorder to "overtreatment" of a disorder, resulting in an injury to the patient. Those cases of negligent treatment resulting in injuries to third parties are covered in the "Duty to Third Parties" section below.

Failure to Take an Adequate History and Failure to Treat

In *Leal v. Simon* (1989), an institutionalized, mentally retarded man had been stabilized on 4 mg haloperidol for self-abusive behavior. He was transferred to a facility in the community, where he began treatment with the defendant psychiatrist. The patient continued to be symptomatically stable for over a year, and the psychiatrist changed his medication to an as-needed basis only (2 mg). The psychiatrist claimed that the discontinuation of medication was required by a state audit regarding the use of medication in the mentally retarded and the potential for tardive dyskinesia, which had not been observed. Within a month of discontinuing the maintenance haloperidol, the patient deteriorated, required hospitalization, with larger does of haloperidol. He had to be returned to the state's developmental center, with contractures of his extremities, and became confined to a wheelchair. At trial, the jury found that the psychiatrist was negligent in failing to review the patient's history, in failing to obtain the patient's complete medical records from the transferring agency, and in so abruptly stopping the medication.

Treatment Not Indicated; Failure to Monitor Treatment for Adverse Effects; Failure to Obtain Informed Consent

In *Clites v. Iowa* (1980), the parents of a mentally retarded male at a state residential facility sued the state for negligence and lack of informed consent for treatment with antipsychotic medication. The patient had been treated by several physicians with antipsychotic medication since age 18 for aggressive and inappropriate sexual behavior toward female staff. Medication continued for 5 years before tardive dyskinesia of the face and extremities was diagnosed. The trial court ruled that (1) medication had been inappropriately used; (2) the patient was improperly monitored for tardive dyskinesia because "he was not regularly visited by a physician and physical exams had not been conducted for a three-year period" (*Clites v. Iowa*, 1982, p. 920); further the attending physician, being "unfamiliar with tardive dyskinesia, should have sought consultations" (p. 920); (3) the patient's parents, his legal guardians, "were never informed of the potential side effects of the use, and prolonged use, of major tranquilizers, nor was consent to their use obtained" (*Clites v. Iowa*, 1982, p. 922), thus violating the standard that requires some form of informed consent prior to the administration of major tranquilizers. Since the parents had not been told of the risks of the treatment program, the trial court rejected the state's argument that the parents had given implied consent to the treatment. The trial court ruled for the plaintiff, awarding $385,165 for future medical expenses, and $375,000 for past and future pain and suffering. The trial court's ruling was later upheld in the Iowa Court of Appeals (*Clites v. Iowa*, 1982).

Failure to Monitor: Cardiopulmonary Arrest

A 35-year-old male patient became violent the morning after he was admitted to a state hospital (*Brown v. State*, 1977). In an upright position, he was treated with 200 mg of chlorpromazine, had to be subdued by the police, and was transferred to another building. He was not monitored in that location for 1¼ hours, was found in respiratory arrest, and could not be resuscitated. The court found negligence for the failure to monitor the patient "during the period of time that the defendant knew serious side effects might have been manifested by the administration of Thorazine" (p. 205).

Overtreatment: Cardiorespiratory Arrest

A female patient in an "extreme manic state" was treated initially through an emergency room with thioridazine and lithium and then in the hospital with haloperidol, chlorpromazine, and diphenhydramine (*Allen v. Kaiser Foundation Hospital*, 1985). She was found without vital signs, but was resuscitated, with residual severe brain damage. At trial, the jury found that there was no negligence in the psychopharmacological regimen or monitoring.

SECLUSION AND RESTRAINTS

General Principles

Seclusion and restraints are commonly used treatments or management techniques for aggressive and destructive psychiatric patients. Their use for geropsychiatric patients has recently attracted considerable attention and controversy (Evans & Strumpf, 1989). Seclusion and restraints in nursing homes and mental health care settings are highly regulated, usually by state statutes and regulations, but also by the state and federal constitutions. Previous litigation in a jurisdiction can also serve to restrict or control the use of seclusion and restraints. Facilities that use seclusion and restraints will have detailed policies and procedures regarding their use. Guidelines from professional societies are available to recommend proper application (American Psychiatric Association, 1985; Tardiff, 1984). The Food and Drug Administration (FDA) considers physical restraint devices to be prescription devices and subject to federal regulation (FDA, 1992).

Typically, there are specific legal and policy rules about the definitions of seclusion and restraint, indications for their use (emergency situations rather than punishment or behavior modification, patient age, diagnosis, symptoms, need for least restrictive alternative), contraindications to their use, physician's responsibilities, nursing staff's responsibilities, need for staff training in their use, patient monitoring procedures, need for consultation or review after extended intervals, need for patient consent, and requirements for documentation.

Litigation Regarding Seclusion and Restraints

While the use of seclusion and restraints is not a frequent source of litigation for psychiatrists and hospitals, liability can occur (Johnson, 1990). Types of potential liabilities include (1) use of seclusion and restraints for an excessive duration or intensity (2) misuse of seclusion or restraints, (3) failure to use seclusion and restraint, or (4) failure to properly monitor a patient in seclusion or restraints. At least in the nursing home setting, liability for inappropriate use exceeds that for failure to use (Kapp, 1992). Failure to use restraints and seclusion can result in injuries to the patient (falls, burns, escapes from custody, accidental or intentional deaths) and injuries to staff or other patients from the patient. The FDA estimates that there are over 100 fatalities yearly due to improper use of restraints, plus injuries such as burns and fractures (FDA, 1992). Most of the deaths occur due to asphyxiation when patients attempt to extricate themselves and strangulate. This is especially a concern for elderly patients in nursing homes who are improperly monitored. However, there are wide variations across facilities in the use of seclusion and restraints (Betemps et al., 1992; Okin, 1985) and thus of injuries due to their use or nonuse.

Psychiatrists incur negligence liability for seclusion and restraints when their overuse or misuse results in injury or death to the patient. In *Clark v. Ohio* (1989), seclusion and restraints were found to have been used for punitive rather than therapeutic reasons. In *Hopper v. Callahan* (1990), in which a female patient died in seclusion, the physicians were alleged to have failed to use professional judgment in ordering the seclusion and in failing to provide necessary medical care. In a case that considered the use of restraint by staff, a 300-pound male attendant knocked a female patient to the ground, fracturing her tibia, in preparing her for an involuntary injection of medication (*Kuster v. New York*, 1989). A plaintiff was awarded $2.5 million against a nursing home when a safety vest was used backwards and the resident slid down in her chair and strangled (*Davis v. Montrose Bay Care Center*, 1989, cited in Kapp, 1992).

In a case of failure to use adequate restraints (as well as alleged failure to diagnose an organic mental disorder), a 67-year-old hospitalized female was restrained with a Posey vest because she was walking the hospital corridor with a sheet over her while waving a knife (*Fleming v. Prince George's County*, 1976). She struck at the nurses and the physician who intervened and was medicated with diazepam and secobarbital. Just 10 minutes after having last been checked by staff, she fell from a window to her death, while apparently attempting to escape from the hospital. The treating physician was alleged to have negligently failed to evaluate her for an organic mental disorder or medication side effect, failed to determine whether restraints were properly applied, and failed to restrain her arms. Failure to properly monitor a patient while restrained was seen in *George v. McIntosh-Wilson* (1991), in which a mentally retarded, paraplegic resident, restrained by a lap belt in his wheelchair, ingested a surgical glove while unattended and suffocated. The resident had been known to have a habit of "mouthing" anything within his grasp.

Perhaps the most well-known legal case involving seclusion and restraints involved constitutional issues in a state facility rather than professional negligence in a private one. In *Youngberg v. Romeo* (1982), the U.S. Supreme Court recognized a committed, mentally retarded person's constitutional right to be free from undue bodily restraint. Profoundly retarded (I.Q. 8–10), Romeo had been committed to Pennhurst state school and hospital in Pennsylvania. He had been injured on at least 63 occasions, either due to self-abuse or abuse by other residents, and was often placed in restraints, even on a routine basis. In his lawsuit against the state, he claimed constitutional rights to freedom of movement, reasonably safe conditions of confinement, and training. While the Court granted these rights to a narrow degree, the case is perhaps more significant for its deference to professional judgment in deciding whether a patient's constitutional rights have been violated by the state in its care of the patient. The Court ruled that

> the decision, if made by a professional, is presumptively valid; liability may be imposed only when the decision by the professional is such a substantial departure from accepted professional judgment, practice or standards as to demonstrate that the person responsible actually did not base the decision on such a judgment. In an action for damages against a professional in his individual capacity, however, the professional will not be liable if he was unable to satisfy his normal professional standards because of budgetary constraints; in such a situation, good-faith immunity would bar liability. (p. 2462)

While the case involved a mentally retarded individual, there is no reason to question its applicability to mentally ill persons, also in public mental health facilities.

Inappropriate or excessive use of seclusion and restraints is often only one of the many forms of substandard mental health care provided to patients in some state psychiatric facilities. Indeed, class action litigation on behalf of state hospital patients over the years has been designed to improve treatment practices in general. In Montana, for example, a class action, civil rights lawsuit was settled for $350,000 for 371 voluntarily hospitalized and civilly committed adults who had been confined on a forensic unit (*Ihler v. Chisholm*, 1991; "Montana Agrees," 1992) without adequate treatment. Patients had allegedly been physically abused, kept in a more restrictive environment than necessary, and routinely or unnecessarily restrained or secluded, even for staff convenience. At Boston State Hospital, patients were secluded contrary to state law in nonemergency situations such as walking nude in the hall, public masturbation, engaging in sexual relations, talking loudly, and to prevent a patient from stealing from another patient (*Rogers v. Okin*, 1979).

CIVIL COMMITMENT

Involuntary Hospitalization

Voluntary or involuntary psychiatric hospitalization is a commonly used treatment strategy for those patients who are judged likely to be violent or attempt suicide if retained in community treatment. Patients may be *voluntarily* hospitalized when they agree to do so, and when they have the requisite mental capacity to consent to do so (Brakel, Parry, & Weiner, 1985; *Zinermon v. Burch, 1990*). Every state in the United States legally provides for *involuntary* hospitalization, though it may be labeled differently (e.g., emergency detention, observational commitment, extended commitment) (Brakel et al., 1985), and all states provide for involuntary outpatient treatment as well (American Psychiatric Association, 1987; McCafferty & Dooley, 1990; Miller, 1985, 1992a). Brief, emergency hospitalizations typically occur on the basis of medical certification alone, or upon administrative rather than judicial authorization. Extended involuntary hospitalization generally requires a formal court hearing with the accompanying legal due process protections available to criminal defendants. These include rights to a hearing, notice of the hearing, attorney (provided by the state if indigent), presentation of evidence and witnesses, cross-examination of the state's witnesses, and appeal. The state bears the legal burden of proving that the person meets the statutory commitment criteria, usually with clear and convincing evidence. Civil commitments are generally time limited, but additional commitment hearings can be held, so that a person may be confined indefinitely.

Prior to the 1970s, with the initiation of these due process protections, civil commitment was accomplished based upon the presence of a mental illness and the patient's need for treatment. In the last two decades, all states have incorporated "dangerousness" to self or others, when it is a result of a mental illness, as a commitment criterion. In some states, mentally ill persons may be civilly committed only when they are judged likely to physically harm themselves or others. In a few states, civil commitment can be predicated upon anticipated property damage or emotional harm to the patient (Miller, 1992b) without treatment. The struggle over legislating civil commitment criteria is chronic, intense, and highly politicized (Bagby & Atkinson, 1988). On the one hand, families, and injured victims, of the mentally ill have lobbied for liberalized commitment criteria, while civil liberties advocates have promoted narrow commitment criteria or abolition of commitment (Chodoff, 1984; Morse, 1982). An important consideration is the additional cost of hospitalizing larger numbers of patients under expanded standards, so that state mental health resources are further strained. This occurred in the state of Washington after its statutory liberalization (Hasebe & McRae, 1987; Pierce, Durham, & Fisher, 1985), an experience that has been widely publicized and has proved to be an incentive to maintain the present narrow criteria.

Two major dilemmas are prompted by the dangerousness standard for civil commitment: (1) those treatment-refusing patients who could benefit from hospitalization but are not sufficiently dangerous to self or others to be involuntarily hospitalized are not receiving appropriate care (Cleveland, Mulvey, Appelbaum, & Lidz, 1989), and (2) those patients who are sufficiently dangerous to others to satisfy legal commitment standards are being committed but are not necessarily treatable. This second concern has prompted a substantial discussion in the literature and deserves elaboration.

Psychiatrists, like much of society, are ambivalent about their social control functions. They prefer to view civil commitment as treatment rather than as preventive detention, which is detention to prevent future criminal violence. Preventive detention in the criminal justice system is limited to certain areas such as setting bail following arrest. Psychiatrists and their organizations have resented the responsibility of managing potentially violent but not treatable individuals, who often are violent because of substance abuse and character disorders. It has been argued that violent or potentially violent patients are more properly the concern of the criminal justice system rather than the mental health system

(Appelbaum, 1988a), though, for many reasons, this shift in responsibility has not been accomplished (Huber, Roth, Appelbaum, & Ore, 1982). Fear about liability for subsequent violence should the patient be allowed to leave the emergency room (or hospital) often drives the psychiatrist to initiate (or prolong) hospitalization for the patient, involuntarily if necessary (Appelbaum, 1988a), even though there is often statutory immunity for release decision making.

The statutory dangerousness commitment criteria typically, and perhaps intentionally, lack clarity. The statutory vagueness permits considerable discretion by the clinician as to whether or not to commit the patient. It may be unclear, for example, as to how imminent or likely the violent conduct must be, or even its type or severity, before commitment can be authorized (Morse, 1982). There is often much uncertainty about whether character-disordered individuals can or should be involuntarily hospitalized when they present some risk of future violence, and how long that hospitalization should be (Huber et al., 1982). Some have proposed greater specificity in commitment criteria to limit dangerousness-based commitments; this could occur by barring personality disorders as the basis for commitment (Brouillette & Paris, 1991; Stone, 1975).

In practice, those patients who are involuntarily hospitalized to prevent future violence under the dangerous-to-others criterion do not necessarily receive adequate treatment. Discussions of violence in psychiatric evaluations are surprisingly meager; it is as if violence were a social problem to be overlooked rather than a biomedical one to be treated (Gondolf, 1992). Patients admitted in crisis because of imminent violence are often discharged as soon as the crisis has passed, without much regard for the longer-term contributing causes to the patient's behavior. Antisocial patients are sometimes discharged from the hospital prematurely due to staff countertransference, patients' lack of motivation for treatment, or their lack of response to treatment (Gabbard & Coyne, 1987; Ogloff, Wong, & Greenwood, 1990). And, there are little data about the efficacy of involuntary hospitalization generally; some literature questions the efficacy of civil commitment in general psychiatric facilities for those who are suicidal (Greenberg, 1974; Siegal & Tuckel, 1987) or antisocial (Gabbard & Coyne, 1987).

Statutory commitment criteria are important predictors of who gets admitted or committed to psychiatric hospitals. For example, there is some empirical evidence that a change in dangerousness-oriented commitment criteria has resulted in an increased number of difficult-to-manage or dangerous patients among those committed (Peters, Miller, Schmidt, & Meeter, 1987). But, as in most social systems, the other forces in the mental health commitment system (e.g., administrators, hearing officers, judges) often attenuate any impact of the changes that might be intended by the reformer, whether from the social control or treatment-oriented perspective (Marx & Levinson, 1988). Due to the intensity of the debate on these issues, for the foreseeable future we are likely to live with a commitment system largely predicated upon dangerousness to self or others.

Involuntary Outpatient Treatment

Involuntary outpatient treatment has been proposed as one solution to the limitations of involuntary hospitalization. Every state has legislatively provided for involuntary treatment on an outpatient basis for civil committees in one form or another (American Psychiatric Association, 1987; McCafferty & Dooley, 1990; Miller, 1985, 1992a). Outpatient commitment has also been successfully used for managing insanity acquittees in the community (Bloom, Williams, & Bigelow, 1991). Outpatient commitment has been advocated as a less restrictive treatment alternative than involuntary hospitalization, one which can promote, if not remedy, the problems created by deinstitutionalization (Mulvey, Geller, & Roth, 1987).

Outpatient commitments occur initially or following a period of involuntary hospitalization. Involuntary outpatient treatment offers an opportunity to supervise outpatients who are noncompliant with clinical interventions such as therapy appointments, abstinence from drug and alcohol use, laboratory monitoring, or psychotropic medication. Enforcement of outpatient commitments is legally and administratively variable, but some noncompliant patients respond favorably to the presence of a court order for outpatient commitment. It may or may not be possible to force psychotropic medication through an outpatient commitment, depending upon applicable law and practice. Noncompliance with the outpatient commitment can prompt a rehospitalization, usually after formal court hearing.

Outpatient commitments are typically underused and are likely to be effective if appropriately attempted (Geller, 1990). Perhaps the most suitable candidate for outpatient commitment is the treatment-responsive, psychotically ill person who refuses outpatient treatment because of the illness and becomes violent. Once treated with antipsychotic medication, the patient can be maintained in the community with appropriate clinical supervision and continued medication.

Outpatient commitment has also been criticized on a number of grounds (Mulvey et al., 1987; Schwartz & Costanzo, 1987). Concern has been raised that outpatient commitment constitutes benevolent state coercion, similar to the criminal justice or child protective systems, which is unlikely to succeed. Outpatient practice often escapes the regulation and oversight characteristic of hospital practice, so more abuses are possible under a system of involuntary outpatient care. Outpatient clinicians may find their roles changing from that of a therapist to that of a social control agent, with a corresponding erosion of the therapeutic alliance. Other concerns are pragmatic; a system of outpatient commitment is unlikely to be adequately funded, given the additional costs of intensive monitoring of noncompliant patients, and outpatient clinicians are typically reluctant to manage difficult and violent patients in the community, especially on an involuntary basis.

RIGHT TO REFUSE TREATMENT

Once hospitalized, patients often refuse part or all of their evaluations and treatments. Refusals of treatment stem from side effects of treatment (e.g., akinesia, akathisia), symptoms of the illness for which the patient was hospitalized, secondary gain (e.g., room and board, disability income), or problems in the therapeutic alliance such as transference and the failure to properly inform the patient about the treatment (Appelbaum, 1982).

Not until the late 1970s did the question of the right to refuse psychiatric treatment receive serious attention (Brakel et al., 1985). In earlier times, physicians forcibly medicated involuntarily hospitalized patients, whether in an emergency or not. Since then, psychiatric patients have been granted various rights to refuse psychotropic medication either by state statutes, state regulations, or case law. Among other bases, the right to refuse treatment has been grounded in constitutional rights to freedom of speech and thought (Winick, 1989).

Treatment Refusals in Emergencies

As in any area of medical practice, physicians are legally permitted to manage medical or psychiatric emergencies in whatever manner they believe necessary, even without the patient's consent. Defining psychiatric emergencies, however, is difficult; the law often relies upon the likelihood of imminent serious physical harm to the patient or another to constitute a psychiatric emergency (i.e., a police emergency). Expanded definitions include imminent psychological deterioration or emotional harm to the patient (i.e., a psychological emergency). While psychotropic medication, or seclusion/restraints, may be involuntarily administered in an emergency, even to a voluntarily hospitalized patient, the duration of the emergency situation may be unclear. A single dose of antipsychotic medication following a patient's assault on another patient may not constitute much in the way of effective treatment of the patient's psychosis. Legally, such emergency medication is viewed more as controlling behavior than psychiatric treatment (Appelbaum & Gutheil, 1991). Once behavior control has been established, the emergency, and the emergency treatment, ceases.

Nonemergency Refusals

The right to refuse psychiatric treatment has been the most controversial in the case of the legally competent, involuntarily hospitalized patient in a nonemergency. One school of thought is that patients are committed to the hospital for treatment, so why should a right to refuse treatment in the hospital be granted? The contrary argument is that patients are committed under dangerousness criteria, and their (and others') safety can be adequately insured with hospitalization, even without treatment. Essentially, two approaches have been taken to this dilemma (Appelbaum, 1988b).

Some jurisdictions grant committed patients a right to object to psychotropic medication in nonemergencies, but not a right to refuse it. In such cases, the treating physician must obtain a second opinion from another physician about the appropriateness of medication, or arrange for an informal administrative hearing during which the patient's objections will be considered. This administrative review process can be completed within days or a few weeks at most. Standards for determining whether the patient's refusal will be overridden include need for treatment, treatability, dangerousness to self or others, or decision-making incapacity.

The second approach, in a growing number of states, grants committed patients a right to refuse treatment unless and until they have been adjudicated incompetent to refuse treatment by a court, following a full due process competency hearing. After a judicial finding of incompetency to refuse treatment, the court, or a court-appointed legal guardian, may order treatment over the patient's refusal by considering the best interests of the patient or what the patient would have decided had he or she been able to do so. An independent clinical review of the treating physician's decision to treat the patient is not provided in this approach.

Empirical studies of these treatment refusal mechanisms have revealed that the judicial review approach has significant disadvantages with uncertain benefits. Given delays in securing court hearings, patients remain unmedicated pending the hearing for weeks to months, with increased risk of patient or staff injury, increased use of seclusion and restraint, longer (and more costly) hospitalizations, and increased chronicity of illness (Hoge et al., 1990). The judicial review system is costly to implement, given the need for attorneys and court personnel. Perhaps surprisingly, courts are apparently *more* willing to override treatment refusals than clinicians, as almost all patients brought before them as incompetent to refuse are medicated involuntarily (Hoge et al., 1990). From most of the available data, it appears that the medical/administrative review process provides better clinical care to treatment-refusing patients, while the costs (e.g., clinical, economic) for formally protecting the competent patient's right to refuse through the judicial review procedure are substantial (Ciccone, Tokoli, Clements, & Gift, 1990).

DUTY TO PROTECT THIRD PARTIES

One of the most frequent and significant medical–legal considerations in the treatment of the aggressive and destructive patient is the potential for injuries to third parties. These can occur while the patient is in the hospital (i.e., injuries to staff, other patients, or visitors), released to the community on temporary pass, escaped from the hospital, or treated in the community. As noted above, in the case of malpractice resulting in injuries to the patient, the clinician is not a guarantor of the public safety. The plaintiff—the injured third party—must still prove negligence in the patient's care to succeed in litigation.

The clinician's obligation to third parties, as opposed to their own patients, is relatively new to the law. In this area, perhaps more than elsewhere in mental health law, the law is still in evolution. In general, individuals bear no affirmative legal duty to control the conduct of others or to warn those who are endangered by others, and thus they have no responsibility for failure to do so. The courts have created exceptions to this rule when the defendant has a "special relationship" to either the actor or the victim. Given the presence of a therapist–patient relationship in or out of the hospital, the special relationship exception, and thus potential liability, is readily satisfied. This third-party liability occurs in cases concerning negligent hospital release or outpatient duty to protect.

Negligent Release

At least since the 1950s, mental health facilities have been alleged to be responsible for injuries to third parties inflicted by former patients. These have been litigated on the grounds that the facility was negligent in releasing the patient from the hospital, either briefly on pass, or absolutely on discharge. Plaintiffs in negligent release cases allege that the facility staff failed to conduct a proper risk assessment for violence, or having done so, failed to adequately manage or treat that risk. Suits for negligent release have been brought against facilities for incidents that occurred months or even years after discharge (*McMillian v. Wallis*, 1990) or in distant locations (*Doyle v. United States*, 1982). Cases have occurred whether the patient was hospitalized voluntarily or involuntarily. Defendants in negligent release cases contend that the patient was adequately evaluated and treated prior to discharge and that the third-party injury resulted from other events following discharge. This is particularly convincing when there was a long interval between release and third-party injury. Usually, but not invariably, the plaintiff in negligent release cases need not prove that there was a specifically identified or readily identifiable foreseeable victim, but only the public at large.

Despite the success of many negligent release suits, defendants have successfully argued that release decision making necessarily involves professional judgment. One court, ruling for the defense, held that the prediction of the future course of a mental illness is a professional judgment of high responsibility and in some instances it involves a measure of calculated risk. If a liability were imposed on the physician or the State each time the prediction of future course of mental disease was wrong, few releases would ever be made and the hope of recovery and rehabilitation of a vast number of patients would be impeded and frustrated. This is one of the medical and public risks which must be taken on balance, even though it may sometimes result in injury to the patient or others. (*Taig v. State of New York*, 1963, pp. 496–497)

Outpatient Duty to Protect

It was not until the California Supreme Court's holding in *Tarasoff v. Regents of the University of California* (1976) that an outpatient therapist was held responsible for an outpatient's violence. Largely through case law throughout the United States, derived from *Tarasoff*, outpatient therapists in most states now have a legal duty to protect foreseeably endangered third parties from their potentially violent outpatients. In the absence of specific case law or statutes on the subject in a particular jurisdiction, therapists are advised to behave as if such law in fact existed.

The *Tarasoff* doctrine, and its legal progeny, have been much criticized. Of concern is that the outpatient therapist, in contrast to the hospital therapist, has little ability or legal authority to control the patient in the community. Psychiatrists have also contended that their inability to predict violence should preclude a legal obligation to do so and legal liability for failing to do so. Finally, protecting a third party may involve breaching the patient's confidentiality, which will undermine the therapeutic alliance with the patient and complicate or obviate the treatment that the patient sought in the first place.

The state legislatures, but not the courts, have been somewhat sympathetic to these considerations. Statutes in nearly half the states limit, but do not obviate, the therapist's third-party liability, usually to situations in which the patient has threatened serious violence toward a specific victim. The statutes specify how therapists can discharge their legal duty to the victim: attempt to hospitalize or commit the patient, implement changes in therapy or medication, involve the intended victim in the treatment process, warn the victim, warn the police, or take any other reasonable steps to prevent the violence (Appelbaum, Zonana, Bonnie, & Roth, 1989). Existing state confidentiality rules or statutes permit a therapist to breach a patient's confidentiality in an emergency situation. In a nonemergency situation (e.g., the threatened violence is not imminent), the duty to protect statutes may provide immunity from suit for breaching confidentiality in discharging the duty to protect.

To a large extent, the duty to protect has been misunderstood as a duty to warn the intended victim. Clinicians are generally advised to first use whatever therapeutic techniques are available to treat the mental disorder that presumably underlies the threatened violence. When being a therapist fails to reduce the risk of violence, then reaching outside the therapeutic relationship to the victim, victim's family, or police may be necessary (Weiner & Wettstein, 1993).

RISK MANAGEMENT

Space does not allow a full consideration of the risk management strategies useful to clinicians who evaluate or treat the aggressive or self-destructive patient. These are amply covered in recently published texts in mental health law (Appelbaum & Gutheil, 1991; Simon, 1992; Weiner & Wettstein, 1993).

It is nevertheless worth noting two fundamental clinical risk management strategies that will serve clinicians well in preventing litigation, as well as minimizing its likelihood of success if it occurs. The first is to obtain consultation in complex cases. Given the increasing knowledge and complexity of clinical practice, consultation with an expert in the area of suicide or violence is often helpful in patient management, as well as risk management. These consultations can be formal, in which the consultant examines the patient, or informal. In the former, the consultant should prepare a written report, outlining his or her sources of information, conclusions or recommendations, and the justification for them. The primary clinician can obtain more than a single consultation, especially when the first consultation is unsatisfactory or offers recommendations that the clinician believes to be inappropriate.

The second general risk management strategy involves documenting clinical decision making. This approach to record keeping does not necessarily require extensive notations in the patient's medical record, but rather a focus on the rationale for why treatment interventions were implemented or not. In this strategy, the clinician "thinks out loud for the record" (Gutheil, 1980) and records his or her assessment of the risks, benefits, and alternatives of a particular course of action, given the inherent uncertainty of clinical care and the need to take calculated risks. At the same time, the clinician writes "for" the plaintiff's attorney, jury, or court who may later review those notations after an adverse result. Of course, it is especially important for the clinician who is evaluating or treating a potentially violent or suicidal patient to document his or her work related to those problems; commonly, the jury is led to believe that if the clinician failed to document an event (e.g., that a proper evaluation of suicide risk in fact occurred), then it never occurred, and the clinician is thereby negligent.

SUMMARY

Contemporary mental health practice is highly regulated, and psychiatrists sometimes feel overwhelmed with the demands placed upon them by the law. Legal regulation of practice guides and limits the profession's behavior. Providing care of the aggressive patient is constrained by rules or law regarding hospitalization, seclusion/restraints, and involuntary medication. The law, and psychiatrists, must secure a balance between the patient's right to treatment, the patient's right to be free from treatment, and the public's right to safety. For the last two decades, there has been an imbalance between these interests, as seen by excessive deference to patients' legal rights at the expense of clinical concerns.

On the other side, tort law deters negligence, thus preventing injuries to patients. While clinicians overestimate their risk of lawsuits, which creates more anxiety and dissatisfaction with practice as well as unnecessary or harmful defensive care practices, such misperceptions also deter negligence (Lawthers et al., 1992). The silver lining is that patients sometimes receive better care than in earlier days when legal sanctions for misconduct, and legal regulation of practice, were less conspicuous.

REFERENCES

Adams v. Murakami, 268 Cal. Rptr. 467 (1990).
Allen v. Kaiser Foundation Hospital, 707 P.2d 1289 (Or. App. 1985).

American Psychiatric Association (1985). *Seclusion and restraint: The psychiatric uses.* Task Force Report #22. Washington, DC: American Psychiatric Press.

American Psychiatric Association (1987). *Involuntary commitment to outpatient treatment: Report of the Task Force on Involuntary Outpatient Commitment* (#26). Washington, DC: American Psychiatric Press.

Appelbaum, P. S. (1982). Clinical aspects of treatment refusal. *Comprehensive Psychiatry, 23*, 560–566.

Appelbaum, P. S. (1988a). The new preventive detention: Psychiatry's problematic responsibility for the control of violence. *American Journal of Psychiatry, 145*, 779–785.

Appelbaum, P. S. (1988b). The right to refuse treatment with antipsychotic medication: Retrospect and prospect. *American Journal of Psychiatry, 145*, 413–419.

Appelbaum, P. S., & Gutheil, T. (1991). *Clinical handbook of psychiatry and the law* (2nd ed.). Baltimore: Williams & Wilkins.

Appelbaum, P. S., Zonana, H., Bonnie, R., & Roth, L. H. (1989). Statutory approaches to limiting psychiatrists' liability for their patients' violent acts. *American Journal of Psychiatry, 146*, 821–828.

Bagby, R. M., & Atkinson, L. (1988). The effects of legislative reform on civil commitment admission rates: A critical analysis. *Behavioral Sciences and the Law, 6*, 45–61.

Betemps, E. J., Buncher, C. R., & Oden, M. (1992). Length of time spent in seclusion and restraints by patients at 82 VA medical centers. *Hospital and Community Psychiatry, 43*, 912–914.

Bloom, J. D., Williams, M. H., Bigelow, D. A. (1991). Monitored conditional release of persons found not guilty by reason of insanity. *American Journal of Psychiatry, 148*, 444–448.

Brakel, S. J., Parry, J., & Weiner, B. A. (1985). *The mentally disabled and the law* (3rd ed.). Chicago: American Bar Foundation.

Brennan, T. A., Leape, L. L., Laird, N. M., Hebert, L., Localio, A. R., Lawthers, A. G., Newhouse, J. P., Weiler, P. C., & Hiatt, H. H. (1991). Incidence of adverse events and negligence in hospitalized patients. *New England Journal of Medicine, 324*, 370–376.

Brouillette, M. J., & Paris, J. (1991). The dangerousness criterion for civil commitment: The problem and a possible solution. *Canadian Journal of Psychiatry, 36*, 285–289.

Brown v. State, 44 N.Y.2d 1006 (1977).

Chodoff, P. (1984). Involuntary hospitalization of the mentally ill as a moral issue. *American Journal of Psychiatry, 141*, 384–389.

Ciccone, J. R., Tokoli, J. F., Clements, C. D., & Gift, T. E. (1990). Right to refuse treatment: Impact of *Rivers v. Katz. Bulletin of the American Academy of Psychiatry and the Law, 18*, 203–215.

Clark v. Ohio Department of Mental Health, 573 N.E. 2d 794 (Ohio Ct.Cl. 1989).

Cleveland, S., Mulvey, E. P., Appelbaum, P. S., & Lidz, C. W. (1989). Do dangerousness-oriented commitment laws restrict hospitalization of patients who need treatment? A test. *Hospital and Community Psychiatry, 40*, 266–271.

Clites v. Iowa, Law #46274, Iowa District Court, Pottawattamie County, August 7, 1980.

Clites v. Iowa, 322 N.W.2d 917 (Iowa 1982).

Doyle v. United States, 530 F. Supp. 1278 (C.D. Cal. 1982).

Evans, L. K., & Strumpf, N. E. (1989). Tying down the elderly: A review of the literature on physical restraint. *Journal of the American Geriatrics Society, 36*, 65–74.

Fishalow, S. E. (1975). The tort liability of the psychiatrist. *Bulletin of the American Academy of Psychiatry and the Law, 3*, 191–229.

Fleming v. Prince George's County, 358 A.2d 892 (Md.App. 1976).

Food and Drug Administration (1992, September). New regulatory controls for patient restraints. *FDA Medical Bulletin*, pp. 5–6.

Gabbard, G. O., & Coyne, L. (1987). Predictors of response of antisocial patients to hospital treatment. *Hospital and Community Psychiatry, 38*, 1181–1185.

Geller, J. L. (1990). Clinical guidelines for the use of involuntary outpatient treatment. *Hospital and Community Psychiatry, 41*, 749–755.

George v. McIntosh-Wilson, 582 So.2d 1058 (Sup.Ct.Ala. 1991).

Gondolf, E. W. (1992). Discussion of violence in psychiatric evaluations. *Journal of Interpersonal Violence, 7*, 334–349.

Greenberg, D. F. (1974). Involuntary psychiatric commitments to prevent suicide. *New York University Law Review, 49*, 227–269.

Gutheil, T. G. (1980). Paranoia and progress notes: A guide to forensically informed psychiatric recordkeeping. *Hospital and Community Psychiatry, 31*, 479–482.

Hasebe, T., & McRae, J. (1987). A ten-year study of civil commitments in Washington State. *Hospital and Community Psychiatry, 38*, 983–987.

Hoge, S. K., Appelbaum, P. S., Lawlor, T., Beck, J. C., Litman, R., Greer, A., Gutheil, T. G., & Kaplan, E. (1990). A prospective, multicenter study of patients' refusal of antipsychotic medication. *Archives of General Psychiatry, 47*, 949–956.

Hopper v. Callahan, 562 N.E.2d 822 (Sup.Jud.Ct. Mass. 1990).

Huber, G. A., Roth, L. H., Appelbaum, P. S., & Ore, T. M. (1982). Hospitalization, arrest, or discharge: Important legal and clinical issues in the emergency evaluation of persons believed dangerous to others. *Law and Contemporary Problems, 45*, 99–123.

Ihler v. Chisholm, No. ADV-88-383 (Mont. Dist. Ct. September 26, 1991).

Imershein, A. W., & Brents, A. H. (1992). The impact of large medical malpractice awards on malpractice awardees. *Journal of Legal Medicine, 13*, 33–49.

Johnson, S. H. (1990). The fear of liability and the use of restraints in nursing homes. *Law, Medicine, and Health Care, 18*, 263–273.

Kapp, M. B. (1992). Nursing home restraints and legal liability. *Journal of Legal Medicine, 13*, 1–32.

Kuster v. State, 560 N.Y.S.2d 301 (A.D. 1989).

Lawthers, A. G., Localio, A. R., Laird, N. M., Lipsitz, S., Hebert, L., & Brennan, T. A. (1992). *Journal of Health Politics, Policy and Law, 17*, 463–482.

Leal v. Simon, 542 N.Y.S.2d 328 (A.D. 1989).

Localio, A. R., Lawthers, A. G., Brennan, T. A., Laird, N. M., Hebert, L. E., Peterson, L. M., Newhouse, J. P., Weiler, P. C., & Hiatt, H. H. (1991). Relation between malpractice claims and adverse events due to negligence. *New England Journal of Medicine, 325*, 245–251.

McCafferty, G., & Dooley, J. (1990). Involuntary outpatient commitment: An update. *Mental and Physical Disability Law Reporter, 14*, 277–287.

McMillian v. Wallis, 567 So.2d 1199 (Ala.Sup.Ct. 1990).

Marx, J. I., & Levinson, R. M. (1988). Statutory change and "street-level" implementation of psychiatric commitment. *Social Science and Medicine, 27*, 1247–1256.

Miller, R. D. (1985). Commitment to outpatient treatment: A national survey. *Hospital and Community Psychiatry, 36*, 265–267.

Miller, R. D. (1992a). An update on involuntary civil commitment to outpatient treatment. *Hospital and Community Psychiatry, 43*, 79–81.

Miller, R. D. (1992b). Need-for-treatment criteria for involuntary civil commitment: Impact in practice. *American Journal of Psychiatry, 149*, 1380–1384.

Montana agrees to pay $350,000 damages for rights violations of state hospital patients. (1992, September). *Hospital and Community Psychiatry, 43*, p. 947.

Morse, S. J. (1982). A preference for liberty: The case against involuntary commitment of the mentally disordered. *California Law Review, 70*, 54–106.

Mulvey, E. P., Geller, J. L., & Roth, L. H. (1987). The promise and peril of involuntary outpatient commitment. *American Psychologist, 42*, 571–584.

Ogloff, J. R. P., Wong, S., & Greenwood, A. (1990). Treating criminal psychopaths in a therapeutic community program. *Behavioral Sciences and the Law, 8*, 181–190.

Okin, R. L. (1985). Variation among state hospitals in use of seclusion and restraint. *Hospital and Community Psychiatry, 36*, 648–652.

Pederson v. Dumouchel, 431 P.2d 973 (Sup.Ct.Wash. 1967).

Peters, R., Miller, K. S., Schmidt, W., & Meeter, D. (1987). The effects of statutory change on the civil commitment of the mentally ill. *Law and Human Behavior, 11*, 73–99.

Pierce, G. L., Durham, M. L., & Fisher, W. H. (1985). The impact of broadened civil commitment standards on admissions to state mental hospitals. *American Journal of Psychiatry, 142*, 104–107.

Rogers v. Okin, 478 F. Supp. 1342 (D. Mass. 1979).

Schwartz, S. J., & Costanzo, C. E. (1987). Compelling treatment in the community: Distorted doctrines and violated values. *Loyola of Los Angeles Law Review, 20*, 1329–1429.

Siegel, K., & Tuckel, P. (1987). Suicide and civil commitment. *Journal of Health Politics, Policy and Law, 12*, 343–360.

Simon, R. (1992). *Clinical psychiatry and the law* (2nd ed.). Washington, DC: American Psychiatric Press.

Stone, A. (1975). *Mental health and the law: A system in transition*. Washington, DC: U.S. Government Printing Office.

Taig v. State of New York, 241 N.Y.S.2d 495 (A.D. 1963).

Tarasoff v. Regents of the University of California, 551 P.2d 334 (Cal.Sup.Ct. 1976).

Tardiff, K. (Ed.). (1984). *The psychiatric uses of seclusion and restraint*. Washington, DC: American Psychiatric Press.

Weiner, B. A., & Wettstein, R. M. (1993). *Legal issues in mental health care*. New York: Plenum.

Wettstein, R. M. (1983). Tardive dyskinesia and malpractice. *Behavioral Sciences and the Law*, *1*, 85–107.

Wettstein, R. M. (1985). Legal aspects of neuroleptic-induced movement disorders. In C. H. Wecht (Ed.), *Legal Medicine 1985* (pp. 117–179). New York: Praeger.

Wettstein, R. M. (1988). Informed consent and tardive dyskinesia. *Journal of Clinical Psychopharmacology*, *8*(Suppl.), 65S–70S.

Winick, B. J. (1989). The right to refuse mental health treatment: A First Amendment perspective. *University of Miami Law Review*, *44*, 1–103.

Youngberg v. Romeo, 102 S.Ct. 2452 (1982).

Zinermon v. Burch, 110 S.Ct. 975 (1990).

CHAPTER 9

Control in the Psychiatric Setting— Adults

MARNIE E. RICE, GRANT T. HARRIS,
AND VERNON L. QUINSEY

INTRODUCTION

Jack was admitted to a secure psychiatric institution after being found not guilty for murder by reason of insanity. He was diagnosed as suffering from paranoid schizophrenia. During the first few years of his stay he was regarded as a "good" patient: he was usually a reliable worker, was compliant with the instructions of ward staff, and was never in a fight. Nevertheless, he frequently exhibited psychotic behavior, asserting that he was a "king of kings," that he had animals in his stomach, and that hospital staff had secret papers about him. Despite the psychotic behavior, and after several years, he eventually earned a transfer to the highest privilege, lowest security ward.

Over the next several months, staff became increasingly dissatisfied with Jack's performance, reporting that he showed poor personal hygiene and poor motivation in the contract workshop. They had him transferred to a ward where security was tighter and that had a token economy program. His hygiene and work behavior quickly came under control, and he earned a transfer back to the less secure ward where privileges were available noncontingently. Immediately thereafter, the staff noted that he had again become "dirty and lazy." They began a practice of sometimes calling him to the ward from activities in order to clean his room, with little positive result. For almost a year, a cyclical pattern continued in which he was sent to the more secure token economy ward, his behavior came under control, and he obtained a transfer to the less secure, nonbehavioral ward. It was clear that the staff on Jack's home ward were completely frustrated in their

---

MARNIE E. RICE and GRANT T. HARRIS • Mental Health Centre, Penetanguishene, Ontario, Canada. **VERNON L. QUINSEY** • Queen's University, Kingston, Ontario, Canada.

Handbook of Aggressive and Destructive Behavior in Psychiatric Patients, edited by Michel Hersen, Robert T. Ammerman, and Lori A. Sisson. Plenum Press, New York, 1994.

attempts to get him to be a "good" patient and believed that the token economy programs on the other ward were having no lasting impact on his behavior.

One day Jack was called back to the ward from the shop and asked to provide a routine blood sample, which he refused to give. The staff member in charge told him to go to his room. As he went, a nearby attendant made a remark, intended to be humorous, the gist of which was that Jack could now spend some time cleaning his messy room.

Jack picked up a cleaner's broom, turned around and started yelling, "You monkeys have no right to keep me here," and attempted to punch the attendant, who backed up and pressed the alarm button. Jack then swung the broom at the staff member in charge and, after missing him, turned around and hit the first attendant with the broom, causing the brush portion to break off. Jack continued to hit him with the handle until it broke into smaller pieces, then tried to stab him in the face with the sharply splintered broken end, causing a cut and scratches. The attendant managed to grab Jack's hands and flip him over his shoulder to the floor, at which point Jack attempted to bite him. More staff responded and helped restrain the patient. Fortunately, no one involved received injuries worse than minor scratches and bruises.

The Incident in Review

Formal incident reports and notes on the clinical record indicated that the clinical staff and supervisory personnel regarded the incident as clearly the direct result of Jack's obvious psychosis. Indeed, in retrospect, a clinician or investigator could have several reactions to the actual incident described above. First, Jack was clearly a very dangerous and a very psychotic man, and one might wonder whether the psychiatric treatment he was receiving was optimal. For example, had the appropriate neuroleptic medication been prescribed in sufficient doses? Second, one wonders about the nondrug treatments provided for Jack. There is considerable evidence that carefully implemented behavioral treatment that provides consequences for both assaultive and prosocial behavior can sharply reduce aggression in psychiatric patients (Liberman, Marshall, & Burke, 1981; Wong, Slama, & Liberman, 1987). The token economy program seemed to be effective while Jack was on it, but there seemed to be no planned weaning from the program when he changed wards. There is no question that all of the above concerns are relevant to the story of Jack and to violence in psychiatric hospitals in general.

In this chapter, however, we present a different way of thinking about such violent incidents as the one described above. We then describe a staff training course based on an innovative view of violence and summarize data supporting effectiveness of the course in reducing violence.

To begin, consider the case of Jack again. To staff on the maximum privilege ward, Jack was a problem: his delusional assertions were distressing and caused staff to label him unpredictable. He was also dirty and untidy. The intervention they attempted was typical of what any lay person might employ in such a situation. When they noticed that his room was messy, they recalled Jack to the ward. They made him aware of their displeasure and they instructed him to get his room in order. When the messiness got beyond their level of tolerance (there was no explicit ward policy), they transferred him off the ward. However, due to day-to-day variations in staff work load and to differences among staff in individual standards of cleanliness, Jack was never in a position to know when he would be recalled and upbraided, or when he would be "demoted" to the more secure ward. Jack's social environment with staff may have been unpredictable and aversive.

However, from the viewpoint of any individual staff person, the situation would have seemed quite different. Staff members would have regarded the difficulties presented by Jack as a routine, albeit frustrating, aspect of the day-to-day job. They would have regarded any instructions to Jack to clean his room or any decision to transfer him to the more structured ward as simply doing the job, and as being entirely consistent with normal standards for deciding these issues.

Jack and the staff, then, had quite divergent views and experiences of the same course of events. The staff involved firmly regarded Jack's violence as another very serious, but completely unpredictable, symptom of psychosis, while Jack regarded himself as the victim of staff authoritarianism and personal bullying. Attending to the distinction between participants' understanding of interpersonal interactions comprises the theoretical basis for our approach to the control of institutional violence. Such a theoretical view leads to the adoption of the principles of social learning theory to teach staff new behaviors to employ in their day-to-day interactions with patients.

RESEARCH ON VIOLENCE IN INSTITUTIONS

Without question, the theoretical perspective adopted by a scientific investigator exerts a powerful influence on the types of variables studied. This observation is as true in the area of violence in psychiatric institutions as it is in any other. For example, studies based on a medical or biological perspective will be likely to investigate the role of such variables as diagnosis, degree of pathology, age, and sex of the violent individual. Conversely, studies based on behavioral or social psychological perspectives are likely to investigate the role of such situational variables as victim characteristics and behaviors, and antecedents and consequences of the violent behavior.

In reviewing the accumulated empirical literature on assaults in psychiatric institutions, we (Rice, Harris, Varney, & Quinsey, 1989) concluded that most investigators have been influenced by the medical or biological view that hospital patients are, by definition, sick. Consequently, most of the published research has concentrated on the characteristics (symptoms, diagnoses) of assaultive patients. The most consistent findings of these studies are that most of the assaults are committed by a minority of patients, that a diagnosis of schizophrenia and evidence of acute distress are each associated with assaultiveness and, within institutions, that assaultive patients are more often those who are young and who have a history of institutional violence. The idea that violence in psychiatric hospitals is due to patient psychopathology severely limits what staff might reasonably do to eliminate it. For example, there is some evidence (Harris, 1989) that a significant proportion of hospitals inpatients are, at best, only partial responders to neuroleptic treatment and that the search for a more effective neuroleptic drug to completely eliminate the symptoms of such patients is likely to fail.

Perhaps inspired by a social psychological or behavioral orientation, some investigators have studied social and environmental factors associated with violence in psychiatric hospitals. Though fewer in number, these studies permit some strong conclusions. Staff are overrepresented as victims of assaults, and some staff characteristics, such as authoritarian behavior, inexperience, and indecision, are associated with being assaulted. Crowding, heat, unstable social environments, lack of supervision by staff, and lack of structured activity for patients are also related to the occurrence of assaults (Rice et al., 1989). Inasmuch as many psychiatric institutions have many of the above conditions, it is not surprising that high levels of violence are reported.

Over a 15-year period, we have conducted a series of investigations aimed at the understanding and control of violence in one psychiatric institution with a maximum security division as well as separate buildings with medium security and completely open psychiatric wards. We have examined the characteristics of assaults and assaulters (Harris & Varney, 1986; Quinsey & Varney, 1977a). We observed a great discrepancy between the reasons staff and patients gave to explain assaults. Patients almost always stated that there was a reason for the assault, and that reason rarely involved psychiatric symptoms or psychopathology. In fact, hallucinations, delusions, or building tension accounted for fewer than 10% of assaults according to patients. Patients reported that the majority of assaults were due to being teased, provoked, ordered to do something, or having a request refused. Although staff also rarely gave hallucinations or delusions as reasons for assaultive behavior, staff most often reported that there was no reason for the assault. These results suggest that violence by inpatients is similar to that which occurs in the general population, inasmuch as the explanations are the same as those given by perpetrators of violence in school yards, bars, or jails and are not different simply because the perpetrators are psychiatric patients. Furthermore, these results are consistent with our other work on released patients (e.g., Rice, Harris, Lang, & Bell, 1990; Rice, Quinsey, & Houghton, 1990) that has shown that the predictors of criminal and violent recidivism of released mentally disordered offenders are the same as those for offenders in general. Because our data suggested that violence among psychiatric patients may not be different from violence among members of the general population, we began to look for methods that have been used to reduce violence in other contexts.

Other areas of our research effort have concentrated on the details of violent altercations between staff and patients (Harris & Rice, 1986) and on the patients' and staff members' views about the strategies employed to control violent behavior (Harris, Rice, & Preston, 1989). In the first study, we found that many injuries staff received in altercations with patients were not due to assaults. Rather, staff were often injured during attempts to control patients with manual restraint. Furthermore, injuries sustained during manual restraint were more serious than those caused by patients' assaults. The second study showed that staff and patients agreed about the relative intrusiveness and aversiveness of various methods hospital staff use to control violent and disruptive behavior (sedative drugs, seclusion, manual restraint, mechanical restraint). However, whereas patients preferred the use of less intrusive methods and believed they were effective, staff favored the use of relatively intrusive methods even though they were pessimistic about their long-term effectiveness.

Aside from some of the behavioral treatments for violent psychiatric patients, the professional and scientific literature on ways to control, reduce, or eliminate institutional violence is surprisingly atheoretical. That is, most accounts of attempts to reduce violence in psychiatric institutions are not based on an articulated theory about the causes of violence.

Traditionally, psychiatric hospital staff have made extensive use of incapacitation as a method of controlling violence. The use of seclusion and mechanical restraint are ubiquitous throughout time and geography. The use of these methods does not depend on any theoretical understanding of the causes of violence. However, despite their universality, remarkably little is known about the long-term effectiveness of seclusion and restraint. There are data on the conditions that occasion frequency of restraint use, characteristics of persons restrained, staff and patient attitudes toward restraint, and institutional policies governing its use (see Rice et al., 1989). However, there are no data to inform those who would employ restraint as a long-term strategy, because there are no data on its effectiveness in reducing future violence. There is some information to suggest that it is possible to use remarkably little restraint and seclusion without experiencing a concomitant increase in patient violence (Davidson, Hemingway, & Wysocki, 1984).

The second traditional approach to the control of violence by psychiatric patients has been the use of drugs. At first glance, it might seem that the use of psychotropic medications is indeed based on the sensible theory that treating psychiatric symptoms with the appropriate pharmacological agent should produce reductions in the violence associated with psychiatric disorders. However, an examination of the existing literature obviates such a conclusion. First, some drugs (neuroleptics) are recommended (and are reportedly effective) in reducing violence regardless of the diagnosis of the patient or the concomitant symptoms. Second, drugs reported to be effective in controlling violence are not those known to ameliorate psychiatric symptoms in general. Thus, lithium (the drug of choice for mania) is reported to reduce aggression in character disorders (Mattes, 1986). Beta-blockers (usually prescribed for hypertension) reportedly reduce violence in persons with brain damage (Greendyke & Kanter, 1986). Although there are other examples (see Rice et al., 1989), the inescapable conclusion is that there are few theories to account for the action most drugs have in reducing violence (cf., Eichelman, 1993).

A STAFF TRAINING COURSE TO CONTROL
VIOLENCE IN INSTITUTIONS

Our empirical work has led us to the conclusion that, although some psychiatric patients are more assaultive than others, insufficient attention has been paid to the nature of staff–patient interactions. In our research, we were strongly influenced by work with police officers and prison guards. Toch (1969), for example, attributed many assaults by citizens on police officers to sharply differing perceptions by the participants in the incidents. Some officers approached people in an authoritarian fashion, but because they treated everyone in the same manner, they regarded their own behavior as routine and "part of the job" and any violent reaction by a citizen as unpredictable and irrational. Conversely, the angry citizen, accustomed to different treatment, regarded the police officer's behavior as arbitrary and personally motivated, and his own reaction as completely understandable under the circumstances.

These observations about violent police–citizen interactions have led some investigators to attempt to reduce such violence by changing the nature of these interactions. Such attempts have concentrated on changing the ways in which police officers deal with members of the public by teaching the officers new interpersonal skills (Goldstein, Monti, Sardino, & Green, 1977; Levens & Dutton, 1980; Miron & Goldstein, 1979; Mulvey & Repucci, 1981). In most cases, this training is in the form of courses in defusing (verbal strategies to prevent violence) and conflict resolution skills.

This view of interpersonal violence had powerful implications for our attempts to eliminate it. Our earliest efforts were operant studies of behavioral inhibition among assaultive patients (Quinsey, 1977), but the social nature of assaults quickly became obvious (Quinsey & Varney, 1977a). Our next efforts were directed at improving the assaultive patients' social skills in provocative situations (Quinsey & Varney, 1977b; Rice, 1983; Rice & Josefowitz, 1983). Although patients acquired new social skills, the social environment was difficult to change, and we found that improvements in social skills did not generalize to the wards (Harris & Rice, 1992). In the end, the intervention that showed the greatest promise was directed not at assaultive patients but at the institution's staff. We developed a staff training course, the goal of which was to eliminate assaults by equipping staff with new interpersonal skills.

Consider again the incident described at the beginning of this chapter. How could training for staff have altered the nature of the social environment and the behavior of the staff and thereby have prevented the incident? First, such training could have alerted staff to the possibility that such an everyday object as a broom can be put to violent purposes, and that the presence of potential weapons can facilitate violence. Second, staff could have been trained to employ different means to get Jack to keep his room clean. The application of a consistently applied intervention that did not depend upon scolding Jack would undoubtedly have been more effective. Third, when Jack was called back to the ward, he believed, of course, that it was to receive yet another reprimand. If the shop personnel had known that the call was for a blood test, Jack could have been so informed and he would not have been anticipating another scolding; he could also have declined the test (as was his right) without leaving the shop. Fourth, the staff member in charge could have sent Jack back to the shop instead of to his room. Undoubtedly, Jack thought he was to be punished for exercising his legal right to decline the blood test. Also, training could have shown how this sequence of events would make almost anyone (whether a psychiatric patient or not) very angry. Fifth, training could have alerted staff to the risks in using humor with someone who is already very upset. Sixth, training could have taught verbal defusing techniques that the attendant could have used to get Jack to put down the weapon before he used it. Seventh, training could have equipped staff members with self-defense skills to be used in such a situation. Also, such training would have emphasized that a physical intervention is a last resort, noting that even experienced co-workers cannot always be counted on for assistance—the staff member in charge of the ward in this case watched the entire incident but never intervened because he "froze" and stood by helplessly. Eighth, interviewing and conflict resolution techniques could have been employed after the incident to resolve the disputes between Jack and the ward staff so that future violence would be less likely.

Our conviction that staff training could reduce patient aggression was bolstered by evidence suggesting that a training course that included both verbal and physical techniques did reduce the number of patient assaults in a psychiatric setting (St. Thomas Psychiatric Hospital, 1976). Other training courses have also been developed for staff in psychiatric settings (Duggan, 1984; Thackrey, 1987), but these courses have not been evaluated and, like the St. Thomas course, they rely heavily on interventions to be used when patients are either in the act of, or very close to, physical violence. The staff training course described here is based on the premise that violence, even among the severely mentally ill, rarely erupts without warning. Instead, in the great majority of cases, patients escalate from a calm state through an anxious state, and then through a hostile state before becoming physically violent. The course emphasizes interventions that can be used with calm or anxious patients, because the use of these techniques reduces the likelihood of violence and yet entails little or no risk of physical or psychological damage. Also included are verbal techniques to be used with hostile patients when violence seems imminent, restraint techniques to be used when physical intervention is absolutely necessary, and self-defense techniques to be used during patient attacks. The course also includes techniques of interviewing and conflict resolution that can be implemented following incidents of aggressive behavior in order to gather information and solve problems so that the risk of a similar escalation in the future is reduced. It is emphasized that the principles of the effective prevention and control of violence apply regardless of the diagnosis or particular psychopathology of the patient. In choosing the techniques that are advocated in the course, we searched the literature so that, as much as possible, we could recommend methods with empirical support. The course and the empirical evidence supporting the techniques chosen are described in more detail elsewhere (Rice et al., 1989).

Preventing Violence

Security

Violence can often be prevented when staff adhere to a sensible and consistently applied set of security guidelines. Such consistency helps make the social environment predictable for staff and patients. Of course, what is sensible depends upon the patient population. Nevertheless, some combination of perimeter security (control over who and what gets in and out of the building) and internal security (control over who is allowed access to what within the building) is necessary. Perimeter security considerations include such things as regular inspection and maintenance by staff of windows, bars, locks, and fences, monitoring of persons and objects coming in and out of the building, and regulations for visitors. Internal security considerations include staff attention to the types of furniture that are purchased for ward areas, staff–patient ratios required for the use of yard areas and for various activities, rules regarding which patients are allowed to roam unescorted within the building, and counting of cutlery and tools.

Although the use of physical hardware is what most readily comes to mind in a discussion of security, the dependence upon physical hardware to maintain security has disadvantages inasmuch as it contributes to a fortress mentality, consumes financial resources, and emphasizes the distinction between those inside and outside the institution. Furthermore, physical hardware devices are short term in nature in the sense that they are not expected to work unless they are being applied, and thus do little to alter a patient's need for extended control in the future. For all of the above reasons, staff must consider other types of control. Other methods include pharmacological control, control through the use of physical and mechanical restraint, control through ward programs and ward rules for determination of privileges, control through the interpersonal skills of staff, and patient self-control. Patient self-control is the ultimate goal of treatments designed to reduce patient aggression.

Calming

The most important component of the training course for the prevention of violence is calming. It is this section of the course that most fundamentally seeks to alter the social environment by teaching staff new and more effective ways of talking to patients. Emphasized in this part of the course is the importance of positive approaches. Using simple verbal techniques with patients on a daily basis, and helping mildly upset patients to express and resolve their concerns, can go a long way toward maintaining a calm environment. A step-by-step procedure consisting of observation, preparation, approach, action, and follow-up can be followed in using calming techniques, as well as for each of the other course sections described below. Observing a patient for signs that calming may be indicated involves looking for such signs as pacing, fidgeting, pupil dilation, sweating, flushing, and lack of eye contact. In preparing to talk to a mildly upset patient, it is important to consider safety by such things as choosing a location within sight of at least one other staff member, to consider patient needs such as privacy by picking a spot out of the earshot of others, and to set aside adequate time (we suggest 10 minutes). In the action phase of calming, simple interviewing skills such as open questions, paraphrasing, and nonverbal listening responses, as well as simply providing information in response to a patient's questions, can assist a patient in identifying and resolving concerns. Follow-up after calming involves such things as writing a brief note for the patient record, and following through with promises (e.g., to get information) made to the patient.

Explosive Situations

When patients become highly upset, the situation must be brought under control quickly and effectively if no one is to be hurt.

Defusing

When patients are very close to physical violence (e.g., when two patients are arguing vehemently, when a patient is kicking furniture), verbal techniques can often be used to de-escalate the situation. Avoiding the use of physical force in such explosive situations is safer for patients and staff, and the use of verbal strategies in such situations also contributes to a more positive social climate in the institution. While mistakes can usually be made in the calming situation without risk of physical injury, mistakes in the defusing situation are likely to result in a physical incident. Observation in the defusing situation includes looking for signs that a patient is about to engage in an act of physical aggression (loud, rapid speech, staring or squinting eyes, flared nostrils, patient standing up) and making mental notes of the location of other staff, potential weapons, and escape routes. Preparation may have to be done very quickly; nevertheless, if staff spend a few moments discussing matters such as who will do the talking and who will do what if a physical altercation breaks out, the likelihood of injury can be minimized. In approaching a highly upset patient, it is important to remember such things as allowing more personal space than at times when the patient is not upset, positioning oneself between the patient and any potential weapons, and standing in a defensive (e.g., hands at waist-to-shoulder height in front of body) but nonthreatening (e.g., not directly in front of the patient) posture. The action phase focuses on the importance of sounding firm but calm, of getting the patient to say "yes," of ordering interventions from lesser to greater intrusiveness, of offering the patient a way to save face, of getting the patients out of eye contact of one another in cases where there is an altercation between two patients, and of trying to get the patient to sit down. Follow-up consists of such things as imposing sanctions on the patient or patients involved, discussing the incident with other staff, and writing a note for the patient record.

Restraint, Seclusion, and Self-Defense

There are rare situations where the use of physical force is unavoidable. An incident that is handled smoothly, efficiently, and in a coordinated fashion is safer for all concerned, and it is less destructive to a positive social environment than a protracted melee or standoff. Sometimes defusing is not possible (e.g., when staff members discover an altercation in progress) or not recommended (e.g., a patient is involved in serious property destruction such as breaking glass or furniture), and sometimes defusing is tried and fails. The restraint, seclusion, and self-defense portion of the course includes time spent in the gym practicing restraint techniques, safe methods of putting a patient into a seclusion room, and self-defense techniques to be used when, for instance, a patient attacks by choking, biting, or pulling hair. In the classroom, the step-by-step procedures of observation (e.g., potential hazards such as chairs obstructing the area required to conduct the restraint), preparation (e.g., who will take hold of what part of the patient's body), approach (e.g., engaging the patient in conversation), action (e.g., how much force to apply), and follow-up (e.g., postrestraint staff discussion to determine possible improvements in the procedure for another time) are discussed. In addition, there is a discussion of legal issues in the management of violent patients (e.g., the legal definition of assault, authority to restrain, the advantages and disadvantages of pressing legal charges against assaultive patients). A final topic reviewed in the course section on explosive situations is hostage-taking.

Following Violent Incidents

After a crisis has subsided, and the patient or patients involved have returned to a calm state, verbal techniques can be used to decrease the likelihood of the same or similar incident occurring in the future.

Interviewing

By gathering as much information as possible from the patient or patients about what triggered the violent incident, staff members will be in a good position to determine whether any environmental modifications would decrease the likelihood of future incidents, what signs staff should watch for at another time, and how their approach to the patients could be altered. In addition, having a complete account of the details of what happened is necessary for conflict resolution. Observation prior to interviewing can establish that patients have returned to a calm state. Preparation for interviewing involves a consideration of issues such as the physical setup (e.g., arranging so that the staff member sits at a table between two patients if two are involved). The action phase involves using techniques to keep control of the interview (especially important when there are two patients), and using recommended strategies (e.g., reflections, pauses, summarizing) and avoiding nonrecommended interviewing techniques (e.g., preaching, offering personal opinions, offering solutions). Follow-up may involve writing a note for the clinical file, or it may be postponed until after conflict resolution.

Conflict Resolution

Negotiation is a way in which two parties (e.g., a patient and a staff member) can, through a process of offering, counteroffering, concession, and compromise, reach a solution to an interpersonal problem or a problem that the patient may have in following the ward rules. Mediation is a procedure whereby a staff member can assist two patients in resolving their disputes (but without imposing a solution). In both cases, the objective is to help patients generate as many ideas as possible for solving their problem, and then to have them select the solution that is most likely to work for them. Especially when two patients are involved, staff must maintain control by laying down and enforcing ground rules about such things as interrupting and name-calling. Staff can also assist patients by such techniques as checking out one patient's solutions with the other patient, encouraging patients to reverse roles to be sure they understand one another, and encouraging patients to examine possible advantages to each party of each proposed solution.

Other Course Topics

Simulations

As each of the above course topics is presented, course participants are given a chance to practice the techniques by doing short role-plays in the classroom by simply breaking up into small groups of three or four and enacting scenes set up in short written scripts. Participants take turns playing the roles of staff and patients. In addition, participants are given additional experience in using the skills taught in the course by spending one whole day in the workplace (an empty ward, if possible) doing more extended role plays. Because it often enables participants to practice many of the skills within one role-play, we often begin with a hostage-taking, emphasizing, however, that such incidents are extremely rare. Other simulations are drawn from typical incidents that occur at our institution. These role-plays are videotaped so that they can be played back and discussed by class participants. This procedure is essentially analogous to social skills training (e.g., Goldstein & Glick, 1987).

Job Stress and Burnout

These issues are discussed as problems that can arise when staff must work in daily contact with assaultive and disruptive patients. Causes, symptoms, and constructive coping techniques are discussed. Discussion during these sessions is often enhanced by a description of a research project or two. For staff who work on minimum security wards, a summary of a research project by Rosenhan (1974), in which eight sane people secretly gained admission to psychiatric hospitals and experienced being labeled and subjected to stereotyping by staff members, can lead to candid discussion of some of the frustrations experienced by both staff and patients working in bureaucratic institutions. For staff who work on secure wards, where the environment has much in common with that in correctional institutions, a similar experience is offered by a discussion of the Stanford Prison Experiment (Zimbardo, Haney, Banks, & Jaffe, 1971). That study, in which college students were randomly assigned the role of prisoner or guard in a simulated prison, stimulates discussion of the way in which power differentials (between staff and inmates/patients) may have a deleterious effect on staff–patient relationships.

Evaluation of Course Effectiveness

To evaluate the course, we employed several strategies and four types of measures. The course evaluation has been described in greater detail elsewhere (Rice et al., 1989; Rice, Helzel, Varney, & Quinsey, 1985). A brief overview is presented here.

Briefly, for some types of measures, a multiple-baseline design was used. For this reason, the course was offered to staff (in groups of seven to nine per class) on three pairs of wards, with 6-month intervals between course administrations to each ward pair. The purpose of this design was to ensure that changes noted before and after the course could be more confidently attributed to the course rather than to other changes that might have occurred throughout the institution.

For other types of measures, a simple pre–post design was used in which the changes made by subjects who took the course were compared with the results of subjects who completed the assessments approximately 1 week apart but who did not take the course during the intervening week.

The first two sets of ward pairs were in Ontario's only maximum security facility. All patients in this facility were male. The third pair of wards comprised a medium and a minimum security ward within a general psychiatric hospital division of the same institution. Patients in this division were both male and female.

The staff ($n = 62$) from the first four wards were all male, and the staff ($n = 26$) from the other two wards were both male and female. All took part voluntarily. Control subjects also came from wards of various security levels and were also primarily male.

Measures of Knowledge and Skill

Four measures were developed to assess verbal and physical knowledge and skill in simulated situations designed to be representative of those discussed in the course.

The Sensitive Situations Skill Test was designed to measure the accuracy of staff members' observations of patient behavior, and their ability to identify effective and ineffective social and physical methods of dealing with potentially violent situations. The test consisted of four videotaped scenes of simulated interactions between patients and staff. Each scene was divided into short segments, and subjects answered questions about each immediately after viewing it.

The Audiotaped Simulations Test consisted of audiotaped scenarios that involved dealing with upset patients. A situation would be described, the "patient" would then say something, and then a tone would sound. The subject was instructed to respond as he or she would if the situation were actually happening. This test was designed to measure calming and defusing skills.

The Physical Skill Test was designed to sample skills taught in the physical section of the course. It consisted of eight situations presented in a fixed order by one trainer to one subject. The trainer began by informing the subject that this was a physical test in which a number of situations that could actually occur would be presented. The trainer then took the role of a patient and either pretended to attack or asked the subject to use restraint techniques. The effectiveness of the subject's response was rated by the trainer on the basis of predetermined criteria.

Finally, the 13-item Self-Defense and Patient Restraint Written Test was designed to measure the ability to verbally describe principles of safety in self-defense and use of patient restraints.

On all four of these measures of knowledge and skill, we were able to demonstrate statistically significant increases that could confidently be attributed to the course. Compared to the control staff who did not take the course, the experimental group showed significant improvements in their abilities to respond verbally in potential crisis situations, to recognize effective and ineffective ways to deal with crises, to defend themselves in the event of attacks, and to restrain patients safely and effectively.

Self-Report Measures

The Course Feedback Questionnaire asked participants to rate how much they enjoyed the course, how good the course was in relation to other courses they had taken at the hospital, and how useful each course topic was. In addition, respondents were asked to indicate how useful the course was in their daily work, and whether they would recommend the course to other staff. This questionnaire was given at the end of the course and again 6 weeks later. Another follow-up questionnaire was given to all staff who had taken the course and who were working on one of the study wards approximately 15 months later. Respondents were asked to answer many of the same questions asked on the original questionnaire as well as whether the course had prevented them, their co-workers, or patients from being injured. These questionnaires were given to experimental subjects only.

The On-Ward Job Reactions Scale allowed staff to indicate how confident and comfortable they felt in their interactions with their patients in a variety of different contexts. It was administered before and 6 weeks after the course to experimental subjects, and at approximately the same intervals to control subjects.

The results obtained on these measures indicated that the course clearly met with the approval of the staff, who judged it to be relevant and useful in their daily work with patients. We were particularly encouraged by the finding that staff still rated the course as very useful 15 months after taking it, and that most stated that it had definitely or probably saved them or co-workers from being injured. These data, as well as informal comments, suggested that the course led to increased levels of self-confidence, which lessened the atmosphere of fear that may seriously interfere with treatment (Paul & Lentz, 1977).

Patient Measures

Originally, we had planned to evaluate the effects of the course on altering the ward environments by asking patients on the wards to complete the Ward Atmosphere Scale (Moos, 1974, 1975). However, this plan had to be abandoned when the union representing the staff objected because they felt it was improper for the patients to be asked questions regarding staff performance, and it was apparent that the entire project would have been in jeopardy had we insisted on this measure. Instead, we decided to ask patients to rate their own self-esteem and mood, on the theory that if the course was successful, staff might change their interactions with patients so that the patients would feel less depressed, less anxious, and have more self-esteem than they did prior to the course. We therefore had every literate patient who consented to do so complete three questionnaires: a modified version of the Coopersmith Self-Esteem Inventory developed for an adult corrections population (Bennett, Sorensen, & Forshay, 1971), a scale including adjectives measuring depression and anxiety from the Adjective Checklist (Gough & Heilbrun, 1965), and a modified version of the Feelings Scale developed by Bradburn and Caplovitz (1965) to measure positive and negative affect in clinical populations. Each questionnaire was given to each patient three times approximately 1 week apart 6 weeks before and 6 weeks after staff on each ward pair were given the course.

Before analysis, the scores on the three questionnaires were added together to form one score that reflected their global affect. We found that patients rated themselves as having significantly more positive affect 6 weeks after the course than 6 weeks before, compared with control patients on wards where staff did not receive the training. For the patients as well as the staff, then, the ward atmosphere seemed to have changed so that they felt better about themselves.

Assault-Related Measures

Data were gathered regarding the number of assaults on patients and staff on the wards involved in the study for each of 18 months before and 18 months after the course. In addition, data were gathered regarding the number of workdays lost due to patient-caused staff injuries. These data were available for staff on study wards as well as nonstudy wards, and data were available for several years prior to the initiation of the study.

For both the assaultive incident data and the number of workdays lost, the data suggested positive effects due to the course. A time-series analysis of the assault data suggested immediate postcourse decreases in the numbers of assaults, followed by gradual increases. Although the gradual increases might be construed as evidence that the course failed to have a long-term effect, other explanations are plausible. One is that the gradual increases could have been due to staff turnover, inasmuch as only half of the staff who had taken the course remained on one of the study wards 1 year later. In addition, it is possible that the increases were due to a more difficult, more assaultive clientele being admitted during the postcourse period. In support of this latter explanation, it was noted that the number of incident reports (filled out on all wards whenever any difficulty was encountered) showed very large increases over the postcourse period in all areas of the hospital (including those wards where the course was not offered). For the work days-lost data, the time-series analyses revealed no consistent trends either before or after the course, but a nonparametric analysis of the number of days lost revealed a significant postcourse reduction for staff on the study wards when compared with staff on nonstudy wards.

The combined results of all our measures support the conclusion that training staff in interpersonal skills and in assault reduction techniques is an important component of an assault reduction strategy in psychiatric institutions. Trainees learned relevant skills, staff and patient morale improved, staff had more confidence in their ability to handle difficult situations with patients, and there were fewer assaults and fewer injuries. Of course, the training approach advocated here should be combined with other strategies (e.g., both social learning and occasionally pharmacological; Rice, Harris, Quinsey, & Cyr, 1990) that target assaultive behavior, and with ward programs that incorporate appropriate contingencies for assaultive behavior and for behaviors that are incompatible with assaultiveness.

SUMMARY

Our research plus that reported by others, combined with an intimate knowledge of the day-to-day life of a psychiatric institution, led us to a social psychological theory to explain the aggressive and destructive behavior exhibited by psychiatric patients. Our theory asserted that assaults are often the result of the ways in which staff members interact with patients. Based on such a view, we developed a staff training course to teach staff new interpersonal skills. The course emphasized verbal strategies and employed techniques from social skills training. Also included in the course were last-resort self-defense and manual restraint techniques. Data collected in evaluating the effectiveness of the course showed that it reduced violence and improved the institution's social environment, thereby providing empirical support for our theory about the etiology of institutional violence.

In considering the story of Jack that began this chapter, one might expect the chapter to end with another example in which staff, equipped with skills acquired in our course, maintain a positive relationship with a disturbed mental patient and effectively employ calming techniques to prevent many assaults. However, such an example is (fortunately) almost impossible to find because the effective prevention of aggression creates no spectacular incidents and few heroes or villains. The competent use of such techniques rarely makes "headlines" and is rarely noted in clinical or personnel records. In an effort both to learn from instances in which serious incidents had been prevented due to good early intervention and to acknowledge and praise the skills of staff involved, staff were encouraged to complete an incident report form whenever calming, defusing, interviewing, or conflict resolution had been used to avoid a physical altercation. However, perhaps because staff members themselves rarely knew when they had prevented an incident, few of these successful cases were recorded. Consequently, institutions often fail to notice and reward those staff members who deal effectively and skillfully with disturbed psychiatric patients. Instead, preference is often given to "great and desperate cures" for the problems patients exhibit (Valenstein, 1986). Alone, a staff training course such as the one described here cannot eliminate violence by psychiatric patients. Institutional administrators must also monitor staff behaviors and reinforce those that are consistent with preventing aggressive and destructive behavior (Harris & Rice, 1992).

ACKNOWLEDGMENTS.   The research described in this chapter was funded by Grant DM421 from the Ontario Ministry of Health. Thanks are due to George Varney and Manuel Helzel for assistance in course design and in conducting the training.

REFERENCES

Bennett, L. A., Sorensen, D. E., & Forshay, H. (1971). The application of self-esteem measures in a correctional setting: 1. Reliability of the scale and relationship to other measures. *Journal of Research in Crime and Delinquency, 8*, 1–9.

Bradburn, N. M., & Caplovitz, D. (1965). *Reports on happiness*. Chicago: Aldine.

Davidson, N. A., Hemingway, M. J., & Wysocki, T. (1984). Reducing the use of restrictive procedures in a residential facility. *Hospital and Community Psychiatry, 35*, 164–167.

Duggan, H. A. (1984). *Crisis intervention*. Lexington, MA: Lexington Books.

Eichelman, B. (1993). Bridges from the animal laboratory to the study of violent or criminal individuals. In S. Hodgins (Ed.), *Mental disorder and crime* (pp. 194–207). Newbury Park, CA: Sage.

Goldstein, A. P., & Glick, B. (1987). *Aggression replacement training*. Champaign, IL: Research Press.

Goldstein, A. P., Monti, P. J., Sardino, T. J., & Green, D. J. (1977). *Police crisis intervention*. Kalamazoo, MI: Behaviordelia.

Gough, H. G., & Heilbrun, A. B., Jr. (1965). *The adjective checklist manual*. Palo Alto, CA: Consulting Psychologists Press.

Greendyke, R. M., & Kanter, D. R. (1986). Therapeutic effects of pindolol on behavioral disturbances associated with organic brain disease: A double-blind study. *Journal of Clinical Psychiatry, 47*, 423–426.

Harris, G. T. (1989). The relationship between neuroleptic drug dose and the performance of psychiatric patients in a maximum security token economy program. *Journal of Behavior Therapy and Experimental Psychiatry, 20* 57–67.

Harris, G. T., & Rice, M. E. (1986). Staff injuries sustained during altercations with psychiatric patients. *Journal of Interpersonal Violence, 1*, 193–211.

Harris, G. T., & Rice, M. E. (1992). Reducing violence in institutions: Maintaining behavior change. In R. DeV. Peters, R. McMahon, & V. L. Quinsey (Eds.), *Aggression and violence through the lifespan* (pp. 263–284). New York: Sage.

Harris, G. T., Rice, M. E., & Preston, D. L. (1989). Staff and patient perceptions of the least restrictive alternatives for the short term control of disturbed behavior. *Journal of Psychiatry and Law, 17*, 239–263.

Harris, G. T., & Varney, G. W. (1986). A ten year study of assaults and assaulters on a maximum security psychiatric unit. *Journal of Interpersonal Violence, 1*, 173–191.

Levens, B. R., & Dutton, D. L. (1980). *The social service role of police-domestic crisis intervention*. Ottawa: Ministry of the Solicitor General.

Liberman, R. P., Marshall, B. D., & Burke, K. L. (1981). Drug and environmental interventions for aggressive psychiatric patients. In R. B. Stuart (Ed.), *Violent behavior: Social learning approaches to prediction, management, and treatment* (pp. 35–67). Washington, DC: American Psychiatric Press.

Mattes, J. A. (1986). Psychopharmacology of temper outbursts: A review. *Journal of Nervous and Mental Disease*, *174*, 464–470.

Miron, M. S., & Goldstein, A. P. (1979). *Hostage*. New York: Pergamon.

Moos, R. H. (1974). *Evaluating treatment environments*. New York: Wiley.

Moos, R. H. (1975). *Evaluating correctional and community settings*. New York: Wiley.

Mulvey, E. P., & Repucci, N. D. (1981). Police crisis intervention training: An empirical investigation. *American Journal of Community Psychology*, *9*, 527–546.

Paul, G. L., & Lentz, R. J. (1977). *Psychosocial treatment of chronic mental patients: Milieu versus social-learning programs*. Cambridge, MA: Harvard University Press.

Quinsey, V. L. (1977). Studies in the reduction of assaults in a maximum security psychiatric institution. *Canada's Mental Health*, *25*, 2–3.

Quinsey, V. L., & Varney, G. W. (1977a). Characteristics of assaults and assaulters in a maximum security psychiatric unit. *Crime and Justice*, *5*, 212–220.

Quinsey, V. L., & Varney, G. W. (1977b). Social skills game: A general method for the modeling and practice of adaptive behaviors. *Behavior Therapy*, *8*, 279–281.

Rice, M. E. (1983). Improving the social skills of males in a maximum security psychiatric setting. *Canadian Journal of Behavioural Science*, *15*, 1–13.

Rice, M. E., Harris, G. T., Lang, C., & Bell, V. (1990). Recidivism among male insanity acquittees. *Journal of Psychology and Law*, *18*, 379–403.

Rice, M. E., Harris, G. T., Quinsey, V. L., & Cyr, M. (1990). Planning treatment programs in secure psychiatric facilities. In D. Weisstub (Ed.), *Law and mental health: International perspectives* (pp. 162–230). New York: Pergamon.

Rice, M. E., Harris, G. T., Varney, G. W., & Quinsey, V. L. (1989). *Violence in institutions: Understanding, prevention, and control*. Toronto: Hans Huber.

Rice, M. E., Helzel, M. F., Varney, G. W., & Quinsey, V. L. (1985). Crisis prevention and intervention training for psychiatric hospital staff. *American Journal of Community Psychology*, *13*, 289–304.

Rice, M. E., & Josefowitz, N. (1983). Assertion, popularity, and social behavior in maximum security psychiatric patients. *Corrective and Social Psychiatry and Journal of Behavior Technology, Methods, and Therapy*, *29*, 97–104.

Rice, M. E., Quinsey, V. L., & Houghton, R. (1990). Predicting treatment outcome and recidivism among patients in a maximum security token economy. *Behavioral Sciences and the Law*, *8*, 313–326.

Rosenhan, D. L. (1974). On being sane in insane places. *Science*, *179*, 250–258.

St. Thomas Psychiatric Hospital. (1976). A program for the prevention and management of disturbed behavior. *Hospital and Community Psychiatry*, *27*, 724–727.

Thackrey, M. (1987). *Therapeutics for aggression: Psychological/physical crisis intervention*. New York: Human Sciences Press.

Toch, H. H. (1969). *Violent men: An inquiry into the psychology of violence*. Chicago: Aldine.

Valenstein, E. S. (1986). *Great and desperate cures*. New York: Basic Books.

Wong, S. E., Slama, K. M., & Liberman, R. P. (1987). Behavioral analysis and therapy for aggressive psychiatric and developmentally disabled patients. In L. H. Roth (Ed.), *Clinical treatment of the violent person* (pp. 20–53). New York: Guilford Press.

Zimbardo, P., Haney, C., Banks, W. C., & Jaffe, D. (1971). *The Stanford Prison Experiment: A simulation study of the psychology of imprisonment* (Available from Phillip G. Zimbardo, Inc., P.O. Box 4395, Stanford, California 94305).

CHAPTER 10

Control in the Psychiatric Setting— Children and Adolescents

Dale J. Hindmarsh

INTRODUCTION

Psychiatric inpatient treatment programs for children and adolescents encounter aggressive behaviors from many of their patients, and it is incumbent upon the professional staff of these programs to have an understanding of the importance of aggressive behavior as a clinical phenomenon and to have a clear approach to the management of violence on the unit. Aggression among hospitalized children and adolescents is multifactorial in etiology. The clinician must weigh the historical and diagnostic antecedents to the child's behavior, as well as the current clinical issues and the inpatient environment itself to unravel the reasons for the child's violent and destructive impulses. Parallel and coexistent with these imperatives are the programmatic needs to maintain a safe, nurturing, and therapeutic environment for all patients, and thus, the need to effectively intervene with aggressive behavior whenever it occurs on the unit. This chapter addresses the factors, clinical and programmatic, relevant to aggressive behavior on child and adolescent units and emphasizes the importance of accurate diagnoses in the evaluation of aggression. It reviews the application of contingency management techniques coupled to child skills training to decrease violent behavior, and it also reviews the psychopharmacological approach to aggression in this age group.

DALE J. HINDMARSH • Division of Child and Adolescent Psychiatry, Department of Psychiatry, Allegheny Neuropsychiatric Institute, Medical College of Pennsylvania, Oakdale, Pennsylvania 15071.

Handbook of Aggressive and Destructive Behavior in Psychiatric Patients, edited by Michel Hersen, Robert T. Ammerman, and Lori A. Sisson. Plenum Press, New York, 1994.

CONTRIBUTING FACTORS TO AGGRESSIVE BEHAVIOR

Diagnostic Factors

There is a temptation to approach aggression on the child or adolescent psychiatric unit as if it were a single behavioral monolith; this is a temptation to be actively avoided. It is imperative for the clinician to appreciate the multifactorial nature of aggressive behavior, and the initial point of departure to achieve a better understanding of violence and destructiveness is establishing an accurate diagnosis. I have been repeatedly impressed how the identification of an affective disorder, an adolescent attention deficit disorder, or an undiagnosed learning disability will shift the conceptualization of aggression from the global rubric of "acting out" to a specific symptom or epiphenomenon of the child's diagnosis.

In children and adolescents the diagnoses of conduct disorders, attention-deficit hyperactivity disorder, and oppositional defiant disorder are heavily represented, the first two more typically demonstrating overt aggression. Children and adolescents are frequently referred for inpatient treatment because of behavior problems that are no longer manageable in the outpatient setting, problems with impulsivity, destructiveness, interpersonal conflicts, fighting, disobedience, and other similarly disruptive behaviors. Children with diagnoses of conduct disorder and attention-deficit hyperactivity disorder (ADHD) often display aggressive behaviors, as well as problems in getting along with their peers, as primary symptoms of their illnesses. Furthermore, the natural history of both conduct disorders (Loeber, 1991; Statton & Magnusson, 1984) and ADHD (Gittelman et al., 1985; Weiss & Hechtman, 1986) demonstrate recurrent patterns of behavior problems frequently persisting into adulthood. These children display the same disruptive symptoms during hospitalizations, and, in a sense, their aggressive acts can be viewed as phenomenological markers that can be monitored in the hospital for frequency and severity as evidence of the patient's response to treatment. There are, however, some preliminary considerations. First, it must be clearly established that beyond carrying the diagnosis of conduct disorder or ADHD, the child or adolescent indeed has violent behavior as an ongoing, recurrent symptom (i.e., the aggression in the hospital is not a new change in the clinical picture). Second, the individual aggressive and/or destructive behaviors of the child can be sufficiently delineated from trends in disruptive behaviors of the unit population as a whole to allow a meaningful individual analysis of the child's behavior patterns.

Children and adolescents with learning disorders can also present with aggressive behaviors, and although the behavior is not used as a diagnostic criterion, it may be an important part of the clinical picture to clarify. In these children aggression can be defensive or reactive in nature. It is often one of the child's responses to recurrent academic frustrations and disappointments. Cantwell (1985) has described an insidious "demoralization syndrome" in children with learning disabilities that often mimics depression and may also have behavioral components. Learning disabilities are also frequently comorbid with diagnoses of conduct disorder and ADHD, in which case the clinician's task is to attempt to determine if the aggression is related more to one disorder than the other. Finally, there is the contribution of the neurocognitive deficits of the child with a learning disability. Children and adolescents with depressed expressive language skills and low verbal I.Q.s, but normal performance intelligence scores, can be tremendously handicapped in verbally mediating social conflicts. In this scenario the child, when faced with an interpersonal conflict, has a relatively normal ability to appreciate the social situation but, due to verbal deficits, is unable to successfully hold his or her own in an argument, and thus resorts to prevailing by force. These young people are also less able than their peers with normal verbal abilities to articulate their frustrations and feelings or to guide their behavior by effectively utilizing internal language, and again may resort to nonverbal physical outbursts.

Bipolar disorder is an important condition to consider in violent children and adolescents. In bipolar disorder with prepubertal onset the clinical presentation can be one of conduct disorder or of a stimulant-resistant hyperactivity disorder. These children are often only retrospectively correctly diagnosed, after they have typically evolved into a rapid cycling and/or a mixed-state adolescent bipolar disorder. Characteristically, these children have increased familial loading for affective disorders and require multiple drug treatment because they are not responsive to lithium alone (Strober et al., 1988). Hypomanic and manic states in adolescence can present with a variety of aggressive behavioral symptoms, including psychomotor agitation, severe affective irritability, and violent impulses. It is important for the staff managing an aggressive and perhaps "obnoxious" manic adolescent to remember that the affective dyscontrol not only results in behavioral acting out but seriously impairs the patient's judgment and concept of physical safety. Teenagers with schizoaffective disorder or schizophrenia can similarly present aggressive behavior on the unit. When a patient is actively psychotic and violent, the treatment team must contain and protect the patient, as well as protect those around him or her, treat the underlying condition, and watch to see if the aggression subsides as the symptoms of the mania or other psychosis resolve.

Depression, more typically an internalizing disorder, may also be related to aggression. There are two, perhaps interacting, models. The first is the depressed child with an impulsive conduct disorder who reacts to his or her unhappiness with destructive behavior. In adolescent males this comorbidity is also associated with violent suicidal acts, especially when alcohol and firearms are available (Brent et al., 1988). The second model is the child whose prevailing mood is irritability instead of sadness. These children and adolescents are chronically miserable and unpleasant to others, and their risk for interpersonal conflicts and fighting is accordingly higher. The salient feature in these dysthymic cases is that the irritability is pervasive and painful.

Children with tic and habit disorders can have associated problems with aggressive behavior, although the prevalence is not as strong as in hyperactivity syndromes. Children with Tourette's disorder are often behaviorally and cognitively impulsive, and if the child has aggressive tendencies the disorder can exacerbate them. Tourette's disorder may arise comorbidly during the stimulant treatment of ADHD, which (as noted above) is strongly related to aggressive behavior. Obsessive–compulsive disorder (OCD) in childhood and adolescence can also be associated with aggression on inpatient units. Patients with severe OCD have increased levels of anxiety and tension related to their impulses to perform rituals, and either as a reaction to their frustration with their disorder or to attempts by staff members to limit or interrupt them, they can become agitated and even explosive. Some adolescents with OCD experience paranoia and may suffer decompensations of psychotic proportions, again increasing the risk for physical outbursts.

Personality disorders in adolescents that are associated with violence and destructiveness on inpatient programs are the antisocial and borderline personality disorders. Antisocial teenagers inevitably come to the program with long histories of antisocial acts and little evidence of either learning from or caring about their past mistakes. Even to experienced clinicians their shallowness and inability to meaningfully relate to the past or future can be startling. Illustrative is one 17-year-old boy in our program who was asked to review a physical outburst from two days before. He regarded the psychiatrist with incredulity and asked why they would want to discuss it, stating "That was Sunday. This is Tuesday." In his mind the incident was now ancient history and meaningless. Aggressive adolescents with borderline personality disorder pose even greater challenges and stress on the treatment program through their characteristic ability to elicit intense and contradictory emotions within the patient community and also within the staff. Making an accurate diagnosis in both of these disorders is immensely helpful in designing individual management strategies that will decrease the occurrence of aggressive acts and help maintain a therapeutic (instead of reactive) approach to the patient by the staff.

Episodic aggression is often a primary reason for the referral of brain-injured children and adolescents to inpatient programs. A thorough diagnostic work up is mandatory to define the interrelationship between the brain injury and the explosive and/or aggressive behavior, and to develop a coherent treatment plan. There are a number of questions to answer.

1. Are there premorbid factors that contribute to the aggressive behavior of the patient?
2. At what age did the brain injury occur, how has it impacted the child's subsequent development, and how does it relate to the child's perception of himself or herself? For example, early injuries predate the inculcation of abilities and adaptive capacities that a child with a later injury can fall back on. A teenager with a traumatic brain injury, on the other hand, may be terribly frustrated by the sense of loss ("I used to be able to do this") he or she suffers when encountering newly acquired handicaps.
3. Is the injury diffuse or localized, and if localized how does injury to this region of the brain contribute to changes in emotions, cognitions, communication, and behavior?
4. Is there epilepsy? If epilepsy is present, does the child or adolescent take anticonvulsants regularly and do the medications have side effects of behavioral toxicity?
5. Is the patient now mentally retarded and how does that impact the patient's life?
6. How does the family view the patient and the episodes of dyscontrol, and how does this affect the patient's behavior?

A careful interdisciplinary evaluation including behavioral observations on the unit, electroencephalographic data, brain-imaging studies for both structure and function, neuropsychological testing, speech and language assessments, classroom observations, and a family evaluation will all enhance the ability of the psychiatrist and the treatment team to develop a clear intervention strategy.

In summary, the first step in controlling a child or adolescent's aggressive behavior on an inpatient unit is to have a well-established criteria-based diagnosis for the patient supplemented by a multidisciplinary evaluation. This will allow the clinician to understand the behavior in a clinical framework, and then to design management strategies that are concordant with the patient's overall treatment plan.

Aggregate Effects and Other Patient Interactions

There are several factors contributing to the occurrence of aggression on child and adolescent units that are more related to the patient population of the unit as a whole than to the individual patient. These are age factors, demographic or diagnosis concentration factors, and the emergence of antitherapeutic groups on the unit.

The ages of the children treated on a psychiatric unit have an immediate impact on the incidence of aggressive behaviors, with younger populations usually demonstrating higher incidences of overt aggressive acts per patient than older populations. In a study of patient aggression and staff counteraggression (i.e., seclusion and restraint) on a child psychiatric unit, Garrison et al. (1990) found younger male patients, age 11 and under, to be especially aggressive and to require frequent use of counteraggressive measures by the staff. This correlation of younger age to aggression was particularly true of assaults. Also, the majority of these children, as is often the case on child psychiatric units, were hospitalized for disruptive behavior disorders, and the most aggressive during the study also had strong histories of aggression prior to hospitalization. Our own experience on an adolescent unit for teenagers 13 to 18 years of age was that the younger adolescents were more active, impulsive, and overtly aggressive than their older peers, especially if they carried diagnoses of ADHD or conduct disorder. When the proportion of 13- and 14-year-olds went up, the unit became more chaotic. There also appeared to be an interactive effect between the age groups, because after we had restructured the program into two separate age cohorts—one for children ages 12 to 15, the other for ages 15 to 18—the level of aggressive behavior in both age cohorts decreased. It was our impression that a proportion of the aggressive behavior shown by young adolescents in a mixed-aged group unit reflects their attempts to maintain their status among the older teenagers. Also, separating the age groups allows for more developmentally specific programming.

Gender is another factor to consider in the occurrence of violent and destructive behavior in inpatient programs, for no other reason than that the clinical picture may be changing. While overt violence continues to be predominated by male perpetrators, there is evidence of a trend toward increased aggressive behavior by female patients. Inamdar, Darrell, Brown, and Lewis (1986) reviewed a random sample of 51 adolescents admitted to an urban adolescent psychiatric unit in 1969 and compared it to a matched group admitted in 1979. There was a significant increase in violence among the female patients, which was not true for the males. The authors had two hypotheses to account for the shift. First, the prevalence of violence in teenagers had increased in general, and violent girls were more likely to be perceived as ill and hospitalized than boys. Second, by 1979 deinstitutionalization had kept a number of psychotic parents in the home who previously would have been in long-term facilities. This resulted in increased family stress, leading to increased acting out. Indeed, the data of Inamdar et al. showed a higher percentage of girls in the 1970s with a psychotic parent in the home (33%) than in the families of girls with similar diagnoses in the 1960s (10%) (Inamdar et al., 1986).

THE TREATMENT PROGRAM IN THE CONTROL OF AGGRESSION

The design of an inpatient program for children or adolescents determines the philosophy and methods for the prevention, reduction, and management of aggressive behaviors. In a thoughtful discussion of the behavioral approach to childhood conduct disorders on inpatient units, Kolko (1992) conceptually divides the approach into three broad components: (1) contingency management; (2) child skills training; and (3) parent, marital, and family skills training. The advantage of this tripartite conceptualization is that it recognizes both the legitimacy and limitations of each of these intervention models, which are much more powerful when used in a coordinated fashion.

Contingency Management

Contingency management refers to the use of explicit consequences for behaviors that are designed to strengthen positive, desirable behaviors or to weaken and decrease the incidence of specific negative, undesirable behaviors. Token systems and privilege-level systems set up tangible or privilege rewards to motivate the patient to behave in a prosocial manner. Undesirable behaviors are "consequenced" with the loss of privileges or the failure to obtain rewards. When the child is admitted to the unit, he or she is given an orientation to the system by the staff. The patient starts at a baseline and then either begins to participate in the unit's token or privilege system, or is given an individually modified form of the system. Kolko (1992) emphasizes the importance of objective and clear definitions of behaviors and expectations in the use of a token economy system with children with conduct disorders. He also notes that careful attention should be given to the practical considerations of running the system, such as monitoring of tokens, providing a diverse range of reinforcers and backup reinforcers, and the relationships between each behavior and its intended consequence. He also encourages the use of certain strategies to enhance the effectiveness of a token program. The staff can help the children by prompting them to engage in prosocial behaviors they might not evidence on their own. Also, the frequency of reinforcers can be varied, being more frequent initially and then gradually faded to promote the development of an increased ability to delay gratification (Kolko, 1992).

In our own experience with an acute care adolescent unit, we went through two extended periods with contrasting privilege-level systems. The first system was a privilege-level economy ("the PLE") that categorized and defined a wide array of behaviors and assigned them either points for prosocial behaviors or fines for negative behaviors. Each patient received a printed "patient version" of the PLE and carried point cards that were scored and initialed by the staff throughout the day and tallied at each day's conclusion. Advancement up the privilege ladder, in theory, was strictly determined by achieved points minus fines. The staff were trained in the PLE using seminars and videotaped examples of specific behaviors for them to identify and give the appropriate consequence. The system was designed not only to clarify the perception of patient behavior, but also to diminish inconsistencies between staff members in their management of acting-out behaviors by the teenagers. It was an elaborate system and went through several revisions. In its final version it was approximately 40 pages in length, addressing all of the possible situations and behaviors pertaining to the patients and the unit itself. To keep the program working effectively required extensive staff energy and close supervision by the program manager. The criticisms of the program were that (1) it was an unwieldily large edifice, (2) it had the effect of forcing the program to emphasize management, arguably at the expense of treatment, and (3) it was perhaps too clear and meticulous in identifying variants of antisocial behavior on the unit. The latter was a "mortal and venial sins" criticism; were we teaching antisocial behaviors as well as treating them?

The second system was more modest while retaining a contingency management component. The unit established a set of 10 expectations and 10 rules. The rules defined general types of behaviors with specific consequences for each rule infraction. The unit expectations encouraged prosocial behavior by youngsters toward their peers on the unit and toward the staff (and to expect similar behavior from others). It encouraged patients to learn about their individual problems and most importantly, to participate to the best of their ability in treatment. There were no specific positive consequences for meeting unit expectations, but advancement in the privilege system was defined by the treatment team's assessment of a patient's involvement in his or her treatment, rather than by good behavior per se. The rules and expectations were displayed prominently on the unit in poster form. Even though the system did not utilize an economy approach, it was more similar to the tripartite program described by Kolko in that the contingency management was coupled to a cognitive-behavioral problem-solving program that required specific child skills training. Moreover, the problem-solving program was the principal means utilized to mediate interpersonal problems on the unit. This same problem-solving technique was generalized across the program, and included the training of parents in the principles of cognitive-behavioral problem solving. This idea is further discussed in the "Child Skills Training" section below. One of the goals of changing from the PLE to the second system was to address the criticism that under the PLE the staff were preoccupied with behavior management (i.e., focusing on good versus bad behaviors, instead of looking at the wider context of psychiatric disorders and their treatment). To help patients place a priority on their own participation in treatment, staff were encouraged to become more knowledgeable about their own patients' disorders and what "patient participation" meant for the individual adolescent. With aggressive patients this started with diagnostic clarity as the initial step and targeting the aggressive behavior as a treatable, rather than correctable, symptom.

Time-Out and Seclusion

On most child and adolescent psychiatric units there is a form of time-out and seclusion utilized, and this may be viewed as a specific category of contingency management. Time-out and seclusion are particularly relevant to the management of aggressive behavior since they serve to isolate the aggressive child or teenager from the presence of other patients, providing protection and lessening the impact of the patient's behavior on the milieu.

The use of time out is relatively noncontroversial, as it is an extension of normal family discipline of noncompliant behavior to the inpatient program. There are well-described guidelines available for the use of time out in the home (Patterson, 1975). A more pertinent issue on the inpatient unit is how a time-out is administered and its duration. Benjamin, Mazzarins, and Kupfersmid (1983), in their study of 13 assaultive children and adolescents, found that the prescribed length of a time-out did not relate to the frequency of subsequent aggressive behavior. In this respect, a time-out of 15 minutes was just as effective as longer time-outs. Additionally, the length of time a child or adolescent took to calm correlated to the length of the time-out (the time-out did not start until the patient was settled), which Benjamin et al. interpreted as a frustration effect. The impact of a longer time-out was that patients were less willing to go to the time-out of their own volition and were more likely to remain disruptive and continue physical violence toward staff. Children facing shorter time-outs tend to settle more quickly, apparently to get the time-out over as soon as possible. In a discussion of behavioral approaches to antisocial adolescents on inpatient units, Lochman, White, Curry, and Rumer (1992) suggest that "patients' perceptions of the procedures (i.e., time-limited and/or somewhat under their control) may be important factors to consider in designing to be an effective treatment procedure (p. 286). Kolko (1992) suggests the following guidelines for designing time-out procedures: (1) provide a warning if possible,

(2) state the reason for the time-out, (3) use backup contingencies for compliance with the time-out to minimize the use of physical force, (4) limit the duration to less than 20 minutes and use a convenient site, (5) provide a clear indication when the time-out is concluded, and (6) use a debriefing period at the conclusion of the time-out to discuss prosocial alternatives. The overall goal of a successful time-out procedure is to provide a consequence for aggressive/disruptive behavior and, at the same time, promote the child or adolescent's feeling of self-control and decision making. In addition, the end of time-out is an opportunity to discuss and encourage future prosocial behavior.

Seclusion, physical restraint, emergent administration of medication (chemical restraint), or combinations of these are utilized when the child or adolescent's behavior has escalated beyond the point that a time-out or verbal intervention is sufficient to manage the situation safely. Also, contrary to time-out, seclusion and restraints represent a level of restrictiveness and control that are beyond normal child management techniques in the home. It is inevitable that the use of these techniques remains a point of controversy. As Gair (1984) points out, child/adolescent inpatient programs can be divided into two types:

> On the one hand is the facility that either will not accept children presenting some of all of these risks [dangerous behavior] or will not keep them if the behavior becomes overt. On the other hand is the facility that will neither exclude patients because of these risks nor discharge them because of such behavior. (p. 73)

This is especially pertinent to adolescents, as their size and strength, and the blurring of psychiatric symptoms versus delinquent behavior, pose difficult clinical and administrative dilemmas.

The decision about which types of restraint to use is an area of clinical controversy. Physical restraint that occurs after the initial encounter with an out-of-control patient can be mechanical (Mazzarins, Payne, & Kupfersmid, 1988) or hands on (Benalcazar-Schmid & Berlin, 1986; Miller, Walker, & Friedman, 1989), and is favored by some authors either for particular safety or therapeutic reasons. In our own experience with an urban university-based acute care psychiatric hospital, there was an institutional bias against using mechanical restraints except in the most extreme circumstance, a position endorsed by the leadership of our adolescent program. On an adolescent unit of up to 28 patients, mechanical restraints were utilized on two occasions in an 8-year period, and one of these two occasions was early in the morning the day following a nursing inservice on "cold wet pack procedures." By contrast, the seclusion rooms were routinely utilized to de-escalate aggressive and destructive behavior, and time limited doses of medications were additionally employed for severe agitation and self-injurious behavior. We considered this a safe and less intrusive approach to physical containment. The following discussion focuses on the utilization of seclusion with children and adolescents with aggressive and destructive behaviors.

Aggression and destruction warranting the use of seclusion is at a level that indicates that safety is the primary immediate issue, and the inpatient program should have a clear policy for (1) the decisions and orders to seclude, (2) the seclusion procedure, (3) the duration of seclusion, (4) the observation and management of patients in seclusion as well as specific documentation guidelines, (5) a procedure for termination of the seclusion, and (6) staff guidelines (authority lines, communication, and notification procedures for all shifts) for dealing with clinical and/or administrative problems that arise during any part of a seclusion. The program should also have an overarching philosophy of the role of seclusion in the treatment of a child or teenager (i.e., how seclusion fits into the overall scheme of the treatment program).

Seclusion, by definition a highly restricted level of care, should be implemented at the time of identification of the behavior it is contingent upon. Seclusions should not be implemented retroactively, such as after a day of staff deliberation over the seriousness of an incident, because the line separating treatment and punishment becomes hopelessly blurred with the passage of time. The staff may believe that a patient who was not secluded has then "gotten away with it," and thus feel unsupported by the program leadership. The dialogue between the line staff and the program leadership on the use and misuse of seclusion is a recurrent and ongoing discussion and educational process. All staff should have training and periodic updates in the procedures of crisis control and safe physical management of uncooperative patients, as well as reviews of the seclusion procedures that are peculiar to their own treatment program. It is also helpful to provide the staff with inservices and case conferences about disruptive behaviors in child and adolescent psychiatric disorders so that aggression and destruction can be seen in a wider clinical context and not only as "bad behavior." Seclusion is, indeed, a microcosm of the inpatient dialectic—control versus treatment—preserving the program function for "all patients" versus striving to tolerate and work with the difficult or dangerous individual. This can be a fruitful tension and over time the program can become therapeutically confident and at the same time comfortable with the principles of appropriate limit setting. A recent report on the use of a quiet room on a children's psychiatric unit is illuminating in this report. In a study of 37 children (Joshi, Capozzoli, & Coyle, 1988), there were 252 instances of use of the quiet room, about one-quarter of which were locked seclusions, while the others were unlocked time-outs. During the hospital stays there was a clear trend toward increasing time intervals between use of the quiet room as the patients progressed through their individual hospital courses. Also, in almost 50% of the instances the use of the quiet room was requested by the child, usually to calm himself or herself down. The authors felt that these trends indicated a therapeutic role for the quiet room on their unit.

There are several distinctions to be made regarding the use of seclusion with children or adolescents. With prepubertal children with disruptive behavior problems (e.g., conduct disorders, oppositional disorders, and hyperactivity syndromes), seclusions should be developmentally and diagnostically appropriate in length, which is often quite brief. The attention span and carry over of many of these children, especially if less than fourth-grade level, is remarkably limited. Also, their ability to differentiate time-limited containment from punishment is poorly developed. For these reasons, the same guidelines that ensure an effective time-out procedure apply to seclusions. The child is informed why he or she is being secluded and for how long (a specified short period after they have calmed). During the seclusion the staff communicate in a calm and matter-of-fact tone how the child can best finish the seclusion, but avoid extended dialogues. When the seclusion ends the staff helps the child review how he or she could have better handled the situation, and the child is reintegrated, if feasible, back into the ongoing activities. Many of the young children admitted to psychiatric units come from disturbed home situations where discipline is often erratic, unpredictable, and sometimes extreme. The staff need to be sensitive to the interpretation a child with this background is apt to draw from the imposition of a seclusion. The staff who are assigned to work with a given child may find it beneficial to discuss sometime later with the child his or her perceptions of what occurred and help the child with any associated misconceptions.

When an adolescent is secluded there are also developmental considerations. Unlike the common practice on adult units of changing secluded patients into hospital pajamas, it is probably best to allow teenagers to keep their clothes, but to turn over (or have removed) shoes and potentially dangerous jewelry, belts, and the like, for the time they are in seclusion. Many of the adolescents on psychiatric units, especially the more violent patients, are victims of previous physical or sexual mistreatment (Monane, Leichter, & Lewis, 1984), and being held down and disrobed by adult staff members or security personnel is unduly intrusive and traumatic. Also, the identity of adolescents is less well established than it is in adulthood and is often closely tied to the adolescent's physical appearance. For these reasons we consider the removal of clothes a more serious event for an adolescent than an adult. At times teenage patients will utilize the rite of seclusion as a countertherapeutic status symbol, and the nursing staff will observe that the patients are "taking turns" in requiring seclusion. This type of observation should make the treatment team suspect that community issues are underlying the misbehavior of the patients, in which case it is better to address the situation at a community-meeting level and consider unitwide plans for intervention. In our experience, the introduction of unitwide control measures is reassuring to the children on the unit and often quietly welcomed by most of them, and it presents an opportunity to reestablish a therapeutic atmosphere between the staff and the patients. Finally, one must always be alert for the playing out of countertransference issues through the use of seclusion: the staff member who complains about feeling like a policeman, but is the first to help physically restrain patients; the staff member who enjoys seclusions or who is the source of recurrent complaints about roughness; or the physician who orders increasingly lengthy seclusions for a borderline adolescent. The administration of discipline is a potentially fertile ground for the expression of countertransference between mental health professionals and aggressive or destructive adolescents. Only constant vigilance, good supervision, and open staff discussion can effectively guard against seclusion becoming a deleterious force within a unit.

Child Skills Training

Several authors have noted the recent emphasis on various skills training programs with children and adolescents in psychiatric settings and in settings for adjudicated delinquents (Henggeler, 1989; Kolko, 1992; Lewis, 1991; Lochman et al., 1992; Petti, 1991). This development has sought to improve upon "the limited generalization and maintenance that often follows exposure to contingency management programs" (Kolko, 1992, p. 214). The use of skills training programs is based on the assumption that behaviorally disturbed children and adolescents, and thus aggressive children and adolescents, have social skills, social communication, and problem-solving deficits that prevent them from successfully negotiating interpersonal situations and conflicts. The goals of these therapies are to teach the child more successful strategies for interacting with peers and adults and to improve their problem-solving abilities, thus expanding their prosocial repertoire. Problem-solving skills programs such as cognitive-behavioral problem solving are particularly attractive for adaptation to inpatient programs because they are relatively specific and definable, they focus on the immediate experience of the child while at the same time encouraging the child to draw on past experiences, they are highly interactive, and they readily adapt to the time limits of acute care psychiatric units. The process of problem-solving skills, that is, its step-by-step approach to an immediate problem, forces the patient to be less impulsive and reactive by even attempting to use problem solving. Finally, cognitive-behavioral problem-solving skills are generalizable to family meetings, the home environment, educational settings, and the community.

At the University of Pittsburgh, the program we instituted for the adolescent inpatient unit is a five-step problem-solving technique based on cognitive-behavioral therapy principles. The steps include the following:

1. The staff assist the patient in identifying the immediate problem the child is facing in clear, concrete terms but in the child's own words.
2. The staff elicit from the child as long a list of possible solutions as the child can generate, even if some are patently unacceptable aggressive solutions. These are recorded without criticism, and, if necessary, the staff coach the child to identify some prosocial possibilities (this is a form of the cognitive therapy tool of "guided discovery").
3. The listed solutions are evaluated by the patient and staff as to the likelihood of their respective successful outcomes.
4. The patient chooses what he or she believes is the best solution and implements it. It is not necessary that the patient and staff agree on which solution is best, and it is preferable that the patient make the final choice as long as it is constructive in spirit.
5. The patient and the staff review the results after the solution is implemented. This is a crucial final step (and the easiest to neglect) that allows the child to learn from the immediate problem-solving exercise, and improve these skills over time.

The problem-solving steps are inculcated into the daily program as prominently as the unit rules and expectations. A poster of the five-step process is prominently displayed on the wall of the unit living space, and the system is used in individual sessions, in community meetings, in groups, and also in the family meetings. When patients are secluded for aggressive outbursts, the debriefing prior to ending the seclusion uses the problem-solving steps to help the patient conceptualize and verbally express more prosocial alternatives. Also, learning and using the problem-solving steps is understood by the patients to be one of the ways of "participating in your treatment" and thus of gaining privileges.

Another type of problem-solving skill, actually a form of social skills training, that is also used within the program is assertiveness training. With adolescents who tend to view themselves as either controlled by others or out of control, assertiveness training is very attractive, and it lends itself well to them-oriented discussion groups.

Other components of cognitive therapy are used with aggressive youths to enhance their self-observation or experimentally check the validity of their perceptions and beliefs. *Self monitoring* is a procedure whereby the patient observes his or her emotions and/or behaviors and tallies the frequency of occurrence of target behaviors or their contingencies (e.g., teasing, time-outs, seclusions, swearing). Kupfersmid et al. (1988) report that the process of keeping track of the occurrence of the patient's own antisocial behavior often results in a prompt decrease in the frequency of the target behaviors. In another self-monitoring program, children are taught the physiological aspects of anger arousal (Lochman et al., 1991) with instruction and videotaped examples. The children are taught first to identify and monitor the continuum of their own anger and then the environmental triggers that make them angry. In group exercises the children experience anger-provoking stimuli, discuss their reactions to them, and explore what helps to diminish them. The combination of self-monitoring of anger followed by group discussion helps children learn the variability in anger from person to person in any given situation.

Task assignment, another standard tool of cognitive-behavioral therapy, is a more active therapeutic intervention than self-monitoring. The patient is assigned a verbal or behavioral task to either verify the accuracy of his or her beliefs, or to experimentally confront a problem with a specific plan of action and observe the results (clearly, a task assignment can be the result of cognitive-behavioral problem solving). Feindler et al. (1986) studied the effectiveness of *group anger-control training* with aggressive, institutionalized male adolescent psychiatric patients in a long-term facility. The subjects had an 8-week training program including relaxation exercises, self-instructions, use of coping statements, assertiveness training, self-evaluations of one's own behavior, self-monitoring of anger and conflict experiences, and problem-solving training. A variety of teaching aides and formats were used over the 12-session training program. The participating patients demonstrated improved self-control, more appropriate verbal and nonverbal techniques in dealing with anger-provoking stimuli, and decreased restrictions for physical aggression and rule violations. At 3-year follow-up, 18 of 21 were discharged from the institution, and only 3 of these had required subsequent psychiatric hospitalizations. It appears that cognitive-behavioral therapies are helpful with managing aggressive behavior on child and adolescent inpatient units, and theoretically they offer better models for postdischarge generalization than contingency management programs alone. It will be interesting to follow the long-term outcomes of aggressive youths treated in multimodal cognitive-behavioral programs, for as Kazdin (1987) has noted in a frequently cited review of the treatment of aggressive young people, there is little solid evidence that any treatment has had long-term generalized positive results.

Parent and Family Treatment

The third component of the inpatient behavioral treatment of aggressive children and adolescents is the involvement of the parents and family. Just as child skills training seeks to inculcate self-assessing abilities and problem-solving skills in order to internalize and generalize self-control and prosocial behaviors, parent and family training seeks to generalize the hospital gains to the home environment. This is accomplished by teaching the parents contingency management strategies, by improving family communications, and by practicing within the family specific cognitive-behavioral methods such as problem-solving techniques. A thorough discussion of this is beyond the scope of this chapter, but there are several comprehensive reviews of parent and family training available (Anastopoulos & Barkley, 1990; Braswell, 1991; Cunningham, 1990; Robin, 1990).

MEDICATION MANAGEMENT OF AGGRESSION IN CHILDREN AND ADOLESCENTS

There are four broad categories for the use of psychopharmacological agents in the management of aggressive behavior in children and adolescents: (1) pharmacological treatment of an underlying psychiatric disorder; (2) the empirical use of medications to treat ongoing violent and/or destructive behaviors, where the relationship of the medication to the patient's diagnosed condition is less specific than in the first condition; (3) preventative administration of medication to provide relief and or tranquilization for a child or teenager when there are signs of impending agitation or violence; and (4) the emergent administration of medication to assist in the control of physical outbursts that are in progress.

There are several conditions in which treatment of the primary disorder with medications can result in a decrease of aggressive behaviors. When aggression is a symptom of attention-deficit hyperactivity disorder (ADHD), stimulants can reduce the incidence of violent and destructive acts by several interactive effects. Children with stimulant responsive ADHD become less impulsive, less overactive, and more able to attend to tasks and directions. Consequently, they are both less apt to get themselves into trouble and more able to check their acting-out impulses when provoked or disciplined. Also, the decrease in hyperactivity and impulsivity may improve their ability to relate successfully with other children and to participate more effectively in group activities. Hechtman, Weiss, and Perlman (1984) found that young adults who had been hyperactive as children and successfully treated with stimulants had fonder memories of childhood, better self-esteem, and better social skills that untreated grown-up hyperactives. The implication is that improvement in self-control allows children to experience more social success, feel better about themselves, and therefore be less likely to engage in physical conflicts with others. Still, medications alone are probably not sufficient treatment for aggressive children with ADHD, although they are usually a necessary component of the child's management. Severely hyperactive children improve, but do not normalize, on stimulants. Satterfield et al. (1981) found that hyperactive boys had less frequent delinquent outcomes if they were treated with a combination of stimulant medication and a treatment team assigned therapy, compared to hyperactive boys treated in a medication clinic alone. The medications should be seen as adjunctive treatments for aggression as well as other symptoms, and not as curative.

In affective disorders, antidepressants and mood-stabilizing agents can help ameliorate associated aggressive symptoms. Irritability, whether related to depression, dysthymic unhappiness, or manic agitation, can respond to appropriate treatment of the mood disorder. We have seen rapid reductions of aggression associated to depressive irritability following the institution of antidepressants, particularly the serotonergic agent fluoxitine. Sometimes the improvement is remarkably rapid, within 48 hours of initiating therapy.

Illustrative is the case of a 13-year-old boy with long-standing conflicts with his parents, who was also perpetually unhappy, sullen, and irritable. He regularly provoked arguments with his father and would escalate them into physical confrontations. At the time of referral these conflicts were occurring on a nightly basis, and the parents were both bewildered and completely exasperated by his violent outbursts. On evaluation he was excruciatingly irritable and socially uncomfortable. He met diagnostic criteria for major depressive disorder with sustained mood disturbance, social withdrawal, anhedonia, hopelessness, frequent crying spells and poor sleep. And, he historically also met criteria for dysthymic disorder. He also displayed prominent obsessive and compulsive symptoms of repeatedly cleaning the lenses of his glasses and avoiding the use of cereal bowls and spoons. He detested boxed cereals and this avoidance of certain dishes and tableware appeared to be a contamination fear. In light of the obsessive–compulsive features and his previous intolerance to side effects of imipramine and clomipramine, we selected the serotonergic antidepressant fluoxitine, which also has a low side effect profile, and started him on 20 mg per day. In two days he had remarkable improvement of his irritability and some decrease of his compulsive behaviors. To the delight and relief of his parents, his relentless arguing also decreased and his violent outbursts ceased.

In the above adolescent, the diagnosis and subtyping of his underlying disorder led to the selection of the particular pharmacological agent that also relieved his symptoms of aggression. Similarly, in prepubertal or adolescent bipolar disorder, treatment of the affective disorder with lithium and/or Tegretol can reduce aggression that is associated to manic states, mixed states, and psychotic agitation, and provide long-term control of aggressive tendencies. Other examples of the treatment of specific disorders that also afford management of associated aggressive behaviors are the use of antipsychotics for schizo-phrenia in adolescence, the use of anticonvulsants for aggressive brain-injured children and adolescents with electroencephalographic evidence of central nervous system irritability, anticonvulsant treatment of complex partial seizure disorder with associated interictal aggression, and occasionally clomipramine or fluoxitine for childhood-onset obsessive–compulsive disorder with aggressive outbursts.

The second category of the psychopharmacology of managing violence and destruc-tive behavior in children and adolescents is the empirical use of medications for ongoing aggressive symptoms per se rather than diagnosis-specific medications. The clearest and largest example of this category are children and teenagers with the diagnosis of conduct disorder. As Lewis (1991) notes,

> conduct disorder is not really a single entity, [therefore] it is not surprising that no single medica-tion or type of medication is especially useful. That is not to say that medication cannot be of enormous help. The choice of which medication or medications to use, however, must rest on the underlying symptoms to be addressed. (p. 570)

Lewis outlines several types of conduct disorder symptoms and the types of medication to try: low-dose antipsychotics for recurrent aggression that is associated with paranoid symptoms, taking care to avoid dystonic reactions; stimulants when the conduct-disordered child has symptoms of hyperactivity and or brain dysfunction; anticonvulsants when there is associated psychomotor epileptic symptomatology; combinations of anticonvulsants and antipsychotics when (as Lewis commonly finds to be the case) there are both psychomotor and psychotic symptomatology; and lithium when the conduct-disordered child also has bipolar disorder.

As in the adult population, brain-injured adolescents with violent aggressive outbursts may be helped by beta-blocking agents such as propranolol, but the results are not predictable. Anticonvulsants are also sensible choices for aggression related to brain injury, particularly carbamazepine. Self-injurious and aggressive behaviors in autistic or mentally retarded children and adolescents may improve with serotonergic agents, especially stereotypic self-injuries. Often a series of empirical trials of different types of medications coupled to behavioral programs is attempted before an optimal regimen is found.

There are several classes of medications that may be used symptomatically or emergently for imminent or actual violent outbursts on child and adolescent units. Short-acting benzodiazepines are often helpful for the tenuous patient who is experiencing acute anxiety or tension. Low-dose antipsychotics are also helpful in these circumstances, but are particularly useful for decreasing paranoia and/or agitation in psychotic adolescents. Clonidine is another useful agent for decreasing agitation and providing temporary calming and sedation. It has the added advantage of not being associated with tardive dyskinesia. It is becoming more commonly used in ADHD children who do not respond to stimulants with reduced arousal and hyperactivity, and in a similar fashion clonidine can be helpful with other aggressive, overactive patients.

The same medications are also applicable to managing the out-of-control patient, usually in conjunction with the institution of seclusion. In these instances, the first deci-sion is whether medication is necessary in addition to the seclusion, either to help relieve patients of some of their acute distress, or for protective reasons. If it is determined that tranquilization is indicated, medication is given orally if possible, following the principle that allowing patients some degree of choice and control helps them to begin regaining their overall control. If necessary, intramuscular medications can be given, and just as in a seclusion there should be a clear procedure for the forced but safe administration of injections. Occasionally one encounters severely agitated and/or violent patients who would require prolonged physical restraint to prevent severe self-injury or property destruction. One such case we encountered was an angry and omnipotent 16-year-old boy weighing over 200 pounds, who, enraged by his placement in seclusion for breaking furniture, began to punch himself violently and repeatedly in the face with both fists. In these extreme circumstances we have successfully utilized droperidal, a highly potent neuroleptic with anesthetic properties, which causes the patient to fall asleep. Usually, as was the case with the described patient, 5 mg is very effective even with large adolescents, 2.5 mg being sufficient for smaller patients. It is prudent to administer an anticholinergic agent such as benztropine at the same time as the droperidal, as droperidal frequently produces dystonic reactions when given alone.

SUMMARY

The treatment of children and adolescents on psychiatric inpatient units inevitably involves treating aggressive patients and managing aggressive and destructive behavior. The predictive factors in aggression in children and teenagers are diagnoses of disruptive behavior disorders, younger age, histories of aggression, histories of family violence and abuse, and male gender, although there is evidence of increasing violence perpetrated by adolescent girls. The foundation for clinically sound and compassionate treatment in the face of these behaviors begins with a commitment to diagnostic clarity, and the existence of a defined unit treatment philosophy and equally well-established procedures for managing impending and actual violence. Contingency management techniques and child skills training programs help decrease the levels of aggression in many patients on the unit, with child skills training aimed at internalizing methods of self-control, improving self-confidence, promoting effective problem solving, and experiencing the benefits of pro-social behavior. Parent and family training seeks to generalize the skills learned by the patient to the rest of the family, thus increasing the chances of extending hospital gains back to the home. The psychopharmacological treatment of aggressive behavior again ultimately rests on the establishment of an accurate diagnosis, for the goal of administering medications is both to be beneficial to the violent child or adolescent and to provide relief to the family and others.

REFERENCES

Amery, B., Minichiello, M. D, & Brown, G. L. (1984). Aggression in hyperactive boys: Response to d-amphetamine. *American Journal of Child and Adolescent Psychiatry*, *23*, 261–269.

Anastopoulos, A., & Barkley, R. A. (1990). Counseling and training parents. In R. A. Barkley (Ed.), *Attention deficit hyperactivity disorder: A handbook for diagnosis and treatment* (pp. 397–431). New York: Guilford Press.

Benalcazar-Schmid, R., & Berlin, I. N. (1986). Violence in the hospitalized adolescent: Some considerations on the management of aggression in the long-term hospital unit. *Bulletin of the Menninger Clinic*, *50*, 480–490.

Benjamin, R., Mazzarins, H., & Kupfersmid, J. (1983). The effect of time-out (TO) duration on assaultiveness in psychiatrically hospitalized children. *Aggressive Behavior*, *9*, 21–27.

Braswell, L. (1991). Involving parents in cognitive-behavioral therapy with children and adolescents. In P. C. Kendall (Ed.), *Child and adolescent therapy: Cognitive-behavioral procedures* (pp. 316–351). New York: Guilford Press.

Brent, D. A., Perper, J. A., Goldstein, C. E., Kolko, D. J., Allan, M. J., Allman, C. J., & Zelenak, J. P. (1988). Risk factors for adolescent suicide: A comparison of adolescent suicide victims with suicidal inpatients. *Archives of General Psychiatry, 45*, 581–588.

Cantwell, D. P. (1985). Paper presented at the Visiting Professor Series, Western Psychiatric Institute and Clinic, Pittsburgh, PA.

Cunningham, C. E. (1990). A family systems approach to parent training. In R. A. Barkley (Ed.), *Attention deficit hyperactivity disorder: A handbook for diagnosis and treatment* (pp 432–461). New York: Guilford Press.

Feindler, E. (1986). Group anger-control therapy for institutionalized psychiatric male adolescents. *Behavior Therapy, 17*, 109–123.

Gair, D. S. (1984). Guidelines for children and adolescents. In K. Tardiff (Ed.), *The psychiatric uses of seclusion and restraint* (pp. 69–85). Washington, DC: American Psychiatric Press.

Garrisson, W. T. (1984). Predicting violent behavior in psychiatrically hospitalized boys. *Journal of Youth and Adolescence, 13*, 225–238.

Garrisson, W. T., Ecker, B., Friedman, M., Davidoff, R., Haeberle, K., & Wagner, M. (1990). Aggression and counteraggression during child psychiatric hospitalization. *Journal of the American Academy of Child and Adolescent Psychiatry, 29*, 242–250.

Gittelman, R., Mannuzza, S., Shenker, R., & Bonagura, N. (1985). Hyperactive children almost grown up. *Archives of General Psychiatry, 42*, 937–947.

Hechtman, L., Weiss, G., & Perlman, T. (1984). Young adult outcome of hyperactive children who received long-term stimulant treatment. *Journal of the American Association of Child and Adolescent Psychiatry, 23*, 261–269.

Henggeler, S. W. (1989). Individual treatment interventions. In Henggeler (Auth.) *Delinquency in adolescence* (pp. 84–94). Newbury Park, CA: Sage Publications.

Henggeler, S. W. (1989). *Delinquency in adolescence* (pp. 84–94). Newbury Park, CA: Sage Publications.

Hunt, R. D., Capper, L., & O'Connell, P. (1990). Clonidine in child and adolescent psychiatry. *Journal of Child and Adolescent Psychopharmacology, 1*, 87–102.

Inamdar, S. C., Darrell, E., Brown, A., & Lewis, D. O. (1986). Trends in violence among psychiatrically hospitalized adolescents: 1969–1979 compared. *Journal of the American Academy of Child and Adolescent Psychiatry, 25*, 704–707.

Joshi, P. T., Capozzoli, J. A., & Coyle, J. T. (1988). Use of a quiet room on an inpatient unit. *Journal of the American Academy of Child and Adolescent Psychiatry, 27*, 642–644.

Kazdin, A. E., Esveldt-Dawson, K., French, N. H., & Unis, A. S. (1987). Effects of parent management training and problem-solving skills training combined in the treatment of antisocial child behavior. *Journal of the American Academy of Child and Adolescent Psychiatry, 26*, 416–424.

Kolko, D. J. (1992). Conduct disorder. In V. B. Van Hasselt & D. J. Kolko (Eds.), *Inpatient behavior therapy for children and adolescents* (pp. 205–237). New York: Plenum.

Kupfersmid, J. (1988). Utilizing mechanical restraints, child and youth services (pp. 153–163). Binghamton, NY: The Haworth Press.

Lewis, D. O. (1991). Conduct disorder. In M. Lewis (Ed.), *Child and adolescent psychiatry—A comprehensive textbook* (pp. 561–573). Baltimore: Williams & Wilkins.

Lochman, J. E., White, K. J., Curry, J. F., & Rumer, R. R. (1992). Antisocial behavior. In V. Van Hasselt & D. J. Kolko (Eds.), *Inpatient behavior therapy for children and adolescents* (pp. 277–312). New York: Plenum.

Loeber, R. (1991). Antisocial behavior: More enduring than changeable? *Journal of the American Academy of Child and Adolescent Psychiatry, 30*, 393–397.

Mazzarins, H., Payne, M., & Kupfersmid, J. (1988). Utilizing mechanical restraints. *Child and Youth Services, 10*, 153–163.

Miller, D., Walker, M. C., & Friedman, D. (1989). Use of a holding technique to control the violent behavior of seriously disturbed adolescents. *Hospital and Community Psychiatry, 40*, 520–524.

Monane, M., Leichter, D., & Lewis, D. O. (1984). Physical abuse in psychiatrically hospitalized children and adolescents. *Journal of the American Academy of Child and Adolescent Psychiatry, 23*, 653–658.

Patterson, G. (1975). *Families* (pp. 73–82). Champaign, IL: Research Press.

Petti, T. A. (1991). Cognitive therapies. In M. Lewis (Ed.), *Child and adolescent psychiatry—A comprehensive textbook* (pp. 831–841). Baltimore: Williams & Wilkins.

Robin, A. L. (1990). Training families with ADHD adolescents. In R. A. Barkley (Ed.), *Attention deficit hyperactivity disorder: A handbook for diagnosis and treatment* (pp. 462–497). New York: Guilford Press.

Satterfield, J. H., Satterfield, B. T., & Cantwell, D. P. (1981). Three-year multimodality treatment study of 100 hyperactive boys. *Journal of pediatrics, 98*, 650–655.

Statton, H., & Magnusson, D. (1984). *The role of early aggressive behavior for the frequency, the seriousness, and the types of later criminal offenses* (No. 618, 1–24). Reports from the Department of Psychology, the University of Stockholm.

Strober, M., Morrell, W., Burroughs, J., (1988). A family study of bipolar I in adolescence: Early onset of symptoms linked to increased familial loading and lithium resistance. *Journal of Affective Disorders*, *15*, 255–268.

Weiss, G. (1991). Attention deficit hyperactivity disorder. In M. Lewis (Ed.), *Child and adolescent psychiatry—A comprehensive textbook* (pp. 544–561). Baltimore: Williams & Wilkins.

Weiss, G., & Hechtman, L. (1986). *Hyperactive children grown up: Empirical findings and theoretical considerations*. New York: Guilford Press.

PART III

ADULT DISORDERS

CHAPTER 11

Organic Mental Disorders

GERALD GOLDSTEIN

DESCRIPTION OF THE DISORDER

Individuals sometimes begin engaging in aggressive behaviors following brain injury or during the development of a degenerative brain disease. Perhaps this phenomenon was first noted clinically in children with encephalitis. Jervis (1959) made the following comment: "Of great diagnostic importance is a certain pattern of behavior which is often observed in postencephalitic children. It is marked by episodes of overactivity, restlessness, impulsiveness, assaultiveness, and wanton destruction" (p. 1305). Another neurological disorder in which aggressive behavior is a commonly observed feature is Huntington's disease. Patients with this disorder are frequently described as "irritable and quarrelsome," "violent," or "excitable." The psychopathology of Huntington's disease has been studied in some detail (Whittier, 1977). Whittier suggests that the aggressive behaviors result from dyscontrol arising from progressive loss of capacity to inhibit.

DSM-III and DSM-III-R do not include organic aggressive syndrome as a specific form of organic mental syndrome, covering the area of aggressive behavior under the diagnosis of organic personality syndrome. One of the criteria for that disorder is "recurrent outbursts of aggression or rage that are grossly out of proportion to any precipitating psychosocial stressors" (p. 115). If that criterion describes the predominant feature of the disorder, the diagnosis of organic personality syndrome, explosive type, is made. Dissatisfaction has been expressed with this formulation, and there have been proposals to include the diagnosis of organic aggressive syndrome in the forthcoming DSM-IV. That suggestion was not adopted for the draft criteria for DSM-IV (American Psychiatric Association, 1993). Indeed, the term Organic Mental Disorder was abandoned and replaced by Delirium, Dementia, Amnestic and Other Cognitive Disorders. Aggressive behavior associated with neurological or other medical conditions can be diagnosed as dementia with behavioral disturbance or as personality change due to a general medical condition. There is an

GERALD GOLDSTEIN • Department of Veterans Affairs, VA Medical Center, Pittsburgh, Pennsylvania 15206.

Handbook of Aggressive and Destructive Behavior in Psychiatric Patients, edited by Michel Hersen, Robert T. Ammerman, and Lori A. Sisson. Plenum Press, New York, 1994.

aggressive type listed under this general category. Apparently, the diagnosis of organic personality syndrome will not be included in DSM-IV. The diagnosis of intermittent explosive disorder is available, but the preliminary criteria suggest that it should not be used if the symptoms are the effects of a substance, or associated with neurological injury.

Despite the probability that this diagnosis will not be included in the final version of DSM-IV, the proposed criteria for the diagnosis are nevertheless of interest. They include the presence of recent aggressive outbursts that are out of proportion to provocation, evidence for an etiologically related organic factor, and lack of association with some other mental disorder. In an extensive review article, Yudofsky, Silver, and Hales (1990) provide a set of distinctions between "organic" aggression and aggression associated with functional disorders such as antisocial personality disorder. To summarize their material, the patient with an organic aggressive disorder typically has outbursts that are not planned, and that are initiated by apparently trivial stimuli. The course is one of brief outbursts followed by long calm periods, and there is presence of concern or embarrassment after an outburst.

The disorder is most commonly observed in individuals who meet diagnostic criteria for dementia, and is seen quite frequently in institutionalized patients suffering from the various presenile and senile dementias. Thus, the clinical phenomenology of the condition often involves the presence of substantially compromised cognitive function in combination with aggressive episodes as described above. Periods of agitation and irritability are commonly observed among patients with Alzheimer's disease and related disorders. A phenomenon has been described called "sundown syndrome," or "sundowning," in which patients with Alzheimer's disease become increasingly confused and agitated during the afternoon or early evening (Evans, 1985). However, a study by Cohen-Mansfield et al. (1989) documented the presence of agitation as a common phenomenon, but it did not seem to have a consistent diurnal pattern across subjects. These patients' poor memories, judgment, and language abilities often make it difficult for them to appreciate the consequences of their aggressive behaviors or to communicate effectively with others about those behaviors. The aggression and irritability of patients who sustained brain trauma has many of the same characteristics, but in rare instances frank episodes of assaultiveness may occur. It is noted that head trauma patients are frequently younger and less feeble than senile dementia patients, and so may be physically capable of inflicting more substantial injuries.

EPIDEMIOLOGY AND ETIOLOGY

In the case of the organic aggressive disorders, epidemiology is inextricably bound to etiology, since prevalence and incidence of the various brain disorders sometimes associated with aggression are highly variable. The frequency of aggressive behaviors within these disorders is also quite variable. Huntington's disease is a rare genetic disorder with symptoms generally appearing during relatively early adulthood. Alzheimer's disease is a common disorder of the elderly. Closed head trauma may occur at any age, but the patient population consists largely of young adults.

While it is assumed that in organic personality disorder a biological basis is present, it is often not specified. The available literature does not deal extensively with the neurology of aggression with reference to this disorder. Mention is frequently made of the significance of the frontal lobes and of the limbic system. There is a very substantial literature on the psychology of aggression much of which involves animal models. An extensive review was written some time ago by Moyer (1971), covering lesion, brain stimulation, neurochemical, endocrinological, and pharmacological studies. The important structures for aggression appear to be certain hypothalamic nuclei, the amygdala, the septum, the limbic system in general, and the frontal lobes. While, ostensibly, these systems and structures are involved in the aggressive behavior of patients, the specific brain and behavior connections as they obtain in particular neuropathological processes do not appear to be well understood. Perhaps our best understanding of correlations between brain dysfunction and aggressive behavior exists in the case of Huntington's disease. That appears to be the case because the neuropathology of Huntington's disease is well understood. Whittier (1977) developed the argument that degeneration of the gamma-aminobutyric acid (GABA) microneurons in the corpus striatum and cortex may well be crucial, because GABA is thought to be an inhibitory neurotransmitter. He suggests that if the pathology of Huntington's disease is relatively specific to cortex and striatum, and this leads to a net reduction in inhibitory capacity, then the psychopathology associated with the disorder may be the consequence of that neuropathology.

In recent years, there has been great interest in the relationship between low serotonin levels and various forms of aggression (Apter et al., 1990). However, there has been no systematic demonstration that the aggression seen in dementia patients is specifically associated with serotonin metabolism, although it has been suggested as a possibility (Gleason & Schneider, 1990). The etiology of aggression following brain trauma is generally thought to be associated with the particular vulnerability of the limbic system and frontal lobes to injury. However, Levin, Benton, and Grossman (1982) report that there are also neurochemical changes following head trauma that may produce sympathetic over-activity and a decrease in cerebral scrotonergic and dopaminergic activity. An important distinction between the agitation seen following head injury and what is seen in Alzheimer's disease is that in the case of head injury the condition may be reversible, but it is not reversible in the case of Alzheimer's disease.

There have been several studies of the prevalence of aggressive behaviors in elderly institutionalized patients. Such behaviors have high prevalence rates. Yudofsky, Silver, and Hales (1990) reviewed several studies, reporting that agitation is shown in about 48% of nursing home residents. Colenda and Hamer (1991) conducted two surveys at a geropsychiatric state hospital in which 42.1% of the patient population carried a dementia diagnosis. They found during the first survey that out of a census of 212, 48 patients committed 199 aggressive events. The second survey, based on a census of 196, found 40 patients who committed 119 aggressive events. The rate of aggressive events was higher among dementia patients than it was among nondementia patients. It would appear that aggressive behaviors among elderly institutionalized patients with dementia is commonplace, and is a significant clinical management problem. A study by Haley, Brown, and Levine (1987) found that agitation was also quite prevalent in home settings, and was rated as being of greater concern than self-care deficits. Problems with aggression among individuals in community settings were also noted by Ware, Fairburn, and Hope (1990), who found that aggression occurred most often during acts of intimate care, such as dressing or shaving the relative with dementia.

AGGRESSION TOWARD SELF AND OTHERS

Huntington himself (1872) described the disease named after him as associated with a tendency toward insanity and suicide. The Huntington's disease patient is still viewed as a suicide risk, and we have seen blatant suicide attempts in individual patients. There have been anecdotal reports of attempted suicide among elderly individuals in the early stages of Alzheimer's disease. These individuals still retain the cognitive function necessary to be aware of the nature of their illness, and choose not to go on with their lives. One can take issue with whether this situation can be appropriately described as aggression against the self. In an unpublished study, we observed a negative correlation between severity of depression and cognitive deficit in elderly patients with known or suspected dementia.

While most of the aggression seen in patients with dementia is against others, that phraseology may also be misleading. Colenda and Hamer (1991) reported that for most of the cases of aggressive events in their surveys, most often, triggering events were rated as "unknown or not observed." It would appear that the aggression of the patient with dementia is often an intrinsically produced behavior that is not necessarily directed against any individual, nor is it directed toward fulfillment of any particular goal. In general, it seems that the dichotomy of aggression against the self or others is not a particularly heuristic one for the area of dementia, because often the aggression is not actually against either of those polarities.

CLINICAL MANAGEMENT

Clinical management of elderly demented patients is made difficult by a number of factors, including the following considerations:

1. Since these patients are elderly, sometimes medically fragile, and suffering from structural brain disease, there are serious limitations imposed on the use of pharmacological agents.
2. The impaired memories, communicative abilities, and reasoning abilities of these patients make behavioral intervention problematic, particularly when the treatments require complex language comprehension, learning of new information, or formation of insights.
3. There would appear to be important differences between treatment of aggressive behaviors that are directed, and perhaps motivated by anger or provocation, and treatment of aggressive behaviors that are not purposive.

Efforts have been made to conceptualize the agitation of patients with dementia (Taft, 1989). There has been a suggestion that it is need fulfilling, but the need may not be evident (Cohen-Mansfield & Billig, 1986). Another theory proposes that agitation represents a stage of disorientation associated with repetitive motion, which is seen as a retreat to prelanguage movements and sounds that provides a self-nurturance function (Zachow, 1984). Cohen-Mansfield, Marx, and Rosenthal (1990) suggested a distinction between the aggressive behaviors of relatively cognitively intact and impaired nursing home residents. Among the intact residents, aggressive behaviors may be seen as coping efforts to protect themselves and their belongings from real or perceived environmental threats. In the case of cognitively impaired residents, aggressive behaviors appear to be directly associated with severity of cognitive impairment. This distinction has clear implications for clinical management of elderly institutionalized patients. Thus, for example, pharmacological treatment may not be called for in the case of the relatively intact agitated patient, since environmental change may be effective.

There is an extensive literature on pharmacological management of aggression in elderly patients. We will not review it in detail here, since that has already been done by competent psychiatrists and pharmacologists (Maletta, 1990; Mattes, 1986; Yudofsky, Silver, & Hales, 1990). In brief summary, many classes of medication have been used, including anticonvulsants, beta-blockers, serotonin-specific antidepressants, lithium, and conventional psychiatric drugs including neuroleptics, psychostimulants, and benzodiazepines. Individual drug studies have been accomplished for carbamazepine (Gleason & Schneider, 1990; Leibovici & Tariot, 1988; Patterson, 1988), lithium (Schiff, Sabin, & Geller, 1982), buspirone (Colenda, 1988), propanolol (Greendyke, Kanter, Schuster, Verstreate, & Woottoon, 1986; Stewart, Mounts, & Clark, 1987), metoprolol (Silver & Yudofsky, 1986), diazepam (Wilkinson, 1985), pindolol (Greendyke & Kanter, 1986), trazodone (Pinner & Rich, 1988), melperone (Fisher, Blair, Shedletsky, Lundell, Napoliello, & Steinberg, 1983), and lorazepam (Bick & Hannah, 1986). Several review articles have compared these medications and have presented proposed indications concerning the types of aggressive behaviors for which several of them are ideally suited.

Yudofsky, Silver, and Hales (1990) made a useful distinction between pharmacological treatment of acute and chronic aggression. In the case of acute aggression, when the patient is clearly agitated and behaving violently, the use of sedation is thought to be appropriate, and drugs such as haloperidol or lorazepam are used. In the case of chronic aggression, the agents must be used for 4 to 8 weeks before therapeutic dose levels are reached. When severe depression is also present, drugs such as propanolol or other beta-blockers, as well as buspirone, are recommended (Yudofsky, Silver, & Hales, 1990).

Probably the most common form of management of aggression in demented elderly patients is restraint. These patients are either kept on locked wards, or kept in such wards with the additional use of protective restraining devices such as restraint jackets, vests and belts, gerichairs, and mitt or wrist devices. While the literature is typically critical of the use of restraining devices (Covert, Rodrigues, & Soloman, 1977; Creighton, 1982; Fletcher, 1990; Johnson, 1990; McHutchion & Morse, 1989; Miller, 1975; Robbins, Boyko, Lane, Cooper, & Jahnigen, 1987), Evans and Stumpf (1989) report that over 500,000 hospitalized older people are tied to their beds or chairs.

While there is an extensive literature concerning behavioral treatment of aggressive disorders, reviewed elsewhere in this volume, we could find very little in print regarding behavioral treatment with organic aggressive disorders. There are several descriptive papers (Brooks & McKinlay, 1983; Cooper & Mendonca, 1989; Hamel et al., 1990; Colenda and Hamer, 1991; Taft, 1989; Ware, Fairburn, & Hope, 1990; Cohen-Mansfield, Marx, & Rosenthal, 1990), and some "advice-giving" papers (Tavani-Petrone, 1986; Levenson, 1985), but we could find few systematic studies of behavioral management of demented elderly individuals. Vaccaro (1990) reported on the use of social skills training with elderly aggressive subjects. Cincirpini, Epstein, and Kotanchik (1980) reported on an intervention method for self-stimulatory and seizure behavior in a child with cerebral palsy. Horton and Sautter (1986) and Goldstein (1990) presented rationales for behaviorally oriented treatment of brain-damaged patients, and provided some examples in the area of aggressive behaviors. Balderston, Negley, Kelly, and Lion (1990) reported on what were described as "data based" interventions to reduce assaultiveness by elderly inpatients. The head injury and mental retardation literatures present some case reports describing methods that may be useful for dementia patients. For example, Crane and Joyce (1991) describe a method they call "cool down," which involves a combination of biofeedback, covert behavior rehearsal, and progressive muscle relaxation. It was used with some success with two adult head-injured clients. Prigatano (1987), Lezak (1978, 1986, 1987), and Brooks (1991) have advocated the application of psychotherapy and counseling to families of brain-damaged patients.

To summarize, clinical management of aggression in brain-damaged patients typically involves some use of physical restraint, pharmacological agents, and, to a lesser extent, behavioral intervention. Without being unduly critical concerning what is obviously an exceedingly difficult treatment and management problem, a number of comments may nevertheless be offered. First, there is clearly no treatment for aggressive behaviors in brain-damaged individuals in a curative, remedial, or rehabilitative sense. Much of the pharmacological treatment is not based on a clear rationale, but rather on the basis of varying degrees of success obtained in studies that are often open and uncontrolled. Thus, the term *management* rather than *treatment* should probably be used in describing these efforts. Management appears to be accomplished through the use of either chemical or physical restraint. Whether it is preferable to use physical restraint, with its consequences for dignity and physical status, or pharmacological agents, with their potential for adverse reactions and impairment of quality of life, is debatable. The major difficulties that beset this area are that the organic mental disorders with which aggression is commonly associated are presently incurable and are often progressive brain diseases, and the cognitive impairment resulting from these diseases generally proscribes application of verbal, insight-oriented therapies. As indicated, the episodes of violence are often unpredictable and without apparent external stimuli. There is also the implicit consideration of a need for protection of other people from the consequences of assaultive behavior.

LONGITUDINAL PERSPECTIVES

The development of aggressive behaviors in patients with dementia follows a reasonably predictable course. It appears to be related to the severity of cognitive impairment and increases to an asymptote at the point at which the final stages of the disorder begin. Verbally agitated behavior persists only as long as the patient has the communication skills and cognitive capacities needed to mediate intelligible language. Cohen-Mansfield, Marx, and Rosenthal (1990) conducted a careful study of the relationship between dementia and agitation, describing the longitudinal course as an increase in physical agitation to the asymptote point described above. The question may be raised as to whether or not the expression of aggression in patients with dementia is related to the premorbid personality. Ware, Fairburn, and Hope (1990), using informant interviews, found that 58% of the informants viewed the aggression noted as an exaggeration of the premorbid personality. However, using objective scales, Burns, Folstein, Brandt, and Folstein (1990) found no correlation between aggression and any premorbid trait in patients with Alzheimer's or Huntington's disease. It appears that the evidence for aggression as premorbid exaggeration is not impressive and is clearly not always the case. In the case of Huntington's disease, Whittier's (1977) review suggests that psychopathology, including aggressive behaviors, may appear years before frank dementia. Whittier quotes a paper by Brothers (1964) containing remarks to the effect that bad temper, violence, and excitability are among the first emotional symptoms of Huntington's disease. Some clinicians believe that depression may, in some cases, be a prodrome of Alzheimer's disease (Caine, 1986).

The situation is somewhat different in head injury. When head-injured patients emerge from coma, they often go into an acute confusional state during which a period of acute agitation sometimes involving yelling and combativeness occurs, followed by a period of disinhibition that could be characterized by sexually aggressive behavior and overreaction to provocation (Levin, Benton, & Grossman, 1982). Brooks and McKinlay (1983) conducted a study of the first year after blunt head injury. Based on relatives' ratings, they found that at 12 months postinjury, judgments concerning the presence of personality change become associated with an increased number of behaviors when compared with 3-month follow-up. Increased irritability was one of the strikingly evident changes noted. The long-term outcome for personality change after head injury is not currently well understood, but we have observed patients clinically that continue to demonstrate irritability and aggressive behaviors many years posttrauma.

In rare cases, the course of aggressive behaviors may be more benign. For example, Crowell, Tew, and Mark (1973) reported on two unusual instances in which patients found to have normal-pressure hydrocephalus engaged in explosive acts of extremely violent behavior. These patients were treated surgically with ventriculoatrial shunting, after which the uncontrolled hostile behavior disappeared. In the past, of course, psychosurgery was used to make patients more sedate and less difficult to manage, but that modality currently is rarely if ever used, having been largely replaced by the use of pharmacological agents (Joschko, 1986).

In summary, the aggression seen in association with brain disease or damage is a chronic condition that rarely remits. In the case of progressive disorders it may become worse during much of the history of the disorder, only to lessen when the patient becomes too enfeebled or impaired to engage in aggressive behaviors. The rate and length of progression are associated with the pathophysiology of the underlying neurological disorder itself. It seems clear that patients with stable, nonprogressive neurological conditions, notably traumatic brain injury, may persist in engaging in aggressive behaviors for some time after the injury, but ultimate outcomes based on long-term follow-up have not been clearly determined.

CASE ILLUSTRATION

We have reported on this case elsewhere (Goldstein & Ruthven, 1983), but will represent the subject here from a somewhat different perspective. The patient was a young man with severe dementia associated with massive traumatic damage, primarily to the frontal lobes. He was confined to a wheelchair, had only very limited ability to speak meaningfully, and apparently had significantly impaired memory, although he could not be tested formally. We (Goldstein & Ruthven, 1983) initially focused on behavioral treatment of his fecal incontinence but provide some additional background and history here. Despite his inability to ambulate, this patient proved capable of physically injuring several staff members through manipulation of his wheelchair. On unpredictable occasions, he would rapidly back his wheelchair into people, thereby frequently inflicting physical injury. His fecal incontinence, which could occur up to 6–7 times a day, in combination with his assaultiveness and dementia made him an exceedingly difficult management problem. He was unresponsive to various medications, including neuroleptics. However, he responded to some extent to diphenhydramine hydrochloride (Benadryl), which appeared to sedate him enough to somewhat reduce the number of assaultive episodes. However, these gains gradually diminished somewhat because the dosages required were rapidly approaching the recommended maximum. In Goldstein and Ruthven (1983) it was shown that despite his severely impaired condition, his incontinence could be reduced behaviorally, using a contingency management program.

This case was briefly presented because (1) it illustrates the unpredictability and severity of aggressive behavior that can be associated with brain damage, (2) it suggests that these conditions may be ameliorated at least temporarily with mild sedation, and (3) it shows that there are some possibilities of behavioral management. We hasten to add that this patient is clearly an extreme case, and most brain-damaged individuals are rarely if ever violent to the extent of assaultiveness.

SUMMARY

Aggression associated with the organic mental disorders is unlike most forms of aggressive behavior. It is typically not purposive behavior motivated out of anger, criminal intent, or the wish to do others harm. It is, correspondingly, unpredictable, and it is often difficult to identify triggering stimuli for aggressive individuals. It appears to occur most often in patients with the dementing diseases of the elderly, Huntington's disease, and following traumatic brain injury. Aggressive behaviors noted range over a broad continuum from mild irritability and verbally expressed hostility to frank assaultiveness. In the case of elderly patients in nursing homes and other institutional facilities, it is a major clinical management problem. In the community, it is often the main reason why elderly individuals are sent to live in institutional settings.

We have expressed the view that treatment of these behaviors is largely based on restraint, which may be exercised physically or chemically. There is typically no definitive cure that transforms aggressive individuals into nonaggressive individuals, and there is very little in the way of rehabilitative and/or behavioral approaches to treatment of aggression associated with the organic mental disorders. However, there are numerous pharmacological agents that appear to be associated with reductions in the incidence of aggressive episodes. The use of physical restraints has been widely criticized, but such criticism has been far from influential with regard to the elimination of this practice. In general, treatment in this area can probably be best described as primitive, with some success at preventing the emission of target behaviors, or their potential unfortunate consequences. There is nothing yet available that can arrest or reverse the processes generating the aggressive behaviors, since they appear to be components of the currently irreversible underlying neurological disorders themselves.

With few exceptions, the potential for aggressive behavior persists through the course of the illness, or, in the case of progressive illnesses, until the patient is no longer capable of engaging in aggressive behaviors. Little is known concerning the long-term outcome of aggressive behavior in head-injured patients, but persistence of such behaviors well beyond the acute confusional state period has commonly been noted.

REFERENCES

American Psychiatric Association (1993). *DSM-IV draft criteria*. Washington, DC: Author.

Apter, A., van Praag, H. M., Plutchik, R., Sevy, S., Korn, M., & Brown, S.-L. (1990). Interrelationships among anxiety, aggression, impulsivity, and mood: A serotonergically linked cluster. *Psychiatry Research, 32*, 191–199.

Balderston, C., Negley, E. N., Kelly, G. R., & Lion, J. R. (1990). Data-based interventions to reduce assaults by geriatric inpatients. *Hospital and Community Psychiatry, 41*, 447–449.

Bick, P. A., & Hannah, A. L. (1986). Intramuscular lorazepam to restrain violent patients. *Lancet, 1*, 206.

Brooks, D. N. (1991). The head-injured family. *Journal of Clinical and Experimental Neuropsychology, 13*, 155–188.

Brooks, D. N., & McKinlay, W. (1983). Personality and behavioural change after severe blunt head injury—A relatives view. *Journal of Neurology, Neurosurgery, and Psychiatry, 46*, 336–344.

Brothers, C. R. D. (1964). Huntington's chorea in Victoria and Tasmania. *Journal of Neurological Science, 1*, 405–420.

Burns, A., Folstein, S., Brandt, J., & Folstein, M. (1990). Clinical assessment of irritability, aggression, and apathy in Huntington's and Alzheimer's disease. *The Journal of Nervous and Mental Disease, 178*, 20–26.

Caine, E. D. (1986). The neuropsychology of depression: The pseudodementia syndrome. In I. Grant & K. M. Adams (Eds.), *Neuropsychological assessment of neuropsychiatric disorders* (pp. 221–243). New York: Oxford University Press.

Cincirpini, P., Epstein, L., & Kotanchik, N. (1980). Behavioral intervention for self-stimulatory, attending and seizure behavior in a cerebral palsied child. *Journal of Behavior Therapy and Experimental Psychiatry, 11*, 313–316.

Cohen-Mansfield, J., & Billig, N. (1986). Agitated behaviors in the elderly: A conceptual review. *Journal of the American Geriatric Society, 34*, 711–721.

Cohen-Mansfield, J., Marx, M. S., & Rosenthal, A. S. (1990). Dementia and agitation in nursing home residents: How are they related? *Psychology and Aging, 5*, 3–8.

Cohen-Mansfield, J., Watson, V., Meade, W., Gordon, M., Leatherman, J., Emor, C. (1989). Does sundowning occur in residents of an Alzheimer's unit? *International Journal of Geriatric Psychiatry, 4*, 293–298.

Colenda, C. C. (1988). Buspirone in treatment of agitated dementia patients. *Lancet, 1*, 1169.

Colenda, C. C., & Hamer, R. M. (1991). Antecedents and interventions for aggressive behavior of patients at a geropsychiatric state hospital. *Hospital and Community Psychiatry, 42*, 287–292.

Cooper, A. J., & Mendonca, J. D. (1989). A prospective study of patient assaults on nursing staff in a psychogeriatric unit. *Canadian Journal of Psychiatry, 34*, 399–404.

Covert, A. B., Rodrigues, T., & Soloman, K. (1977). The use of mechanical and chemical restraints in nursing homes. *Journal of the American Geriatrics Society, 25*, 85–89

Crane, A. A., & Joyce, B. G. (1991). Brief report: Cool down: A procedure for decreasing aggression in adults with traumatic head injury. *Behavioral Residential Treatment, 6*, 65–75.

Creighton, H. (1982). Are siderails necessary? *Nursing Management, 13*, 45–48.

Crowell, R. M., Tew, J. M., Jr., & Mark, V. H. (1973). Aggressive dementia associated with normal pressure hydrocephalus. *Neurology, 23*, 461–464.

Evans, L. K. (1985). Sundown syndrome in the elderly: A phenomenon in search of exploration. *Center for the Study of Aging Newsletter, 7*, 7.

Evans, L. K., & Stumpf, N. (1989). Tying down the elderly: A review of the literature on physical restraint. *Journal of the American Geriatrics Society, 37*, 65–74.

Fisher, R., Blair, M., Shedletsky, R., Lundell, A., Napoliello, M., & Steinberg, S. (1983). An open dose finding study of Melperone in treatment of agitation and irritability associated with dementia. *Canadian Journal of Psychiatry, 28*, 193–196.

Fletcher, K. R. (1990). Restraints should be a last resort. *RN, 90*, 52–56.

Gleason, R. P., & Schneider, L. S. (1990). Carbamazepine treatment of agitation in Alzheimer's outpatients refractory to neuroleptics. *Journal of Clinical Psychiatry, 51*, 115–118.

Goldstein, G. (1990). Behavioral neuropsychology. In A. S. Bellack, M. Hersen, & A. E. Kazdin (Eds.), *International handbook of behavior modifications and therapy* (2nd ed.). New York: Plenum.

Goldstein, G. & Ruthven, L. (1983). *Rehabilitation of the brain-damaged adult*. New York: Plenum.

Greendyke, R. M., & Kanter, D. R. (1986). Therapeutic effects of Pindolol on behavioral disturbances associated with organic brain disease: A double-blind study. *Journal of Clinical Psychiatry, 47*, 423–426.

Greendyke, R. M., Kanter, D. R., Schuster, D. B., Verstreate, S., & Wootton, J. (1986). Propanolol treatment of assaultive patients with organic brain disease: A double-blind crossover, placebo-controlled study. *The Journal of Nervous and Mental Disease, 174*, 290–294.

Haley, W. E., Brown, S. L., & Levine, E. G. (1987). Family caregiver appraisals of patient behavioral disturbance in senile dementia. *Clinical Gerontologist, 6*, 25–34.

Hamel, M., Gold, D. P., Andres, D., Reis, M., Dastoor, D., Grauer, H., & Bergman, H. (1990). Predictors and consequences of aggressive behavior by community-based dementia patients. *The Gerontologist, 30*, 206–211.

Horton, A. M., Jr., & Sautter, S. W. (1986). Behavioral neuropsychology: Behavioral treatment for the brain-injured. In D. Wedding, A. M. Horton, Jr., & J. Webster (Eds.), *The neuropsychology handbook: Behavioral and clinical perspectives* (pp.). New York: Springer.

Huntington, G. (1872). On chorea. *The Medical and Surgical Reporter, 26* 317–321.

Jervis, G. A. (1959). The mental deficiencies. In S. Arieti (Ed.), *American handbook of psychiatry* (Vol. 2). New York: Basic Books.

Johnson, S. H. (1990). The fear of liability and the use of restraints in nursing homes. *Law, Medicine, and Health Care, 18*, 263–273.

Joschko, M. (1986). Clinical and neuropsychological outcome following psychosurgery. In I. Grant & K. M. Adams (Eds.), *Neuropsychological assessment of neuropsychiatric disorders* (pp. 300–320). New York: Oxford University Press.

Leibovici, A., & Tariot, P. N. (1988). Carbamazepine treatment of agitation associated with dementia. *Journal of Geriatric Psychiatry and Neurology, 1,* 110–112.

Levenson, J. L. (1985). Dealing with the violent patient: Management strategies to avoid common errors. *Postgraduate Medicine, 78,* 329–335.

Levin, H. S., Benton, A. L., & Grossman, R. G. (1982). *Neurobehavioral consequences of closed head injury.* New York: Oxford University Press.

Lezak, M. D. (1978). Living with the characteriologically altered brain injured patient. *Journal of Clinical Psychiatry, 39,* 529–598.

Lezak, M. D. (1986). Psychological implications of traumatic brain damage for the patient's family. *Rehabilitation Psychology, 3,* 241–250.

Lezak, M. D. (1987). Brain damage is a family affair. *Journal of Experimental and Clinical Neuropsychology, 10,* 111–123.

Maletta, G. J. (1990). Pharmacologic treatment and management of the aggressive demented patient. *Psychiatric Annals, 20,* 446–455.

Mattes, J. A. (1986). Psychopharmacology of temper outbursts. *The Journal of Nervous and Mental Disease, 174,* 464–470.

McHutchion, E., and Morse, J. M. (1989). Releasing restraints: A nursing dilemma. *Journal of Gerontological Nursing, 15,* 16–21.

Miller, M. (1975). Iatrogenic and nursigenic effects of the prolonged immobilization of the ill aged. *Journal of the American Geriatrics Society, 23,* 360–369.

Moyer, K. E. (1971). *The physiology of hostility.* Chicago: Markham Publishing.

Patterson, J. F. (1988). A preliminary study of Carbamazepine in the treatment of assaultive patients with dementia. *Journal of Geriatric Psychiatry and Neurology, 1,* 21–23.

Pinner, E., & Rich, C. L. (1988). Effects of Trazodone on aggressive behavior in seven patients with organic mental disorders. *American Journal of Psychiatry, 145,* 1295–1296.

Prigatano, G. P. (1987). Personality and psychosocial consequences after brain injury. In M. J. Meier, A. L. Benton, & L. Diller (Eds.), *Neuropsychological rehabilitation* (pp. 355–378). Edinburgh: Churchill Livingstone.

Robbins, L., Boyko, E., Lane, J., Cooper, D., and Jahnigen, D. (1987). Binding the elderly: A prospective study of the use of mechanical restraints in an acute care hospital. *Journal of the American Geriatrics Society, 35,* 290–296.

Schift, H. B., Sabia, T. D., and Gener, A. (1982). Lithium in aggressive behavior. *American Journal of Psychiatry, 139,* 1346–1348.

Silver, J. M., & Yudofsky, S. C. (1986). Propanolol in the treatment of chronically hospitalized violent patients. In C. Shagass, R. C. Josiassen, W. H. Bridger, (Eds.), *Proceedings of the IVth World Congress of Biological Psychiatry* (1885) (pp. 174–176). New York: Elsevier.

Stewart, J. T., Mounts, M. L., & Clark, R. L., Jr. (1987). Aggressive behavior in Huntington's disease: Treatment with Propranolol. *Journal of Clinical Psychiatry, 48,* 106–108.

Taft, L. B. (1989). Conceptual analysis of agitation in the confused elderly. *Archives of Psychiatric Nursing, 3,* 102–107.

Tavani-Petrone, C. (1986). Psychiatric emergencies. *Emergency Medicine for the Primary Care Physician, 13,* 157–167.

Vaccaro, F. J. (1990). Application of social skills training in a group of institutionalized aggressive elderly subjects. *Psychology and Aging, 5,* 369–378.

Ware, C. J. G., Fairburn, C. G., & Hope, R. A. (1990). A community-based study of aggressive behaviour in dementia. *International Journal of Geriatric Psychiatry, 5,* 337–342.

Whittier, J. R. (1977). Hereditary chorea (Huntington's chorea); A paradigm of brain dysfunction with psychopathology. In C. Shagass, S. Gershon, & A. J. Friedhoff (Eds.), *Psychopathology and brain dysfunction* (pp. 267–277). New York: Raven Press.

Wilkinson, C. J. (1985). Effects of diazepam (Valium) and trait anxiety on human physical aggression and emotional state. *Journal of Behavioral Medicine, 8,* 101–115.

Yudofsky, S. C., & Silver, J. M., & Hales, R. E. (1990). Pharmacologic management of aggression in the elderly. *Journal of Clinical Psychiatry, 51* (Suppl. 10), 22–28.

Zachow, H. M. (1984). Helen, can you hear me? *Journal of Gerontological Nursing, 10,* 18–22.

CHAPTER 12

Psychoactive Substance Abuse

HOWARD B. MOSS, IHSAN M. SALLOUM, AND BARRY FISHER

DESCRIPTION OF THE DISORDER

Substance use disorders are the most prevalent psychiatric conditions among the general population (Robins, Helzer, Weissman, Orvaschel, Gruenberg, Bruke, & Regier, 1984). These conditions constitute a major public health problem and result in enormous economic costs to society (National Institute on Alcohol Abuse and Alcoholism [NIAAA], 1991). Numerous definitions and taxonomic schemata have been advanced to characterize these disorders (Hill, 1985; Meyer, 1986). The two most widely accepted ones, the World Health Organization's (WHO) International Classification of Diseases (ICD) (World Health Organization [WHO], 1977) and the American Psychiatric Association's *Diagnostic and Statistical Manual of Mental Disorders* (DSM) (American Psychiatric Association, 1987), are periodically modified. These periodic changes in definition highlight the many uncertainties that surround the criteria for these disorders.

The current diagnostic frameworks (DSM-III-R and DSM-IV) are enhanced by the adoption of operationalized criteria to improve the reliability of those constructs and their validity. The DSM-III-R diagnostic system conceptualizes substance abuse disorders as follows:

> This diagnostic class deals with symptoms and maladaptive behavioral changes associated with more or less regular use of psychoactive substances that affect the central nervous system. These behavioral changes would be viewed as extremely undesirable by almost all cultures (APA, 1987, p. 165).

The psychoactive substance abuse disorders in the DSM-III-R approximate that of the WHO's ICD-9, and they are derived from the conceptualization of the alcohol "dependence syndrome" originally proposed by Edwards and Gross (1976). Although this typology was originally proposed for alcohol use only, it has been adopted for all other categories of

HOWARD B. MOSS, IHSAN M. SALLOUM, AND BARRY FISHER • Comprehensive Alcohol and Drug Abuse Program, Western Psychiatric Institute and Clinic, University of Pittsburgh School of Medicine, Pittsburgh, Pennsylvania 15213.

Handbook of Aggressive and Destructive Behavior in Psychiatric Patients, edited by Michel Hersen, Robert T. Ammerman, and Lori A. Sisson. Plenum Press, New York, 1994.

psychoactive substance use disorders in DSM-III-R. The dependence syndrome is characterized by the presence of specific cognitive, behavioral, and physiological symptoms. These symptoms are operationalized within nine criteria that apply to all of the psychoactive substances. Any three of these criteria have to be met, in addition to a duration of the disturbance for a period of one month, in order to meet diagnostic criteria for psychoactive substance dependence. The nine criteria explore three major domains of psychopathology reflecting physical or psychological dependence. These include (1) inability to stop or regulate use of the substance, (2) primacy of use over social and role obligations, and (3) presence of physical signs of dependence. DSM-III-R also includes criteria for rating severity of the disorder. Severity ratings are based on the number of symptoms and the resultant impairment in psychosocial functioning.

In addition to psychoactive substance dependence diagnoses, DSM-III-R includes a category for psychoactive substance *abuse*. Criteria for this disorder are met when there is a maladaptive pattern of use that does not meet the criteria for dependence. Under the current diagnostic schema, psychoactive substance abuse is reduced to a residual category. The validity of these constructs has yet to be established. Revisions of both the dependence and abuse categories have been undertaken for the DSM-IV (Frances, Pincus, Widiger, Davis, & First, 1990). The term Psychoactive Substance Use Disorder has been broadened to Substance-Related Disorders in DSM-IV.

Although the basic construct of the dependence syndrome remains similar to the DSM-III-R version, greater emphasis has been placed on items describing physical dependence. Physical dependence items are listed in DSM-IV as the first and second criteria. Evidence of physiological dependence is still not essential for the definition of the disorder. However, a qualification of the dependence syndrome, as either with or without physical dependence, is now required. Other changes in the dependence syndrome include shortening the number of criteria to seven and providing more detailed modifiers to describe the course of the disorder (APA, 1993).

The DSM-IV version of the substance abuse syndrome is intended to sharpen the distinction between nonpathological use and abuse and between dependence and abuse. Items included are those that pertain to the consequences of use and are considered clinically significant. The number of criteria have increased from two in DSM-III-R to four. These criteria describe a wide range of maladaptive patterns of use, including "failure to fulfill major role obligations, repeated use in situations in which it is physically hazardous, recurrent substance-related legal problems, and continued use despite recurrent social or interpersonal problems" (APA, 1993). The presence of one criterion is still sufficient to meet the diagnosis of substance abuse in DSM-IV.

The duration of the disturbance for both the dependence and the abuse syndromes have been substantially increased to twelve months instead of the one month required under the DSM-III-R (APA, 1993).

In DSM-III-R and DSM-IV, drugs of abuse are subdivided into nine classes of specific substance-related dependence or abuse syndromes. These include alcohol, amphetamines (and similarly acting psychomimetics), cannabis, cocaine, hallucinogens, inhalants, opioids, phencyclidine (and similarly acting arylcyclohexylamine), sedatives, hypnotics, anxiolytics, and a category for nicotine dependence but not for nicotine abuse.

Substance abuse disorders frequently have a chronic relapsing course with periods of exacerbations and remissions. Males are more commonly affected than females, with age of onset ranging from late teens to 40 years of age. Males usually have an earlier age of onset than females, especially in regard to pathological use of alcohol. The age of onset of drug abuse other than alcohol is usually earlier and with less pronounced differences between the sexes. For example, cocaine abuse has an earlier age of onset among females than males (Griffin, Weiss, Mirin, & Lange, 1989).

Associated features of these disorders include repeated episodes of intoxication, intensification of mood and personality disturbances, and development of accentuation of antisocial behavior. Mood lability and suspiciousness may be induced by chronic drug use and may thereby lead to aggressive or suicidal behavior.

EPIDEMIOLOGY

Substance use disorders are among the most prevalent psychiatric conditions among both community-dwelling and clinical populations (Robins et al., 1984; Regier, Farmer, Rae, Locker, Keith, Judd, & Goodwin, 1990).

The best estimates of the prevalence rates of substance abuse disorders in the United States are provided by the National Institute of Mental Health Epidemiologic Catchment Area (ECA) study (Regier et al., 1990). This study has revealed a lifetime prevalence across all psychoactive substance abuse disorders of 16.7%. The prevalence rate for alcohol abuse or dependence disorders combined is reported to be 13.5%. The prevalence rate of any psychoactive substance abuse except alcohol is reported to be 6.1%. Prevalence rate for marijuana abuse is 4.3%, cocaine abuse 0.2%, opiate abuse 0.7%, barbiturate abuse 1.3%, amphetamine abuse 1.7%, and hallucinogen abuse 0.3% (Regier et al., 1990).

Comorbidity of substance use with other psychiatric disorders has received increasing recognition as a major mental health problem. The mentally ill have a 30–55% prevalence rate of psychoactive substance abuse disorders (Crowley, Chesluk, Dilts, & Hart, 1974; Hesselbrock, Meyer, & Keener, 1985; Helzer & Pryzbeck, 1988). Half of the individuals with a substance abuse disorder other than alcohol have at least one additional mental disorder. Most prominent among comorbid conditions is antisocial personality disorder, with 83.6% meeting diagnostic criteria for substance abuse or dependence (Regier et al., 1990).

Polysubstance abuse is an increasingly severe problem, especially among the younger age group (Watkins & McCoy, 1980). The prevalence rate for comorbidity of alcohol abuse with other types of drug abuse is 47% (Regier et al., 1990). Interestingly, 84% of cocaine abusers are found to have an additional alcohol abuse diagnosis, making this type of polysubstance abuse an important clinical problem.

Longitudinal epidemiological data on substance use disorders are mainly derived from surveys of high school seniors, reports from medical examiners, and records from emergency room visits (Johnston, O'Malley, & Bachman, 1989; National Institute on Drug Abuse [NIDA], 1988). According to these sources, current rates of drug abuse are declining. The cocaine abuse epidemic peaked in 1985 and is now on the decline. Amphetamines, hallucinogens, and phencyclidine use have had a steady decline after being popular during the 1960s and 1970s. Also, medical and nonmedical abuse of sedatives, hypnotics, and anxiolytics (including the benzodiazepines), peaked in the mid-seventies and declined thereafter (Du Pont, 1988). Marijuana use, considered by some to be a "gateway" drug for other illicit substance abuse (Clayton & Voss, 1981), has also declined from a peak in the late 1970s. The number of opioid abusers has remained relatively stable at approximately half a million people (Frances & Franklin, 1989). Inhalant use has also remained relatively stable, with little fluctuation over time (Johnston et al., 1989). Alcohol has remained the most widely used psychoactive substance (Gallant, 1985). There are an estimated 10 million adults in the United States who have major medical or psychiatric disorders related to alcohol use (Mendelson & Mello, 1985). Death and disabilities related to trauma and traffic accidents (Heise, 1934; Maull, 1982; Perrine, 1975), violence and crime (Moss, 1987), and suicide are reported to be highly associated with alcohol use, with death due to suicide among alcoholics reported at 15 times that of the general population (Hawton, 1987).

Cocaine, despite reports of a decline in general use, is associated with increased morbidity and mortality. Deaths due to cocaine use have increased dramatically in recent years. This increase is attributed, in part, to the toxicity of cocaine preparations, such as "crack" and "freebase" (Karan, Haller, & Schnoll, 1991).

ETIOLOGY

The spectrum of etiological factors that ultimately result in the production of a psychoactive substance abuse disorder remains to be fully elucidated. Consequently, a host of factors derived from several disparate perspectives have been proposed in an attempt to address the origins of substance abuse.

From a sociological perspective, factors such as low socioeconomic status (Cahalan & Room, 1974), ethnicity (Vaillant, 1983), religious affiliation (Mandlebaum, 1965), magnitude of religiosity (Tennant, Detels, & Clark, 1975), availability of psychoactive substances (Smart, 1980), tolerance for deviance and unconventionality (Jessor & Jessor, 1977), parental substance abuse (Huba & Bentler, 1980), and peer group use of drugs (Jessor & Jessor, 1975) have all been linked to risk for a substance abuse disorder.

From a psychological perspective, several specific behavioral characteristics have also been found to be linked to risk for substance abuse. These high-risk behavioral characteristics include hyperactivity, impulsivity, aggressivity (Hechtman, Weiss, Perlman, & Angel, 1984; McCord & McCord, 1960), antisocial behavior (Robins, 1966), the pursuit of novel experiences or "sensation seeking" behavior (Zuckerman, 1972), the existence of negative mood states and psychological distress (Bry, McKeon, & Pandina, 1982; Gomberg, 1982), a disinhibitory psychopathic state (Gorenstein & Newman, 1980), and the presence of deviant temperament traits (Tarter, Kabene, Escallier, Laird, & Jacob, 1990).

Interestingly, epidemiological investigations have demonstrated that antisocial personality disorder is the most common comorbid psychiatric diagnosis among substance abusers (Regier et al., 1990). Individuals with antisocial personality frequently display a lifelong pattern of irritable and aggressive behavior as core features of their disorder. Thus, aggressivity is linked to vulnerability for substance abuse, and may therefore be a behavioral precursor.

From the biological perspective, several studies have suggested that individual organismic variations may be associated with enhanced risk for substance abuse disorders. These include low platelet MAO activity (Alexopoulos, Lieberman, & Frances, 1983), altered hormonal responses to alcohol (Schuckit, Parker, & Rossman, 1983), an altered hormonal response to thyrotropin-releasing hormone (Moss, Guthrie, & Linnoila, 1986), a diminished perception of the degree of intoxication (Schuckit, 1980), variations in neurophysiological measures such as the P300 component of the event-related potential (Begleiter, Porjesz, Bihari, & Kissin, 1984), autonomic hyperreactivity (Pihl, Finn, & Peterson, 1989), and an enhanced physiological "stress-dampening" response to alcohol consumption (Sher & Levenson, 1982).

Numerous studies have demonstrated that alcoholism, drug abuse, criminality, and antisocial personality run in families, and that these disorders are more frequently found among males (Cotton, 1979). These studies have resulted in speculation as to the role of family environment in augmenting risk for substance abuse, as well as stimulating an interest in potential genetic mechanisms of substance abuse etiology (Murray, Clifford, Gurling, Topham, Clow, & Bernadt, 1983).

A potentially nomothetic approach that joins these disparate perspectives on substance abuse etiology has evolved from more recent twin studies of the genetics of human behavior. Specifically, this method involves the disaggregation of putative contributory factors for a given phenotype (in this case, substance abuse) into three influential domains. These domains can be statistically evaluated to determine the proportion of phenotypic variance they explain. Thus, the following three domains relevant to substance abuse etiology can be estimated from genetic studies: (1) genetic influences, (2) influences of the shared family environment, and (3) the influences of the unique nonfamilial environment of the individual (Plomin, DeFries, & Fulker, 1988). Theoretically, sociological factors may be subsumed under either shared familial or unique nonfamilial environmental influences, while biological factors may be more closely associated with genetic influences. Behavioral, psychiatric, or personality variables may be parceled out to both genetic and environmental influences (Reiss, Plomin, & Hetherington, 1991; Tellegen, Bouchard, Wilcox, Segal, Lykken, & Rich, 1988).

Using twin cross-adoption studies, and monozygotic/dizygotic twin studies, several important findings about substance abuse etiology have emerged. First, it appears that the genetic factors that contribute to alcohol drinking behavior overlap with those that contribute to drug use behavior. Furthermore, antisocial personality disorder has a heritable component, and the genes that are associated with antisocial personality overlap with those contributing to alcohol and drug abuse (Grove, Eckert, Heston, Bouchard, Segal, & Lykken, 1990). Second, genetic factors appear to have only a modest effect on risk for alcoholism or drug abuse for both men and women. For men, risk for alcoholism is predominantly associated with shared familial environmental factors, while for women the nonfamilial unique environment of the individual is chiefly associated with alcoholism risk. Third, risk for other drug abuse disorders in men is associated predominantly with common family environmental factors, and to a lesser extent, genetic factors. For women, risk of drug abuse is again predominantly associated with unique nonfamilial environmental factors (Pickens, Svikis, McGue, Lykken, Heston, & Clayton, 1991).

In summary, the etiology of substance abuse remains obscure and controversial. Dispositional aggressivity may precede substance abuse and be etiologically linked to the development of psychoactive substance abuse through association with antisocial personality disorder. Emerging research has suggested that etiological factors for the development of a substance abuse disorder may differ between men and women. Although genetic factors play a role in the development of substance abuse, environmental factors generally have greater importance. For men, the shared environment of the family may contribute most to risk of becoming a substance abuser. For women, peers and one's interactions with the external environment may be most influential. Behavioral propensities may enhance risk through both genetic mechanisms and interactions with nonfamilial environmental factors. Antisocial personality disorder has a unique association with vulnerability for substance abuse in that this condition frequently occurs comorbidly with substance abuse, is associated with aggressive behavior, and may be genetically linked to alcohol and drug abuse.

AGGRESSION TOWARD SELF

Alcoholism and drug abuse are known risk factors for suicide (Hawton, 1987), and the association between psychoactive substance use and suicidal behavior has been widely reported (Fowler, Rich & Young, 1986; Kosten & Rounsaville, 1988; Petronis, Samuels, Moscicki, & Anthony, 1990; Robins, Murphy, Wilkinson, Gassner, & Kayes, 1959; Tunving, 1988). A substantial rate of suicide is attributed to alcoholism, and studies of completed suicide have demonstrated a high prevalence of alcoholism among suicide victims. It is estimated that 22% of all suicides are due to alcoholism (Robins, 1986), and the lifetime prevalence of suicide among alcoholics approximates the 15% prevalence of suicide among patients with depressive disorders (Murphy, 1986). While earlier studies of completed suicide involved subjects who were of an older age group and had mainly alcoholism as a substance abuse disorder (Barraclough, Bunch, Nelson, & Sainsbury, 1974; Dropat & Ripley, 1960; Robins et al., 1959), more recent studies demonstrate a significant association between substance abuse and suicide among the younger age group. Fowler et al. (1986) studied 133 suicides among patients younger than 30 years of age. Of their sample, 53% had a principal diagnosis of substance abuse. The younger suicide victims had the highest rate of substance abuse. Specifically, the rate of substance abuse in those suicidals who were younger than 30 was 67% as opposed to 40% in those who were over 30 years of age (Murphy, 1988). It is hypothesized that the high incidence of substance abuse may be contributing to the currently increasing incidence of suicide among the young (Fowler et al., 1986).

Several studies have reported an increased frequency of suicide among nonalcoholic drug abusers (Barraclough et al., 1974; Chynoweth, Tonge, & Armstrong, 1980; Dropat & Ripley, 1960; Robins et al., 1959). It is estimated that one out of every four addicts commits suicide (Hasstrup & Jepsen, 1984; James, 1967). Suicidal behavior in opioid addicts is reported to be from 5 to 20 times higher than that of the general population. Kosten and Rounsaville (1988) studied suicidality among 263 opioid addicts over a 2.5-year period. Of these patients, 17% had a positive history of a previous suicide attempt. Of those attempters, 43% were men, with white males being overrepresented. One-fifth of the subjects who had no prior history of suicidality developed suicidal intent over the follow-up period. Of these patients, 27% had reported an actual suicide attempt. The overall incidence of suicide attempts among these patients over the 2.5-year period was 5.5%. There was no correlation between the presence of suicidality and a history of overdose on opiates, suggesting that overdoses among these patients are largely accidental.

The recent ECA study (Regier et al., 1990) confirmed an association between cocaine abuse and suicide. Cocaine abusers had estimated relative odds of 62 times the general population for making a suicide attempt. This was higher than that of major depression or alcoholism, which have relative odds of 41 and 18 respectively (Petronis et al., 1990). There was no associated increased risk for suicide attempt among marijuana, amphetamine, or sedative–hypnotics abusers.

Risk Factors for Suicide among Substance Abusers

There are several important risk factors that link alcohol and drug abuse to suicidal behavior. First, alcohol and drug intoxication frequently occur prior to a suicide attempt (Chiles, Strosahi, Cowden, Graham, & Lineham, 1986). An elevated blood alcohol level has been found in 30% of successful suicide victims independent of the diagnosis of alcoholism (Evans, 1980). This suicide is frequently carried out within hours after alcohol ingestion (Goodwin, 1973). Intoxication with LSD (Bowers, 1977) or phencyclidine (PCP) (Yago, Pitts, Burgoyne, Aniline, Yago, & Pitts, 1981) has also been linked to suicide. Chronic use or withdrawal from some drugs, such as alcohol or psychostimulants (Ellinwood, 1970), may produce a psychosis or delirium that could also contribute to risk for suicide.

Second, the disease of addiction itself has been linked to suicide. Robins et al. (1959) demonstrated that suicide typically occurs late in the course of an active addictive career. The mean duration of abusive drinking among suicidal alcoholics has been reported to be about 20 years. Similarly, Fowler et al. (1986) documented a 9-year history of chronic substance abuse among young suicidals. In all probability, the psychosocial consequences of addiction contribute to this risk for suicide. For example, disruptions of interpersonal relationships and subsequent conflicts are frequent among alcoholics and drug abusers, and significant interpersonal losses, such as marital separation, divorce, or estrangement from the family, have been found with great frequency among alcoholic and other substance-abusing suicide victims (Murphy & Robins, 1967; Rich, Fowler, Fogarty, & Young, 1988).

Third, psychiatric comorbidity occurs commonly among substance abusers who engage in suicidal behavior (Barraclough et al., 1974; Drop & Ripley, 1960; Robins et al., 1959; Sanborn, Sanborn & Cimbolic, 1973). While depressive disorders occur most frequently among alcohol-addicted (Berglund, 1984; Hesselbrock, Hesselbrock, Syzmanski, & Weidenman, 1988; Murphy, Armstrong, Hermel, Fischer, & Clendenin, 1979) and opiate-addicted suicides (Kosten & Rounsaville, 1988), other psychiatric comorbid disorders, such as antisocial personality, phobic conditions, panic disorder, and obsessive–compulsive disorder, have also been linked to suicidal behavior among substance abusers.

Other risk factors associated with suicide among substance abusers include a history of previous suicide attempts; significant lethality in a previous attempt; poor state of health; limited financial, occupational, or social resources; family history of suicide or other mental illness; geographic and occupational instability; and an apparent uncooperative attitude during a clinical interview (Motto, 1980; Sonneck, 1982).

AGGRESSION TOWARD OTHERS

Although there are clear correlations between the use of alcohol or other drugs and aggressive, destructive, and sometimes criminal behaviors, there has been little agreement as to the factors responsible for this association. Direct pharmacological actions of drugs such as alcohol on the central nervous system have, for many years, been the primary explanation for the production of aggressive behavior in some substance abusers. The facilitation of aggression produced by alcohol ingestion, for example, has been attributed to alcohol-induced behavioral disinhibition (Muehlberger, 1956). However, as noted by Blum (1969), drugs may only modify the judgment and self-control of the user, who in a given specific situation may then become violent. Furthermore, experimental evidence suggests that the direct pharmacological effects of drugs alone are not necessary or sufficient for such behaviors to manifest themselves in humans or animals (Eichelman, 1978). An additional confound is the observation that substance abusers may be premorbidly antisocial or lead antisocial lifestyles that may include aggressive and violent behavior that occurs independently of the pharmacological effects of drugs (Schuckit, 1973). Furthermore, there is evidence to suggest that primarily younger addicts tend to be involved in violent crimes, and that there exists a process of "maturing out" of both one's addiction and associated violent criminality (Hanlon, Nurco, Kinlock, & Duszynski, 1990). Thus, current approaches to understanding the link between drugs and aggression suggest that the resultant aggressive behavior is mediated through the complex interaction of (1) the pharmacological effects and dose of the drug, (2) the individual psychological and biological characteristics of the substance abuser, and (3) the situational context in which the drug use occurs. This interactive schema has been most frequently applied to alcohol-related aggression (Permanen, 1976); however, it is salient in understanding the effects produced by other drugs as well. Therefore, we now review several specific pharmacological agents of abuse, including alcohol, with attention directed toward the elucidation of interplay between direct pharmacological factors and individual and situational variables.

Alcohol and Aggression

The effects of alcohol on aggression represent one of the most widely investigate pharmacological–behavioral associations. These studies are in response to the observation of a correlation between the conduct of violent crimes, such as murder (Virkkunen, 1974; Wolfgang & Strohm, 1956) and rape (Rada, 1975), and the frequent use of alcohol by violent offenders (Permanen, 1976). As previously noted, the conventional wisdom was that alcohol produced behavioral disinhibition that directly contributed to violence and aggression. Consequently, experimental laboratory research initially proceeded with attempts to identify direct pharmacological parameters, such as dose–response relationships between alcohol consumption and laboratory models of aggression. These investigations suggested that alcohol ingestion did indeed increase aggressive responding in a dose-dependent fashion such that the expression of aggression was related to the quantity of alcohol consumed. However, subsequent investigations of the effects of low doses of alcohol were more controversial and inconsistent. Low doses of alcohol were reported to be *without an effect* on aggression (Shuntich & Taylor, 1972), associated with an *increase* in provoked aggression (Cherek, Steinberg, & Vines, 1984), or a *decrease* in aggression (Taylor & Gammon, 1975). Furthermore, several reports suggested that alcohol alone may not be responsible for the aggressive responses noted. For example, the type of alcoholic beverage consumed was found to be a relevant factor in aggressive outcomes. Vodka was shown to have a more pronounced effect on aggression than bourbon, despite equivalent alcohol concentrations (Taylor & Gammon, 1975). Male liquor drinkers were found to be more aggressive than male beer drinkers (Murdoch & Pihl, 1985; Pihl, Smith, & Farrell, 1984), while female beer drinkers were more aggressive than female liquor drinkers, despite equivalent blood alcohol concentrations (Murdoch, Pihl, & Ross, 1988). Although congeners in different alcoholic beverage types could account for these discrepancies, a more compelling argument is that nonpharmacological factors may interact with pharmacological effects, producing differential outcomes.

The role of learned cognitive expectancies in mediating many of alcohol's subjective effects are generally well accepted (Marlatt & Rohsenow, 1980). However, the specific role of learned expectancies in alcohol-related aggression is more controversial. The balanced placebo design experiment is one approach that allows for the separate evaluation of expectancy versus drug effects through the provision of differing instructional sets concerning the identity of authentic drug or placebo. Although a clear expectancy effect for alcohol-related aggression was initially demonstrated using this technique (Lang, Goeckner, Adesso, & Marlatt, 1975), a subsequent study failed to find an expectancy effect on checklist endorsements of aggression or concurrent observation of aggressive behavior during intoxication (Murdock & Pihl, 1985). A subsequent experiment that used the balanced placebo design to manipulate alcohol dose levels, as well as the authenticity of drug, was also unable to replicate the original finding of Lang and colleagues (Gustafson, 1985). However, other investigators using a different experimental approach were able to demonstrate that the expectation of alcohol to cause aggression moderates the interaction between one's drinking habits and frequency of aggressive behavior. Consequently, this study confirmed a role for expectancy in the relationship between alcohol and aggression (Dermen & George, 1989). The magnitude of the effect of such cognitive expectancies on aggressive outcomes has yet to be definitively addressed.

Situational variables also appear to be relevant with respect to the production of aggressive behavior under the influence of alcohol. Provocation may be one such situational variable. Zeichner and Pihl (1980) demonstrated that intoxicated individuals were more aggressive in response to the magnitude of provocation without regard to whether or not the instigator was perceived as being malicious or neutral. Similarly, it has been demonstrated that although aggressive responses correlated with the intensity and frequency of provocation, and that high doses of alcohol in themselves produced increases in aggressive responses to provocation, no interactions between alcohol and provocation conditions could be found (Kelly, Cherek, Steinberg, & Robinson, 1988). However, the threat of a punishing retaliatory response by an instigator was found to inhibit aggressive responses in intoxicated individuals (Gustafson, 1986). Thus, intoxicated individuals may modulate their aggressive behavior in response to specific social contingencies.

Despite the initial observation that social pressure from an observer would only minimally reduce aggressive responses by intoxicated individuals (Taylor & Gammon, 1976), subsequent studies suggest that application of a socially established nonaggressive norm moderates aggressive responses by those who are intoxicated (Jeavons & Taylor, 1985). Social pressures for increased aggression, however, will augment aggressive responding by intoxicated individuals (Taylor & Sears, 1988). Clearly, the impact of such social cues on alcohol-associated behavior is salient to the observation that specific social drinking environments are more conducive to the production of aggressive behavior (Graham, La Rocque, Yetmen, Ross, & Guistra, 1980). Furthermore, they provide insight into the role of societal norms in regard to the link between aggression and alcohol use.

Individual characteristics are also clearly relevant to the production of alcohol-related aggression. One such unique individual variation is the controversial clinical entity referred to as "pathological intoxication." This disorder has been described as "an extraordinarily severe response to alcohol, especially to small amounts, marked by apparently senseless violent behavior, usually followed by exhaustion, sleep, and amnesia for the episode" (Maletzky, 1976, p. 1216). Furthermore, the violent consequences of alcohol ingestion are described as being atypical of the person when not intoxicated. Only a limited number of laboratory investigations have systematically attempted to precipitate aggressive violence through alcohol administration to individuals suspected of having this condition, and those few studies have yielded inconsistent results (Bach-Y-Rita, Lion, & Ervin, 1970; Maletzky, 1976). Despite the absence of significant empirical evidence as to the existence of this disorder, it remains in the current psychiatric taxonomy as "Alcohol Idiosyncratic Intoxication" (APA, 1987). It is therein described as being associated with some types of brain injury (or temporal lobe epilepsy) that somehow make the brain more sensitive to alcohol effects.

Individual emotional factors may also relate to the development of aggressive behavior in those intoxicated with alcohol. Individuals in the sober state who are anxious, unhappy, unfriendly, or are quick to anger may be at greater risk for aggressive behavior while intoxicated. Consequently, some subjective effects of intoxication may be mediated by one's baseline emotional state (Pihl, Zacchia, & Zeichner, 1982; Russel & Mehrabian, 1975).

Individuals with specific psychobiological characteristics may also be at risk for alcohol-associated aggressive behavior. Specifically, alterations in the serotonergic system have been linked to alcoholism, aggression toward others, and suicidal behavior. Cerebrospinal fluid concentrations of the major metabolite of serotonin, 5-hydroxyindoleacetic acid (CSF 5-HIAA), have been found to be low in alcoholic men (Ballenger, Goodwin, Major, & Brown, 1979), and to inversely correlate with histories of aggressive behavior and measures of psychopathic deviance (Brown, Goodwin, Ballenger, Goyer, & Major, 1979; Brown, Ebert, Goyer, Jimerson, Klein, Bunney, & Goodwin, 1982; Roy, Adinoři, & Linnoila, 1988). Hormonal responses to a serotonin agonist, m-chlorophenylpiperazine, have also been found to inversely correlate with aggression scores among antisocial substance-abusing men (Moss, Yao, & Panzak, 1990). In addition, a host of investigations has linked suicidality with low CSF 5-HIAA (Asberg, Traskman, & Thoren, 1976), reduced brain serotonin content (Beskow, Gottfries, Roos, & Winblad, 1976), and increased brain serotonin receptor binding (Mann, Stanley, McBride, & McEwen, 1986). Thus, reduced serotonergic neurotransmission may be related to human aggression as a biological trait. Laboratory investigations of how alcohol intoxication directly affects individuals with altered serotonergic functioning, and trait aggressivity, remain to be conducted.

In summary, alcohol has been the most intensely studied drug with respect to its systematic associations with aggressive behavior. Empirical evidence supports a complex interaction of various pharmacological, situation, and individual factors in the development of aggressive behavior in response to alcohol consumption.

Amphetamine and Aggression

Contemporary amphetamine abuse in the United States peaked in the early 1970s and is now apparently in a decline. However, there is increasing concern that a new amphetamine epidemic may be imminent due to the appearance on the streets of West Coast cities of a drug called "Ice," which is crystallized pure d-methamphetamine that can be smoked (Cho, 1990). Thus, lessons gleaned from the amphetamine epidemics of the past may be highly salient with respect to future associations between Ice abuse and aggression and violence.

Amphetamine abuse was initially observed to be associated with violent aggression in Japan during the post–Korean War amphetamine epidemic. At that time, it was reported that of "the 60 murder cases . . . during May and June of 1954, 31 convicted murderers had some connection with amphetamine abuse" (Angrist & Gershon, 1969, p. 197). Of these amphetamine-linked cases, the majority were associated with the clinical development of paranoid psychoses by chronic users. Later, in the 1960s, amphetamine abuse became widespread in the United States. Among the counterculture, use of amphetamine ("speed") was associated with unpredictable and violent behavior and was deemed responsible for the end of the "peace and love" era typified by the hippie movement. Hippies were warned away from the use of amphetamines because "speed kills," while the use of amphetamines became firmly entrenched in the antisocial motorcycle culture of the Hell's Angels and others.

As with other forms of illicit drug abuse, a substantial proportion of amphetamine abusers had a history of antisocial or criminal behavior. In a study of amphetamine abusers admitted to Bellevue Psychiatric Hospital in New York City from 1966 to 1968, two-thirds of these patients had significant police records (Angrist & Gershon, 1969). However, most of these subjects had histories of behavioral problems and poor psychosocial functioning prior to amphetamine use. Aggressive behavior was noted primarily among those who became psychotic as a consequence of chronic self-administration of amphetamine. Suicide attempts and destructive or assaultive behavior was documented in about 13% of patients presenting with amphetamine-induced paranoid psychoses.

Interestingly, clinical associations between amphetamine use and aggressivity are not supported by controlled laboratory investigations, which use normal volunteers and acute doses. In two studies by Cherek and colleagues (1986, 1987), aggressive responding by normal males was generally *decreased* by high-dose amphetamine administration, in a manner analogous to the reduction of aggressive behavior produced by amphetamine in attention deficit disordered children. Of course, none of the subjects suffered an amphetamine-induced paranoid psychosis, nor did they have histories of assaultive or sociopathic behavior. Sociopathy has been suggested by some to increase the probability of aggressive reactions to amphetamine (Jones, 1973), although experimental demonstrations of this association are lacking. Since repetitive use of high doses of amphetamine has been most frequently associated with the induction of a paranoid psychosis, and because aggressive behavior is a frequent concomitant of amphetamine psychosis, it is not surprising that aggressive reactions did not occur with acute doses administered to normals.

As with other drug–aggression interactions, the production of aggression is probably influenced by (1) pharmacological factors, such as amphetamine dose and chronicity; (2) individual factors, such as the presence of a paranoid psychosis or the existence of predisposing sociopathy or aggressiveness; and (3) the situational context in which the drug is used, as in the case of antisocial or criminal subcultures.

Cocaine and Aggression

The recent epidemic of cocaine abuse in the United States provides a further example of the complex interactions between social contextual factors, direct pharmacological effects of the drug, and individual dispositional characteristics of the user that may result in aggressive behavior. At the time of this writing, there are no published reports of laboratory investigations of the direct effects of acute or chronic cocaine use on human aggression. However, it has been clinically established that chronic cocaine use may produce a paranoid psychosis that is clinically similar to that produced by amphetamine and that can result in aggressive behavior. However, as with amphetamines, preclinical investigation supports a direct aggression-reducing effect of acute cocaine administration in animal models (Darmani, Hadfield, Carter, & Martin, 1990). Also similar to amphetamines, the human societal experience with cocaine has been quite the opposite of the attentuation of aggressive behavior seen in the laboratory. Recent reports from coroners and medical examiners have linked cocaine use to volent homicides in several urban areas, such as Memphis (Harruff, Francisco, Elkins, Phillips, & Fernandez, 1988), Philadelphia (Lindenbaum, Carroll, Daskal, & Kapusnick, 1989), Los Angeles (Budd, 1989), New York (Tardiff, Gross, Wu, Stajic, & Millman, 1989), and Detroit (Hood, Ryan, Monforte, & Valentour, 1990). Interestingly, a differential effect of the type of cocaine formulation on violent behavior has also been reported. Smokers of crack cocaine are reported to be more violent than freebase cocaine smokers (which is, in essence, a homemade version of crack), who are in turn more violent than intravenous and intranasal cocaine users (Honer, Gewirtz,

& Tukey, 1987). Variations in cocaine pharmacokinetics could account for some of these differences; however, it seems more likely that sociocultural, environmental, and individual dispositional factors are involved. Societal factors are probably more influential than direct drug effects in the production of violent aggression among cocaine users. Public demand for cocaine, the profitability of the illicit drug trade, the successful marketing of crack cocaine, and its ubiquitous availability are among the factors that have stimulated the development of an extensive criminal subculture (frequently linked to urban street gangs) involved in the importation, sale, and distribution of the drug. Disputes over cocaine resources, territory, and money are common sources of discord among individuals (and gangs) in the cocaine trade. These disputes are not infrequently "resolved" through the use deadly force (Goldstein, 1985). Furthermore, individuals who are dispositionally aggressive and/or violent are commonly gang leaders or "enforcers" within the criminal subculture. Individuals who are dependent upon cocaine may also resort to criminally violent activities as a means to obtain funds to purchase cocaine.

Phencyclidine and Aggression

The phencyclidine (PCP) abuse epidemic dating from the late 1970s through the mid-1980s, resulted in this drug acquiring a singular reputation for producing assaultive and violent behavior. The vast majority of the clinical reports of violence associate with PCP abuse have been described among patients with prolonged abuse of PCP who have developed a resultant psychosis (Fauman, Aldinger, & Fauman, 1976; Luisada & Brown, 1976). Four types of PCP-related violent acts have been described by Fauman and Fauman (1979). They are (1) reality and goal-directed acts committed by individuals with a clear sensorium but whose capacity is diminished by the drug; (2) unexpected impulsive acts of violence committed by individuals with a decreased reality orientation due to PCP abuse; (3) unexpected, bizarre, or idiosyncratic violence that is independent of reality-based goals; and (4) severely disorganized and psychotic violence that is uncoordinated and chaotic and that is usually committed by individuals with markedly impaired cognitive functioning. These four varieties of PCP-induced violence may be viewed on a continuum of severity with an associated PCP-induced organic brain syndrome (Fauman, 1978).

Interestingly, aggression associated with PCP abuse does not appear to be related to an individual's prior history of violence (Fauman & Fauman, 1979), nor are postdetoxification abusers of PCP any more aggressive or violent than clinically matched heroin addicts (Khajawall, Erickson, & Simpson, 1982). Thus, individual dispositional characteristics of the user may be less relevant in PCP-associated aggression. Inconsistencies in the association between violence and PCP abuse may be explained by variations in dose, pharmacokinetic factors, cognitive factors, and the context in which the drug is used. Controlled human laboratory studies of the effects of PCP on aggression have yet to be reported.

Opiates and Aggression

The popular press has long portrayed the heroin addict as an individual who commits desperate acts of criminal violence to acquire the money necessary to support his or her drug habit (Inciardi, 1986). In particular, the use of heroin was thought to transform healthy, normal "good citizens" into aggressive and irrational predatory criminals. However, systematic investigations into the relationship between heroin abuse and criminality did not support the causal role of heroin in the development of criminality, nor did they confirm the image of all heroin addicts being violent criminals. Specifically, studies have demonstrated that a large proportion of heroin abusers had extensive criminal careers prior to the initiation of heroin use (Stephens & McBride, 1976). Thus, heroin use per se was not causal in the initiation of these individuals into a life of crime. Furthermore, other investigations documented that heroin addicts were overrepresented in nonviolent crimes against property and were comparatively underrepresented in crimes directed against people (McBride & Swartz, 1990). Thus, assaultive violence appears not to be a necessary component of the otherwise antisocial lifestyle of the heroin addict.

Laboratory investigations also do not support the contention that opiate intoxication produces aggressive behavior. Morphine chronically administered to volunteer drug abusers was found to produce sedation without any sign of increased aggressivity, emotional lability, or psychopathology (Haertzen & Hooks, 1969). Although pharmacological factors do not explain violence associated with opiate abuse, violence between addicts is not uncommon. For example, it was found that the majority of street drug abusers' deaths in Miami, Florida, were due to homicides that took place during a drug deal (McBride & Swartz, 1990). Some authors have suggested that the situational context of a heroin purchase transaction is fraught with suspicion and ambiguity such that it sets the scene for potential violence between addicts (Agar, 1973; Fiddle, 1976). Thus, violence associated with heroin addiction (as with cocaine abuse) may best be ascribed to a social artifact of the illegal heroin trade, its distribution network, and the high cost of obtaining the illegal drug. Individual predispositions to violence may also accentuate the risk for an aggressive or violent interaction.

Cannabis and Aggression

As is the case with heroin, surveys of the research literature do not support a pharmacological enhancement of aggression by cannabis (Abel, 1977). In fact, an ethnographic study of the effects of smoking marijuana on human social behavior suggested that cannabis produces "calmness, passivity, and social harmony" (Pliner, Cappell, & Miles, 1972), which are clearly antithetical to the augmentation of aggression. A more recent laboratory study of the effects of three doses of marijuana on provoked human aggression indicated that marijuana *reduces* aggressive responding to provocation in a dose-dependent fashion (Myerscough & Taylor, 1985). Preclinical investigations also support the notion that cannabis reduces, rather than augments, aggression across a wide range of doses (Miczek & Krsiak, 1979). It appears that delta-1-tetrahydrocannabinol is the cannabinoid constituent that is most strongly implicated in the aggression-reducing effects of marijuana (van Ree, Niesink, & Nir, 1984).

However, there may be unique circumstances in which cannabis increases hostility and aggression. The phenomenon of cannabis psychosis is well described, although etiologically controversial. Reported symptoms of cannabis psychosis include emotional lability, paranoia, delusions, and confusion (Chopra & Smith, 1974). These symptoms could result in the production of poorly organized, violent behavior. Despite the high prevalence of marijuana use in the West, cannabis psychosis is much more commonly reported in Asian cultures. Grinspoon (1977) has suggested that this differential presentation is due to the fact that oral ingestion of cannabis is more common in Asia than the West. Oral administration of cannabis results in a pattern of cannabinoids and metabolites different from that produced by smoking (Ohlsson, Lindgren, Wahlen, Agurell, Hollister, & Gillespie, 1980). Thus, sociocultural and pharmacological factors interact to produce a higher prevalence of cannabis psychosis in the East, where oral consumption of cannabis is a more customary route of administration.

CLINICAL MANAGEMENT

Assessment and Management of the Suicidal Substance Abuser

Consistent with the assessment of any suicidal patient, the interviewer must incisively evaluate for the presence of suicidal ideation, the nature and timing of the suicidal behavior, the lethality of the act, and the magnitude of the intent. For substance abusers, impulsive suicide attempts should be regarded as being quite as lethal as premeditated attempts. In the intoxicated state, patients may demonstrate poor judgment or have "blackouts" such that a relatively minor, but impulsive, suicide gesture could result in a fatal outcome.

The assessment of the suicidal substance abuser is complicated by the acute effects of alcohol and/or drugs of abuse. At the time of the interview, special attention should be paid to the evaluation for the presence of intoxication or withdrawal states. If an altered mental state is in evidence or suspected, a urine drug screen and blood alcohol determination should be obtained immediately. This is especially important because the patient may have already ingested a lethal dose of some substance prior to the interview. Such patients should be kept under constant observation with vital signs monitored, because drug-induced complications may ensue and emergency medical care may be necessary.

The substance abuser's psychosocial environment and status are quite important in determining risk for suicide. As mentioned earlier, interpersonal losses are frequently associated with risk for suicide among substance abusers and should be the subject of detailed inquiry. In addition, chronic medical illness with subsequent loss of function as well as employment (Roy, 1989) is also a risk factor for suicide that should be carefully explored. Comorbidity with a psychiatric illness also places the substance abuser at greater risk for suicide, as does having family members with positive histories of suicide.

If, in the clinician's judgment, there are concerns about the patient being a continued danger to himself or herself, psychiatric hospitalization should be implemented. This is done not only to protect the patient but also to provide an opportunity for medical management of any potential drug withdrawal states and to allow for a drug-free interval in which to conduct a psychiatric evaluation. Particularly during the early phases of hospitalization, constant observation and other suicide precautions should be implemented. Certain drug withdrawal states (e.g., the cocaine "crash") may place the patient at greater suicide risk.

Aftercare is critical for substance-abusing patients in general, and is particularly important for those with comorbid psychiatric disorders. Particularly effective are those programs that provide both psychiatric and substance abuse treatment modalities concurrently.

Acute Management of the Aggressive Substance Abuser

In general, the acute management of the aggressive substance abuser involves (1) behavioral stabilization, (2) medical stabilization, and (3) a diagnostic assessment of the origins and sequelae of the presenting complaint. Only after these three pragmatic but critical tasks have been accomplished should a disposition for the patient be decided upon.

As with any patient in whom the potential for violence is a concern, one should approach the possibly violent substance abuser cautiously. Basic rules of behavior such as maintaining reasonable interpersonal distance from the patient, avoiding disagreements, behaving in a manner that does not arouse suspicions or the perception of threat, and judiciously applying pharmacological and physical restraint are all important in one's approach to the potentially violent substance abuser. Such patients should be assessed in quiet rooms that are well lit in order to minimize stimulation, illusions, or visual hallucinations. Constant nursing observation is a must since the behavior of such patients is unpredictable. For a comprehensive review of the clinical interview of the potentially violent patient see Shea (1988).

Once it is established that the patient is not imminently violent or is less dangerous, a general assessment of the patient can proceed. As is often the case, such patients may be under the influence of alcohol, drugs, or both, and are therefore unable or unwilling to provide an accurate history. Collateral information from family or friends becomes invaluable in clarifying the sequence of events leading to the hospital or clinic visit, as well as eliciting a recent and past history of substance use, and a substance abuse treatment history.

A central historical issue to be explored is when the aggressive behavior occurred and if a change in mental status was observed prior or during the incident. A determination of the patient's whereabouts during the time prior to admission can also be quite important. Clearly, it must then be determined whether alcohol and other drugs were consumed in temporal association with the violent episode. An awareness of patient's usual pattern of alcohol or drug abuse and any changes in that pattern (such as a recent decrease in alcohol consumption) might lead one to conclude that the altered mental status is secondary to a withdrawal state. Lastly, when dealing with substance abusers, it is important that the clinician regard historical data concerning illicit drugs skeptically. Information about the patient's drug-taking history may be disguised and distorted to protect the patient and his or her friends from legal trouble. In addition, the presence of adulterants or substitutions may result in inaccurate reporting of drug ingestion. Information concerning alcohol and drug consumption may also be inaccurate due to the direct effects of these drugs on learning and memory, and the clinical phenomenon of "denial," in which problematic use is defensively minimized.

Simultaneous with the history-taking procedure, the astute clinician should be performing as comprehensive a mental status examination as is allowed by the condition and cooperation of the patient. Careful attention should be paid to critical elements such as patient appearance; his or her orientation to person, place and time; quality of speech production; assessment of memory functioning; presence of paranoid or other delusions; and presence of hallucinatory behavior. The patient must also be evaluated for suicidality, even if aggression toward others is the presenting complaint.

The physical exam (including a good neurological evaluation) is clearly a more objective source of information regarding a drug-related aggressive episode. During the physical exam special attention should be given to five general areas: (1) vital signs, (2) autonomic dysfunction, (3) heart and lung dysfunction, (4) localizing neurological signs as well as evidence of head trauma, and (5) abnormalities of the pupils and oculomotor functioning (Shea, 1988).

Concurrent with the physical examination, various laboratory tests may assist in the assessment of the aggressive substance-abusing patient. Obviously, a routine toxicology screen that includes the major drugs of abuse should be obtained. It is advisable that a member of the hospital staff be present when a urine sample is obtained from the patient to ensure the validity of the specimen. If alcohol intoxication is suspected a breathalyzer or blood alcohol administration can be utilized. A low blood alcohol level in a markedly delirious patient raises the possibility of a pathological alcohol intoxication state. Of course, intoxication with an additional substance should also be considered because concomitant use of alcohol with other drugs is common. Additional laboratory tests, such as electrolyte and metabolic screens, and complete blood counts may assist in determining whether delirium is secondary to metabolic derangements or infectious processes indirectly related to substance abuse. Often, such abnormalities coexist with substance abuse, such as in the malnourished alcoholic who develops pneumonia or the intravenous drug abuser who acquires septicemia or hepatitis. Brain-imaging techniques or EEGs may be necessary to rule out structural or physiological abnormalities.

Medical management of the medically ill or traumatically injured aggressive substance abuser may require venous access through an indwelling intravenous line. The clinician is advised to be cautious of the use of intravenous solutions containing only dextrose in water. Those patients who are nutritionally depleted as a consequence of alcoholism may develop an acute episode of Wernicke–Korsakoff's syndrome precipitated by the intravenous carbohydrate load. This eventuality can be avoided by the addition of thiamine and other soluble B-vitamins to all intravenous solutions administered to suspected substance abusers in an acute setting.

The alcohol withdrawal state is characterized by a general state of autonomic arousal with diaphoresis tachycardia, hypertension, and hyperthermia, as well as hyperreflexia, jitteriness, abdominal discomfort with nausea and vomiting, insomnia, and tremor. With the more serious form of alcohol withdrawal, namely, delirium tremens (DTs), disorientation, a changing mental status, hallucinations, nightmares, and delusions may additionally occur. The risk for DTs is usually greatest within the first 72–96 hours after the last alcohol ingestion or significant reduction in consumption (Mirin & Weiss, 1983). Benzodiazepines remain the treatment of choice for alcohol withdrawal states.

In general, the management of depressant drug intoxication or withdrawal is similar to that of the management of alcohol withdrawal; however, the potential for rapid progression from a state of intoxication to coma requires aggressive management in the emergency room. In the conscious patient, urine and blood levels should be obtained and gastric lavage attempted. In the patient who is becoming stuporous or comatose, management should be directed toward preventing cardiopulmonary collapse. The withdrawal syndrome usually occurs 12–16 hours after the last ingestion or reduction in dose and is similar to the withdrawal syndrome associated with alcohol. The pentobarbital tolerance test is usually administered to determine the amount of phenobarbital required to prevent a serious withdrawal syndrome (Mirin & Weiss, 1983).

In the acute setting, the amphetamine- or cocaine-intoxicated patient is likely to present with restlessness, anxiety, irritability, lability of mood, tremor, and at times confusion; the patient may appear manic. In chronic stimulant abusers, a syndrome similar to paranoid schizophrenia may complicate an accurate diagnosis. Tactile hallucinations may occur when prolonged high-dose usage has occurred. For the acute treatment of psychotic symptoms, neuroleptics are the treatment of choice. If psychotic or manic symptoms do not remit after a stimulant-free period of 24 hours, an underlying mood or thought disorder may be present. Besides the acute stimulant intoxication state, one must also be aware of the poststimulant dysphoric syndrome (known as the "crash"). While the typical stimulant withdrawal syndrome includes symptoms of dysphoria, fatigue, hypersomnia, and hyperphagia, it is usually limited to 1–2 days (Weddington, Brown,

Haertzen, Cone, Dax, Herning, & Michaelson, 1990). Such patients are at increased risk for suicidal ideation and behavior during this time interval. Recovery of mood usually returns after two prolonged evenings of sleep. Close observation of the patient during this period of time is recommended to prevent suicidal behavior. If depressive symptoms persist, one must consider the presence of a primary mood disorder and think about treatment with an antidepressant medication (Gawin & Ellinwood, 1989).

Mild PCP intoxication (5 mg or less) is typically identified in the emergency room by symptoms of muscular incoordination, numbness of the extremities, vertical or horizontal nystagmus, and impaired perception of pain. At higher doses (5–10 mg) increased muscle tone or rigidity may be accompanied by hyperreflexia and ataxia. When greater than 20 mg has been ingested, hypertensive crisis, rigidity seizures, coma, and death may occur; delirium and psychotic symptoms may also occur. The potential for violent behavior while delirious is more worrisome given the patient's relative analgesia. Such patients are unable to perceive painful stimuli associated with aggression against the self or others. Overstimulation exacerbates this delirious state; hence, these patients should be hospitalized and placed in a "quiet room" with minimal stimulation. Acidification of urine should be instituted to increase the excretion of drug. For acute psychosis, a high-potency neuroleptic with minimal anticholinergic side effects may be used.

While many detoxification techniques can be implemented in an emergency room setting, ongoing concern regarding the patient's potential aggressivity usually warrants hospitalization on a unit equipped to first detoxify and then provide a drug-free interval, which is necessary to adequately rule out a comorbid psychiatric disorder. During the early phases of hospitalization the use of seclusion and restraint to prevent violent behavior may be necessary. The provision of adequate nursing observation and attention to vital functions and mental status changes are also an absolute requirement for patient management.

Long-Term Management of the Aggressive Substance Abuser

The long-term management of aggressive substance abusers requires the application of treatment modalities that address three underlying etiological factors contributing to both substance abuse and aggression:

1. The premorbid characteristics of the patient.
2. The environmental stimuli in which the violent behavior occurs.
3. The pharmacological actions of the drugs of abuse.

Long-term approaches for reducing aggressive behavior associated with substance abuse must focus on cessation of substance abuse, acquisition of prosocial behaviors, and environmental manipulations. For cessation of substance abuse, typical therapeutic modalities employed in this context include pharmacological interventions, psycho-educational programs, participation in peer-oriented self-help groups, and behavioral skill training. Violent substance-abusing criminals may also require vocational training and supplemental education to improve their long-term outcomes.

While outpatient substance abuse rehabilitation programs may be utilized, residential rehabilitation programs may be most effective for those patients who require a structured environment to support them in achieving abstinence. Although many aggressive substance abusers may enter treatment only under legal coercion or civil commitment, contrary to the conventional wisdom, research has demonstrated that such treatment is efficacious (Anglin,

1988). Following participation in a structured rehabilitation setting, many criminal substance abusers benefit from a long-term structured living situation, such as a half-way house or a therapeutic community, which provides a prosocial environment and diminishes the threat of relapse.

Twelve-step programs such as Alcoholics Anonymous and Narcotics Anonymous focus on helping the individual maintain abstinence from the abused substance and provide a drug-free peer network to support recovery. Recently, a prison self-help group for incarcerated drug abusers called CASH was cited as being a highly useful therapeutic measure for the rehabilitation of this population (Hamm, 1990).

Postdetoxification pharmacological approaches include the use of medications to mitigate craving for drugs (e.g., methadone for heroin addiction), drugs that reduce the rewarding effects of the abused substance (e.g., naltrexone for opiate abuse), and drugs that cause an aversive reaction when taken with the drug of abuse (e.g., disulfiram for alcohol addiction). Pharmacological treatments can have benefits beyond simply altering drug abuse associated behavior. Methadone maintenance programs have been demonstrated not only to assist in reduction of opioid and nonopioid drug use but also to promote more prosocial behavior in patients participating in these programs (Dole & Joseph, 1989; Simpson, Joe, & Bracy, 1989).

Several programs also utilize behavioral techniques for the reduction of aggressive behavior among substance abusers, such as anger management training (Moon & Eisler, 1983), problem-solving skill training (Intagliata, 1978), and social skills training (Hawkins, Catalano, Gillmore, & Wells, 1989) to diminish frustration and provide an alternative prosocial behavior for the habitually assaultive.

LONGITUDINAL PERSPECTIVES

Longitudinal studies suggest an excess mortality among drug addicts as compared to the general population (Hasstrup & Jepson, 1984; Joe, Lehman, & Simpson, 1982; Vaillant, 1970, 1973). A sizable proportion of this death rate is due to suicidal or violent acts. In a 10-year prospective study, Tunving (1988) reported an 11.8% mortality rate from drug-related causes in a sample of 524 young opiate, amphetamine, and mixed-drug addicts. The death rate due to suicide or accidents and violent acts was 5.4%, while that due to overdoses or intoxication accounted for 6.7% of the sample.

Aggression toward self and suicidal behavior may constitute one of the long-term complications of addiction. Retrospective studies have shown that suicidal behavior occurs after years of an established addiction career. Berglund (1984) reported on 1,312 alcoholics who were hospitalized over a 20-year period and then followed for 11 years. Approximately 7% of the sample killed themselves during the follow-up period. The median length of time from admission to suicide was 5 years. Similar to other suicidal groups studied prospectively, suicidal patients in this sample had a high prevalence of psychiatric comorbidity, especially major depressive disorder (Borg & Stahl, 1982).

Beck, Steer, and Trexler (1989) reported on a sample of 161 subjects with alcohol abuse diagnosis hospitalized for suicide attempt. Over 11% of the sample completed suicide over the 5- to 10-year follow-up period. Most patients who completed suicide did so within 5 years of the index episode. One-third completed suicide during the first year, and half committed suicide within the first 3 years.

Crime, assault, and violent acts have been widely reported to be associated with drug use; however, there is a dearth of empirical data regarding the long-term effects of drug and alcohol use on aggressive behavior. Available longitudinal studies have dealt mainly with criminal activities among opiates addicts. Criminality is known to accompany the addiction careers, especially among narcotic addicts (Ball, Rosen, Flueck, & Nurco, 1982; Inciardi, 1986; Shaffer, Nurco, & Kinlock, 1984). Prospective investigations have focused on levels and patterns of criminal activity among narcotic addicts during addiction and nonaddiction phases of their addiction careers. Although criminal activities are reported to be more frequent during the addiction phases than during the nonaddiction phases of addicts careers (McGlothlin, Anglin, & Wilson, 1978; Nurco, Schaffer, Ball, Kinlock, & Langrod, 1986), a somewhat contrasting longitudinal association between criminal activities and addiction has been reported. Hanlon, Nurco, Kinlock, and Duszynski (1990) studied 132 narcotic addicts, who had multiple periods of relapse and abstinence, over an average of 15 years. They noted a pattern of significant decrease in crime activities over successive periods of addiction, especially for theft, violence, drug distributions, and gambling. These addicts had highest levels of criminal activity during the first periods of addition. A decrease in crimes of violence was also reported for consecutive nonaddiction periods, but it fell short of statistical significance. This is consistent with a "maturing out" of criminal behavior occurring as a developmental process.

A heterogenous group, narcotics addicts differ in terms of level, type, and pattern of criminal activity (Nurco, Schaffer, Ball, & Kinlock, 1984). Addiction, it appears, also has a differential effect on criminal behavior relative to the individual's preaddiction level of criminality. In one study, a group of 214 addicts were divided into low-crime and high-crime groups according to their histories of criminal activity prior to becoming addicts. The criminal behavior of these two groups was compared during subsequent periods of addiction and nonaddiction. It was found that the impact of the addiction was much more pronounced in the low-crime group, with a significant decrease in criminal behavior during the nonaddiction period. Interestingly, violent crimes were more frequent among the high-crime group, especially during the preaddiction period (Nurco, Hanlon, Kinlock, & Duszynski, 1988).

It also appears that addiction differentially affects criminal behavior among members of various ethnic groups. A recent study demonstrated a significantly greater decrease in criminal activity among Hispanic addicts during nonaddiction periods than among whites or blacks (Hanlon et al., 1990). Interestingly, a decrease in criminal activities among Hispanics addicts in treatment was previously reported by Kosten, Rounsaville, and Kleber (1987).

Taken together, these longitudinal studies suggest that preaddiction levels of criminal activity, age of addicts relative to the duration of their addiction, and ethnicity may be important interactive parameters to consider in implementing effective intervention strategies to reduce crime connected with narcotics addiction.

CASE ILLUSTRATION

A 19-year-old male with unkept hair and a torn T-shirt, accompanied by several close friends, was brought by the police to the psychiatric emergency room at 4 a.m. The young man's friends told the psychiatric resident on duty that he had been acting strangely ever since they returned from a rock concert that evening. He was unable to sleep and kept pacing around the room screaming unintelligibly. When they approached him he became agitated and lashed out, hitting two of his friends in the jaw and apparently bruising his fist. Surprisingly, he did not seem to be in pain. The friends, alarmed at his behavior, called the police, who brought him to the psychiatric emergency room. When the friends were asked by the psychiatric resident about recent use of drugs, they said that he had only smoked a "few joints" and drank a few beers at the concert.

The resident conducted a brief mental status examination, which revealed that the patient was at times alert but had difficulty attending to questions and would often stare into space. He would become intermittently agitated and uncooperative. At one point he threatened to hit an attendant. He was disoriented as to place and time, but not to person. His speech was generally disorganized and nongoal directed. At times he was referential. He would not cooperate for testing of memory or intellectual functioning. He denied suicidal or homicidal ideation or intent.

Physical exam revealed a blood pressure of 160/100 mm Hg and a pulse rate of 130 beats/min, suggesting autonomic hyperactivity. His deep tendon reflexes were increased, and he had a diminished response to painful stimuli. On neurological examination, vertical nystagmus was demonstrated.

While the only drugs reported to have been consumed were alcohol and marijuana, the patient appeared to have the symptoms of a drug induced delirium. PCP-induced delirium was suspected because of the presence of vertical nystagmus. Therefore, a urine drug screen was ordered to evaluate this hypothesis. While waiting on the results of the drug screen, the patient was placed in a well-lit, quiet room under constant nursing observation. After one hour, his agitation escalated into aggressive threatening behavior. Therefore, to protect both the patient and the staff, he was placed in restraints and given 5 mg of haloperidol intramuscularly. After several hours of continued agitation and paranoia, he was admitted to the seclusion room of an inpatient psychiatric unit. There he was maintained under constant nursing observation. The urine drug screen returned positive for both PCP and marijuana. He was treated for several days with oral haloperidol, his agitation improved, and gradually his sensorium cleared. On careful history taking, he then revealed daily use of marijuana and frequent drinking of over a case of beer each weekend.

Upon discharge from the hospital, the patient was referred to an outpatient program specializing in the care of individuals with comorbid mental health and substance abuse problems to provide follow-up care and further evaluation.

This case demonstrates several important clinical points:

1. The importance of conducting both mental status and physical exams.
2. The need to obtain historical information from collateral informants if the patient is uncooperative.
3. The importance of maintaining low stimulation for the patient.
4. The importance of the drug screen in confirming the diagnosis, especially if adulteration or drug substitution is suspected.
5. The appropriate use of physical restraints and neuroleptics for delirious or psychotic aggression.
6. The importance of constant nursing observation.
7. The importance of an adequate referral for long-term treatment of the patient's addiction and assessment of psychopathology.

SUMMARY

Both aggression against the self and aggression against others are closely associated with psychoactive substance abuse. These behaviors are a result of the complex interactions between the pharmacodynamics of the drug of abuse, the dispositional characteristics of the individual, and the situational context in which intoxication occurs. The astute clinician appreciates these associations and is prepared to diagnose and treat both the aggressive behavior and the substance abuse disorder. Optimal assessment includes acquisition of a comprehensive psychosocial history, a detailed evaluation of the patient's physical and mental status, and a thorough substance use history collaborated by additional informants. In most instances, failure to address all components of the clinical presentation doom the patient to an unsatisfactory outcome.

REFERENCES

Abel, E. L. (1977). The relationship between cannabis and violence: A review. *Psychological Bulletin, 84*, 193–211.

Agar, M. (1973). *Ripping and running: A formal ethnography of urban heroin addicts.* New York: Academic Press.

Alexopoulos, G., Lieberman, K., & Frances, R. (1983). Platelet MAO activity in alcoholic patients and their first-degree relatives. *American Journal of Psychiatry, 140*, 150–154.

Anglin, M. D. (1988). The efficacy of civil commitment in treating narcotics addiction. In C. G. Leukefeld & F. M. Tims (Eds.), *Compulsory treatment of drug abuse: Research and clinical practice* (NIDA Research Monograph, pp. 8–34). Rockville, MD: National Institute on Drug Abuse.

Angrist, B. M., & Gershon, S. (1969). Amphetamine abuse in New York City—1966–1968. *Seminars in Psychiatry, 1*, 195–207.

Asberg, M., Traskman, L., & Thoren, P. (1976). 5-HIAA in the cerebrospinal fluid: A biochemical suicide predictor? *Archives of General Psychiatry, 38*, 1193–1197.

American Psychiatric Association (1987). *Diagnostic and statistical manual of mental disorders*, 3rd Edition, Revised. Washington, DC: American Psychiatric Association.

American Psychiatric Association (1993). *DSM-IV draft criteria.* Washington, DC: Author.

Bach-Y-Rita, G., Lion, J. R., & Ervin, F. R. (1970). Pathological intoxication: Clinical and electroencephalographic studies. *American Journal of Psychiatry, 127*, 698–703.

Ball, J. C., Rosen, L., Flueck, J. A., & Nurco, D. N. (1982). Lifetime criminality of heroin addicts in the United States. *Journal of Drug Issues, 11*, 225–239.

Ballenger, J., Goodwin, F., Major, L., & Brown, G. (1979). Alcohol and central serotonin metabolism in man. *Archives of General Psychiatry, 36*, 224–227.

Barraclough, B., Bunch, J., Nelson, B., & Sainsbury, P. (1974). A hundred cases of suicide: Clinical aspects. *British Journal of Psychiatry, 125*, 355–373.

Beck, A. T., Steer, R. A., & Trexler, L. D. (1989). Alcohol abuse and eventual suicide: A 5- to 10-year prospective study of alcohol-abusing suicide attempters. *Journal of Studies on Alcohol, 50*, 202–209.

Begleiter, H., Porjesz, B., Bihari, B., & Kissin, B. (1984). Event-related brain potentials in boys at risk for alcoholism. *Science, 225*, 1493–1496.

Berglund, M. (1984). Suicide in alcoholism: A prospective study of 88 suicides. I. The multidimensional diagnosis at first admission. *Archives of General Psychiatry, 41*, 888–891.

Beskow, J., Gottfries, C. G., Roos, B. E., & Winblad, B. (1976). Determination of monoamine and monoamine metabolites in the human brain: Postmortem studies in a group of suicides and in a control group. *Acta Psychiatrica Scandinavia, 53*, 7–20.

Blum, R. J. (1969). Drugs and violence. In D. J. Mulhill, M. M. Tunin, & L. A. Curtis (Eds.), *Crimes of violence* (pp. 1461–1523). National Commission for the Prevention of Violence.

Borg, S. E., & Stahl, M. (1982). Prediction of suicide: A prospective study of suicides and controls among psychiatric patients. *Acta Psychiatrica Scandinavia, 65*, 221–232.

Bowers, M. B. (1977). Psychoses precipitated by psychomimetic drugs. *Archives of General Psychiatry, 34*, 832–835.

Brown, G., Ebert, M., Goyer, P., Jimerson, D., Klein, W., Bunney, W., & Goodwin, F. (1982). Aggression, suicide, and serotonin: Relationships to CSF amine metabolites. *American Journal of Psychiatry, 139*, 741–746.

Brown, G., Goodwin, F., Ballenger, J., Goyer, P., & Major, L. (1979). Aggression in humans correlates with cerebrospinal fluid metabolites. *Psychiatry Research, 1*, 131–139.

Bry, B. H., McKeon, P., & Pandina, R. (1982). Extent of drug use as a function of number of risk factors. *Journal of Abnormal Psychology, 91*, 273–279.

Budd, R. D. (1989). Cocaine abuse and violent death. *American Journal of Alcohol and Drug Abuse, 15*, 375–382.

Cahalan, D., & Room, R. (1974). *Problem drinking among American men.* New Brunswick, NJ: Rutgers Center for Alcohol Studies.

Cherek, D. R., Steinberg, J. L., Kelly, T. H., & Robinson, D. E. (1986). Effects of d-amphetamine on human aggressive behavior. *Psychopharmacology, 88*, 381–386.

Cherek, D. R., Steinberg, J. L., Kelly, T. H., & Robinson, D. (1987). Effects of d-amphetamine on aggressive responding of normal male subjects. *Psychiatry Research, 21*, 257–265.

Cherek, D. R., Steinberg, J. L., & Vines, R. V. (1984). Low doses of alcohol affect human aggressive responses. *Biological Psychiatry, 19*, 263–267.

Chiles, J. A., Strosahi, K., Cowden, L., Graham, R., & Lineham, M. (1986). The 24 hours before hospitalizations: Factors related to suicide attempting. *Suicide and Life-threatening Behavior, 16*, 335–342.

Cho, A. K. (1990). Ice: A new dosage form of an old drug. *Science, 249*, 631–634.

Chopra, G. S., & Smith, J. W. (1974). Psychotic reactions following cannabis use in East Indians. *Archives of General Psychiatry, 30*, 24–27.

Chynoweth, R., Tonge, J. I., & Armstrong, J. (1980). Suicide in Brisbane: A retrospective psychosocial study. *Australian and New Zealand Journal of Psychiatry, 14*, 37–45.

Clayton, R. R., & Voss, H. L. (1981). *Young men and drugs in Manhattan: A causal analysis* (NIDA Research Monograph No. 39). Washington, DC: U.S. Government Printing Office.

Cotton, N. (1979). The familial incidence of alcoholism. A review. *Journal of Studies of Alcohol, 40*, 89–116.

Crowley, T. J., Chesluk, D., Dilts, S., & Hart, R. (1974). Drug and alcohol abuse among psychiatric admissions. *Archives of General Psychiatry, 30*, 13–20.

Darmani, N. A., Hadfield, M. G., Carter, W. H., & Martin, B. R. (1990). Acute and chronic effects of cocaine on isolation-induced aggression in mice. *Psychopharmacology* (Berlin), *102*, 37–40.

Dermen, K. H., & George, W. H. (1989). Alcohol expectancy and the relationship between drinking and physical aggression. *The Journal of Psychology, 123*, 153–161.

Dole, V. P., & Joseph, H. (1970). Long term outcomes of patients treated with methadone. *Annals of the New York Academy of Sciences, 311*, 181–189.

Dropat, T. L., & Ripley, H. S. (1960). A study of suicide in the Seattle area. *Comprehensive Psychiatry, 1*, 349–359.

Du Pont, R. L. (1988). Abuse of Benzodiazepines: The problems and the solutions. *American Journal of Drug and Alcohol Abuse, 14*(Suppl. 1), 1–69.

Edwards, G., & Gross, M. M. (1976). Alcohol dependence: Provisional description of a clinical syndrome. *British Medical Journal, 1*, 1058–1061.

Eichelman, B. (1978). Animal models: Their role in the study of aggressive behavior in humans. *Progress in Neuro-Psychopharmacology, 2*, 663–643.

Ellinwood, E. H. (1970). Assault and homicide associated with amphetamine abuse. *American Journal of Psychiatry, 127*, 1170–1175.

Evans, C. M. (1980). Alcohol, violence and aggression. *British Journal on Alcohol and Alcoholism, 15*, 104–117.

Fauman, B., Aldinger, G., & Fauman, M. (1976). Psychiatric sequelae of phencyclidine abuse. *Clinical Toxicology, 9*, 529–538.

Fauman, M. A. (1978). Treatment of the agitated patient with an organic brain disorder. *Journal of the American Medical Association, 240*, 380–382.

Fauman, M. A., & Fauman, B. J. (1979). Violence associated with phencyclidine abuse. *American Journal of Psychiatry, 136*, 1584–1586.

Fiddle, S. (1976). Sequences in addiction. *Addictive Diseases, 2*, 553–568.

Fowler, R. C., Rich, C. L., & Young, D. (1986). San Diego suicide study. II. Substance abuse in young cases. *Archives of General Psychiatry, 43*, 962–965.

Frances, A., Pincus, H. A., Widiger, T. A., Davis, W. W., & First, M. D. (1990). DMS-IV. Work in progress. *American Journal of Psychiatry, 147*, 1439–1448.

Frances, R. J., & Franklin, J. E. (1989). *A concise guide to treatment of alcoholism and addiction.* Washington, DC: American Psychiatric Press.

Gallant, D. M. (1985). Alcoholism: The most common psychiatric illness. *Alcoholism: Clinical and Experimental Research, 9*, 297.

Gawin, F. H., & Ellinwood, E. H. (1989). Stimulants: Actions, abuse and treatment. *New England Journal of Medicine, 381*, 1173–1183.

Goldstein, P. J. (1985). The drugs/violence nexus: A tripartite conceptual framework. *Journal of Drug Issues, 13*, 493–506.

Gomberg, E. (1982). The young male alcoholic: A pilot study. *Journal of Studies on Alcohol*, *43*, 683–700.

Goodwin, D. W. (1973). Alcohol in suicide and homicide. *Quarterly Journal of Studies on Alcohol*, *34*, 144–156.

Gorenstein, E. E., & Newman, J. P. (1980). Disinhibitory psychopathy: A new perspective and a model for research. *Psychological Review*, *87*, 301–315.

Graham, K., La Rocque, L., Yetman, R., Ross, T. J., & Guistra, E. (1980). Aggression and barroom environments. *Journal of Studies on Alcohol*, *41*, 277–292.

Griffin, M. L., Weiss, R. D., Mirin, S. M., & Lange, U. (1989). A comparison of male and female cocaine abusers. *Archives of General Psychiatry*, *46*, 122–126.

Grinspoon, L. (1977). *Marihuana reconsidered*. Cambridge, MA: Harvard University Press.

Grove, W. M., Eckert, E. D., Heston, L., Bouchard, T. J., Segal, N., & Lykken, D. T. (1990). Heritability of substance abuse and antisocial behavior: A study of monozygotic twins reared apart. *Biological Psychiatry*, *27*, 1293–1304.

Gustafson, R. (1985). Alcohol and aggression: Pharmacological versus expectancy effects. *Psychological Reports*, *57*, 955–966.

Gustafson, R. (1986). Threat as a determinant of alcohol-related aggression. *Psychological Reports*, *58*, 287–297.

Haertzen, C. A., & Hooks, N. T. (1969). Changes in personality and subjective experience associated with the chronic administration and withdrawal of opiates. *Journal of Nervous and Mental Disease*, *148*, 606–614.

Hamm, M. S. (1990). Addicts helping addicts to help themselves: The Baltimore City Jail Project. In R. Weisheit (Ed.), *Drugs, crime and the criminal justice system* (pp. 361–381). Cincinnati, OH: Anderson Publishing.

Hanlon, T. E., Nurco, D. N., Kinlock, T. W., & Duszynski, K. R. (1990). Trends in criminal activity and drug use over an addiction career. *American Journal of Drug and Alcohol Abuse*, *16*, 223–238.

Harruff, R. C., Francisco, J. T., Elkins, S. K., Phillips, A. M., & Fernandez, G. S. (1988). Cocaine and homicide in Memphis and Shelby county: An epidemic of violence. *Journal of Forensic Science*, *33*, 1231–1237.

Hasstrup, S., & Jepsen, P. W. (1984). Seven year follow-up of 300 young drug abusers. *Acta Psychiatrica Scandinavica*, *70*, 503–509.

Hawkins, J., Catalano, R., Gillmore, R., & Wells, E. (1989). Skills training for drug abusers: Generalization, maintenance, and effects on drug use. *Journal of Consulting and Clinical Psychology*, *57*, 415–427.

Hawton, K. (1987). Assessment of suicide risk. *British Journal of Psychiatry*, *150*, 145–153.

Hechtman, L., Weiss, G., Perlman, T., & Angel, R. (1984). Hyperactives as young adults: Past and current substance abuse and antisocial behavior. *American Journal of Orthopsychiatry*, *54* 415–425.

Heise, H A. (1934). Alcohol and automobile accidents. *Journal of the American Medical Association*, *103*, 739–741.

Helzer, J. E., & Pryzbeck, T. R. (1988). The co-occurrence of alcoholism with other psychiatric disorders in the general population and its impact on treatment. *Journal of Studies on Alcohol*, *49*, 219–224.

Hesselbrock, M. N., Meyer, R. E., & Keener, J. J. (1985). Psychopathology in hospitalized alcoholics. *Archives of General Psychiatry*, *42*, 1050–1055.

Hesselbrock, M., Hesselbrock, V., Syzmanski, K., & Weidenman, M. (1988). Suicide attempts and alcoholism. *Journal of Studies on Alcohol*, *49*, 436–442.

Hill, S. Y. (1985). The disease concept of alcoholism: A review. *Drug and Alcohol Dependence*, *16*, 193–214.

Honer, W. G., Gewirtz, G., & Tukey, M. (1987). Psychosis and violence in cocaine smokers. *The Lancet*, *II*, 451.

Hood, I., Ryan, D., Monforte, J., & Valentour, J. (1990). Cocaine in Waybe County Medical Examiner's cases. *Journal of Forensic Science*, *35*, 591–600.

Huba, G. J., & Bentler, P. M. (1980). The role of peer and adult models for drug taking at different stages in adolescence. *Journal of Youth and Adolescence*, *9*, 449–465.

Inciardi, J. A. (1986). *The war on drugs*. Palo Alto, CA: Mayfield.

Intagliata, J. (1978). Increasing the interpersonal problem-solving skills of an alcoholic population. *Journal of Consulting and Clinical Psychology*, *46*, 489–498.

James, I. P. (1967). Suicide and mortality amongst heroin addicts in Britain. *British Journal of Addiction*, *62*, 391–398.

Jeavons, C. M., & Taylor, S. P. (1985). The control of alcohol-related aggression: Redirecting the inebriate's attention to socially appropriate conduct. *Aggressive Behavior*, *11*, 93–101.

Jessor, R., & Jessor, S. (1975). Adolescent development and the onset of drinking: A longitudinal study. *Journal of Studies on Alcohol*, *36*, 27–51.

Jessor, R., & Jessor, S. L. (1977). *Problem behavior and psychosocial development*. New York: Academic Press.

Joe, G. W., Lehman, W., & Simpson, D. D. (1982). Addict rates during a four-year post-treatment follow-up. *American Journal of Psychiatric Health*, *72*, 703–709.

Johnston, L. D., O'Malley, P. M., & Bachman, J. G. 1989). *National trends in drug use and related factors among*

American high school students and young adults, 1975–1988 (DHHS Publication No. ADM 87-1535). Washington, DC: U.S. Government Printing Office.

Jones, R. T. (1973). Mental illness and drugs: Pre-existing psychopathology and response to psychoactive drugs. In *Drug use in America: Problem in perspective* (pp. 373–397). Washington, DC: National Commission on Marihuana & Drug Abuse.

Karan, L. D., Haller, D. L., & Schnoll, S. H. (1991). Cocaine. In R. J. Frances & S. I. Miller (Eds.), *Clinical textbook of addictive disorders* (pp. 122–123). New York: Guilford Press.

Kelly, T. H., Cherek, D. R., Steinberg, J. L., & Robinson, D. (1988). Effects of provocation and alcohol on human aggressive behavior. *Drug and Alcohol Dependence, 21*, 105–112.

Khajawall, A. M., Erickson, T. B., & Simpson, G. M. (1982). Chronic phencyclidine abuse and physical assault. *American Journal of Psychiatry, 139*, 1604–1606.

Kosten, T. R., & Rounsaville, B. J. (1988). Suicidality among opioid addicts: 2.5 year follow-up. *American Journal of Drug and Alcohol Abuse, 14*, 357–369.

Kosten, T. R., Rounsaville, B. J., & Kleber, H. D. (1987). A 2.5 year follow-up of cocaine use among treated opioid addicts: Have our treatments helped? *Archives of General Psychiatry, 44*, 281–284.

Lang, A. R., Goeckner, D. J., Adesso, V. J., & Marlatt, G. A. (1975). Effects of alcohol on aggression in male social drinkers. *Journal of Abnormal Psychology, 84*, 508–518.

Lindenbaum, G. A., Carroll, S. F., Daskal, I., & Kapusnick, R. (1989). Patterns of alcohol and drug abuse in an urban trauma center: The increasing role of cocaine abuse. *Journal of Trauma, 29*, 1654–1658.

Luisada, P. C., & Brown, B. I. (1976). Clinical management of the phencyclidine psychosis. *Clinical Toxicology, 9*, 539–545.

Maletzky, B. M. (1976). The diagnosis of pathological intoxication. *Journal of Studies on Alcohol, 37*, 1215–1228.

Mandelbaum, D. (1965). Alcohol and culture. *Current Anthropology, 6*, 281–293.

Mann, J. J., Stanley, M., McBride, A., & McEwen, B. S. (1986). Increased serotonin-2 and beta-adrenergic receptor binding in the frontal cortices of suicide victims. *Archives of General Psychiatry, 43*, 954–959.

Marlatt, G. A., & Rohsenow, D. J. (1980). Cognitive processes in alcohol use: Expectancy and the balanced placebo design. In N. K. Mellon (Ed.), *Advances in substance abuse: Behavioral and biological research* (pp. 159–199). Greenwich, CT: JAI Press.

Maull, K. I. (1982). Alcohol abuse. Its implications in trauma care. *Southern Medical Journal, 75*, 794–798.

McBride, D. C., & Swartz, J. A. (1990). Drugs and violence in the age of crack cocaine. In R. Weisheit (Ed.), *Drugs, crime and the criminal justice system* (pp. 141–169). Cincinnati, OH: Anderson Publishing.

McCord, W., & McCord, J. (1960). *Origins of alcoholism.* Stanford, CA: Stanford University Press.

McGlothlin, W. H., Anglin, M. D., & Wilson, B. D. (1978). Narcotic addiction and crime. *Criminology, 16*, 293–316.

Mendelson, J. H., & Mello, N. K. (1985). Diagnostic criteria for alcoholism and alcohol abuse. In J. H. Mendelson and N. K. Mello (Eds.), *The diagnosis & treatment of alcoholism* (pp. 2–18). New York: McGraw-Hill.

Meyer, R. E. (1986). How to understand the relationship between psychopathology and addictive disorders: Another example of the chicken and the egg. In R. E. Meyer (Ed.), *Psychopathology and addictive disorders* (pp. 3–16). New York: Guilford Press.

Miczek, K. A., & Krsiak, M. (1979). Drug effects on agonistic behavior. In P. B. Dews (Ed.), *Advances in behavioral pharmacology* (pp. 88–163). New York: Academic Press.

Mirin, S., & Weiss, R. (1983). Substance abuse. In E. L. Bassuk, S. C. Schoonover, & A. J. Gelenbert (Eds.), *The practitioner's guide to psychoactive drugs* (2nd ed.) (pp. 271–291). New York: Plenum.

Moon, J., & Eisler, R. (1983). Anger control: An experimental comparison of three behavioral treatments. *Behavior Therapy, 14*, 493–505.

Moss, H. B. (1987). Serotonergic activity and disinhibitory psychopathy in alcoholism. *Medical Hypotheses, 23*, 353–361.

Moss, H. B., Guthrie, S., & Linnoila, M. (1986). Enhanced thyrotropin response to thryrotropin releasing hormone in boys at risk for the development of alcoholism. *Archives of General Psychiatry, 43*, 1137–1141.

Moss, H. B., Yao, J. K., & Panzak, G. L. (1990). Serotonergic responsivity and behavioral dimensions in antisocial personality disorder with substance abuse. *Biological Psychiatry, 28*, 325–338.

Motto, J. A. (1980). Suicide risk factors in alcohol abuse. *Suicide and Life-threatening Behavior, 10*, 230–238.

Muehlberger, C. W. (1956). Medicolegal aspects of alcohol intoxication. *Michigan State Bar Journal, 35*, 38–42.

Murdoch, D. D., Pihl, R. O., & Ross, D. (1988). The influence of dose, beverage type and sex of interactor on female bar patron's verbal aggression. *International Journal of Addictions, 23*, 953–966.

Murdock, D., & Pihl, R. O. (1985). Alcohol and aggression in group interaction. *Addictive Behaviors, 10*, 97–101.

Murphy, G. E. (1986). Suicide in alcoholism. In A. Roy (Ed.), *Suicide* (pp. 89–96). Baltimore: Williams & Wilkins.

Murphy, G. E. (1988). Suicide and substance abuse. *Archives of General Psychiatry*, *45*, 593–594.

Murphy, G. E., & Robins, E. (1967). Social factors in suicide. *Journal of the American Medical Association*, *199*, 303–308.

Murphy, G. E., Armstrong, J. W., Hermel, S. L., Fischer, J. R., & Clendenin, W. W. (1979). Suicide and alcoholism: Interpersonal loss confirmed as predictor. *Archives of General Psychiatry*, *36*, 65–69.

Murray, R. M., Clifford, C. A., Gurling, H. M. D., Topham, A., Clow, A., & Bernadt, M. (1983). Current genetic and biological approaches to alcoholism. *Psychiatric Developments*, *2*, 179–192.

Myerscough, R., & Taylor, S. (1985). The effects of marijuana on human physical aggression. *Journal of Personality and Social Psychology*, *49*, 1541–1546.

National Institute on Alcohol Abuse and Alcoholism. (1991). Estimating the economic cost of alcohol abuse. *Alcohol Alert*, *11* (p. 293). Washington, DC: D.H.H.S.

National Institute on Drug Abuse (1988). 1987 annual data. *Drug Abuse Warning Network* (DAWN) (DHHS Publication No. ADM 88-1584). Washington, DC: D.H.H.S.

Nurco, D. N., Hanlon, T. E., Kinlock, T. W., & Duszynski, K. R. (1988). Differential criminal patterns of narcotic addicts over an addiction career. *Criminology*, *26*, 407–423.

Nurco, D. N., Shaffer, J. W., Ball, J. C., & Kinlock, T. W. (1984). Trends in the commission of crime among narcotic addicts over successive periods of addiction and nonaddiction. *American Journal of Drug and Alcohol Abuse*, *10*, 481–489.

Nurco, D. N., Shaffer, J. W., Ball, J. C., Kinlock, T. W., & Langrod, J. (1986). A comparison by ethnic group and city of the criminal activities of narcotic addicts. *Journal of Nervous and Mental Disease*, *174*, 112–116.

Ohlsson, A., Lindgren, J. E., Wahlen, A., Agurell, S., Hollister, L, E,, & Gillespie, B. A. (1980). Plasma delta-9-tetrahydrocannabinol concentrations and clinical effects after oral and intravenous administration and smoking. *Clinical Pharmacology and Therapeutics*, *28*, 409–416.

Permanen, K. (1976). Alcohol and crimes of violence. In B. Kissin & H. Begleiter (Eds.), *The biology of alcoholism* (pp. 351–444). New York: Plenum.

Perrine, M. W. (1975). Alcohol involvement in highway crashes. *Clinics in Plastic Surgery*, *2*, 11–34.

Petronis, K. R., Samuels, J. F., Moscicki, E. K., & Anthony, J. C. (1990). An epidemiologic investigation of potential risk factors for suicide attempts. *Social Psychiatry of Epidemiology*, *25*, 193–199.

Pickens, R. W., Svikis, D. S., McGue, M., Lykken, D. T., Heston, L. L., & Clayton, P. J. (1991). Heterogeneity in the inheritance of alcoholism. A study of male and female twins. *Archives of General Psychiatry*, *48*, 19–28.

Pihl, R. O., Finn, P., & Peterson, J. (1989). Autonomic hyperreactivity and risk for alcoholism. *Progress in Neuro-Psychopharmacology and Biologic Psychiatry*, *13*, 489–496.

Pihl, R. O., Smith, M., & Farrell, B. (1984). Alcohol and aggression in men: A comparison of brewed and distilled beverages. *Journal of Studies on Alcohol*, *45*, 278–282.

Pihl, R. O., Zacchia, C., & Zeichner, A. (1982). Predicting levels of aggression after alcohol intake in men social drinkers: A preliminary investigation. *Journal of Studies on Alcohol*, *43*, 599–602.

Pliner, P., Cappell, H., & Miles, C. G. (1972). Observer judgments of intoxicated behavior during social interaction: A comparison of alcohol and marijuana. In J. M. Singh, L. H. Miller, & H. Lal (Eds.), *Drug addiction* (pp. 59–67). Mt. Kisco, NY: Futura Publishing.

Plomin, R., DeFries, J. C., & Fulker, D. W. (1988). *Nature and nurture during infancy and early childhood*. New York: Cambridge University Press.

Rada, R. T. (1975). Alcoholism and forcible rape. *American Journal of Psychiatry*, *132*, 444–446.

Regier, D. A., Farmer, M. E., Rae, D. S., Locker, B. Z., Keith, S. J., Judd, L. L., & Goodwin, F. K. (1990). Comorbidity of mental disorders with alcohol and other drugs of abuse. Results from the Epidemiologic Catchment Area (ECA) Study. *Journal of the American Medical Association*, *264*, 2511–2518.

Reiss, D., Plomin, R., & Hetherington, E. M. (1991). Genetics and psychiatry: An unheralded window on the environment. *American Journal of Psychiatry*, *148*, 283–291.

Rich, C. L., Fowler, R. C., Fogarty, L. A., & Young, D. (1988). San Diego suicide study: III. Relationships between diagnosis and stressors. *Archives of General Psychiatry*, *45*, 589–592.

Robins, E. (1986). Completed suicide. In A. Roy (Ed.), *Suicide*. Baltimore, MD: Williams & Wilkins.

Robins, E., Murphy, G. E., Wilkinson, R. H., Gassner, S., & Kayes, J. (1959). Some clinical considerations in the prevention of suicide based on a study of 134 successful suicides. *American Journal of Public Health*, *49*, 888–899.

Robins, L. N. (1966). *Deviant children grown up: A sociological and psychiatric study of sociopathic personality*. Baltimore, MD: Williams & Wilkins.

Robins, L. N., Helzer, J. E., Weissman, M. M., Orvaschel, H., Gruenberg, E., Bruke, J. D., & Regier, D. A. (1984). Lifetime prevalence of specific psychiatric disorders in three sites. *Archives of General Psychiatry*, *41*, 949–958.

Roy, A. (1989). Suicide. In H. Kaplan (Ed.), *Comprehensive textbook of psychiatry V* (pp. 1414–1427). Baltimore, MD: Williams & Wilkins.

Roy, A., Adinoff, G., & Linnoila, M. (1988). Acting out hostility in normal volunteers: Negative correlation with levels of 5-HIAA in cerebrospinal fluid. *Psychiatry Research*, *24*, 189–194.

Russel, J. A., & Mehrabian, A. (1975). The mediating role of emotions in alcohol use. *Journal of Studies on Alcohol*, *36*, 1508–1536.

Sanborn, D. E., Sanborn, C. J., & Cimbolic, P. (1973). Two years of suicide: A study of adolescent suicide in New Hampshire. *Child Psychiatry and Human Development*, *3*, 234–242.

Schuckit, M. A. (1973). Alcoholism and sociopathy—Diagnostic confusion. *Quarterly Journal of Studies on Alcohol*, *34*, 157–164.

Schuckit, M. A. (1980). Self-rating of alcohol intoxication by young men with and without family histories of alcoholism. *Journal of Studies on Alcohol*, *41*, 242–249.

Schuckit, M. A., Parker, D., & Rossman, L. (1983). Ethanol-related prolactin responses and risk for alcoholism. *Biological Psychiatry*, *18*, 1153–1159.

Shaffer, J. W., Nurco, D. N., & Kinlock, T. W. (1984). A new classification of narcotic addicts based on type and extent of criminal activity. *Comprehensive Psychiatry*, *25*, 315–328.

Shea, S. C. (1988). Exploring suicidal and homicidal ideation. In *Psychiatric interviewing: The art of understanding*. Philadelphia, PA: Saunders.

Sher, K. J., & Levenson, R. W. (1982). Risk for alcoholism and individual differences in the stress-response-dampening effect of alcohol. *Journal of Abnormal Psychology*, *91*, 350–367.

Shuntich, R. J., & Taylor, S. P. (1972). The effects of alcohol on human physical aggression. *Journal of Experimental Research on Personality*, *6*, 34–38.

Simpson, D. D., Joe, G. W., & Bracy, S. A. (1989). Six year follow-up of opioid addicts after admission to treatment. American Psychiatric Association Task Force (Eds.), *Treatment of psychiatric disorders* (Vol. 2) (pp. 1218–1241). Washington, DC: American Psychiatric Association.

Smart, R. G. (1980). Availability and the prevention of alcohol-related problems. In T. C. Harford, D. A. Parker, & L. Light (Eds.), *Normative approaches to the prevention of alcohol abuse and alcoholism* (pp. 123–157). Rockville, MD: National Institute on Alcohol Abuse and Alcoholism.

Sonneck, G. (1982). Crisis interventions and suicide preventions. III. Recidivism. *Psychiatric Clinical* (Basel), *15*, 60–96.

Stephens, R. C., & McBride, D. C. (1976). Becoming a street addict. *Human Organization*, *35*, 87–94.

Tardiff, K., Gross, E., Wu, J., Stajic, M., & Millman, R. (1989). Analysis of cocaine-positive fatalities. *Journal of Forensic Science*, *34*, 53–63.

Tarter, R. E., Kabene, M., Escallier, E. A., Laird, S. B., & Jacob, T. (1990). Temperament deviation and risk for alcoholism. *Alcoholism: Clinical and Experimental Research*, *14*, 380–382.

Taylor, S. P., & Gammon, C. B. (1975). Effects of type and dose of alcohol on human physical aggression. *Journal of Personality and Social Psychology*, *32*, 169–175.

Taylor, S. P., & Gammon, C. B. (1976). Aggression behavior of intoxicated subjects: The effect of third-party intervention. *Journal of Studies on Alcohol*, *37*, 917–930.

Taylor, S. P., & Sears, J. D. (1988). The effects of alcohol and persuasive social pressure on human physical aggression. *Aggressive Behavior*, *14*, 237–243.

Tellegen, A., Bouchard, T. J., Wilcox, K. H., Segal, N. L., Lykken, D. T., & Rich, S. (1988). Personality similarity in twins reared apart and together. *Journal of Personality and Social Psychology*, *54*, 1031–1039.

Tennant, F. S., Detels, R., & Clark, V. (1975). Some antecedents of drug and alcohol abuse. *American Journal of Epidemiology*, *102*, 377–384.

Tunving, K. (1988). Fatal outcome in drug addiction. *Acta Psychiatrica Scandinavica*, *77*, 551–566.

Vaillant, G. E. (1970). The natural history of narcotic addiction. *Seminars in Psychiatry*, *2*, 486–498.

Vaillant, G. E. (1973). A twenty-year follow-up of New York narcotic addicts. *Archives of General Psychiatry*, *29*, 237–241.

Vaillant, G. (1983). *The natural history of alcoholism*. Cambridge, MA: Harvard University Press.

van Ree, J. M., Niesink, R. J., & Nir, I. (1984). Delta l-tetrahydrocannabinol but not cannabidiol reduces contact and aggressive behavior of rats tested in dyadic encounters. *Psychopharmacology* (Berlin), *84*, 561–565.

Virkkunen, M. (1974). Alcohol as a factor precipitating aggression and conflict behavior leading to homicide. *British Journal of Addiction*, *69*, 149–154.

Watkins, V. M., & McCoy, C. B. (1980). Drug use among urban Appalachian youths. In V. M. Watkins & C. B. McCoy (Eds.), *Drug abuse patterns among young poly-drug abusers and urban Appalachian youths* (NIDA Services Research Report, DHHS Publication No. 801002, pp. 17–34). Washington, DC: U.S. Government Printing Office.

Weddington, W., Brown, B., Haertzen, C., Cone, E., Dax, E., Herning, R., & Michaelson, B. (1990). Changes in mood, craving, and sleep during short-term abstinence reported by male cocaine addicts. *Archives of General Psychiatry*, *47*, 861–868.

Wolfgang, M. E., & Strohm, R. B. (1956). The relationship between alcohol and criminal homicide. *Quarterly Journal of Studies on Alcohol*, *17*, 411–425.

World Health Organization (1977). *Manual of the international statistical classification of diseases, inquirer and causes of death* (9th rev. ed.). Geneva: World Health Organization.

Yago, K. B., Pitts, F. N. Jr., Burgoyne, R. N., Aniline, O., Yago, L. S., & Pitts, A. F. (1981). The urban epidemic of phencyclidine (PCP) use. Clinical and laboratory evidence from a public psychiatric hospital emergency service. *Journal of Clinical Psychiatry*, *42*, 193–196.

Zeichner, A., & Pihl, R. O. (1980). Effects of alcohol and instigator intent on human aggression. *Journal of Studies on Alcohol*, *41*, 265–276.

Zuckerman, M. (1972). Drug usage as one manifestation of "sensation seeking." In W. Keup (Ed.), *Drug abuse: Current concepts and research* (pp. 154–163). Springfield, IL: Charles C. Thomas.

CHAPTER 13

Schizophrenia

WILLIAM C. WIRSHING, DONNA AMES,
STEPHEN R. MARDER, AND TARA HICKS-GRAY

DESCRIPTION OF THE DISORDER

Schizophrenia is a major psychiatric illness whose definition has varied with respect to both time and country. Thus, the "schizophrenia" referred to in the American literature of the late 1960s was different from that defined by the British psychiatric profession of the same era and different also from the accepted definitions in the United States today. This evolution of the schizophrenia construct makes it problematic to apply the literature from disparate places and eras to the modern schizophrenia patient.

Broadly speaking, American psychiatrists have historically tended to emphasize disturbances in certain psychological processes (the "Bleulerian" approach), while British psychiatrists have focused more on a deteriorating course (the dementia praecox of Emil Kraepelin), and pathognomonic symptoms (e.g., Schneiderian first-rank symptoms). These various theoretical postures have resulted in a historic American schizophrenia that is more broadly inclusive, heterogeneous, and prevalent than its British or European counterpart.

Fortunately, the definitions of schizophrenia converged in the early 1980s, and most modern literature is comparable across national boundaries. The present definition will undoubtedly change as new discoveries and technologies allow for a more profound understanding of the entity. Currently, schizophrenia is defined in terms of both phenomenology and historical course. In the active phase of the illness—which must last at least one week—psychotic symptoms must be present. These symptoms include bizarre delusions (e.g., "I am being controlled by an electronic device that was planted in my neck by an alien race"); prominent hallucinations (usually auditory, but other sensory modalities can be

WILLIAM C. WIRSHING, DONNA AMES, STEPHEN R. MARDER, AND TARA HICKS-GRAY •
Department of Psychiatry and Biobehavioral Sciences, UCLA School of Medicine, and West Los Angeles
Veterans Affairs Medical Center, Los Angeles, California 90073.

Handbook of Aggressive and Destructive Behavior in Psychiatric Patients, edited by Michel Hersen, Robert T.
Ammerman, and Lori A. Sisson. Plenum Press, New York, 1994.

involved); a marked disturbance of interactive style (e.g., incoherence, grossly inappropriate affect, or frank catatonia). In addition to this acute phase, there must be a decline in function in such areas as work, social relations, and/or self-care to a point markedly below the highest level achieved before the onset of the disturbance (or, when the onset is in childhood or adolescence, failure to advance to an expected level of development). The disturbance must be manifest for at least 6 months and must not be secondary to any organic etiology or to a major disturbance in mood.

The lifetime prevalence of schizophrenia so defined is slightly less than 1% and appears consistent across cultural and ethnic boundaries. There is no gender difference in prevalence, but males tend to develop the illness earlier (15–25 years old) than females (25–40 years old) and have a more disabling, chronic, and treatment-unresponsive course.

Genetics plays an important and complex role in schizophrenia. For example, children with a single schizophrenic parent have a 10% chance of developing the condition themselves (i.e., 10 times the risk of a child with nonschizophrenic parents); the rate rises to 30%–50% when both parents are afflicted. In monozygotic twin studies, the rate of discordance for schizophrenia varies between 22% and 67%. Thus, genetics strongly influences, but is not the sole determinant of, schizophrenia.

Other risk factors that have been investigated include perinatal complications, winter births, high-stress lifestyles, and viral infections. None of these, though, is universally accepted, and none carries the weight of the genetics factor. It has been suggested that males may have a schizophrenia that is more environmentally determined (e.g., birth trauma, viral brain infections, etc.) than females. Such a theoretical possibility will become important in the discussion below of aggression in the neurologically impaired schizophrenic patient.

Schizophrenia begins, on average, in late adolescence or early adulthood. It follows a variable course and can be relentlessly progressive, relapsing and remitting, chronic without worsening, or it can even remit permanently. Generally though, schizophrenia is a lifelong condition, and individuals so afflicted are notoriously sensitive to stress—even if that stress is idiosyncratically perceived. They usually require long-term treatment with antipsychotic medications and will frequently need to be hospitalized during periods of acute exacerbations.

Since the early 1950s, the mainstay of treatment has been antipsychotic medications—also called neuroleptics or major tranquilizers. This class of drugs blocks dopamine—a chemical in the brain that functions as a type of molecular messenger between neurons in certain areas of the central nervous system. These medications are particularly effective in reducing the so-called positive symptoms of schizophrenia (e.g., hallucinations, delusions, and disorders of communication), but they are only marginally useful in treating negative symptoms (apathy, amotivation, avolition, and social withdrawal). About 70% of those with schizophrenia will benefit from treatment with neuroleptics.

These medications, however, have a number of untoward endocrinologic and neurological side effects. The endocrine disturbances can cause amenorrhea, galactorrhea, and sexual dysfunction in females, and gynecomastia, erectile incompetence, and decreased libido in males. Prominent among the possible neurological consequences of these agents are parkinsonism, dystonia, akathisia (a profound internal state of restlessness coupled with an inability to sit or stand still), and tardive dyskinesia. This latter condition is a hyperkinetic, usually choreic disorder that occurs after months of treatment and may be irreversible—even if the causal agent is discontinued.

EPIDEMIOLOGY

Aggression toward Self

The fact that schizophrenics attempt and commit suicide with alarming frequency is undisputed. Between 0.5% and 1% of the general population will die by suicide; 10% of schizophrenics will die by their own hand (Roy, 1986; Winokur & Tsuang, 1975). The majority of these suicides will occur in the first decade after the illness is diagnosed (Nyman & Jonsson, 1986; Roy, 1982; Warnes, 1968). In a recent prospective study of 79 schizophrenic subjects who were early in the course of their disease, 8% had committed suicide after 2 years of follow-up, and 10% had suicided by year 5 (Carone, Harrow, & Westermeyer, 1991).

Demographically, few consistent characteristics have emerged to differentiate those schizophrenics who are self-destructive from those who are not. Generally, the suicides occur before age 45 (Cohen, Leonard, Farberow, & Shneidman, 1964; Levy & Southcombe, 1953; Yarden, 1974), and male suicides predominate in most controlled studies (Breier & Astrachan, 1984; Cheng, Leung, Lo, & Lam, 1990; Roy, 1982; Warnes, 1968). Some observers have suggested that whites may be at greater risk than other races (Breier & Astrachan, 1984), but in most studies, no clear race differences have emerged (Shaffer, Perlin, Schmidt, & Stephens, 1974). Patients who suicide tend to have more education than their nondestructive counterparts (Farberow, Shneidman, & Leonard, 1961; Salama, 1988).

The rate of attempted suicides (parasuicides) is higher still—18% to 55% (Cohen et al., 1964; Levy, Kurtz, & Kling, 1984; Planansky & Johnston, 1971; Roy, 1982, 1986; Roy, Mazonson, & Pickar, 1984). The lifetime risk for parasuicide in a schizophrenic is over 20 times that of the overall population (Dyck, Bland, Newman, & Orn, 1988). In the general population, female parasuicides outnumber male suicides two to one; among schizophrenic parasuicides, though, the sexes are equally represented (Drake, Gates, & Cotton, 1986; Wilkinson & Bacon, 1984). Compared with those who complete suicide, attempters make fewer explicit suicide threats, are more likely to live with their families, are less depressed, and express less suicidal ideation (Drake et al., 1986).

Aggression toward Others

The image of the psychotic killer is common in both lay notions and pop cultural depictions of schizophrenia. Early reports on the subsequent dangerousness of schizophrenics convicted of criminal activity suggested, however, that even this violent subgroup of schizophrenics was significantly less dangerous than the average person (Pollock, 1938). Other reports, however, indicated that schizophrenics were overrepresented in psychiatrically impaired individuals arrested for violent crimes (Benezech, Bourgeois, & Yesavage, 1980; Lanzkron, 1963; Oltman & Friedman, 1941; Rollin, 1965; Silverman, 1943; Taylor & Gunn, 1984; Tennent, Loucas, Fenton, & Fenwick, 1974) and were more likely than the general population to commit subsequent violent acts against others (Rappeport & Lassen, 1965; Zitrin, Hardesty, Burdock, & Drossman, 1976). The cognitive disorganization that accompanies the schizophrenic illness might make schizophrenics more liable to detection in the commission of crimes and thus artificially raise their prevalence in arrested or convicted populations (Robertson, 1988).

Among the noncriminal psychiatric population, the most common diagnosis associated with violence is schizophrenia (Krakowski, Convit, & Volavka, 1988; Shader, Jackson, Harmatz, & Appelbaum, 1977; Tardiff & Sweillam, 1980, 1982). In surveys of psychiatrists, 42% had been assaulted by patients at some point in their careers, and schizophrenics accounted for 63% of these assaults (Madden, Lion, & Penna, 1976). While prevalence estimates vary widely and depend on the type of population studied (e.g., acute or chronic inpatient, private or public hospital, etc.) and on the method of the study (e.g., history by interview, chart reviews, prospective study, etc.), anywhere from 18% to 46% of hospitalized schizophrenics may manifest overt violence toward others (Craig, 1982; Greenfield, McNiel, & Binder, 1989; Karson & Bigelow, 1987; Tardiff, 1984; Tardiff & Sweillam, 1980, 1982). Demographically, those factors that are associated with violence in the population at large also cluster in the violent schizophrenic, that is, youth, maleness, and a history of abuse as a child (Madden et al., 1976; Pearson, Wilmot, & Padi, 1986; Tardiff & Sweillam, 1979, 1980, 1982). Also, those patients that carry the secondary diagnoses of drug or alcohol abuse, mental retardation, and seizure disorder are more likely to be violent. Finally, some studies (Addad, Benezech, Bourgeois, & Yesavage, 1981; Blackburn, 1968; Planansky & Johnston, 1977; Rossi, Jacobs, Monteleone, Olsen, Surber, Winkler, & Wommack, 1986; Tardiff & Sweillam, 1980), but not all (Shader et al., 1977; Tardiff & Sweillam, 1982; Yesavage, 1983), have shown that the paranoid subtype is relatively more violent.

ETIOLOGY

The etiology of aggressive behavior in schizophrenia is a heterogeneous mixture of social, psychological, and biological factors. Certain predisposing characteristics, current psychopathology, and environmental qualities will codetermine whether aggressive behavior to the self or others will occur (Volavka & Krakowski, 1989).

The clinical circumstances that surround the suicidal act in the schizophrenic—youth, male gender, refractory course, depression, occurrence in the postpsychotic period (see "Aggression toward Self" section below)—suggest that a secondary reactive depressive process plays a role. It is possible, for instance, that an awareness of psychosocial decline, the inadequacy of treatment, and the inevitability of continued illness overwhelm the young schizophrenic's coping capacity and lead to a pervasive sense of hopeless despondency. These highly disturbed psychological states are commonly associated with suicidal acts in all patients. While speculative, such an explanation is not without precedent in chronic debilitating diseases in young patients (e.g., AIDS and cancer).

A variety of more biologically based hypotheses have been advanced to account for schizophrenic aggression. It has long been suspected that derangements in brain amine metabolism account for the protean schizophrenic symptoms. Dopamine and to a lesser extent serotonin neurotransmitter systems have been most strongly implicated. Dopamine excess can cause psychosis in humans and self-destructive behavior in animals. However, dopamine hyperfunction has not been demonstrated in schizophrenics who violently suicide (Roy, Ninan, Mazonson, Pickar, Van Kammen, Linnoila, & Paul, 1985). Further, the relative decoupling of the acute psychosis and the suicidal behavior (i.e., schizophrenics do not suicide when maximally psychotic) (Drake, Gates, Whitaker, & Cotton, 1985) indicates that dopamine excess alone does not account for both conditions.

The bulk of suicides follow treatment with neuroleptics—agents that are known to block dopamine transmission. It is possible, therefore, that dopamine hyperfunction causes the psychosis, and a relative, neuroleptic-induced depletion of dopamine in the posttreatment period accounts for the depression and subsequent suicide. It has been suggested that these medications may contribute to the high suicide rate in schizophrenics (Beisser & Blanchette, 1961; Hussar, 1962). In addition to causing depression, antipsychotic agents might exert such an effect by causing akathisia (Van Putten, 1975; Van Putten, Mutalipassi, & Malkin, 1974), which would account for the restlessness and agitation that has been frequently noted in the immediate presuicide period (Farberow et al., 1961; Planansky & Johnston, 1971; Warnes, 1968). These untoward effects, however, are probably impacting only a minority of patients, because studies of groups of schizophrenics who suicide suggest that neuroleptics confer some measure of protection (Cohen et al., 1964; Warnes, 1968).

Hypofunction of the serotonergic neurotransmitter system has also been suggested to causally account for depressive symptoms, suicidal behavior, and violence toward others. Some investigators have noted a positive relationship between low levels of serotonin (or its major metabolite, 5-hydroxyindoleacetic acid) and violence in animals (Eichelmann, 1987) and with violent suicides in schizophrenics (Ninan, Van Kammen, Scheinin, Linnoila, Bunney, & Goodwin, 1984). This relationship has not been shown consistently (Roy et al., 1985), and the exact role that serotonin plays in the schizophrenic condition is far from clear (Lemus, Lieberman, Johns, Pollack, Bookstein, & Cooper, 1990; Van Praag, 1983, 1986).

In addition to these putative neurochemical derangements, some have suggested that concomitant neurological abnormalities may predispose schizophrenics to act violently. Violent behavior seems related to the severity of both psychotic symptoms (Yesavage, Werner, Becker, Holman, & Mills, 1981) and overall course (Volavka & Krakowski, 1989). A greater prevalence of minor neurological abnormalities has been seen in this more severe group (e.g., poorer premorbid adjustment, greater number of relapses, and relative treatment resistance) (Manscheck & Ames, 1984; Quitkin, Rifkin, & Klein, 1976; Tucker, Campion, & Silberfarb, 1975). Krakowski et al. (1988) demonstrated that repetitively violent schizophrenics could be distinguished from nonviolent schizophrenics by performance on a neurological and neuropsychological test battery. They found that performance on tests of integrative sensory function and complex coordination of motor activity most clearly differentiated the groups.

Aggressive behavior in animals and humans can be elicited by electrical stimulation of limbic, brain-stem, and even paleocerebellar structures, and it can be blocked—in animals—by destruction of the amygdala (Piacente, 1986). Thus, violent behavior in schizophrenics might be the result of a subclinical seizure-like phenomenon. Schizophrenics have abnormal electroencephalograms (EEGs) at 2 to 3 times the rate of the normal population. This rate is even higher when there is a family history of psychosis, an earlier onset of illness, or treatment resistance (Kaplan & Sadock, 1989; Neppe, 1983). As these characteristics also cluster in the repetitively violent schizophrenic group, EEG abnormalities and violence may be correlated (Neppe, 1988). Such an overt relationship, however, has not been demonstrated (Krakowski et al., 1988).

Environmental factors may also causally contribute to aggressive behavior. A variety of noxious stimuli—crowding, noise, and disturbing companions—may encourage violence. Poorly trained and inadequately staffed ward environments tend to have more acts of violence, use more sedating medications, and more frequently resort to the use of seclusion and restraints (Campbell & Simpson, 1986). Aggressive behavior may be positively reinforced in such hospital settings, where little else can draw the attention of harried staff members. These environments can further promote violent behavior in patients if the behavior is "rewarded" by staff allowing such patients to be dismissed from normal ward tasks (Wong, Woolsey, Innocent, & Liberman, 1988).

AGGRESSSION TOWARD SELF

There is some evidence to support the utility of conceptualizing at least three distinct forms of self-directed violence in the schizophrenic patient: suicides, parasuicides, and nonlethal self-mutilations. While there is no doubt overlap of these populations, forcing them into separate categories may facilitate their study, enhance clinical sensitivity to their existence, and ultimately improve their detection, prediction, and prevention.

Schizophrenic patients who commit suicide generally do not do so in the midst of a psychotic episode or in response to command hallucinations. Indeed, when compared to their nonsuicidal counterparts, they tend to have less overt psychotic symptomatology (Roy, 1982; Warnes, 1968). A history of parasuicide is present in 40% to 70% of suicide completers, but this is only slightly different from that of the general schizophrenic population (20–50%). Thus, a history of parasuicide or even a recent attempt is probably of little predictive value (Drake et al., 1985; Roy, 1982). As mentioned above, only youth and male gender consistently emerge as demographic distinctions in the suicide group. This group, though, does tend to have a more chronic course of illness with more frequent exacerbations and remissions (Cheng et al., 1990; Roy, 1982). Those who suicide also tend to have more depression (Cheng et al., 1990; Cohen et al., 1964; Nyman & Jonsson, 1986; Roy 1982), hopelessness, and a greater awareness of their impairments (Farberow et al., 1961; Warnes, 1968). They have been reported to have reached a higher level of premorbid functioning but to have fewer family supports at the time of death (Drake et al., 1985). The suicides cluster around the time of discharge from a hospital (Cohen et al., 1964; Farberow et al., 1961; Warnes, 1968; Yarden, 1974). The patients are commonly described as agitated, restless, and even hostile before they commit suicide (Farberow et al., 1961; Planansky & Johnston, 1971; Warnes, 1968).

Taken together, a high-risk composite can be constructed. The young, male patient with a relatively good premorbid history and refractory course appears to be especially vulnerable during the first 10 years of illness. An awareness of psychosocial deterioration, hopelessness about the future, depression, agitation, restlessness, and lack of family support compound this risk, particularly around times of relapse and hospitalization.

The parasuicide group is much larger than the suicide group, and probably amounts to about 40% of all schizophrenics over the lifetime course of this illness (Roy, 1986). Compared with the suicide group, the parasuicide group has more females, the patients are younger, and the attempts are associated with more intense psychotic activity and anxiety (Drake et al., 1986; Nyman & Jonsson, 1986). The most common method used is poisoning with prescribed and nonprescribed medications (75%), and of these attempts, about 25% result in some type of coma (Wilkinson & Bacon, 1984).

The self-mutilations in schizophrenic patients are distinct from the repetitive, stereotypical, and self-injurious behaviors of the mentally retarded or characterologically disturbed individual (Winchel & Stanley, 1991). Self-mutilations in the schizophrenic subject are sporadic, bizarre, and dramatic: autocastration, self-enucleation, autoamputation of digits and limbs, autocannibalism, and autosurgery These unusual events (the incidence is unknown but presumably very low) occur during intensely psychotic periods and may be complicated by alcohol or illicit drug use (Greilsheimer & Groves, 1979).

AGGRESSION TOWARD OTHERS

The violence of schizophrenia seems, at first glance, as unfathomable as the psychosis that defines the disease. It varies from vague threats to actual homicide, can occur at any point in the course of the illness, is most often unpredictable, and is sometimes unpreventable even in the most controlled and technically advanced medical environments (Krakowski et al., 1988). Upon closer inspection, though, some recognizable order takes form.

In inpatient studies, the largest fraction of violent schizophrenics commit acts that are nondeadly, and the frequency of acts peaks shortly after hospital admission and falls off rapidly after the first 2 weeks of hospitalization (Myers & Dunner, 1984; Planansky & Johnston, 1977). The violence during this acute period is correlated with severity of psychotic disorganization (Yesavage et al., 1981) and appears to be disproportionately enacted by paranoid subtype schizophrenics (Addad et al., 1981; Blackburn, 1968; Planansky & Johnston, 1977; Rossi et al., 1986; Tardiff & Sweillam, 1980).

Following the acute treatment period, a much smaller cadre of schizophrenic patients (perhaps 3–5%) continues to be repetitively violent (Barber, Hundley, Kellogg, Glick, Godleski, Kerler, & Vieweg, 1988). This recidivistically violent group tends to carry nonparanoid diagnoses (Shader et al., 1977; Tardiff & Sweillam, 1982), to be refractory to pharmacological treatment, to have concomitant neurological impairment (Barber et al., 1988; Krakowski et al., 1988), and to have had an earlier onset of schizophrenia (Krakowski et al., 1988).

Outside the hospital, the paranoid subtype again accounts for a lopsided share of the violence. This violence usually follows "logically" from the delusion, is generally directed at a significant individual in the patient's life, is often preceded by longstanding resentment, and can be quite deadly (Virkkunen, 1974). The violent acts of the nonparanoid but psychotically disorganized patient, on the other hand, are usually less targeted, less premeditated, and often less deadly (Krakowski, Volavka, & Brizer, 1986).

The core distillation from these various clinical observations is that the violence of schizophrenia is a direct consequence of psychotic derangement. It does not stem from a sense of hopeless despair, as appears to be the case with schizophrenic suicides. Neither is it the manipulative tool of the prototypic violent sociopath. Rather, it appears to be an integral part—though certainly not an obligatory one—of the schizophrenic process.

CLINICAL MANAGEMENT

Aggression toward Self

The cumulative clinical experience with self-destructive behavior in schizophrenics implies that it is common, unpredictable, and unaffected by advances in medical technologies. Even with all the changes in conceptualization, diagnosis, and treatment, the rate of completed suicide has remained constant at about 10% over the last 80 years (Carone et al., 1991; Rennie, 1939). While sobering, these data also suggest that such a constant process, like earthquakes in California, can be anticipated—even if not actually predicted—and prepared for.

The drama and finality of the suicidal act obscures the complexity and multiplicity of factors that go into the "decision" to take one's life. Any single intervention, even if consistently and uniformly applied, would be expected to have little impact on the overall behavior of the schizophrenic group. A systems approach, however, that recognizes the multifactorial nature of the act and at once addresses the biological, psychological, and sociological deficits of these patients could decrease the forces that favor the completed suicide.

Because depression appears to be a common antecedent of suicide, efforts should be made to diagnose and correct it, particularly in the young male patient. Depressive symptoms may occur as a core manifestation of the illness, as in schizoaffective disorder; as an undesirable consequence of neuroleptic treatment, as in akinesia (Klein & Davis, 1969; Rifkin, Quitkin, & Klein, 1975; Van Putten & May, 1978); or as a symptom complex that manifests after the acute psychosis has remitted, that is, the so-called postpsychotic depression (Bowers & Astrachan, 1967; Docherty, Van Kammen, Siris, & Marder, 1978; Donlon & Blacker, 1973; Johnson, 1981; MacKinnon, 1977; McGlashan & Carpenter, 1976; Rada & Donlon, 1975; Roth, 1970; Semrad, 1966). This latter condition, which seems most correlated with suicide, always warrants close attention; when unremitting, it requires pharmacological intervention. Tricyclic (or atypical) antidepressants (TCA) should be added to the neuroleptic and advanced to the usual antidepressant levels after optimizing the neuroleptic treatment and ruling out the possibility that the observed depressive syndrome is not neuroleptic-induced akinesia. Care should be taken with markedly agitated patients because there is some suggestion that TCAs may exacerbate the underlying psychosis in these individuals (Siris, Van Kammen, & Docherty, 1978). Patients on such combined therapy must be observed closely for the development of toxic adverse reactions, since competitive metabolism can increase the blood levels of both agents.

Temporally, most suicides occur around the time of hospital discharge (Cohen et al., 1964; Farberow et al., 1961; Warnes, 1968; Yarden, 1974) and these patients have fewer family supports (Drake et al., 1985). These demographics suggest that the transition back to the community should be a gradual one and that patient and family education should be an integral part of discharge planning—particularly early in the course of the illness. The focus of such education should be on the nature of the illness, the avoidance of stress, the importance of medications in reducing relapse, and the development of realistic family and patient expectations. Vocational rehabilitation should not be instituted until the psychotic disorganization has adequately remitted; however, its early introduction may offset the hopeless despair that frequently precedes suicide (Farberow et al., 1961; Warnes, 1968).

All suicide attempts should be taken seriously by the clinician and efforts made to comprehend the milieu that bred the aberrant behavior. The approach to the patient depends on whether the attempt was a consequence of psychotic disorganization, a despairing reaction to perceived hopelessness, or a dysfunctional attempt to manipulate or communicate with the social environment. Treatment would then target the underlying cause of the behavior—the psychosis, depression, or disordered communication/coping style.

Aggression toward Others

The treatment of other-directed violence in the schizophrenic patient is, in essence, the treatment of schizophrenia itself. If the perceptual disturbance is controlled, the violence will usually abate. For the majority (circa 70%) of patients, this will mean treatment with conventional neuroleptics alone. These medications do not, however, work quickly and may not exert any significant effects for several weeks. The time immediately after hospital admission is therefore a highly volatile one in which the majority of violent acts occur. Nonpharmacological approaches that can help minimize these events include high staff-to-patient ratios, avoidance of crowding, use of only experienced staff in the acute units, and a structured milieu that maximizes scheduled therapeutic interactions that encourage pro-social behaviors. Even the most experienced, prepared, and diligent staff will not prevent all violent acts, and staff denial of this violent potential may paradoxically encourage its emergence (Lion & Pasternak, 1973).

A wide range of neuroleptics has been elaborated in a number of different classes (e.g., phenothiazines, thioxanthenes, butyrophenones, etc.). None (except clozapine) has been shown to be clearly superior in the acutely psychotic patient. Such treatment equivalency conclusions, however, are based on group data and cannot be strictly applied to individual cases. It is possible, for instance, that a given patient may respond well to one drug and be unaffected or even worsened by another. Thus, historical documentation of positive or negative responsivity should be seriously weighed in the choice of a neuroleptic.

The equal-efficacy data apply to the primary effects of these agents, but not to the secondary or side effects. When neuroleptics are used to treat aggressive behavior acutely, it is often the sedative side effects of these drugs, and not the antipsychotic properties, that are being utilized. Hence, patients with chronic difficulties with aggression may be treated with chronic sedation, that is, chemical restraint. This places the patient at risk of developing many untoward side effects. Generally, when compared to the low-potency neuroleptics, the high-potency compounds like fluphenazine, haloperidol, and droperidol have less sedation, less anticholinergic effects, and fewer cardiovascular effects (e.g., orthostatic hypotension), but at a cost of producing more acute extrapyramidal side effects (e.g., akathisia, drug-induced parkinsonism, and dystonia). The choice then of which neuroleptic to use is generally made by considering which particular constellation of side effects would be least harmful or most beneficial to a given patient.

Despite massive clinical and research experience with these agents compiled over the last three and a half decades, the question of appropriate dosage has not yet been clearly and completely answered. Some studies have reported an inverse correlation between violent episodes and neuroleptic drug level (Yesavage, 1982). There seems to be a therapeutic window of efficacy for neuroleptic medication, however, because patients treated with haloperidol at doses exceeding 20 mg per day demonstrated more violent behavior than patients treated with lower doses of this medication, as well as patients treated with a low-potency neuroleptic—clozapine (Herrera, Sramek, Costa, Roy, Heh, & Nguyen, 1988). These and other data (see Baldessarini, Cohen, & Teicher, 1988, for a comprehensive review) indicate that a curvilinear relationship exists between dose and response; that is, low doses (less than 250 mg of chlorpromazine equivalents) lead to suboptimal clinical response, midrange doses (400–1,200 mg) result in the maximum drug-mediated response, and high doses (over 1,200 mg) are associated with some falloff in positive clinical effect. This high-end degradation in response may be secondary to an intervening neurotoxicity (e.g., akathisia) (Diamond, 1985; Keepers, Clappison, & Casey, 1983; Marder, Van Putten, Mintz, McKenzie, Labell, Faltico, & May, 1984; Simpson, Varga, & Haber, 1976; Teicher & Baldessarini, 1985) that in turn leads to psychotic worsening, violent behavior (Herrera et al., 1988), or noncompliance (Quitkin, Rifkin, & Klein, 1975; Van Putten, Marder, May, Poland, & O'Brien, 1985).

In the patient who remains agitated, psychotic, and potentially (or actually) violent in spite of apparently adequate neuroleptic treatment (i.e., appropriate doses for about 4 weeks) alternate pharmacological methods should be attempted. The most common clinical choice for the treatment-unresponsive patient is high-dose neuroleptic therapy. The literature has a number of anecdotal (Fouks, 1967) and controlled reports that support the use of very large doses (up to 60,000 mg per day of chlorpromazine equivalents) in a treatment-resistant population. However, a study by Quitkin et al. (1975) blindly compared two fixed doses of fluphenazine (1,200 mg vs. 30 mg per day) in a nonchronic but treatment-resistant group. The outcome results favored the standard dose above the "megadose." Thus, while experience would support a high-dose trial for the treatment-resistant patient, it would also predict little benefit of such an approach.

Lithium has been used for over two decades to effectively treat the symptoms of bipolar illness. When combined with neuroleptics it has also been reported to benefit patients with excited schizoaffective illness (Biederman, Lerner, & Belmaker, 1979) and schizophreniform illness (Hirschowitz, Casper, & Garver, 1980). Small, Kellams, Milstein, and Moore (1975), showed that combining lithium and neuroleptics in a chronically hospitalized and relatively treatment-refractory population somewhat reduced symptomatology. It therefore seems reasonable to try lithium in the neuroleptic-refractory patient, but, as with the high dose, little optimism is warranted.

Propranolol has been suggested as an additional treatment since Atsmon, Blum, Wijsenbeek, Maoz, Steiner, and Ziegelman (1971) anecdotally reported that adjunctive high-dose propranolol positively influenced acute schizophrenia. Subsequently some studies (Lindstrom & Persson, 1980; Pugh, Steinert, & Priest, 1983; Sheppard, 1979; Yorkston, Zaki, Pitcher, Gruzelier, Hollander, & Sergeant, 1977), but not all (Myers, Campbell, Cocks, Flowerdew, & Muir, 1981), have reported improvement with the addition of propranolol (400–2,000 mg per day) to standard neuroleptic regimens. These results hint that high-dose propranolol might be a useful adjunctive agent, but they do little to guide the clinician in the choice of a target dose. A dose of 1,000 mg is probably a reasonable (Rifkin & Siris, 1987) middle-ground choice, but support for even higher doses (up to 2,000 mg) can be found (Lindstrom & Persson, 1980). Because propranolol, like the antidepressants, elevates neuroleptic (and metabolite) levels (Kahn, Schultz, Perel, & Alexander, 1990; Peet, Bethell, Coates, Khamnee, Hall, Cooper, King, & Yates, 1981), care should be exercised in monitoring for an increase in neuroleptic-induced neurotoxic or endocrinologic side effects.

Anticonvulsant medication has been used to treat schizophrenics with aggressive behavior based on the theory that aggressive behavior is caused by "kindling" phenomenon that may occur in limbic structures (Neppe, 1988). When used alone, carbamazepine (the most frequently used anticonvulsant in schizophrenic individuals) has little to recommend it for stable but refractory schizophrenics. There is even some suggestion that it may destabilize some of these patients (Sramek, Herrera, Costa, Heh, Tran-Johnson, & Simpson, 1988). However, there is some evidence from controlled studies that indicates that when combined with neuroleptics, carbamazepine may have benefits over neuroleptics alone in "excited psychoses," including schizophrenia (Klein, Bental, Lerer, & Belmaker, 1984). Additional anecdotal reports and uncontrolled studies have indicated that it may be of adjunctive utility in schizophrenics with evidence of temporal lobe EEG abnormalities (Neppe, 1983; Hakola, & Laulumaa, 1982) or violence (Luchins, 1984). Other studies, however, have found no benefit or even some worsening in nonexcited but refractory schizophrenics (Kidron, Averbuch, Klein, & Belmaker, 1985). Kidron and colleagues hypothesized that the measured reduction in neuroleptic plasma levels caused by the addition of carbamazepine (presumably through induction of hepatic metabolic enzymes) caused this clinical worsening. In those patients who do improve, it is possible that this decrease in neuroleptic levels may result in a decrease in neuroleptic side effects, for example, akathisia, which may itself have led to the aggressive behavior (Van Putten, 1975; Van Putten et al., 1974). In spite of the uncertainty with carbamazepine, it is still probably reasonable to try it (at typical anticonvulsant levels) in refractory subjects with either known EEG abnormalities or violent clinical manifestations. In addition to the usual hematologic, hepatic, and dermatologic concerns one has when using carbamezepine, one must also be alert to the possibility that it may necessitate increasing the neuroleptic dose.

Although the literature on the use of benzodiazepines in schizophrenia is divided (Arana, Ornstein, Kanter, Friedman, Greenblatt, & Shader, 1986; Keats & Mukherjee, 1988; Salzman, Green, Rodriguez-Villa, & Jaskiw, 1986), it is heavily skewed to the left (i.e., negative or null effect). Some investigators have been mildly encouraging (Kellner, Wilson, Muldawer, & Pathak, 1975; Lingjaerde, 1982; Jimerson, Van Kammen, Post, Docherty, & Bunney, 1982), but others have been frankly negative (Gundlach, Engelhardt, Hankoff, Paley, Rudorfer, & Bird, 1966; Hollister, Bennett, Kimbell, Savage, & Overall, 1963; Karson, Weinberger, Llewellyn, & Wyatt, 1982). Karson and colleagues not only reported a lack of efficacy for adjunctive clonazepam, but described the new development of violent behaviors in 4 of 13 patients during treatment. Thus, benzodiazepines should probably be reserved for those cases that fail all other adjunctive modalities or in whom clear anxious symptoms predominate. There may be some benefit to the use of these highly sedating agents during acutely agitated moments, but their effects are somewhat unpredictable.

The demonstration that clozapine has superior antipsychotic efficacy and fewer neurologic side effects (Kane, Honigfeld, Singer, Meltzer, & the Clozaril Collaborative Study Group, 1988) suggests that this agent may be the treatment of choice for unresponsive and violence-prone schizophrenics. Its expense and hematologic side effect profile (it causes granulocytopenia in 1% to 2%) will, however, make it unusable in many patients. The existence of an atypical agent like clozapine has forever altered the conventional wisdom that held all neuroleptics to be equally efficacious and uniformly neurotoxic. The pharmacological legacy of clozapine promises to provide clinicians with biological therapies that are at once safe, effective, and easy to administer.

The acute management of a violent patient may require behavioral techniques in addition to pharmacological management. Seclusion and restraint are frequently employed, but behavioral treatment also involves positive reinforcement for nonaggressive behavior. The basic goal of behavioral treatment is to change an unstructured hospital environment (which may foster violent behavior among patients) into a structured program that will provide therapeutic activities aimed at decreasing violent behavior and increasing prosocial behavior (Tardiff, 1989). Components of a behavioral approach to the aggressive schizophrenic include withdrawal of positive reinforcement for and ignoring undesirable behavior. Social skills training may also be beneficial in that it may help teach disturbed, violent patients to use social skills such as solicitation, persuasion, and negotiation rather than aggression to obtain their needs.

LONGITUDINAL PERSPECTIVES

Only half of schizophrenics who suicide (5%) will have heralded their death with a prior suicide attempt. Although 40% of all schizophrenics will attempt suicide, only about 12.5% of this parasuicide group will ultimately die by suicide. Since the risk of suicide in the non-parasuicide schizophrenic is about 8.3% (i.e., 5 out of 60), a history of parasuicide carries a relative risk of suicide of only 1.5. It is, therefore, of little predictive utility in judging which patients will die by suicide. Parasuicides are recidivistic—about 75% will repeat a suicide attempt. A history of parasuicide in a young patient (i.e., less than age 30), therefore, carries a relative risk for a future attempt of about 2. This relative risk for future suicide attempts—compared to patients with no history of parasuicide—rises dramatically with age. About 80% of first attempts occur before age 30, and virtually all will have taken place by age 40 (Nyman & Jonsson, 1986). The age at which subsequent attempts are made seems to have no clear falloff (Wilkinson & Bacon, 1984). Thus, a patient without a history of parasuicide who is above age 35 is very unlikely to demonstrate self-destructive tendencies in the future. A patient with such a history, however, continues to be at risk into old age.

Violence directed at others, like suicide, tends to be manifest in young males, and like parasuicide, past violence predicts future violence. The paranoid schizophrenic patient with little conceptual disorganization and with a crystallized delusional system is at greatest risk for inflicting deadly violence. The object of such violence is usually a relative or friend, and the hostility that antedates the actual violence is generally longstanding (Virkkunen, 1974). The degree to which the psychotic symptoms respond to treatment (usually pharmacological) and the compliance of the patient with this treatment will determine the recidivism of the violence. Those patients who respond well to treatment and who comply with successful pharmacological regimens will likely remain violence-free in the future, even if they have a violent past. The violent paranoid patient who is either treatment-unresponsive or noncompliant, though, will likely commit violent acts into old age.

The treatment-resistant, nonparanoid patient is also likely to continue to demonstrate violence. This is particularly true if the illness is confounded by neurological impairment or mental retardation. The acts themselves, however, will generally be of a minor nature. There is no clear evidence suggesting that these acts become more dangerous as the subject ages. Indeed, if there is an intervening dementing illness in the senescence, the violent acts will likely become less dangerous still (Krakowski et al., 1986).

CASE ILLUSTRATION

Mr L. was a 21-year-old single, white male when he originally presented for psychiatric evaluation. Pertinent symptoms at that time included constant, loud, third-person auditory hallucinations, marked conceptual disorganization, profound agitation, and a complex and difficult-to-follow delusional system that involved ideas of demonic possession. He was, during that first hospitalization, given the diagnosis of acute undifferentiated schizophrenia (the symptoms had been present for over 8 months by his family's account). He was initially treated with haloperidol (a high-potency neuroleptic), but this had little effect on his psychotic symptoms. He was frequently so disruptive and agitated that locked seclusion and leather restraints were necessary to control him. His behavior eventually improved somewhat on higher medication doses, but he remained delusional, hallucinating, and moderately disruptive even at the time of discharge.

During the next several years, he required frequent rehospitalization, continued to be relatively unresponsive to a wide range of conventional neuroleptics and adjunctive treatments (e.g., propranolol, carbamazepine, benzodiazepines, lithium, etc.), and was chronically disruptive and verbally threatening. Three years after his original diagnosis, he enucleated himself bilaterally in response to what he said was a demon's command that he "pluck his eyes out." Following this dramatic event his psychiatric condition was unchanged, but his care was markedly complicated by his blind status.

One year later he was begun on the atypical neuroleptic clozapine. Although he had some side effects (drooling, weight gain, tachycardia, and constipation), he did have a clear diminution in his psychotic symptoms, threatening behavior, and subjective dysphoria. After 4 years on this agent alone, he still has the residual symptoms of mild, nondisturbing hallucinations and idiosyncratic notions of spirits controlling the world. He is no longer threatening, disruptive, or tortured by his symptoms and has remained out of the hospital during this time.

This case underscores the tenet that improvement in violent tendencies follows improvement in psychotic symptoms. It further indicates the potential utility of clozapine in violent patients who fail to respond to conventional treatment.

SUMMARY

The problem of self and other-directed violence is common and recurrent in the schizophrenic patient. Few factors are of help in predicting where and when such violence will emerge. In general, though, the young, male patient with a relatively good premorbid history, a tendency toward depressive reactions, and a refractory course is at greatest risk for suicide during the first 10 years of illness. Prevention strategies in such cases should focus on the assiduous elimination of remediable neuroleptic-induced side effects; effective treatment of any underlying depression; and the design of an outpatient program that is comprehensive, interactive, and stresses skills training and vocational rehabilitation when appropriate.

Other-directed violence is also more of a concern in the young male patient. This violence usually occurs in the context of significant psychotic symptoms, and in the paranoid individual it follows logically from the delusional misinterpretations. It is only as treatable as the underlying psychotic symptoms; when the primary symptoms are unresponsive, the violence tends to recur. In the nonparanoid individual, aggression toward others also occurs in proportion to the degree of psychotic disorganization. Unlike the paranoid individual, the violence of the disorganized schizophrenic tends to be undirected, senseless, and unpredictable. Treatment efforts should be directed toward the amelioration of the psychotic symptoms and treatable medication side effects. Pharmacologically this includes a variety of adjunctive strategies as well as a trial of newer atypical agents. Behaviorally, a well-staffed, controlled, highly structured, and predictable environment that promotes prosocial behaviors can be of assistance in modifying all but the most recalcitrant violent offenders.

REFERENCES

Addad, M., Benezech, M., Bourgeois, M., & Yesavage, J. (1981). Criminal acts among schizophrenics in French mental hospitals. *Journal of Nervous and Mental Disease*, *169*, 289–293.

Arana, G. W., Ornstein, M. L., Kanter, F., Friedman, H. L., Greenblatt, D. J., & Shader, R. I. (1986). The use of benzodiazepines for psychotic disorders: A literature review and preliminary clinical findings. *Psychopharmacology Bulletin*, *22*, 77–87.

Atsmon, A., Blum, I., Wijsenbeek, H., Maoz, B., Steiner, M., & Ziegelman, G. (1971). Short-term effects of adrenergic-blocking agents in a small group of psychotic patients: Preliminary clinical observations. *Psychiatria, Neurologia, Neurochirurgia, 74*, 251–258.

Baldessarini, R. J., Cohen, B. M., & Teicher, M. H. (1988). Significance of neuroleptic dose and plasma level in the pharmacological treatment of psychoses. *Archives of General Psychiatry, 45*, 79–90.

Barber, J. W., Hundley, P., Kellogg, E., Glick, J. L., Godleski, L., Kerler, R., & Vieweg, W. V. R. (1988). Clinical and demographic characteristics of 15 patients with repetitively assaultive behavior. *Psychiatric Quarterly, 59*, 213–224.

Beisser, A. R., & Blanchette, J. E. (1961). A study of suicides in a mental hospital. *Diseases of the Nervous System, 22*, 365–369.

Benezech, M., Bourgeois, M., & Yesavage, J. (1980). Violence in the mentally ill: A study of 547 patients at a French hospital for the criminally insane. *Journal of Nervous and Mental Disease, 168*, 698–700.

Biederman, J., Lerner, Y., & Belmaker, R. H. (1979). Combination of lithium carbonate and haloperidol in schizo-affective disorder: A controlled study. *Archives of General Psychiatry, 36*, 327–333.

Blackburn, R. (1968). Emotionality, extraversion and aggression in paranoid and nonparanoid schizophrenic offenders. *British Journal of Psychiatry, 114*, 1301–1302.

Bowers, M. B., & Astrachan, B. M. (1967). Depression in acute schizophrenic psychosis. *American Journal of Psychiatry, 123*, 976–979.

Breier, A., & Astrachan, B. M. (1984). Characterization of schizophrenic patients who commit suicide. *American Journal of Psychiatry, 141*, 206–209.

Campbell, R., & Simpson, G. M. (1986). Alternative approaches in the treatment of psychotic agitation. *Psychosomatics, 27*, 23–26.

Carone, B. J., Harrow, M., & Westermeyer, J. F. (1991). Posthospital course and outcome in schizophrenia. *Archives of General Psychiatry, 48*, 247–253.

Cheng, K. K., Leung, C. M., Lo, W. H., & Lam, T. H. (1990). Risk factors of suicide among schizophrenics. *Acta Psychiatrica Scandinavica, 81*, 220–224.

Cohen, S., Leonard, C. V., Farberow, N. L., & Shneidman, E. S. (1964). Tranquilizers and suicide in the schizophrenic patient. *Archives of General Psychiatry, 11*, 312–321.

Craig, T. J. (1982). Violence among psychiatric inpatients: An epidemiologic study of problems associated with violence among psychiatric inpatients. *American Journal of Psychiatry, 139*, 1262–1266.

Diamond, R. (1985). Drugs and the quality of life: The patient's point of view. *Journal of Clinical Psychiatry, 42*, 636–637.

Docherty, J. P., Van Kammen, D. P., Siris, S. G., & Marder, S. R. (1978). Stages of onset of schizophrenic psychosis. *American Journal of Psychiatry, 135*, 420–426.

Donlon, P. T., & Blacker, K. H. (1973). Stages of schizophrenia decompensation and reintegration. *Journal of Nervous and Mental Disease, 157*, 200–208.

Drake, R. E., Gates, C., Whitaker, A., & Cotton, P. G. (1985). Suicide among schizophrenics: A review. *Comprehensive Psychiatry, 26*, 90–100.

Drake, R. E., Gates, C., & Cotton, P. G. (1986). Suicide among schizophrenics: A comparison of attempters and completed suicides. *British Journal of Psychiatry, 149*, 784–787.

Dyck, R. J., Bland, R. C., Newman, S. C., & Orn, H. (1988). Suicide attempts and psychiatric disorders in Edmonton. *Acta Psychiatrica Scandinavica, 77* (Suppl. 338), 64–71.

Eichelmann, B. (1987). Neurochemical bases of aggressive behavior. *Psychiatric Annals, 17*, 371–374.

Farberow, N. L., Shneidman, E. S., & Leonard, C. V. (1961). Suicide among schizophrenic mental hospital patients. In N. L. Farberow & E. S. Shneidman (Eds.), *The cry for help* (pp. 78–109). New York/Toronto/London: McGraw-Hill Books.

Fouks, L. (1967). Originalite et specificite de la fluphenazine. In *Proceedings of the Fifth International Congress of Neuropsychopharmacology* (International Congress Series #192, pp. 1128–1134). Amsterdam: Exerpta Medica Foundation.

Greenfield, T. K., McNiel, D. E., & Binder, R. L. (1989). Violent behavior and length of psychiatric hospitalization. *Hospital and Community Psychiatry, 40*, 809–814.

Greilsheimer, H., & Groves, J. E. (1979). Male genital self-mutilation. *Archives of General Psychiatry, 36*, 441–446.

Gundlach, R., Engelhardt, D. M., Hankoff, L., Paley, H., Rudorfer, L., & Bird, E. (1966). A double-blind outpatient study of diazepam (Valium) and placebo. *Psychopharmacology, 9*, 81–92.

Hakola, H. P. A., & Laulumaa, V. A. (1982, June 12). Carbamazepine in treatment of violent schizophrenics. *Lancet*, p. 1358.

Herrera, J. N., Sramek, J. J., Costa, J. F., Roy, S., Heh, C. W., & Nguyen, B. N. (1988). High potency neuroleptics and violence in schizophrenia. *Journal of Nervous and Mental Disease, 176*, 558–561.

Hirschowitz, J., Casper, R., & Garver, D. L. (1980). Lithium response in good prognosis schizophrenia. *American Journal of Psychiatry*, *137*, 916–920.

Hollister, L. E., Bennett, J. L., Kimbell, I., Jr., Savage, C., & Overall, J. E. (1963). Diazepam in newly admitted schizophrenics. *Diseases of the Nervous System*, *24*, 746–750.

Hussar, A. E. (1962). Effect of tranquilizers on medical morbidity and mortality in a mental hospital. *Journal of the American Medical Association*, *179*, 682–686.

Jimerson, D. C., Van Kammen, D. P., Post, R. M., Docherty, J. P., & Bunney, W. E., Jr. (1982). Diazepam in schizophrenia: Preliminary double-blind trial. *American Journal of Psychiatry*, *139*, 489–491.

Johnson, D. A. W. (1981). Studies of depressive symptoms in schizophrenia: I. The prevalence of depression and its possible causes. *British Journal of Psychiatry*, *139*, 89–101.

Kahn, E. M., Schulz, S. C., Perel, J. M., & Alexander, J. E. (1990). Change in haloperidol level due to carbamazepine: A complicating factor in combined medication for schizophrenia. *Journal of Clinical Psychopharmacology*, *10*, 54–57.

Kane, J., Honigfeld, G., Singer, J., Meltzer, H., & the Clozaril Collaborative Study Group. (1988). Clozapine for the treatment-resistant schizophrenic: A double-blind comparison with chlorpromazine. *Archives of General Psychiatry*, *45*, 789–796.

Kaplan, H. I., & Sadock, B. J. (Eds.). (1989). *Comprehensive textbook of psychiatry* (Vol. 5). Baltimore: Williams & Wilkins.

Karson, C., & Bigelow, L. B. (1987). Violent behavior in schizophrenic inpatients. *Journal of Nervous and Mental Disease*, *175*, 161–164.

Karson, C. N., Weinberger, D. R., Llewellyn, B., & Wyatt, R. J. (1982). Clonazepam treatment of chronic schizophrenia: Negative results in a double-blind, placebo-controlled trial. *American Journal of Psychiatry*, *139*, 1627–1628.

Keats, M. M., & Mukherjee, S. (1988). Antiaggressive effect of adjunctive clonazepam in schizophrenia—Associated with seizure disorder. *Journal of Clinical Psychiatry*, *49*, 117–118.

Keepers, G. A., Clappison, V. J., & Casey, D. E. (1983). Initial anticholinergic prophylaxis for neuroleptic-induced extrapyramidal syndromes. *Archives of General Psychiatry*, *40*, 1113–1117.

Kellner, R., Wilson, R. M., Muldawer, M. D., & Pathak, D. (1975). Anxiety in schizophrenia: Responses to chlordiazepoxide in an intensive design study. *Archives of General Psychiatry*, *32*, 1246–1254.

Kidron, R., Averbuch, I., Klein, E., & Belmaker, R. H. (1985). Carbamazepine-induced reduction of blood levels of haloperidol in chronic schizophrenia. *Biological Psychiatry*, *20*, 219–222.

Klein, D. F., & Davis, J. M. (1969). *Diagnosis and drug treatment of psychiatric disorders*. Baltimore: Williams & Wilkins.

Klein, E., Bental, E., Lerer, B., & Belmaker, R. H. (1984). Carbamazepine and haloperidol *v* placebo and haloperidol in excited psychoses: A controlled study. *Archives of General Psychiatry*, *41*, 165–170.

Krakowski, M., Volavka, J., & Brizer, D. (1986). Psychopathology and violence: A review of literature. *Comprehensive Psychiatry*, *27*, 131–148.

Krakowski, M., Convit, A., & Volavka, J. (1988). Patterns of inpatient assaultiveness: Effect of neurological impairment and deviant family environment on response to treatment. *Neuropsychiatry, Neuropsychology, and Behavioral Neurology*, *1*, 21–29.

Lanzkron, J. (1963). Murder and insanity: A survey. *American Journal of Psychiatry*, *119*, 754–758.

Lemus, C. Z., Lieberman, J. A., Johns, C. A., Pollack, S., Bookstein, P., & Cooper, T. B. (1990). CSF 5-hydroxy-indoleacetic acid levels and suicide attempts in schizophrenia. *Biological Psychiatry*, *27*, 926–929.

Levy, A. B., Kurtz, N., & Kling, A. S. (1984). Association between cerebral ventricular enlargement and suicide attempts in chronic schizophrenia. *American Journal of Psychiatry*, *141*, 438–439.

Levy, S., & Southcombe, R. H. (1953). Suicide in a state hospital for the mentally ill. *Journal of Nervous and Mental Disease*, *117*, 504–514.

Lindstrom, L. H., & Persson, E. (1980). Propranolol in chronic schizophrenia: A controlled study in neuroleptic-treated patients. *British Journal of Psychiatry*, *137*, 126–130.

Lingjaerde, O. (1982). Effect of the benzodiazepine derivative estazolam in patients with auditory hallucinations: A multicentre double-blind, cross-over study. *Acta Psychiatrica Scandinavica*, *65*, 339–354.

Lion, J. R., & Pasternak, S. A. (1973). Countertransference reactions to violent patients. *American Journal of Psychiatry*, *130*, 207–210.

Luchins, D. J. (1984). Carbamazepine in violent non-epileptic schizophrenics. *Psychopharmacology Bulletin*, *20* 569–571.

MacKinnon, B. L. (1977). Postpsychotic depression and the need for personal significance. *American Journal of Psychiatry*, *134*, 427–429.

Madden, D. J., Lion, J. R., & Penna, M. W. (1976). Assaults on psychiatrists by patients. *American Journal of Psychiatry*, *133*, 422–425.

Manscheck, T. C., & Ames, D. (1984). Neurologic features and psychopathology in schizophrenic disorders. *Biological Psychiatry*, *19*, 703–719.

Marder, S. R., Van Putten, T., Mintz, J., McKenzie, J., Labell, M., Faltico, G., & May, P. R. A. (1984). Costs and benefits of two doses of fluphenazine. *Archives of General Psychiatry*, *41*, 1025–1029.

McGlashan, T. H., & Carpenter, W. T. (1976). An investigation of the postpsychotic depressive syndrome. *American Journal of Psychiatry*, *133*, 14–19.

Myers, D. H., Campbell, P. L., Cocks, N. M., Flowerdew, J. A., & Muir, A. (1981). A trial of propranolol in chronic schizophrenia. *British Journal of Psychiatry*, *139*, 118–121.

Myers, K. M., & Dunner, D. L. (1984). Self and other directed violence on a closed acute-care ward. *Psychiatric Quarterly*, *56*, 178–188.

Neppe, V. M. (1983). Carbamazepine as adjunctive therapy in nonepileptic chronic inpatients with EEG temporal lobe abnormalities. *Journal of Clinical Psychiatry*, *44*, 326–331.

Neppe, V. M. (1988). Carbamazepine in nonresponsive psychosis. *Journal of Clinical Psychiatry*, *49*, 22–28.

Ninan, P. T., Van Kammen, D. P., Scheinin, M., Linnoila, M., Bunney, W. E., Jr., & Goodwin, F. K. (1984). CSF 5-hydroxyindoleacetic acid levels in suicidal schizophrenic patients. *American Journal of Psychiatry*, *141*, 566–569.

Nyman, A. K., & Jonsson, H. (1986). Patterns of self-destructive behaviour in schizophrenia. *Acta Psychiatrica Scandinavica*, *73*, 252–262.

Oltman, J. E., & Friedman, S. (1941). A psychiatric study of one hundred criminals—with particular reference to the psychological determinants of crime. *Journal of Nervous and Mental Disease*, *93*, 16–41.

Pearson, M., Wilmot, E., & Padi, M. (1986). A study of violent behavior among in-patients in a psychiatric hospital. *British Journal of Psychiatry*, *149*, 232–235.

Peet, M., Bethell, M. S., Coates, A., Khamnee, A. K., Hall, P., Cooper, S. J., King, D. J., & Yates, R. A. (1981). Propranolol in schizophrenia. I. Comparison of propranolol, chlorpromazine and placebo. *British Journal of Psychiatry*, *139*, 105–111.

Piacente, G. J. (1986). Aggression. *Neuropsychiatry*, *9*, 329–339.

Planansky, K., & Johnston, R. (1971). Occurrence and characteristics of suicidal preoccupation and acts in schizophrenia. *Acta Psychiatrica Scandinavica*, *47*, 473–483.

Planansky, K., & Johnston, R. (1977). Homicidal aggression in schizophrenic men. *Acta Psychiatrica Scandinavica*, *55*, 65–73.

Pollock, H. M. (1938). Is the paroled patient a menace to the community? *The Psychiatric Quarterly*, *12*, 236–244.

Pugh, C. R., Steinert, J., & Priest, R. G. (1983). Propranolol in schizophrenia: A double blind, placebo controlled trial of propranolol as an adjunct to neuroleptic medication. *British Journal of Psychiatry*, *143*, 151–155.

Quitkin, F., Rifkin, A., & Klein, D. F. (1975). Very high dosage vs. standard dosage fluphenazine in schizophrenia: Double-blind study of nonchronic treatment-refractory patients. *Archives of General Psychiatry*, *32*, 1276–1281.

Quitkin, F., Rifkin, A., & Klein, D. F. (1976). Neurologic soft signs in schizophrenia and character disorders. *Archives of General Psychiatry*, *33*, 845–853.

Rada, R. T., & Donlon, P. T. (1975). Depression and the acute schizophrenic process. *Psychosomatics*, *16*, 116–119.

Rappeport, J. R., & Lassen, G. (1965). Dangerousness—Arrest rate comparisons of discharged patients and the general population. *American Journal of Psychiatry*, *121*, 776–783.

Rennie, T. (1939). Follow-up study of five hundred patients with schizophrenia admitted to the hospital from 1913 to 1923. *Archives of Neurology*, *42*, 877–891.

Rifkin, A., & Siris, S. (1987). Drug treatment of acute schizophrenia. In H. Y. Meltzer (Ed.), *Psychopharmacology: The third generation of progress* (pp. 1095–1101). New York: Raven Press.

Rifkin, A., Quitkin, F., & Klein, D. F. (1975). Akinesia, a poorly recognized drug-induced extrapyramidal behavioral disorder. *Archives of General Psychiatry*, *32*, 672–674.

Robertson, G. (1988). Arrest patterns among mentally disordered offenders. *British Journal of Psychiatry*, *153*, 313–316.

Rollin, H. R. (1965). Unprosecuted mentally abnormal offenders. *British Medical Journal*, *1*, 831–835.

Rossi, A. M., Jacobs, M., Monteleone, M., Olsen, R., Surber, R. W., Winkler, E. L., & Wommack, A. (1986). Characteristics of psychiatric patients who engage in assaultive or other fear-inducing behaviors. *Journal of Nervous and Mental Disease*, *174*, 154–160.

Roth, S. (1970). The seemingly ubiquitous depression following acute schizophrenic episodes, a neglected area of clinical discussion. *American Journal of Psychiatry, 127*, 91–98.

Roy, A. (1982). Suicide in chronic schizophrenia. *British Journal of Psychiatry, 141*, 171–177.

Roy, A. (1986). Depression, attempted suicide, and suicide in patients with chronic schizophrenia. *Psychiatric Clinics of North America, 9*, 193–206.

Roy, A., Mazonson, A., & Pickar, D. (1984). Attempted suicide in chronic schizophrenia. *British Journal of Psychiatry, 144*, 303–306.

Roy, A., Ninan, P., Mazonson, A., Pickar, D., Van Kammen, D., Linnoila, M., & Paul, S. M. (1985). CSF monoamine metabolites in chronic schizophrenic patients who attempt suicide. *Psychological Medicine, 15*, 335–340.

Salama, A. A. (1988). Depression and suicide in schizophrenic patients. *Suicide and Life-Threatening Behavior, 18*, 379–384.

Salzman, C., Green, A. I., Rodriguez-Villa, F., & Jaskiw, G. I. (1986). Benzodiazepines combined with neuroleptics for management of severe disruptive behavior. *Psychosomatics, 27*, 17–21.

Semrad, E. V. (1966). Long-term therapy of schizophrenia. In E. L. Usdin (Ed.), *Psychoneuroses and schizophrenia* (pp. 155–156). Philadelphia: J. B. Lippincott.

Shader, R. I., Jackson, A. H., Harmatz, J. S., & Appelbaum, P. S. (1977). Patterns of violent behavior among schizophrenic inpatients. *Diseases of the Nervous System, 38*, 13–16.

Shaffer, J. W., Perlin, S., Schmidt, C. W., & Stephens, J. H. (1974). Prediction of suicide in schizophrenia. *Journal of Nervous and Mental Disease, 159*, 349–355.

Sheppard, G. P. (1979). High-dose propranolol in schizophrenia. *British Journal of Psychiatry, 134*, 470–476.

Silverman, D. (1943). Psychoses in criminals: A study of five hundred psychotic prisoners. *Journal of Criminal Psychopathology, 4*, 703–723.

Simpson, G. M., Varga, E., & Haber, E. J. (1976). Psychotic exacerbations produced by neuroleptics. *Diseases of the Nervous System, 37*, 367–369.

Siris, S. G., Van Kammen, D. P., & Docherty, J. P. (1978). Use of antidepressant drugs in schizophrenia. *Archives of General Psychiatry, 35*, 1368–1377.

Small, J. G., Kellams, J. J., Milstein, V., & Moore, J. (1975). Placebo-controlled study of lithium combined with neuroleptics in chronic schizophrenic patients. *American Journal of Psychiatry, 132*, 1315–1317.

Sramek, J., Herrera, J., Costa, J., Heh, C., Tran-Johnson, T., & Simpson, G. (1988). A carbamazepine trial in chronic, treatment-refractory schizophrenia. *American Journal of Psychiatry, 145*, 748–750.

Tardiff, K. (1984). Characteristics of assaultive patients in private hospitals. *American Journal of Psychiatry, 141*, 1232–1235.

Tardiff, K. (1989). *Concise guide to assessment and management of violent patients.* Washington, DC: APA Press.

Tardiff, K., & Sweillam, A. (1979). The relation of age to assaultive behavior in mental patients. *Hospital and Community Psychiatry, 30*, 709–711.

Tardiff, K., & Sweillam, A. (1980). Assault, suicide, and mental illness. *Archives of General Psychiatry, 37*, 164–169.

Tardiff, K., & Sweillam, A. (1982). Assaultive behavior among chronic inpatients. *American Journal of Psychiatry, 139*, 212–215.

Taylor, P. J., & Gunn, J. (1984, June 30). Violence and psychosis. I. Risk of violence among psychotic men. *British Medical Journal, 288* (Abstracts from *Clinical Research 1945–1952*).

Teicher, M. H., & Baldessarini, R. J. (1985). Selection of neuroleptic dosage. *Archives of General Psychiatry, 42*, 636–637.

Tennent, G., Loucas, K., Fenton, G., & Fenwick, P. (1974). Male admissions to Broadmoor Hospital. *British Journal of Psychiatry, 125*, 44–50.

Tucker, G. J., Campion, E. W., & Silberfarb, P. M. (1975). Sensorimotor functions and cognitive disturbance in psychiatric patients. *American Journal of Psychiatry, 132*, 17–21.

Van Praag, H. M. (1983, October 22). CSF 5-HIAA and suicide in nondepressed schizophrenics. *Lancet*, pp. 977–978.

Van Praag, H. M. (1986). (Auto) aggression and CSF 5-HIAA in depression and schizophrenia. *Psychopharmacology Bulletin, 22*, 669–673.

Van Putten, T. (1975). The many faces of akathisia. *Comprehensive Psychiatry, 16*, 43–47.

Van Putten, T., & May, P. R. A. (1978). Akinetic depression in schizophrenia. *Archives of General Psychiatry, 35*, 1101–1107.

Van Putten, T., Marder, S. R., May, P. R. A., Poland, R. E., & O'Brien, R. P. (1985). Plasma levels of haloperidol and clinical response. *Psychopharmacology Bulletin, 21*, 69–72.

Van Putten, T., Mutalipassi, L. R., & Malkin, M. D. (1974). Phenothiazine-induced decompensation. *Archives of General Psychiatry, 30* 102–105.

Virkkunen, M. (1974). Observations on violence in schizophrenia. *Acta Psychiatrica Scandinavica, 50,* 145–151.

Volavka, J., & Krakowski, M. (1989). Schizophrenia and violence. *Psychological Medicine, 19,* 559–562.

Warnes, H. (1968). Suicide in schizophrenics. *Disease of the Nervous System, 29,* 35–40.

Wilkinson, G., & Bacon, N. A. (1984). A clinical and epidemiological survey of parasuicide and suicide in Edinburgh schizophrenics. *Psychological Medicine, 14,* 899–912.

Winchel, R. M., & Stanley, M. (1991). Self-injurious behavior: A review of the behavior and biology of self-mutilation. *American Journal of Psychiatry, 148,* 306–317.

Winokur, G., & Tsuang, M. (1975). The Iowa 500: Suicide in mania, depression, and schizophrenia. *American Journal of Psychiatry, 132,* 650–651.

Wong, S. E., Woolsey, J. E., Innocent, A. J., & Liberman, R. P. (1988). Behavior treatment of violent psychiatric patients. *Psychiatric Clinics of North America, 11,* 569–580.

Yarden, P. E. (1974). Observations on suicide in chronic schizophrenics. *Comprehensive Psychiatry, 15,* 325–333.

Yesavage, J. A. (1982). Inpatient violence and the schizophrenic patient: An inverse correlation between danger-related events and neuroleptic levels. *Biological Psychiatry, 17,* 1331–1337.

Yesavage, J. A. (1983). Inpatient violence and the schizophrenic patient: A study of Brief Psychiatric Rating Scale scores and inpatient behavior. *Acta Psychiatrica Scandinavica, 67,* 353–357.

Yesavage, J. A., Werner, P. D., Becker, J., Holman, C., & Mills, M. (1981). Inpatient evaluation of aggression in psychiatric patients. *Journal of Nervous and Mental Disease, 169,* 299–302.

Yorkston, N. J., Zaki, S. A., Pitcher, D. R., Gruzelier, J. H., Hollander, D., & Sergeant, H. G. S. (1977, September 17). Propranolol as an adjunct to the treatment of schizophrenia. *Lancet,* pp. 575–578.

Zitrin, A., Hardesty, A. S., Burdock, E. I., & Drossman, A. K. (1976). Crime and violence among mental patients. *American Journal of Psychiatry, 133,* 142–149.

CHAPTER 14

Affective Disorders

Alec Roy

DESCRIPTION OF THE DISORDER

The diagnostic inclusion criteria for the major depressive episode in the *Diagnostic and Statistical Manual of Mental Disorders* (DSM-IV) (American Psychiatric Association, 1993) are listed below.

A. At least five of the following symptoms have been present during the same two-week period and represent a change from previous functioning; at least one of the symptoms is either (1) depressed mood or (2) loss of interest or pleasure.

    1. Depressed mood most of the day, nearly every day, as indicated by either subjective report (e.g., feels sad or empty) or observation made by others (e.g., appears tearful). Note: in children and adolescents, can be irritable mood.

    2. Markedly diminished interest or pleasure in all, or almost all activities most of the day, nearly every day (as indicated either by subjective account or observation made by others).

    3. Significant weight loss or weight gain when not dieting (e.g., more than 5% of body weight in a month), or decrease or increase in appetite nearly every day. Note: in children, consider failure to make expected weight gains.

    4. Insomnia or hypersomnia nearly every day.

    5. Psychomotor agitation or retardation nearly every day (observable by others, not merely subjective feelings or restlessness or being slowed down).

    6. Fatigue or loss of energy nearly every day.

    7. Feelings of worthlessness or excessive or inappropriate guilt (which may be delusional) nearly every day (not merely self-reproach or guilt about being sick).

ALEC ROY • Department of Psychiatry, University of Medicine and Dentistry, New Jersey Medical School, Newark, New Jersey 07103-2770.

Handbook of Aggressive and Destructive Behavior in Psychiatric Patients, edited by Michel Hersen, Robert T. Ammerman, and Lori A. Sisson. Plenum Press, New York, 1994.

8. Diminished ability to think or concentrate, or indecisiveness, nearly every day (either by subjective account or as observed by others).
9. Recurrent thoughts of death (not just fear of dying), recurrent suicidal ideation without a specific plan, or a suicide attempt or a specific plan for committing suicide.

B. The symptoms cause clinically significant distress or impairment in social, occupational, or other important areas of functioning.

C. Not due to the direct effects of substance (e.g., drugs of abuse, medication) or a general medical condition (e.g., hypothyroidism).

D. Not occurring within two months of the loss of a loved one (except if associated with marked functional impairment, morbid preoccupation with worthlessness, suicidal ideation, psychotic symptoms, or psychomotor retardation).

EPIDEMIOLOGY

Depression is the most common of all mental disorders. At any one time, about 5% of the population is suffering from a major depression. About 10% of the general population will experience a major depression at some time in their lifetime. Suicide accounts for at least 25,000 deaths each year in the United States. About 12 out of 100,000 people in the United States commit suicide each year—about one person every 20 minutes, one adolescent every 90 minutes, or approximately 73 people a day. The number one suicide site in the United States is the Golden Gate Bridge—over 900 people have jumped to their deaths since the bridge opened.

Mood disorder is the diagnosis most commonly associated with suicide. In the general population study of Robins, Murphy, and Wilkinson (1959), 45% of the suicide victims were diagnosed as having had primary depression, as were 30% in the study of Dorpat and Ripley (1960); 64% of Barraclough, Bunch, Nelson and Sainsbury's (1974) 100 suicide victims had primary depression, and 17% of them had bipolar disorder. The age-adjusted suicide rates for patients suffering from either major mood disorder or dysthymia have recently been estimated to be 400 and 190 per 100,000, respectively, for males, and 180 and 70 per 100,000 for female patients.

More male depressives commit suicide than females, and the chance of depressed persons killing themselves is increased by being single, separated, divorced, widowed, or recently bereaved. Depressives in the community who commit suicide tend to be middle-aged or elderly. For example, of the 60 mood-disordered suicide victims in the study of Robins et al., only 5 were under 40 years of age, and the onset of illness occurred after 40 years of age in 75% of the subjects. In Barraclough et al. (1974), the mean age of the 64 primary depressive suicide victims was 54 years. In the recent San Diego study of Rich et al. (1986), affective disorder diagnoses were found more among suicides aged 30 or over than among those under 30 years of age.

Follow-up studies of depressed patients have reported that about one in six (15%) died by committing suicide, though many of these studies were carried out before lithium prophylaxis was available (see Table 1). Goodwin and Jamison (1990) recently reviewed 30 studies of suicide among a total of 9,389 manic-depressive patients. They found a range of 9% to 60% of deaths due to suicide; the mean was 18.9%. They also reviewed 15 studies of attempted suicide among manic-depressive patients. They found that between 25% and 50% of such patients attempt suicide at least once. Female manic-depressives are more likely to attempt suicide than men. Goodwin and Jamison examined the eight studies that

TABLE 1. Death by Suicide in Affective Disorder

	Cases (no.)	Follow-up (years)	Dead (no.)	Suicide (no.)	Death due to suicide (%)
Langeluddecke, 1941	341	40	268	41	15.3
Slater, 1938	138	30	59	9	15.3
Lundquist, 1945	319	20	119	17	14.3
Schulz, 1949	2,004	5	492	66	13.6
Stendstedt, 1952	216	10	42	6	14.3
Pitts & Winokur, 1964	56	death	56	9	16.0

Note. From Sainsbury (1986). Adapted from Robins et al. (1959).

compared unipolar and bipolar disease among a total of 3,089 patients. There were no significant differences for rates of suicide or attempted suicide.

ETIOLOGY

Over the years there have been many theories about the etiology of affective disorders. The original catecholamine hypothesis was introduced a quarter of a century ago and posited a synaptic deficiency of the neurotransmitter norepinephrine. This hypothesis derived from observations that treatment of hypertension with reserpine, which depletes nerve terminals of catecholamines, led to depression in approximately 15% of patients, and that tricyclic medications that blocked neuronal norepinephrine re-uptake, and thus led to an increase in the synapse, were effective antidepressants. Conversely, mania was hypothesized to be due to an excess of norepinephrine. Since then, other catecholamine theories have been suggested involving the catecholamines serotonin and dopamine. A cholinergic theory has also been proposed and the amino acid gamma-aminobutyric acid (GABA) has been implicated in a GABAergic theory of depression. Most recently, investigations suggesting a depression-related hypersecretion of corticotropin-releasing hormone (CRH) from the hypothalamic paraventricular nucleus have led to the formulation of a CRH theory of depression.

Genetic theories about the etiology of depression have been supported by family, twin, and adoption studies. There have been reports of linkage to chromosomes 5 and 11 and the sex chromosome. There have also been other nonbiological theories. Life stress models have been suggested, and an excess of life events preceding the onset of depression is a well-replicated finding. Brown and Harris (1978) have described social vulnerability factors for depression including early parental loss, unemployment, a poor marital relationship, and having three or more children under the age of 14 years at home. Personality factors such as low self-esteem and high neuroticism have also been implicated in the etiology of depression.

AGGRESSION TOWARD SELF

Clinical Studies

A few studies have investigated increased suicide risk in mood-disorder patients. Barraclough and Pallis (1975) compared 64 community depressive suicide victims with 128 depressed patients referred to psychiatric services. The striking findings were that significantly more of the depressed suicide victims than the living depressives had made a previous suicide attempt (41% vs. 4%), and significantly more of them were unmarried and lived alone. This finding suggests that, among depressed patients, social isolation enhances a suicidal tendency. This is in accord with data showing that persons who commit suicide tend to be less well integrated in society.

When they examined psychiatric symptoms, Barraclough's group found that the rank order of the frequency of the 10 leading affective symptoms was the same in depressed suicide victims as in living depressives. The three symptoms that differed in the two groups were insomnia, self-neglect, and impaired memory. All three symptoms were significantly more common among depressives who had committed suicide than among the living ones.

NIMH Collaborative Study

The National Institute of Mental Health (NIMH) Collaborative Program on the Psychobiology of Depression involves 954 affective disorder patients. Over the first 8 years of follow-up, 32 (3%) of the 954 patients committed suicide. Thirteen (41%) of these 32 suicides occurred during the first year of follow-up (short-term suicides), and 19 (59%) after the first year (long-term suicides). Fawcett, Scheftner, Fogg, Clark, Young, Hedeker, and Gibbons (1990) examined prospective predictors of suicide in this sample. They found that nine clinical features were associated with suicide. Six of these—panic attacks, severe psychic anxiety, diminished concentration, global insomnia, moderate alcohol abuse, and severe loss of interest or pleasure (anhedonia)—were associated with suicide within 1 year; three others—severe hopelessness, suicidal ideation, and past attempts—were associated with suicide occurring after 1 year. They suggested that the anxiety symptoms related to short-term risk may be modifiable with medication or psychotherapeutic intervention.

Depressed Suicide Attempters

It is of interest to consider whether depressed patients who attempt suicide differ from depressed patients who do not attempt suicide. Bulik, Carpenter, Kupfer, and Frank (1990) compared 67 recurrent depressives who had attempted suicide with 163 recurrent depressives who had never attempted suicide. Significantly more of the attempters had bipolar II disorder (19% vs. 9%, $p < .05$), a history of alcohol abuse (20% vs. 7%, $p < .01$), and schizotypal features (17% vs. 7%, $p < .01$). At baseline assessment, depressives with a history of attempts were more severely depressed and had more current suicidal ideation, weight and appetite loss, insomnia, and irritability. Also, significantly more of the attempters were single, separated, or divorced (58% vs. 32%, $p < .005$).

Family History of Suicide

There are five main lines of evidence implicating genetic factors in suicide.

Clinical Studies

Pitts and Winokur (1964) found that among 748 consecutive inpatients 37 reported a possible or definite suicide in a first-degree relative (4.9%). In 25 of the 37 (68%) the diagnosis was an affective disorder; the statistical probability of this distribution occurring by chance was less than .02. When the probable diagnoses in the cases of the first-degree relatives who committed suicide were considered, in 24 of the 237 patient–relative pairings, both members had affective disorders. Roy (1983) reported that among 5,845 consecutive inpatients, 243 had a family history of suicide (4.2%). More than half (56.4%) of patients with a family history of suicide had a primary diagnosis of an affective disorder, and more than a third (34.6%) had recurrent affective disorder. A family history of suicide was found to significantly increase the risk for an attempt at suicide in various diagnostic subgroups of affective disorder patients (Table 2).

Recently, Linkowski, de Maertelaer, and Mendlewicz (1985) found that 123 of 713 depressed inpatients (17%) had a first- or second-degree relative who had committed suicide. A family history of suicide significantly increased the probability of a suicide attempt among depressed patients, especially the risk for a violent suicide attempt. Linkowski et al. concluded that "a positive family history for violent suicide should be considered as a strong predictor of active suicidal attempting behavior in major depressive illness" (p. 237). Approximately 10% of depressed patients have a family history of suicide (Roy, 1982, 1985a, 1985b, 1986).

Iowa-500 Study

The Iowa-500 study is a 30- to 40-year follow-up of 685 selected psychiatric patients and surgical controls hospitalized in Iowa City between 1933 and 1944. Follow-up revealed that there had been 30 suicides—29 among the 525 psychiatric patients (5.5%) and 1 among the 160 controls (0.6%). Tsuang (1983) followed up the first-degree relatives of the Iowa-500 study. Relatives of patients were found to have a risk of suicide almost 3 times greater than relatives of controls. When only deceased relatives were considered, relatives of psychiatric patients were found to have a risk of suicide almost 6 times greater than the risk among deceased relatives of controls. First-degree relatives of the 29 patients who committed suicide had a 4 times greater risk of committing suicide compared with relatives of patients who did not commit suicide. Among the deceased relatives, the suicide rate was 3 times greater.

When individual psychiatric diagnoses were examined, risk of suicide was significantly greater among first-degree relatives of depressed patients than it was among relatives of either manic or schizophrenic patients. When the relatives of patients who committed

TABLE 2. Attempted Suicides of Depressed Inpatients Admitted
to the Clarke Institute of Psychiatry between January, 1974 and June 1981

Diagnostic subgroup	Second- or first-degree relative suicided		No family history of suicide	
	Number (%) attempted	Number of attempts	Number (%) attempted	p
Unipolar	13/32 (41.6)	24	50/372 (13.4)	<.0001
Bipolar	22/58 (37.9)	48	56/405 (13.9)	<.0001
Depressive neurosis	26/47 (55.3)	45	221/715 (30.9)	<.0001

Note. From Roy (1983). Reproduced with permission of *Archives of General Psychiatry.*

suicide were compared, the suicide risk was equally high among the relatives of both depressed and manic patients.

Twin Studies

If the propensity to commit suicide is genetically transmitted, concordance for suicide should be found more frequently among identical than fraternal twins. Roy, Segal, Centerwall, and Robinette (1990) reported on 176 twin pairs in which one twin had committed suicide. In nine of these twin pairs, both twins had committed suicide. Seven of these nine pairs concordant for suicide were found among the 62 identical twin pairs, while two pairs concordant for suicide were found among the 114 fraternal twin pairs. This twin group difference for concordance for suicide (11.3% vs. 1.8%) is statistically significant.

Combining the 176 twin pairs of Roy et al. with the 149 twin pairs described by Haberlandt (1965, 1967), the 73 twin pairs described by Juel-Nielsen and Videbech (1970), and the one twin pair described by Zaw (1981) yields 399 twin pairs—129 identical twin pairs (17/129 [13.2%] concordant for suicide) and 270 fraternal twin pairs (2/270 [0.7%] concordant for suicide). These combined data demonstrate that identical twin pairs show significantly greater concordance for suicide, relative to fraternal twin pairs.

The Amish Study

Egeland and Sussex (1985) reported on the 26 suicide victims among the Old Order Amish of Lancaster County in southeastern Pennsylvania over the 100 years from 1880 to 1980. They found that 24 of 26 suicide victims met Research Diagnostic Criteria for a major affective disorder. Eight had bipolar I, 4 bipolar II, and 12 unipolar affective disorder. An additional case had minor depression. Furthermore, most of the suicide victims had a heavy family loading for affective disorders.

A second important finding was that almost three-quarters of the 26 suicide victims clustered in four family pedigrees, each of which contained a heavy loading for affective disorders and suicide. Interestingly, the converse was not true since there were other family pedigrees with heavy loadings for affective disorder but without suicides. Thus, a familial loading for affective disorders was not in itself a predictor for suicide.

The third finding was that only 6 of 26 suicide victims (23%) had received psychiatric treatment despite the fact that 24 of them had severe affective disorders. Egeland and Sussex (1985) concluded that

> our study replicates findings that indicate an increased suicidal risk for patients with a diagnosis of a major affective disorder and a strong family history of suicide. Bipolar and unipolar illness conveys a high risk as a diagnostic pattern in pedigrees. The number not receiving adequate treatment for manic-depressive illness (among the suicides) supports the common belief that intervention for these patients at risk is recommended. . . . it appears most warranted in those families in which there is a family history of suicide. The clustering of suicides in Amish pedigrees follows the distribution of affective illness in the kinship and suggests the role of inheritance. (p. 918)

Danish-American Adoption Studies

The strongest evidence for the role of genetic factors in suicide comes from the adoption studies carried out in Denmark by Schulsinger, Kety, Wender, and Rosenthal

(1979). The Psykologisk Institut has a register of the 5,483 adoptions that occurred in greater Copenhagen between 1924 and 1947. A screening of the registers of causes of death revealed that 57 of these adoptees eventually committed suicide. They were matched with adopted controls. Searches of the causes of death revealed that 12 of the 269 biological relatives of these 57 adopted suicides had themselves committed suicide, compared with only 2 of the 269 biological relatives of the 57 adopted controls. This is a highly significant difference for suicide between the two groups of relatives. None of the adopting relatives of either the suicide or control group had committed suicide. Because the suicides were largely independent of the presence of psychiatric disorder, Schulsinger et al. proposed that there may be a genetic predisposition for suicide independent of, or additive to, the major psychiatric disorders associated with suicide.

Wender, Kety, Rosenthal, Schulsinger, Ortmann, and Lunde (1986) went on to study another group of the Danish adoptees. These were the 71 adoptees identified by the psychiatric case register as having suffered from an affective disorder. They were matched with 71 control adoptees without affective disorder. The results of this study showed that, when contrasted with controls, significantly more of the adoptees with affective disorder had a relative who had committed suicide.

Of particular interest was the type of affective disorder suffered by the suicide victim. Adoptee suicide victims with the diagnosis of "affect reaction" had significantly more biological relatives who had committed suicide than controls. The diagnosis of affect reaction is used in Denmark to describe an individual who has affective symptoms accompanying a situational crisis—often an impulsive suicide attempt. These findings led Kety (1986) to suggest that a genetic factor in suicide may be an inability to control impulsive behavior, which has its effect independent of, or additive to, psychiatric disorder. Affective disorder, or environmental stress, may serve "as potentiating mechanisms which foster or trigger the impulsive behavior, directing it toward a suicidal outcome" (Kety, 1986, p. 44). Kety also noted that there has been much recent work on the biology of impulsivity and that disturbances in central serotonin systems have been described in relation to suicidal behavior.

Biological Studies

Serotonin

The first study of central serotonin systems in depressed patients exhibiting suicidal behaviors was by Asberg, Traskman, and Thoren (1976). They found a bimodal distribution of levels of the serotonin metabolite 5-hydroxyindoleacetic acid (5-HIAA) in the lumbar cerebrospinal fluid (CSF) of 68 depressed patients. Asberg et al. also noted that significantly more of the depressed patients in the low CSF 5-HIAA group had attempted suicide in comparison with those in the high CSF 5-HIAA group. This led to the proposal by Asberg et al. that low CSF 5-HIAA levels may be associated with suicidal behavior. Among depressed patients, Van Praag (1982) confirmed the observation that suicide attempts were found significantly more often among patients with low CSF 5-HIAA levels. Other studies of CSF 5-HIAA levels in relation to suicidal behavior (shown in Table 3) have been extensively reviewed elsewhere (Roy & Linnoila, 1988).

Over the years, postmortem brain studies of suicide victims have focused on the serotonin system. Some, but not all, neurochemical studies report modest decreases in

**TABLE 3.   Studies Examining the Relationships
between Suicidal Behavior and CSF Amine Metabolites**

Study	Diagnosis	CSF amine metabolites		
		5HIAA	HVA	MHPG
1. Vestergard et al., 1978	Unipolar depression	NS	—	—
	Bipolar depression			
2. Agren, 1980	Unipolar depression	↓	NS	↓
	Bipolar depression	NS	NS	NS
3. Leckman et al., 1981	Affective and schizophrenic psychoses	↓ [a]	NS	NS
4. Banki et al., 1982	Major depression	↓	NS	—
5. Montgomery and Montgomery, 1982	Depression and personality disorder	↓	↓	—
6. Agren, 1983	Unipolar depression	↓	NS	↓
	Bipolar depression	NS	NS	NS
7. Palaniappan et al., 1983	Depression	↓	↓	NS
8. Ninan et al., 1984	Schizophrenia	↓	—	—
9. Berrettini et al., 1985	Euthymic bipolar depression	NS	NS	—

Note. From Brown and Goodwin (1986).
[a]Suicidal ideation.
↓ = decrease; NS = nonsignificant change; dashes mean parameter not measured (see study for details).

serotonin itself, or in its metabolite 5-HIAA, in either the brain stem or frontal cortex. Four of five postmortem receptor studies, using ^{3}H imipramine as the ligand, have reported significant decreases in the presynaptic binding of this ligand to serotonin neurons in suicide victims (reviewed in Stanley, Mann, and Cohen, 1986). Stanley and Mann (1983), using ^{3}H spiroperidol as the ligand, have also reported a significant increase in postsynaptic serotonin-2 (5-HT$_2$) binding sites in suicide victims who used violent methods to end their lives.

Taken together, these neurochemical and receptor studies tend to support the hypothesis that diminished central serotonin turnover, as evidenced by reduced presynaptic imipramine binding, reduced levels of 5HT and 5-HIAA, and upregulation of the postsynaptic 5HT$_2$ receptor, is associated with suicide.

Dopamine

Some studies have also reported lower CSF levels of the dopamine metabolite homovanillic acid (HVA) among depressed patients who have attempted suicide (see Table 3) (Traskman, Asberg, Bertilsson, and Sjostrand, 1981). Agren (1983) also reported that low CSF HVA levels were associated with the potential lethality of past suicide attempts made by depressed patients and that the contribution of CSF 5-HIAA was quite minimal. Furthermore, Montgomery and Montgomery (1982) found a highly significant relationship between CSF HVA levels and a history of attempting suicide ($p < .001$) and that the relationship with low CSF 5-HIAA levels was less strong ($p < .05$). In a recent study, depressed patients who had attempted suicide were found to have significantly lower CSF HVA levels than either depressed patients who had never attempted suicide or controls (Roy, Agren, Pickar, Linnoila, Doran, Cutler, & Paul, 1986). There were no significant differences between the groups for CSF 5-HIAA levels.

Norepinephrine

There have been relatively few studies examining the noradrenergic system in relationship to suicidal behavior. Brown, Goodwin, Ballenger, Goyer, and Major (1979) reported that personality-disordered patients who had attempted suicide, compared with those who had not, showed significantly higher CSF levels of the norepinephrine (NE) metabolite 3-methoxy-4-hydroxyphenylglycol (MHPG). Brown et al. also noted a significant positive correlation between aggression scores and CSF MHPG levels. However, other studies have shown decreases in CSF MHPG (Table 3). Agren (1980), studying depressed patients, also found significant correlations between CSF MHPG levels and various aspects of suicidality (Table 3).

Studies of peripheral indices of noradrenergic activity have produced conflicting results (reviewed in Roy & Linnoila, 1990). Among postmortem studies, low NE levels have been reported in the putamen of suicide victims by Beskow, Gottfries, Roos, and Winblad (1976). Mann, Stanley, McBride, and McEwen (1987), like Zanko and Biegon (1983), found a significant increase in B-adrenergic receptor binding in the frontal cortex of suicide victims compared with controls, suggesting that there may be a degree of noradrenergic dysregulation in suicide victims.

Lethality

It is of note that low CSF 5-HIAA levels have been particularly associated with violent suicide attempts. In fact, in an early study, Traskman et al. (1981) reported that CSF 5-HIAA levels were significantly lower only among those patients who had made a violent suicide attempt (hanging, drowning, shooting, gassing, several deep cuts), and that levels were not reduced among those who had made a nonviolent suicide attempt (overdosage). More recently, Banki et al. (1984) also found that among 141 female psychiatric patients suffering from depression and other disorders, levels of CSF 5-HIAA were significantly lower in the violent suicide attempters in all four diagnostic categories.

AGGRESSION TOWARD OTHERS

Other studies in violent offenders suggest that low CSF 5-HIAA levels may be associated with a tendency toward impulsive violent behavior, which may manifest itself either as violence toward others or as attempts at suicide (see Table 4). Some investigators have reported correlations between monoamine levels and various measures of personality. Brown, Ebert, Goyer, Jimerson, Klein, Bunney and Goodwin (1982) noted a strong negative correlation between CSF 5-HIAA levels and lifetime aggression scores. This observation has been recently extended to include deviant childhood behavioral variables, which also correlate negatively with CSF 5-HIAA levels (Brown, Kline, Goyer, Minichiello, Kreusi, and Goodwin, 1985). Van Praag (1982) has shown that depressives with low CSF 5-HIAA levels have higher hostility scores on a variety of measures. Roy, Adinoff, and Linnoila (1988) noted that CSF 5-HIAA levels were significantly negatively associated with hostility scores.

Such observations are of interest because they suggest how biological abnormality may influence enduring behavioral patterns through an effect on personality. There is also an extensive animal literature suggesting a role for monoamines in self-destructive animal behavior.

TABLE 4.   Studies Examining the Relationship
between Aggressive/Impulsive Behavior, Suicidal Behavior and CSF 5HIAA

		CSF 5HIAA	
Study	Diagnosis	Aggressive/Impulsive behavior	Suicidal behavior
1. Brown et al., 1979	Personality disorders (military)	↓	↓
2. Bioulac et al., 1978, 1980	Personality disorders XYY (prisoners)	↓ [a]	?
3. Brown et al., 1982	Borderline disorders (military)	↓	↓
4. Linnoila et al., 1983	Personality disorders (prisoners)	↓	↓
5. Lidberg et al., 1984	Murderers of own children (forensic)	↓ [b]	↓
6. Lidberg et al., 1985	Murderers—depression anxiety, personality disorders (forensic)	↓ [b,c]	↓

Note. From Brown and Goodwin (1986).
[a]Postprobenecid
[b]Not necessarily a history of aggressivity/impulsivity.
[c]Only if victims were sexual partners and subjects were not alcoholics.
1 of 4 studies in which CSF HVA was examined found it lower in more aggressive subjects.
1 of 3 studies in which CSF MHPG was examined found it higher in more aggressive subjects.
↓ = decrease; ? = not reported (see study for details).
Branchey et al., 1984 (alcoholics)— ↓ plasma tryptophan/neutral amino acids in more aggressive subjects.

CLINICAL MANAGEMENT

Current evidence suggests that depression is poorly recognized, undertreated, and/or inappropriately treated by the health care system. Successful management of suicidally depressed individuals depends on recognition, adequate assessment, and initiating and maintaining the appropriate treatment interventions. Suicidal depressives can be recognized because they are, in general, in contact with the health services.

Prevention of suicide in depressives requires not only recognition but also full assessment. The main factors affecting suicide risk are outlined in Table 5. Treatment intervention in suicidal depressives invariably involves somatic treatment and supportive psychotherapy. Somatic treatment usually involves antidepressant medication or electro-convulsive therapy (ECT). The decisions as to whether to admit the patient, and whether to admit to an open or closed unit, usually stem from the full assessment of suicide risk (see Table 5). In general, severely suicidally depressed patients should be admitted to a closed unit.

Whether somatic treatment influences long-term mortality in affective-disordered patients has been examined. For example, Black, Winokur, Mohandoss, Woolson, and Nasrallah (1989) reported on 1,076 depressed inpatients who were divided into four treatment groups determined by the type of treatment they received during their index admission. Follow-up revealed that there had been 36 suicides. However, there was no significant difference in the risk of suicide between patients who were acutely treated with ECT, adequate antidepressants, inadequate antidepressants, or neither treatment.

However, there are increasing data suggesting that long-term prophylactic treatment with lithium may reduce the suicide rate among manic-depressive patients. The International Group for the Study of Lithium-Treated Patients has recorded deaths among 813 affective-disordered patients who were given lithium prophylactically between 1976 and 1989. Forty deaths were observed among these patients compared with the 49 deaths shown

TABLE 5. Assessment of the Suicidal: Some Factors Affecting the Risk

1. Personal and social
   M > F: aged over 40
   Marital status; widowed, divorced, or separated
   Immigrant
   Mode of living: alone, does not belong to a domestic group
   Occupation: unoccupied or unemployed, works in recreational services, retired
   District: socially disorganized urban areas, resort towns
2. Previous history
   Family history of affective disorder, suicide, alcoholism
   Previous history of affective disorder, alcoholism
   Previous suicide attempt
   Soon after onset: at the beginning of treatment, 6/12 following discharge from active treatment
3. Life stresses
   Bereavement and separations, moving, loss of job
   In alcoholics, domestic and social complications of drinking
   Incapacitating terminal illness in elderly
4. Personality
   Cyclothymic, sociopathic (impulsive, violent, capricious, delinquent)
   Excessive drinking and drug dependency
5. Psychiatric illness
   Depression, notably manic-depressive and recurrent depression
   Alcoholism and other addictions
   Early dementia and confusional states in elderly
   Organic brain syndromes (epilepsy and head injury)
   Combinations of the above
6. Symptoms
   Depressive: persistent insomnia; dejected appearance and loss of weight, slowed speech
   Loss of usual interests, listlessness and social withdrawal
   Hopelessness and pessimism
   Ideas of unworthiness
   Agitation and restlessness
   Suicidal thoughts
   Alcoholics: medical and CNS complications
7. Circumstances of an attempt
   Precautions taken against discovery
   Prepatory acts: procuring means, affairs in order, warning statements, suicide note
   Violent methods and more lethal drugs/poisons

From Sainsbury (1986).

by life-table analysis to be expected in the general population (Muller-Oerlinghausen, Volk, Grof, Grof, Schorr, Vestergaard, Lenz, Thou, & Wolf, 1991). Muller-Oerlinghausen et al. speculated that possible mechanisms might include the mood-stabilizing effects of lithium as well as improved serotonergic neurotransmission leading to lithium's antiaggressive effects.

LONGITUDINAL PERSPECTIVES

Few studies have examined the relationship of suicide to longitudinal course of illness. In one such study, Roy-Byrne, Post, Hambrick, Leverich, and Rosoff (1988) reported on suicide and course of illness among 87 affective-disordered patients seen at the NIMH.

Of the 87 patients, 49 (56%) had attempted suicide. Patients with and without an attempt did not differ for prior course of illness, past history of psychotic affective episodes, peak severity of depression or psychosis at NIMH, or course of illness at NIMH. However, patients who had a history of suicide attempt had significantly more severe suicidal ideation in the year prior to their NIMH admission than patients who had never attempted.

In a recent longitudinal study, Duggan, Sham, Lee, and Murray (1991) carried out an 18-year follow-up of suicidal behavior in 88 depressed patients. They found that five patients (6%) had committed suicide, and that almost half of the sample (48%) either attempted or completed suicide during the 18 years after the index admission. In addition, suicidal behavior was significantly predicted by severe dysphoria at baseline and two risk factors relating to comorbidity: past alcoholism and chronic physical illness. However, the frequency of attempting was significantly related to severe dysphoria, past suicide attempts, and early parental separation. Thus, Duggan et al. concluded that different aspects of long-term suicidal behavior may have different determinants.

Roy, DeJong, and Linnoila (1989) carried out the first 5-year follow-up of suicidal behavior in depressed patients in relationship to CSF concentrations of 5-HIAA and HVA. After the index NIMH admission, all 27 patients were discharged back to the care of their referring psychiatrist. Before their index NIMH admission, 19 of 27 depressed patients (70.4%) had made a suicide attempt. Of these 19 patients, 7 (36.8%) reattempted suicide during the 5-year follow-up. When patients who reattempted during follow-up ($n = 7$) were compared with the remaining patients ($n = 20$), depressives who reattempted showed significantly lower CSF levels of both 5-HIAA (mean, 66.9 ± 28.8 vs. 98.7 ± 32.6 pmol/ml; $t = 2.28$; $df = 25$; $p < .03$) and HVA (mean, 83.1 ± 51.4 vs. 151.5 ± 76.7 pmol/ml; $t = 2.18$; $df = 25$; $p < .04$).

When, the three melancholic groups that did ($n = 6$) or did not ($n = 11$) reattempt suicide during follow-up or never attempted ($n = 5$) were contrasted, there were highly significant differences for CSF levels of both 5-HIAA ($p < .009$) and HVA ($p < .004$). Melancholic reattempters had significantly lower CSF levels of both 5-HIAA and HVA than melancholics who never attempted ($p < .01$ and $p < .01$, respectively) and lower CSF levels of 5-HIAA than melancholics who did not reattempt ($p < .05$). These follow-up results suggest that among depressed patients who have previously attempted suicide, measures of CSF 5-HIAA and HVA may be predictive markers of an increased risk of further suicidal behavior.

CASE ILLUSTRATION

David was a 26-year-old single male admitted to NIMH because his major depressive episode had not responded to treatment as an outpatient. He had recently left home and moved to a new job in a new city. He had had five previous episodes of depression over the 7.5-year duration of his recurrent unipolar affective disorder that had begun when he was 19 years old. He had had two previous admissions for depression. He had made two previous serious suicide attempts by drug overdosage. His grandfather had committed suicide. His father had been treated for three separate episodes of major depression, for one of which he received a course of electroconvulsive therapy.

During his inpatient stay at NIMH, David had a lumbar puncture and assay that revealed a low CSF 5-HIAA concentration of 42 pmol/ml. David was difficult to engage in psychotherapy and showed no response to treatment with antidepressant medication, which was increased until he was receiving the high dose of imipramine of 450 mg per day. He reported feeling very hopeless and on one occasion left the ward, purchased a large amount of aspirin at a local pharmacy, and made a very serious suicide attempt. Later during this admission he made a dramatic recovery with lithium augmentation of the imipramine treatment. He was discharged back to the care of his psychiatrist in his local community. Follow-up 5 years later revealed that he had continued on lithium and remained well except for one recurrence of affective disorder when he discontinued lithium. During that depression he again attempted suicide and was hospitalized.

SUMMARY

Suicidal behavior among patients with affective disorders is a serious public health problem. It is probably best conceptualized as a multidetermined behavior. Social, psychiatric, psychodynamic, genetic, personality, and biological factors all play a part. Suicidal behavior among depressed patients is largely state dependent. If the patient is not depressed the risk of suicide is greatly reduced. Thus, the prevention of suicide among affective-disordered patients depends largely on both the recognition, assessment, and treatment of current affective episodes and the long-term prophylactic management of patients with recurrent affective disorder.

REFERENCES

Agren, H. (1980). Symptom patterns in unipolar and bipolar depression correlating with monoamine metabolites in the cerebrospinal fluid, II: Suicide. *Psychiatry Research, 3,* 225–236.

Agren, H. (1983). Life at risk: Markers of suicidality in depression. *Psychiatric Developments, 1,* 87–140.

American Psychiatric Association (1987). *Diagnostic and statistical manual of mental disorders,* 3rd Edition, Revised. Washington, DC: Author.

American Psychiatric Association (1993). *DSM-IV draft criteria.* Washington, DC: Author.

Asberg, M., Traskman, L., & Thoren, P. (1976). 5-HIAA in the cerebrospinal fluid: A biochemical suicide predictor? *Archives of General Psychiatry, 33,* 1193–1197.

Banki, C., Arato, M., Papp, Z., & Kurez, M. (1984). Biochemical markers in suicidal patients: Investigations with cerebrospinal fluid amine metabolites and neuroendocrine tests. *Journal of Affective Disorders, 6,* 341–350.

Barraclough, B., & Pallis, D. (1975). Depression followed by suicide: A comparison of depressed suicides with living depressives. *Psychological Medicine, 5,* 56–61.

Barraclough, B., Bunch, J., Nelson, B., & Sainsbury, P. (1974). A hundred cases of suicide: Clinical aspects. *British Journal of Psychiatry, 125,* 355–373.

Berrettini, W., Nornberger, J., Linnoila, M., Narrow, W., Scheinin, M., Seppala, T., Simmons-Alling, S., & Gershon, S. (1985). CSF and plasma monoamines and their metabolites in eurythnic bipolar patients. *Biological Psychiatry, 20,* 257–275.

Beskow, J., Gottfries, G., Roos, B., & Winblad, B. (1976). Determination of monoamine and monoamine metabolites in the human brain: Postmortem studies in a group of suicides and a control group. *Acta Psychiatrica Scandinavica, 53,* 7–20.

Bioulas, B., Benezech, M., Renaud, B., Roche, D., Noel, B. (1978). Biogenic amines in 47, XYY syndrome. *Neuropsychopharmacology, 4,* 366–370.

Black, D., Winokur, G., Mohandoss, E., Woolson, R., & Nasrallah, A. (1989). Does treatment influence mortality in depressives? A follow-up of 1076 patients with major affective disorders. *Annals of Clinical Psychiatry, 1,* 165–173.

Brown, G. W., & Harris, T. (1978). *Social origins of depression.* New York: Free Press.

Brown, G., Ebert, M., Goyer, P., Jimerson, D., Klein, W., Bunney, W., & Goodwin, F. (1982). Aggression, suicide, and serotonin: Relationship to CSF amine metabolites. *American Journal of Psychiatry, 139,* 741–746.

Brown, G., Goodwin, F., Ballenger, J., Goyer, P., & Major, L. (1979). Aggression in humans correlates with cerebrospinal fluid metabolites. *Psychiatry Research*, *1*, 131–139.

Brown, G., Kline, W., Goyer, P., Minichiello, M., Kruesi, P., & Goodwin, F. (1985). Relationship of childhood characteristics to cerebrospinal fluid 5-hydroxyindoleacetic acid in aggressive adults. In C. Shagass, R. Josiassen, W. Bridger, K. Weiss, D. Stoff, & G. Simpson (Eds.), *Proceedings of world congress of biological psychiatry* (pp. 177–179). Amsterdam, the Netherlands: Elsevier Science Publishers.

Bulik, C., Carpenter, L., Kupfer, D., & Frank, E. (1990). Features associated with suicide attempts in recurrent major depression. *Journal of Affective Disorders*, *18*, 29–37.

Dorpat, T., & Ripley, H. (1960). A study of suicide in the Seattle area. *Comprehensive Psychiatry*, *1*, 349–359.

Duggan, C., Sham, P., Lee, S., & Murray, R. (1991). Can future suicidal behavior in depressed patients be predicted? *Journal of Affective Disorders*, *22*, 111–118.

Egeland, J., & Sussex, J. (1985). Suicide and family loading for affective disorders. *Journal of the American Medical Association*, *254*, 915–918.

Fawcett, J., Scheftner, W., Fogg, L., Clark, D., Young, M., Hedeker, D., & Gibbons, R. (1990). Time-related predictors of suicide in major affective disorder. *American Journal of Psychiatry*, *147*, 1189–1193.

Goodwin, F., & Jamison, K. (Eds.), (1990). Suicide. In *Manic depression* (pp. 227–244). Baltimore: Williams & Wilkins.

Guze, S., & Robins, E. (1970). Suicide and primary affective disorders. *British Journal of Psychiatry*, *117*, 437–483.

Haberlandt, W. (1965). Der suizid als genetisches problem (zwillings and familien analyse). *Anthropol Anz*, *29*, 65–89.

Haberlandt, W. (1967). Aportacion a la genetica del suicide. *Folia Clinica Int*, *17*, 319–322.

Juel-Nielsen, N., & Videbech, T. (1970). A twin study of suicide. *Acta Geneticae Medicae et Gemellologiae (Roma)*, *19*, 307–310.

Kety, S. (1986). Genetic factors in suicide. In A. Roy (Ed.), *Suicide* (pp. 41–45). Baltimore: Williams & Wilkins.

Langeluddecke, A. (1941). Uber Lebenserwartung and Ruckssfallhaufigkeit bei Manisch-depressiven. *Psychiatrica Hyg*, *13*, 1–14.

Leckman, J., Charrey, D., Nelson, C., Heninger, G., & Bowels, M. (1981). CSF tryptophan, 5-HIAA and HVA in 132 patients characterized by diagnosis and clinical state. *Recent Advances in Neuropsychopharmacology*, *31*, 289–297.

Lidberg, L., Tuck, J., Asberg, M., Scalia-Tombra, G., Bertilson, L. (1985). Homicide, suicide, and CSF 5-HIAA. *Acta Psychiatrica Scandinavica*, *71*, 230–236.

Lidberg, L., Ashberg, M., & Sungrvist-Stensman, V. (1984). 5-hydroxyindoleacetic acid levels in attempted suicides who have killed their children. *Lancet*, *2*, 98.

Linkowski, P., de Maertelaer, V., & Mendlewicz, J. (1985). Suicidal behavior in major depressive illness. *Acta Psychiatrica Scandinavica Copenhagen*, *72*, 233–238.

Linnoila, M., Virkkven, M., Soheinin, M., Nuutila, A., Riman, R., & Goodwin, F. (1983). Low cerebrospinal fluid 5-hydroxyindoleacetic acid concentrations differentiates impulsive from nonimpulsive violent behavior. *Life Science*, *33*, 2609–2614.

Lundquist, G. (1945). Prognosis and course in manic-depressive psychosis. *Acta Psychiatrica Neurologica Scandinavica*, *35*(Supplement), 1–96.

Mann, J., Stanley, M., McBride, P., & McEwen, B. (1987). Increased serotonin$_2$ and B-adrenergic receptor binding in the frontal cortices of suicide victims. *Archives of General Psychiatry*, *43*, 954–959.

Montgomery, S., & Montgomery, D. (1982). Pharmacological prevention of suicidal behaviour. *Journal of Affective Disorders*, *4*, 291–298.

Muller-Oerlinghausen, B., Volk, J., Grof, P., Grof, E., Schorr, M., Vestergaard, P., Lenz, G., Thou, K., & Wolf, R. (1991). Reduced mortality of manic-depressive patients in lithium treatment: An international long-term collaborative study by IGSLI. *Psychiatry Research*, *36*, 329–331.

Ninian, P., van Kammen, D., Scheinin, M., Linnoila, M., Barney, W., & Goodwin, F. (1984). CSF 5-hydroxy-indoleacetic acid in suicidal schizophrenic patients. *American Journal of Psychiatry*, *141*, 566–569.

Palanioappan, V., Ramachandran, V., Somasundaram, O. (1983). Suicidal ideation and biogenic amines in depression. *Indian Journal of Psychiatry*, *25*, 286–292.

Pitts, F., & Winokur, G. (1964). Affective disorder. Part III (Diagnostic correlates and incidence of suicide). *Journal of Nervous and Mental Disorders*, *139*, 176–181.

Rich, C., Young, D., & Fowler, R. (1986). San Diego Suicide Study, I, young vs. old subjects. *Archives of General Psychiatry*, *43*, 577–582.

Robins, E., Murphy, G., & Wilkinson, R. (1959). Some clinical considerations in the prevention of suicide based on a study of 134 successful suicides. *American Journal of Public Health*, *49*, 888.

Roy, A. (1982). Risk factors for suicide in psychiatric patients. *Archives of General Psychiatry*, *39*, 1089.

Roy, A. (1983). Family history of suicide. *Archives of General Psychiatry*, *40*, 971.

Roy, A. (1985a). Family history of suicide in manic-depressive patients. *Journal of Affective Disorders*, *8*, 187–189.

Roy, A. (1985b). Family history of suicide in affective disorder patients. *Journal of Clinical Psychiatry*, *46*, 317–319.

Roy, A. (1986). Genetics of suicide. In J. Mann & M. Stanley (Eds.), *Psychobiology of suicidal behavior* (pp. 97–105). New York: Annals of the New York Academy of Sciences.

Roy, A., & Linnoila, M. (1988). Suicidal behavior, impulsiveness, and serotonin. *Acta Psychiatrica Scandinavica*, *78*, 529–535.

Roy, A., & Linnoila, M. (1990). Monoamines and suicidal behavior. In H. van Praag, R. Plutchik, and A. Apter, *Violence and Suicidality* (pp. 41–183). New York: Brunner Mazel.

Roy, A., Adinoff, B., & Linnoila, M. (1988). Acting out hostility in normal volunteers: Negative correlations with levels of 5-HIAA in cerebrospinal fluid. *Psychiatry Research*, *24*, 187–194.

Roy, A., Agren, H., Pickar, D., Linnoila, M., Doran, A., Cutler, N., & Paul, S. (1986). Reduced CSF concentration of homovanillic acid and homovanillic acid to 5-hydroxyindoleacetic acid ratios in depressed patients: Relationship to suicidal behavior and dexamethasone nonsuppression. *American Journal of Psychiatry*, *143*, 1539–1545.

Roy, A., DeJong, J., & Linnoila, M. (1989). Cerebrospinal fluid monoamine metabolites and suicidal behavior in depressed patients: A five-year follow-up study. *Archives of General Psychiatry*, *46*, 609–612.

Roy, A., Segal, N., Centerwall, B., & Robinette, D. (1991). Suicide in twins. *Archives of General Psychiatry*, *48*, 29–32.

Roy-Byrne, P., Post, R., Hambrick, D., Leverich, G., & Rosoff, A. (1988). Suicide and course of illness in major affective disorder. *Journal of Affective Disorders*, *15*, 1–8.

Sainsbury, P. (1986). Depression, suicide, and suicide prevention. In A. Roy (Ed.), *Suicide* (pp. 73–88). Baltimore: Williams & Wilkins.

Schulsinger, F., Kety, S., Rosenthal, D., & Wender, P. (1979). A family study of suicide. In M. Schou & E. Stromgren (Eds.), *Origins, prevention and treatment of affective disorders* (pp. 277–287). New York: Academic Press.

Schulz, B. (1949). Sterblichkeit endogen Geiteskranker und lher Eltern. *Z Menschl Vererb Konstitutions Lehr*, *29*, 338–367.

Slater, E. (1938). Zur Erbpathologic des manish-de-pressiven lrreseins: Die Eltern and Kindern von Manisch Depressiven. *Z Gesamte Neurol Psychiatrica*, *163*, 1–47.

Stanley, M., Mann, J. (1983). Increased serotonin-2 binding sites in frontal cortex of suicide victims. *Lancet*, 214–216.

Stanley, M., Mann, J., & Cohen, S. (1986). Serotonin and serotonergic receptors in suicide. In *Psychobiology of Suicidal Behavior* (pp. 122–127). New York: Annals of New York Academy of Sciences.

Stendstedt, A. (1952). A study in manic-depressive psychoses. *Acta Psychiatrica Neurologica Scandinavica Supplement*, *35*, 1–96.

Traskman, L., Asberg, M., Bertilsson, L., & Sjostrand, L. (1981). Monoamine metabolites in CSF and suicidal behavior. *Archives of General Psychiatry*, *38*, 631–636.

Tsuang, M. (1983). Risk of suicide in the relatives of schizophrenics, manics, depressives, and controls. *Journal of Clinical Psychiatry*, *44*, 396–400.

Van Praag, H. (1982). Depression, suicide and the metabolism of serotonin in the brain. *Journal of Affective Disorders*, *4*, 275–290.

Vestegaard, P., Sorensen, T., Hoppe, E. et al. (1978). Biogenic amine metabolites in cerebrospinal fluid in patients with affective disorders. *Acta Psychiatrica Scandinavica*, *58*, 88–96.

Wender, P., Kety, S., Rosenthal, D., Schulsinger, F., Ortmann, J., & Lunde, I. (1986). Psychiatric disorders in the biological and adoptive families of adopted individuals with affective disorders. *Archives of General Psychiatry*, *43*, 923–929.

Zanko, M., & Biegon, A. (1983). Increased B-adrenergic receptor binding in human frontal cortex of suicide victims. *Abstract of the Annual Meeting of the Society for Neuroscience*, Boston, MA.

Zaw, K. (1981). A suicidal family. *British Journal of Psychiatry*, *189*, 68–69.

CHAPTER 15

Dissociative Disorders

RICHARD P. KLUFT

The dissociative disorders consist of dissociative identity disorder (DID) (formerly multiple personality disorder [MPD]), dissociative fugue (DF) (formerly psychogenic fugue [PF]), dissociative amnesia (DA) (formerly psychogenic amnesia [PA]), depersonalization disorder (DD), and a variety of allied conditions subsumed under the rubric of dissociative disorder not otherwise specified (DDNOS). Although they were studied in great depth and detail in the era of Charcot and Janet, dissociative disorders received minimal attention for nearly 80 years thereafter (Ellenberger, 1970). Due to a number of factors reviewed elsewhere (Kluft, 1987a, 1988), a renaissance of interest in these conditions is currently underway, and they are once again becoming mainstream concerns of the mental health sciences. Unfortunately, the drama and lay interest that surround them often give rise to polarized reactions of fascination and skepticism, both of which have proven impediments to their becoming the subject of rational scientific exploration. Virtually no funds have been made available for their systematic investigation. As a consequence, although the clinical literature with regard to dissociative identity disorder (virtually all written using the multiple personality disorder nomenclature) has burgeoned and become rather sophisticated, controlled studies about the basic phenomena of the dissociative disorders are relatively few. Efforts often are made to extrapolate from laboratory studies of hypnosis, but these are fraught with peril because dissociation and hypnosis are partially overlapping rather than identical constructs (Carlson & Putnam, 1989; Frankel, 1990). Therefore, this chapter must draw upon such sources as are available, and qualify its observations repeatedly. Since dissociative amnesia is unique in being described as a symptom of other disorders (Loewenstein, 1991), it is difficult to discuss it in the current context as a freestanding disorder. The modern literature on dissociative fugue, depersonalization disorder, and dissociative disorder not otherwise specified is minimal. Because the vast preponderance of recent publications in this field have studied DID (MPD), observations relevant to this condition dominate this chapter.

RICHARD P. KLUFT • The Institute of Pennsylvania Hospital, Philadelphia, Pennsylvania, 19139, and Department of Psychiatry, Temple University School of Medicine, Philadelphia, Pennsylvania 19140.

Handbook of Aggressive and Destructive Behavior in Psychiatric Patients, edited by Michel Hersen, Robert T. Ammerman, and Lori A. Sisson. Plenum Press, New York, 1994.

DESCRIPTION OF THE DISORDER

The dissociative disorders are characterized by disturbances or alterations of the normally integrative functions of memory, identity, or consciousness (American Psychiatric Association, 1987). Therefore, for a time certain information is not associated or integrated with other information as it normally or logically would be (West, 1967). Dissociation itself is a complex psychophysiological process with psychodynamic triggers that produces alterations in a person's consciousness during which these failures of integration occur (Putnam, 1985). Different states of mind may be involved, each with a characteristic organization and phenomenology (Putnam, 1988). Viewed from an information-processing perspective, dissociation involves the segregation of certain types of information from other types of information in a relatively rule-bound manner (Spiegel, 1986a). Consequences of this segregation are compromised cognition and cognitive structures (Fine, 1988, 1990) and an impoverishment of the ability of the mental apparatus to approach situations with optimal and appropriate access to all information and skills that may be relevant for optimal assessment, self-awareness, self- control, and problem solving (Kluft, 1990a, 1990b). "Dissociation has an implicitly paradoxical element in that information is unavailable to consciousness, yet indicates its presence" (Spiegel, 1991, p. 261). Dissociation is usually thought of in terms of what is ablated, but it refers as well to the intrusion of unintegrated elements (Braun, 1988a, 1988b). It is important to realize that dissociation in and of itself is not invariably associated with mental illness (Kluft, 1988). It involves a spectrum of phenomena (Hilgard, 1986; Putnam, 1991a; Spiegel, 1991) many of which are normal and found in surveys of nonpatient populations (Ross, Joshi, & Currie, 1990, 1991). A high capacity for experiencing hypnosis overlaps with and usually co-occurs with high dissociativity (Carlson & Putnam, 1989; Frankel, 1990).

The clinical dissociative disorders are highly correlated with histories of antecedent trauma and/or stress (Putnam, 1985; Spiegel, 1991). They offer an immediate and ongoing anodyne:

> Dissociative defenses, which allow individuals to compartmentalize perceptions and memories, seem to perform a dual function. They help victims separate themselves from the full impact of a physical trauma while it is occurring, and, by the same token, they may delay the necessary working through and putting into perspective of these traumatic experiences once they have occurred. They help the trauma victim maintain a sense of control during an episode of physical helplessness, but then become a mechanism by which the individual feels psychologically helpless once he or she has regained physical control. (Spiegel, 1991, p. 261)

In essence, most of the dissociative disorders can be understood as posttraumatic and/or as indications of profound intrapsychic conflict (Kluft, 1987a; Putnam, 1985, 1991a; Spiegel, 1984, 1986b, 1991).

Dissociative Identity Disorder/Multiple Personality Disorder

Dissociative identity disorder (DID), or multiple personality disorder (MPD), the paradigmatic dissociative disorder, is a complex and chronic dissociative psychopathology (Kluft, 1987a) characterized by disturbances of memory and identity (Nemiah, 1980). "It is distinguished from other mental disorders by the ongoing coexistence of relatively consistent but alternating subjective identities and recurrent episodes of memory distortion, frank amnesia, or both" (Kluft, 1991a, p. 161). According to patients' given histories, it is invariably a sequel to overwhelming childhood experiences, usually involving intentionally inflicted child abuse (Putnam, Guroff, Silberman, Barban, & Post, 1986; Ross, Norton, Wozney, 1989; Schultz, Braun, & Kluft, 1989). The DSM-III-R diagnostic criteria for multiple personality disorder were as follows:

> A. The existence within the person of two or more distinct personalities or personality states (each with its own relatively enduring pattern of perceiving, relating to, and thinking about the environment and self). B. At least two of these personalities or personality states recurrently take full control of the person's behavior. (American Psychiatric Association, 1987, p. 272)

DSM-IV will offer the following criteria for DID/MPD:

> A. The presence of two or more distinct identities or personality states (each with its own relatively enduring pattern of perceiving, relating to, and thinking about the environment and self). B. At least two of these identities or personality states recurrently take control of the person's behavior. C. Inability to recall important personal information that is too extensive to be explained by ordinary forgetfulness. D. Not due to the direct effects of a substance (e.g., blackouts or chaotic behavior during alcohol intoxication) or a general medical condition (e.g., complex partial seizures). Note: In children, the symptoms are not attributable to imaginary playmates or other fantasy play. (American Psychiatric Association, 1993, p. N:1)

The new criteria are not likely to prove more restrictive in limiting the frequency with which this diagnosis is made because of over 95% of contemporary DID/MPD cases fulfil them and many of the most published scientific investigators have been using even more stringent criteria since 1984.

Despite years of being considered a rarity, DID/MPD is not uncommon. Newer diagnostic methods (reviewed in Kluft, 1987b, 1991a) have facilitated the identification of these patients, who are usually misdiagnosed for 6.8 years and receive over three previous diagnoses before their identification (Putnam et al., 1986). Screening clinical populations with such instruments reveals that approximately 4% of psychiatric patients suffer from previously undiagnosed DID/MPD (Ross, 1991; Saxe et al., 1993). In identified clinical populations, women predominate at a ratio of 8–9:1 (Kluft, 1991a). However, males with DID/MPD are not uncommon. It long had been assumed that women with DID/MPD attack themselves and are identified within clinical populations, while men attack others and might be found in prison populations. While there is some evidence to sustain this line of reasoning (Bliss & Larson, 1985; Kluft, 1985), more recent studies indicate that males are found in clinical populations when sensitive observers have a suitable index of suspicion and diagnostic sophistication (Loewenstein & Putnam, 1990; Ross & Norton, 1989b). It is typical for DID/MPD patients to present with a polysymptomatic and pleiomorphic picture that fluctuates over time and makes diagnosis difficult (Kluft, 1985). Symptoms characteristic of psychosis, neurosis, character disorder, and other conditions are commonly found to coexist with DID/MPD (Bliss, 1980).

Dissociative Amnesia and Dissociative Fugue

A distinction between DA, DF, DDNOS, and DID is absent from much of the earlier studies of DA and DF. Dissociative fugue and dissociative amnesia occur at a baseline rate within civilian populations, and are found in much greater number under difficult and traumatic circumstances (Kluft, 1988; Loewenstein, 1991; Putnam, 1985). Under such circumstances, it is difficult to distinguish between dissociative amnesia per se, post-traumatic stress disorder (of which amnesia is a symptom), and the newly created entity, brief reactive dissociative disorder. In military populations exposed to combat, the severity of combat exposure is a determinant of the prevalence of amnesia thereafter. However, a small group of soldiers with personal or family histories of fugue or conversion symptoms seemed differentially vulnerable, and demonstrated amnesia or fugue with lesser combat exposure. In civilian populations, young women are most likely to appear as amnestic; no reliable data exist for the gender distribution of fugues. In the first systematic study of a modern series of civilian amnesia cases, Coons and Milstein (1989, 1992) found that 72% had a history of child abuse, with 52% having suffered sexual abuse and 40% physical abuse. It is relevant that Briere and Conte (1989) found that 59.6% of 468 subjects with histories of childhood sexual abuse had had an inability to remember the abuse at some time during their lives. Amnesia is linked with more serious episodes of abuse (Briere & Conte, 1989; Herman & Schatzow, 1987). Abuse histories are believed to be less common in those who have fugues. This may relate to a basic difference between civilian DA and DF populations, or the lack of systematically studied series. Coons and Milstein's discovery of the high degree of abuse histories in DA patients represents a novel finding; the earlier literature described occasional DA cases with abuse backgrounds, but had not studied this issue in detail. The literature as a whole concurs that "the psychosocial environment out of which psychogenic amnesia and fugue develop are massively stressful, with the patient experiencing intolerable emotions of shame, guilt, despair, rage, frustration, and conflict experienced as unresolvable without suicide or flight" (Loewenstein, 1991, pp. 199–200).

The DSM-III-R diagnostic criteria for psychogenic amnesia were: "A. The predominant disturbance is an episode of sudden inability to recall important personal information that is too extensive to be explained by normal forgetfulness. B. The disorder is not due to Multiple Personality Disorder or to an Organic Mental Disorder (e.g., blackouts during Alcohol Intoxication)" (American Psychiatric Association, 1987, p. 275). There are several subtypes of amnesia (American Psychiatric Association, 1987; Loewenstein, 1991). The diagnostic criteria for psychogenic fugue were: "A. The predominant disturbance is sudden, unexpected travel away from home or one's customary place of work, with inability to recall one's past. B. Assumptions of a new identity (partial or complete). C. The disturbance is not due to Multiple Personality Disorder or to an Organic Mental Disorder (e.g., partial complex seizures in temporal lobe epilepsy)" (American Psychiatric Association, 1987, p. 273). DSM-IV diagnostic criteria for dissociative amnesia are:

> A. The predominant disturbance is one or more episodes of inability to recall important personal information, usually of a traumatic or stressful nature, that is too extensive to be explained by ordinary forgetfulness. B. The disturbance does not occur exclusively during the course of Dissociative Identity Disorder and is not due to the direct effects of a substance (e.g., drugs of abuse, medication) or a general medical condition (e.g., Amnestic Disorder due to head trauma). (American Psychiatric Association, 1993, p. N:1)

The new definition acknowledges the frequent connection between dissociation and trauma, and acknowledges the increasingly recognized role of head trauma in neuropsychiatric evaluation. The diagnostic criteria for dissociative fugue in DSM-IV are:

> A. The predominant disturbance is sudden, unexpected travel away from home or one's customary place of work, with inability to recall one's past. B. Confusions about personal identity or assumption of a new identity (partial or complete). C. The disturbance does not occur exclusively during the course of Dissociative Identity Disorder and is not due to the direct effects of a substance (e.g., drugs of abuse, medication) or a general medical condition (e.g., temporal lobe epilepsy). (American Psychiatric Association, 1993, p. N:1)

This revision attempts to correct problems with the DSM-III-R criterion B, which was widely disputed, and for which there was little evidence, and, as do the criteria for DA, acknowledges the importance of considering DID/MPD in every differential diagnosis involving dissociative phenomena.

Depersonalization Disorder

Depersonalization disorder is a difficult condition to discuss. Although the literature on the subject of depersonalization is large, and depersonalization is a common symptom in many psychiatric disorders, there remains significant disagreement as to whether or not DD constitutes an autonomous entity (Steinberg, 1991). This question is in the process of clarification in Steinberg's ongoing research. There is a broad spectrum of depersonalization symptoms, ranging from common and mild to abnormal and chronic. Its link to trauma is through its high incidence in traumatized populations, such as concentration camp survivors and those exposed to life-threatening events (Putnam, 1985; Steinberg, 1991). However, there appears to be a significant diversity to its etiology. Kluft (1988) proposed that there were at least two subgroups of depersonalization disorder, one of which involved classic dissociative and hypnotic phenomena, and another of which emerged from a diverse group of psychodynamic processes that estrange one from one's identity. The DSM-III-R diagnostic criteria were:

> A. Persistent or recurrent experiences of depersonalization as indicated by either (1) or (2): (1) an experience of feeling detached from, and as if one is an outside observer of, one's mental processes or body (2) an experience of feeling like an automaton or as if in a dream. B. During the depersonalization experience, reality testing remains intact. C. The depersonalization is sufficiently severe and persistent to cause marked distress. D. The depersonalization experience is the predominant disturbance and is not a symptom of another disorder, such as Schizophrenia, Panic Disorder, or Agoraphobia without History of Panic Disorder but with limited symptom attacks of depersonalization, or temporal lobe epilepsy. (American Psychiatric Association, 1987, pp. 276–277)

The DSM-IV criteria for depersonalization disorder are the following:

> A. Persistent or recurrent experiences of feeling detached from, as if one is an outside observer of, one's mental processes or body (e.g., feeling like one is in a dream). B. During the depersonalization experience, reality testing remains intact. C. The depersonalization causes clinically significant distress or impairment in social, occupational, or other important areas of functioning. D. The depersonalization experience is not better accounted for by another disorder, such as Schizophrenia, Dissociative Identity Disorder, or Panic Disorder, and is not due to the direct effects of a substance (e.g., drugs of abuse, medication) or a general medical condition (e.g., temporal lobe epilepsy). (American Psychiatric Association, 1993, p. N:2)

Dissociative Disorder Not Otherwise Specified

DDNOS is a category for "disorders in which the predominant feature is a dissociative symptom (i.e., a disturbance or alteration in the normal integrative functions of identity, memory, or consciousness) but the criteria are not met for any specific Dissociative Disorder" (American Psychiatric Association, 1993, p. N:2). However, it is important in this context because many patients with the inner structure of DID/MPD are thus diagnosed, as well as those with fugues in which there is no second identity, trance states following trauma, and dissociative states resulting from periods of prolonged and intense coercive persuasion. It may be used in the future to classify those individuals who have been influenced by antisocial applications of hypnosis that have been studied by intelligence operatives (e.g., Scheflin, 1991).

EPIDEMIOLOGY

The dissociative disorders have been redefined and reclassified throughout the last century, and have been explored within a multitude of theoretical paradigms, each of which emphasized the importance of certain types of information at the expense of others. There-fore, it is difficult to combine and compare the studies of one generation of scholars with those of another (Kluft, 1988). Furthermore, contemporary scientific investigators often use mutually incompatible methods of data collection and presentation (Kluft, 1991a). With respect to the study of aggression and destructive behavior in the dissociative disorders, the available information is fragmentary and widely dispersed throughout the literature.

Dissociative Identity Disorder/Multiple Personality Disorder

Dissociative identity disorder (DID), or multiple personality disorder (MPD) is highly associated with antecedent experiences of child abuse. Putnam et al. (1986) found that 97% of 100 DID/MPD patients reported histories of childhood abuse, predominantly sexual abuse (83%, with 68% reporting incest), repeated physical abuse (75%), and witnessing of a violent death (45%), and both physical and sexual abuse (68%); an average of 3.2 types of childhood traumata were reported per patient. Ross, Norton, and Wozney (1989) found that 88.5% of 236 patients had been either physically or sexually abused, and that 11.1% were uncertain as to whether or not they had been abused. Sexual abuse was reported by 79.2% and physical abuse by 74.9%. Ross et al. concluded that the absence of abuse might occur in as few as 3.6% of male and 4.3% of female DID/MPD patients. Schultz, Braun, and Kluft (1989) found that childhood abuse was reported by 98% of 355 DID/MPD patients. In a multicenter study of MPD, Ross, Miller, et al. (1990) found that 95.1% of 102 DID/MPD patients had suffered childhood physical and/or sexual abuse. Of the 50 DID/MPD patients examined by Coons, Bowman, and Milstein (1988), 96% had suffered physical and/or sexual abuse. Most of these series also noted the occurrence of neglect, abandonment, psychological abuse, and witnessing violent deaths. There is a consensus within the field that DID/MPD patients are almost invariably overwhelmed in childhood, usually by abuse (Kluft, 1984, 1991a). However, several surveys and case reports indicate the possibility of onset with adult traumatic exposures. Many experts doubt that such cases are truly without antecedent childhood traumatization.

Self-directed aggression is a common finding in DID/MPD patients. Their treatments are often punctuated with episodes of suicidality and self-mutilation (Kluft, 1983). Putnam et al. (1986) reported that 1 of the 100 patients they studied had suicided, but that 61% made serious suicide attempts and 71% had made suicide gestures. Fifty-three percent reported attempts at "internal suicide" (i.e., the attempt of one personality to kill another). In 34%, one or more personalties would mutilate the body to punish another alter. In the MPD patients studied by Ross et al. (1989), 72% attempted suicide, and 2.1% suicided. In their multicenter study, Ross, Miller, et al. (1990) found that 92% had recurrent thoughts of death and suicide, wanted to be dead, or had attempted suicide. Coons and Milstein (1990) noted that 48% of 50 DID/MPD patients self-mutilated. Loewenstein and Putnam (1990) found that 100% of their male and 88% of their female DID/MPD patients demonstrated suicidality and 23% of the males and 36% of the females were self-mutilators. Putnam et al. (1986) and Kluft (in press-a) note that surveys of DID/MPD patients that show a low rate of successful suicide should not be misunderstood to indicate a low lethality. Survey methods make it unlikely that most DID/MPD suicides will be reported to investigators.

It is difficult to assess the true degree of aggression toward others demonstrated by DID/MPD patients. Unlike suicide attempts and self-mutilation, much of which can be documented, many DID/MPD reports of aggression, much as many DID/MPD reports of childhood abuse, are not documented. Also, a special problem exists. Relatively recently many DID/MPD patients have reported being both victims and involved with ritual abuse, usually described as satanic in variety. In such settings a variety of lethal practices are said to have been pursued. As of this writing, the veracity of such accounts remains to be proven or disproven (Kluft, 1989). The interested reader is referred to Ganaway (1989), Van Benschoten (1990), Jones (1991), Lanning (1991), Putnam (1991b), and Young, Sachs, Braun, and Watkins (1991) for further details of this controversial area.

The available literature indicates that aggression against others is reported in patients' given histories. Putnam et al. (1986) found that 70% of DID/MPD patients described at least one alter as assaultive or destructive, and 29% attributed actual homicidal behavior to an alter. Six percent stated that they had committed actual homicides and 20% stated they were involved in a sexual assault on another individual. Coons et al. (1988) found that 32% of DID/MPD patients they studied had engaged in crimes including shoplifting, assault and battery, prostitution, burglary, robbery, and child abuse. They noted a marked gender difference, as only 28% of females but 75% of males had committed crimes, all of which were violent or potentially violent. This gender difference was studied by Loewenstein and Putnam (1990), who found it to be a trend, albeit not statistically significant. They found that 47% of males and 35% of females engaged in unspecified criminal behaviors; 19% of the males and 7% of the females reported the perpetration of a homicide. They noted 60% of men and 36% of women were involved in drunk driving. Gender difference was also studied by Ross and Norton (1989b), who found that 28.6% of males with DID/MPD had been convicted of crimes, as opposed to 9.7% of women ($p < .01$).

Dell and Eisenhower (1990) reported 36% (all female) of their adolescents with DID/MPD were "violent" or threatened violence to others; Kluft (1985) reported aggressive and assaultive behavior in four adolescent males, ranging from property destruction to arson and dangerous assault. Kluft (1987c) studied 75 mothers with DID/MPD and found that 16% of them were physically assaultive to at least one of their children, and 1% had sexually seduced one of their children. Bliss and Larson (1985) studied 33 convicted and incarcerated sex offenders who had admitted their crimes, thereby eliminating any who claimed amnesia for the offenses. Two-thirds had dissociative symptoms. Seven (21.2%) had DID/MPD, and another six (18%) were suspected of DID/MPD.

Apart from the data of these studies, DID/MPD is often associated with aggression because of the notoriety of forensic cases celebrated in the media (e.g., "The Hillside Strangler" and Billy Milligan). The interested reader is referred to specialized discussions (Allison, 1984; Coons, 1991; Kluft, 1987d; Lewis & Bard, 1991; Orne, Dinges, & Orne, 1984; Watkins, 1984), and a book-length account (Keyes, 1981) of these topics.

Dissociative Amnesia and Dissociative Fugue

These conditions are the subject of an excellent review by Loewenstein (1991). The literature relating dissociative amnesia (DA) to aggressive behavior is curious for its apparent unacknowledged division into three areas, which often are described independently— amnesia in combat soldiers, civilian populations, and criminals. The first relates to situations in which one may expect to be both the victim and perpetrator of aggression, the second refers to populations in which aggression is unanticipated, and the third deals with allegations of memory difficulties among those who have committed violent offenses.

In wartime, amnestic syndromes are relatively common, and dissociative amnesia and dissociative fugue are often not distinguished. It is likely that many older reports that focused on amnesia as a major symptom would, if they were written today, focus on posttraumatic stress disorder, of which amnesia is a symptom. Of veterans, 5–20% report amnesia for their combat experiences (Archibald & Tuddenham, 1965; Henderson & Moore, 1944); in the Second World War, amnestic syndromes accounted for 5–14% of psychiatric casualties (Putnam, 1985). Sargent and Slater (1941) found that 14.4% of 1,000 patients had amnesia as a prominent symptom. They found that 35% of those who endured sustained combat under fire had amnestic syndromes, while these were found in only 13% of those under periodic fire or intermittent combat, and in only 6% of those in a base camp. Those with amnesia with lesser combat exposure often had families in which amnestic or conversion symptoms were reported. It must be understood that head trauma and other organic causes may account for some of the combat statistics. Over 50% of Henderson and Moore's (1944) combat group had been rendered unconscious.

Fugues in connection with combat have long been reported (Ellenberger, 1970). In one combat-related case described by Fisher and Joseph (1949), a merchant seaman's fugue was related to his helping a critically injured friend die with less pain. This man came from an abusive home, but was not noted to have been abused himself.

Among civilian populations, abused populations frequently report having had amnesia for their abuse at some time in their lives. Fifty-nine percent of 468 clinical subjects studied by Briere and Conte (1989) gave such accounts. The only contemporary series of dissociative amnesia cases has been collected by Coons and Milstein (1992). These authors found that possible precipitants were child abuse (60%), marital trouble (24%), disavowed sexual behavior (16%), criminal behavior (12%), and several less common and unknown factors. Unfortunately, they did not specify whether the criminal behavior was antecedent to the amnesia or committed during the time for which the patient was amnestic. The Coons and Milstein study is a landmark in many ways, and has contributed several novel observations, especially the high association of amnesia with antecedent abuses. Prior studies had stressed the importance of intrapsychic and interpersonal conflicts, but a number of authors had noted abnormalities (usually unspecified) in their subjects' childhoods or family lives (Kluft, 1988; Putnam, 1985).

A final group of individuals with amnestic complaints is found in the criminal justice system. Dissociative amnesia is claimed by as many as 30–40% of perpetrators of homicides, and is alleged by a lower percentage of perpetrators of other violent crimes (Kopelman, 1987a, 1987b). Amnesia primarily for the criminal act is alleged. Kopelman (1987b) states that in those cases thought to be genuine, the individuals had been in a state of high emotional arousal and launched an unpremeditated attack upon a close relative. Unfortunately, the art of distinguishing true from malingered dissociative amnesia is not well advanced (Kopelman, 1987b; Schacter, 1986). Furthermore, it is difficult to ascertain the point at which deliberate deception gives way to unconscious defensive processes (Kopelman, 1987b; Lishman, 1987).

ETIOLOGY

The dissociative disorders literature is difficult to review in connection with the etiology of aggressive/destructive behavior in dissociative disorder patients. For the most part, these patients are described as being the victims of such behavior from others, or as developing their difficulties in the aftermath of such experiences. Little attention is devoted to the etiology of the aggressive/destructive behavior itself. With few exceptions, the study of such phenomena in dissociative disorder patients is restricted to the modern literature on DID/MPD.

Aggressive/destructive behavior in DID/MPD patients is usually attributed to one of the following mechanisms:

1. Behavior of particular personalities toward external others.
2. Behavior of particular personalities toward external others in the service of battles between the personalities.
3. Behaviors of personalities toward one another with the body as a battlefield.
4. Reenactments of past traumata.
5. Co-occurring psychopathology and/or neurological conditions.
6. Self-destruction due to despair over intrapsychic pain or abandonment, self-hatred, etc.
7. Addiction to trauma.

Several of these appear to be directly related to antecedent childhood abuse. They may be understood as forms of responding to the experience of past victimization by taking a role corresponding to that of their prior abusers (i.e., rendering active what had been endured passively and employing the mechanism of identification with the aggressor). Sometimes DID/MPD patients recapitulate their relationships with their abusers in their systems of personalities, and the personalities reenact the abusive relationships among themselves and with external others (Kluft, Braun, & Sachs, 1984).

In DID/MPD the various personalities may have significant differences in memory, identity, and cognitive functioning. Because they think, form their opinions, and rationalize their understandings and actions on the basis of different data bases and different cognitive styles and operations, they live, in effect, in subjectively different worlds, which they endorse with a conviction of delusional intensity. This absence of a consensual understanding of their histories and circumstances is closely correlated with their irresponsible autonomy under certain circumstances. Although some DID/MPD patients can control the actions of the various alters, many cannot. In fact, in many DID/MPD patients, the personalities are not aware of one another's existence. This sets the stage for the emergence and behavior of alters that embody and enact ideas and urges that, were they under the aegis of a central ego with overarching synthetic and controlling functions, might never achieve uncontrolled and unmodified expression. There is dyscontrol by default. Since many of the personalities developed in connection with mistreatment, it is hardly unexpected that many behave as if they were those (or were like those) who had abused the patient; still others are based on real or imagined rescuers and/or protectors and may behave in accordance with such an ascribed identity.

Behavior of the personalties toward external others may take several forms. For example, one woman with DID/MPD had a 14-year-old alter that was an identification with a brother who had abused her when he was that age. That alter molested the patient's 6-year-old daughter. Another patient had a "protector" alter that assaulted a therapist who asked questions that upset the personality being interviewed. A male patient had an alter based on an abuser that periodically became assaultive to demonstrate its strength, and another that perpetrated rapes whenever the patient felt inadequate. Another woman funneled all of her anger into one alter. On the rare occasions that it emerged it was very prone to violence.

The personalities often constitute an inner society with its own complex rules and relationships. At times a personality will take action against another person in connection with inner battles among the alters. The author once was assaulted by a hospitalized DID/MPD patient in a personality that was trying to prevent the others from making revelations about the mistreatment perpetrated by the individual with whom that alter was identified. This alter knew that such an assault would lead to the patient's discharge from the specialized program directed by the author, and thereby hoped to sabotage treatment. The inner battles between two alters in a male with DID/MPD led one to commit a violent offense and remain on the scene until the police arrived. The offending alter then "stepped back," leaving the other alter in the grips of the police and unable to explain its circumstances.

It is not uncommon for alters' disputes with one another to take the form of assaults upon the body, which is used as the battlefield. Each alter sees the body as belonging to the other and not to itself. The author has seen dozens of instances in which different alters had control of the right and left arms, respectively, and rained blows on the other limb, the face, and the trunk, each alter firm in the subjective belief that it was a complete person involved in an altercation with a completely separate individual. Because alters often cannot accept the fact that they are all aspects of a single person, and may have self-representations that deny their participation in the patient's body and life, they may attempt "internal homicide," that is, try to kill one another. The body will be assaulted as if it belonged to a completely separate foe. In a similar manner, one alter may hurt or mutilate the body to punish or disfigure another, oblivious to the fact that all alters will face the consequences of such acts.

Reenactments of past traumata are a major cause of self-directed aggressive/destructive behavior. They infrequently harm others, because what is reenacted usually constitutes aspects of a victimization scenario. It often takes the form of compulsive unconscious flashbacks (Blank, 1985). Patients may place themselves at risk, either passively or provocatively, exemplifying the "sitting duck syndrome" (Kluft, 1990a).

Co-occurring phenomena may also be responsible for aggressive/destructive behavior. Although it remains unclear to what extent the pleiomorphic and polysymptomatic picture of DID/MPD represents epiphenomena of DID/MPD or constitutes genuine concurrent mental or neurological disorders (Kluft, 1991b), it is clear that in certain individual cases comorbidity plays an essential role. The author has seen a male with DID/MPD and bipolar disorder whose overt interpersonal aggression was confined to certain alters when the man went into irritable and paranoid manic phases. Fichtner, Kuhlman, Gruenfeld, and Hughes (1990) studied a woman whose coexisting episodic dyscontrol syndrome was associated with a rhythmic midtemporal discharge pattern and was correlated with violence in certain alters. Both of these patients' aggressive behaviors responded well to effective pharmacotherapy of the comorbid condition. Many DID/MPD patients with coexisting major depression are very self-destructive until the affective disorder is treated.

DID/MPD patients are often depressed both within and across alters. They often are extremely masochistic. They are overwhelmed by the pain of their abuse, the desolation and loneliness of their lives, and the unpleasant nature of their circumstances. They see no end to their misery except to destroy themselves, and often are preoccupied with such ideas for protracted periods of time. Often they are inclined to respond to virtually all manner of life events by turning aggression against themselves and finding themselves to blame for their circumstances. This often is associated with a forlorn hope that by attacking themselves they are rehabilitating the images of family members who have abused them and paving the way for a reconciliation. Hence an episode of self-injury may relieve the DID/MPD patient subjectively. The dynamics of these episodes are often quite unique, but the above features are relatively commonplace.

The model of addiction to trauma is thought by many to be important in DID/MPD, especially for those patients who are involved in repetitive self-injury or provoking attack upon themselves. For example, van der Kolk and Greenberg (1987) proposed that traumatized organisms become addicted to the endogenous opiates that are liberated in response to hurt and injury and thereafter seek out circumstances in which they will again experience such a release. Therefore, the addiction to endogenous opiates will take the behavioral form of an addiction to trauma, which will create the circumstances under which the opiates are released. There are a number of anecdotal clinical studies (Braun, 1989) that suggest a role for such a mechanism.

AGGRESSION TOWARD SELF

Dissociative Identity Disorder/Multiple Personality Disorder

As noted in the section "Epidemiology," self-destructive behavior is very common among DID/MPD patients. Coons and Milstein (1990) and Ross and Norton (1989a) have attempted to study this phenomenon. Coons and Milstein found that 48% of a sample of DID/MPD patients had engaged in self-mutilation. Thirty percent had made cuts on their extremities, 6% had cut their faces, 4% had cut their abdomens, and 4% had wounded their vaginas; 6% hit themselves or a wall, 4% inflicted burns, and 2% were involved with hairpulling, neurotic excoriation, tongue abrasion, and nail biting. Ross and Norton (1989) unfortunately did not supply data on self-mutilation for DID/MPD patients who did not attempt suicide. However, of 167 who did attempt suicide, 85.4% had overdosed, 68.7% had inflicted cigarette burns or other self-injuries, and 60.4% had slashed their wrists.

To describe the full spectrum of self-destructive behaviors in an DID/MPD cohort, the author will share data on a series of 40 DID/MPD patients being studied for another purpose (Kluft, in press-b). Of this group, all but 2 of whom are female, 27 (or 65%) had made at least one serious and potentially lethal suicide attempt, and 1 had killed herself; 75% had at least one episode of self-mutilation, and 35% had mutilated themselves repetitively (over six times, range: 6 to >200 times).

Among the suicide attempters, all but three (or 89%) (60% of the whole cohort) had made at least one serious attempt by ingestion with prescription drugs. One patient had attached herself to an intravenous setup and injected a bolus of barbiturates, but she recovered. This patient also injected herself intravenously with fecal material. Six attempted suicide by vehicle: three drove into solid structures at high speed, one drove her car into deep water, and two engaged in reckless racing and games of "chicken," hoping to die in the process. Of the cohort, 73% inflicted cuts on their bodies, but 33% inflicted cuts with severe lethal potential and premeditated suicidal intent. A number of suicide attempts related to suffocation (35%) were reported: six (15%) ran their cars in enclosed areas in an attempt to die by carbon monoxide poisoning; three (8%) attempted to kill themselves with gas ovens; five (13%) tried to hang or otherwise asphyxiate themselves with ligatures, occasionally combined with plastic bags over their heads. Twenty percent had attempted to throw themselves in front of vehicles or eloped from the hospital with such plans and were stopped by staff or the police before they had succeeded in doing so. Four (10%) attempted to kill themselves by beating their head against hard surfaces for protracted periods; one actually inflicted considerable brain damage. Two tried to shoot themselves, but were stopped when spouses they thought were asleep interrupted their efforts. Several deliberately made themselves available to sexual partners known or suspected to be very violent, and three (8%) attempted to have intercourse with HIV-infected partners. One (3%) left the hospital lightly clad in the dead of winter and walked 30 miles in the hopes of dying of exposure. One patient arranged for a weight to fall upon her from considerable height. One patient attempted to perform a hysterectomy upon herself. A number of the patients attempted to kill themselves by avoiding recommended medical attention or by increasing their risk factors, but this was difficult to quantify. Ten (25%) stated that they had attempted to starve themselves to death, and most had required medical hospitalization in that connection. Conversely, three (8%) had attempted to kill themselves by gaining so much weight that their death would be hastened.

In terms of self-mutilation, 75% had inflicted some harm upon themselves, and 53% had inflicted over six self-injuries (range 6 to >200 self-injuries). As noted, cutting, which involved 73%, was the most frequent mechanism, and invariably involved the wrists and forearms. However, 25% had cut the abdomen, 18% the thighs, 18% the genitals, 15% the breasts, 5% the neck, and 5% the face. Forty-five percent repetitively struck the body or struck hard surfaces in an attempt to harm parts of the body. Several patients had alters who were alleged to cause the body to fall, often down stairs. Ten (25%) had inflicted burns with cigarettes or boiling water. Caustic burns were not inflicted by members of this series but occurred in an earlier cohort the author had examined several years previously. A considerable number abused the body by periodic self-starvation (48%) or laxative/enema abuse (25%). Twenty percent had worked as prostitutes; this compares to a figure of 19.1% in the series of Ross et al. (1989).

These figures, drawn from the author's current practice, appear to offer a reasonable approximation of the occurrence of these types of behaviors in DID/MPD patients, and strongly suggest that this is a profoundly self-destructive group.

Dissociative Amnesia and Dissociative Fugue

There are little data with regard to self-directed aggression for these states. Coons and Milstein (1990) indicate that 29% of their dissociative amnesia cases had histories of self-mutilation, and there were no such incidents in their dissociative fugue states; in a later series (1992) they reported a 20% incidence. However, it should be noted that these are the first series including so called "nonclassical" dissociative amnesia, that is, the long time gaps of childhood periods in abuse victims (Loewenstein, 1991). The authors correlate self-mutilation largely with those patients who have had abuse backgrounds (Coons, personal communication, 1991).

Depersonalization Disorder

As reviewed by Coons and Milstein (1990), depersonalization is not uncommon in those who self-harm, and some who feel depersonalized may inflict self-harm to counter their distressing numbed and detached state of mind. However, attempts to study the literature on self-harm and depersonalization are stymied by the fact that it is a common symptom of many conditions (Steinberg, 1991). As of yet, no series of depersonalization disorder patients diagnosed by modern criteria has been systematically studied.

Dissociative Disorder Not Otherwise Specified

No organized body of data addresses this group of patients. Clinical experience suggests that those DDNOS patients who most resemble DID/MPD suffer self-injury at a rate similar to but somewhat lower than actual DID/MPD patients. An inherent problem in this connection is that most DID/MPD patients spend most of their lives without florid DID/MPD phenomena, and that any DDNOS series is likely to include many patients who will be openly DID/MPD at other times in their lives (Kluft, 1985).

AGGRESSION TOWARD OTHERS

Apart from the epidemiological data reported above and a handful of sensationalized forensic cases involving patients with DID/MPD, there is little actually known about the aggressive behaviors of dissociative disorder patients toward others. The limited information in the literature consists in the main of undocumented statements made by patients. It is important to realize that psychiatric patients' accounts of their criminal activities are not necessarily accurate. Convit, O'Donnell, and Volavka (1990) compared 41 psychiatric inpatients' self-reports of arrests with official arrest records. Sixty-six percent gave accurate reports, 12% denied officially documented arrests, and 22% reported arrests that had not occurred.

Dissociative Identity Disorder/Multiple Personality Disorder

Of Loewenstein and Putnam's (1990) male subjects, 19% reported committing a homicide and 13% stated that they had perpetrated a rape; 10% of their female subjects stated that they had killed someone. Of Coons and Milstein's (1988) series of 50 DID/MPD patients, 32% had engaged in a variety of criminal behaviors, including child abuse, but only one subject, a male, had perpetrated a rape. No homicides were reported. Specific criminal behaviors were not included in the Ross et al. (1989) survey. It is difficult to reconcile the available studies. Loewenstein and Putnam's data suggest that DID/MPD patients are a dangerous and potentially lethal group. Coons and Milstein's data paint a less disturbing picture. Clinicians familiar with DID/MPD are not impressed that either series is definitive. Furthermore, as mentioned above, when patients' descriptions of aggressive behavior involve allegations of satanic ritualistic abuse, there is no way at present to confirm or deny such possibilities.

Although a series drawn from a single practitioner's practice is inevitably skewed, and may not include the most violent of individuals, it may offer an additional perspective. The allegations of aggressive behavior of 40 DID/MPD patients (from the author's practice) were tabulated. Of these patients, 21 (53%) said that they had attacked, killed, raped, or abused someone. However, 18 (45%) stated that these offenses had occurred in connection with their participation in satanic ritual abuse. In all, it was possible to document aggressive behavior on the part of eight patients (20%), four of whom alleged additional undocumented satanic ritual abuse experiences. Three patients had struck their husbands on a number of occasions as certain alters attempted to undermine their marriages. One inpatient with coexisting bipolar disorder and mild organic brain damage abruptly struck out at a fellow patient, and delivered a single punch before she was controlled. One patient had a history of assaultiveness to staff on psychiatric units but had never been aggressive under other circumstances. One patient had a long history of fights with her siblings, and had a jail record stemming from one of these incidents. She had refused to desist when the police arrived, and had become involved in an altercation with them. She had assaulted and strangled a psychiatric nurse during one hospital stay. One patient had attacked two intrusive and provocative fellow patients during a hospital stay. The final patient repetitively took an aggressive posture toward hospital staff, and attacked a friend after discharge. Three patients, all of whom alleged satanic ritual abuse histories, attacked the author during therapy sessions when they misperceived him as a past abuser associated with a satanic cult. None of these attacks was sustained or terribly serious.

In this series, then, were it not for allegations of participation in violent behavior in the suppositional context of ritualistic abuse, DID/MPD would not appear to be a very dangerous condition. Hopefully, future studies will clarify the discrepancies and unresolved issues surrounding interpersonal aggression in DID/MPD patients.

Information about interpersonal aggression in patients diagnosed with psychogenic amnesia, psychogenic fugue, depersonalization disorder, or dissociative disorder not otherwise specified is unavailable.

CLINICAL MANAGEMENT

The treatment of aggressive and destructive behavior in dissociative disorder patients is intrinsically interwoven with the reintegration of disavowed mental contents and structures, and with the management of coexistent psychopathologies and organic disorders. A major concern in the treatment of any dissociative disorder patient is providing the patient with alternative coping mechanisms, so that dissociation will be less likely to be the first or second response to stressful circumstances. Ego strengthening through all available therapeutic techniques is of use. It also is particularly useful to teach the patient about the mechanisms of dissociation, so that the patient can appreciate and interdict its incipient phases. Often, helping the patient restructure his or her dissociative experience, and coaching the patient in autohypnotic methods to interrupt uncontrolled dissociation, is useful. Spiegel and Spiegel (1978; also see Spiegel, 1991) offer several excellent and relevant contributions in their discussion of the management of the individual who is highly hypnotizable. In brief, these authors suggest that by teaching such patients to induce and curtail autohypnotic experiences, they can be helped to achieve a form of mastery over their dissociative diathesis.

Dissociative Identity Disorder/Multiple Personality Disorder

The recent literature offers several excellent outlines for the treatment of DID/MPD (Braun, 1986; Kluft, 1991a; Putnam, 1989; Ross, 1989). In essence, establishing an atmosphere of safety and socializing the patient to therapy is followed by a stage of preliminary interventions in which the patient is stabilized and strengthened through contracting with the alters, providing symptomatic relief, collaborating in the use of techniques that will be applied throughout the therapy, and deepening the therapeutic alliance. Thereafter, history-gathering and exploring the system of alters and working with the issues of the individual alters take place. Only then is there a stage of metabolizing the traumatic antecedents of the condition. Thereafter, as the material is discussed and worked through across alters, and their relationships improve, facilitation of further closeness characterizes moving toward integration. Next, the alters are brought to integration. Thereafter, the patient must learn new coping skills, solidify gains, and do still more working through before being placed on a follow-up status (Kluft, 1991a).

The management of aggressive and destructive behavior depends on its mechanism.

When it is due to the behavior of particular personalities toward external others, an initial approach involves attempting to contract with the involved alters to curtail such behavior, and to avoid contact with the external others. This is often quite difficult, because often some alters endorse positive and affectionate ties to persons others see as abusers and wish to attack. The patient is informed of the therapist's Tarasoff obligations, and told that the therapist will under no circumstances testify at a later date that any future such behavior would qualify for a not guilty by reason of insanity defense. In most cases this resolves matters abruptly. If a patient will not contract, and the therapist assesses that genuine danger is likely, that patient should be hospitalized, involuntarily if necessary, and treatment carried out in a structured setting. In essence, the therapist must access the involved alters, discover their reasons for being, abreact the antecedents and affects that drive their behavior, and bring the alters to the point at which they will contract for safety.

When the potential for danger is driven by the behavior of particular personalities toward external others in the service of battles between the personalities, the same basic conditions apply. However, it often is possible to find hypnotic and imagery interventions that refocus the alters away from external others, and to address the conflicts that led to such problems by working with conflicting alters.

In situations in which the alters use the body as a veritable battlefield, attempts are made to access the involved alters and to help them find avenues of expression for their concerns that do not involve self-harm. DID/MPD patients are often reluctant to give up self-harm, rationalizing that it hurts no one else and that they do not wish to stop. Frequently they argue that self-harm terminates dysphoric states, is not felt as painful, and "is better than killing myself or hurting someone else." In such situations, the therapist attempts to achieve contracts against such behavior for limited periods of time, and scrupulously renews them. Work with the alters to resolve their issues and to abreact any traumata that may fuel such episodes will be necessary to effect a lasting resolution. If initial efforts are unavailing, treatment may have to occur in an inpatient setting.

The reenactments of past traumata may involve a flashback per se, or the re-creation of destructive scenarios in the fantasy structure of the alters' world or with persons in the patient's environment. The detection and explication of these episodes is essential. Often the past events that drive such reenactments must be abreacted completely across all involved alters before they can be curtailed.

When aggression toward self or others is fueled by co-occurring psychopathology and/or neurological conditions, the treatment of choice is the control of the co-occurring condition; alters alleged to be the vehicles of such behaviors can be dealt with concomitantly. Often the co-occurring autonomous condition can be mimicked, consciously and/or unconsciously, by the involved alters, so that the control of the comorbid condition results in suboptimal control of the problem behavior. Thus, Fichter et al. (1990) achieved excellent but incomplete reduction in the violence of an DID/MPD patient with episodic dyscontrol treated by carbamazepine.

Not uncommonly, self-destructive behaviors (including the provocation of others to hurt one's self) are due to despair over some form of intrapsychic pain, abandonment, or self-hatred. The dynamics of such behavior are quite varied from individual to individual, but usually involve distraction from a subjectively intolerable pain by the creation of another pain; achieving a perverse mastery by actively inflicting a pain by choice as a diversion from a pain caused by another, and endured helplessly; or making an offer of contrition in the hopes of appeasing some other. Treatment involves working with the concerned alters on the relevant dynamics, helping patients more accurately appreciate their interpersonal circumstances (especially with regard to whether the relationship with which the patient is preoccupied is appropriate), and work through the painful loss of preferred but inaccurate perceptions of others. It is not uncommon for such issues to be difficult to resolve, because they may require the renunciation of lifelong wishes. Recurrent brief hospital stays may be necessary to restabilize such patients. Much work may be necessary to help such patients develop a support system and connect with nonabusive others.

A final approach involves the perspective of addiction to trauma (van der Kolk & Greenberg, 1987). Braun (1990, and personal communications, 1987–91) has been involved with the psychopharmacological treatment of DID/MPD patients with severe and repetitive self-destructive patterns. He has pioneered the use of narcotic antagonists, and reported some impressive preliminary anecdotal successes. However, his work remains unpublished, and must be regarded as highly experimental.

Dissociative Amnesia and Dissociative Fugues

The treatment of violence and aggression in connection with these disorders is difficult to describe, because the destructive episodes almost invariably antedate the onset of the condition and the patient's receiving clinical attention. Treatment is to better understand the events in question, and to prevent the occurrence of additional such episodes by recognizing and resolving the problematic dynamics and experiences that made them likely to occur. In essence, recent reviews of the treatment of such patients emphasize the importance of establishing a solid relationship with the patient before proceeding. Disavowed material is reintegrated into memory at a permissive pace well within the patient's tolerance, and the relevant dynamics must be worked with and processed (Kluft, 1988; Loewenstein, 1991). Hypnosis and drug-facilitated interviews may be quite invaluable; it often is useful to tape or videotape such sessions, and review them with the patient when the patient is ready to do so. It is very helpful to make such patients aware of their dissociative potential, and teach them how to control their dissociative diathesis (Spiegel, 1988; Spiegel & Spiegel, 1978). When the material to be retrieved and reintegrated is known to be difficult, or this is discovered in the course of the explorations under hypnosis or during a drug-facilitated interview, it is best to be gentle and permissive with respect to how much the patient is able to absorb at once. If hypnosis is used, it is helpful to make suggestions that the patient will recover the material only at a rate that is tolerable. The same suggestions may be made to the patient in a drug-facilitated interview. Pressuring the patient to absorb such material too rapidly may lead to regressions and suicide attempts. A patient's apparently healthy wish to "know it all and face it" may prove counterphobic or frankly masochistic, and should be regarded with caution rather than welcomed as a sign of excellent motivation.

Depersonalization Disorder

A recent review of the treatment of depersonalization disorder was contributed by Steinberg (1991). This author's literature review did not discover any information about the treatment of aggression in this clinical population, nor did the author's efforts to obtain anecdotal accounts from dissociative disorder patients bear fruit. In this author's limited clinical experience, when such patients feel quite estranged from themselves and self-injure to test their own reality, they usually have done so in the context of actual perceived interpersonal rejection, in connection with which they feel even more estranged from themselves than usual.

Dissociative Disorder Not Otherwise Specified

Although there is virtually no relevant literature with respect to aggression and DDNOS, it is important to be aware that this diagnostic category is increasingly used for patients who have the structure of DID/MPD but are not presenting floridly. However, most DID/MPD patients spend most of their lives making a DDNOS appearance (Kluft, 1985, 1991a, 1991b). Therefore, the remarks under DID/MPD above may be relevant to this population.

LONGITUDINAL PERSPECTIVES

The author's literature review uncovered minimal longitudinal data relevant to the manifestations of aggressive and destructive behaviors in dissociative disorder patients. With regard to DID/MPD, however, some information is available due to the author's follow-up of a large cohort of DID/MPD patients over time (Kluft, 1985). Clinical experience is an imperfect but valuable source of data. The author's study of 75 DID/MPD mothers included several (16%) who had been abusive to their children. As their DID/MPD resolved with psychotherapy, the abuse ceased. As of last follow-up, none who remained integrated ever abused again, but one who has still not achieved integration has been abusive intermittently. Also, the author has followed several men with histories of violent behavior through integration and beyond. Thus far, the only legal infraction on follow-ups of 8 or more years in this group was a single episode of driving while intoxicated.

On the surface, this would suggest that, with treatment, offenders with dissociative disorders may be able to be removed from the ranks of recidivist criminals, an argument made earlier by Bliss and Larson (1985). However, any population of offenders that sought treatment in the private sector and remained treatment adherent for years without external compulsion is a most unusual and highly motivated self-selected group from which no generalizations should be inferred because they may be quite atypical. Nonetheless, such findings, should they be confirmed by others, would suggest that the intensive psychotherapeutic treatment of dissociative-disordered individuals with problematic aggressive behaviors is a worthwhile endeavor.

CASE ILLUSTRATION

Incontrovertible evidence demonstrated that William Baney (a pseudonym), a construction worker and volunteer fireman, was responsible for setting a series of fires. He came into psychiatric treatment when he insisted that although he could not deny that his guilt was proven, he had no recollection of doing what he was known to have done. Those who knew him well vouched for his character and could not believe that the had committed arson. He submitted to psychiatric assessment. Although his psychiatric and neurological assessment was without positive findings, he was diagnosed as suffering from psychomotor epilepsy and placed on a series of anticonvulsants, including caramazepine. These medications did not prevent further firesetting.

After additional encounters with the legal system, and his acquittal on all charges on medical grounds, another episode led to his evaluation by a person familiar with dissociative disorders. Over the next 2 years, the following history was reconstructed from the patient and a variety of ancillary sources (mother, aunt, uncle, older sister, a long-time neighbor, and his girlfriend). Although the informants often differed as to details, they agreed in all major particulars.

Bill was the oldest son of a highly skilled machinist, who, although well regarded in the community and at work, was a severe alcoholic who was brutally abusive to his wife and his children. Bill's father beat him several times a week throughout his childhood. He had suffered several fractures as a child, the causes of which were not revealed to treating physicians. As he grew older, and tried to protest the beatings given his mother and sister, his father beat him more severely. His behavior outside of his home was very unruly. His mother also used liberal corporal punishment, and on occasion burned his fingers for stealing. Powerful, large, and quick, Bill initially appeared to be destined for athletic greatness. However, his unreliable attendance at practices, his apparent forgetting of plays his coaches took efforts to teach him, and his gratuitous violence in practices limited his potential. Soon he quit all teams and worked after school. He was considered a good worker unless he had conflicts with his supervisors. At such times he often became extremely vituperative and threatened physical violence. He often was puzzled when he was fired, and said that he could not recall the alleged angry events. His minister often helped him find other jobs, and valued him as an effective and pious Sunday-school teacher.

At times Bill was observed to be childlike and playful, and to refer to himself as "Billy," but this was regarded as volitional "fooling around" behavior by family and friends alike. When Bill was 16, his father taunted him about this type of behavior and Bill began to cry. Then, abruptly, he appeared to go into an intensely rageful state. His father, unaccustomed to such behavior in Bill, hit him in the face. His mother, who witnessed the event, states that Bill shouted, "You'll never hurt Billy again," grabbed a chair, and thrashed his father. Thereafter Bill had a headache, and could not recall what had occurred. His father disbelieved him, but never struck him again. His father died later that year of complications of alcoholism.

Bill graduated high school, and had no trouble getting work. However, he rarely lasted more than a few months, because of altercations with his bosses. On two occasions he reported for work only to be told he had been fired the day before for behavior that Bill could neither recall nor believe. On one of these jobs he met an older man who took a fatherly interest in him, and suggested that he join a volunteer fire company in which he was active. This man's positive influence on Bill greatly reduced his outbursts, and he became more stable in work situations.

However, Bill found himself increasingly in conflict with his mother, who tried to curtail his dating and social behaviors. She was quite concerned about him, and became very intrusive. Soon Bill was having angry outbursts at home and disappearing for periods of time. He never gave an account of these missing hours, but retrospectively it is possible to reconstruct that at those times he switched to an alter that gave vent to his rage at his mother in acts of vandalism against property. Over the course of a year or so, as he became increasingly involved in the volunteer fire company, these acts became arson. This proved to be determined by his mother's use of burning as a punishment when he was young and by his love of the fireman work. He became increasingly knowledgeable about how to start fires inventively, and then enjoyed getting to the company rapidly to participate in putting them out.

Bill's guilt and shame about his ways of venting his anger were intense. The alter who taught Sunday school thought that the alters that set the fires had to be punished. Gradually, that alter came to delay Bill's leaving the scene of his arsons and to interfere with his covering his tracks. Consequently, he was apprehended at or near the scene of several fires, and arrested. He had attempted suicide after a number of these arrests.

Bill proved to have a number of personalities, many of which were relevant to aggressive aspects of his behavior. He had a child alter, Billy, who was terrified of grown men like his father. A violent alter, Duke, was modeled on his assaultive father, contained Bill's rage at his father, and saw himself as Billy's protector. He had beaten his father and been inappropriately aggressive at work when he felt the patient had been offended. Still another personality, Deacon, came from his identification with his mother's religiosity and the influence of his minister. Deacon taught Sunday school and arranged for the "bad" alters to be caught. The damage to property and the arson was done by Jerry (the name being a masculine congener of his mother's name), who held Bill's anger at his mother, who was abusive in her own way. "Bad William" was full of self-hatred on the basis of Bill's perception that his parents did not value or love him. He was always ready to hurt himself in contrition and atonement. This was not appreciated until therapy was well advanced, when it became apparent that "Bad William" often was involved in provoking fights in which Bill would have no chance to win, and would be hurt. For example, after one confrontation with mother over his dating, "Bad William" felt so guilty that he initiated a bar fight with several toughs, by whom he was thrashed. This describes only a fraction of Bill's system of alters.

Bill's treatment involved the gradual identification of the alter system and the bringing of the alters into agreement to be in therapy and to abstain from further antisocial and self-injurious behaviors. Minor tranquilizers were used liberally to reduce anxiety. As therapy progressed over a period of months, there were no further episodes of arson and he rarely got into fights. However, as Bill, Billy, and other alters previously unaware that the destructive behaviors actually were related to them in any way came to understand that the behaviors in fact had been performed by other aspects of the mind of which they all were a part, they became suicidal.

After several brief hospital stays failed to stabilize the patient, it was determined to carry out the remainder of the memory retrieval and processing in the structure of an inpatient setting. In the course of a 3½-month stay, Bill nearly succeeded in hanging himself on two occasions, and inflicted several minor cuts to his wrists, but finally was able to face what had to be faced. It was difficult and humiliating for Bill to accept his abuse history. He was much better able to deal with what he himself had done actively. Many of the alters would rather see themselves as tough and bad, rather than as the helpless (and unmanly) victims of child abuse. A number of them spoke of attacking the therapist who was "causing them so much pain" by making them remember the assaults they had passively endured. Safety contracts were repeatedly renegotiated. After a few weeks it was possible to retrieve, abreact, and work through the abuse experiences, and own and accept responsibility for the actions of the many alters. This therapy was vigorous and tricky. Some alters wanted to be restrained in session, lest they become destructive. However, it was possible to arrange ways of continuing the treatment without resorting to this measure.

Bill's outstanding criminal charges were resolved in a manner that postponed judicial action, but reserved the right to reinitiate proceedings should further offenses occur. He was prohibited from participating in voluntary fire companies and admonished to remain in treatment, which was recommended, but not mandated. Bill sublimated his considerable aggression with the purchase of an outlandishly macho motorcycle and leather paraphernalia. For several years he chose to do farm labor, working for men with whom he could get along well.

Bill's intense treatment lasted approximately 3 years, after which he was seen in follow-up periodically. He took no medications after the first year of therapy. He has been steadily employed, and now can work quite smoothly with others. He has remained affiliated with his church. His relationship with his family was quite tense for a while, but improved when he became involved with a young woman of whom his mother approved. On 10-year follow-up, there have been no further problems with aggressive dyscontrol, and no legal difficulties. He has been a good father to his two young children, and a caring husband to his wife. He now drives a station wagon.

SUMMARY

The study of aggressive and destructive behavior in dissociative disorder patients is in its infancy. Most of these conditions have not been explored systematically from the perspective of violence. The recent literature on multiple personality disorder has addressed a number of relevant concerns, however. Several mechanisms have been found that appear to underlie the violence against self and others perpetrated by these patients. Current therapeutic strategies allow for the successful treatment of many such patients. For those DID/MPD patients who commit themselves to definitive psychotherapy, the diminution and cessation of their dysfunctional aggression appears to occur in the course of treatment. Attention to comorbid psychopathology and organic disease is essential. The fragmentary evidence available to date suggests that this may be a subgroup of aggressive and destructive patients many of whose problem behaviors can be resolved by available but not widely practiced therapeutic approaches.

REFERENCES

Allison, R. B. (1984). Difficulties in diagnosing the multiple personality syndrome in a death penalty case. *International Journal of Clinical and Experimental Hypnosis, 32*, 102–117.

American Psychiatric Association (1987). *Diagnostic and statistical manual of mental disorders*, 3rd Edition, Revised. Washington, DC: Author.

American Psychiatric Association (1991). *DSM-IV options book: Work in progress 9/1/91*. Washington, DC: Author.

American Psychiatric Association (1993). *DSM-IV draft criteria*. Washington, DC: Author.

Archibald, H. C., & Tuddenham, R. D. (1965). Persistent stress reaction after combat. *Archives of General Psychiatry, 12*, 475–481.

Blank, A. S. (1985). The unconscious flashback to the war in Viet Nam veterans: Clinical mystery, legal defense, and community problem. In S. M. Sonnenberg, A. S. Blank, & J. A. Talbott (Eds.), *The trauma of war: Stress and recovery in VietNam veterans* (pp. 293–308). Washington, DC: American Psychiatric Press.

Bliss, E. L. (1980). Multiple personality: A report of fourteen cases with implications for schizophrenia and hysteria. *Archives of General Psychiatry, 37*, 1388–1397.

Bliss, E. L., & Larson, E. M. (1985). Sexual criminality and hypnotizability. *Journal of Nervous and Mental Disease, 173*, 522–526.

Braun, B. G. (1986). Issues in the psychotherapy of multiple personality disorder. In. B. G. Braun (Ed.), *Treatment of multiple personality disorder* (pp. 1–28). Washington, DC: American Psychiatric Press.

Braun, B. G. (1988a). The BASK (behavior, affect, sensation, knowledge) model of dissociation. *Dissociation, 1*(1), 4–23.

Braun, B. G. (1988b). The BASK model of dissociation: Clinical applications. *Dissociation, 1*(2), 16–23.

Braun, B. G. (1989, October). *Psychology and brain chemistry in the programming of human beings*. Paper presented at the Sixth International Conference on Multiple Personality Dissociative States, Chicago.

Briere, J., & Conte, J. (1989, August). *Amnesia in adults molested as children: Testing theories of repression*. Paper presented at the annual meeting of the American Psychological Association, New Orleans.

Carlson, E. B., & Putnam, F. W. (1989). Integrating research on dissociation and hypnotizability: Are there two pathways to hypnotizability? *Dissociation, 2*, 32–38.

Convit, A., O'Donnell, J., & Volavka, J. (1990). Validity of self-reports of criminal activity in psychiatric inpatients. *Journal of Nervous and Mental Disease, 178*, 48–51.

Coons, P. M. (1991). Iatrogenesis and malingering of multiple personality disorder in the forensic evaluation of homicide defendants. *Psychiatric Clinics of North America*, *14*, 757–769.

Coons, P. M., & Milstein, V. (1989, October). *Psychogenic amnesia: A clinical study of 50 cases*. Paper presented at the Sixth International Conference on Multiple Personality/Dissociative States, Chicago.

Coons, P. M., & Milstein, V. (1990). Self-mutilation associated with dissociative disorders. *Dissociation*, *3*, 81–87.

Coons, P. M., & Milstein, V. (1992). Psychogenic amnesia: A clinical study of 50 cases. *Dissociation*, *5*, 73–79.

Coons, P. M., Bowman, E. S., & Milstein, V. (1988). Multiple personality disorder: A clinical investigation of fifty cases. *Journal of Nervous and Mental Diseases*, *176*, 519–527.

Dell, P. F., & Eisenhower, J. W. (1990). Adolescent multiple personality disorder. *Journal of the American Academy of Child and Adolescent Psychiatry*, *29*, 359–366.

Ellenberger, H. F. (1970). *The discovery of the unconscious*. New York: Basic Books.

Fichter, C. G., Kuhlman, D. T., Gruenfeld, M. J., & Hughes, J. R. (1990). Decreased episodic violence and increased control of dissociation in a carbamazepine-treated case of multiple personality. *Biological Psychiatry*, *27*, 1045–1052.

Fine, C. G. (1988). Thoughts on the cognitive-perceptual substrates of multiple personality disorder. *Dissociation*, *1*(4), 5–10.

Fine, C. G. (1990). The cognitive sequelae of incest. In R. P. Kluft, (Ed.), *Incest-related syndromes of adult psychopathology* (pp. 161–182). Washington, DC: American Psychiatric Press.

Fisher, C., & Joseph, E. D. (1949). Fugue with awareness of loss of personal identity. *Psychoanalytic Quarterly*, *18*, 480–493.

Frankel, F. H. (1990). Hypnotizability and dissociation. *American Journal of Psychiatry*, *147*, 823–829.

Ganaway, G. K. (1989). Historical truth versus narrative truth: Clarifying the role of exogenous trauma in the etiology of multiple personality disorder and its variants. *Dissociation*, *2*, 205–220.

Henderson, J. L., & Moore, M. (1944). The psychoneuroses of war. *New England Journal of Medicine*, *230*, 273–279.

Herman, J. L., & Schatzow, E. (1987). Recovery and verification of memories of childhood sexual trauma. *Psychoanalytic Psychology*, *4*, 1–14.

Hilgard, E. R. (1986). *Divided consciousness: Multiple controls in human thought and action* (expanded edition). New York: Wiley.

Jones, D. P. H. (1991). Ritualism and child sexual abuse. *Child Abuse and Neglect*, *15*, 163–170.

Keyes, D. (1981). *The minds of Billy Milligan*. New York: Bantam.

Kluft, R. P. (1983). Hypnotherapeutic crisis intervention in multiple personality. *American Journal of Clinical Hypnosis*, *26*, 205–220.

Kluft, R. P. (1984). The treatment of multiple personality disorder: A study of 33 cases. *Psychiatric Clinics of North America*, *7*, 9–29.

Kluft, R. P. (1985). The natural history of multiple personality disorder. In R. P. Kluft (Ed.), *Childhood antecedents of multiple personality* (pp. 197–238). Washington, DC: American Psychiatric Press.

Kluft, R. P. (1987a). An update on multiple personality disorder. *Hospital and Community Psychiatry*, *38*, 363–373.

Kluft, R. P. (1987b). Making the diagnosis of multiple personality disorder. In F. F. Flach (Ed.), *Diagnostic and psychopathology* (pp. 207–225). New York: Norton.

Kluft, R. P. (1987c). The parental fitness of mothers with multiple personality disorder: A preliminary study. *Child Abuse and Neglect*, *11*, 272–280.

Kluft, R. P. (1987d). The simulation and dissimulation of multiple personality disorder. *American Journal of Clinical Hypnosis*, *30*, 104–118.

Kluft, R. P. (1988). The dissociative disorders. In J. A. Talbot, R. E. Hales, & S. C. Yudofsky (Eds.), *The American psychiatric press textbook of psychiatry* (pp. 557–584). Washington, DC: American Psychiatric Press.

Kluft, R. P. (1989). Reflections on allegations of ritual abuse. *Dissociation*, *2*, 191–193.

Kluft, R. P. (1990a). Incest and subsequent revictimization: The case of therapist-patient sexual exploitation, with a description of the sitting duck syndrome. In R. P. Kluft (Ed.), *Incest-related syndromes of adult psychopathology* (pp. 263–287). Washington, DC: American Psychiatric Press.

Kluft, R. P. (1990b). Dissociation and revictimization: A preliminary study. *Dissociation*, *3*, 167–173.

Kluft, R. P. (1991a). Multiple personality disorder. In A. Tasman & S. M. Goldfinger (Eds.), *The American psychiatric press annual review of psychiatry* (vol. 10) (pp. 161–188). Washington, DC: American Psychiatric Press.

Kluft, R. P. (1991b). Clinical presentations of multiple personality. *Psychiatric Clinics of North America*, *14*, 605–630.

Kluft, R. P. (in press-a). Treatment trajectories in multiple personality disorder. *Dissociation.*

Kluft, R.P. (in press-b). Completed suicides in multiple personality disorder patients: A study of five cases. *Dissociation.*

Kluft, R. P., Braun, B. G., & Sachs, R. G. (1984). Multiple personality disorder, intrafamilial abuse, and family psychiatry. *International Journal of Family Psychiatry, 5,* 283–301.

Kopelman, M. D. (1987a). Amnesia: Organic and psychogenic. *British Journal of Psychiatry, 150,* 428–442.

Kopelman, M. D. (1987b). Crime and amnesia: A review. *Behavioral Sciences and the Law, 5,* 323–342.

Lanning, K. V. (1991). Ritual abuse: A law enforcement perspective. *Child Abuse and Neglect, 15,* 171–173.

Lewis, D. O., & Bard, J. S. (1991). Multiple personality and forensic issues. *Psychiatric Clinics of North America, 14,* 741–756.

Lishman, W. A. (1987). *Organic psychiatry* (2nd ed.). Cambridge, MA: Blackwell Scientific.

Loewenstein, R. J. (1991). Psychogenic amnesia and psychogenic fugue: A comprehensive review. In A. Tasman & S. M. Goldfinger (Eds.), *The American Psychiatric Press Annual Review of Psychiatry* (Vol. 10) (pp. 189–22). Washington, DC: American Psychiatric Press.

Loewenstein, R. J., & Putnam, F. W. (1990). The clinical phenomenology of males with multiple personality disorder. *Dissociation, 3,* 135–143.

Nemiah, J. C. (1980). Dissociative disorders. In H. Kaplan, A. Freedman, & B. Sadock (Eds.), *Comprehensive textbook of psychiatry* (3rd ed.) (pp. 1544–1561). Baltimore: Williams and Wilkins.

Orne, M. T., Dinges, D., & Orne, E. C. (1984). On the differential diagnosis of multiple personality in the forensic context. *International Journal of Clinical and Experimental Hypnosis, 32,* 118–190.

Putnam, F. W. (1985). Dissociation as a response to extreme trauma. In R. P. Kluft (Ed.), *Childhood antecedents of multiple personality* (pp. 66–97). Washington, DC: American Psychiatric Press.

Putnam, F. W. (1988). The switch process in multiple personality disorder and other state-change disorders. *Dissociation, 1*(1), 24–32.

Putnam, F. W. (1989). *Diagnosis and treatment of multiple personality disorder.* New York: Guilford.

Putnam, F. W. (1991a). Dissociative phenomena. In A. Tasman & S. M. Goldfinger (Eds.), *American Psychiatric Press Review of Psychiatry* (Vol. 10) (pp. 145–160). Washington, DC: American Psychiatric Press.

Putnam, F. W. (1991b). The satanic ritual abuse controversy. *Child Abuse and Neglect, 15,* 175–179.

Putnam, F. W., Guroff, J. J., Silberman, E. K., Barban, L., & Post, R. M. (1986). The clinical phenomenology of multiple personality disorder: Review of 100 recent cases. *Journal of Clinical Psychiatry, 47,* 285–293.

Ross, C. A. (1989). *Multiple personality disorder: Diagnosis, clinical features, and treatment.* New York: Wiley.

Ross, C. A. (1991). The epidemiology of multiple personality disorder and dissociation. *Psychiatric Clinics of North America, 14,* 503–517.

Ross, C. A., & Norton, G. R. (1989a). Suicide and parasuicide in multiple personalty disorder. *Psychiatry, 52,* 365–371.

Ross, C. A., & Norton, G. R. (1989b). Differences between men and women with multiple personality disorder. *Hospital and Community Psychiatry, 40,* 186–188.

Ross, C. A., Joshi, S., & Currie, R. (1990). Dissociative experiences in the general population. *American Journal of Psychiatry, 147,* 1547–1552.

Ross, C. A., Joshi, S., & Currie, R. (1991). Dissociation in the general population: Identification of three factors. *Hospital and Community Psychiatry, 42,* 297–301.

Ross, C. A., Miller, S. D., Reagor, P., Bjornson, L., Fraser, G. A., & Anderson, G. (1990). Structured interview data on 103 cases of multiple personality disorder from four centers. *American Journal of Psychiatry, 147,* 596–601.

Ross, C. A., Norton, G. R., & Wozney, K. (1989). Multiple personality disorder: An analysis of 236 cases. *Canadian Journal of Psychiatry, 34,* 413–418.

Sargent, W., & Slater, E. (1941). Amnesic syndromes in war. *Proceedings of the Royal Society of Medicine, 34,* 757–764.

Saxe, G. N., van der Kolk, B. A., Berkowitz, R., Chinman, G., Hall, K., Lieberg, G., & Schwartz, J. (1993). Dissociative disorders in psychiatric patients. *American Journal of Psychiatry, 150,* 1037–1042.

Schacter, D. L. (1986). Amnesia and crime: How much do we really know? *American Psychologist, 41,* 286–295.

Scheflin, A. (1991, April). *Antisocial uses of hypnosis in declassified government documents.* Paper presented at the annual meeting of the American Society of Clinical Hypnosis, St. Louis, MO.

Schultz, R., Braun, B. G., & Kluft, R. P. (1989). Multiple personality disorder: Phenomenology of selected variables in comparison to major depression. *Dissociation, 2,* 45–51.

Spiegel, D. (1984). Multiple personality as a posttraumatic stress disorder. *Psychiatric Clinics of North America, 7,* 101–110.

Spiegel, D. (1986a). Dissociating damage. *American Journal of Clinical Hypnosis*, *29*, 123–131.

Spiegel, D. (1986b). Dissociation, double binds, and post-traumatic stress in multiple personality disorder. In B. G. Braun (Ed.), *Treatment of multiple personality disorder* (pp. 61–77). Washington, DC: American Psychiatric Press.

Spiegel, D. (1988). Dissociation and hypnosis in post-traumatic stress disorders. *Journal of Traumatic Stress*, *1*, 17–33.

Spiegel, D. (1991). Dissociation and trauma. In A. Tasman & S. M. Goldfinger (Eds.), *American psychiatric press review of psychiatry* (Vol. 10) (pp. 261–267). Washington, DC: American Psychiatric Press.

Spiegel, H., & Spiegel, D. (1978). *Trance and treatment*. New York: Basic Books.

Steinberg, M. (1991). The spectrum of depersonalization: Assessment and treatment. In A. Tasman & S. M. Goldfinger (Eds.), *American psychiatric press review of psychiatry* (Vol. 10) (pp. 223–247). Washington, DC: American Psychiatric Press.

Van Benschoten, S. C. (1990). Multiple personality disorder and ritual abuse: The issue of credibility. *Dissociation*, *3*, 22–30.

van der Kolk, B. A., & Greenberg, M. S. (1987). The psychobiology of the trauma response: Hyperarousal, constriction, and addiction to traumatic reexposure. In B. A. van der Kolk (Ed.), *Psychological trauma* (pp. 63–88). Washington, DC: American Psychiatric Press.

Watkins, J. G. (1984). The Bianchi (L.A. Hillside Strangler) case: Sociopath or multiple personality? *Journal of Clinical and Experimental Hypnosis*, *32*, 67–101.

West, L. J. (1967). Dissociative reaction. In A. M. Freedman & H. I. Kaplan (Eds.), *Comprehensive textbook of psychiatry* (pp. 885–898). Baltimore: Williams & Wilkins.

Young, W. C., Sachs, R. B., Braun, B. G., & Watkins, R. T. (1991). Patients reporting ritual abuse in childhood: A clinical syndrome. Report of 37 cases. *Child Abuse and Neglect*, *15*, 181–189.

CHAPTER 16

Sexual Deviations

Nathaniel McConaghy

Sexual deviations can result in both physical and psychological aggression toward victims, as well as self-destructive consequences for the perpetrator. Subjects with deviations of sex role behaviors also suffer physical and psychological aggression. The DSM-III-R (American Psychiatric Association, 1987) classified sexual deviations as paraphilias because it was considered this term correctly emphasized that the deviation (para) lay in that to which the person was attracted (philia). This appears inconsistent with its later statement that the imagery in a paraphilic fantasy is frequently the stimulus for sexual excitement in people without a paraphilia. The term paraphilia is retained in the DSM-IV draft criteria (APA, 1993), although the older term sexual deviation would seem more appropriate, as it emphasizes that the activity is carried out by a minority. No changes of significance were made in the DSM-IV draft criteria for the individual paraphilias from the criteria in the DSM-III-R.

DESCRIPTION OF THE DISORDER

Exhibitionism is the commonest of the deviations and results in the subject exposing his penis, not necessarily erect, to one or a few females, most commonly strangers, at or just past puberty. He may masturbate during or following the act, which is usually carried out in secluded areas or from an automobile. It has a strong compulsive quality and may be carried out several times a day. Untreated offenders are frequently charged repeatedly. Apart from the presence of the deviant behavior, exhibitionists appear unremarkable. The majority of 21 seeking treatment reported that they were happily married, and most of the remainder were having satisfactory heterosexual relationships (McConaghy, Armstrong, & Blaszczynski, 1985; McConaghy, Blaszczynski, & Kidson, 1988). Ten patients reported sex offenses or charges additional to exhibitionism, mainly heterosexual pedophilia, which could reflect the tendency of exhibitionists to choose victims around the age of puberty. One

NATHANIEL MCCONAGHY • The Prince of Wales Hospital, Randwick, N.S.W. Australia.

Handbook of Aggressive and Destructive Behavior in Psychiatric Patients, edited by Michel Hersen, Robert T. Ammerman, and Lori A. Sisson. Plenum Press, New York, 1994.

reported voyeurism and one, sexual assault. Voyeurism appears a closely related offense, in that not infrequently exhibitionists report having carried out occasional acts of voyeurism and vice versa. Voyeurism appears equally compulsive, with both exhibitionists and voyeurs commonly reporting marked excitement and physiological concomitants of high arousal, such as increased heart rate and sweating prior to carrying out the offense. The commonest form of voyeurism is peeping, the observing of a woman undressing (usually a stranger). While observing the women the offender frequently masturbates. Seeking opportunities for peeping often leads the offender to enter private property, which can lead to the commission of further offenses (in particular sexual assault and theft). The personality of voyeurs appears unremarkable, and most are married by the time they are convicted or seek treatment. A related offense is going into women's lavatories to see or hear a woman urinating or defecating.

Pedophilia, sexual activity with a child, at times is carried out by women, unlike exhibitionism and voyeurism, which are almost invariably carried out by men, although instances involving women are very rarely reported. O'Connor (1987) stated that he could find no systematic studies of female sex offenders. The heterosexual male pedophiles (i.e., men who offended against female children) studied by Groth and Birnbaum (1978) were attracted to adult women, and most were married. Their victims were related or well known to them. At the time of the offense, they may have been sexually deprived. Heterosexual pedophiles molest one or a few girls repeatedly. In contrast, homosexual male pedophiles commonly molest a considerable number of boys on one or a few occasions. Their victims are usually strangers or casual acquaintances. Most homosexual pedophiles, though of average intelligence or above, are not attracted socially or sexually to adults of their own age of either sex. They are single and may spend much of their leisure time in pinball arcades or other places where young boys congregate. Heterosexual pedophiles, compared to homosexual pedophiles, were found more likely to be heavy drinkers, to be of lower socioeconomic class, to have had little schooling, and to have committed other criminal offenses (Lukianowicz, 1972; Swanson, 1968). Heterosexual pedophiles, who, in my experience, do not show evidence of antisocial behavior or low ethical standards, commonly report complete lack of awareness of any attraction to prepubertal girls prior to their offense. Such offense tends to occur impulsively in relation to an unexpected opportunity, such as a girl wrestling with them in a pool or cuddling with them.

Sadomasochists are sexually aroused by infliction of physical pain or psychological domination or humiliation. The sadist is aroused by performing the act and the masochist by being its victim. Commonly the same person enjoys both roles, and masochists may inflict pain on themselves. Sadomasochists rarely seek help but have been investigated by questionnaires given to members of clubs or sent to subjects advertising in magazines for partners. Of respondents, 20–30% were women, few of whom were paid for their services (Breslow, Evans, & Langley, 1985; Moser & Levitt, 1987). More of the women were bisexual and submissive than the men, most of whom were heterosexual. The majority of respondents were both sadistic and masochistic, were above average in intelligence and social status, and wished to continue sadomasochistic activities. Some men seek treatment for bondage (the urge to tie up their sexual partner) in the absence of other sadomasochistic practices. Sexual asphyxia is considered a form of masochism in some classifications. Subjects with this condition increase their sexual arousal by temporary suffocation, using devices such as nooses, masks, or plastic bags. Knowledge concerning sexual asphyxia has mainly been obtained from the study of resulting accidental deaths. Of 132 subjects of such deaths reported by Hazelwood, Dietz, and Burgess (1983), 37 were teenagers and 5 were female. Sexual asphyxia is distinguished from suicide by features found at the scene of the fatality. The apparatus used to produce suffocation may show signs of regular use and of a failsafe procedure that proved ineffective. There is evidence of autoerotic activity, such as erotic literature, exposure of the genitals, presence of seminal ejaculate, and at times of cross-dressing, fetishism, bondage, and/or pain-producing devices, such as nipple clamps.

The DSM-IV draft criteria for sexual sadism remain those of the DSM-III-R. No changes were proposed in the DSM-IV options book (APA, 1991) in regard to the different diagnosis of sexual sadism from rape and other sexual assault, which included as a form of sexual sadism those rapes and sexual assaults in which the suffering inflicted on the victim is far in excess of that necessary for compliance, and the visible pain of the victim is sexually arousing. These were considered to be carried out by less than 10% of rapists. The DSM-III-R made the further statement that some rapists are sexually aroused by forcing a person to engage in intercourse, but not by the victim's suffering, so that they are not regarded as sadists. Present evidence would question that such rapists exist. In a series of studies, about 40% of university students reported some likelihood of raping a woman if they could be assured no one would know and that they could in no way be punished (Malamuth, 1989). When investigated by a male experimenter, students acknowledging this likelihood reported greater arousal to descriptions of sexual assault when the woman experienced pain than when she did not (Malamuth & Check, 1983). Of 50 single undergraduate men, 19 reported more than one episode where their dating partners had expressed dissatisfaction because the men had exceeded the sexual limits the partner preferred. These 19 men compared to the remainder reported that pictures of distressed women in bondage were more sexually stimulating than those of similar women displaying positive effect (Heilbrun & Leif, 1988).

In their study of 1,000 consecutive rape victims, Bowie, Silverman, Kalick, and Edbril (1990) found two predominant types of rape, similar to those described by Burgess and Holmstrom (1980) as blitz and confidence rapes. Blitz rapes were sudden surprise attacks by unknown assailants. Confidence rapes involved some nonviolent interaction between the rapist and the victim before the attacker's intention to commit rape became apparent. Blitz rapes generally occurred in settings the victims assumed to be secure, with significantly more occurring in their homes. Blitz rape victims were more likely to have experienced actual threats to their lives and were twice as likely as confidence rape victims to have seen a weapon or had the presence of one implied by the rapist. Blitz victims resisted their assailants less frequently than confidence victims and attempted to flee the situation only half as often. Confidence rape victims were three times more likely than blitz victims to have consumed alcohol or other drugs. The rape was more likely to have taken place in the rapist's home, where the victim had spent some time, or in an automobile in which she was in transit with the assailant. Confidence rape victims waited significantly longer before seeking medical help. Some, particularly victims of date rapes, were unclear that the assault constituted rape. Confidence rape assailants were more likely to be of the same race as their victims, to have known the victim's name and/or address, to have consumed alcohol or other drugs before committing the rape, and to have prolonged the incident beyond 5 hours. In a comparison of rapes reported with those not reported to the police, Holmstrom (1985) found that the more the features were those of blitz rape the more likely it was to be reported. This was consistent with Ageton's (1983) findings in her study of sexual assault of a representative sample of adolescents. Most of the assailants were boyfriends or dates in the victims' age range. Only 5% were reported to the police, mainly those carried out by unknown or multiple assailants, involving threats or employment of violence. Over two-thirds of victims told their friends but over three-quarters did not inform their parents.

In most studies of rape it is taken for granted that only women are victims. Groth and

Burgess (1980) described 22 cases of male rape. Most had occurred when the men were engaged in solitary out-of-doors activities, or hitchhiking. They were usually intimidated by threat of physical harm or were suddenly hit or overpowered. Three were entrapped by the offender getting them drunk. The majority were sexually penetrated, and in half the cases the offender attempted to get the victim to ejaculate. All the offenders were male and half were known to the victims. Sarrel and Masters (1982) reported a series of rapes of men by women.

Fetishists are sexually aroused by nonliving objects, commonly clothing, shoes, or gloves; or by parts of the body that are not secondary sexual characteristics, usually feet, hands, or hair. They frequently masturbate while holding, rubbing, or smelling the fetish. Fetishists at times enter private property to obtain their fetishes, and may assault a resident if discovered. Frotteurism, the pressing of the subject's penis against the body of an unknown women, usually in crowded situations such as public transport; toucheurism, the intimate touching of an unknown woman; and obscene telephone calling can be psychologically distressing to women victims.

Deviations of sex-linked behaviors are sufficiently recognized by the lay public to have attracted the labels sissiness and tomboyism. Strangely, no scientific terms have replaced these labels. In its extreme form in young boys, sissy behaviors include dressing in female clothes at every opportunity, using cosmetics and jewelry, and walking and posturing like girls. Prospective studies have shown that the majority of these boys self-identify as homosexual in adulthood (Green, 1987; Zuger, 1966, 1984). Workers studying extreme sissiness have ignored less extreme forms or considered that they were categorically different (Zuger & Taylor, 1969). However, in retrospective studies, both patient (Bieber, 1962) and nonpatient subjects (Evans, 1969; Saghir & Robins, 1973) who self-identified in adulthood as homosexual, compared to heterosexual subjects, reported that as children they were significantly more likely to be fearful of physical injury. They also avoided fights and involvement in competitive sport. These behaviors are included in the lay concept of sissy behaviors. The behaviors were also found to correlate with the degree of homosexual feelings reported by subjects, most of whom were predominantly heterosexual (McConaghy, 1987). Tomboyism in girls incorporates strong involvement in competitive sport, initiation of physical fighting, and preference for boys' clothes. Its association with identification as homosexual in adulthood has been less investigated, but would appear to be weaker than the equivalent association in boys. Women high in masculinity on the Bem (1974) Sex-Role Inventory, retrospectively reported higher levels of tomboyism in their girlhoods than those low in masculinity (McConaghy & Zamir, submitted). They showed no increased likelihood of identifying as homosexual. Sissy behaviors in boys are associated with their victimization (Harry, 1989), and high masculinity in both male and female university students with their being sexually coercive (McConaghy & Zamir, in press).

Deviations of sexual identity can be associated with urges to cross-dress—the condition originally termed transvestism. The development of an operation to convert male to female genitalia made it apparent that two conditions were involved. Male cross-dressers who sought the operation reported a sustained opposite sex identity and wished to live permanently as women. They were termed transsexuals (Benjamin, 1954). Those who did not seek the operation were satisfied with episodes of cross-dressing, during which they usually adopted a female first name and enjoyed appearing to pass as women in company. The term transvestite was retained for these subjects. No women with compulsion to cross-dress equivalent to that of male transvestites have been described. About 30% of transsexuals are women. Both transsexuals and transvestites commence cross-dressing in childhood. At puberty, cross-dressing produces sexual arousal in transvestites, so that at this stage their condition appears to be a form of fetishism. Fetishism of female underwear or transvestism has been reported in many of the rare subjects who carry out sexual or sadistic murders (Brittain, 1970; Revitch, 1980). Most were reported to be poorly educated, from lower social classes, socially isolated, emotionally flattened, weird in personality, overtly or latently psychotic, to have convictions for nonsexual offenses, and to express hatred, contempt, and fear of women. They appear to be very different from the typical self-identified sadomasochists.

EPIDEMIOLOGY

Several surveys of representative community samples investigated the prevalence of most mental disorders but did not include sexually deviant behaviors, so this information is limited. In response to a inventory about sexual experiences and fantasies, 4% of male university students reported having exhibited their body in public in the last 3 months (Person, Terestman, Myers, Goldberg, & Salvadori, 1989). The study's implication that this was sexual exposure was not clarified. Exhibitionism accounted for a third of sexual convictions for sexual offenses in the United States, Canada, England, and Germany, but was less frequent in France and Italy (Rooth, 1973). The majority of subjects charged with sex-related crimes reported by Beck, Borenstein, and Dreyfus (1986) were accused of exhibitionism. Exhibitionists made up 21 of 45 sex offenders consecutively seeking treatment (McConaghy et al., 1985, 1988). Thirty percent of women reported being victims of exhibitionists (DiVasto, Kaufman, Jackson, Christy, Pearson, & Burgett, 1984). Less data are available to indicate the prevalence of voyeurism, but substantially fewer voyeurs than exhibitionists seek treatment or are charged with sex offenses. Voyeurs made up 4 of the 45 offenders in the studies of McConaghy et al. (1985, 1988).

The prevalence of sexual molestation of children, particularly girls, has been intensively studied. Due to the infrequency with which such molestation is reported, its prevalence has been determined from retrospective questioning of adults. Differences in definition and methods of collecting information has led to considerable variation in the findings. Studies that used trained women in face-to-face interviews to ask a number of questions about situations where abuse may have occurred have reported the highest figures. Using this approach, Russell (1986) found that 28% of San Francisco women had experienced sexual abuse before the age of 14 years: 12% from a relative and 20% from a non-relative (some of these women were victims of abuse from both a relative and nonrelative). Sexual abuse was defined as any sexual contact or attempted contact with a relative 5 years or more older, whether or not the child considered it neutral or positive. Using a similar approach, Wyatt (1985) found the highest prevalence yet reported; 62% of Los Angeles women experienced sexual abuse prior to the age of 18 years. Wyatt and Peter's (1986) conclusion that failure to use face-to-face interview and multiple probing questions is associated with markedly lower prevalence rates is supported by more recent surveys. As part of the Los Angeles Epidemiologic Catchment Area Project, Siegel, Sorenson, Golding, Burnam, and Stein (1987) interviewed 1,645 women, of whom about a quarter were Hispanic and the remainder largely non-Hispanic whites. They were asked once if anyone had tried to pressure or force them to have sexual contact. Seven percent reported such experiences before the age of 16 years. Non-Hispanic white women under 40 years reported a prevalence of 15%. Prepubertal experiences with postpubertal partners not obtained by force or pressure were not classified as abusive, which would have further reduced the prevalence in relation to other studies. The assailant's relationship to the victim was similar to that found by Russell. Strangers comprised 22%, acquaintances 56%, and relatives 23%, of whom 13% were parents. Continued assault was more likely to be carried out by a relative, and 93% of the assailants were male.

No studies have used trained interviewers to employ a series of probing questions to retrospectively determine the prevalence of sexual abuse of male children. A U.S. national survey reported that 27% of women and 16% of men were molested in childhood (Finkelhor & Lewis, 1988). The Los Angeles Epidemiologic Catchment Area (ECA) Project found that 3.8% of the total sample of 1,480 men and 6.5% of those who were non-Hispanic whites under 40 years of age reported being pressed or forced into sexual contacts (Siegel et al., 1987). A national survey of 2,000 adults in Canada found that 22% of women and 9% of men had experienced serious and unwanted sexual abuse before the age of 18 (Carver, Stalker, Stewart, & Abraham, 1989). In contrast to these figures from community surveys, in which about half as many male as female children were sexually abused, a National Incidence Study that collected data on all cases known to professionals in the United States (Alter-Reid, Gibbs, Lachenmeyer, Sigal, & Massoth, 1986) found 83% of victims to be female. Alter-Reid et al. quoted similar findings from an equivalent United Kingdom study. Also, the annual national statistics on sexually abused children provided by the U.S. child protection system consistently reported male cases to be 20% less than female cases (Faller, 1989). Faller reported 373 cases of sexual abuse referred to Michigan child protection agencies between 1979 and 1986. Twenty-eight percent were male—the highest percentage reported in clinical studies.

In national reported child protection cases, 23% of boys and 14% of girls were sexually abused outside the home (Faller, 1989). Faller's study reported comparable figures: 37% of boys and 11% of girls suffered extrafamilial abuse. Faller pointed out that the incidence of extrafamilial abuse is higher in both males and females investigated in community surveys. In Finkelhor's 1979 and 1984 studies, 83% and 77% of boys and 56% and 66% of girls were abused by nonfamily members. It is likely that the proportion of extrafamilial to intra-familial abuse increases with the age of the victim and that extrafamilial abuse is less likely to be reported. This would account for child victims being younger in clinical than community studies. In Faller's study the mean age at onset of abuse of boys was 6.3 years and for girls, 5.5 years. In a study of 566 sexually abused children seen at a sexual assault crisis center of an inner-city hospital, the male victims showed one modal peak at age 7, while the female distribution showed modal peaks at ages 6 and 15 with a sharp decrease in reported cases between 6 and 11 (Alter-Reid et al., 1986). The mean age of those at first assault in the community Los Angeles area project (Siegel et al., 1987) was 9.5 years. However, for victims of continued assault, it was 8.5 years, the assaults tending to end at the age of 13.1 years. In regard to the age of victims at the onset of sexual abuse, Faller (1989) commented on the inconsistency in the literature concerning whether the mean age at onset of abuse was higher in boys or girls.

No community surveys have attempted to establish the prevalence of pedophile sex offenders. Women have been reported to be perpetrators in from 4% (Russell, 1983) to 19% (Finkelhor, 1985) of offenses against girls and in 17% (Finkelhor, 1985) to 75% (Fromuth & Burkhart, 1989) of offenses against boys. The majority of male victims of females do not regard the experience as negative, so very few women are charged with the offense. Women were convicted of 1% of sex offenses and 1.5% of acts of indecency against children in Britain (O'Connor, 1987). If on average there are between one and two female victims of a pedophile, if 90% of pedophiles are male, if 30% of women are their victims, and if there are about four times as many adults as children, then 5% of men and 0.5% of women would molest girls. Since at least twice as many girls are molested as boys, and since homosexual pedophiles molest a considerable number of boys, the number of homosexual pedophiles must be much less than that of heterosexual pedophiles. About 15% of male and 2% of female university students in the United States and Australia reported some likelihood of having sexual activity with a prepubertal child if they could do so without risk (Malamuth, 1989; McConaghy & Zamir, in press).

Few data are available concerning the prevalence of sadomasochistic behaviors in community samples. In a U.S. national survey of 2,000 subjects (Hunt, 1974), 4.8% of men and 2.1% of women reported obtaining sexual pleasure by inflicting pain, and 2.5% of men and 4.6% of women reported obtaining sexual pleasure by receiving pain, most having carried out the behaviors in the previous year. In Person et al.'s (1989) investigation of university students' sexual experiences in the previous 3 months, 4–6% of women reported sexual acts of being forced to submit, bound, and degraded, and 1% of being tortured, beaten, whipped, or torturing a partner. A smaller percentage of men reported similar experiences. Though it was not stated that the subjects consented to the acts, this was implied by their being described as sadomasochistic and being presented in relation to reports of a much higher percentage of the students having sexual fantasies of these acts The DSM-III-R included mutilation and murder in the definition of sadomasochism, along with the typical acts of dominance and submission. Though sadistic murders attract extensive media coverage, they make up less than 1% of homicides between acquaintances and sexual partners (Swigert, Farrell, & Yoels, 1976). A survey of child murder showed that 3 of 83 victims had been killed in a sexual assault (Quinsey, 1986). Hazelwood et al. (1983) speculated that sexual asphyxia results in 500 to 1,000 deaths in the United States and Canada yearly.

The prevalence of rape reported in the FBI national crime statistics doubled from 1971 and 1981 to reach 34.4 of every 100,000 women, still less than a hundredth of the prevalence reported in community studies. No male victims were included. Koss and Oros (1982) developed a Sexual Experiences Survey to investigate the concept that rape represented an extreme behavior on a continuum with normal male sexual behavior. The survey investigated two continua: one of men's sexual experiences obtained by verbal coercion, threat of and use of force, and one of women's experiences as victims of such coercion. McConaghy and Zamir (in press) modified the survey so that both men and women could report experiences as aggressors and as victims of coercion. Koss and Oros (1982) investigated Kent State University students, and McConaghy and Zamir, University of New South Wales medical students. Thirty-three percent of Kent State women, 14% of Sydney women, and 13% of Sydney men reported experiences in which their partners were so aroused they could not stop them even though they did not want intercourse. Twenty-three percent of Kent State men, 11% of Sydney men, and 6% of Sydney women reported that they were so aroused they could not stop, although their partner did not want intercourse. Two percent of Kent State men and Sydney men and women reported the use of force to attempt to obtain sexual intercourse. Six percent of Kent State women and 2% of Sydney women reported having been raped. No Sydney men reported having raped or been raped. Three percent of Kent State men reported obtaining sexual intercourse by physical force when the women didn't want it. These data support the concept that sexual assault is dimensional.

When the prevalence of rape, like child molestation, is determined by trained interviewers who ask a series of probing questions in face-to-face interviews, experiences the subject may not report as sexual assault in answers to a single question are likely to be revealed as sexual assaults. With this method, Russell (1986) found a high prevalence of sexual assault in a community sample of San Francisco women. Using the narrowest definition of rape, viz., forced intercourse or intercourse obtained by physical threat or completed when the woman was unable to consent, 24% reported being victims of rape and 44% of attempted rape. Two studies supplementary to NIMH Epidemiologic Catchment Area surveys used a broader definition of sexual assault (any pressured or forced touching of the victim's or offender's sexual parts). In North Carolina, 7% of women 44 years of age or younger and 3% of women 45–64 years of age reported having been sexually assaulted (Winfield, George, Swartz, & Blazer, 1990). In Los Angeles, 13% of women reported having been sexually assaulted in adulthood (Sorenson, Stein, Siegel, Golding, & Burnam, 1987). This study also investigated male subjects, 7% of whom reported having been sexually assaulted in adulthood. Sexual assaults were reported more often by white non-Hispanic younger men and women. The most recent assault involved a male assailant in 75% of cases, who acted alone in 90% of cases and was acquainted with but not related to the victim in 77% of cases. Of assaults on women, 13% were by spouses and 13% by lovers; 6% of assaults of men were by spouses and 18% by lovers. The sex of the victims of the 25% of women assailants was not reported. In reviewing explanations as to why younger and more educated subjects reported higher rates of sexual assault, Sorenson et al. did not consider the possibility that these subjects may have been more prepared to recognize excessive pressure for sexual activity as assaultive. Most rapes of women in these surveys occurred when the women were younger than 20 years. Ageton (1983) concluded from her representative study of adolescents that from 5% to 7% of teenage girls were sexually assaulted yearly.

ETIOLOGY

The most widely accepted theories of etiology of sexual deviations are stimulus control and cognitive models. Stimulus control models propose that deviant behaviors are motivated by sexual arousal to the related deviant stimuli. They were initially supported by findings that sexually deviant males showed penile circumference responses (PCRs) to the deviant cues for their behaviors equal to or greater than their PCRs to cues for consenting sexual activity. For example, rapists, as compared to controls, showed greater PCRs to audiotaped descriptions of rape but equal or reduced PCRs to descriptions of consenting intercourse. These findings were obtained with small numbers of subjects. Later studies using larger numbers failed to replicate them. Baxter, Barbaree, and Marshall (1986) found no difference between the PCRs of rapists and nonrapists; Nagayama, Hall, Procter, and Nelson (1988) found no difference between the PCRs of child molesters and normals. One possible explanation for these negative findings was that PCR assessment of sexual arousal is of limited validity. McConaghy (1989) pointed out that it had never been adequately validated but had relied on studies that validated penile volume responses (PVRs) as providing an accurate measure of individual subjects' degree of homosexual and heterosexual feelings. The PVRs were assessed in the 10 or 20 seconds immediately following the exposure to a moderately strong sexual stimulus, a male or female nude. PCRs are assessed over 2 to 5 minutes following exposure to a variety of sexual stimuli, so it is possible subjects can more easily modify PCRs by deliberate use of sexual fantasy.

Many workers continue to accept the validity of PCR assessment (McAnulty & Adams, 1992). To do so and also accept the findings that the majority of rapist and child molesters are not more sexually aroused by rape and child stimuli than nonoffenders has forced some behavior therapists, previously the strongest proponents of the deviant sexual stimulus control model, to abandon it. Marshall and Barbaree (1990a) decided that the majority of exhibitionists, child molesters, and rapists were not sexually aroused by the situations or stimuli associated with their deviant behaviors. This view requires acceptance of the paradox that deviant subjects are not aroused by the stimuli for their behavior, which many normals find sexually arousing in fantasy (Crepault & Couture, 1980; Price & Miller, 1984). However, the view does account for the finding that a number of adult offenders report generalized arousal rather than sexual excitement when carrying out their deviant acts. To preserve the stimulus control model, while accounting both for this finding and an additional one, the author advanced the behavior completion hypothesis (McConaghy, 1980). The additional finding was that following aversive therapy for compulsive homosexuality, subjects reported that they could control behaviors previously experienced as compulsive, such as spending more time than they wished seeking encounters on beats. However, they showed no reduction in their homosexual arousal, either as assessed by their PVRs to pictures of nude men or subjectively, so they could enjoy desired homosexual experiences as before (McConaghy, 1976). Based on work of the neo-Pavlovian physiologists Sokolov and Anohkin, it was suggested that behavior completion mechanisms (BCMs) are established in the brain for these behaviors that are carried out repeatedly. When a cue for a habitual behavior is encountered in reality or imagination, the BCM for that behavior is activated. The BCM then monitors incoming stimuli that indicate the activity is being completed. If the subject delays completing the activity, the incoming stimuli are not received by the BCM, which activates the brain arousal system so that the subject experiences a high level of general arousal, increased heart rate, sweating, and a feeling of tension that may be sufficiently aversive as to compel the subject to complete the activity. Given the significant percentage of normals who experience some sexual arousal to deviant fantasies it could be expected that in adolescence, when sexual arousal is high and subjects are exploring their sexuality, some by chance and others deliberately would encounter situations where they act on their deviant urges. Some who repeat the deviant behaviors will with increasing maturity wish to cease them. They may find this impossible, since BCMs have become established, rendering the behaviors compulsive.

Cognitive models propose that deviant behaviors are motivated by attitudes and beliefs of the perpetrator. One consequence of the primary role of the women's movement in increasing public awareness of sexual assault has been widespread acceptance of the feminist perspective that rape is an act of social control by which patriarchal society intimidates and dominates women. Rape is seen as normative male behavior and rapists as conforming to a socially encouraged perception of the male sex role. Proponents of the theory (Herman, 1990) ignore the evidence that men are victims of a third of sexually coercive acts and that a significant percentage of women carry them out. Regarding rape as an act of social control led many feminists to argue that it is not sexually motivated and indicates nothing about male sexuality. Palmer (1988) critically reviewed and rejected the arguments supporting this position. He did not include the evidence discussed subsequently that reduction of rapists' level of the sex hormone testosterone is effective in reducing the likelihood of their reoffending. The major empirical support for the social control theory of rape was provided by cross-cultural studies that showed that cultures that idealize war and male toughness, encourage interpersonal violence, and give women little political or economic power are associated with high levels of rape (Herman, 1990; Stermac, Segal, & Gillis, 1990). It was considered that these features characterized U.S. society and that the rate of reported rape was higher in the United States than in other Western societies. As discussed previously, reported rape provides a poor index of its prevalence in the community, and more studies of this prevalence in various societies are required. Students in Australia as compared to the United States did report markedly lower rates of sexual coercion and rape (McConaghy and Zamir, in press).

Less radical cognitive approaches accept that not all men are equally likely to rape and attribute the difference to the degree to which they hold rape-supportive cognitions. These include "rape myths," for example, the belief that many women have an unconscious wish to be raped and unconsciously set up situations in which rape is likely, or the idea that a women who goes to a man's apartment on their first date implies she is willing to have sex. Burt (1980) found in both men and women that agreement with rape myths correlated with acceptance of other cognitions considered supportive of rape, viz., interpersonal violence, sex role stereotyping, and the belief that sexual interactions between men and women were adversarial. Acceptance of all four sets of beliefs was greater in older and less educated subjects. Empirical support that these cognitions are causal in sexual assault is lacking. Both incarcerated rapists (Stermac et al., 1990) and sexually assaultive adolescents (Ageton, 1983) did not differ from controls in prevalence of rape-supportive cognitions. Koss and Dinero (1988) investigated an approximately representative national sample of 2,972 male students at 32 U.S. institutions of higher education. Though the subjects' rape-supportive cognitions correlated with their sexually coercive behaviors, their early exposure to family violence, childhood sexual abuse, and early age of sexual initiation predicted their later sexually aggressive behaviors equally well, suggesting that their cognitions and sexually aggressive behaviors were both secondary to the childhood experiences, or to genetic determinants of these experiences. It is possible that rape-supportive cognitions may not differentiate rapists from nonrapists, but yet alter the climate of society so as to increase the prevalence of rape.

The psychiatric-psychopathological etiological theory of sex offenses, commonly considered to have been discarded (Scully & Marolla, 1985), is supported by a considerable amount of empirical evidence. In this model, offenders are regarded as driven by irresistible sexual impulses, as psychologically disordered, or as acting under the influence of alcohol; some victims are considered to be vulnerable to the offense. The theory was rejected from a feminist perspective as removing offenses against women and children from the realm of the everyday or normal world.

Characteristics of some victims of sex offenders may influence their likelihood of being victimized, though this should not be interpreted as in any way justifying their victimization. Prior to their assault, victims, as compared to controls, showed increased evidence of delinquency (Ageton, 1983) and higher prevalences of major depression, alcohol and drug abuse, antisocial personality, and phobias (Burnam, Stein, Golding, Siegel, Sorenson, Forsythe, & Telles, 1988). Koss and Dinero (1988) also found victims of assault as compared to controls to show higher use of alcohol prior to the assault. Lesbian and gay students were two to three times as likely to report having sex against their will as their heterosexual colleagues (Duncan, 1990).

In relation to the concept of irresistible sexual impulses, Scully and Marolla (1985) argued that a study of reported rapes showed that 71% were premeditated and so could not be impulsive. However, subjects' reports of irresistible impulses to carry out apparently premeditated behaviors such as gambling and shoplifting are accepted, and the behaviors are classified in the DSM-IV draft criteria (APA, 1993) as disorders of impulse control. Following treatment, subjects gain control of these disorders (McConaghy, 1988; Mc-Conaghy & Blaszczynski, 1988) and of sexually assaultive behaviors (McConaghy, 1990a), demonstrating that they were previously uncontrollable. The most consistent finding concerning the psychological disorders of sex offenders is that a high percentage show behaviors characteristic of antisocial or psychopathic personality disorder. Ageton (1983) cited reports that from 20% to 43% of men arrested for rape and sexual assault had previous convictions for other offenses, and Knight et al. (1985) found both convicted rapists and child molesters had previous convictions for nonsexual offenses. Marshall and Barbaree (1990a) pointed out that the greater exposure to parental violence in the childhood of sex offenders was similar to that of people with antisocial personalities. Herman (1990) concluded that many convicted sex offenders met the diagnostic criteria for sociopathic, schizoid, paranoid, and narcissistic personality disorders. She stated incorrectly that there was no evidence that these disorders were more common in undetected sexually aggressive males than in the total male population. Ageton (1983), in her study of a representative sample of adolescents, found that males who had committed sexual assaults, compared to the remainder, were basically delinquent youths. Koss and Dinero (1988) found that sexual aggression of male college students was associated with family violence in childhood, current use of alcohol, and poor relationships that reinforced highly sexualized views of women, consistent with the presence of antisocial personality traits. Additional evidence of the possible role of alcohol in relation to sex offenses were findings that police and victims confirmed alcohol intoxication in 70% of rapists (Marshall & Barbaree, 1990a). In contrasting the more common confidence and rarer blitz rapes, Bowie et al. (1990) found that prior to confidence rapes the assailants and victims were much more likely to have spent time together consuming alcohol or other drugs. In Ageton's (1983) study, about half the males who reported carrying out sexual assaults noted that they had been drinking or taking drugs prior to the event. Victims considered that the offender being drunk was a major factor precipitating the assault.

An etiological theory of sexual deviations that incorporates the current empirical evidence is that they are motivated by sexual arousal to cues for the deviant behaviors, but that social attitudes, fortuitous circumstances, personality factors, drug use, and physiological mechanisms maintaining habitual behaviors interact to determine whether such motivation is expressed in behaviors, and if it is, whether the behaviors are carried out rarely or repeatedly and compulsively.

AGGRESSION TOWARD SELF

The shame and guilt associated with the revelation of sexually deviant behavior may lead to attempted or successful suicide. There appears to be no published information concerning its prevalence. In the author's experience it has been more likely in extrafamilial heterosexual pedophiles. More commonly, offenders deal with their shame or other reactions to community hostility by leaving their place of residence to live in another suburb, or another town, if the town is small. Of the 29 adolescents identified as homosexual by Remafedi (1987), all but 1 had contemplated suicide and 10 had attempted it at least once. Some of the fatalities associated with sexual asphyxia might be prevented with more community awareness of the condition. Associates of the dead perpetrator not infrequently report some knowledge of the behavior that presumably out of embarrassment they failed to discuss with him, losing the opportunity to warn him concerning the danger and to suggest the need for treatment. A significant minority of sadomasochists reported self-bondage and pain infliction during masturbation (Breslow et al., 1985; Moser and Levitt, 1987), but reports of their needing to seek medical help appear rare, though this has been necessary in subjects who have inserted objects into their bladder or rectum for sexual stimulation.

AGGRESSION TOWARD OTHERS

The major studies of child sexual abuse classified as abusive acts that ranged from exposure and forced kissing to anal and vaginal penetration. Most studies provided little information concerning the frequency of the various acts. In Russell's (1986) study of San Francisco women, in almost half the cases of abuse by stepfathers and a quarter of those by biological fathers, the abuse was in the very serious category, which ranged from forceful penile-vaginal penetration to nonforceful attempted fellatio, cunnilingus, analingus, and anal intercourse. Herman (1985) reported that abuse of daughters usually began with fondling and proceeded to oral-genital activities, with vaginal intercourse not usually attempted until the child reached puberty. Of an approximately representative national sample of male students who were molested before 14 years of age, roughly a third reported exhibitionism, a third, fondling, and a third, attempted or successful penetration, as the most serious experience (Risin & Koss, 1987). Gomes-Schwartz, Horowitz, and Sauzier (1985) investigated 112 children who attended a family crisis program for sexually abused children. The most serious sexual acts were vaginal or anal intercourse in 28%, oral-genital contact or penetration by a foreign object in 38%, and fondling in 23%. Younger children were abused for a shorter time and were less likely to have experienced intercourse. The threat or use of force was not mentioned. Freund, Heasman, and Roper (1982) pointed out the enormous discrepancy in reported incidence of the use of force in sexual abuse of children, ranging from 0% to 50%. They attributed the discrepancy to the different samples of victims studied. None of the 18,000 persons interviewed by the Kinsey group claimed to have been sadistically victimized as a child (Quinsey, 1986). Berliner (1985) pointed out the common absence of physical evidence in reported cases of child abuse. Finkelhor and Lewis (1988) considered that most child sexual abuse did not involve violent attack on children but the use of authority or misrepresentation.

Much more attention has been given to the psychological effects of sexual abuse of children. In the 1950s, incestuous abuse was considered to occur in one family in a million (Weinberg, 1955). The discovery in the 1970s that it was nearer to one in ten (Hunt, 1974) was made in the context of the emphasis placed by the women's movement on sexual assault as a form of male domination of women. Rather than oppose the sexual abuse of children as exploitation of their inability to make an informed choice, it was opposed on the grounds of its harmful psychological effects. This required reversal of views expressed in the 1970s that these effects were often slight. Constantine (1981) reviewed 30 studies of the effects, finding that 20 reported some subjects without ill effect, 13 concluding that there was essentially no harm for the majority of subjects, and 6 identifying some subjects for whom the experience was "positive or beneficial." Workers convinced of the marked harmful effects of all childhood sexual abuse reacted by labeling workers who attempted to critically evaluate their evidence as skeptics, enabling the evaluations to be rejected without further discussion (Finkelhor and Browne, 1988). In other fields, skepticism is seen as essential to the scientific process. The major criticism concerns to what extent the symptoms following sexual abuse can be attributed to the abuse itself or to the concomitants of abuse, such as family pathology and the handling of the abusive experience.

Evidence of the immediate or short-term harmful effects of sexual abuse can be investigated only in the children who come to the attention of mental health professionals. These children could include those with more serious immediate effects. Asher (1988) reviewed evidence of the effects of recent abuse, pointing out that many victims are too young to verbalize information concerning their abuse and that it was imperative that professionals be aware of the signs and symptoms of abuse. In the preschool child these included sudden weight loss or gain, abdominal pain, vomiting, and urinary tract infections. More clearly indicative were perineal bruising and tears, pharyngeal infections, and venereal disease. Behavioral symptoms included sleep disturbance, nightmares, compulsive masturbation, precocious sex play, loss of toilet training, finger sucking, and clinging. These behaviors were generally interpreted as due to fear and anxiety concerning being punished, rejected from the family, or not believed if they revealed the abuse. Asher pointed out that many of these symptoms were typical of other emotional disorders of childhood. The attitude of the professional concerning whether it is potentially more damaging to fail to diagnose child sexual abuse when it is present or to diagnose it when it is absent will be a major factor in deciding whether to attribute nonspecific symptoms to such abuse and to report it to authorities as is mandatory. There are problems in interpreting even apparently specific features of abuse. Hobbs and Wynne (1989) diagnosed anal sexual abuse in 83% of boys and 29% of girls in whom a diagnosis of probable or confirmed sexual abuse was made, apparently at times on the basis of the anal changes, in particular anal dilatation. McCann, Voris, Simon, and Wells (1989) emphasized the need for normative data, finding anal dilatation in 50% of children screened to exclude possible cases of sexual abuse.

Long-term effects of sexual abuse of children and of sexual assault of adolescents and adults have been identified and intensively studied. Like the short-term effects, the long-term effects of childhood sexual abuse were not found to be specific (Finkelhor & Browne, 1988). Asher (1988) advised that the adolescent or adult victim's report of sexual abuse should not be discounted just because she presented with symptoms that were not typical. This type of presentation would seem infrequent in the light of the statement Asher also made pointing out the myriad of symptoms that have been attributed to childhood sexual abuse. These included depression, self-destructive behavior, anxiety and tension, anger and hostility, poor self-esteem, feelings of isolation and stigma, fear of and difficulty trusting others especially men, homosexuality, promiscuity, physical and sexual revictimization, marital and relationship problems, sexual difficulties, sleep disturbances including nightmares, eating disorders, drug and alcohol abuse, multiple and borderline personality disorders, schizophrenia, and murder (Asher, 1988; Finkelhor & Browne, 1988; Mzarek & Mzarek, 1981). The few studies that investigated male adult victims of childhood sexual abuse report a similar prevalence of similar effects (Briere, Evans, Runtz, & Wall, 1988; Johnson & Shrier, 1987). Before it can be accepted that symptoms in adults reporting childhood abuse in clinical studies are actually the effects of the abuse, it needs to be ascertained whether subjects who are vulnerable to psychiatric conditions are more likely to remember or interpret events in childhood as abusive. One group who may report falsely that they have been victims of child abuse are child molesters, as this could advance their legal disposition (Freund, Watson, & Dickey, 1990). To doubt the report of other subjects, including, for example, those with borderline personality who may gain much from the attention given victims, has itself been considered to be a form of abuse (Armsworth, 1989). Little evidence of pathology was found in male and female university students who reported at least one experience of childhood sexual abuse as compared to the remainder who did not (Fromuth, 1986; Fromuth & Burkhart, 1989).

In the studies they reviewed, Browne and Finkelhor (1986) found that duration of childhood sexual abuse, age at which it occurred, and whether or not it was incestuous, involved intercourse, or the victim felt compelled to keep it a secret were not consistently associated with severity of long-term symptoms. In regard to the degree of force employed, they stated that they were inclined to give credence to the studies that showed force to be a major traumagenic influence, despite the fact that a number of studies did not find an association. They concluded it was difficult to establish the severity of the risk of child sexual abuse being followed by significant long-term effects. When tests developed to assess the adjustment of members of the normal population were used to investigate victims of child sexual abuse, most victims appeared normal or only slightly impaired. Browne and Finkelhor considered that such standardized tests were not sensitive to more subtle forms of discomfort and difficulty.

In regard to the effect of sadistic behaviors on others, the DSM-III-R added to the usual behaviors of sadists, viz., infliction of humiliation and pain, the acts of rape, mutilation and murder. This inclusion and the DSM-III-R statement that the severity of sadistic acts increases over time, reinforce the stereotype that sadomasochism as a minority sexual practice is frequently associated with sexual violence. Studies of self-identified sado-masochists (Breslow et al., 1985; Moser & Levitt, 1987) found that beating, bondage, and fetishistic practices were common, but more extreme or dangerous practices were rare. Most subjects studied wished to continue sadomasochistic activities. The rarity with which self-identified sadomasochists seek psychological help or medical attention indicates that few find their condition emotionally distressing or suffer significant physical harm from their activities. In interviews with club members, Gosselin and Wilson (1980) concluded that most sadists had no wish to hurt their partners in "sex games" more than what was enjoyed or at least accepted by the partners. There is no evidence that self-identified sadists show an increased likelihood of raping nonconsenting subjects and, as discussed earlier, the personality and behavior of the very rare sex murderers is very different from those of sadomasochists investigated.

Possibly to emphasize that all sexually coercive behaviors are a form of rape, the degree of physical harm inflicted in investigations of sexual assaults is rarely specified. Palmer (1988) concluded that excessive force is used in only a minority of cases. He found that 15–20% of victims of rape reported to the police required hospital treatment of physical injuries and that severe lasting physical injuries were rare. Reported rapes constitute only a small percentage of total sexual assaults, mainly blitz rapes, but are likely to include most cases in which significant physical injury was inflicted. Quinsey and Upfold (1985) investigated 95 completed rapes and 41 attempts made by 72 men referred to a maximum security psychiatric institution. Sixty-nine victims were not injured, eight were treated in a clinic and released, seven were hospitalized overnight, and two were killed. Swift (1980) estimated that less than 1 rapist in 500 is convicted. Those convicted are likely to overrepresent rapists who severely injure their victims. In Ageton's (1983) study of a representative sample of adolescents, 27% of the sexually assaulted women experienced some pushing, slapping, and mild roughness; the majority were successful in deterring the assault. Of the assaults, 5% were reported to the police, mainly blitz rapes; that is, those carried out by unknown or multiple assailants and involving threats or employment of violence. In the Los Angeles ECA study of the prevalence of sexual assault (Sorenson et al., 1987), verbal pressure was used with 62% of the male and 27% of the female victims and harm or threat of harm with 37% of the female and 9% of the male victims. Of the victims, 83% tried to resist, and the outcome was some form of intercourse in 50% of women and 39% of men. Kaufman, Divasto, Jackson, Voorhees, and Christy (1980) considered the severity of rape may need to be greater for men to report it. Of the 14 males and 100 female victims who presented to a sexual assault team in New Mexico, 7 of the males and 23 of the females had been attacked by more than one assailant; 9 of the males were beaten, 5 so severely that they suffered more physical trauma than the 11 females who were beaten. Five of the males did not report their sexual assault during their initial contact with emergency department staff, preferring to seek treatment solely for their nongenital trauma. In a study of lifetime victimization of women by sexual or physical assault or robbery, Kilpatrick, Best, Saunders, and Veronen (1988) found that women sexually assaulted by husbands or dates sustained more physical injury than those assaulted by strangers.

More information is available concerning the psychological and behavioral effects of sexual assault. Apart from the study of Ageton (1983), the immediate effects have been studied only in subjects who report the assault or seek treatment. They were considered to suffer from a rape trauma syndrome (Burgess & Holmstrom, 1985). This is characterized by an initial acute or disruptive phase in which the victim reexperiences the trauma in daytime imagery, dreams, and nightmares; suffers numbing of responsiveness; and may show hyperalertness, sleep disturbance, guilt, impairment of memory and concentration, avoidance of situations reminiscent of the assault, and symptoms related to it, in particular sexual dysfunctions. In addition, she may experience compound reactions, depression, psychosis, psychosomatic disorders, suicidal behavior and drug use, and a delayed response to earlier unresolved sexual trauma. Similar responses were found in male victims (Groth & Burgess, 1980). Following this acute phase which may last days or weeks, a second phase of long-term reorganization occurs in which the victim has the task of restoring order to and control over her life. This phase could last months or years. In reviewing studies of longer-term effects of sexual assault of adult women, Nadelson, Notman, Zackson, and Gornick (1982) found some studies to report that most victims had recovered within a year, but in other studies a third to a half of the victims still experienced rape-related adjustment problems, including decreased social activities and worsening sexual relations with their partners, which persisted for years. In regard to individual symptoms following sexual assault, psychosexual dysfunctions appear to be the most commonly reported in clinical studies both in women victims of male assailants (Foley, 1985) and male victims of male (Groth & Burgess, 1980) and female assailants (Sarrel & Masters, 1982). Ellis (1983) reviewed studies that investigated relationships between the severity of victims' reactions and circumstances of the rape, including the degree of force and whether a weapon was used. No consistent relationships were revealed. Prior victimization, economic stress, and lack of social support were associated with slower recovery, as was a history of prior psychiatric or physical health problems and suicidal ideation or attempt. Ellis concluded that these findings were consistent with a crisis theory model of response to rape. The outcome of a crisis is not solely determined by antecedent factors such as the nature of the stress. The victim's previous experience and personality or character structure load the dice in favor of a positive or negative outcome. If this theory is correct, studies of community samples of rape victims would show the majority recovering fairly rapidly, whereas clinical studies would report high percentages with slow and minimal recovery.

Ageton (1983) was able to investigate the effects of recent sexual assaults in a community sample of adolescents. She concluded that the typical assault, a date rape, generated few negative reactions that persisted for 6 months. Reactions to the assault were not differentiated by race, age, social class, number of offenders, relationship to the offender, or the amount of force experienced. Only completion of the assault had a significant influence, being associated with more negative reactions in the following year. In contrast to this community study, clinical studies of adolescent victims of sexual assault reported severe effects, including depression and suicidal attempts (Asher, 1988). Mann (1981) found that the emotional impact of rape of adolescents who sought treatment was rated by health professionals as more severe on the parents than the victims.

Although homosexuality is no longer regarded as a sexual deviation, the opposite-sex-linked behaviors or effeminacy that in men precedes homosexuality in childhood and to some extent continues to accompany it into adolescence and adulthood is, when marked, classified as disorder of gender identity. A number of male homosexuals report physical and psychological abuse in childhood and adolescence in relation to sissy or effeminate behaviors. Harry (1989) pointed out the consistent findings of negative relationships of homosexual men with their fathers and found that homosexual as opposed to heterosexual male undergraduates reported experiencing more parental physical abuse in adolescence, the extent correlated with features of childhood femininity. There is less evidence as to whether tomboyism causes girls to suffer abuse. McConaghy and Silove (1992) found that opposite-sex behaviors in both male and female students correlated with negative relations with parents. Considerable media attention has been given to "gay bashings," the occasionally fatal physical assaults of homosexual men, particularly following the identification of homosexual activity with increased risk of HIV infection. Of 289 gay men and lesbians who answered a questionnaire (Anderson, 1982), 72% reported verbal harassment, 23% physical assault, and 6% (including 10 men) rape, because of their sexual orientation. Of those assaulted, 9% reported the incident to the police, 22% talked to a friend, and 66% took no action. Empirical support does not appear to have been sought for speculations that the perpetrators of gay bashings are in part motivated by conscious or unconscious fears of their own homosexual feelings.

CLINICAL MANAGEMENT

Despite evidence of lack of validity for the use of penile circumference responses (PCRs) to assess sexually abusive and assaultive males, discussed earlier, it remains central to the assessment of sex offenders in most treatment programs in North America (Quinsey & Earls, 1990). However, some workers are questioning its value (Marshall & Barbaree, 1990b). The author considers subjects' self-reports to provide the most valid information, supplemented where possible by information from their social contacts and victims, and records of past offenses. Sex offenders' self-reports of reduction in the strength of their deviant urges correlated strongly with reduction in their serum testosterone levels produced by medroxyprogesterone therapy (McConaghy et al., 1988). Both offenders and interviewer were unaware of the levels.

Current treatment programs for sexually abusive and assaultive offenders in North America mainly use multimodal approaches, though modification of inappropriate sexual arousal remains the central aim (Quinsey & Earls, 1990). This is usually attempted by use of an aversive procedure. With this procedure cues for the deviant arousal are presented followed by an unpleasant or aversive stimulus. The stimulus may be real, as in electric shock aversive therapy, or imagined in a state of relaxation, as in covert sensitization. Evidence that aversive therapy reduced deviant sexual interest was based on use of the invalid PCR assessment of homosexual interest (McConaghy, 1977, 1990b). As discussed earlier, the author's research indicated that aversive therapy does not reduce sexual interest but does give subjects control over compulsive urges (McConaghy, 1976). This finding led to the development of the behavior completion hypothesis. On the basis of this hypothesis, a treatment termed imaginal desensitization was developed and shown to be more effective than electric shock aversive therapy (McConaghy, Armstrong, Blaszczynski, & Allcock, 1983) and covert sensitization (McConaghy et al., 1985) in giving subjects control over compulsive urges. With imaginal desensitization, subjects are briefly trained to relax and then instructed to visualize being in situations where they have carried out deviant behaviors in the past but to visualize not completing the behaviors and leaving the situations while remaining relaxed. The behavior completion hypothesis also led to modification of medroxyprogesterone acetate (MPA) therapy of sex offenders. As introduced, 200 mg was given intramuscularly two to three times weekly before being reduced to 100 mg weekly to monthly. Patients generally became impotent for some period of time (Gagne, 1981), justifying the label of chemical castration. In the modified form (McConaghy et al., 1988), patients were given 150 mg every 2 weeks for 2 months and then monthly injections, for 4 months. The aim was to reduce their serum testosterone levels sufficiently to weaken the deviant urges while allowing their sexual arousal to physical stimulation to remain unimpaired so they could continue acceptable sexual activities. As they continued to experience cues for deviant activities without acting in response to them, the behavior completion mechanisms for the deviant acts gradually weakened, so when the therapy was ceased the subjects no longer experienced deviant urges as compulsive.

A program was developed and aimed at maximal use of minimal resources, enabling two part-time therapists to treat over 100 subjects yearly (McConaghy, 1990a). The subjects were given the choice of a week's inpatient treatment of 14 sessions of imaginal desensitization or 8 outpatient sessions in each of which they received an injection of MPA. If one treatment was not sufficiently effective they received the second. In the course of interviewing the patients, cognitive correction was attempted where appropriate and referral to community services made if treatment modules such as anxiety management or assertive or social skills training seemed indicated. Few patients made use of these resources, but the dropout from the basic program was very low. Multimodal programs in use in North America appear to incorporate these additional modules routinely and more intensively, making the programs more demanding of therapy resources. Studies comparing multimodal programs with those based primarily on a single therapy have not been carried out. In a comparison study of imaginal desensitization and MPA, 30 sex offenders were randomly allocated, 10 to one of two procedures and 10 to both. Differences in response of the three groups was not significant. A year following treatment, 28 had ceased deviant behavior, 2 of the 28 having required aversive therapy in addition. In the following 2 to 5 years, 3 relapsed but responded to reinstitution of MPA. This response was in the same range as that in more intensive programs (McConaghy, 1990a, 1990b).

A number of programs have been described for the management of both the immediate and long-term reactions of victims of child sexual abuse and sexual assault. Outcome data are rarely presented. Play therapies appear to be the most common treatments of younger child victims. Walker and Bolkovatz (1988) reviewed the use of different forms, seeing them as assisting the child heal from the experience, preventing or reversing the development of shame, providing a trust experience, and enabling the child to regain personal power. Gomes-Schwartz et al. (1985) considered that with young children who exhibit little manifest distress, repetitive probing into the details of the abuse should be avoided. A nationwide survey of 553 child sexual abuse programs (Keller, Cicchinelli, & Gardner, 1989) found that although over 88% focused on the victim, the majority took a family-oriented approach, and only 15% focused on the child and 6% on the adult victim exclusively. Incest cases were most often emphasized. In relation to treatment of the incest victim, Furness (1983) found that intervention should be aimed at changing family relationships and the underlying dynamics that led to and maintained the incest. However, Herman (1990) warned against regarding incest as merely a symptom of family dysfunction, stressing its criminal and addictive nature. She recommends crisis intervention, using an active and directive approach. In the postcrisis period, she found that the family was so fragmented that family therapy was not possible, but that group therapy for mothers, fathers, and child victims was far more promising. Giarretto (1978, 1981) developed a treatment program from a humanistic psychology perspective. He also decided against conjoint family therapy immediately following disclosure of incest and recommended individual counseling for mother, father, and daughter, succeeded by mother–daughter, then marital and father–daughter, and finally group counseling. His program was independently evaluated by Kroth (1979), who found a recidivism rate of 0.6%, compared with an average of 2% reported by other programs. The outcome of 0.6% needs to treated with caution, since 40% of the treated families said they might not reveal further child abuse if it occurred. Conte and Berliner (1988) criticized the distribution of services to abused children, stating that it was unduly influenced by the assertiveness of the child's caseworker and class, race, and economic factors rather than the severity of the child's problem.

In treating adult victims of childhood sexual abuse, Courtois and Sprei (1988) recommended an eclectic approach, incorporating gestalt, psychodrama, psychodynamic, cognitive, behavioral, social learning, transactional analytic, and humanistic strategies along with bibliotherapy. Controversy between supporters (Rychtarik, Silverman, Van Landingham, & Prue, 1984) and critics (Kilpatrick & Best, 1984) of a behavioral approach indicates the need for empirical data derived from comparative evaluations of different programs.

With regard to the treatment of rape victims who disclose the assault, Burgess and Holmstrom (1985) recommended immediate crisis intervention, considering the speed of its commencement crucial in improving the prognosis. Along with recognition and management of the emotional trauma, Hochbaum (1987) discussed the need for assessment and treatment of physical injuries, prevention of venereal disease and pregnancy, and appropriate collection of evidence. He pointed out the discomfort therapists could experience in the latter role, leading to its neglect. McCombie and Arons (1980) discussed the emotional problems rape counselors may need to resolve in relation to anger toward the aggressor, or shame and guilt concerning their own rape fantasies. The counselor should accept the role of a nonjudgmental, noncontrolling interviewer, who identifies and supports the victim's ego strengths and does not encourage regression. Steketee and Foa (1987) reviewed alternative multimodal cognitive-behavioral approaches. In a 4- to 6-hour Brief Behavioral Intervention Program used immediately after the rape, the victim is encouraged to recall the rape events in imagery and to experience and express emotional reactions to it. Feelings of guilt and responsibility for the rape are reduced by discussion of societal expectations and rape myths. Coping skills, such as self-assertion, relaxation, thought stopping and methods for resuming normal activities, are then taught. In the treatment of adolescent rape, the most common form, Mann (1981) found that crisis workers spent more time counseling and calming the parents than the adolescents. Burgess and Holmstrom (1985) followed therapy of the acute phase of posttraumatic stress disorder with rape work to treat the second phase of long-term reorganization. In this phase the victim has the task of restoring order to an control over his or her life. They point out that this phase could last months or years.

LONGITUDINAL PERSPECTIVES

Development of programs to prevent sexual aggression is a recent initiative, and there is little evidence of their efficacy. They include school programs to reduce children's fear of saying no to a family member or friend and increase their awareness of what constitutes appropriate and inappropriate touching. Brassard, Tyler, and Kehle (1983) recommended that the latter issue be included in accompanying parent education programs. Films and video presentations are available to accompany such programs or for presentation on public television, where there may be resistance to presenting sensitive material. Without evaluation, some uncertainty must exist concerning what content is appropriate. Asher (1988) believes that programs aimed at empowering children by teaching them what to do when approached by strangers may instill fear of men and further reinforce the concept of men as powerful, as well as implicitly convey that children are in part responsible for their own victimization.

Swift (1985) was critical of conventional approaches to prevention of sexual assaults that advise women to restrict such activities as going alone to parks or being out alone at night. Bart and O'Brien (1984) investigated assaulted women in the Chicago area to determine differences between those who were raped and those who had avoided rape. Over 80% of women who fled from the rapist avoided being raped, as did almost 70% of women who fought their attacker. Women who avoided rape were taller and heavier, played football or another contact sport often in childhood, and engaged in sport regularly. The finding supports the value of training women in physical resistance, a rape prevention strategy currently widely sponsored by feminist groups and police departments.

Swift (1985) pointed out that few efforts have been directed at reducing men's likelihood of sexually coercing women, except by treatment after they have offended. Herman (1990) recommended that boys and young men be considered a priority for preventive work and organized male groups that foster traditional sexual attitudes targeted, including athletic teams, college fraternities, and the military. I believe the little acknowledged information that a significant number of men are capable of being sexually aroused by female children should be emphasized in education programs. The initial offenses of many molesters of children occurs in response to an unexpected opportunity in which they experience arousal, of which they were previously unaware they were capable. Herman (1990) argues that vigorous enforcement of existing criminal laws prohibiting sexual assault might be expected to have some preventive effect. In a cross-cultural study, Otterbein (1979) found a correlation between severity of punishment and frequency of rape of $-.68$. Swift (1985) pointed out that research had confirmed that punishment reduced crime only in relation to its certainty and that 90% of cases of rape are unreported. She concluded that in 1,000 cases only two convictions resulted. Attitudes of law enforcement agencies to rape victims will need to be changed in order for more women first to report the rape and then not withdraw from the subsequent trial due to the trauma involved (Murphy, 1980).

CASE ILLUSTRATION

X was a cherubic-looking boy who was small for his 13 years. He attended with his mother to consult me concerning a charge of attempted rape of a 60-year-old woman 2 months previously. He was to attend court a few days later for sentencing. The woman had been crossing a pedestrian bridge at a railway station when he forced her to the ground, pulled her dress up and her underclothing down and pulled his pants down and attempted to get on top of her. He stated he was sure he did not have an erection. An adult man intervened, rescued the woman, and informed the police. X said that he had never had an impulse to act in this way before or since. Twelve months previously he had been reported to the police for exposing his erect penis to an adult woman in a parking lot. He was given a warning. He had experienced puberty a few years previously and masturbated a few times weekly with fantasies of sexual activity with good-looking women around the age of 20 years. He believed his peers had similar fantasies concerning women of this age. He denied any fantasies involving violence or exposure. He experienced a strong impulse to expose himself about weekly and did so about once a month in the street, to good-looking girls about 15 years of age. Apparently they never reported his behavior to the police, as in view of his record it would seem likely the police would have interviewed him.

He was the eldest of four siblings and his parents were well and in their 40s. He reported a happy, uneventful childhood and was in the appropriate class at school for his age. He enjoyed school and was not considered difficult in his behavior by his teachers, although he said he belonged to a group of five boys who cut up in class at times. He had no history of truanting. He had a group of friends with whom he associated at and away from his school. His academic performance was somewhat above average and his knowledge of current events reasonable. He played soccer and tennis competently. He denied any tendency to excessive aggression in his interactions with peers, in conformity with his school counselor's report. He was not dating a girl and denied any sexual relationships. He suffered from asthma for which he inhaled salbutamol sulfate about weekly.

He had seen a psychiatrist on a few occasions since his offense and the psychiatrist referred him to me for another opinion. I suggested that he receive a week's treatment with imaginal desensitization and continue to attend his school counselor. At his court appearance he agreed to be on good behavior for 3 years and to accept treatment. Following the week's treatment he reported marked reduction in the urge to expose. A few months later he reported occasional urges to expose that he could control. He also said that one night in bed he thought of attempting to rape a woman in a park. Following this he did not attend for a few months and then reported that he had exposed himself on a few occasions over that period. He had continued to attend the counselor. In discussion with his parents it was agreed that it could be detrimental to his schooling to take a week off, so it was agreed that a course of medroxyprogesterone be started. Blood was taken for a baseline serum testosterone estimation, and he received an initial injection of 150 mg. He received three more injections at 2-week intervals followed by four at monthly intervals. He exposed once more 8 days after the first injection but a few days later he noticed marked diminution in urges to expose and they disappeared by the third injection. He reported that his frequency of erections remained unchanged. His serum testosterone prior to treatment was 9.7 nmol/L, toward the bottom of the laboratory normal range of 8.4 to 34. Following usual practice, another level was not taken because he was showing a satisfactory response. After a few months his counselor informed me that X was not keeping appointments, and in discussion X said he was embarrassed to be seen coming into class late after attending the counselor.

It was agreed that he could attend the counselor early and avoid this. His school work, involvement in sports, and social life was progressing well. Two months following cessation of the medroxyprogesterone, he reported no return of deviant sexual urges and he had no deviant fantasies in masturbation. A few months later he reported experiencing a strong exposure urge to the usual cue of seeing a woman alone in the street. Although he did not act on the urge it was suggested that he have a further course of imaginal desensitization during his school vacation. He continued to experience occasional strong urges to expose until he completed this course, following which he reported their disappearance. He ceased attending the counselor at this time. In the subsequent 2½ years he has continued to report no deviant urges or fantasies of exposure or sexual assault and has had no further charges. It is not possible to establish the relative importance of counseling and behavioral and chemical treatments in this patient. However, marked reported reduction in urges followed immediately after both weekly sessions of behavioral treatment and 10 days after introduction of medroxyprogesterone, suggesting these treatments had specific effects. The need for more than one course of these treatments is consistent with my experience in treating adolescent as compared with adult offenders (McConaghy et al., 1989).

SUMMARY

Exhibitionism, voyeurism, pedophilia, sadomasochism, sexual asphyxia, fetishism, and deviations of sexual identity, all of which can be associated with psychological or physical aggression, are briefly described, as are sexual assault and murder. Studies of the prevalence of these behaviors in clinical and community populations are reviewed. Stimulus control, cognitive, and psychiatric-psychopathological theories of the etiology of sexual aggression are discussed. The effects of sexual aggression upon the perpetrator and the victim are reported. The psychological effects of child sexual abuse and sexual assault of adolescents and adults have been studied much more intensively than the harmful physical effects. Programs for treatment of sex aggressors and their victims are described as are those being initiated and aimed at the prevention of child molestation and sexual assault. A case of an adolescent exhibitionist and sexually assaultive male who required repeated treatment to respond successfully is reported.

REFERENCES

Ageton, S. S. (1983). *Sexual assault among adolescents*. Lexington: Lexington Books.

Alter-Reid, K., Gibbs, M. S., Lachenmeyer, J. R., Sigal, J., & Massoth, N. A. (1986). Sexual abuse of children: A review of the empirical findings. *Clinical Psychology Review, 6*, 249–266.

American Psychiatric Association (1987). *Diagnostic and statistical manual of mental disorders*, 3rd Edition, Revised. Washington, DC: Author.

American Psychiatric Association (1991). *DSM-IV options book: Work in progress 9/1/91*. Washington, DC: Author.

American Psychiatric Association (1993). *DSM-IV draft criteria*. Washington, DC: Author.

Anderson, C. L. (1982). Males as sexual assault victims: Multiple levels of trauma. In J. S. Gonsiorek (Ed.), *Homosexuality and psychotherapy* (pp. 145–162). New York: Haworth Press.

Armsworth, M. W. (1989). Therapy of incest survivors: Abuse or support? *Child Abuse and Neglect, 13*, 549–562.

Asher, S. J. (1988). The effects of childhood sexual abuse: A review of the issues and evidence. In L. E. A. Walker (Ed.), *Handbook on sexual abuse of children* (pp. 3–18). New York: Springer.

Bart, P. B., & O'Brien, P. H. (1984). Stopping rape: Effective avoidance strategies. *Signs: Journal of Women in Culture and Society, 10*, 83–101.

Baxter, D. J., Barbaree, H. E., & Marshall, W. L. (1986). Sexual responses to consenting and forced sex in a large sample of rapists and non-rapists. *Behaviour Research and Therapy, 24*, 513–520.

Beck, J. C., Borenstein, N., & Dreyfus, J. (1986). The relationship between verdict, defendant characteristics, and type of crime in sex-related criminal cases. *Bulletin of the American Academy of Psychiatry and Law, 13*, 141–146.

Bem, S. L. (1974). The measurement of psychological androgyny. *Journal of Consulting and Clinical Psychology, 42*, 155–162.

Benjamin, H. (1954). Transsexualism and transvestism as psychosomatic and somatopsychic syndromes. *American Journal of Psychotherapy, 8*, 219–230.

Berliner, L. (1985). The child and the criminal justice system. In A. W. Burgess (Ed.), *Rape and sexual assault* (pp. 199–208). New York: Garland Publishing.

Bieber, I. (1962). *Homosexuality*. New York: Basic Books.

Bowie, S. I., Silverman, D. C., Kalick, S. M., & Edbril, S. D. (1990). Blitz rape and confidence rape: Implications for clinical intervention. *American Journal of Psychotherapy, 44*, 180–188.

Brassard, M. R., Tyler, A. H., & Kehle, T. J. (1983). School programs to prevent intrafamilial child sexual abuse. *Child Abuse and Neglect, 7*, 241–245.

Breslow, N., Evans, L., & Langley, J. (1985). On the prevalence and roles of females to the sadomasochistic subculture: Report of an empirical study. *Archives of Sexual Behavior, 14*, 303–319.

Briere, J., Evans, D., Runtz, M., & Wall, T. (1988). Symptomatology in men who were molested as children: A comparison study. *American Journal of Orthopsychiatry, 58*, 457–461.

Brittain, R. P. (1970). The sadistic murderer. *Medicine, science and the law, 10*, 198–207.

Browne, A., & Finkelhor, D. (1986). Impact of child sexual abuse: A review of the research. *Psychological Bulletin, 99*, 66–77.

Burgess, A. W., & Holmstrom, L. L. (1980). Rape typology and the coping behavior of rape victims. In S. L. McCombie (Ed.), *Rape crisis intervention handbook* (pp. 27–42). New York: Plenum.

Burgess, A. W., & Holmstrom, L. L. (1985). Rape trauma syndrome and post traumatic stress response. In A. W. Burgess (Ed.), *Rape and sexual assault* (pp. 46–60). New York: Garland Publishing.

Burnam, M. A., Stein, J. A., Golding, J. M., Siegel, J. M., Sorenson, S. B., Forsythe, A. B., & Telles, C. A. (1988). Sexual assault and mental disorders in a community population. *Journal of Consulting and Clinical Psychology, 56*, 843–850.

Burt, M. R. (1980). Cultural myths and support for rape. *Journal of Personality and Social Psychology, 38*, 217–230.

Carver, C. M., Stalker, C., Stewart, E., & Abraham, B. (1989). The impact of group therapy for adult survivors of childhood sexual abuse. *Canadian Journal of Psychiatry, 34*, 753–758.

Constantine, L. L. (1981). The effects of early sexual experiences. In L. L. Constantine and F. M. Martinson (Eds.), *Children and sex* (pp. 217–244). Boston: Little, Brown.

Conte, J. R., & Berliner, L. (1988). The impact of sexual abuse on children: Empirical findings. In L. E. A. Walker (Ed.), *Handbook on sexual abuse of children* (pp. 72–93). New York: Springer.

Courtois, C. A., & Sprei, J. E. (1988). Retrospective incest therapy for women. In L. E. A. Walker (Ed.), *Handbook on sexual abuse of children* (pp. 270–300). New York: Springer.

Crepault, C., & Couture, M. (1980). Men's erotic fantasies. *Archives of Sexual Behavior, 9*, 565–581.

DiVasto, P. V., Kaufman, L. R., Jackson, R., Christy, J., Pearson, S., & Burgett, T. (1984). The prevalence of sexually stressful events among females in the general population. *Archives of Sexual Behavior, 13*, 59–67.

Duncan, D. F. (1990). Prevalence of sexual assault victimization among heterosexual and gay/lesbian university students. *Psychological Reports, 66*, 65–66.

Ellis, E. M. (1983). A review of empirical rape research: Victim reactions and response to treatment. *Clinical Psychology Review, 3*, 473–490.

Evans, R. B. (1969). Childhood parental relationships of homosexual men. *Journal of Consulting and Clinical Psychology, 33*, 129–135.

Faller, K. C. (1989). Characteristics of a clinical sample of sexually abused children: How boys and girl victims differ. *Child Abuse and Neglect, 13*, 281–291.

Finkelhor, D. (1979). *Sexually abused children*. New York: Free Press.

Finkelhor, D. (1974). *Child sexual abuse: New theory and research*. New York: Free Press.

Finkelhor, D. (1985). Sexual abuse of boys. In A. W. Burgess (Ed.), *Rape and sexual assault* (pp. 97–103). New York: Garland Publishing.

Finkelhor, D., & Browne, A. (1988). Assessing the long-term impact of child sexual abuse: A review and conceptualization. In L. E. A. Walker (Ed.), *Handbook on sexual abuse of children* (pp. 55–71). New York: Springer.

Finkelhor, D., & Lewis, I. A. (1988). An epidemiologic approach to the study of child molestation. *Annals of the New York Academy of Sciences*, *528*, 64–78.

Foley, T. S. (1985). Family response to rape and sexual assault. In A. W. Burgess (Ed.), *Rape and sexual assault* (pp. 159–188). New York: Garland Publishing.

Freund, K., Heasman, G. A., & Roper, V. (1982). Results of the main studies of sexual offenses against children and pubescents (a review). *Canadian Journal of Criminology*, *24*, 387–397.

Freund, K., Watson, R., & Dickey, R. (1990). Does sexual abuse in childhood cause pedophilia: An exploratory study. *Archives of Sexual Behavior*, *19*, 557–568.

Fromuth, M. E. (1986). The relationship of childhood sexual abuse with later psychological and sexual adjustment in a sample of college women. *Child Abuse and Neglect*, *10*, 5–15.

Fromuth, M. E., & Burkhart, B. R. (1989). Long-term psychological correlates of childhood sexual abuse in two samples of college men. *Child Abuse and Neglect*, *13*, 533–542.

Furness, T. (1983). Mutual influence and interlocking professional-family process in the treatment of child sexual abuse and incest. *Child Abuse and Neglect*, *7*, 207–223.

Gagne, P. (1981). Treatment of sex offenders with medroxyprogesterone acetate. *American Journal of Psychiatry*, *138*, 644–646.

Giarretto, H. (1978). Humanistic treatment of father-daughter incest. *Journal of Humanistic Psychology*, *18*, 62–76.

Giarretto, H. (1981). A comprehensive child sexual abuse treatment program. In P. B. Mrazek & C. H. Kempe (Eds.), *Sexually abused children and their families* (pp. 179–197). Oxford: Pergamon.

Gomes-Schwartz, B., Horowitz, J. M., & Sauzier, M. (1985). Severity of emotional distress among sexually abused preschool, school-age, and adolescent children. *Hospital and Community Psychiatry*, *36*, 503–508.

Gosselin, C., & Wilson, G. (1980). *Sexual variations* London: Faber and Faber.

Green, R. (1987). *The "Sissy boy syndrome" and the development of homosexuality*. Yale: Yale University Press.

Groth, A. M., & Birnbaum, H. J. (1978). Adult sexual orientation and attraction to underage persons. *Archives of Sexual Behavior*, *7*, 175–181.

Groth, A. N., & Burgess, A. W. (1980). Male rape: Offenders and victims. *American Journal of Psychiatry*, *137*, 806–810.

Harry, J. (1989). Parental physical abuse and sexual orientation in males. *Archives of Sexual Behavior*, *18*, 251–261.

Hazelwood, R. R., Dietz, P. E., & Burgess, A. W. (1983). *Autoerotic fatalities*. Lexington: Lexington Books.

Heilbrun, A. B., & Leif, D. T. (1988). Erotic value of female distress in sexually explicit photographs. *Journal of Sex Research*, *24*, 47–57.

Herman, J. L. (1985). Father-daughter incest. In A. W. Burgess (Ed.), *Rape and sexual assault* (pp. 83–96). New York: Garland Publishing.

Herman, J. L. (1990). Sex offenders. A feminist perspective. In W. L. Marshall, D. R. Laws, & H. E. Barbaree (Eds.), *Handbook of sexual assault* (pp. 177–193). New York: Plenum.

Hobbs, C. J., & Wynne, J. M. (1989). Sexual abuse of English boys and girls: The importance of anal examination. *Child Abuse and Neglect*, *13*, 195–210.

Hochbaum, S. R. (1987). The evaluation and treatment of the sexually assaulted patient. *Emergency Medical Clinics of North America*, *5*, 601–622.

Holmstrom, L. L. (1985). The criminal justice system's response to the rape victim. In A. W. Burgess (Ed.), *Rape and sexual assault* (pp. 189–198). New York: Garland Publishing.

Hunt, M. (1974). *Sexual behavior in the 1970's*. New York: Dell Publishing.

Johnson, R. L., & Shrier, D. (1987). Past sexual victimization by females of male patients in an adolescent medicine clinic population. *American Journal of Psychiatry*, *144*, 650–652.

Kaufman, A., Divasto, P., Jackson, R., Voorhees, D., & Christy, J. (1980). Male rape victims: Noninstitutionalized assault. *American Journal of Psychiatry*, *137*, 221–223.

Keller, R. A., Cicchinelli, L. F., & Gardner, D. M. (1989). Characteristics of child sexual abuse treatment programs. *Child Abuse and Neglect*, *13*, 361–368.

Kilpatrick, D. G., & Best, C. L. (1984). Some cautionary remarks on treating sexual assault victims with implosion. *Behavior Therapy*, *15*, 421–423.

Kilpatrick, D. G., Best, C. L., Saunders, B. E., & Veronen, L. J. (1988). Rape in marriage and in dating relationships: How bad is it for mental health? *Annals of the New York Academy of Sciences*, *528*, 335–344.

Knight, R. A., Rosenberg, R., & Schneider, B. A. (1985). Classification of sex offenders: Perspective, methods, and validation. In A. W. Burgess (Ed.), *Rape and sexual assault* (pp. 222–293). New York: Garland.

Koss, M. P., & Dinero, T. E. (1988). Predictors of sexual aggression among a national sample of male college students. *Annals of the New York Academy of Sciences*, *528*, 133–147.

Koss, M. P., & Oros, C. J. (1982). Sexual experiences survey: A research instrument investigating sexual aggression and victimization. *Journal of Consulting and Clinical Psychology*, *50*, 455–457.

Kroth, J. A. (1979). Family therapy impact on intrafamilial child sexual abuse. *Child Abuse and Neglect*, *3*, 297–302.

Lukianowicz, N. (1972). Incest I: Paternal incest II: Other types of incest. *British Journal of Psychiatry*, *120*, 301–313.

Malamuth, N. M. (1989). The attraction to sexual aggression scale: Part two. *Journal of Sex Research*, *26*, 324–354.

Malamuth, N. M., & Check, J. V. P. (1983). Sexual arousal to rape depictions: Individual differences. *Journal of Abnormal Psychology*, *92*, 55–67.

Mann, E. M. (1981). Self-reported stresses of adolescent rape victims. *Journal of Adolescent Health Care*, *2*, 29–33.

Marshall, W. L., & Barbaree, H. E. (1990a). An integrated theory of the etiology of sexual offending. In W. L. Marshall, D. R. Laws, & H. E. Barbaree (Eds.), *Handbook of sexual assault* (pp. 257–275). New York: Plenum.

Marshall, W. L., & Barbaree, H. E. (1990b). Outcome of comprehensive cognitive-behavioral treatment programs. In W. L. Marshall, D. R. Laws, & H. E. Barbaree (Eds.), *Handbook of sexual assault* (pp. 363–385). New York: Plenum.

McAnulty, R. D., & Adams, H. E. (1992). Validity and ethics of penile circumference measures of sexual arousal: A reply to McConaghy. *Archives of Sexual Behavior*, *21*, 177–186.

McCann, J., Voris, J., Simon, M., & Wells, R. (1989). Perianal findings in prepubertal children selected for nonabuse: A descriptive study. *Child Abuse and Neglect*, *13*, 179–193.

McCombie, S. L., & Arons, J. H. (1980). Counseling rape victims. In S. L. McCombie (Ed.), *The rape crisis intervention handbook* (pp. 145–171). New York: Plenum.

McConaghy, N. (1976). Is a homosexual orientation irreversible? *British Journal of Psychiatry*, *129*, 556–563.

McConaghy, N. (1977). Behavioral treatment in homosexuality. In M. Hersen, R. M. Eisler, & P. M. Miller (Eds.), *Progress in behavior modification* (vol. 5, pp. 309–380). New York: Academic Press.

McConaghy, N. (1980). Behavior completion mechanisms rather than primary drives maintain behavioral patterns. *Activitas Nervosa Superior* (Praha), *22*, 138–151.

McConaghy, N. (1987). Heterosexuality/homosexuality: Dichotomy or continuum. *Archives of Sexual Behavior*, *16*, 411–424.

McConaghy, N. (1988). Assessment and management of pathological gambling. *British Journal of Hospital Medicine*, *40*, 131–135.

McConaghy, N. (1989). Validity and ethics of penile circumference measures of sexual arousal: A critical review. *Archives of Sexual Behavior*, *18*, 357–369.

McConaghy, N. (1990a). Assessment and management of sex offenders: The Prince of Wales Program. *Australian and New Zealand Journal of Psychiatry*, *24*, 175–182.

McConaghy, N. (1990b). Sexual deviation. In A. S. Bellack, M. Hersen, & A. E. Kazdin (Eds.), *International handbook of behavior modification therapy* (2nd ed., pp. 565–580). New York: Plenum.

McConaghy, N., & Blaszczynski, A. (1988). Imaginal desensitization: A cost-effective treatment in two shop-lifters and a binge-eater resistant to previous therapy. *Australian and New Zealand Journal of Psychiatry*, *22*, 78–82.

McConaghy, N., & Silove, D. (1992). Do sex-linked behaviors in children influence their relationships with their parents? *Archives of Sexual Behavior*.

McConaghy, N., & Zamir, R. (submitted). Sissiness, tomboyism, sex role, identity and orientation.

McConaghy, N., & Zamir, R. (in press). Non-sexist sexual experiences survey and attraction to sexual aggression scale. *Australian and New Zealand Journal of Psyciatry*.

McConaghy, N., Armstrong, M. S., & Blaszczynski, A. (1985). Expectancy, covert sensitization and imaginal desensitization in compulsive sexuality. *Acta Psychiatrica Scandinavica*, *72*, 1176–187.

McConaghy, N., Armstrong, M. S., Blaszczynski, A., & Allcock, C. (1983). Controlled comparison of aversive therapy and imaginal desensitization in compulsive gambling. *British Journal of Psychiatry*, *142*, 366–372.

McConaghy, N., Blaszczynski, A., Armstrong, M. S., & Kidson, W. (1989). Resistance to treatment of adolescent sexual offenders. *Archives of Sexual Behavior*, *18*, 97–107.

McConaghy, N., Blaszczynski, A., & Kidson, W. (1988). Treatment of sex offenders with imaginal desensitization and/or medroxyprogesterone. *Acta Psychiatrica Scandanavica*, *77*, 199–206.

Moser, C., & Levitt, E. E. (1987). An exploratory-descriptive study of a sadomasochistically oriented sample. *Journal of Sex Research*, *23*, 322–337.

Mrazek, P. B., & Mrazek, D. A. (1981). The effects of child sexual abuse: Methodological considerations. In P. B. Mrazek & C. H. Kempe (Eds.), *Sexually abused children and their families* (pp. 235–245). Oxford: Pergamon.

Murphy, P. J., III. (1980). The police investigation. In S. L. McCombie (Ed.), *Rape crisis intervention handbook* (pp. 69–78). New York: Plenum.

Nadelson, C. C., Notman, M. T., Zackson, H., & Gornick, J. (1982). A follow-up study of rape victims. *American Journal of Psychiatry, 139,* 1266–1270.

Nagayama Hall, G. C., Proctor, W. C., & Nelson, G. M. (1988). Validity of physiological measures of pedophilic sexual arousal in a sexual offender population. *Journal of Consulting and Clinical Psychology, 56,* 118–122.

O'Connor, A. A. (1987). Female sex offenders. *British Journal of Psychiatry, 150,* 615–620.

Otterbein, K. F. (1979). A cross-cultural study of rape. *Aggressive Behavior, 5,* 425–435.

Palmer, C. T. (1988). Twelve reasons why rape is not sexually motivated: A skeptical examination. *Journal of Sex Research, 25,* 512–530.

Person, E. S., Terestman, N., Myers, W. A., Goldberg, E. L., & Salvadori, C. (1989). Gender differences in sexual behaviors and fantasies in a college population. *Journal of Sex and Marital Therapy, 15,* 187–198.

Price, J. H., & Miller, P. A. (1984). Sexual fantasies of black and of white college students. *Psychological Reports, 54,* 1007–1014.

Quinsey, V. L. (1986). Men who have sex with children. In D. N. Weisstub (Ed.), *Law and mental health. international perspectives* (Vol. 2, pp. 140–172). New York: Pergamon.

Quinsey, V. L., & Earls, C. M. (1990). The modification of sexual preferences. In W. L. Marshall, D. R. Laws, & H. E. Barbaree (Eds.), *Handbook of sexual assault* (pp. 279–295). New York: Plenum.

Quinsey, V. L., & Upfold, D. (1985). Rape completion and victim injury as a function of female resistance strategy. *Canadian Journal of Behavioral Science, 17,* 40–50.

Remafedi, G. (1987). Adolescent homosexuality: Psychosocial and medical implications. *Pediatrics, 79,* 331–377.

Revitch, E. (1965). Sex murder and the potential sex murderer. *Diseases of the Nervous System, 26,* 640–648.

Revitch, E. (1980). Gynocide and unprovoked attacks on women. *Correctional and Social Psychiatry, 26,* 6–11.

Risin, L. I., & Koss, M. P. (1987). Sexual abuse of boys: Prevalence and descriptive characteristics of childhood victimization. *Journal of Interpersonal Violence, 2,* 309–319.

Rooth, F. G. (1973). Exhibitionism outside Europe and America. *Archives of Sexual Behavior, 2,* 351–363.

Russell, D. E. H. (1983). The incidence and prevalence of intrafamilial and extrafamilial sexual abuse of female children. *Child Abuse and Neglect, 7,* 133–146.

Russell, D. E. H. (1986). *The secret trauma. Incest in the lives of girls and women.* New York: Basic Books.

Rychtarik, R. G., Silverman, W. K., Van Landingham, W. P., & Prue, D. M. (1984). Further considerations in treating sexual assault victims with implosion. *Behavior Therapy, 15,* 423–426.

Saghir, M., & Robins, E. (1973). *Male and female homosexuality: A comprehensive investigation.* Baltimore: Williams & Wilkins.

Sarrel, P., & Masters, W. (1982). Sexual molestation of men by women. *Archives of Sexual Behavior, 11,* 117–133.

Scully, D., & Marolla, J. (1985). Rape and vocabularies of motive: Alternative perspectives. In A. W. Burgess (Ed.), *Rape and sexual assault* (pp. 294–312). New York: Garland Publishing.

Siegel, J. M., Sorenson, S. B., Golding, J. M., Burnam, M. A., & Stein, J. A. (1987). The prevalence of childhood sexual assault. *American Journal of Epidemiology, 126,* 1141–1153.

Sorenson, S. B., Stein, J. A., Siegel, J. M., Golding, J. M., & Burnam, M. A. (1987). The prevalence of adult sexual assault. *American Journal of Epidemiology, 126,* 1154–1164.

Steketee, G., & Foa, E. B. (1987). Rape victims: Post-traumatic stress responses and their treatment. *Journal of Anxiety Disorders, 1,* 69–86.

Stermac, L. E., Segal, Z. V., & Gillis, R. (1990). Social and cultural factors in sexual assault. In W. L. Marshall, D. R. Laws, H. E. Barbaree (Eds.), *Handbook of sexual assault* (pp. 143–159). New York: Plenum.

Swanson, D. W. (1968). Adult sexual abuse of children. *Diseases of the Nervous System, 29,* 677–683.

Swift, C. F. (1985). The prevention of rape. In A. W. Burgess (Ed.), *Rape and sexual assault* (pp. 413–433). New York: Garland Publishing.

Swigert, V. L., Farrell, R. A., & Yoels, W. C. (1976). Sexual homicide: Social, psychological and legal aspects. *Archives of Sexual Behavior, 5,* 391–401.

Walker, L. E. A., & Bolkovatz, M. A. (1988). Play therapy with children who have experienced sexual assault. In L. E. A. Walker (Ed.), *Handbook of sexual abuse of children* (pp. 249–269). New York: Springer.

Weinberg, S. K. (1955). *Incest behavior.* New York: Citadel Press.

Winfield, I., George, L. K., Swartz, M., & Blazer, D. G. (1990). Sexual assault and psychiatric disorders among a community sample of women. *American Journal of Psychiatry, 147,* 335–341.

Wyatt, G. E. (1985). The sexual abuse of Afro-American and white-American women in childhood. *Child Abuse and Neglect, 9*, 507–519.

Wyatt, G. E., & Peters, S. E. (1986). Methodological considerations in research on the prevalence of child sexual abuse. *Child Abuse and Neglect, 10*, 241–251.

Zuger, B. (1966). Effeminate behavior present in boys from early childhood. I. The clinical syndrome and follow-up studies. *Journal of Pediatrics, 69*, 1098–1107.

Zuger, B. (1984). Early effeminate behavior in boys. Outcome and significance for homosexuality. *Journal of Nervous and Mental Disease, 172* 90–97.

Zuger, B., & Taylor, P. (1969). Effeminate behavior present in boys from early childhood. II. Comparison with similar symptoms in non-effeminate boys. *Pediatrics, 44*, 375–380.

CHAPTER 17

Impulse Control Disorder

Robert M. Stowe

DESCRIPTION OF THE DISORDER

The term *impulse control disorder*, as used in the revised third edition of the *Diagnostic and Statistical Manual of Mental Disorders* (American Psychiatric Association, 1987), subsumes a variety of conditions in which there is a failure to resist the drive or temptation to commit acts potentially harmful to the patient or others. These include psychoactive substance use disorders, paraphilias, kleptomania, pyromania, pathological gambling, trichotillomania, and "intermittent explosive disorder" (IED). The section on impulse control disorders not elsewhere classified in DSM-IV is not expected to differ significantly from DSM-III-R and, unless otherwise noted, references to DSM-III-R elsewhere in this chapter should be considered applicable to DSM-IV as well.

In keeping with the theme of this handbook, the focus of this chapter will be on IED and related disorders of impulse control manifested primarily by episodically violent behavior.

Intermittent explosive disorder (IED) is defined by transient loss of impulse control restricted to repetitive, episodic, violent and/or destructive behavior that is grossly disproportionate to any "provoking" events, and which the subject typically later regrets. The diagnostic criteria for IED outlined in DSM-III-R include multiplicity of episodes, serious injury to others or property damage, disproportionality to "precipitating psychosocial stressors," and absence of more general impulsive or aggressive tendencies. Important exclusion criteria include diagnoses of concurrent psychosis or intoxication with psychoactive substances, "organic personality syndrome," and antisocial, borderline personality, or conduct disorders. An alternative term, *episodic dyscontrol syndrome* (EDS), has been widely used in the past, and the two terms are sometimes used synonymously. However, since studies of episodic dyscontrol syndrome have not excluded patients with etiologically relevant neurological and psychiatric disorders, the term "syn-

ROBERT M. STOWE • Neurobehavioral Unit Program, Department of Veterans Affairs, VA Medical Center, and University of Pittsburgh School of Medicine, Pittsburgh, Pennsylvania 15206.

Handbook of Aggressive and Destructive Behavior in Psychiatric Patients, edited by Michel Hersen, Robert T. Ammerman, and Lori A. Sisson. Plenum Press, New York, 1994.

drome" is appropriately used to refer to such studies, whereas we will restrict our use of intermittent explosive disorder to characterize the few studies in which DSM-III-R inclusion and exclusion criteria were followed. In the DSM-III-R description of IED, the cautionary statement is made that "this category has been retained . . . despite the fact that many doubt the existence of a clinical syndrome characterized by episodic loss of control" independent of these excluded disorders (American Psychiatric Association, 1987). Such skepticism is not without basis. Literature frequently cited in support of EDS is largely based on clinical series that are anecdotal and poorly controlled (there are, for example, no studies that prospectively and systematically exclude relevant personality disorders by formal rating instruments, or the presence of coexistent central nervous system pathology by neurological and neuropsychological examination or neuroimaging procedures). Many reports have included individuals referred for medicolegal evaluation and/or facing serious legal charges, or who were intoxicated at the time of the episode prompting referral. For example, in one monograph frequently cited as a reference for the clinical phenomenology of episodic dyscontrol (Mark & Ervin, 1970), the authors state frankly that of their 108 patients, nearly half had enuresis persisting past age 7, about half had a history of cruelty to animals, and a quarter had a history of firesetting as children, characteristics associated with antisocial personality disorder.

These nosological and methodological caveats aside, there appears to be a generally held consensus in the literature as to the clinical phenomenology of EDS and IED. Patients reportedly experience paroxysmal outbursts or "spells," at times preceded by various pro-dromal symptoms or "auras," which may include heightened anxiety and/or irritability, drowsiness, headache, paresthesias, and staring. At times patients may be able to abort "attacks" by withdrawing from social contact at this stage. The prodrome is followed by extreme violence directed at people and/or objects, often leading to severe injury and/or property destruction. Although patients appear to maintain contact with the environment, partial or total amnesia and drowsiness is often claimed to follow episodes (American Psychiatric Association, 1987; Bach-Y-Rita, Lion, Climent, & Ervin, 1971; Elliot, 1990; Mark & Ervin, 1970).

Frequently reported characteristics of patients with episodic dyscontrol include spouse and child abuse, pathological intoxication with alcohol (Bach-Y-Rita, Lion, & Ervin, 1970), dangerously aggressive driving practices leading to multiple traffic accidents and moving violations, and sexual impulsivity and/or violence.

EPIDEMIOLOGY

Epidemiological data are sorely lacking. Although complaints of "temper control problems" are not uncommon in clinical practice, IED is said to be "very rare" in DSM-III-R. This apparent discrepancy is resolved by the observation that the vast majority of patients referred to neurologists and psychiatrists for evaluation of such problems have outbursts that are strongly context-dependent and/or have coexistent psychopathology, psychosocial stressors, substance abuse, and/or neurological disorders that may be etio-logically salient, thereby excluding a diagnosis of IED.

In Bach-Y-Rita et al.'s (1971) study of 130 voluntary, nonschizophrenic patients presenting to the authors for psychiatric evaluation in the Boston City and Massachusetts General Hospital emergency rooms with impulsive violence, the average age was 28 (range 16–60 years), and 90% were male. The majority were either unemployed or in semiskilled or unskilled jobs, and gave psychosocial histories portraying childhood deprivation and social maladjustment and alcohol abuse (and amphetamine abuse in 12 patients). Since patients frequenting inner-city emergency rooms are unlikely to be a representative cross section of the population, and a control sample was not obtained, the epidemiological validity of these observations is uncertain at best. Low socioeconomic status, younger age, and male sex were independently correlated with the incidence of self-reported violent behavior in the NIMH Epidemiological Cachement Area study (Swanson, Holzer, Ganju, & Jono, 1990), which did not, however, distinguish between instrumental violence and the non-goal-directed violence of IED/EDS. An opposite bias of ascertainment is probably reflected in Elliot's (1982) reported experience with 286 EDS patients seen in his private practice, "almost all" of whom were middle or upper class.

ETIOLOGY

For a detailed discussion of etiological considerations, the reader is referred to Part I of this volume. Space permits only a cursory review here.

Psychological and Learning Theories

Menninger (1963), who is credited with coining the term "episodic dyscontrol," and who described a variety of types of explosive aggressive behavior in his book *The Vital Balance*, viewed such behavior as symptomatic of "ego rupture," and the resulting discharge of aggressive drives as a last-ditch defense against total ego disintegration and psychosis.

The high incidence of abnormal psychodevelopmental histories in explosively violent patients is noted in many clinical reports, and have been repeatedly cited as evidence of psychodynamic and behavioral models of etiology. Featured prominently are physical and/or sexual abuse in childhood (Lewis & Pincus, 1989), emotional deprivation (Bach-Y-Rita et al., 1971), violent parental conflict (Tardiff, 1987), and parental alcoholism (Linnoila, DeJong, & Virkkunen, 1989).

Nevertheless, many individuals who grow up in dysfunctional and violent home environments do not become violent, and some patients with EDS have been raised in apparently normal families. The association between being exposed to explosive parental violence in childhood and being violent as an adult could equally be explained by a genetic hypothesis. Selective breeding studies in several animal species clearly demonstrate that genetic factors can strongly influence aggressivity (Elliot, 1990; Goldstein, 1974), and certain heritable disorders in humans such as Klinefelter (Baker et al., 1970) and Wolfram (Swift, Sadler, & Swift, 1990) syndromes are associated with an increased incidence of aggressive behavior.

Biological Theories

A large body of experimental literature links limbic structures in the hypothalamus and the frontal and temporal lobes, and areas in the brainstem reticular formation, with the regulation and expression of aggressive behavior (Goldstein, 1974; see also Chapter 1 of this volume). Theoretically, from a biological perspective such behavior could reflect (1) an increase in aggressive drives, (2) enhanced emotional reactivity to environmental stimuli, and/or (3) impaired inhibitory mechanisms. Bilateral lesions in the ventromedial hypothalamus have been associated with unprovoked aggressive behavior in both animals and humans, and would appear to represent an example of the first instance (Weiger & Bear, 1988). Another example might be the interictal irritability and aggressivity reported in a subset of patients whose seizures originate in limbic or paralimbic mesocortical regions ("temporolimbic epilepsy"—see Spiers, Schomer, Blume, & Mesulam, 1985). While the topic of interictal personality changes in epilepsy is complex and remains controversial, there is considerable evidence that at least some patients with temporolimbic epilepsy (TLE) develop heightened anger, irritability, and aggressivity interictally (Bear & Fedio, 1977; Devinsky & Bear, 1984), which may be noticeably more pronounced prior to a seizure and remit for some time postictally (Fenwick, 1989). Aggressivity in TLE may also represent an instance of the second putative mechanism, where limbic kindling (particularly in the amygdala—the most easily kindled brain structure and an important site of sensory–limbic interaction) may result in inappropriately intense emotional responses to affectively neutral stimuli (Bear, 1979; Bear, Schenk, & Benson, 1981). Enhanced emotional reactivity to novel or threatening stimuli is also seen in rats following medial septal lesions (Mesulam, 1985), and tumors which invade or compress this region have been associated with aggressive behavior in isolated cases (Elliot, 1990; Goldstein, 1974).

Prefrontal lesions, particularly those involving the orbitofrontal cortex in nonhuman primates (Iversen & Mishkin, 1970) and/or mesial frontal areas in humans (Leimkuhler & Mesulam, 1985; Lhermitte, 1986; Lhermitte, Pillon, & Serdaru, 1986; Verfaellie & Heilman, 1987) produce a deficit in the ability to inhibit inappropriate or "automatic" responses to stimuli. Single-unit recordings from the prefrontal cortex of rhesus monkeys have also revealed neurons whose firing rates are specifically correlated with "no-go" trials in a go/no-go paradigm, in which the animal is required to selectively withhold a response under certain stimulus conditions (Watanabe, 1986). It may not be coincidental that areas 6, 9, and 10 of the prefrontal cortex are the only neocortical sites projecting directly to the brainstem dorsal raphe nuclei that provide serotonergic input to the entire cortex and limbic system (Nieuwenhuys, Voogd, and van Huijzen, 1988). A rapidly growing body of literature suggests an important role for serotonin in the modulation of aggressivity and impulsivity, with consistent findings of correlations between low CSF 5-HIAA (the major metabolite of serotonin) and impulsive destructive behavior (see, for example, Brown & Linnoila; Coccaro, Siever, Klar, Maurer, Cochrane, Cooper, Mohs, & Davis, 1989; Miczek, Mos, & Olivier, 1989). Thus, impulsive aggression and "temper outbursts" seen following damage to the mesial and/or inferior prefrontal regions (Price, Daffner, Stowe, & Mesulam, 1989), commonly observed in the setting of head trauma (Filley, Cranberg, Alexander, & Hart, 1987; Mattson & Levin, 1990), may reflect an example of the third putative mechanism (impaired inhibitory mechanisms). In a study of 15 convicted murderers awaiting execution, all reportedly had histories of significant head injury, and 5 had major neurological findings on examination and/or EEG abnormalities (Lewis, Pincus, Feldman, Jackson, & Bard, 1986). It is also likely that prefrontal dysfunction contributes to aggressive behavior in schizophrenia, and neurological abnormalities (independent of medication effects) have been found to increase the risk of violence in young schizophrenic inpatients (Convit, Jaeger, Pin Lin, Meisner, Brizer, & Volavka, 1988). The prefrontal cortex sends dense projections to the caudate nucleus, which is in turn involved in a complex striato-pallido-thalamic circuit possibly functioning to modulate bidirectional information flow between the medial dorsal thalamic nucleus and the prefrontal region (Alexander, DeLong, & Strick, 1986). This may explain the disinhibited and impulsively aggressive behavior associated with Huntington's disease, in which early findings include prominent loss of medium-sized striatal projection interneurons and atrophy of the medial caudate and ventral putamen (DiFiglia, 1990).

Uncontrolled studies of patients with EDS have revealed a high incidence of neuro-developmental abnormalities and acquired neurological disease, thus supporting the hypothesis that this syndrome may have a neurobiologic etiology. Of Bach-Y-Rita et al.'s (1971) 130 patients with EDS (see above), 55% had past histories of unconsciousness due to head injury or illness; 58% of those questioned (29/50) reported hyperactivity as children; 27% had nocturnal enuresis past age 5; two had Klinefelter's syndrome, and 23% had had either febrile convulsions or seizures in adulthood (not attributable to alcohol withdrawal or eclampsia). EEGs in almost half of the 79 patients in whom they were obtained were abnormal, 20 because of epileptiform abnormalities (including 13 who had not previously been diagnosed to have temporal lobe epilepsy). In Elliot's (1982) series of 286 patients referred for neurological evaluation of EDS (which excluded patients with major psychoses, mental retardation, and those with drug-related, strongly provoked, and instrumental aggression), only 18 had "no demonstrable organicity"; the most common diagnoses were "minimal brain dysfunction" in 42%, head injury in 18%, and epilepsy in 16%, the vast majority of whom had complex partial seizures (criteria for diagnoses were not specified, but apparently included evidence of learning disabilities, attention deficit disorder, and/or multiple "soft neurological signs"). EEGs were abnormal in 149/245 patients (61%), and CT scans in 61/148 (41%). All 11 patients with cerebral infarction had right-hemisphere lesions. Consistent with other reports linking lesion-associated aggressive behavior in humans and animals to limbic lesions, 12 of 13 tumors found with CT scans involved limbic structures directly. Right-hemisphere tumors were overrepresented, as were lesions involving the cingulate region and the hypothalamus (one left sphenoid wing and four right parasagittal meningiomas, one left frontal and two right temporal gliomas, and two epidermoid cysts involving the midline hypothalamic region). The right hemisphere predominance may be a chance finding, as the numbers are small, but neuropsychiatric manifestations of right hemisphere lesions such as impulsivity, egocentricity, paranoia (Levine & Grek, 1984; Price & Mesulam, 1985), and receptive aprosodia (the inability to perceive the affective state of others in voice, gesture, and facial expression; Ross, 1985) could help to explain this apparent association.

Since limbic discharges, particularly those involving the amygdala, may result in directed aggression (Fenwick, 1989; Mark & Ervin, 1970), the reported high incidence of temporolimbic epilepsy in patients with EDS, the paroxysmal and unprovoked nature of outbursts, and claims of partial or total amnesia for episodes and drowsiness afterwards raise the possibility that IED and EDS may result from seizures involving limbic and paralimbic areas. In reviewing the clinical histories of 111 patients with epileptiform scalp EEG abnormalities during admissions to a psychiatric ward of a community general hospital, Bridgers (1987) noted a significantly increased incidence of epileptiform abnormalities in the EEGs of patients (not previously identified as epileptic) under the age of 25 presenting with explosive outbursts (9.4%, or 8/85 patients, compared with an overall incidence of 4.1% in all patients in this age group). This association remained significant even when drug effects could be excluded. Of course, such an association between epileptiform abnormalities on routine EEGs and episodes of explosive violence is weak evidence for the hypothesis that the episodes represent epileptiform seizures, since to prove the latter would require recording seizure activity on EEG during episodes. It is possible, for example, that both the EEG abnormalities and the violent behavior are both independent manifestations of limbic system dysfunction, or that repeated seizures lead to enhanced interictal aggressivity (perhaps via kindling). Video EEG monitoring of violent patients with seizures provides a more direct way of testing this hypothesis. In an influential study, a panel of 18 epileptologists from the United States, Canada, Germany, and Japan reviewed 33 seizures captured by video EEG from 19 patients selected for suspected ictal aggressive behavior from a total population of over 5,400 from multiple epilepsy clinics (Delgado-Escueta, Mattson, King, Goldensohn, Spiegel, Madsen, Crandall, Dreifuss, & Porter, 1981). Only 7 of these 19 patients manifested directed violence (including kicking, boxing, and attempts to grab and scratch the face of an observer), which lasted an average of only 29 seconds. Aggression occurred without warning or provocation and was stereotyped and unpremeditated; all patients could be easily restrained, and only one patient's behavior would have been likely to result in serious injury to others. Furthermore, six of these seven patients were intellectually or neurologically impaired (compared with none of the six patients rated as showing only minimal or no aggression), and five manifested interictal aggressive behavior as well, raising the possibility that impaired impulse control could have been involved in addition to "ictal rage." We have seen a middle-aged senior executive who, after successful resection of a large, right parasagittal meningioma, developed fleeting but intense, inexplicable feelings of paroxysmal rage during which he would feel a compelling urge to strangle anyone within eyesight (including complete strangers), but which he was able to resist. Episodes resolved on carbamazepine. By contrast, another of our patients with a history of idiopathic mental retardation, frequent complex partial seizures, a strikingly vicious, sarcastic, and angry affect, and poor impulse control, judgment, and insight, also had paroxysmal urges to strangle strangers, which he had acted on on several occasions, causing serious injury to one of his victims.

Several factors suggest that Delgado-Escueta et al.'s (1981) report may have underestimated the possibility that episodic aggression may be the result of ictal events. Their report did not indicate how many patients presenting to the contributing clinics because of aggressive behavior were excluded because they were judged too destructive during episodes (because of potential danger to equipment and personnel) to be monitored; because no episodes were recorded during the monitoring period; or because scalp EEG recordings were normal during episodes. Studies of scalp EEG (even prolonged recording to maximize the likelihood of capturing an episode) in EDS are likely to underestimate the incidence of ictal violence, since depth-electrode recordings have demonstrated that brief seizures which originate in, and remain localized to, deep mesial structures in the limbic system, such as the amygdala and the cingulate gyrus, may occur without apparent changes in scalp-recorded EEG activity. Since intracranial EEG recording techniques are invasive procedures generally reserved for patients being investigated for epilepsy surgery, there is no reliable information about the incidence of this phenomenon. Furthermore, as Pincus (1981) and Fenwick (1989) have pointed out, the EEG monitoring suite is a highly controlled and artificial environment. Limbic seizures which induce anger or fear may be much more likely to result in violence in "real-life" social situations in the community.

AGGRESSION TOWARD SELF

Acts of self-directed aggression are not commonly reported in IED/EDS. Self-mutilating behaviors arc frequently seen in borderline personality disorder (see Chapter 18, this volume), where impulsive cutting and suicide attempts are often seen; autism; and in some patients with mental retardation, particularly the Lesch-Nyhan syndrome (where lip-biting is often prominent and severe).

AGGRESSION TOWARD OTHERS

Patients with IED may be quite assaultive, both verbally and physically, to others during episodes. To meet diagnostic criteria for IED, the assaultive behavior should be unprovoked, or grossly disproportionate to the evoking circumstances, and, as discussed earlier, needs to be differentiated from the instrumental or goal-directed use of violence as a manipulative act. Helpful, but not essential, corollaries are the presence of genuine remorse and concern for the victim afterwards (in other words, the violence is ego-dystonic) and insight into the inappropriateness of the behavior and its potential moral and legal consequences. The spouses and children of patients with IED are frequently victims, but when frequent acts of explosive violence occur solely in the privacy of the patient's home, the diagnosis of IED should probably not be made, since such circumstances suggest that the patient is capable of controlling violent impulses in other contexts. In such situations, the conferral of a diagnosis of an "impulse control disorder" can be perceived to a certain extent to relieve the patient of responsibility for his or her abusive behavior, a potentially very countertherapeutic strategy (spouse- and child-battering are considered later in Part V, Chapters 26 and 27).

CLINICAL MANAGEMENT

Differential Diagnosis

The differential diagnosis of aggressive behavior is extensive; a less-than-exhaustive list is outlined in Table 1. The most common causes within each diagnostic category are printed in bold type, whereas those disorders (however rare) in which violence is fairly frequently observed are marked with an asterisk. Thus, for example, while violent behavior is considerably less common in Alzheimer's than in Pick's disease, Alzheimer's is a more common cause of impaired control of aggressive impulses because its prevalence is at least 10 to 20 times higher than that of Pick's disease. (For a discussion of aggressive behavior in dementia, refer to Chapter 11, "Organic Mental Disorders").

Although this list is intimidating, the reader should keep in mind that relatively few patients with any of the disorders listed in Table 1 will have episodes consistent with IED; when a careful history can be obtained from reliable observers, violence will usually be seen to occur in response to perceived provocation (nonetheless sometimes relatively mild) rather than spontaneously; extreme autonomic arousal and selective amnesia associated with the incident or subsequent drowsiness are infrequent; and violence does not escalate into a destructive frenzy, lasting only seconds instead, with a fairly rapid return of self-control, even though anger may persist. In the author's experience, when episodes truly resembling those of IED are reported, the important diagnostic considerations are substance abuse; mania; mental retardation (frequently in association with a seizure disorder); conduct disorder in adolescents; spouse-battering; and structural brain injury, particularly closed head injury (with frontal lobe contusions, if the disorder is chronic) and large right-hemisphere infarctions; and complex partial epilepsy (with or without secondary generalized seizures).

TABLE 1.   Disorders Associated with Aggressive Behavior

Dementias
   Alzheimer's, Pick's,[a] **Huntington's**[a] **dementias**
   Multiinfarct dementia,[a] Parkinsonism-dementia
   Normal pressure hydrocephalus
   AIDS dementia complex
   Rarely others
Chromosomal/Genetic Disorders
   Klinefelter's syndrome,[a] possibly XYY karyotype
   Lesch-Nyhan, Rett, Sanfilippo, Wolfram[a] syndromes
   Metachromatic leukodystrophy, Spielmeyer-Vogt syndrome
   Wilson's disease
   Phenylketonuria
Developmental/Pediatric Disorders
   Conduct disorder[a]
   Mental retardation[a] (multiple causes)
   Attention-deficit disorder/"minimal brain dysfunction"
   Pervasive developmental disorder
   Tourette's syndrome
   Autism[a]
   Klein-Levin syndrome
   Neuronal migration abnormalities, aqueduct stenosis
Psychiatric and Personality Disorders
   Schizophrenia[a]
   Mania[a]
   Antisocial, borderline personality disorders[a]
   Narcissistic, paranoid personality disorders
   Intermittent explosive disorder[a]
Substance Abuse/Medication Toxicity
   Alcohol[a]
   Stimulants (**amphetamines, cocaine,**[a] methylphenidate, pemoline)
   Phencyclidine[a]
   Benzodiazepines, steroids, bronchodilators
Neurological Disorders
   Head injury[a]
   Dementia[a] (see heading above)
   Complex partial epilepsy
   Focal limbic lesions[a] (including **infarction**, tumor, subdural and intracerebral hemorrhage, hamartomas,
     AVMs, vasculitis, encephalitis)
   Paraneoplastic limbic encephalitis
Toxic/Metabolic Disorders
   Acute confusional state[a] (multiple causes)
   Organotin,[a] manganese, cholinesterase poisoning
   Cushing's disease
   Acute intermittent porphyria

Note. Disorders in boldface type represent the most common diagnostic entities associated with violent behavior within each
category.
[a]Aggressive behavior occurs with fairly high frequency.

    While DSM-III-R does not allow a diagnosis of IED to be made in the presence of
conduct or personality (e.g., antisocial or borderline) disorders in which aggressive
behavior may be prominent, from the standpoint of clinical management, the specific
characteristics of violence and the situations under which violence occurs are more
important than the presence of a potentially salient Axis II disorder. For example, not all
patients with antisocial personality disorder are impulsively aggressive. In those who are,

EDS-like episodes may benefit from treatment strategies used in IED, whereas when violence is being used instrumentally, for sadistic pleasure, or after trivial provocation because of a total lack of concern for rules of conduct or legal consequences, pharmacological interventions in particular are not likely to be helpful.

Investigation

A carefully obtained history, including a detailed description of episodes, psychodevelopmental and psychosocial histories, and neurological and psychiatric review of systems, is the most informative diagnostic procedure. In evaluating episodes, it is important to explore not only the patient's behavior before, during and after these, but also psychological, physical, and social precipitants, the settings in which violence typically occurs, and whether the patient derives gratification or a sense of relief from the violence (Reid & Balis, 1987). In addition, one should inquire about possible clues to developmental etiologies and early brain damage, such as anomalous hand and foot preference; pre- or perinatal complications; febrile or nonfebrile convulsions, "staring spells," auras, or episodes of loss of consciousness; academic, athletic, or behavioral/social dysfunction in school; head injury, meningitis, or encephalitis; family history of alcoholism, affective disorder, birth defects, dementia, epilepsy, learning disabilities, mental retardation, or antisocial behavior; substance abuse; headaches, changes in memory, focal neurological symptoms, or personality change; dysphoria, irritability (between episodes), or neurovegetative symptoms.

The neurological and mental status examinations should include tests of attention, language, memory, constructions, and abstract reasoning, geared to the patient's estimated level of intellectual ability and educational achievement; primitive or "release" reflexes (grasp, root, snout, suck); examination for hemihypoplasia of the face, thumb and great toe nail beds and foot size, and "soft" neurological signs such as mirror movements and impaired coordination and fine finger dexterity.

A variety of neuropsychological tests can be used to assess impulsivity (Weintraub & Mesulam, 1985); two commonly used instruments are the Stroop Color/Word Test and the Continuous Performance Test ("AX" and "CPT double" forms). A "go/no-go" paradigm, which is sometimes abnormal in patients with pathological impulsivity resulting from frontal lobe damage (Leimkuhler & Mesulam, 1985), can be administered without specialized tools. The patient is asked to raise and then lower his or her dominant index finger in response to crisp tapping sounds delivered by the examiner with a ruler or pen (out of view of the patient) about every 2 seconds—once for one tap, twice for two (when two stimuli are presented, the second tap follows immediately after the first). After this is rehearsed for about a minute, the patient is then told to continue to respond to one tap, but no longer to two. The sensitivity of the procedure can be increased by using pseudo-random sequences that contain runs of four or five "go" trials before some of the "no-go" trials. While normals may make one or two errors in the first 10 trials, their error rate diminishes rapidly. Impulsive patients, on the other hand, remain unable to withhold a response consistently on "no-go" trials, even though they will often be aware that they are making errors and even comment on them as they continue to respond inappropriately. Unfortunately, neuropsychological tests of frontal lobe function, including response inhibition, frequently fail to predict real-life performance. Thus, individuals who are impulsive on the Stroop or the go/no-go tests may or may not have problems with impulse control in social situations, whereas some patients with flawless performance in the highly structured setting of the physician's or psychologist's office may show major deficits in the ability to inhibit aggressive impulses in the face of relatively minor provocation at home or elsewhere in the community. History and behavioral observations therefore should not be discounted when formal mental status examination is unremarkable, particularly in otherwise high-functioning individuals.

The recently described Carolina Nosology of Destructive Behavior (Eichelman & Hartwig, 1990) classifies patients along Medical Diagnostic (primary vs. secondary disorders), Psychological Correlative, Biological Correlative, and Moral/Cultural axes, and includes a 10-category checklist for codifying salient features of destructive episodes. The Overt Aggression Scale (Yudofsky, Silver, Jackson, Endicott, & Williams, 1986) may be useful to follow treatment responses, particularly in an inpatient setting.

A complex partial seizure disorder should be suspected if any of the following features are associated with episodes: olfactory, gustatory, or autonomic hallucinations (fear, an epigastric "rising" sensation, vertigo, déjà vu); onset with a fixed stare and/or pupillary dilatation or oscillation during which the patient is unresponsive; piloerection; tonic head and eye deviation, focal tremor or myoclonic jerking; repetitive, semipurposeful stereotypical behavior or automatisms that do not occur when the patient appears fully alert and responsive; incontinence; or confusion and drowsiness after episodes. A diagnosis of epilepsy should generally not be made without confirmatory evidence of epileptiform (as opposed to more nonspecific) abnormalities on EEG, particularly when subjective symptoms or reports of an apparent change in consciousness by the patient or untrained observers are the only clinical evidence for a seizure disorder. The yield of EEG recordings is increased by sleep deprivation and the use of nasopharyngeal, sphenoidal and minisphenoidal, or anterior temporal lead placements. If cyclicity is apparent, EEGs should be timed to coincide with phases when episodes occur most frequently; for example, both complex partial seizures (Herzog, Seibel, Schomer, Vaitukaitis, & Geschwind, 1986) and EDS (Elliot, 1990) in women may be exacerbated in the premenstrual period. When episodes are reliably induced by specific stimuli, it may be helpful to try to reproduce these in the EEG lab. If episodes are occurring more than once a week or are reliably provoked by specific stimuli, ambulatory cassette EEG or even inpatient monitoring should be considered if there is ambiguity about the diagnosis. Appropriate precautions should be taken to minimize potential risks to equipment and personnel.

Common causes of new-onset temper outbursts in the elderly include confusional states (sometimes superimposed on early dementia), cerebral infarction, and affective disorders. These patients in particular require thorough medical and neurological evaluation.

When episodes are of recent onset and are unexplained by changes in the patient's circumstances, substance abuse or medications, or are accompanied by personality changes, endocrine dysfunction, or by focal abnormalities on EEG, neuropsychological or neurological examinations, then a neuroimaging procedure should be performed. Contrast-enhanced magnetic resonance imaging (MRI) scanning is the procedure of choice because it provides better imaging than CT scanning of important limbic areas such as mesial temporal and orbitofrontal regions, and it has higher sensitivity for developmental (neuronal migration) abnormalities and scarring (gliosis) following brain injury.

Drug screens for the abusable substances listed in Table 1 should be considered in every case.

Psychological/Behavioral/Family Therapies

While psychotherapy, family therapy, and behavioral therapies are important modalities of management of the patient with situationally related temper outbursts, even when these are related to neurological disorders such as traumatic brain injury (Franzen & Lovell, 1987), their role is probably limited in "true" IED. Counseling and family therapy may help the patient and significant others to achieve a better understanding of the disorder and to take appropriate precautionary measures, such as removing weapons from the home environment (the administration of clear instructions on this point should be documented in writing). If there is a prodromal period of irritability, the patient and family should be helped to identify this and to take appropriate "evasive action." Relaxation therapy may help some patients to abort attacks in this phase.

Pharmacological Treatment

The psychopharmacology of EDS and IED has been reviewed in several useful monographs (Mattes, 1986; Yudofsky, Silver, & Schneider, 1987). As in much of the literature in this area, most studies are anecdotal, poorly controlled, and unblinded. Since IED is rare, and the clinician will far more commonly encounter the problem of treating patients with "secondary" disorders, the following discussion will deal with drug treatment of episodic aggressive behavior in general. The principal classes of medications that have been used include anticonvulsants, beta-adrenergic receptor blocking drugs, antidepressants, hormones, lithium, and neuroleptics.

It must be kept in mind that many of the drugs used to treat agitation and aggressive behavior can induce or worsen confusion in patients with compromised CNS function. The most common cause of aggressive behavior in patients referred to our neurobehavioral unit is a confusional state, and attempts to treat the agitation with a variety of these agents (often two or three in combination when the first was ineffective) has typically made it worse. Stopping all psychotropic medications in such a situation requires patience and an empathetic and supportive nursing staff familiar with the use of environmental measures (such as frequent reorientation and reassurance, minimization of extraneous stimulation, and sometimes gentle restraint). But this approach, and treatment of any precipitating medical illnesses, will most often result in substantial improvement within a few days to a week. Medications with anticholinergic side effects are frequent offenders in such situations.

Anticonvulsants

Phenytoin was the first anticonvulsant to be tried in the treatment of EDS, with controversial results (Goldstein, 1974); several double-blind, placebo-controlled studies found it ineffective (Yudofsky et al., 1987). Subsequently, carbamazepine has been widely used to treat aggressivity in neuropsychiatrically heterogeneous populations of patients; many case reports and uncontrolled studies testify to its efficacy. However, placebo-controlled, double-blind studies in IED/EDS have not been reported. While carbamazepine (CBZ) is frequently employed to treat patients with complex partial epilepsy and psychiatric comorbidity, presence or absence of EEG abnormalities does not reliably predict response in patients with EDS (Mattes, 1986, 1990). Our tendency is to use carbamazepine first when patients with impulsive aggressive behavior also display affective lability, rapid mood cycling, or behavioral changes resembling mania or hypomania (Post, 1989) following frontal lobe injury; borderline personality characteristics (Gardner & Cowdry, 1986); or complex partial epilepsy. There is no evidence that blood levels between 4 and 12 μg/dL (the range within which seizures are typically controlled) are relevant for treatment of IED/EDS. Because CBZ is a potent inducer of the hepatic microsomal enzyme oxidizing system, it can be difficult to achieve therapeutic levels at lower doses in some patients, and metabolism of other drugs (including oral contraceptives) may be increased. In our experience the effective daily dose may be anywhere from 500 mg to as high as 1,800 mg and is best given every 8 hours. Our approach is to start at 100 mg BID and to increase the dose in 100-mg increments every 3 days (CBZ is very sedating initially, and most patients will not tolerate much more rapid increases in dose) until a therapeutic response is achieved or dose-related side effects (peak-dose diplopia, "dizziness," nausea, sedation) supervene. Other side effects include rash, mild leukopenia, hepatic enzyme induction, hyponatremia (common) and hepatitis, aplastic anemia, agranulocytosis, and a variety of involuntary movement disorders (rare). We check CBC, liver function tests, and serum sodium about a week after a daily dose of 600 mg is reached, and repeat these after substantial increases in dosage are made. Significant bioavailability differences among different formulations of CBZ can produce peak-dose toxicity when brands are changed. Some children and adolescents with a history of hyperactivity and conduct disorder become irritable and affectively labile, particularly on higher doses (Evans & Gualtieri, 1985).

Valproic acid has recently shown promise in the treatment of complex partial epilepsy and of some psychiatric disorders in which CBZ has also been effective, including typical and atypical bipolar syndromes (Brown, 1989; Calabrese & Delucchi, 1989; McElroy, Keck, Pope, & Hudson, 1988, 1989); like CBZ, valproic acid has potent antikindling activity (Post, 1989; Silver, Shin, & McNamara, 1991), suggesting that it might be useful in patients who have developed increased anger and aggressivity interictally. However, we are unaware of any published experience on its use in EDS/IED. Benzodiazepine anticonvulsants, such as clonazepam, are best avoided in our view, since chronic administration of benzo-diazepines may lead to disinhibition, irritability, and dependence (Yudofsky et al., 1987).

Beta-Adrenergic Receptor Blocking Drugs

Propranolol was first reported to be efficacious in the treatment of "rage outbursts" by Elliot (1977), in patients with acute brain injuries, and since then a number of anecdotal reports and small series have been published. A double-blind controlled study in neuro-logically impaired patients with aggressive behavior showed moderate to marked improve-ment in 7 of 10 patients at a mean daily dose of 520 mg (Greendyke, Kantner, Schuster, Verstreate, & Wooton, 1986). A retrospective study in eight Mayo Clinic patients with "intermittent explosive disorder" (all of whom had neurological impairment) found that five improved substantially or completely. Similar efficacy was reported in a retrospective study of 30 children and adolescents with "organic brain dysfunction" (Williams, Mehl, Yudofsky, Adams, & Roseman, 1982). Mattes (1990) compared carbamazepine and propranolol in an uncontrolled study of 80 patients with temper outbursts of diverse etiologies, 51 of whom were randomly assigned, and found equivocal evidence for efficacy with both drugs, with patients with attention-deficit disorder showing greater benefit from propranolol. We use propranalol first in patients with typical episodes of IED/EDS (particularly when accompanied by signs of extreme autonomic arousal) in whom complex partial epilepsy can be excluded.

Effective doses of propranolol range from 200 to 800 mg/day, given in three divided doses, starting at 20 mg TID and increasing by 60 mg/day. Common side effects include bradycardia, orthostatic hypotension, bronchospasm, fatigue, and depression. A therapeu-tic effect may not be seen for 1–2 months after beginning treatment.

More limited evidence suggests efficacy for other beta-blockers, such as metoprolol, a cardioselective (beta-1 receptor) antagonist (Mattes, 1984) and pindolol (Greendyke & Kantner, 1986). The mechanism of action of these drugs is unknown, but may be independent of their effects on noradrenergic receptors (Mattes, 1986). All are lipophilic and therefore cross the blood–brain barrier easily.

Antidepressants

A newer approach to the treatment of violent behavior is the use of antidepressants, particularly those with serotonergic properties. As mentioned earlier, the serotonin system seems to have a particular role in controlling impulsivity and aggressivity. Trazadone, an atypical, nontricyclic antidepressant, has been reported anecdotally to be effective in the behavioral management of agitation in several demented (Gelenberg, 1987) and mentally retarded (Simpson & Foster, 1986) patients. We have similarly observed favorable responses in patients with agitation, aggressivity, and irritability in association with dementia syndromes, cerebral infarction, and head injury, often in the absence of self-reported dysphoria or tearfulness, and at relatively low doses (50–125 mg daily, given at bedtime or BID). The effect may be observed within 1 to 2 days of treatment and does not appear related to trazadone's sedating properties. One major advantage of this medication is its lack of significant cardiotoxicity, anticholinergic blockade (which often produces cognitive deterioration in patients with compromised cortical function), or other major side effects; however, priapism may be a serious problem in males. We try trazadone initially when irritability is prominent between episodes of dyscontrol and/or mild dysphoria or neuro-vegetative symptoms of depression are evident.

Buspirone, a nonbenzodiazepine anxiolytic with mild antidepressant properties that chronically increases firing of serotonergic dorsal raphe neurons (Aghajanian, Sprouse, Sheldon, and Rasmussen, 1990), has been reported in a case review to help 9 of 14 retarded and/or autistic adults with anxiety and aggressive behavior directed at themselves and/or others (Ratey, Sovner, Mikkelsen, & Chmielinski, 1989). Fluoxetine, a selective inhibitor of serotonin re-uptake, was recently reported to improve impulsive aggression in three patients with personality disorders (Coccaro, Astill, Herbert, & Schut, 1989), although the evidence presented is weak, and recent media attention to lawsuits involving isolated cases where increased suicidal and homicidal ideation was attributed to the drug suggest that it would be prudent to avoid using this drug in patients with borderline and antisocial personality features (for medicolegal reasons alone).

While the literature has focused on antidepressants with serotonergic effects, we and colleagues have also observed good responses to noradrenergic antidepressants on occasion.

Hormones

Antiandrogens, estrogens, and even castration have been used in isolated cases to reduce aggressivity (Mattes, 1986). Their use cannot generally be recommended due to unacceptable side effects and ethical/legal considerations.

Neuroleptics

Dopamine-receptor blocking drugs are very commonly used to treat aggressive behavior. While they are undoubtedly effective in the context of an acute schizophrenic or manic psychosis, there are few methodologically sound studies to suggest efficacy in IED/ EDS or other patient populations, although a few such studies suggest that aggressive behavior will respond to neuroleptics in about a third of demented patients (Wragg & Jeste, 1988). We and others who treat patients with agitation and aggressive outbursts in the context of a confusional state, head injury, dementia, or stroke have been impressed with how frequently neuroleptics actually induce behavioral, as well as cognitive and motor, deterioration in this population (Yudofsky et al., 1987). In addition to drug-induced parkinsonism (the most frequent complication), tardive dyskinesia, urinary retention, weight gain, neuroleptic malignant syndrome, hypotension, arrhythmias, seizures, and angle-closure glaucoma are potential complications. In treating neurologically impaired patients, we generally reserve neuroleptics for those with other target symptoms for these drugs (e.g., paranoid delusions or manic-like excitement) and use low doses of agents with low anticholinergic blocking properties (e.g., haloperidol, 0.5 mg BID to TID). When sedation is desirable or the patient has a seizure disorder, we use molindone, 10 mg BID to TID. In violent younger patients with intact cognitive function, the use of more anticholinergic neuroleptics (e.g., thioridazine, chlorpromazine) might be considered, since there is suggestive evidence that cholinergic hyperactivity can produce irritability and aggressivity in both animals and man (Weiger & Bear, 1988).

Lithium

The use of lithium in the treatment of behavioral dyscontrol has been reviewed by Glenn and Joseph (1987). This drug was first reported to reduce the incidence of aggressive behavior in studies (including some conducted using placebo controls and blinded ratings) in assaultive inmates and incarcerated conduct-disordered adolescents in the 1970s. Subsequently, it has been reported efficacious in case reviews of 14 mentally retarded adolescents (Dostal & Zvolsky, 1970), and in 10 patients with "organic brain syndrome" of diverse etiology (Williams & Goldstein, 1979). Luchins and Dojka (1989) compared lithium and propranolol for aggressive behavior directed at self and others in a retrospective review of 17 mentally retarded patients and found evidence of efficacy for both drugs (responses rates of 64% for lithium and 82% for propranolol, the difference not reaching statistical significance). Our limited experience with lithium in brain-damaged patients has not been encouraging; even at low therapeutic levels (0.5–0.7 mg/dL), attentional deficits and agitation have frequently worsened. Lithium should be used with extreme caution in patients with seizure disorders. We generally reserve lithium for patients with psychomotor agitation in whom the premorbid history, and/or a strong family history, is suggestive of bipolar affective disorder.

LONGITUDINAL PERSPECTIVES

Information about the long-term course and prognosis of EDS/IED is lacking.

CASE ILLUSTRATION

A 55-year-old salesman presented for evaluation and treatment of stereotyped episodes of emotional dyscontrol, which were typically precipitated by particular sounds, including the wrinkling of a newspaper, and the sound of high-heeled shoes clicking on the floor. He would then develop a "difficult-to-describe" feeling in his head, and increasing anxiety and irritability, culminating in rage, during which he would yell uncontrollably and at times would throw and break objects. Episodes began 5 years earlier after he underwent coronary bypass surgery, which was complicated by the development of an ICU psychosis and postoperative depression. Episodes were refractory to numerous medications, including haloperidol, thioridazine, phenytoin, lorazepam, and amitriptyline. The patient reported a history of rheumatic fever in childhood and migrainous headaches. One son was autistic, while another had hydrocephalus and seizures. On examination, the patient was anxious, slightly irritable, and had a tendency to keep returning to the same themes repeatedly in conversation. There was a slight left pronator drift, left-sided hyperreflexia, and bilateral posturing on complex gait maneuvers (left more than right). Neuropsychological testing showed mild impairment of auditory/verbal attention and verbal memory. CT scan was normal. MRI revealed a small area of increased signal intensity on T2-weighted images in the left lateral temporal lobe, thought possibly to be a cortical vein. An EEG showed an isolated right midtemporal sharp wave during drowsiness, and a mild left temporal theta dysrhythmia. A sleep-deprived EEG with nasopharyngeal leads did not show epileptiform activity. He was started on carbamazepine, and the frequency of episodes decreased from one or more per week to less than one per month, and their severity and duration were also much attenuated, on 200 mg TID of CBZ, which produced a blood level of 7.2 μg/dL. The patient found higher doses too sedating. When he transiently discontinued CBZ about a year later, he had a 2-day episode of extreme irritability and dyscontrol that responded to reinstitution of the drug.

SUMMARY

Intermittent explosive disorder, as defined in DSM-III-R, is a rare condition. Most patients with episodically violent behavior have contributory psychopathology and/or neurological disease. In the latter instance, limbic system and/or prefrontal dysfunction, whether due to structural lesions, degenerative disease, epilepsy, or metabolic derangements, appears to be a common denominator. A thorough history and a neurobehaviorally oriented mental status and neurological examination are the keys to differential diagnosis and management. Rational pharmacotherapy is based on the phenomenology of episodes and on etiological considerations and may include the use of antidepressants, carbamazepine, beta-blockers, and lithium.

REFERENCES

Aghajanian, G. K., Sprouse, J. S., Sheldon, P., & Rasmussen, K. (1990). Electrophysiology of the central serotonin system: Receptor subtypes and transducer mechanisms. In P. M. Whitaker-Azmitia & S. J. Peroutka (Eds.), The neuropharmacology of serotonin. *Annals of the New York Academy of Sciences, 600*, 93–103.

Alexander, G. E., DeLong, M. R., & Strick, P. L. (1986). Parallel organization of functionally segregated circuits linking basal ganglia and cortex. *Annual Review of Neuroscience, 9*, 357–381.

American Psychiatric Association (1987). *Diagnostic and statistical manual of mental disorders*, 3rd Edition, Revised. Washington, DC: Author.

American Psychiatric Association (1993). *DSM-IV draft criteria*. Washington, DC: Author.

Bach-Y-Rita G., Lion, J. R., & Ervin, F. R. (1970). Pathological intoxication: Clinical and electroencephalographic studies. *American Journal of Psychiatry, 127*, 158–163.

Bach-Y-Rita, G., Lion, J. R., Climent, C. E., & Ervin, F. R. (1971). Episodic dyscontrol: A study of 130 violent patients. *American Journal of Psychiatry, 127*, 1473–1478.

Baker, D., Telfer, M. A., Richardson, C. E., & Clark, G. R. (1970). Chromosome errors in men with antisocial behavior. *Journal of the American Medical Association, 214*, 869–878.

Bear, D. (1979). Temporal lobe epilepsy: A syndrome of sensory-limbic hyperconnection. *Cortex, 15*, 357–384.

Bear, D. M., & Fedio, P. (1977). Quantitative analysis of interictal behavior in temporal lobe epilepsy. *Archives of Neurology, 38*, 454–467.

Bear, D. M., Schenk, L., & Benson, H. (1981). Increased autonomic responses to neutral and emotional stimuli in patients with temporal lobe epilepsy. *American Journal of Psychiatry, 138*, 843–845.

Bridgers, S. L. (1987). Epileptiform abnormalities discovered on electroencephalographic screening of psychiatric inpatients. *Archives of Neurology, 44*, 312–316.

Brown, G. L., & Linnoila, M. I. (1990). CSF serotonin metabolite (5-HIAA) studies in depression, impulsivity, and violence. *Journal of Clinical Psychiatry, 51[4, Suppl.]*, 31–43.

Brown, R. (1989). U.S. experience with valproate in manic depressive illness: a multicenter trial. *Journal of Clinical Psychiatry, 50*(Suppl. 3), 13–16.

Calabrese, J. R., & Delucchi, G. A. (1989). Phenomenology of rapid cycling manic depression and its treatment with valproate. *Journal of Clinical Psychiatry, 50* (Suppl. 3), 30–34.

Coccaro, E. F., Astill, J. L. Herbert, J. L., & Schut, A. G. (1990). Fluoxetine treatment of impulsive aggression in DSM-III-R personality disorder patients (letter). *Journal of Clinical Psychopharmacology, 10*, 373–375.

Coccaro, E. F., Siever, L. J., Klar, H. M., Maurer, G., Cochrane, K., Cooper, T. B., Mohs, R. C., & Davis, K. L. (1989). Serotonergic studies in patients with affective and personality disorders: Correlates with suicidal and impulsive aggressive behavior. *Archives of General Psychiatry, 46*, 587–599.

Convit, A., Jaeger, J., Pin Lin, S., Meisner, M., Brizer, D., & Volavka, J. (1988). Prediction of violence in psychiatric inpatients. In T. E. Moffitt & S. A. Mednick (Eds.), *Biological contributions to crime causation* (pp. 223–245). Boston: M. Nijhoff.

Delgado-Escueta, A. V., Mattson, R. H., King, L., Goldensohn, E. S., Spiegel, H., Madsen, J., Crandall, P., Dreifuss, F., & Porter, R. J. (1981). The nature of aggression during epileptic seizures. *New England Journal of Medicine, 305*, 711–716.

Devinsky, O., & Bear, D. (1984). Varieties of aggressive behavior in temporal lobe epilepsy. *American Journal of Psychiatry, 141*, 651–656.

DiFiglia, M. (1990). Excitotoxic injury of the neostriatum: A model for Huntington's disease. *Trends in Neurosciences, 13*, 286–289.

Dostal, T., & Zvolksy, P. (1970). Antiaggressive effects of lithium salts in severe mentally retarded adolescents. *International Pharmacopsychiatry, 5*, 203–207.

Eichelman, B., & Hartwig, A. (1990). The Carolina Nosology of Destructive Behavior (CNDB). *Journal of Neuropsychiatry and Clinical Neurosciences, 2*, 288–296.

Elliot, F. A. (1977). Propranolol for the control of belligerent behavior following acute brain damage. *Annals of Neurology, 1*, 489–491.

Elliot, F. A. (1982). Neurological findings in adult minimal brain dysfunction and the dyscontrol syndrome. *Journal of Nervous and Mental Disease, 170*, 680–687.

Elliot, F. A. (1990). Neurology of aggression and episodic dyscontrol. *Seminars in Neurology, 10*, 303–312.

Evans, R. W., & Gualtieri, C. T. (1985). Carbamazepine: A neuropsychological and psychiatric profile. *Clinical Neuropharmacology, 8*, 221–241.

Fenwick, P. (1989). The nature and management of aggression in epilepsy. *Journal of Neuropsychiatry and Clinical Neurosciences, 1*, 418–425.

Filley, C. M., Cranberg, L. D., Alexander, M. P., & Hart, E. J. (1987). Neurobehavioral outcome after closed head injury in childhood and adolescence. *Archives of Neurology, 44*, 194–198.

Franzen, M. D., & Lovell, M. R. (1987). Behavioral treatments of aggressive sequelae of brain injury. *Psychiatric Annals, 17*, 389–396.

Gardner, D. L., & Cowdry, R. W. (1986). Positive effects of carbamazepine on behavioral dyscontrol in borderline personality disorder. *American Journal of Psychiatry, 143*, 519–522.

Gelenberg, A. J. (Ed.). (1987). Trazadone (Desyrel): Unique properties? *MGH Newsletter Biological Therapies in Psychiatry, 10*, 15–16.

Glenn, M. B., & Joseph, A. B. (1987). The use of lithium for behavioral and affective disorders after traumatic brain injury. *Journal of Head Trauma Rehabilitation, 2*, 68–76.

Goldstein, M. (1974). Brain research and violent behavior: A summary and evaluation of the status of biomedical research on brain and aggressive behavior. *Archives of Neurology, 30*, 1–35.

Greendyke, R. M., & Kantner, D. R. (1986). Therapeutic effects of pindolol on behavioral disturbances associated with organic brain disease: A double-blind study. *Journal of Clinical Psychiatry*, *47*, 423–426.

Greendyke, R. M., Kantner, D. R., Schuster, D. B., Verstreate, S., & Wooton, J. (1986). Propranolol treatment of assaultive patients with organic brain disease. *Journal of Nervous and Mental Disease*, *174*, 290–294.

Herzog, A. G., Seibel, M. M., Schomer, D. L., Vaitukaitis, J. L., & Geschwind, N. (1986). Reproductive endocrine disorders in women with partial seizures of temporal lobe origin. *Archives of Neurology*, *43*, 341–346.

Iversen, S. D., & Mishkin, M. (1970). Perseverative interference in monkeys following selective lesions of the inferior frontal convexity. *Experimental Brain Research*, *11*, 376–386.

Leimkuhler, B., & Mesulam, M.-M. (1985). Reversible go-no-go deficits in a case of frontal lobe tumor. *Annals of Neurology*, *18*, 617–619.

Levine, D. N., & Grek, A. (1984). The anatomic basis of delusions after right cerebral infarction. *Neurology*, *34*, 577–582.

Lewis, D. O., & Pincus, J. H. (1989). Epilepsy and violence: Evidence for a neuropsychotic-aggressive syndrome. *Journal of Neuropsychiatry and Clinical Neurosciences*, *1*, 413–418.

Lewis, D. O., Pincus, J. H., Feldman, M., Jackson, L., & Bard, B. (1986). Psychiatric, neurological, and psychoeducational characteristics of 15 death row inmates in the United States. *American Journal of Psychiatry*, *143*, 838–845.

Lhermitte, F. (1986). Human autonomy and the frontal lobes. Part II: Patient behavior in complex social situations: The environmental dependency syndrome. *Annals of Neurology*, *19*, 335–343.

Lhermitte, F., Pillon, B., & Serdaru, M. (1986). Human autonomy and the frontal lobes. Part I: Imitation and utilization behavior: A neuropsychological study of 75 patients. *Annals of Neurology*, *19*, 326–334.

Linnoila, M., DeJong, J., & Virkkunen, M. (1989). Family history of alcoholism in violent offenders and impulsive fire setters. *Archives of General Psychiatry*, *46*, 613–616.

Lion, J. R. (1972). *Evaluation and management of the violent patient*. Springfield, IL: Charles C. Thomas.

Luchins, D. J., & Dojka, D. (1989). Lithium and propranolol in aggression and self-injurious behavior in the mentally retarded. *Psychopharmacology Bulletin*, *25*, 372–375.

Mark, V. H., & Ervin, F. R. (1970). *Violence and the brain*. Hagerstown, MD: Harper & Row.

Mattes, J. A. (1984). Metroprolol for intermittent explosive disorder. *American Journal of Psychiatry*, *142*, 1108–1109.

Mattes, J. A. (1986). Psychopharmacology of temper outbursts: A review. *The Journal of Nervous and Mental Disease*, *174*, 464–470.

Mattes, J. A. (1990). Comparative effectiveness of carbamazepine and propranolol for rage outbursts. *Journal of Neuropsychiatry and Clinical Neurosciences*, *2*, 159–164.

Mattson, A. J., & Levin, H. S. (1990). Frontal lobe dysfunction following closed head injury: A review of the literature. *Journal of Nervous and Mental Disease*, *178*, 282–291.

McElroy, S. L., Keck, P. K., Jr., Pope, H. G., Jr., & Hudson, J. I. (1988). Valproate in the treatment of rapid-cycling bipolar disorder. *Journal of Clinical Psychopharmacology*, *8*, 275–279.

McElroy, S. L., Keck, P. K., Jr., Pope, H. G., Jr., & Hudson, J. I. (1989). Valproate in psychiatric disorders: Literature review and clinical guidelines. *Journal of Clinical Psychiatry*, *50* (Suppl. 3), 23–29.

Menninger, K. (1963). *The vital balance: The life process in mental health and illness*. New York: Viking Press.

Mesulam, M.-M. (1985). Patterns in behavioral neuroanatomy: Association areas, the limbic system, and hemispheric specialization. In M-M. Mesulam (Ed.), *Principles of behavioral neurology* (pp. 1–70). Philadelphia: F. A. Davis.

Miczek, K. A., Mos, J., & Olivier, B. (1989). Brain 5-HT and inhibition of aggressive behavior in animals: 5-HIAA and receptor subtypes. *Psychopharmacology Bulletin*, *25*, 399–403.

Monroe, R. R. (1985). Episodic behavioral disorders and limbic ictus. *Comprehensive Psychiatry*, *26*, 466–479.

Nieuwenhuys, R., Voogd, J., & van Huijzen, C. (1988). *The human central nervous system: A synopsis and atlas* (3rd revised edition). New York: Springer-Verlag.

Ozer, I. J. (1989). Epilepsy and the violent mind in literature. *American Epilepsy Digest*, *6*, 1.

Pincus, J. (1981). Violence and epilepsy. *New England Journal of Medicine*, *305*, 696–699.

Post, R. M. (1989). Use of anticonvulsants in the treatment of manic-depressive illness. In R. M. Post, M. R. Trimble, & C. E. Pippenger (Eds.), *Clinical use of anticonvulsants in psychiatric disorders* (pp. 113–152). New York: Demos.

Price, B., Daffner, K., Stowe, R. M., & Mesulam, M.-M. (1989). The compartmental learning disabilities of early frontal damage. *Brain*, *113*, 1383–1393.

Price, B. H., & Mesulam, M.-M. (1985). Psychiatric manifestations of right hemisphere infarctions. *Journal of Nervous and Mental Disease*, *173*, 610–614.

Ratey, J. J., Sovner, R., Mikkelsen, E., & Chmielinski, H. E. (1989). Buspirone therapy for maladaptive behavior and anxiety in developmentally disabled persons. *Journal of Clinical Psychiatry, 50*, 382–384.

Reid, W. H., & Balis, G. U. (1987). Evaluation of the violent patient. *American Psychiatric Association Annual Review, 6*, 491–509.

Ross, E. D. (1985). Modulation of affect and non-verbal communication by the right hemisphere. In M.-M. Mesulam (Ed.), *Principles of behavioral neurology* (pp. 239–257). Philadelphia: F. A. Davis.

Silver, J. M., Shin, C., & McNamara, J. O. (1991). Antiepileptogenic effects of conventional anticonvulsants in the kindling model of epilepsy. *Annals of Neurology, 29*, 356–363.

Simpson, D. M., & Foster, D. (1986). Improvement in organically disturbed behavior with trazadone treatment. *Journal of Clinical Psychiatry, 47*, 191–103.

Spiers, P. A., Schomer, D. L., Blume, H. W., & Mesulam, M.-M. (1985). Temporolimbic epilepsy and behavior. In M.-M. Mesulam (Ed.), *Principles of behavioral neurology* (pp. 289–326). Philadelphia: F. A. Davis.

Swanson, J. W., Holzer, C. E., III, Ganju, V. K., & Jono, R. T. (1990). Violence and psychiatric disorder in the community: Evidence from the Epidemiological Catchment Area surveys. *Hospital and Community Psychiatry, 41*, 761–770.

Swift, R. G., Sadler, D. B., & Swift, M. (1990). Psychiatric findings in Wolfram syndrome homozygotes. *Lancet, 336*, 667–669.

Tardiff, K. (1987). Determinants of human violence. *American Psychiatric Association Annual Review, 6*, 451–463.

Verfaellie, M., & Heilman, K. M. (1987). Response preparation and response inhibition after lesions of the medial frontal lobe. *Archives of Neurology, 44*, 1265–1271.

Watanabe, M. (1986). Prefrontal unit activity during delayed conditional go/no-go discrimination in the monkey. II. Relation to go and no-go responses. *Brain Research, 382*, 15–27.

Weiger, W. A., & Bear, D. M. (1988). An approach to the neurology of aggression. *Journal of Psychiatric Research, 22*, 85–98.

Weintraub, S., & Mesulam, M.-M. (1985). Mental state assessment of young and elderly adults in behavioral neurology. In M.-M. Mesulam (Ed.), *Principles of behavioral neurology* (pp. 71–123). Philadelphia: F. A. Davis.

Williams, D. T., Mehl, R., Yudofsky, S. C., Adams, D., & Roseman, B. (1982). The effect of propranolol on uncontrolled rage outbursts in children and adolescents with organic brain dysfunction. *Journal of the American Academy of Child Psychiatry, 21*, 129–135.

Williams, K. H., & Goldstein, G. (1979). Cognitive and affective responses to lithium in patients with organic brain syndrome. *American Journal of Psychiatry, 136*, 800–803.

Woodcock, J. H. (1986). A neuropsychiatric approach to impulse disorders. *Psychiatric Clinics of North America, 9*, 341–352.

Wragg, R. E., & Jeste, D. V. (1988). Neuroleptics and alternative treatments: Management of behavioral symptoms and psychosis in Alzheimer's disease and related conditions. *Psychiatric Clinics of North America, 11*, 195–213.

Yudofsky, S. C., Silver, J. M., Jackson, W., Endicott, J., & Williams, D. (1986). The Overt Aggression Scale for the objective rating of verbal and physical aggression. *American Journal of Psychiatry, 143*, 35–39.

Yudofsky, S. C., Silver, J. M., & Schneider, S. E. (1987). Pharmacologic treatment of aggression. *Psychiatric Annals, 17*, 397–407.

CHAPTER 18

Borderline Disorder

JENNIFER WALTZ

DESCRIPTION OF THE DISORDER

Perhaps more than any other diagnostic category, borderline personality disorder (BPD) is associated with destructive behaviors, particularly parasuicide. Helping patients change these behaviors represents one of the most challenging clinical problems that professionals face. Due to the severity of the potential consequences of these behaviors, they often need to be addressed quickly. However, because of the histories that have shaped thcm, they are likely to be difficult to change. Other characteristics BPD patients present with, such as interpersonal problems and intense negative affect, make maintaining an effective therapeutic relationship, within which the destructive behaviors can be addressed, especially difficult.

This chapter reviews research on parasuicide and aggressive behavior in borderline patients. A biosocial conceptualization of BPD (Linehan, 1993), and its implications for understanding parasuicidal and aggressive behavior in BPD patients are presented. This approach provides a conceptual framework for understanding BPD, based primarily on behavioral theory, that attempts to account for the currently available research evidence on the characteristics of people meeting criteria for BPD who also engage in parasuicide.

The history of the label "borderline" as used in psychiatric and psychological circles, as well as our understanding of the behavioral patterns currently identified with that label, is lengthy and complicated. The term *borderline* has had many different meanings and in some cases has referred to issues that are quite unrelated to its current use. Historically, the meaning of the label has been complicated by the use of theory-specific symptomatology associated with it. A comprehensive description of this history is impossible here, but interested readers are referred to Stone (1980).

The term *borderline* was first used by Knight (1953) to refer to patients whose symptoms could not be categorized simply as "neurotic" or "psychotic," but instead seemed to fall somewhere between these two ends of the spectrum. This usage of the term,

JENNIFER WALTZ • Department of Psychology, University of Montana, Missoula, Montana 59812-1075.
Handbook of Aggressive and Destructive Behavior in Psychiatric Patients, edited by Michel Hersen, Robert T. Ammerman, and Lori A. Sisson. Plenum Press, New York, 1994.

to refer to people whose maladaptive behavior did not fit clearly into either the psychotic or neurotic category, is probably the most widely recognized origin of the current concept of BPD. However, the maladaptive behavioral patterns seen in people meeting DSM-III-R criteria for BPD were earlier described by other writers using other terms (Deutsch, 1942; Federn, 1952; Stern, 1938, Zilboorg, 1941). In addition, a separate body of literature on the topic of parasuicide (variously called "wrist-slashing," "self-mutilation," "manipulative suicide attempt" and others) has also grown up (Graff & Mallin, 1967; Grunebaum & Klerman, 1967; Rinzler & Shapiro, 1968; Rosenthal, Rinzler, Wallsh, & Klausner, 1972). Clinical descriptions of these patients suggest that they are likely to have been people who would meet the current criteria for BPD. There have thus been several independent lines of work addressing what can be understood to be a single population of people who would currently be classified as having BPD.

A plethora of symptoms have at one point or another been associated with the term borderline. A review of symptoms described by five major theorists (Knight, Kernberg, Grinker, Gunderson and Singer) done in 1978 (Perry & Klerman) found that across the theorists, 104 separate symptoms were noted. Of these, one-half were mentioned by an isolated theorist, suggesting a wide divergence in understanding of what the term borderline referred to at that time. In a separate study, a total of 129 different symptoms were included in a checklist used to try to differentiate BPD patients from other psychiatric patients (Perry & Klerman, 1980). Of these, 81 were found to discriminate patients diagnosed as having BPD from others.

Borderline personality disorder, as described by the proposed DSM-IV criteria, is characterized by "a pervasive pattern of instability of interpersonal relationships, self-image, affects, and control over impulses" (American Psychiatric Association, 1993). The proposed criteria for BPD include nine behavioral and/or affective maladaptive patterns. To receive a diagnosis, a person must exhibit at least five of them. Of the nine patterns, two reflect interpersonal difficulties: "frantic efforts to avoid real or imagined abandonment" and "unstable and intense interpersonal relationships" in which other people are viewed in black and white ways. Two reflect behavioral difficulties: "impulsivity in at least two areas that are potentially self-damaging (e.g., spending, sex . . .)," and "recurrent suicidal behavior."

One pattern reflects difficulties in the realm of sense of self: "identity disturbance: persistent and markedly disturbed, distorted, or unstable self-image." Difficulties in the realm of affect are reflected in three of the patterns: "affective instability due to a marked reactivity of mood," "chronic feelings of emptiness," and "inappropriate, intense anger or lack of control of anger." The final symptom, "transient, stress-related paranoid ideation or severe dissociative symptoms" is a proposed change from DSM-III-R to DSM-IV, included to reflect the observation that many people with BPD characteristics experience paranoid thoughts or dissociative symptoms when under stress.

One of the most striking aspects of these criteria is their diversity. Any two people meeting criteria for BPD may have very few maladaptive behaviors in common. There has been considerable debate about the utility of classifying people meeting these criteria under a single diagnostic label, with the implicit assumption that thinking of them as a group will lead to more effective treatments. However, there is mounting evidence supporting the notion that BPD is a discrete clinical entity. Sheehy, Goldsmith, and Charles (1980) found that patients diagnosed as borderline could be differentiated from those diagnosed as schizophrenic, neurotic, or other personality disorder, particularly on the dimensions of "impulsivity, affectivity and overvaluation/derogation of others" (p. 1374).

Perry and Klerman (1980) also were able to distinguish patients diagnosed with BPD from other patients on a variety of symptoms.

Development of reliable instruments used to assess BPD has enhanced researchers' ability to identify relatively homogeneous groups of people meeting criteria for this disorder. For example, the Diagnostic Interview for Borderlines (Gunderson, Kolb, & Austin, 1981) has been demonstrated to be a reliable measure. It is a structured interview that assesses Gunderson's criteria for BPD. Measures like the Structured Clinical Interview for DSM-III (SCID) (Spitzer, Williams, Gibbon, & First, 1990) diagnose BPD using DSM-III criteria.

EPIDEMIOLOGY

According to a recent review (Widiger & Frances, 1989), estimates of the prevalence of BPD in the population have ranged from .2% using DSM-III criteria (Merikangas & Weissman, 1986) to 15% using Kernberg's criteria (Gunderson, 1984). A community survey (Swartz, Blazer, George, & Winfield, 1990) of 1,541 people found that 1.8% of the respondents met the study's criteria for BPD using the Diagnostic Interview Schedule/Borderline Index. In addition, in a study of 797 first degree relatives of normal controls and patients, Zimmerman and Coryell (1989) found that 1.6% of the subjects met criteria for BPD. These studies suggest that somewhere around 2% of the population meet criteria for BPD. Based on their review, Widiger and Frances (1989) also estimate that approximately 11% of outpatients and 19% of all inpatients would meet criteria for BPD.

Concerning the sex ratio for people meeting criteria for BPD, again based on a review of a large number of studies (Widiger & Frances, 1989), it appears that about 74% of BPD patients are female. Swartz et al. (1990) found that 73.2% of the people meeting criteria for BPD in their sample were female. Little data about the relationship of socioeconomic factors to BPD are available; however, it has been found that borderlines, like other personality-disordered people, tend to be younger than non-personality-disordered control groups (Akhtar, Byrne, & Doghramji, 1986).

Parasuicide

Parasuicide is perhaps the hallmark behavior of BPD. In fact, it is one of the best single predictors of whether a person will meet criteria for the disorder (Gunderson & Kolb, 1978). A fair amount of research has been directed at discovering what clusters of behaviors most effectively define this disorder, including looking at the prevalence of parasuicide among people meeting criteria for the disorder. Some of this work, as well as studies that report actual prevalence rates of parasuicide among people meeting criteria for BPD, is reviewed here.

In one of the first empirical studies to systematically examine the behavior patterns of people who had been diagnosed as having BPD, Gunderson (1977) compared BPD, schizophrenic, and neurotic patients. BPD patients were found to more frequently report "self-mutilation" and were judged more frequently to have engaged in a "manipulative suicide attempt."

Perry and Klerman (1980) compared patients who met criteria for BPD to those who did not at a psychiatric emergency service. Patients who were diagnosed as having BPD by the admitting staff were found to score higher on the items "has slashed wrists," "has mutilated self in other ways," "has made suicide attempts," and "suicide attempts were deemed manipulative."

In a replication of Gunderson's (1977) work, Soloff and Ulrich (1981) compared clinically identified borderlines with patients meeting Research Diagnostic Criteria (RDC) (Spitzer, Endicott, & Robins, 1975) for schizophrenia and another group meeting RDC for major depression. All subjects were given the Diagnostic Interview for Borderlines (Gunderson, Kolb, & Austin, 1981). Borderline patients were found to score higher on "slashed wrist, self-mutilation," and "manipulative suicide threat or effort" than both the schizophrenic and depressed groups.

A recent study of 100 male psychiatric inpatients compared people who were nonsuicidal to suicide ideators and those who had made a suicide attempt (Raczek, True, & Friend, 1990). This study found that "borderline personality traits" were twice as likely to be found in suicide ideators and people who had parasuicided than in the nonsuicidal group.

In a study of 20 outpatients meeting DSM-III criteria for BPD, Clarkin et al. (1983) found that 75% of the sample had a history of parasuicide, as compared to 36% of a control group of outpatients with some other personality disorder. Interestingly, parasuicide was not the symptom most predictive of meeting BPD criteria in this sample. Impulsivity was found in 100% of the BPD patients, affective instability in 95%, unstable and/or intense relationships in 90%, and anger problems in 90%.

It is clear from this body of research that parasuicide is more common among patients who meet criteria for BPD than among other patient populations. Other BPD symptoms that are extremely common among those receiving the diagnosis (i.e., impulsivity, affective instability, etc.) are behaviors that are related to parasuicide, in the sense that many parasuicides occur in the context of extreme affect, and are carried out impulsively. It may be that presence of parasuicide represents a more extreme version of similar behavioral patterns.

Violence toward Others

There has been less research devoted to assessing the presence of violence toward others among people who meet criteria for borderline personality disorder. Based on the research that has been done, however, it appears that this behavior is less common than parasuicide (Gunderson & Kolb, 1978). As is the case with parasuicide, several studies have compared presence of violent behavior among people meeting criteria for BPD to members of other diagnostic groups. It is unfortunate that little actual prevalence data are reported.

Several of the studies described above also included assessment of violent behavior (Gunderson, 1977; Perry & Klerman, 1980; Soloff & Ulrich, 1981). Gunderson (1977) found no significant difference on "trouble with the law, assaultiveness, or other antisocial impulse-action patterns" between BPD, schizophrenic, and depressed patients. Soloff and Ulrich (1981), in their replication of Gunderson, did find a significant difference between borderlines and these two other groups, with borderlines committing more of these aggressive behaviors. Perry and Klerman (1980) found no difference between borderlines and other emergency psychiatric patients on physical assaults of another person or threats of violence to another person, but did find a higher rate of destruction of property among the borderline group.

In a study conducted in our own laboratory, 48 women reporting for therapy who met

DSM-III-R and Gunderson's (Gunderson, Kolb, & Austin, 1981) criteria for BPD were studied. This subject sample only included women who had a history of at least two instances of parasuicide in the preceding 5 years, at least one of which had occurred in the previous 8 weeks. Subjects who met criteria for current diagnoses of substance dependence, bipolar disorder, or schizophrenia were excluded. No control group was included in this study. All subjects completed the Diagnostic Interview for Borderlines. Three types of violent behavior were assessed: (1) assaults on other people, (2) threats to be violent toward another person, and (3) violence to property. The percentages of subjects who had engaged in each type of behavior were as follows: assaultive behavior, 38%; threatened violence, 35%; violence to property, 63%. These results suggest that at least among borderline patients who engage in parasuicide, rates of aggressive behavior are quite high, with destruction of property being much more common than threatening or actually being violent toward another person; however, it should be noted that the subject sample was not representative of BPD patients, as all subjects had histories of multiple parasuicides. In addition, "assaults" done in self-defense were included.

Finally, in a study by Snyder, Pitts, and Pokorny (1986), of 4,800 psychiatric inpatients, a subscale of the Brief Psychiatric Rating Scale (Overall & Gorham, 1962) was used to develop a borderline subscale. Subjects also reported on recent violent behavior. The results demonstrated a positive correlation between number of borderline items endorsed and recent violent behavior, both in and out of the hospital.

Overall, currently available results are mixed, but seem to lend tentative support to the notion of a relationship between meeting criteria for BPD and engaging in violent or aggressive behavior. The relationship is less clear than that between BPD and parasuicide. There are several problems involved in interpreting the existing data. One is that problems with anger is one of the criteria used to diagnose BPD. So the selection process for being identified as a borderline and the assessment of violent behavior are not independent.

Another major flaw with all of the studies reported on in this section is that none reported whether the violent behavior was done in self-defense. Since many people meeting criteria for BPD come from families that are sexually and/or physically abusive, it may be that some portion of the aggressive behavior being reported on has been done in self-defense. This is an important distinction to be taken into account when assessing aggressive behavior. Clearly, more research is needed to get a better picture of the function of the violence being reported by persons with BPD.

ETIOLOGY

There is currently no widely accepted understanding of the etiology of borderline personality disorder, or of the various behaviors such as parasuicide and violent behavior that seem to be part of it. Several theories attempting to explain the various maladaptive behaviors seen in this population exist. Historically, psychoanalytic (Adler & Buie, 1979; Gunderson, 1984; Kernberg, 1967; Masterson, 1976) and biological (Cowdry & Gardner, 1988; Leone, 1982; Serban & Siegel, 1984; Soloff, 1981) perspectives have been most concerned with BPD. More recently, behavioral and cognitive theorists have begun addressing BPD.

One such theory, proposed by Linehan (1987), is a biosocial model of borderline personality disorder. This theory, as well as its application to parasuicide and violent behavior, will be explained in some detail below. Linehan's model proposes that BPD is primarily a disorder of emotion regulation. Such dysregulation of emotion is comprised of emotion vulnerability and inadequate emotion regulation capacity.

Emotion vulnerability includes four components. Emotionally vulnerable people are highly sensitive to emotional stimuli, they tend to have intense responses to these stimuli, they are not good at modulating these emotional responses, and they have a slow return to baseline. An example would be a person who is exposed to some moderate emotional cue, such as low-level criticism. The emotionally vulnerable person is likely to be very sensitive to such a stimulus, to have an intense reaction, to be unable to reduce the strong affect produced, and to feel that emotion for a longer period of time than a nonemotionally vulnerable person.

The focus on emotion as a key component of borderline personality disorder is supported by the features making up the disorder: emotional lability, high levels of anger, fear of abandonment, problems with feelings of emptiness and boredom. It is also phenomenologically consistent with therapists' experiences with borderline patients. The extremes of emotion and difficulty modulating extreme emotions are frequently seen by therapists working with BPD patients. In addition, many borderline patients have coexisting affective disorders, including major depression, bipolar disorder, and the like (Perry, 1985; Plakun, Burkhardt, & Muller, 1985; Widiger & Frances, 1989).

Linehan's theory does not specify one particular way in which a person would come to have emotion dysregulation problems. It is likely that there are many ways that emotion dysregulation may be produced, because the emotion system is very complex and involves many different physiological systems. For example, for some people the source may be genetically based; for others, it may be the result of some prenatal trauma.

Human emotional responses are related to many other behaviors and experiences. The acquisition of an ability to moderate or control emotion is one of the most important tasks of childhood development. Almost all other behaviors are dependent on the person's ability to regulate his or her emotional responses. The ability to modulate affect has been found to be related to a broad range of behaviors including delay of gratification, perceptions of control, and descriptions of self. A sense of self is largely based on one's observations of one's own behavior across settings, and on others' reactions to oneself. Lability in emotional responding makes it difficult to form a consistent view of oneself.

The interpersonal problems seen in borderlines can also be understood as resulting from emotional dysregulation. Relationships are inherently the source of much emotionally laden stimuli, both positive and negative. In order to maintain relationships effectively, individuals must have the capacity to modulate their responses to emotions produced by the other person's behavior. This includes tolerating emotional pain, modulating expression of emotion, and being able to delay emotional expression in favor of responding to the other person's needs. Borderlines' experiencing of extreme emotions and limited capacity to modify them make their interpersonal relationships difficult.

Linehan's biosocial theory also postulates that the presence of certain characteristics of the environment interact in an ongoing way with emotion dysregulation problems to exacerbate the difficulty regulating effect. The type of environment hypothesized to exacerbate problems produced by emotion dysregulation difficulties is one that is characterized by invalidation from others. The distinguishing characteristic of these environments is that they respond inappropriately and inconsistently to the child's emotional experiences. They tend to underrespond to emotional experiences that are private and not publicly displayed, while overresponding to public displays of emotion. So, for example, if the child has some experience that is likely to produce sadness, the invalidating family would not be sensitive to what the child was experiencing. They would ignore the event, tell the child to "put on a smile," or downplay the importance of the event. On the other hand, if the child cries, the family overreacts. This creates a discrepancy between the child's inner experience and the environmental reaction.

Environmentally invalidating families also tend to emphasize internal control of emotions (i.e., "just don't think about it and it will be OK"). They do not teach the child to label and modulate arousal. They are likely to teach the child that her own emotional responses are not valid indicators of what is happening in the world around her, forcing her to scan the environment to make choices, as opposed to looking inward at her own emotions (i.e., "why are you so upset, it's no big deal.").

In addition to general invalidation from their environments, there is a growing body of evidence attesting to a high prevalence rate of sexual abuse in the histories of borderline patients (Herman, Perry, & Van der Kolk, 1989). Among inpatients with BPD, 71–86% report histories of childhood sexual abuse, as compared to 22–34% of inpatients not diagnosed with BPD (Bryer, Nelson, Miller, & Kroll, 1987; Ogata et al., 1990). In outpatient samples diagnosed as borderline, similar prevalence rates are found (Herman, 1986; Herman, Perry, & Van der Kolk, 1989). Briere and Zaidi (1989) found that among emergency psychiatric patients, 37% who reported a history of childhood sexual abuse had been diagnosed with BPD or had borderline traits. Only 7% of those who had not been sexually abused had been diagnosed with BPD. Linehan and Wagner (in press) found that in a sample of women reporting for outpatient therapy who met DSM-III criteria for BPD and had a history of parasuicide, 76% reported histories of sexual abuse. Childhood trauma such as sexual abuse may exacerbate emotion dysregulation problems or reduce the child's capacity to learn emotion regulation skills, as well as producing other symptoms typical of posttraumatic stress disorder (PTSD).

Linehan's model is also a behavioral one. From a behavioral perspective, any attempt to understand a particular behavior must be contextual; that is, it necessarily involves an assessment of the context within which the behavior occurs. Each instance of a behavior may have a different function, depending on the context. There is therefore no one explanation for the cause of different occurrences of a behavior. There may be some broad generalizations or themes that can be described, based on multiple instances of the behavior. In this chapter, a method for understanding behaviors like parasuicide and violence toward others, as well as information about variables commonly observed to be related to these behaviors, is described. It must be emphasized, however, that on an individual basis, each instance of the behavior must be examined idiographically to be understood.

The process whereby behaviors such as parasuicide and violence toward others are understood is critical. This process involves an analysis of the function of the behavior. To understand any particular instance of the behavior, one must know the environmental events occurring before the behavior, the patient's cognitive and affective states, as well as other behaviors they were engaging in, relevant aspects of the person's history and any other relevant contextual variables. One must also understand the consequences of the behavior for the individual; in other words, what were the reinforcers and/or punishers involved? Reinforcers do not just involve attention from others; they include such consequences as reduction of negative affect, induction of affect when the person is feeling nothing, removal of the person from an aversive environment, reduction of guilt, blackouts that allow the avoidance of negative emotions or difficult situations, and so forth.

Obviously, to gather information about all of these factors surrounding a particular behavior, a tremendous amount of careful assessment is required. This point cannot be overemphasized. Behavioral approaches are assessment based. Probably the most frequently made mistake in using behavioral analysis to understand a behavior is the making of assumptions about some important aspect of that behavior or context, rather than use of thorough assessment.

From a behavioral perspective, it is of primary importance to gather information that allows for an understanding of what is maintaining or eliciting a particular behavior. For any one instance of parasuicide, there may be many factors present. To understand which factors are maintaining the behavior, it is important to do thorough assessment across multiple instances of the behavior, to determine which factors stand out as consistently present. These are the factors that can then be addressed by interventions chosen.

AGGRESSION TOWARD SELF

The term *parasuicide* refers to any acute, intentional, self-injurious behavior or action that puts the individual at risk of injury or loss of life (Kreitman, 1977). This definition includes behaviors that run the range of severity (e.g., scratching oneself to shooting oneself with a gun). It also includes behaviors accompanied by the entire range of intent to result in death (e.g., no intent to die, to full intent to die).

Some of the common ways in which parasuicide functions are reviewed in this section. This information has been derived from clinical experience with borderlines participating in research/therapy under the direction of Dr. Marsha Linehan. These various functions are not mutually exclusive; that is, any one instance of parasuicide may involve more than one of the following. In addition, they are presented for descriptive purposes, not as a comprehensive list of the functions of parasuicide. No typology or list can replace thorough assessment of an individual instance of the behavior; however, the following list is intended to provide some possible leads and ways to think about the behavior.

It has frequently been noted that one of the primary functions of parasuicide in borderlines seems to be for affect regulation. Parasuicide is an extraordinarily effective means of reducing certain types of painful affect, including anger or rage, shame, guilt, sadness, or fear. Given the emotional climate of the borderline's life described in the theory section above (i.e., they respond to mild affective stimuli, their affective responses are extreme, their ability to modulate emotion is limited, and their return to baseline is slow), it is clear why powerful affect regulation behaviors, such as parasuicide, might come to strength. The effectiveness of parasuicide as an affect regulator makes it very difficult to eliminate. The alternative behaviors and skills available are usually not as effective in modulating affect, particularly at first.

Some parasuicides seem to function as avoidance behavior. The avoidance may be of emotions, thoughts, interpersonal problems, or of some combination thereof. An example would be a patient who overdoses and blacks out when she experiences flashbacks of sexual abuse. The result of the overdose is that she avoids the flashbacks and concomitant emotions, even if only temporarily. Another example would be a client whose parasuicides occur in the context of interpersonal problems in her living situation. If the parasuicide results in hospitalization, the client avoids the interpersonal problems at home.

As described earlier, many borderlines have grown up in environments in which people tend to ignore private experiences, such as emotional experiences that are not expressed, and to overreact to public expressions, such as crying. When something happens that is likely to produce an emotion, important others are unlikely to take the child's experience seriously. Many borderlines have therefore not learned to respond to their own emotions in a validating way. They have learned that only public expressions are "real" and to be taken seriously. In some cases, then, parasuicide may be a communication behavior. It must be remembered, however, that this does not mean that the pain being communicated is not real. It is, however, being communicated in a destructive way that is uncomfortable for others and potentially dangerous to the patient.

In some cases in which the parasuicide functions as communication behavior, it may also have the effect of getting other people to act in a particular way. For example, for a client who is being pushed by her therapist to get a job, the parasuicide may convince the therapist that the client is not ready to get a job and cause the therapist to stop pushing. Therapists and others working with BPD patients have a tendency to focus primary attention on this aspect of parasuicide and to assume that all instances of the behavior function in this way, that is, to get other people to do something. From a behavioral perspective, the client is not seen as parasuiciding to get some desired result from others; instead, the fact that others respond in certain ways sometimes reinforces parasuicide and thereby *maintains* the behavior.

In some cases, parasuicides are actual attempts to suicide that fail. Although some writers emphasize that persons with BPD in actuality "do not wish to die" (Walsh & Rosen, 1988), in our experience most borderlines experience extreme ambivalence about their desire to live. It is a mistake to adopt their black-and-white thinking and assume that someone either wants to die or does not want to die. Seldom is it that clear; however, some parasuicides are outright attempts at suicide.

Finally, some parasuicides are attempts to control dissociation or to induce emotion when the client is feeling numb. These parasuicides may function to reduce feelings of depersonalization. As with its effect on other types of emotions, parasuicide seems to be quite effective in this area.

AGGRESSION TOWARD OTHERS

Understanding aggressive behavior in patients with BPD necessitates some exploration of the experience of anger in these patients. As described in Linehan (1993), many BPD patients attempt to inhibit feelings of anger, sometimes out of fear that if they begin to feel angry they will escalate and lose control. This type of patient may have a history of such experiences, and he or she is faced with two challenges: learning to modulate the expression of anger (i.e., inhibiting aggressive or hostile behavior) and learning to experience anger instead of attempting to block it.

The escalation of anger may reflect a variety of things for the patient. For some patients, it may serve as a way to cope with other intense emotions, such as shame, worthlessness, or despair. These emotions may be more painful to experience than anger. Unfortunately, a cycle may result whereby the patient's coping strategy (i.e., escalating anger and aggressive behavior) provides temporary relief from feelings such as shame, but ultimately serves to produce even greater shameful feelings.

An escalation of anger may also reflect feelings of fear or lack of safety. For example, intense fear of abandonment may be experienced as "threatening," because of the emotional consequences of a relationship loss for the patient. Escalating anger or aggressive behavior may function as an attempt at "self-protection" in this situation, although for obvious reasons this approach is not likely to be effective.

Relatedly, some patients' aggressive behavior occurs in a context of feelings of powerlessness. Many borderlines have experienced abusive family situations in which they were powerless (e.g., being physically, sexually, or emotionally abused as children). Their relationships with others (and particularly the therapy relationship) are often experienced as painful. From the patient's perspective, the other person in the relationship may be perceived as having the ability to reduce the patient's pain, but withholding of whatever it is that might reduce the pain. For example, a patient may desire more frequent contact with his or her therapist because greater support would be likely to make the patient feel less isolated and depressed. If the therapist decides not to provide the increased frequency of contact, the patient may feel powerless to have influence in the relationship. This experience of powerlessness may set off a chain of feelings and behaviors that ultimately end in anger or hostility. Some patients may have histories characterized by modulating of use of aggression to respond to situations in which one feels powerless.

Aggression by BPD patients may function as self-defense in response to threats or actual assaults by others. Some patients have physically aggressive family members, partners, or spouses, and their own histories of aggression include aggressive behavior that has served as a means of self-defense. In some cases, patients recognize cues from others who have previously been physically abusive that indicate that violence from that person is imminent or highly likely. The patient may then act aggressively him- or herself. Although the patient in this situation may be the first to be physically aggressive, the function of the behavior may be the same as in cases where he or she responds to aggressive behavior with aggression; that is, the function may still be self-defense because the patient is responding to cues that violence is imminent.

For some patients, violent behavior may be a PTSD response. An event or stimulus in the current context may trigger a flashback which then leads to aggressive behavior. For example, a patient who has a flashback in response to an unexpected physical touch by her husband may respond aggressively.

Like parasuicide, aggressive behavior, particularly destruction of property, may be a communication behavior. Again, it should be emphasized that although one function of the behavior may be communication, this does not mean that patients' emotions are not real or to be taken seriously. Patients may have learned that they must escalate to the point of aggression in order for their feelings to be recognized by others.

CLINICAL MANAGEMENT

The treatment of parasuicide and violent behavior is a major issue for therapists and other treatment providers working with borderlines. Because both of these behaviors can have very serious consequences, treatment providers are under pressure to deal with them effectively. Particularly in the case of parasuicide, however, the behavior tends to be very difficult to eliminate. For many borderlines, it has been their primary, sometimes only, effective means of reducing intense negative affect and is therefore very difficult to replace with more adaptive behaviors that are less effective in the short run.

The clinical approach described in this section is based on a Dialectical Behavior Therapy (DBT) approach, developed by (Linehan, 1993). This is the only treatment that has been tested empirically and found to effectively reduce parasuicide in borderline patients (Linehan, Armstrong, Suarez, Allmon, & Heard, 1991). Its effectiveness in addressing violence toward others has not been tested; however, no other treatment modalities have been empirically examined in terms of their effectiveness in reducing violent behavior in borderlines. It is impossible to provide a complete description of this treatment in the space of several pages, so the description to follow focuses primarily on how parasuicide and violent behavior are specifically addressed. Interested readers should consult Linehan (1993) for a more thorough coverage of Dialectical Behavior Therapy.

DBT is a treatment approach designed for patients with BPD who engage in parasuicide. The DBT approach is based on the notion that change-oriented and acceptance-oriented therapeutic strategies must be balanced. The central change-oriented therapeutic strategies are based on behavioral theory and include behavioral analysis of maladaptive behaviors and solution analysis. Other behaviorally based strategies include contingency management, contingency clarification, and psychoeducational skills training. The central acceptance-oriented strategies involve the therapist validating the patient's thoughts, feelings, or behaviors; encouraging or cheerleading the client; and suggesting to the patient the notion of accepting reality as it is.

The DBT model includes a hierarchy of therapeutic targets or goals. Sessions are structured in such a way that behaviors or problems higher on the hierarchy are the focus of the session if they are currently an issue or have occurred since the previous session. Parasuicide is the top treatment target, followed by therapy-interfering behaviors, quality-of-life-interfering behaviors, skills training, PTSD, and other individual goals of the client.

The approach to parasuicidal behaviors in DBT involves several components. First, the client must make a commitment to stopping the behavior to be accepted into therapy. This commitment is very important, as the therapist is likely to need to draw on it throughout the therapy. Second, the behavior is always addressed when it occurs; it is not ignored. Addressing the behavior means doing a behavioral analysis of the parasuicide, and then carrying out a solution analysis. Training in behavior therapy is necessary to learn to conduct thorough behavioral analyses. Briefly, in this instance, a behavioral analysis involves talking through the events, thoughts, feelings, and behaviors that led up to the parasuicide and those that were consequences of it, as described in the theory section above. This analysis must be carried out in an extremely detailed way, with the therapist avoiding making any assumptions about the events and behaviors involved. It is an assessment-based intervention.

A solution analysis involves determining at what point in the chain of events and behaviors of the parasuicide a change or intervention could most effectively be made. If the solution analysis suggests that the behavior was the result of some skills deficit, such as parasuicides precipitated by interpersonal problems or emotion regulation deficits, the solution analysis would point to skills training as the intervention of choice. If the client has the skills needed, but the contingencies are not reinforcing the use of them, contingency management is implicated. For example, if the client has other behaviors in her repertoire that will bring about closeness with the therapist, but parasuicide is more effective in getting the therapist to focus attention on her, the contingencies favor parasuicide. The intervention would involve making contact with the therapist, such as phone calls, contingent on not parasuiciding. Finally, if the client has the skills and the contingencies favor using them, but the behavior is being blocked by emotions such as fear or guilt, an exposure-based intervention would be the treatment of choice.

The approach to aggressive behavior used in DBT takes into account the nature of the aggressive behavior, including the frequency, severity, potential consequences, and function. For example, aggressive behavior toward others would likely be addressed differently than aggressive behavior that involves destruction of the patient's own property in a way that does not endanger anyone. Of course, adhering to ethical and legal guidelines must be the primary consideration in situations where safety may be at risk. The following discussion of clinical management of aggressive behavior will focus on interventions designed to help patients eliminate aggressive behavior. It will not review risk assessment or the ethical and legal guidelines relevant to aggressive behavior. However, it should be emphasized that clinicians working with BPD patients should have a thorough knowledge of these guidelines.

There are some important similarities in the types of interventions used to address parasuicide and those likely to be used to address aggressive behavior from a DBT perspective. These reflect similarities in the two types of behavior. Both behaviors are likely to occur in the context of intense negative affect. Some of the functions they serve may be similar. For example, both may be a means to communicate distress, to influence other people's behavior, or to temporarily reduce negative affect. Both are likely to result in feelings of shame, guilt, or humiliation. Both parasuicide and aggressive behavior are likely to occur when the patient is unable to generate other means to resolve problems and both are likely to occur in the context of interpersonal difficulties.

The behavioral analysis and solution analysis approaches, as described above, would likely be used to address aggressive behavior, in order to understand the situations, feelings, thoughts, events, and behaviors related to the behavior, and to determine what type of intervention is most appropriate. For example, if the behavioral analysis suggests that the aggressive behavior was an anger or frustration response, the therapist may choose interventions designed to address emotion regulation. The therapy may also focus on the patient working on appropriate expression of anger, assertiveness training, anger management techniques, and the like. Other interpersonal skills may also need to be addressed if the client becomes aggressive in the context of interpersonal difficulties.

If the aggressive behavior serves as a means to avoid other types of affect, such as shame or guilt, interventions may be introduced to increase the patient's ability to tolerate those types of affect; for example, working on the patient's ability to identify his or her own emotions and using gradual exposure to those emotions to increase his or her ability to tolerate them. For instance, the therapist and patient may discuss whatever set of circumstances or events set off the shame or guilt initially, very gradually increasing the intensity of feelings generated by the discussions over time. This type of exposure must be done in the context of validation and support by the therapist. Cognitive interventions may also be useful—for example, if the client feels guilty or responsible for some negative event that he or she was not responsible for.

If the patient possesses the skills needed to eliminate aggressive behavior, the behavior may continue whether the contingencies support it or not. In this case, contingency management would be needed. For example, if the therapist primarily attends to the patient's painful affect after the patient has escalated to the point of an aggressive outburst, the contingencies favor maintenance of that behavior. One way to change these contingencies would be for the therapist to find additional ways to focus on and acknowledge the patient's painful affect in the absence of aggressive behavior, and reduce such focus when aggressive behavior has occurred.

It is important to keep in mind that the meaning of a given aggressive behavior may differ for different patients. For one patient, breaking a plate may represent an "adaptive" alternative to cutting herself, if parasuicide would have been her typical response in the same situation. Although breaking a plate may not be the ultimate goal as a means of coping, depending on where the patient is at in her therapy, it may be a step in the right direction for her. For another patient, this same behavior might represent a less adaptive means of coping than she is typically capable of, and would not be viewed as progress for her. The point here is that the meaning of the behavior for a given patient must be taken into account when making a decision regarding what interventions are appropriate.

If the aggressive behavior occurred in the context of therapy, it would be viewed as a therapy-interfering behavior. Since part of the DBT approach is therapist observation of his or her own limits, the therapist may need to clarify with the client the effect such behavior has on the therapist and what the consequences of future occurrences will be. For example, one client threatened her therapist's family. Since that behavior was unacceptable to that therapist, given her own individual limits, she discussed that with the client and let her know what the consequence for such threats would be in the future. It must be emphasized that according to the DBT model, each therapist has his or her own limits. These are not defined by the treatment protocol but must be discovered by each therapist independently. Arbitrary contingencies are to be avoided, while observation of one's own natural limits and the consequences of going past those are to be employed.

LONGITUDINAL PERSPECTIVES

A fair amount of research on the course of borderline personality disorder has been conducted; however, these studies are seriously limited in a number of ways. Perhaps most importantly, they have primarily been conducted on hospitalized samples of patients. It is therefore impossible to generalize to nonhospitalized people meeting criteria for BPD. In addition, because many of these studies include use of a time-one assessment while the patient is hospitalized, they either include only retrospective data on prehospitalized level of functioning, or have no information about that period of time. Because of the recency of the delineation of reliably measurable criteria for BPD, studies carried out before 1980 are very difficult to interpret. Many did not include clear inclusion and exclusion criteria (Stone, 1989).

Some conclusions can be drawn across studies, however. Results from a comprehensive review (Stone, 1989) are described here. Most of the patients in studies reviewed by Stone were hospitalized in their late teens or early twenties. According to his review, an estimated 3–10% of BPD patients will have committed suicide during a 2- to 5-year follow-up period. In fact, BPD patients are at high risk for suicide across follow-up periods. A history of parasuicide does seem to be related to eventual completed suicide (Kotila & Lonnquist, 1987). In one study, BPD patients who had previously engaged in parasuicide were twice as likely to eventually suicide than nonparasuicidal borderlines (Stone, 1989). The remaining patients "will continue to show major impairment in work, social, and close personal spheres, so that at two- or five-year follow-up they can scarcely be distinguished functionally from schizophrenic patients of similar age" (p. 119). At 8- to 10-year follow-up, when patients are entering their 30s, a stabilization in functioning is frequently seen, often associated with development of a primary relationship. Stone's review suggests that up to two-thirds of patients will be quite stable at this point in terms of occupational functioning. A return to previously poor levels of functioning is common when some life stress occurs, particularly loss of an important relationship.

Longitudinal studies conducted to date have revealed some factors predictive of course of the disorder. Indicators of poor prognosis include "substance abuse, aggressivity, parental victimization via incest or cruelty, having all eight BPD criteria, antisociality" (Stone, 1989, p. 119). Some factors that were unrelated to outcome were presence of an eating disorder, presence of narcissistic personality traits, presence of schizotypal personality traits, or presence of a major affective disorder.

It is important to note that both parasuicide and aggressive behavior toward others have been identified empirically as poor prognostic indicators for borderlines, parasuicide being predictive of eventual suicide and aggressive behavior being predictive of continued poor functioning. It may be said that these behaviors represent some of the more extreme responses to emotion dysregulation problems.

CASE ILLUSTRATION

Background Information

"Peg," a 36-year-old Caucasian female, was referred by her case manager. She had a history of multiple hospitalizations in adolescence and adulthood for suicidality. She met DSM-III criteria for BPD and also had a history of bulimia. At the time she entered therapy, Peg was living with her boyfriend and supporting herself on a part-time job at a gas station.

Peg came from a working-class family background. She was the oldest of five children. Her father left her mother when she was an infant and she never knew him. Peg's childhood was chaotic, with many moves and several father-figures who were in and out of her life. One of Peg's mother's boyfriends was physically abusive to Peg. As a result, Peg ran away from home and was raised in foster homes from age 15 on.

Parasuicide

Peg began parasuiciding at age 14. Her parasuicide methods have included burning and cutting herself. At the time she entered therapy, she was engaging in these behaviors approximately once every two or three months. Her parasuicides were generally moderate in lethality, yet quite physically harmful.

Violence toward Others

Peg had been aggressive toward others on several occasions. She had a history of being physically aggressive with her best friend, particularly when they were in their late teens. She has been physically aggressive toward her current boyfriend twice. Peg's physically aggressive behavior with her best friend and boyfriend had consisted of shoving or pushing them. Neither of them had a history of initiating physical aggression toward Peg, although they had responded aggressively when she became aggressive. She also had been destructive of property on several occasions.

Treatment

Peg entered a DBT program, which included individual therapy twice a week and group skills training once a week. Peg's individual and group therapists both participated in a DBT consultation group on a weekly basis, an important part of the DBT model of therapy.

Establishing a strong therapeutic relationship was an early goal of treatment. The nature of this relationship was heavily influenced by the overriding principle of balancing acceptance and change. The therapist provided both a great deal of support and validation and communicated expectations that the client could and must change her behavior. For example, when Peg expressed that she believed she would never be able to stop parasuiciding, her therapist responded both with validation ("of course you feel that way, it makes perfect sense to feel that way.") and with confidence that Peg could meet the challenges of therapy ("I know you can do it; you can get through this.").

Reducing Peg's parasuicidal behavior was the first treatment goal in the individual component of the therapy. Therapy began with the therapist orienting the client to the treatment approach and expectations and a commitment by the client to the goal of eliminating parasuicide. Behavioral analyses revealed that Peg's parasuicides were frequently precipitated by a series of events, which included interpersonal problems, extreme negative affect that Peg was unable to modulate, cognitions that seemed to maintain the negative affect, and reinforcement of parasuicide through reduction of negative affect.

For example, in one instance, Peg had a series of disagreements with her best friend, "Julie," who she often experienced as controlling. Peg made increased efforts to please her friend in order to avoid conflict and possible rejection, all the while resenting things her friend was doing. Eventually Peg "blew up" at Julie, and Julie left in disgust. Peg felt intense feelings of guilt, humiliation, and hopelessness, and had thoughts that she would never be able to repair things with Julie again. She ruminated on all the relationship failures she had experienced in her life, feeling more and more worthless. The various things Peg tried in order to change her affective state were ineffective, and her negative feelings escalated to the point that she felt she "couldn't take it anymore" and then cut herself. After cutting, Peg felt much calmer and more in control. She phoned Julie and made amends with her, promising never to lose her temper again.

This brief description of some of the factors related to Peg's parasuicide suggest areas of potential intervention that were addressed in therapy with Peg. First, addressing interpersonal deficits became an important aspect of therapy, since it was clear that interpersonal difficulties were frequent precipitants of parasuicides. This included skills training, use of role play, and use of the therapeutic relationship as a setting for practicing more adaptive interpersonal behaviors. Second, the behavioral analysis suggested that intense, negative emotions often precipitated Peg's parasuicides; therefore, emotion regulation training was used both in group and individual therapy. In addition, interventions were introduced to help Peg learn to more effectively tolerate negative affect.

A similar approach to that described above was used to develop an understanding of Peg's aggressive behavior toward others and to work toward changing it. Peg made a commitment toward eliminating her aggressive behavior. Several of the factors described above, in particular interpersonal problems, were also important aspects of the chain of events leading up to aggressive behavior. Peg's aggressive behavior almost always occurred in the context of high levels of anger or frustration resulting from interpersonal difficulties. Again, interpersonal skills training were key in helping Peg behave more assertively in her relationships so that she would be less likely to reach the point of "blowing up." Anger management strategies were useful in improving Peg's ability to inhibit her aggressive behavior when she was angry. In addition, the therapist worked to help Peg identify and experience her feelings of anger.

Perhaps most important, the therapist applied a dialectical approach to understanding Peg's aggressive behavior. This involved balancing acceptance of Peg's feelings with a concomitant insistence that Peg change. She validated the feelings and needs underlying

Peg's aggressive behavior, communicating that her fear that Julie would leave her, a desire for a greater sense of "safety" in the relationship, and anger toward Julie made sense. She also maintained a firm stance that Peg needed to change her aggressive behavior.

SUMMARY

This chapter reviewed research evidence addressing the relationship between BPD and presence of a history of parasuicide or aggressive behavior toward others. These data suggest a strong relationship between BPD and parasuicide. They are less clear regarding the relationship between BPD and aggressive behavior toward others. The evidence supporting the notion that people meeting criteria for BPD are likely to have been violent toward property is stronger than that supporting a link between BPD and violence toward other people. None of the available data addresses the issue of whether the aggressive behavior was carried out in self-defense.

This chapter also reviewed Linehan's biosocial theory of borderline personality disorder, and presented an application of the theory to parasuicide and aggressive behavior in BPD individuals. Linehan's model stresses the importance of understanding these behaviors within the context in which they have occurred. Context includes both environmental factors (e.g., life events, interactions with other people) and factors such as the person's affective state and his or her history. All of these variables must be assessed to understand the function of a given instance of the behavior. Common precipitating factors for parasuicide and aggressive behavior toward others, drawn from the clinical experience of the author and the Linehan clinical group, were presented.

Finally, clinical issues around addressing parasuicide and aggressive behavior toward others in BPD patients were discussed from a Dialectical Behavior Therapy perspective. A case example was presented demonstrating the use of the relevant therapeutic approaches and interventions. The importance of thorough assessment was stressed. Interventions need to be tailored to the individual, based on the results of the assessment. For example, if the assessment suggests, on the one hand, that a skills deficit problem is precipitating the behavior, therapy would include skills training. On the other hand, if the assessment suggested that appropriate reinforcement is only available upon occurrence of the parasuicide or aggressive behavior, contingency management would be the intervention of choice.

As is the case with many aspects of BPD, our understanding of the etiology of these behaviors is limited. Empirical evidence is scant. New evidence showing a high prevalence of childhood sexual abuse in the histories of BPD patients may provide a better understanding of the etiology of such extreme behaviors as parasuicide and aggression toward others. However, many victims of childhood sexual abuse do not go on to develop BPD symptoms, so it is clear that other factors are operating. Given the prevalence of BPD in psychiatric populations, and the importance of these particular behaviors, the need for more applied research on how to address these behaviors is great.

REFERENCES

Adler, G., & Buie, D. H. (1979). Aloneness and borderline psychopathology: The possible relevance of child development issues. *International Journal of Psychoanalysis*, *60*, 83–96.

Akhtar, S., Byrne, J., & Doghramji, K. (1986). The demographic profile of borderline personality disorder. *Journal of Clinical Psychiatry*, *47*, 196–198.

American Psychiatric Association (1987). *Diagnostic and statistical manual of mental disorders*, 3rd Edition, Revised. Washington, DC: American Psychiatric Association.

American Psychiatric Association (1993). *DSM-IV draft criteria*. Washington, DC: Author.

Briere, J., & Zaidi, L. Y. (1989). Sexual abuse histories and sequelae in female psychiatric emergency room patients. *American Journal of Psychiatry, 146*, 1602–1606.

Bryer, J. B., Nelson, B. A., Miller, J. B., & Kroll, J. B. (1987). Childhood sexual and physical abuse as factors in adult psychiatric illness. *American Journal of Psychiatry, 144*, 1426–1430.

Clarkin, J., Widiger, T., Frances, A., Hurt, S., & Gilmore, M. (1983). Prototypic typology and the borderline personality disorder. *Journal of Abnormal Psychology, 92*, 263–275.

Cowdry, R. W., & Gardner, D. S. (1988). Pharmacotherapy of borderline personality disorder: Alprazolam, carbamazepine, trifluoperazine and tranylcypromine. *Archives of General Psychiatry, 45*, 111–119.

Deutsch, H. (1942). Some forms of emotional disturbance and their relationship to schizophrenia. *Psychoanalytic Quarterly, 11*, 301– 321.

Federn, P. (1952). *Ego psychology and the psychoses*. New York: Basic Books.

Graff, H., & Mallin, R. (1967). The syndrome of the wrist cutter. *American Journal of Psychiatry, 124*, 74–80.

Grunebaum, H. V., & Klerman, G. L. (1967). Wrist slashing. *American Journal of Psychiatry, 124*, 113–120.

Gunderson, J. G. (1977). Characteristics of borderlines. In P. Hartocollis (Ed.), *Borderline personality disorders* (pp. 173–192). New York: International Universities Press.

Gunderson, J. (1984). *Borderline personality disorder*. Washington, DC: American Psychiatric Press.

Gunderson, J. G., & Kolb, J. E. (1978). Discriminating features of borderline patients. *American Journal of Psychiatry, 135*, 792–796.

Gunderson, J. G., Kolb, J. E., & Austin, V. (1981). The diagnostic interview for borderline patients. *American Journal of Psychiatry, 138*, 896–903.

Herman, J. I. (1986). Histories of violence in an outpatient population. *American Journal of Orthopsychiatry, 36*, 137–141.

Herman, J. L., Perry, J. C., & Van der Kolk, B. A. (1989). Childhood trauma in borderline personality disorder. *American Journal of Psychiatry, 146*, 490–495.

Kernberg, O. (1967). Borderline personality organization. *American Journal of Psychoanalysis, 15*, 641–685.

Knight, R. (1953). Borderline states. *Bulletin of the Menninger Clinic, 17*, 1–12.

Kotila, L., & Lonnquist, J. (1987). Adolescents who make suicide attempts repeatedly. *Acta Psychiatrica Scandinavica, 76*, 386–393.

Kreitman, N. (1977). *Parasuicide*. London: Wiley.

Leone, N. F. (1982). Response of borderline patients to loxapine and chlorpromazine. *Journal of Clinical Psychiatry, 43*, 148–150.

Linehan, M. M. (1987). Dialectical behavior therapy for Borderline personality disorder: Theory and method. *Bulletin of the Menninger Clinic, 53*, 261–276.

Linehan, M. M. (1993). Cognitive-behavioral treatment for Borderline Personality Disorder: The dialectics of effective treatment. New York: Guilford Press.

Linehan, M. M., Armstrong, H. E., Suarez, A., Allmon, D., & Heard, H. L. (1991). Cognitive-behavioral treatment of chronically parasuicidal borderline patients. *Archives of General Psychiatry, 48*(12), 1060–1064.

Linehan, M. M., & Wagner, A. W. (in press). Relationship between childhood sexual abuse and topography of parasuicide among women with borderline personality disorder. *Journal of Personality Disorders*.

Masterson, J. (1976). *Psychotherapy of the borderline adult*. New York: Brunner/Mazel.

Merikangas, K., & Weissman, M. (1986). Epidemiology of DSM-III Axis II personality disorders. In A. Frances & R. Hales (Eds.), *Psychiatry update American Psychiatric Association annual review, vol 5*. (pp. 258–278). Washington, DC: American Psychiatric Press.

Ogata, S. N., Silk, K. R., Goodrich, S., Lohr, N. E., Westin, D., & Hill, E. M. (1990). Childhood sexual and physical abuse in adult patients with borderline personality disorder. *American Journal of Psychiatry, 147*, 1008–1013.

Overall, J. E., & Gorham, D. R. (1962). The Brief Psychiatric Rating Scale. *Psychiatric Reports, 12*, 799–812.

Perry, J. C. (1985). Depression in Borderline personality disorder: Lifetime prevalence at interview and longitudinal course of symptoms. *American Journal of Psychiatry, 142*, 15–21.

Perry, J. C., & Klerman, G. L. (1978). The borderline patient: A comparative analysis of four sets of diagnostic criteria. *Archives of General Psychiatry, 35*, 141–152.

Perry, J. C., & Klerman, G. L. (1980). Clinical features of the borderline personality disorder. *American Journal of Psychiatry, 137*, 165–173.

Plakun, E., Burkhardt, P., & Muller, J. (1985). Fourteen-year follow-up of borderline and schizotypal personality disorders. *Comparative Psychiatry*, *26*, 448–455.

Raczek, S. W., True, P. K., & Friend, R. C. (1990). Suicidal behavior and personality traits. *Journal of Personality Disorders*, *3*, 345–351.

Rinzler, C., & Shapiro, D. (1968). Wrist-cutting and suicide. *Journal of Mount Sinai Hospital, New York*, *25*, 485–488.

Rosenthal, R. J., Rinzler, C., Wallsh, R., & Klausner, E. (1972). Wrist-cutting syndromes: The meaning of a gesture. *American Journal of Psychiatry*, *128*, 47–52.

Serban, G., & Siegel, S. (1984). Response of borderline and schizotypal patients to small doses of thiothixene and haloperidol. *American Journal of Psychiatry*, *141*, 1455–1458.

Sheehy, M., Goldsmith, L., & Charles, E. (1980). A comparative study of borderline patients in a psychiatric outpatient clinic. *American Journal of Psychiatry*, *137*, 1374–1379.

Snyder, S., Pitts, W. M., & Pokorny, A. D. (1986). Selected behavioral features of patients with borderline personality traits. *Suicide and Life-Threatening Behavior*, *16*, 28–39.

Soloff, P. H. (1981). A comparison of borderline with depressed and schizophrenic patients on a new diagnostic interview. *Comparative Psychiatry*, *22*, 291–300.

Soloff, P. H., & Ulrich, M. S. (1981). Diagnostic interview for borderline patients: A replication study. *Archives of General Psychiatry*, *38*, 686–692.

Spitzer, R. L., Endicott, J., & Robins, E. (1975). *Research diagnostic criteria*. New York: Biometrics Research.

Spitzer, R. L., Williams, J. B. W., Gibbon, M., & First, M. B. (1990). Structured clinical interview for DSM-III-R. Washington, DC: American Psychiatric Press.

Stern, A. (1938). Psychoanalytic investigation and therapy in the borderline group of neuroses. *Psychoanalytic Quarterly*, *1*, 467–489.

Stone, M. H. (1980). *The borderline syndrome*. New York: McGraw-Hill.

Stone, M. H. (1989). The course of borderline personality disorder. In A. Tasman, R. E. Hales, & A. J. Frances (Eds.), *Annual review of psychiatry, Vol. 8* (pp. 103–122). Washington, DC: American Psychiatric Press.

Stone, M. H. (1989). *Long-term follow-up of borderline patients: The P.I.-500*. New York: Guilford Press.

Swartz, M., Blazer, D., George, L., & Winfield, I. (1990). Estimating the prevalence of Borderline personality disorder in the community. *Journal of Personality Disorders*, *4*, 257–272.

Walsh, B. W., & Rosen, P. M. (1988). *Self mutilation: Theory, research & treatment*. New York: Guilford Press.

Widiger, T. A., & Frances, A. J. (1989). Epidemiology, diagnosis, and comorbidity of borderline personality disorder. In A. Tasman, R. G. Hales, & A. J. Frances (Eds.), *American Psychiatric Press Review of Psychiatry*. Washington, DC: American Psychiatric Press, Inc.

Zilboorg, G. (1941). Ambulatory schizophrenia. *Psychiatry*, *4*, 149–155.

Zimmerman, M., & Coryell, W. (1989). DSM-III Personality disorder diagnoses in a non-patient sample. *Archives of General Psychiatry*, *46*, 682–689.

PART IV

CHILD AND
ADOLESCENT DISORDERS

CHAPTER 19

Mental Retardation

LORI A. SISSON

DESCRIPTION OF THE DISORDER

Definition of Mental Retardation

A universally accepted definition of mental retardation has been elusive due to the highly relative and culturally determined nature of this disorder (Tyson & Favell, 1988). In 1983, the American Association on Mental Deficiency (AAMD) [now the American Association on Mental Retardation (AAMR)] set forth the most widely endorsed definition currently in use. The standards for diagnosis included (1) an I.Q. score two standard deviations or more below the relevant age and sex mean on a standardized intelligence test, (2) impairments in adaptive behavior, and (3) onset before age 18 (Grossman, 1983). This multidimensional approach to definition is in keeping with other recognized systems, such as the *Diagnostic and Statistical Manual of Mental Disorders* (American Psychiatric Association, 1987, 1993). A number of professional groups, including the American Psychiatric Association, have adopted it.

The intellectual functioning of persons with mental retardation usually is assessed via the Stanford–Binet Intelligence Scale or one of the Wechsler Scales (WPPSI, WISC-R, or WAIS-R). Alternatively, for individuals who function in the severe or profound ranges of mental retardation, tests that measure nonverbal behavior, such as the Peabody Picture Vocabulary Test-Revised, the Slosson Intelligence Test, the Leiter International Performance Scale, or the Bayley Scales of Infant Development, are used (see Anastasi, 1976). Adaptive skill levels typically are derived from the AAMD Adaptive Behavior Scales, although the Vineland Adaptive Behavior Scale, among other measures, may be employed (Meyers, Nihira, & Zetlin, 1979). It is this latter component of the definition of mental retardation that is most attacked by critics who contend that the notion of adaptive behavior is vaguely defined and not reliably measured. Zigler, Balla, and Hodapp (1984), for example, advocate the sole use of an I.Q. of at least two standard deviations below the

LORI A. SISSON • Western Pennsylvania School for Blind Children, Pittsburgh, Pennsylvania 15213.

Handbook of Aggressive and Destructive Behavior in Psychiatric Patients, edited by Michel Hersen, Robert T. Ammerman, and Lori A. Sisson. Plenum Press, New York, 1994.

mean, along with considerations of etiology. However, adaptive behavior measurement has served to cross-validate the findings of intellectual measures and has improved the foundation for initial treatment prescription by clarifying relative strengths and weaknesses in both basic and more elaborate skills (Matson, 1988).

The population of individuals who are mentally retarded often is further classified into four levels of functioning, based on I.Q. score: (1) mild mental retardation, 50–70; (2) moderate mental retardation, 35–49; (3) severe mental retardation, 20–34; and (4) profound mental retardation, below 20 (Grossman, 1983). An alternate classification system has been used by special educators who refer to students with mild mental retardation as educable mentally retarded, those with moderate mental retardation as trainable mentally retarded, and persons with severe and profound mental retardation as severely handicapped (MacMillan, 1982). It is widely recognized that many children and adults with mental retardation have at least one other disability in addition to a primary diagnosis of mental retardation. These may include sensory impairments, physical disabilities, neurological problems, or psychiatric disorders (Tyson & Favell, 1988).

The AAMR recently developed a new terminology and classification manual (American Association on Mental Retardation, 1992). This new manual redefines mental retardation in the context of a political climate that is critical of traditional assessment practices and that focuses on educational programming and social supports as limiting (or enhancing) factors in overall functioning level. In brief, the new definition of mental retardation is applied in a three-step process. First, the practitioner determines that the person's intellectual functioning level is below I.Q. 70–75, that there are significant deficits in at least two of ten adaptive skill areas, and that the age of onset is 18 years or below. The subcategories of mental retardation, listed above, are eliminated. Step two consists of describing the individual's (1) strengths and weaknesses in reference to psychological/emotional considerations; (2) overall physical health, indicating the condition's etiology; and (3) current environment as well as the optimal environment that would facilitate growth and development. Third, the pattern and intensity of supports that the person needs in adaptive, emotional, health, and environmental areas are identified. Although much effort has been put forth in developing and refining the new classification system, the literature already documents that there is professional disagreement with regard to both its philosophical/theoretical basis and its practical applications (e.g., Jacobson & Mulick, 1992). Clearly, the definition is too new to know its usefulness in terms of diagnosis, prevention, or treatment.

Epidemiology and Etiology of Mental Retardation

The rate of mental retardation, as reflected in incidence and prevalence figures, varies across cultures and times. This variation occurs because the instruments used to measure the condition, as well as the professional communities' conceptualization of the problem, fluctuate considerably. The earliest estimates place the prevalence rate at approximately 3% of the total population (see Matson, 1988). However, these figures were based on I.Q. alone. With the inclusion of adaptive behavior deficits in the diagnosis, recognition that most cases are undetected until well into the school years (when academic failure is noted), the fact that many persons are no longer considered to be mentally retarded upon leaving school, and the finding that persons functioning at the lowest levels tend to have a relatively high mortality rate, it appears that the 3% figure may be too high. Indeed, more recent research has supported a prevalence rate of closer to 1% (Grossman, 1983; Tarjan,

Wright, Eyman, & Keeran, 1973). Interestingly, individuals who are of school age, male, rural residents, in the lower socioeconomic groups, and members of minority groups are more frequently found to be mentally retarded (MacMillan, 1982).

With regard to etiological considerations, persons with mental retardation often are assigned to one of two basic categories: (1) cultural-familial, in which the condition has no clear organic cause, and (2) organic, in which a known organic cause can be identified (Zigler, 1967). Although exact prevalence estimates are difficult to obtain, it appears that from 50% to 75% of all persons with mental retardation are of the cultural-familial type, whereas the remaining 25% to 50% suffer from organic mental retardation (Zigler & Hodapp, 1986). At present, the cause of mental retardation in the first group remains unclear. Zigler and Hodapp (1991) have summarized several hypotheses: (1) persons with this condition receive fewer genes for high intelligence from their parents (polygenic factors); (2) these individuals grow up in unstimulating environments (environment factors); and (3) some combination of polygenic and environmental factors account for the mental retardation. Individuals in the culture-familial group generally have I.Q.s in the 50–70 range and exhibit few biological or behavioral characteristics that distinguish them from nonretarded individuals (Matson, 1988; Zigler & Hodapp, 1991). The second group is comprised of persons whose condition has a clear organic cause, whether of prenatal, perinatal, or postnatal origin. Prenatal factors include all of the genetic syndromes (e.g., Down's syndrome, fragile-X syndrome), rubella, thalidomide, and other conditions causing damage to the developing fetus. Perinatal factors include anoxia, prematurity, and other birth-related events. Meningitis, head trauma, or other insults in the childhood years constitute the postnatal causes of organic mental retardation. Grossman (1983) estimated that there are over 200 types of organic mental retardation. A general consensus exists that organic causes for mental retardation are most likely to be found for persons functioning in the severe or profound ranges (Matson, 1988). Recent research has documented not only that there are learning and behavioral characteristics that distinguish this group from the nonretarded population, but also that individuals with organic mental retardation demonstrate etiology-specific behavioral profiles (Zigler & Hodapp, 1991).

Behavioral Functioning

Mental retardation is most frequently conceptualized and described in terms of a limited repertoire of functional responses, or deficits in adaptive skills. The new AAMR definition (American Association on Mental Retardation, 1992) specifically lists 10 adaptive skill areas considered to be important to independent functioning: communication, self-care, home living, social skills, community use, self-direction, health and safety, functional academics, leisure, and work. Accordingly, considerable research and clinical practice has been devoted to developing procedures to increase both the variety and complexity of the behavior of individuals with mental retardation (e.g., Reid, Wilson, & Faw, 1983; Sisson & Van Hasselt, 1989). Yet there is another facet that often characterizes persons with mental retardation. That is, they frequently demonstrate behavioral excesses, such as disruption, stereotyped movements, self-injury, and aggression, that can be severely debilitating in a functional sense (Rojahn & Sisson, 1990; Schroeder, Mulick, & Schroeder, 1979; Van Hasselt, Ammerman, & Sisson, 1990). Consequently, reduction of these behaviors becomes a significant aspect of most prescriptive treatment programs. With this brief background on mental retardation, the focus is shifted to a more detailed discussion of self-injury and aggression, which are the topics of this volume.

EPIDEMIOLOGY OF SELF-INJURY
AND AGGRESSION IN MENTAL RETARDATION

As noted above, it has been widely recognized that a significantly higher rate of problem behavior occurs among persons with mental retardation than among comparably aged nonretarded peers. However, estimated prevalence rates vary from study to study, due not only to wide disparity in definitions and inclusiveness of target behavior(s), but also to discrepancies in the populations and settings investigated (Schroeder et al., 1979). One of the most frequently cited epidemiological studies is that of Rutter, Tizard, and Whitmore (1970), which was conducted in 1964–1965 on the entire population of 9- to 11-year-old children on the Isle of Wight just off the southern coast of England. Rutter et al. found that nearly 3% of the children sampled were mentally retarded, and that 20% of these had a "psychiatric disability." More recently, Jacobson (1982) reported data on a large number of individuals with mental retardation residing in the state of New York. Approximately 14% of children and 17% of adults were diagnosed with a concomitant psychiatric impairment. Nearly 48% of the total sample were estimated to display 1 of 29 problem behaviors, including assault upon others, property destruction, self-injury, hyperactivity, stereotypical movements, and temper tantrums. The results of a national interview study of residents with mental retardation across the United States (Hill & Bruininks, 1984) established that 36% of individuals in public residential facilities and 19% of residents in community settings exhibited at least one of four categories of maladaptive behavior (self-injury, aggression, property destruction, disruptive responding) to a degree considered to require some type of intense or systematic intervention. This prevalence rate for persons with mental retardation living in institutions was corroborated in a study of maladaptive responses of residents of a large hospital in England (Tutton, Wynne-Willson, & Piachaud, 1990). These authors documented that approximately 30% had at least one problematic behavior.

A few epidemiological investigations have focused on prevalence rates for specific behaviors, including self-injury and aggression. With regard to self-injury, prevalence rates from about 2% (among noninstitutionalized persons with mental retardation living in West Germany) (Rojahn, 1986) to about 66% (among individuals with severe or profound mental retardation residing in a large institution in that same country) (Rojahn, 1984) have been reported. However, a majority of recent, large-scale studies have found more modest numbers, such as those reported by Hill and Bruininks (1984): 11% of community residents versus 22% of facility residents exhibited self-injurious behavior. The numbers documented for aggression are similarly disparate. Ross (1972) found that "antisocial acts" occurred on a daily, weekly, or monthly basis among 27% of persons with mental retardation institutionalized in California. Griffin, Williams, Stark, Altmeyer, and Mason (1986) reported that aggression was a problem for 55% of a similar sample in Texas. Finally, Hill and Bruininks (1984) noted that 16% of their national sample of community residents with mental retardation injured others, while 30% of public facility residents engaged in the same type of behavior.

The data summarized above suggest that both self-injury and aggression are more likely to be displayed by persons with mental retardation living in institutional settings rather than in community residences. Other data show that high ratings on measures of maladaptive behavior are associated with low I.Q. and social age scores, inability to ambulate, infrequent opportunities for functional activities, and being male (Duker, van Druenen, Jol, & Oud, 1986; Maisto, Baumeister, & Maisto, 1978; Ross, 1972; Schroeder, Schroeder, Smith, & Dalldorf, 1978). The relationship between maladaptive behavior and chronological age is rather unclear. For self-injury, high rates of the target behavior have been found in younger versus older samples (Maisto et al., 1978), in older versus younger groups (Eyman & Call, 1977), and in individuals about 15 years old versus those younger or older (Berkson, McQuiston, Jacobson, Eyman, & Borthwick, 1985). It appears that persons with mental retardation who exhibit the most problematic aggressive responding often are males in the adolescent and young adult age ranges, perhaps because of their size and physical strength (Duker et al., 1986).

ETIOLOGY OF SELF-INJURY AND AGGRESSION IN MENTAL RETARDATION

A number of clinicians and researchers have speculated about the etiology of self-injurious and aggressive behaviors in mental retardation; however, in reality, very little is known about the causes of these responses. Some cases of self-injury and aggression are closely associated with medical conditions, most notably the Lesch-Nyhan and Cornelia de Lange syndromes. Study of these syndromes suggests that maladaptive responding may result from decreases in certain neurotransmitters, specifically serotonin and dopamine, necessary for basic brain functioning (Cataldo & Harris, 1982). Other brain chemicals, particularly the endorphins, also have been implicated in the origin and maintenance of self-injury. Physical stress, including intense stereotypy or self-injurious responding, has been related to endorphin release. Endorphin release, in turn, results in euphoric sensations, much like those produced by morphine and heroin, and can potentially act as an internal reinforcer (Lewis & Baumeister, 1982). Further, it appears to be feasible that early endorphin release, with its associated opiate receptor activity, can result in permanent changes in sensitivity to pain, which may further promote occurrence of severe self-injury by removing pain as a deterrent (Cataldo & Harris, 1982). Interestingly, DeLissovoy (1963) linked early bouts of otitis media to both head banging in infancy and self-injurious responding later in life, leading recent writers to speculate on the relationship between self-injury during critical periods of brain development and alteration of pain thresholds (Cataldo & Harris, 1982). Finally, other brain dysfunction, manifested in seizure disorders, has been implicated in both severe self-injury (Gedye, 1989) and aggression (Eyman, Moore, & Capes, 1970; Rodin, 1973; Williamson, Spencer, Spencer, Novelly, & Mattson, 1985). Although each of these organic theories is plausible, a paucity of systematic, empirical investigations of the mechanisms or processes responsible for destructive behavior, conflicting and nonconclusive results, and apparent applicability to only a small percentage of the population of mentally retarded persons who display self-injury or aggression, preclude their widespread acceptance.

Another possible explanation for self-injurious behavior, especially that which is rhythmic, has been advanced. The underlying assumption of this theory is that organisms naturally strive for the maintenance of a balanced level of central nervous system activation. According to the theory of homeostatic balance, the low levels of stimulation experienced by many persons with mental retardation, due perhaps to long periods of institutionalization or to sensory, physical, and/or cognitive impairments, are thought to trigger stereotypy and/or self-injury as compensatory mechanisms (Berkson & Davenport, 1962; Guess, 1966). Alternatively, rhythmic activity might reduce high levels of arousal associated with frustration, stress, or anxiety (Hutt & Hutt, 1970; Zentall & Zentall, 1983). Although satisfying in their parsimony, the evidence for arousal-increasing and arousal-decreasing hypotheses in human beings is limited to a few accounts (see Baumeister & Forehand, 1973; Guess & Carr, 1991). Further, these explanations may apply more to stereotypical behavior in general than to self-injury in particular (Carr, 1977).

A third major approach to the understanding of self-injurious and aggressive responding derives from the experimental analysis of behavior. Within this framework, destructive behavior is viewed as an operant response, affected by its consequences and controlled by antecedent stimuli that signal differential consequences. Specifically, four conditions have been discussed with regard to the origin and maintenance of self-injury, and three of these appear to apply also to aggression. One behavioral explanation states that self-injury and aggression are shaped and maintained by social attention as a consequence. This attention may be in the form of empathetic statements (Lovaas, Freitag, Gold, & Kassorla, 1965), physical restraint (Favell, McGimsey, Jones, & Cannon, 1981), vigorous scolding (Taylor et al., 1993), or any other social interaction (Favell, Azrin, et al., 1982). Less well documented is the role that tangibles (e.g., toys, food, activities) can play in the display of destructive responding by individuals with mental retardation. Lovaas and Simmons (1969) found that providing their subject with access to preferred play activities contingent on self-injurious behavior resulted in increased frequencies of the behavior, and more recent evidence has documented that self-injury and aggression may be evoked when preferred foods or activities are denied—a response pattern resembling an "extinction burst" (Durand & Crimmins, 1988; Edelson, Taubman, & Lovaas, 1983). Together, these observations suggest that, for some individuals, severe problem behavior may serve to gain access to tangible rewards.

While social attention and tangibles may serve to positively reinforce self-injury and aggression, escape from aversive situations may be involved in the negative reinforcement of these behaviors. In other words, individuals may engage in self-injurious or aggressive responses in order to remove themselves from unpleasant situations (e.g., academic tasks). Evidence for the escape hypothesis has come primarily from investigations of the effect of task demands on destructive behavior. Carr, Newsom, and Binkoff (1976) and Weeks and Gaylord-Ross (1981), for example, studied self-injurious behavior in the presence of easy versus difficult task demands. They found that destructive responding by their subjects was more frequent with difficult task demands. Finally, a fourth motivating condition for self-injury concerns the sensory feedback provided by the behavior. It has been suggested that this sensory feedback (involving auditory, visual, or tactile modalities) may be reinforcing, and therefore self-injury in some individuals may be maintained by sensory rather than (or in addition to) social, tangible, or escape consequences (Durand, 1988; Favell, McGimsey, & Schell, 1982; Rincover & Devany, 1982). Research has shown that particular topographies of self-injurious behavior (e.g., eye gouging) may provide a specific type of sensory feedback (e.g., visual). Removing this feedback (Rincover & Devany, 1982) or providing alternative ways of obtaining it (Favell, McGimsey, & Schell, 1982) may result in reductions in targeted maladaptive responding. Although causal relationships between environmental stimuli and self-injurious or aggressive behaviors are not well established, the evidence is accumulating for such factors in the maintenance of disruptive responses.

AGGRESSION TOWARD SELF

Self-injurious behavior is a term referring to a broad array of responses that result in physical damage to the individual displaying the behavior. In addition, in mental retardation research and clinical practice, self-injurious behavior tends to be characterized as repetitive and chronic, that is, occurring at frequencies ranging from hundreds of times an hour to several times a month over a sustained period (Favell, Azrin et al., 1982). In an extensive review of the literature, an Association for Advancement of Behavior Therapy (AABT) Task Force (Favell, Azrin, et al., 1982) identified several generic forms of self-injury, including self-striking (e.g., face slapping, head banging); biting; pinching, scratching, poking, or pulling various body parts (e.g., eye poking, hair pulling); repeated vomiting or vomiting and reingesting food (i.e., rumination); and consuming nonedible substances (e.g., pica, or eating objects; coprophagia, or eating feces). The physical damage sustained by such behavior varies. Some individuals produce only minor lesions with few permanent conse-quences. Others, however, exhibit behaviors that result in serious, permanent damage to themselves, such as blindness, loss of limb, severe bleeding, or concussion. The latter group of individuals often are chemically or physically restrained (e.g., given tranquilizing medications, placed in arm splits or helmets, tied down to their beds or chairs), to avoid further injury or even death. Interestingly, it has been observed that persons with mental retardation who exhibit self-injury often display other, perhaps related behaviors, such as stereotyped self-stimulation (repetitive, chronic behaviors that do not produce bodily harm) (Barron & Sandman, 1984; Schroeder et al., 1978) and outward-directed aggression including verbal and physical abuse of nearby people (Dizmang & Cheatham, 1970).

Self-injurious behavior has commanded a great deal of attention from clinicians and researchers primarily because it carries the risk of serious bodily injury (Carr, 1977; Durand & Carr, 1985). As suggested above, the wide range of self-injurious actions can result in pain, tissue and organ damage, infections, body disfigurement, and poisoning due to ingestion of toxic substances. Further, the chemical or physical restraints that are used for protection may themselves result in physical damage, as in tendon shortening caused by prolonged immobility (Favell, Azrin, et al., 1982). However, there are several other reasons that professionals may feel an urgency to address self-injurious behavior. Because of the sometimes all-consuming nature of self-injury, the restrictiveness of many preventative measures, and the negative effects this behavior has on others, individuals may be unable to benefit from habilitative or humanizing activities, which have become mandates for appropriate treatment and care. Also, the referral for special services or institutionaliza-tion is caused more by the occurrence of destructive behavior among persons with mental retardation than by level of impairment. The additional staff and programming efforts required to work effectively with such individuals may result in costs of $100,000 or more per year. In addition, there are a number of indirect costs associated with self-injury, such as the costs of not being able to participate in supported or competitive employment (which results in the need for income maintenance or other subsidies), and the costs to families trying to maintain a family member at home (which results in lost economic opportunities by precluding the employment of family members who must stay at home to care for their relative with self-injurious behavior) (U.S. Department of Health and Human Services, 1989).

AGGRESSION TOWARD OTHERS

As used here, the term aggression refers to those acts that are explicitly disruptive, harmful to others, or otherwise have an adverse effect upon the environment (Forehand & Baumeister, 1976). Fighting, property damage, physical and verbal assault, stealing, excessive screaming, crying, and tantrum behavior are included in this category. Clearly, the range of effects upon others or the environment varies considerably. For example, in many instances, aggressive behavior results in little more than annoying others and requires only the interruption of the act and redirection to a more appropriate response. However, more severe aggressive behavior, such as physical assault, can cause pain as well as physical and emotional injury to the receiver of the attack, and necessitates a more programmatic approach to its elimination.

In contrast to self-injury, which has been a topic of many scholarly articles and research investigations, dangerous destructive behavior toward others has remained under-researched and undertreated (Foxx, Zukothyski, & Williams, in press). Foxx (1992) has suggested that this is because of the fact that the only danger that self-injury poses is to the self-injurer, while therapists and interventionists become potential victims when individuals are aggressive toward others. Thus, although the clinical, political, philosophi-cal, legal, and ethical issues surrounding aggressive behavior are perhaps more straightfor-ward given that the major concern is the rights of others to be protected from danger, the chosen course of action is more likely to be a restrictive environment and/or a pharmaco-logical intervention (designed mainly to contain the individual) rather than a behavioral treatment (designed to reduce the target behavior and provide adaptive alternatives). Nonetheless, aggressive responding demands consideration by professionals within the field of mental retardation for a number of the same reasons that self-injury does. Negative behaviors, including biting, hitting, screaming, whining, and crying, on the part of persons with mental retardation have been shown to result in reduced social and instructional interactions with teachers as well as a restricted range of functional activities and learning opportunities (Carr, Taylor, & Robinson, 1991). Many clinical researchers have viewed the elimination of aggressive behaviors as a prerequisite, or at least an essential, component of programs that are designed to generate more socially adaptive behaviors (Foxx, McMorrow, Bittle, & Bechtel, 1986; Taylor, Sisson, McKelvey, & Trefelner, 1993). Restrictive "treat-ments" may preclude community-based educational and habilitative efforts (U.S. Depart-ment of Health and Human Services, 1989). And, attempts to place individuals with severe destructive behavior in community residential and work settings often are problematic (Eyman & Borthwick, 1980), with resulting increased costs for specialized services and care (U.S. Department of Health and Human Services, 1989).

CLINICAL MANAGEMENT

It is apparent from a previous section that there are a number of theories regarding the etiology of self-injury, and, albeit to a lesser extent, aggression. In contrast, treatments for severe disruptive behavior can generally be grouped into only two categories: medical approaches and behavioral approaches (U.S. Department of Health and Human Services, 1989). Further, the vast majority of scientific research points to the efficacy of behavioral over all other types of interventions in treating self-injury and aggression, at least over the short term, regardless of the hypothesized etiology of the problem behavior (Favell, Azrin, et al., 1982; Repp & Singh, 1990; Singh & Millichamp, 1985). It has been suggested that this is because the factors that are responsible for the onset of disruptive behavior (whether medical, homeostatic, or behavioral) may be quite different from those that subsequently maintain the behavior (Favell, McGinsey, et al., 1982; Matson & Gardner, 1991), with the implication that maintaining factors usually are environmental. Certainly, any therapeutic intervention should explicitly include an attempt to analyze the biological and environmental factors that caused, *as well as those that now maintain*, the problem behavior, and arrange for the elimination or alteration of those conditions.

Medical Approaches

As already noted, a variety of medical disorders are associated with self-injurious behavior in mental retardation, for example, the Lesch-Nyhan syndrome (Nyhan, 1976), Cornelia de Lange syndrome (Bryson, Sakati, Nyhan, & Fish, 1971), and otitis media (DeLissovoy, 1963). Similarly, evidence suggests that seizure disorders may be causal in some instances of aggressive responding (Eyman, Moore, & Capes, 1970; Martin & Agran, 1985). Investigation related to these and other medical conditions not only holds promise in possible prevention and treatment of the severe disruptive behavior correlated with these syndromes, but also in uncovering biological mechanisms that may underlie other instances of such responding (Cataldo & Harris, 1982). Yet, while thorough medical examination is recommended to identify, and if possible, to control biological factors associated with problem behavior, currently we are not able to remediate many of these conditions in an attempt to eliminate self-injurious or aggressive responding. Further, even when a cure is available, such as with otitis media, self-injury or aggression often continues, requiring additional treatment (Carr & McDowell, 1980).

Psychopharmacological agents frequently are used to reduce destructive behavior in persons with mental retardation (Singh, Guernsey, & Ellis, 1992). This is in contrast to the typical use of drug treatment in individuals without mental retardation, where medications are prescribed with the specific therapeutic intent of ameliorating a psychiatric condition. For about 30–50% of persons with mental retardation residing in institutions and about 2–7% of children and 14–36% of adults with mental retardation living in the community, chemical intervention is the major treatment for behavior disorders, including aggression, hyperactivity, self-injury, excitability, and screaming (Aman & Singh, 1988). The drugs used to reduce these types of responding, directly or indirectly, include neuroleptics (e.g., chlorpromazine, thioridazine, haloperidol), sedative-hypnotics (barbiturates), stimulants (d-amphetamine, methylphenidate), antianxiety drugs (benzodiazepines), antidepressants and mood stabilizers (imipramine, lithium), anticonvulsants (carbamazepine, phenytoin, phenobarbital), antihypertensives (beta-adrenergic blocking agents such as propranolol and pindolol), and opiate antagonists (naloxone, naltrexone). The psychopharmacological agents most frequently prescribed for destructive behavior are the neuroleptics, with thioridazine being the most widely used (Aman & Singh, 1983; Farber, 1987; Rivinus, Grofer, Feinstein, & Barrett, 1989; U.S. Department of Health and Human Services, 1989).

It is remarkable that pharmacological approaches to managing severely destructive behavior continue to be so prevalent given that numerous reviews of the literature describe not only a paucity of investigations of drug effects for persons with mental retardation but also inadequate research methodology in studies evaluating the effectiveness of medications (Aman & Singh, 1983; Farber, 1987; Rivinus et al., 1989; Singh & Millichamp, 1985). Further, equivocal results in terms of suppression of specific symptoms, such as self-injury and aggression (Lennox, Miltenberger, Spengler, & Erfanian, 1988); conflicting findings both within and across reports (Ruedrich, Grush, & Wilson, 1990); undesirable short- and long-term side effects, including (but not limited to) increased maladaptive responding, decreased cognitive and adaptive functioning, and movement disorders (Aman, 1984; Handen, Feldman, Gosling, Breaux, & McAuliffe, 1991); and limited data as to the efficacy of medication over months or years (U.S. Department of Health and Human Services, 1989), should deter the widespread use of chemical interventions. Unfortunately, it seems that pharmacological agents may often be prescribed simply because they can suppress motor activity, which, in turn, will incidentally diminish self-injurious and aggressive behavior (Aman, 1987; U.S. Department of Health and Human Services, 1989). Given these observations, an in-depth review of the literature addressing drug effects in mental retardation is unwarranted for the purposes of the present chapter, and the interested reader is referred instead to several recent publications (Aman & Singh, 1982; Barrett, Payton, & Burkhart, 1988; Ruedrich et al., 1990; Singh & Winton, 1984; Zingarelli, Ellman, Hom, Wymore, Heldorn & Chicz-DeMet, 1992) and the review articles cited above.

It should be mentioned that the research to date implies that the promise of psychotropic medications in controlling maladaptive responding may lie in their use for identified cases of mental disorder, rather than for behavior modification per se (Singh, Guernsey, & Ellis, 1992). Indeed, persons with mental retardation experience the full range of medical and psychiatric disorders evident in the general population. Further, the medications indicated and prescribed for these conditions are the same as those for persons who are not mentally retarded. However, Bates, Smeltzer, and Arnoczky (1986) found that while specific psychiatric diagnoses were assigned unanimously by multidisciplinary teams in 242 cases of institutionalized persons receiving psychotropic medication, only 45% of the diagnosis–medication combinations were considered to be appropriate. This suggests that, for a significant proportion of individuals with mental retardation receiving chemical intervention, their medications may be inappropriate for their diagnosis.

A new and potentially fruitful approach to pharmacological treatment is represented by the use of specific agents to address suspected underlying neurobiological disorders that result in severe problem behaviors, including self-injury and aggression. For example, administration of narcotic antagonists, such as naloxone and the longer-acting naltrexone, has been based on the premise that for some individuals self-injury has been shown to raise the level of endogenous beta-endorphin, a naturally occurring narcotic and, therefore, a potent reinforcer. By blocking the reinforcing effect of this internal opiate, the narcotic antagonists hypothetically produce an extinction phenomenon, thus leading to a reduction of the target maladaptive behavior (Singh, Singh, & Ellis, 1992). Although initial reports are conflicting (Zingarelli et al., 1992), the approach to understanding and ameliorating self-injury and aggression that has been adopted by researchers in this area should serve as an example for future endeavors.

Behavioral Approaches

The efficacy of behavioral interventions for reducing or eliminating, at least temporarily, problem behavior displayed by individuals with mental retardation has been documented repeatedly over a number of years (Favell, Azrin, et al., 1982; Forehand & Baumeister, 1976; Repp & Brulle, 1981; Van Hasselt, et al., 1990). Until recently, most approaches to the reduction of such responding were characterized by the identification of a single target behavior and the manipulation of the consequences of that behavior (i.e., reinforcers and punishers). In addition, some professionals have argued that there was an overreliance on behavior change techniques that involve pain or the potential for social humiliation (Durand, 1988). Perhaps because of the questionable long-term efficacy of conventional approaches to behavior management (Donnellan, LaVigna, Negri-Schoultz,

& Fassbender, 1988), the need to develop procedures that can be used in community settings increasingly frequented by persons with mental retardation (Dunlap, 1990), and enhanced sensitivity to the rights and feelings of individuals with disabilities (Horner et al., 1990), new procedures for dealing with challenging behaviors are emerging. The most important and exiting elements of this new approach to behavior management are its emphasis on multicomponent interventions that affect broad behavioral patterns (Dunlap, 1990), consideration of an expanded range of variables when designing treatments (Donnellan et al., 1988; Favell, Azrin et al., 1982), and the precise implementation of positive intervention strategies (Horner et al., 1990). In the interest of reviewing a vast literature in only a few pages, promising new strategies for the treatment of self-injury and aggression are highlighted in this section, while the use of more intrusive, yet commonly used interventions (such as time-out, physical restraint, and overcorrection) will be given only brief consideration.

Functional Assessment

One of the first steps in behaviorally oriented treatment for severe disruptive behavior is the identification of antecedent and consequent events that are temporally contiguous to the target response and that occasion and maintain it (Axelrod, 1987; Durand, 1987). Presumably, an understanding of the controlling variables, achieved through a functional assessment of the aberrant response, will lead to the selection of more effective treatments (Parrish, Iwata, Dorsey, Bunck, & Slifer, 1985; Slifer, Ivancic, Parrish, Page, & Burgio, 1986). For example, a functional assessment may pinpoint antecedent conditions that evoke the self-injurious or aggressive behavior. By either removing these conditions or altering their characteristics, the practitioner can prevent the response (Touchette, MacDonald, & Langner, 1985). Alternatively, a functional assessment may identify the reinforcing consequences of self-injury or aggression, which can then lead the clinician to eliminate their occurrence following the behavior (Rincover & Devany, 1982; Taylor et al., 1993). Furthermore, information obtained from a functional assessment may aid in the identification of a more appropriate but functionally equivalent (resulting in the same reinforcing consequences) alternative to the target behavior (Bird, Dores, Moniz, & Robinson, 1989; Durand & Carr, 1991).

There are three methods of conducting a functional assessment of self-injury or aggression in applied settings (Lennox & Miltenberger, 1989). The *behavioral interview* is designed to obtain an informant's (teacher, staff member, or parent) report of the topography of the problem behavior, its antecedent and consequent events, and other information necessary to isolate maintaining variables and to select appropriate interventions. Behavior rating scales, checklists, and questionnaires can help structure the process of obtaining information by focusing attention on relevant variables. For example, Durand and Crimmins (1988) have developed the Motivation Assessment Scale, which consists of 16 questions designed to determine whether a target response is reinforced by attention, tangibles, escape-avoidance, or sensory stimulation. While in some cases, the behavioral interview may be the main source of information, it is more likely to be part of a more thorough assessment that includes direct observation, or even experimental analysis (Taylor et al., 1993). In *direct observation*, an observer (teacher, staff member, parent, or independent party) records descriptive accounts of both the target behavior and temporally related environmental events. This narrative is then analyzed to ascertain antecedent–behavior–consequence (A-B-C) sequences. Over time, such data may reflect a correlational relationship that leads to hypotheses about potentially important events (Cooper, Heron, & Heward, 1987). The third method of functional assessment involves the *experimental manipulation* of controlling variables (Axelrod, 1987). By recording behavioral changes associated with the systematic introduction and withdrawal of various antecedent and consequent events, the variables that are functionally related to the target behavior can be determined. While gaining control of potential variables often is difficult and time consuming, at least one group of clinical researchers is working on strategies to make experimental analysis manageable in applied settings (Derby, Wacker, Sasso, Steege, Northup, Cigrand, & Asmus, 1992). Indeed, the cost effectiveness of a well-designed functional assessment has been demonstrated in a number of recent reports that have evaluated treatments for self-injurious behavior and/or aggression displayed by children and adults with mental retardation (Durand & Carr, 1992; Iwata, Dorsey, Slifer, Bauman, & Richman, 1982; Taylor et al., 1993).

Teaching Adaptive Behavior

Perhaps the one new behavior management approach to spark the most interest among clinicians and researchers is teaching individuals with mental retardation more effective and socially acceptable ways of getting their needs met and of coping with unpleasant situations. This focus is based on the premise that persons with mental retardation often use maladaptive responding, including self-injury and aggression, to communicate desires ("I want help," "I need a break") and to express unpleasant feelings (boredom, frustration, anger). At least two variations on this general theme have been elaborated. The first involves instruction in a specific skill that serves the same function as the problem behavior. A major example involves identifying the communicative function of the challenging response and then building communication skills that will achieve the same end in a more acceptable manner. In several clinical and research demonstrations, enhanced communication abilities have been associated with the reduction in levels of self-injury or aggression exhibited by persons with mental retardation (Bird et al., 1989; Durand & Carr, 1992; Durand & Kishi, 1987).

Teaching adaptive behavior also has been used to reduce self-injurious and aggressive responding by developing alternative, functionally related (although not directly equivalent) skills. One rapidly growing research emphasis in this area is teaching choice-making behavior. Most people with mental retardation have little control over their lifestyles or daily activities. Their choices tend to be limited, even with regard to small matters, such as the sequence of morning routines, what to eat for dinner, or what activity to engage in during "free" time. Research has shown that even individuals who have profound disabilities and severely restricted communication can be taught to make choices (Green, Reid, Canipe, & Gardner, 1991; Wacker, Berg, Wiggins, Muldoon, & Cavanaugh, 1985). These persons may show their preferences for available options by pointing, using gestures, altering their facial expressions, or even pressing microswitches. Early work on choice making has demonstrated that opportunities to select activities can help reduce the serious problem behavior of individuals with mental retardation (Dyer, Dunlap, & Winterling, 1990).

Manipulating Antecedent Events and Contextual Factors

Increasingly, interventions for self-injury and aggression reflect attention to a broad array of antecedent and contextual events. These factors range from environmental conditions (such as room temperature, noise level, social density, and the predictability of daily activities) to instructional methods (including the type of requests, tasks, and materials used) to a person's physiological status (e.g., the amount of sleep, exercise, hunger, or anxiety) (LaVigna et al., 1989). When such stimuli are identified, behavioral improvements can be attained by removing or ameliorating the events that produce undesirable responses or by presenting stimuli that are associated with acceptable behavior. There is some preliminary evidence that this approach can result in immediate and durable treatment effects for persons with mental retardation (Dunlap, Kern-Dunlap, Clarke, & Robbins, 1991; Horner, Day, Sprague, O'Brien, & Heathfield, 1991). For example, one positive strategy that has been used in the treatment of aggressive responding related to demand situations is to introduce requests that have a high probability of receiving an appropriate response. Such requests may include "Give me five," "Shake hands," and "Say your name." When persons comply with these commands, they are then more likely to respond appropriately to subsequent statements like "Make your bed," and aberrant behavior is reduced (Horner et al., 1991). Lately, creative scheduling of functional activities also has received much attention as a behavior-change strategy (Brown, 1991; Durand & Kishi, 1987). In this approach, the typical activities of persons with mental retardation (which may include repetitious sorting, assembling, and packaging tasks) are hypothesized to be so removed from the interests, needs, and potential of these individuals that they result in problem behavior. In contrast, a schedule of activities that are important to everyday functioning, that provide some payoff for the person, and that increase access to a wide variety of relevant and interesting situations may remove the conditions that are discriminative for aberrant responses.

Differential Reinforcement

Several techniques employed in the treatment of self-injury and aggression rest on the principle of differential reinforcement. Differential reinforcement means that relatively more reinforcement is provided for positive behaviors and less, or no, reinforcement is accrued following the occurrence of destructive responding. The result is an increase in more appropriate alternative behaviors and a decrease in the undesired ones. Differential reinforcement is programmed in two major ways. In differential reinforcement of other behavior (DRO), preferred stimuli are delivered at the end of a period during which no instances of the aberrant behavior are displayed (Luiselli, Myles, Evans, & Boyce, 1985). Thus, the individual receives reinforcement for refraining from self-injury or aggression. In a second procedure, called differential reinforcement of incompatible behavior (DRI), reinforcement is delivered for a specific behavior (such as manipulating toys) that is impossible for the individual to perform at the same time as the response targeted for reduction (such as hand biting) (McClure, Moss, McPeters, & Kirkpatrick, 1986). With both DRO and DRI procedures, occurrences of self-injury or aggression typically delay reinforcement. Further, as the target response decreases, the time between reinforcements is extended gradually until the individual's behavior and rate of reinforcement approximates that of his or her peers. Generally, differential reinforcement is not used alone, but is carried out at the same time as the practitioner trains the person in functionally equivalent or related adaptive responses, alters stimuli that provoke problem behavior, or applies some consequences following self-injury or aggression. Although a small body of literature attests to the efficacy of DRO or DRI alone, a more extensive literature supports the use of these procedures combined with other techniques (Favell, Azrin et al., 1982).

Traditional Strategies

At this point, not enough information is available to assert that positive approaches are capable of decreasing self-injury or aggression in all cases. The question, then, is this: What should be done when teaching adaptive responses, manipulating antecedents, and differential reinforcement do not work or are not working quickly enough to reduce disruptive or harmful behavior? The answer is not clear; rather, the issue has been emotionally debated in the professional literature (Guess, Turnbull, & Helmstetter, 1990; Mulick, 1990a, 1990b). Despite conflicting views, it can be stated that more intrusive strategies are warranted when (1) all least restrictive interventions have been proven to be ineffective (Matson & DiLorenzo, 1984); (2) the intrusiveness of the treatment can be justified by the benefit anticipated for the person with mental retardation (Lovaas & Favell, 1987); (3) rigorous procedures for evaluation of treatment application and outcome are in place (Favell, Azrin et al., 1982); and (4) to the extent possible, the intervention maintains the personal dignity of the individual who is receiving it (Horner, Dunlap, & Koegel, 1988).

A traditional approach to behavior management offers several consequence-based strategies that are designed to reduce problem behavior, including time-out (removing the subject from a reinforcing situation) (Luiselli, Myles, & Littman-Quinn, 1983; Sisson, Van Hasselt, Hersen, & Aurand, 1988), manual or physical restraint (restricting the individual's movement for a period of time) (Slifer, Iwata, & Dorsey, 1984), and overcorrection (manually guiding the person through repetitive actions) (Barton & LaGrow, 1983; Sisson, Van Hasselt, & Hersen, 1993). In the past, providers of care in educational, residential, and work settings serving persons with mental retardation have been quick to apply such contingencies to inappropriate behavior, especially when less restrictive approaches are ineffective or when the offending response is severe. In fact, there is precedence for the use of these procedures in a vast literature that supports their efficacy (Repp & Brulle, 1981; Schroeder, Schroeder, Rojahn, & Mulick, 1981; Van Hasselt, et al., 1990). The use of aversive electrical stimulation (delivery of a physically harmless but subjectively noxious electrical stimulus) (Foxx et al., 1986) and the delivery of other punishers (e.g., aromatic ammonia, water mist, and lemon juice) (Altman, Haavik, & Cook, 1978; Dorsey, Iwata, Ong, & McSween, 1980; Sajwaj, Libet, & Agras, 1974), although effective (Favell, Azrin et al., 1982), are described only rarely in the contemporary literature, perhaps because of the current clinical practice of applying least restrictive (positive) alternatives first, and the trend away from the use of aversive procedures whenever possible (Lennox et al., 1988).

LONGITUDINAL PERSPECTIVES

The course of self-injury and aggression over the lifetime of the individual with mental retardation is unclear. As described earlier, the relationship between maladaptive behavior and chronological age has not been established. Thus, epidemiological data provide little insight into the question of whether topography and/or frequency of destructive behavior will change over time. However, anecdotal clinical observations suggest that both self-injurious and aggressive responding tend to be chronic. Further, the treatment literature provides scarce indication of whether the effects of medication regimens or behavior modification strategies will maintain over time (Favell, Azrin et al., 1982; Lennox et al., 1988; Matson & Gorman-Smith, 1986). Indeed, at present, it appears that improvements in self-injury or aggression are limited to only those situations in which treatment is applied, with the implication that interventions must be administered throughout each day, carried out in all environments in which the individual lives, and continued over a lengthy, perhaps indefinite, period. This situation has served as the impetus for the design and evaluation of the new approaches to deceleration of maladaptive behavior, described above. For example, it is hoped that by teaching adaptive responses that serve the same function as the destructive ones, treatment effects will generalize across situations and over time. This is because the new behaviors will evoke positive consequences from the environment without explicit training; thus, they will be continued (Durand, 1987; Durand & Carr, 1992). Although the theory and preliminary work is exciting, it is too soon to judge the long-term efficacy of these strategies.

CASE ILLUSTRATION

Beth, a young woman who is blind, deaf, profoundly mentally retarded, and non-ambulatory as a result of maternal rubella, had a long history of engaging in a variety of maladaptive behaviors. Some of these responses, such as public masturbation, were simply socially inappropriate. Others, however, such as repetitive face punching and gagging to the point of vomiting, were of great concern because they resulted in tissue damage in the targeted facial area and throat.

Because of the nature and severity of Beth's problem behaviors, coupled with the fact that she resided in a well-staffed residential school for individuals with visual impairment and multiple disabilities, a number of treatment approaches had been systematically applied and evaluated in the past. For example, she had been exposed to a differential reinforcement program. Preferred stimuli (chocolate candies) were delivered according to a DRO paradigm, in which Beth received reinforcement for very short intervals (gradually expanded from 3 seconds to 1 minute) without occurrences of self-injury. Unfortunately, Beth was virtually nonresponsive to this approach, and a brief (10-second) contingent physical restraint (manually holding her hands down) was added. Although rates of self-injury were decreased by over 50% with this combination of procedures, the fact that the intensity of the program precluded its use across the day, as well as the observation that significant amounts of self-injury remained (20%), led to discontinuation of the procedures. It should be noted that DRO plus contingent aversive olfactory stimuli (vinegar) also was ineffective in reducing self-injurious face punching and gagging. Additionally, over the past decade, classroom and residential staff had attempted to manage self-stimulation and self-injury through a variety of consequence-based procedures, including extinction, time-out, and overcorrection (arm exercises), with little or no success. Finally, Beth's multidisciplinary team, including her parents, resorted to the use of arm splints to prohibit her from seriously injuring herself. Clearly, Beth's already limited interactions with her environment were further restricted in this way.

Beth also had received a psychiatric evaluation due to what appeared to be cyclical patterns of disruptive behavior over time (including extreme agitation, sobbing, and self-injury), coupled with nonresponsiveness to behavioral interventions. As a result, two medications were evaluated, first an antidepressant (imipramine) and then a mood stabilizer (lithium). Again, treatment was terminated, in the first case because of no positive behavioral effects, and in the second case because of the appearance of frequent pants wettings, considered to be a drug side effect.

Interviews with Beth's teacher and caretakers at the time of the current referral to a behavioral treatment team revealed that she exhibited self-injurious and self-stimulatory behaviors continuously when she was not wearing her physical restraints. Because of their potential for harm or social embarrassment, Beth's maladaptive responses typically were followed by staff intervention, including covered signed admonishments (i.e., signing "No, that's wrong!", while holding her hands) and manual restraint until she was calm. An empirical functional analysis suggested that interaction with adults, as well as brief respites from the demands of tasks, reinforced Beth's problem behavior, especially when Beth was in an unstimulating, boring environment. A close look at Beth's classroom routine showed that there was a significant amount of "down" time during which the needs of other classmates with serious handicaps were being met. Problems in this situation were exacerbated because Beth had no appropriate leisure skills, and her sensory impairments precluded her from benefiting from observations of classroom activities in which she was not directly involved. Furthermore, the tasks that she was assigned (such as putting pegs in boards and bagging large plastic "nuts and bolts") typically were nonfunctional ones that she had been doing for many years.

Thus, the first step in treating Beth was to revamp her daily schedule so it offered experiences with more age-appropriate and meaningful activities and capitalized on her preferences whenever possible. For example, because Beth enjoyed water play, she was involved daily in dishwashing, cleaning tables, and washing her wheelchair. When she was not engaged in tasks designed to meet her individual educational goals, the staff were instructed to include her in the activities of others by placing her near them and periodically communicating to her about what they were doing using simple signs while holding Beth's hands. By making her daily activities more functional and encouraging her participation in the group, the staff reduced Beth's self-injurious responses from an average of 70 or more incidents per day to fewer than 20 (similar reductions were evidenced for self-stimulation). At present, Beth wears her restraints only when it is impossible for a staff member to be near her, such as when they are caring for the personal hygiene needs of other individuals, and for no more than 1 hour per day. Indeed, functional activities programming has provided a "window of opportunity" for the institution of other, more specific instructional procedures. Training in leisure skills, so Beth can occupy herself in an acceptable manner, and instruction in communication strategies, using an auditory attention-seeking signal and simple tactile communication board, have been initiated recently and may further reduce her problem behaviors.

SUMMARY

It is estimated that persons with mental retardation make up about 1% of the total population. Problem behavior, including self-injury and aggression, appears to be significantly more prevalent in this group than among individuals without mental retardation, particularly for those that reside in institutions, are lower functioning, and have limited access to functional activities. Indeed, self-injury and, to a lesser extent, aggression have captured the attention of practitioners and researchers in the field. Clearly these responses have the potential to interfere with not only the well-being of the client and others in the environment, but also habilitative programming, which has become a mandate for appropriate treatment and care. Although several theories that account for self-injury and aggression have been presented in the literature, only one approach has had a substantial impact on the treatment of these behaviors in individuals with mental retardation. Within a behavioral framework, destructive behavior is viewed as an operant response, affected by its consequences and controlled by antecedent stimuli that signal differential consequences. Although causal relationships between environmental stimuli and self-injurious or aggressive behaviors are not well established, recent work has pointed directly to such factors in the maintenance of disruptive responses. As a result, and due to their demonstrated efficacy, the most widely used treatments are behavioral. These strategies, which are applied on the basis of data from a functional assessment, include training adaptive responses that replace or circumvent problem behavior, altering antecedent or contextual variables, using differential reinforcement paradigms, and arranging punishing consequences for self-injurious or aggressive responses. While clearly effective over the short term, more work must be done to develop procedures and strategies that produce effects that generalize across situations and over time.

REFERENCES

Altman, K., Haavik, S., & Cook, J. (1978). Punishment of self-injurious behavior in natural settings using contingent aromatic ammonia. *Behaviour Research and Therapy, 16,* 85–96.

Aman, M. G. (1984). Drugs and learning in mental retardation. In G. D. Burrows & J. S. Werry (Eds.), *Advances in human psychopharmacology* (Vol. 3) (pp. 121–163). Greenwich, CT: JAI Press.

Aman, M. G. (1987). Overview of pharmacotherapy: Current status and future directions. *Journal of Mental Deficiency Research, 31,* 121–130.

Aman, M. G., & Singh, N. N. (1982). Methylphenidate in severely retarded residents and the clinical significance of stereotypic behavior. *Applied Research in Mental Retardation, 3,* 345–348.

Aman, M. G., & Singh, N. N. (1983). Pharmacologic intervention. In J. L. Matson & J. A. Mulick (Eds.), *Handbook of mental retardation* (pp. 317–337). Elmsford, NY: Pergamon Press.

Aman, M. G., & Singh, N. N. (1988). Patterns of drug use: Methodological considerations, measurement techniques, and future trends. In M. G. Aman & N. N. Singh (Eds.), *Psychopharmacology of the developmental disabilities* (pp. 1–28). New York: Springer-Verlag.

American Association on Mental Retardation (1992). *Mental retardation: Definition, classification, and systems of supports* (9th ed.). Washington, DC: Author.

American Psychiatric Association (1987). *Diagnostic and statistical manual of mental disorders,* 3rd Edition, Revised. Washington, DC: Author.

American Psychiatric Association (1993). *DSM-IV draft criteria.* Washington, DC: Author.

Anastasi, A. (1976). *Psychological testing* (4th ed.). New York: Macmillan.

Axelrod, S. (1987). Functional and structural analyses of behavior. Approaches leading to reduced use of punishment procedures? *Research in Developmental Disabilities, 8,* 165–178.

Barrett, R. P., Payton, J. B., and Burkart, J. E. (1988). Treatment of self-injury and disruptive behavior with carbamazepine (Tegretol) and behavior therapy. *Journal of the Multihandicapped Person, 1,* 79–91.

Barron, J. L., & Sandman, C. A. (1984). Self-injurious behavior and stereotypy in an institutionalized mentally retarded population. *Applied Research in Mental Retardation, 5,* 499–511.

Barton, L. E., & LaGrow, S. J. (1983). Reducing self-injurious and aggressive behavior in deaf-blind persons through overcorrection. *Journal of Visual Impairment and Blindness, 77,* 221–242.

Bates, W. J., Smeltzer, D. J., & Arnoczky, S. M. (1986). Appropriate and inappropriate use of psychotherapeutic medications for institutionalized mentally retarded persons. *American Journal on Mental Deficiency, 90,* 363–370.

Baumeister, A. A., & Forehand, R. (1973). Stereotyped acts. In N. R. Ellis (Ed.), *International review of research in mental retardation* (Vol. 6) (pp. 55–96). New York: Academic Press.

Berkson, G., & Davenport, R. K. (1962). Stereotyped movements in mental defectives: I. Initial survey. *American Journal of Mental Deficiency, 94,* 37–48.

Berkson, G., McQuiston, S., Jacobson, J. W., Eyman, R. K., & Borthwick, S. (1985). The relationship between age and stereotyped behaviors. *Mental Retardation, 23,* 31–33.

Bird, F., Dores, P. A., Moniz, D., & Robinson, J. (1989). Reducing severe aggressive and self-injurious behaviors with functional communication training: Direct, collateral and generalized results. *American Journal of Mental Retardation, 94,* 37–48.

Brown, F. (1991). Creative daily scheduling: A nonintrusive approach to challenging behaviors in community residences. *Journal of the Association for Persons with Severe Handicaps, 2,* 75–84.

Bryson, Y., Sakati, N., Nyhan, W., & Fish, C. (1971). Self-mutilative behavior in the Cornelia de Lange Syndrome. *American Journal of Mental Deficiency, 76,* 319–324.

Carr, E. G. (1977). The motivation of self-injurious behavior: A review of some hypotheses. *Psychological Bulletin, 84,* 800–916.

Carr, E. G., & McDowell, J. J. (1980). Social control of self-injurious behavior of organic etiology. *Behavior Therapy, 11,* 402–409.

Carr, E. G., Newsom, C. D., & Binkoff, J. A. (1976). Stimulus control of self-destructive behavior in a psychotic child. *Journal of Abnormal Child Psychology, 4,* 139–153.

Carr, E. G., Taylor, J. C., & Robinson, S. (1991). The effects of severe behavior problems in children on the teaching behavior of adults. *Journal of Applied Behavior Analysis, 24,* 523–535.

Cataldo, M. F., & Harris, J. (1982). The biological basis for self-injury in the mentally retarded. *Analysis and Intervention in Developmental Disabilities, 2,* 21–39.

Cooper, J. O., Heron, T. E., & Heward, W. L. (1987). *Applied behavior analysis.* Columbus, OH: Merrill.

DeLissovoy, V. (1963). Head banging in early childhood: A suggested cause. *Journal of Genetic Psychology, 102,* 109–114.

Derby, K. M., Wacker, D. P., Sasso, G., Steege, M., Northup, J., Cigrand, K., & Asmus, J. (1992). Brief functional assessment techniques to evaluate aberrant behavior in an outpatient setting: A summary of 79 cases. *Journal of Applied Behavior Analysis, 25,* 713–721.

Dizmang, L., & Cheatham, C. (1970). The Lesch-Nyhan Syndrome. *American Journal of Psychiatry, 127,* 671–677.

Donnellan, A. M., LaVigna, G. W., Negri-Schoultz, N., & Fassbender, L. L. (1988). *Progress without punishment: Effective approaches for learners with behavior problems.* New York: Teachers College Press, Columbia University.

Dorsey, M. F., Iwata, B. A., Ong, P., & McSween, T. E. (1980). Treatment of self-injurious behavior using a water mist: Initial response suppression and generalization. *Journal of Applied Behavior Analysis, 13,* 343–353.

Duker, P., van Druenen, C., Jol, K., & Oud, H. (1986). Determinants of maladaptive behavior of institutionalized mentally retarded individuals. *American Journal of Mental Deficiency, 91,* 51–56.

Dunlap, G. (1990). Choice-making as a management strategy. *American Association in Mental Retardation News and Notes, 3,* 3–8.

Dunlap, G., Kern-Dunlap, L., Clarke, M., & Robbins, F. R. (1991). Functional assessment and curricular revision in solving the serious behavior challenges of a student with multiple disabilities. *Journal of Applied Behavior Analysis, 24,* 387–397.

Durand, V. M. (1987). "Look Homeward Angel": A call to return to our (functional) roots. *Behavior Analyst, 10,* 299–302.

Durand, V. M. (1988). Towards acceptable and effective intervention for severe behavior problems. In R. H. Horner & G. Dunlap (Eds.), *Behavior management and community integration for individuals with developmental disabilities and severe behavior problems* (pp. 83–96). Eugene: Specialized Training Program, University of Oregon.

Durand, V. M., & Carr, E. G. (1985). Self-injurious behavior: Motivating conditions and guidelines for treatment. *School Psychology Review, 14,* 171–176.

Durand, V. M., & Carr, E. G. (1991). Functional communication training to reduce challenging behavior: Maintenance and application in new settings. *Journal of Applied Behavior Analysis, 24,* 251–264.

Durand, V. M., & Carr, E. G. (1992). An analysis of maintenance following functional communication training. *Journal of Applied Behavior Analysis, 25,* 777–794.

Durand, V. M., & Crimmins, D. B. (1988). Identifying the variables maintaining self-injurious behavior. *Journal of Autism and Developmental Disorders, 18,* 99–117.

Durand, V. M., & Kishi, G. (1987). Reducing severe behavior problems among persons with dual sensory impairments: An evaluation of a technical assistance model. *Journal of The Association for Persons with Severe Handicaps, 12,* 2–10.

Dyer, K., Dunlap, G., & Winterling, V. (1990). The effects of choice-making on the problem behaviors of students with severe handicaps. *Journal of Applied Behavior Analysis, 23,* 515–524.

Edelson, S. M., Taubman, M. T., & Lovaas, O. I. (1983). Some social contexts of self-destructive behavior. *Journal of Abnormal Child Psychology, 11,* 299–312.

Eyman, R. K., & Borthwick, S. A. (1980). Patterns of care for mentally retarded persons. *Mental Retardation, 18,* 63–66.

Eyman, R. K., & Call, T. (1977). Maladaptive behavior and community placement of mentally retarded persons. *American Journal of Mental Deficiency*, 82, 137–144.

Eyman, R. K., Moore, B. D., & Capes, L. (1970). Maladaptive behavior of institutional retardates with seizures. *American Journal of Mental Deficiency*, 74, 651–659.

Farber, J. M. (1987). Psychopharmacology of self-injurious behavior in the mentally retarded. *Journal of the American Academy of Child and Adolescent Psychiatry*, 26, 296–302.

Favell, J. E., Azrin, N. H., Baumeister, A. A., Carr, E. G., Dorsey, M. F., Forehand, R., Foxx, R. M., Lovaas, O. I., Rincover, A., Risley, T. R., Romanczyk, R. G., Russo, D. E., Schroeder, S. R., & Solnik, J. V. (1982). The treatment of self-injurious behavior. *Behavior Therapy*, 13, 529–554.

Favell, J. E., McGimsey, J. F., & Schell, R. M. (1982). Treatment of self-injury by providing alternate sensory activities. *Analysis and Intervention in Developmental Disabilities*, 2, 83–104.

Favell, J. E., McGimsey, J. F., Jones, M. L., & Cannon, P. R. (1981). Physical restraint as positive reinforcement. *American Journal of Mental Deficiency*, 85, 425–432.

Forehand, R., & Baumeister, A. A. (1976). Deceleration of aberrant behavior among retarded individuals. In M. Hersen, R. M. Eisler, & P. M. Miller (Eds.), *Progress in behavior modification* (Vol. 2) (pp. 223–278). New York: Academic Press.

Foxx, R. M. (1992). Saying vs. doing: Some frequently discussed and underresearched issues. *Psychology in Mental Retardation and Developmental Disabilities*, 18, 1–4.

Foxx, R. M., McMorrow, M. J., Bittle, R. G., & Bechtel, D. R. (1986). The successful treatment of a dually diagnosed deaf man's aggression with a program that included contingent electric shock. *Behavior Therapy*, 17, 170–186.

Foxx, R. M., Zukothyski, G., & Williams, D. E. (in press). Measurement and evaluation of treatment outcomes with extremely dangerous behavior. In T. Thompson & D. Gray (Eds.), *Treatment of destructive behavior in developmental disabilities* (Vol. 2). Newbury Park, CA: Sage Publications.

Gedye, A. (1989). Extreme self-injury attributed to frontal lobe seizures. *American Journal on Mental Retardation*, 94, 20–26.

Green, C. W., Reid, D. H., Canipe, V. S., & Gardner, S. M. (1991). A comprehensive evaluation of reinforcer identification processes for persons with profound multiple handicaps. *Journal of Applied Behavior Analysis*, 24, 537–552.

Griffin, J. C., Williams, D. E., Stark, M. T., Altmeyer, B. K., & Mason, M. (1986). Self-injurious behavior: A state-wide prevalence survey of the extent and circumstances. *Applied Research in Mental Retardation*, 7, 105–116.

Grossman, H. J. (Ed.). (1983). *Classification in mental retardation*. Washington, DC: American Association on Mental Deficiency.

Guess, D. (1966). The influence of visual and ambulation restrictions on stereotyped behavior. *American Journal of Mental Deficiency*, 70, 542–547.

Guess, D., & Carr, E. (1991). Emergence and maintenance of stereotypy and self-injury. *American Journal on Mental Retardation*, 96, 299–319.

Guess, D., Turnbull, H. R., & Helmstetter, E. (1990). Science, paradigms, and values: A response to Mulick. *American Journal on Mental Retardation*, 95, 157–163.

Handen, B. L., Feldman, H., Gosling, A., Breaux, A. M., & McAuliffe, S. (1991). Adverse side effects of methylphenidate among mentally retarded children with ADHD. *Journal of the American Academy of Child and Adolescent Psychiatry*, 30, 241–245.

Hill, B. K., & Bruininks, R. H. (1984). Maladaptive behavior of mentally retarded individuals in residential facilities. *American Journal of Mental Deficiency*, 88, 380–387.

Horner, R. H., Day, M., Sprague, J. R., O'Brien, M., & Heathfield, L. T. (1991). Interspersed requests: A nonaversive procedure for decreasing aggression and self-injury during instruction. *Journal of Applied Behavior Analysis*, 24, 265–278.

Horner, R. H., Dunlap, G., & Koegel, R. L. (1988). *Generalization and maintenance: Life-style changes in applied settings*. Baltimore: Paul H. Brookes.

Horner, R. H., Dunlap, G., Koegel, R. L., Carr, E. G., Sailor, W., Anderson, J., Albin, R. W., & O'Neill, R. E. (1990). Toward a technology of "nonaversive" behavioral support. *Journal of The Association for Persons with Severe Handicaps*, 15, 125–132.

Hutt, C., & Hutt, S. J. (1970). Stereotypes and their relation to arousal: A study of autistic children. In S. J. Hutt & C. Hutt (Eds.), *Behavior studies in psychiatry*, (pp. 175–204). New York: Pergamon Press.

Iwata, B. A., Dorsey, M. F., Slifer, K. J., Bauman, K. E., & Richman, G. S. (1982). Toward a functional analysis of self-injury. *Analysis and Intervention in Developmental Disabilities*, 2, 1–20.

Jacobson, J. W. (1982). Problem behavior and psychiatric impairment within a developmentally disabled population I: Behavior frequency. *Applied Research in Mental Retardation, 3,* 121–139.

Jacobson, J. W., & Mulick, J. A. (1992). Behavior modification and technologies: A new definition of MR or a new definition of practice? *Psychology in Mental Retardation and Developmental Disabilities, 18,* 9–14.

LaVigna, G. W., Willis, T. J., & Donnellan, A. M. (1989). The role of positive programming in behavioral treatment. In E. Cipani (Ed.), *Behavioral approaches in the treatment of aberrant behavior* (pp. 59–83). Washington, DC: American Association on Mental Deficiency.

Lennox, D. B., & Miltenberger, R. G. (1989). Conducting a functional assessment of problem behavior in applied settings. *Journal of The Association for Persons with Severe Handicaps, 14,* 304–311.

Lennox, D. B., Miltenberger, R. G., Spengler, P., & Erfanian, N. (1988). Decelerative treatment practices with persons who have mental retardation: A review of five years of the literature. *American Journal on Mental Retardation, 92,* 492–501.

Lewis, M. H., & Baumeister, A. A. (1982). Stereotyped mannerisms in mentally retarded persons: Animal models and theoretical analyses. In N. R. Ellis (Ed.), *International review of research in mental retardation* (Vol. 11) (pp. 123–161). New York: Academic Press.

Lovaas, O. I., & Favell, J. E. (1987). Protection for clients undergoing aversive/restrictive interventions. *Education and Treatment of Children, 10,* 311–325.

Lovaas, O. I., & Simmons, J. Q. (1969). Manipulation of self-destruction in three retarded children. *Journal of Applied Behavior Analysis, 2,* 143–157.

Lovaas, I., Freitag, G., Gold, V. J., & Kassorla, I. C. (1965). Experimental studies in childhood schizophrenia: Analysis of self-destructive behavior. *Journal of Experimental Child Psychology, 2,* 67–84.

Luiselli, J. K., Myles, E., & Littman-Quinn, J. (1983). Analysis of a reinforcement/time-out treatment package to control severe aggressive and destructive behaviors in a multihandicapped, rubella child. *Applied Research in Mental Retardation, 4,* 65–78.

Luiselli, J. K, Myles, E., Evans, T. P., & Boyce, D. A. (1985). Reinforcement control of severe dysfunctional behavior of blind, multihandicapped students. *American Journal of Mental Deficiency, 90,* 328–334.

MacMillan, D. L. (1982). *Mental retardation in school and society.* Boston: Little, Brown.

Maisto, C. R., Baumeister, A. A., & Maisto, A. A. (1978). An analysis of variables related to self-injurious behavior among institutionalized retarded persons. *Journal of Mental Deficiency Research, 22,* 27–35.

Martin, J. E., & Agran, M. (1985). Psychotropic and anticonvulsant drug use by mentally retarded adults across community residential and vocational placements. *Applied Research in Mental Retardation, 6,* 33–49.

Matson, J. L. (1988). Mental retardation in adults. In V. B. Van Hasselt, P. S. Strain, & M. Hersen (Eds.), *Handbook of developmental and physical disabilities* (pp. 353–369). New York: Pergamon.

Matson, J. L., & DiLorenzo, T. M. (1984). *Punishment and its alternatives: A new perspective for behavior modification* (Vol. 13). New York: Springer.

Matson, J. L., & Gardner, W. I. (1991). Behavioral learning theory and current applications to severe behavior problems in persons with mental retardation. *Clinical Psychology Review, 11,* 175–183.

Matson, J. L., & Gorman-Smith, D. (1986). A review of treatment research for aggressive and disruptive behavior in the mentally retarded. *Applied Research in Mental Retardation, 7,* 95–103.

McClure, J. T., Moss, R. A., McPeters, J. W., & Kirkpatrick, M. A. (1986). Reduction of hand mouthing by a boy will profound mental retardation. *Mental Retardation, 24,* 219–222.

Meyers, C. E., Nihira, K., & Zetlin, A. (1979). The measurement of adaptive behavior. In N. Ellis (Ed.), *Handbook of mental deficiency: Psychological theory and research* (pp. 131–164). Hillsdale, NJ: Lawrence Erlbaum Associates.

Mulick, J. A. (1990a). The ideology and science of punishment in mental retardation. *American Journal of Mental Deficiency, 95,* 142–156.

Mulick, J. A. (1990b). Ideology and punishment reconsidered. *American Journal on Mental Retardation, 95,* 173–181.

Nyhan, W. L. (1976). Behavior in the Lesch-Nyhan Syndrome. *Journal of Autism and Childhood Schizophrenia, 6,* 235–252.

Parrish, J. M., Iwata, B. A., Dorsey, M. F., Bunck, T. J., & Slifer, K. J. (1985). Behavior analysis, program development, and transfer of control in the treatment of self-injury. *Journal of Behavior Therapy and Experimental Psychiatry, 16,* 159–168.

Reid, D. H., Wilson, P. G., & Faw, G. D. (1983). Teaching self-help skills. In J. L. Matson & J. A. Mulick (Eds.), *Handbook of mental retardation* (pp. 429–442). New York: Pergamon.

Repp, A. C., & Brulle, A. R. (1981). Reducing aggressive behavior of mentally retarded persons. In J. L. Matson & J. R. McCartney (Eds.), *Handbook of behavior modification with the mentally retarded* (pp. 177–210). New York: Plenum.

Repp, A. C., & Singh, N. N. (1990). *Perspectives on the use of nonaversive and aversive interventions for persons with developmental disabilities*. Sycamore, IL: Sycamore.

Rincover, A., & Devany, J. (1982). The application of sensory extinction procedures to self-injury. *Analysis and Intervention in Developmental Disabilities, 2*, 67–81.

Rivinus, T. M., Grofer, L. M., Feinstein, C., & Barrett, R. P. (1989). Psychopharmacology in the mentally retarded individual: New approaches, new directions. *Journal of the Multihandicapped Person, 2*, 1–23.

Rodin, E. A. (1973). Psychomotor epilepsy and aggressive behavior. *Archives of General Psychiatry, 29*, 210–213.

Rojahn, J. (1984). Self-injurious behavior in institutionalized, severely/profoundly retarded adults—Prevalence data and staff agreement. *Journal of Behavioral Assessment, 6*, 13–27.

Rojahn, J. (1986). Self-injurious and stereotypic behavior of noninstitutionalized mentally retarded people: Prevalence and classification. *American Journal of Mental Deficiency, 91*, 268–276.

Rojahn, J., & Sisson, L. A. (1990). Stereotyped behavior. In J. L. Matson (Ed.), *Handbook of behavior modification with the mentally retarded* (2nd ed.) (pp. 191–223). New York: Plenum.

Ross, A. (1972). Behavioral correlates of levels of intelligence. *American Journal of Mental Deficiency, 76*, 545–549.

Ruedrich, S. L., Grush, L., & Wilson, J. (1990). Beta adrenergic blocking medications for aggressive or self-injurious mentally retarded persons. *American Journal on Mental Retardation, 95*, 110–119.

Rutter, M., Tizard, J., & Whitmore, K. (1970). *Education, health and behavior*. New York: Wiley.

Sajwaj, T., Libet, J., & Agras, S. (1974). Lemon-juice therapy: The control of life-threatening rumination in a six-month infant. *Journal of Applied Behavior Analysis, 7*, 557–563.

Schroeder, S. R., Mulick, J., & Schroeder, C. (1979). Management of severe behavior problems of the retarded. In N. Ellis (Ed.), *Handbook of mental deficiency* (2nd ed.) (pp. 341–366). New York: Erlbaum.

Schroeder, S. R., Schroeder, C. S., Rojahn, J., & Mulick, J. A. (1981). Self-injurious behavior: An analysis of behavior management techniques. In J. L. Matson & J. R. McCartney (Eds.), *Handbook of behavior modification with the mentally retarded* (pp. 61–115). New York: Plenum.

Schroeder, S. R., Schroeder, C. S., Smith, B., & Dalldorf, J. (1978). Prevalence of self-injurious behavior in a large state facility for the retarded. *Journal of Autism and Developmental Disorders, 8*, 261–269.

Singh, N. N., & Millichamp, J. (1985). Pharmacological treatment of self-injurious behavior in mentally retarded persons. *Journal of Autism and Developmental Disorders, 15*, 257–267.

Singh, N. N., & Winton, A. S. W. (1984). Behavioral monitoring of pharmacological interventions for self-injury. *Applied Research in Mental Retardation, 5*, 161–170.

Singh, N. N., Guernsey, T. F., & Ellis, C. R. (1992). Drug therapy for persons with developmental disabilities: Legislation and litigation. *Clinical Psychology Review, 12*, 665–679.

Singh, N. N., Singh, Y. N., & Ellis, C. R. (1992). Psychopharmacology of self-injury. In J. K. Luiselli, J. L. Matson, & N. N. Singh (Eds.), *Self-injury: Assessment, analysis and treatment* (pp. 307–351). New York: Springer-Verlag.

Sisson, L. A., & Van Hasselt, V. B. (1989). Feeding disorders. In J. K. Luiselli (Ed.), *Behavioral medicine and developmental disorders* (pp. 45–73). New York: Springer-Verlag.

Sisson, L. A., Van Hasselt, V. B., & Hersen, M. (1993). Behavioral interventions to reduce maladaptive responding in youth with dual sensory impairment: An analysis of direct and concurrent effects. *Behavior Modification, 17*, 164–188.

Sisson, L. A., Van Hasselt, V. B., Hersen, M., & Aurand, J. C. (1988). Tripartite behavioral intervention to reduce stereotypic and disruptive behaviors in young multihandicapped children. *Behavior Therapy, 19*, 503–526.

Slifer, K. J., Ivancic, M. T., Parrish, J. M., Page, T. J., & Burgio, L. D. (1986). Assessment and treatment of multiple behavior problems exhibited by a profoundly retarded adolescent. *Journal of Behavior Therapy and Experimental Psychiatry, 17*, 203–213.

Slifer, K. J., Iwata, B. A., & Dorsey, M. J. (1984). Reduction of eye gouging using a response interruption procedure. *Journal of Behavior Therapy and Experimental Psychiatry, 15*, 369–375.

Tarjan, G., Wright, S. W., Eyman, R. K., & Keeran, C. V. (1973). Natural history of mental retardation: Some aspects of epidemiology. *American Journal of Mental Deficiency, 77*, 369–379.

Taylor, J. C., Sisson, L. A., McKelvey, J. L., & Trefelner, M. F. (in press). Situation specificity in attention seeking problem behavior: A case study. *Behavior Modification, 17*, 474–477.

Touchette, P. E., MacDonald, R. F., & Langner, S. N. (1985). A scatter plot for identifying stimulus control of problem behavior. *Journal of Applied Behavior Analysis, 18*, 343–351.

Tutton, C., Wynne-Willson, S., & Piachaud, J. (1990). Rating management difficulty: A study into the prevalence and severity of difficult behaviour displayed by residents in a large residential hospital for the mentally handicapped. *Journal of Mental Deficiency Research, 34*, 325–339.

Tyson, M., & Favell, J. E. (1988). Mental retardation in children. In V. B. Van Hasselt & M. Hersen (Eds.), *Handbook of developmental and physical disabilities* (pp. 336–352). New York: Pergamon.

U.S. Department of Health and Human Services. (1989). *Treatment of destructive behaviors in persons with developmental disabilities: National Institutes of Health consensus development conference statement* (Vol. 7, Number 9, pp. 1–41). Bethesda, MD: Author.

Van Hasselt, V. B., Ammerman, R. T., and Sisson, L. A. (1990). Physically disabled persons. In A. E. Kazdin, A. S. Bellack, & M. Hersen (Eds.), *International handbook of behavior modification and therapy* (2nd ed.) (pp. 831–855). New York: Plenum.

Wacker, D. P., Berg, W. K., Wiggins, B., Muldoon, M., & Cavanaugh, J. (1985). Evaluation of reinforcer preferences for profoundly handicapped students. *Journal of Applied Behavior Analysis, 18*, 173–178.

Weeks, M., & Gaylord-Ross, R. (1981). Task difficulty and aberrant behavior in severely handicapped students. *Journal of Applied Behavior Analysis, 14*, 449–463.

Williamson, P. D., Spencer, D. D., Spencer, S. S., Novelly, R. A., & Mattson, R. H. (1985). Complex partial seizures of frontal lobe origin. *Annals of Neurology, 18*, 497–504.

Zentall, S. S., & Zentall, T. R. (1983). Optimal stimulation: A model of disordered activity and performance in normal and deviant children. *Psychological Bulletin, 94*, 446–471.

Zigler, E. (1967). Familial mental retardation: A continuing dilemma. *Science, 155*, 292–298.

Zigler, E., & Hodapp, R. M. (1986). *Understanding mental retardation*. New York: Cambridge University Press.

Zigler, E., & Hodapp, R. M. (1991). Behavioral functioning in individuals with mental retardation. *Annual Review of Psychology, 42*, 29–50.

Zigler, E., Balla, D., & Hodapp, R. (1984). On the definition and classification of mental retardation. *American Journal of Mental Deficiency, 89*, 215–230.

Zingarelli, G., Ellman, G., Hom, A., Wymore, M., Heldorn, St., Chicz-DeMet, A. (1992). Clinical effects of naltrexone on autistic behavior. *American Journal on Mental Retardation, 97*, 57–63.

CHAPTER 20

Attention-Deficit Hyperactivity Disorder

STEPHEN P. HINSHAW AND CASSANDRA SIMMEL

DESCRIPTION OF THE DISORDER

Attention-deficit hyperactivity disorder (ADHD) is a prevalent, persistent, and often perplexing behavioral disturbance of childhood. The typical clinical picture is that of a child with normal intelligence—most often a boy—who shows patterns of attentional deployment, impulse control, and behavioral regulation that (1) are severely deficient for his age or general developmental level, (2) have persisted since early childhood, (3) appear in multiple settings (e.g., school and home), and (4) are not explicable on the basis of other severe psychopathology (American Psychiatric Association, 1993). Thus, despite normal appearance and intellectual capacity, such a child has great difficulties negotiating the developmental tasks of childhood. Through overzealousness, disruptive tendencies, and lack of judgment, he exasperates parents and teachers alike. Furthermore, most peers actively reject him, largely because of an immature and aggressive behavioral style (see Erhardt, 1991; Pelham & Bender, 1982). In many cases, difficulties with schoolwork are salient, accumulating over time to precipitate academic failure (Hinshaw, 1992). Low self-esteem and frustration are common, as vicious cycles of negative interaction patterns ensue in home, school, and community settings.

Many different terms have been used to describe this disorder—for example, minimal brain dysfunction (MBD), hyperkinesis, and hyperactivity (see Hinshaw, 1987a, for a review). With more recent emphasis on these children's difficulties in sustaining attention

The writing of this chapter was supported by Grant No. 45064 from the National Institute of Mental Health. Correspondence should be addressed to Stephen P. Hinshaw, Department of Psychology, Tolman Hall, University of California, Berkeley, CA 94720.

STEPHEN P. HINSHAW and CASSANDRA SIMMEL • Department of Psychology, University of California at Berkeley, Berkeley, California 94720.

Handbook of Aggressive and Destructive Behavior in Psychiatric Patients, edited by Michel Hersen, Robert T. Ammerman, and Lori A. Sisson. Plenum Press, New York, 1994.

(e.g., Douglas, 1983), further changes in official nomenclature were made during the 1980s, with the terms attention deficit disorder (American Psychiatric Association, 1980) and ADHD (American Psychiatric Association, 1987) now supplanting earlier labels. (We use the terms attentional deficits, hyperactivity, and ADHD interchangeably in this chapter). Despite changes in nomenclature, however, heated debate still continues as to the primacy of attention, behavioral, motoric, or motivational factors in the genesis and maintenance of the disorder (e.g., Barkley, 1990; Sergeant, 1989).

ADHD currently is listed, along with oppositional-defiant disorder (ODD) and conduct disorder (CD), under the heading of disruptive (externalizing) behavior disorders in the *Diagnostic and Statistical Manual of Mental Disorders* (American Psychiatric Association, 1993). ODD and CD are marked by a variety of age-inappropriate aggressive and antisocial symptoms, ranging from defiance and impertinence in younger children (ODD) to assault and theft in preadolescents and adolescents (CD). This diagnostic linkage of ADHD with categories earmarked by aggressive features corresponds to the many empirical investigations in which dimensions of attentional problems/hyperactivity are correlated with interpersonal aggression, negative affect, and antisocial tendencies (Quay, 1986). In fact, in second-order factor analyses, narrower hyperactivity and aggression factors typically load together on broad-band externalizing dimensions (Achenbach & Edelbrock, 1983). The overlap of attentional deficits/hyperactivity with aggression is further indicated by the presence of significant aggressive features in a majority of ADHD children (Hinshaw, 1987b; Szatmari, Boyle, & Offord, 1989).

Yet these dimensions are not alternate names for the same phenomenon. As indicated above, they comprise distinct factors in empirical investigations; more importantly, they have distinct correlates. For one thing, family histories tend to differ, with aggression tied to antisocial features or substance abuse and attentional deficits linked with language and learning problems (e.g., August & Stewart, 1983; Lahey et al., 1988). In addition, developmental and environmental concomitants are distinct: ADHD is associated preferentially with language and other developmental delays, whereas conduct problems are linked selectively with disturbed family interactions and social disadvantage (Szatmari, Boyle, & Offord, 1989). Importantly, they also may diverge with respect to long-term course, with aggressive behavior in childhood more predictive of delinquent behavior and severe maladjustment (e.g., Loney, Kramer, & Milich, 1981; but see also Schachar, 1991). When the two types of problems are combined, the dual-diagnosis group of youngsters with both ADHD and aggression tends to have academic, interpersonal, and behavioral problems that are far worse than the single disorders (see reviews in Hinshaw, 1987b; Moffitt, 1990). A key aim of this chapter is to elucidate the linkages between these often overlapping domains.

Whereas attentional difficulties were, in the recent past, thought to be limited in duration by puberty, methodologically sound follow-up investigations have documented the persistence of these youngsters' attentional, behavioral, and interpersonal problems into adolescence and young adulthood (Barkley, Fischer, Edelbrock, & Smallish, 1990; Gittelman, Mannuzza, Shenker, & Bonagura, 1985; Satterfield, Hoppe, & Schell, 1982; Weiss & Hechtman, 1986). We have noted above that the dysregulated behavioral style of the ADHD child leads to troublesome parent–child interactions, frequent confrontations with classroom rules, noteworthy difficulties with academic achievement, and severe rejection by agemates (Barkley, 1990; Pelham & Bender, 1982; Whalen, 1989). Given the strong predictive power of difficulties in these domains for subsequent pathology (see Barkley et al., 1990; Parker & Asher, 1987; Stattin & Magnusson, 1989), the persistence of ADHD and its sequelae are hardly surprising. A lingering question involves the role of the "core" symptoms of inattention, impulsivity, and overactivity versus the "secondary" features of aggression and its correlates in predicting and mediating such a troublesome life course.

As with all psychiatric disorders, ADHD encompasses a wide spectrum of severity, from children with relatively mild attentional and learning problems that are limited to classroom settings to youngsters with severe, cross-situational problems of dysregulation and explosiveness. In addition, the presenting picture varies markedly, from children with an exuberant, carefree style to those with significant internalizing tendencies of withdrawal, dysphoria, and anxiety. Whereas space does not permit extensive portrayal of this range of disturbance, vivid descriptions of the behavioral presentation and phenomenology of ADHD and more thorough reviews can be found in Barkley (1990), Ross and Ross (1982), Schachar (1991), and Whalen (1989).

EPIDEMIOLOGY

Prevalence estimates for ADHD have varied widely, chiefly because of differences of opinion and approach regarding the defining characteristics of the disorder, the levels of severity thought to warrant diagnosis, and the instruments chosen to make assessments. Furthermore, consistent standards have not been kept on both sides of the Atlantic. British definitions typically define "hyperkinesis" as a rare (e..g, less than 0.1%; Rutter, Tizard, & Whitmore, 1970) condition of cross-situational dysregulation often compounded by intellectual retardation, whereas American investigations include a broader symptom picture and less stringent criteria, yielding prevalence estimates in the neighborhood of 5–10% (cf. American Psychiatric Association, 1987). Sophisticated epidemiological work in Canada—namely, the Ontario Child Health Study by Szatmari, Offord, and colleagues—both validates the broader conception of ADHD as a viable disorder and provides an intriguing look at attentional problems and their relation to aggressive behavioral phenomena.

Using the criteria for attention deficit disorder in DSM-III (American Psychiatric Association, 1980) and combining data from parents and teachers (and, in the case of adolescents, self-reports), Szatmari, Offord, and Boyle (1989b) found that the overall prevalence of the disorder among 4- to 16-year-olds was 6.3%, with a threefold increase in the rate for males (9.0%) over females (3.3%). Because their definition included only cross-sectional information—neglecting data regarding age of onset or duration—these estimates may somewhat overinflate rates of persistent attentional deficits. The highest overall prevalence rate (8.6%) occurred for children aged 8–9 years. Also noteworthy is the finding that more often than not attentional deficits were associated with either "emotional" (internalizing) symptoms, conduct problems, or both. Indeed, approximately 57% of the hyperactive children (aged 4–11) also qualified for a diagnosis of conduct disorder. This rate of overlap is particularly noteworthy given the nonclinical, epidemiological nature of the sample under investigation.

As highlighted above, the Ontario reports revealed that attention deficit disorder (but not conduct disorder) was associated with several developmental variables of interest, for example, language delay, clumsiness, and low birth weight (Szatmari, Offord, & Boyle, 1989a). Aggression/conduct problems, on the other hand, showed clear relationships with psychosocial disadvantage (Szatmari, Boyle, & Offord, 1989). Intriguingly, the comorbid subgroup with both attentional problems and aggression displayed some characteristics of each "pure" disorder but could not be considered to constitute a simple combination of the single-disorder categories (see also Moffitt, 1990). Other recent investigations, however, indicate that although children with the combination of hyperactivity and aggression are quantitatively more disturbed on a number of dimensions than is either single-disorder category, they do not necessarily show a qualitatively different profile of correlates or medication response (e.g., Barkley, McMurray, Edelbrock, & Robbins, 1989; Hinshaw, Henker, Whalen, Erhardt, & Dunnington, 1989).

These Canadian data are representative of recent epidemiological investigations in the United States, which reveal that samples of ADHD children defined on the basis of parent and/or teacher instruments are relatively prevalent (upwards of 5% of the child population) and usually deserving of clinical services (for a review, see Brandenberg, Friedman, & Silver, 1990). There are consistent findings of higher prevalence rates for boys than for girls; the male:female ratios are on the order of 2:1 or 3:1 in community surveys but as high as 8:1 or more in clinic samples. These greater gender disparities among clinic attendees probably reflect the greater likelihood that ADHD children with comorbid aggression—who are far more likely to be boys—are selectively referred for services.

ETIOLOGY

Because even cursory coverage of current conceptions as to the etiology of ADHD would take more pages than are allotted for the entire chapter, we provide the sparest of outlines regarding this broad topic (for recent reviews, see Barkley, 1990; Schachar, 1991; Whalen, 1989). In the first place, clear consensus exists that ADHD is not a unitary disorder and that multiple causal pathways may converge to lead to the development of persistent inattention, impulsivity, and overactivity (Whalen, 1989). Second, many of the putative causal agents or factors for ADHD also are likely to result in other behavioral or emotional disturbance; thus, primary or specific etiologic factors have not yet been identified. Third, much extant etiologic research has been hampered by the tendency in the field to confound ADHD and aggression in samples of "hyperactive" children (see Hinshaw, 1987b). Such diagnostic heterogeneity has rendered the search for specific etiologic routes to attentional deficits versus aggressive behavior extremely problematic.

As for plausible causal mechanisms, recent twin studies have revealed rather strong heritability for clinically meaningful inattentive and hyperactive behavior (Goodman & Stevenson, 1989a). Yet such genetic predisposition is, of course, influenced by familial and environmental factors in precipitating symptomatology (cf. Goodman & Stevenson, 1989b). Although a plausible end product of deviant genetic inheritance may be deficient or faulty neurotransmission in catecholaminergic systems, few replicable data have been obtained in the neurochemical or neuroanatomic domain (Zametkin & Rapaport, 1987). A host of nongenetic biological factors may also contribute to ADHD, including environmental lead; maternal ingestion of alcohol, tobacco, or other drugs during pregnancy; and a host of birth and perinatal complications. None of these causal factors, however, has been specifically linked with ADHD; they may rather set the stage for a wide range of externalizing (and even internalizing) symptomatology. Furthermore, the compelling data of Werner and Smith (1982) serve as reminders that risks incurred by perinatal complications are mediated strongly by subsequent familial and psychosocial factors. Thus, biological predispositions (either heritable or nonheritable) interact with the psychosocial milieu in forging pertinent symptomatology.

As for other potential causal factors, despite wide speculation and fervent intervention efforts, dietary factors or allergic mechanisms seem to pertain to only an extremely small minority of ADHD youngsters. In addition, an intriguing report that ADHD is precipitated by poor attachment in infancy and by inappropriate mother–child interactions early in life mandates replication (Jacobvitz & Sroufe, 1987). Furthermore, the known linkages between ADHD and underachievement have led to various causal theories as to the nature of this relationship. Recently, McGee and Share (1988) contended that reading failure is, in fact, causative of the symptomatology associated with ADHD. Yet, inattention/hyperactivity is correlated with academic readiness deficiencies early in life, usually before the onset of schooling; therefore, a host of neurodevelopmental, language-related, and familial "third variables" are likely to predispose to the comorbid pattern (Hinshaw, 1992).

In summary, etiologic theories abound for ADHD, but the field is plagued with diagnostic unclarity, problematic measures of possible causal mechanisms, and a host of nonreplicated findings. Furthermore, aside from divergent family histories (see Schachar, 1991) and a preferential linkage of poverty and psychosocial disadvantage with antisocial tendencies (Szatmari, Boyle, & Offord, 1989), there is no clear separability of causal factors for conduct problems/aggression versus attentional problems/hyperactivity. Much work remains to be performed in this key area.

AGGRESSION TOWARD SELF

There is an almost complete dearth of systematic data on the topic of self-directed aggression among ADHD populations. Yet some suggestive evidence does exist. First, with respect to depression, at least one investigative team has revealed a strong prevalence of affective disturbance in family members of children with ADHD (Biederman, Faraone, Keenan, & Tsuang, 1991). Presumably, such family histories could place at least a subset of children with ADHD at risk for subsequent self-destructive actions. Second, there is clear evidence that ADHD is linked with increased rates of such self-injurious acts as accidental poisonings and bone fractures in childhood (see Szatmari, Offord, & Boyle, 1989a); it also is associated with increased risk for substance abuse (particularly alcohol, tobacco, and marijuana) and for such careless, impulsive acts as increased traffic violations during adolescent and young adult years (Gittelman et al., 1985; Weiss & Hechtman, 1986). Whether such behaviors and actions are indexes of subclinical self-destructive tendencies or are manifestations of an impulsive, sensation-seeking style—or, in some cases, both—is indeterminate. Third, although self-destructive acts per se are not documented, recent investigations have begun to report the prevalence of depressive symptoms in children with attentional deficits (e.g., Brown, Borden, Clingerman, & Jenkins, 1988). A major question is whether sad mood and other depressive symptoms in these children are secondary to the attentional deficits and behavioral disturbance or vice versa.

Another slant on this topic would be to ascertain the risk for suicidal, self-destructive behavior in ADHD youngsters who have reached adulthood. One provocative finding in this regard was made in the systematic, prospective investigation of Weiss and Hechtman (1986). It was found that a small subgroup of ADHD youngsters (approximately 10%) displayed serious psychiatric disturbance in young adulthood, with a portion of these individuals having made suicide attempts. Severe antisocial tendencies, personality disorders, and social isolation tended to characterize this subgroup.

We should note that clinically significant depression does covary with conduct disturbances in preadolescence and adolescence (e.g., Puig-Antich, 1982), fueling speculation that outwardly directed aggression may be closely related to depression (and possibly self-destructive tendencies) in teenage youngsters. Given the frequent comorbidity of ADHD and conduct disturbance, depressive outcomes may therefore be associated with attentional problems because of the linkage of the latter with aggression.

In short, although no evidence yet exists that links ADHD with clearly suicidal or self-destructive behavior, (1) children and adolescents with attentional deficits are likely to have serious accidents, to ingest substances, and to commit impulsive, dangerous acts, all of which may lead to harmful outcomes; (2) some ADHD youngsters show clear depressive symptomatology; (3) a small subgroup of ADHD youngsters shows evidence of severe psychopathology in early adulthood, with suicide attempts noted in this group; and (4) by some accounts interpersonal aggression and antisocial behavior in adolescence show substantial comorbidity with major depression. As additional longitudinal investigations of youngsters with ADHD extend into the adult years, it will be important to take note of increased risk for major depression and/or suicidal tendencies in these individuals (Barkley, personal communication, September, 1991).

AGGRESSION TOWARD OTHERS

We have highlighted that a major concomitant of ADHD is interpersonal aggression. Indeed, it is aggression that usually precipitates clinical referral for children with inattentive behavior patterns and/or learning difficulties (e.g., Shaywitz, Shaywitz, Fletcher, & Escobar, 1990). In this section we discuss the overlap of ADHD and aggression, the development of aggression in at-risk youngsters, and pertinent subcategories of aggressive and antisocial behavior.

First, we must reiterate that clinically significant aggression is a frequent concomitant of ADHD. Indeed, half or more of children formally classified as having attentional deficits also receive diagnoses of oppositional-defiant or conduct disorders (see review of Hinshaw, 1987b). In a recent, sophisticated attempt to discern the underlying relationship between these two disorders, Fergusson, Horwood, and Lloyd (1991) tested, via confirmatory factor analysis, several models relating dimensions of attention deficit and conduct disorder in a birth cohort of 9- and 10-year-old children in New Zealand (Christchurch Child Development Study). Optimal support was found for a model in which attention deficits and conduct disorders were indeed distinct factors but with a massive intercorrelation (approximately $r = .88$). Because of the greater precision of confirmatory factor models, this association is considerably higher than the correlations (e.g., $r = .5$ to .6) found in more typical exploratory factor analytic investigations. Thus, despite the findings that such dimensions have unique correlates (e.g., McGee et al., 1985) and that subgroups of purely hyperactive, purely aggressive, and mixed hyperactive–aggressive children differ with respect to family history, developmental and environmental criteria, peer status, and course (see Hinshaw, 1987b), substantial empirical overlap does exist between these domains.

What conditions may "tip the scales" toward the development of frank aggression in children with predispositions for externalizing behavior? First, as noted earlier, conduct problems are associated with lower social class and impoverished living conditions. Yet discordant family environments appear to be a more specific predictor of aggressive child behavior than is social class per se (Paternite, Loney, & Langhorne, 1976). In this regard, the seminal work of Patterson (1982) on coercive family process is of central importance. From extensive, in-home observations that test social learning models of family interchange, Patterson and colleagues have found that a series of escalating, negatively reinforcing contingencies between parents and child—termed *coercion*—promote the rapid intensification of antisocial acts. In brief, the defiant child is negatively reinforced by parental capitulation to his escalating tantrums and demands; and parents are similarly rewarded for aggressive and even abusive parenting by their child's ultimate compliance with high-level punishments (see extensive data in Patterson, 1982). Recent work of this research team has linked the expression of such an incompetent parenting style with parental stress and depression and with the subsequent development of achievement difficulties, poor peer relationships, and self-esteem deficits in the aggressive child (e.g., Patterson, de Baryshe, & Ramsey, 1989).

We can speculate that the child at risk for ADHD—who typically shows a difficult temperament during infancy and a resistant, oppositional style during the preschool years (e.g., Campbell, 1990) and who is at risk for motoric and other neurodevelopmental delay (Moffitt, 1990)—may be particularly vulnerable to becoming victimized by a coercive parental style, especially given the likelihood of finding impulsive, antisocial features in parents of externalizing youngsters (see Lahey et al., 1988). This scenario would, in many cases, exemplify gene–environment correlation, whereby shared hereditary predispositions toward difficult, oppositional behavior would be compounded by the discordant family environment characterizing the home setting of such parents. Such intertwined and intransigent causal factors lead to extreme difficulty in promoting lasting change in children who are both hyperactive and aggressive (see also Hinshaw, Lahey, & Hart, 1993, and later section on "Clinical Management").

At this point, we must mention that aggression is far from a unitary construct. Indeed, recent empirical work has fueled theoretical contentions on the meaningfulness and separability of several subtypes of aggressive/antisocial behavior. First, aggressive interchanges can be verbal or physical, with the latter type quite prevalent in preschool years but fading to low levels in normal youngsters with continued development (e.g., Parke & Slaby, 1983). The continued presence of high rates of physical aggression during the grade-school years not only leads to peer rejection and ostracism but also portends a bleak prognosis (e.g., Robins, 1979). Second, youngsters may direct aggression toward adults or toward their peers, and a provocative report by Johnston and Pelham (1986) suggests that adult-directed defiance and aggression may be associated with continued social difficulties during the elementary school years. Third, recent research has examined the distinction between proactive or instrumental aggression—in which the child initiates aggressive activity in order to meet personal goals—versus reactive or retaliatory aggression, where the child reacts (or overreacts) to a real or perceived threat by striking back (see Dodge & Coie, 1987). Importantly, only reactive aggression is characterized by such key social information-processing difficulties as impulsive social judgment and attribution of hostile intent toward ambiguous interpersonal conflicts (see Price & Dodge, 1989).

Another distinction of theoretical and clinical importance is the separation of behaviors that are overtly aggressive (e..g, fighting, bullying) from those that are covertly antisocial (lying, stealing, truancy, substance abuse). Both factor analytic and multidimensional scaling investigations support the empirical distinctiveness of these two types of antisocial behavior (Loeber & Schmaling, 1985; Loeber, Lahey, & Thomas, 1991). Importantly, children who are primarily covert in their display of antisocial behavior may have family interaction patterns (which are marked by poor monitoring rather than harsh coercion) and prognoses (such youngsters are *more* likely to display subsequent delinquency) that diverge from those of children who show exclusively overt aggression (see discussion in Hinshaw, Heller, & McHale, 1992). Furthermore, the development of more serious conduct disorders in children with early signs of ADHD or oppositional-defiant disorder is apparently marked by the development of "transitional" covert behaviors (e.g., lying, petty stealing) in early to middle childhood (Hinshaw, Lahey, & Hart, 1993). Although diversely antisocial youngsters—those who are both "stealers" and "fighters"—have the worst prognoses of all, it is important both clinically and theoretically to carve the domain of aggressive/ antisocial behavior for greater precision in ascertaining causal factors and in predicting outcome.

In sum, a variety of aggressive and antisocial behaviors may come to mark the "careers" of children with attentional deficits, and these features may relate to either increased genetic loading for externalizing deviance, pre- and perinatal risk, discordant home environments, or a combination of all three. The joint presence of attentional deficits and severe aggression portends a bleak future (see Farrington, Loeber, & van Kammen, 1990; Magnusson, 1987), as we continue to highlight below.

CLINICAL MANAGEMENT

The most frequently used treatment modality for children with ADHD is stimulant medication, which has been shown to provide clinically significant benefit in ADHD youngsters both with and without concomitant aggression (Barkley et al., 1989). Indeed, in children with attentional deficits, directly observed aggressive behavior often is reduced dramatically with stimulant treatment (see review by Hinshaw, 1991). Recent evidence points to the conclusions that (1) covert antisocial behaviors are reduced with stimulant medication (Hinshaw et al., 1992), and (2) medication improves sociometric status in hyperactive children (Whalen et al., 1989). Despite such encouraging findings, there are clear reasons to question the adequacy of this intervention strategy for ADHD.

In the first place, medications are not successful with all children who have ADHD: 20–30% either do not show a favorable response or reveal problematic side effects, and alternative interventions are needed for this subgroup. Second, even among "positive responders," stimulant actions are rarely clinically sufficient (see Pelham & Hinshaw, 1992). For example, the benefits of stimulant medication last only a few hours, and important after-school and weekend periods—which may be fertile ground for parent–child conflict and aggressive interaction with peers—are typically not "covered" by medication. Third, although not truly experimental in design, long-term follow-up investigations reveal that despite important short-range benefits that accrue from medication treatment, adolescent and adult functioning is not altered appreciably by stimulant intervention (e.g., Weiss & Hechtman, 1986). It seems clear that medications must be combined with psychosocial intervention if lasting benefit is to be obtained.

Indeed, consensus in the field is converging on the contention that combinations of medication with behavioral parent-management strategies, academic tutoring, family therapy, and classroom consultation are necessary to effect maximum benefit (see, for example, Barkley, 1990; Hinshaw & Erhardt, 1991; Pelham & Murphy, 1986). Given the diverse areas in which ADHD children show problems—socially, academically, interpersonally—we should expect that treatments must be wide ranging. Furthermore, given the problems that even the most efficacious interventions for ADHD (e.g., stimulant medications plus behavioral programs) have in promoting lasting change, combination treatments will need to be delivered for long durations. Rigorous research investigations regarding the efficacy of multiple-component interventions are just beginning to be performed (see review in Hinshaw & Erhardt, 1991); their results will be important in determining whether the difficult group of children with ADHD and aggression can show meaningful, lasting improvement with multimodality treatment.

LONGITUDINAL PERSPECTIVES

We have noted repeatedly that ADHD children—and particularly those with concomitant aggression—are at high risk for long-term difficulties. Indeed, the various manifestations of aggressive and antisocial behavior are, in their extreme forms, quite stable over time (e.g., Caspi & Moffitt, in press; Olweus, 1979) and quite predictive of negative outcome in children with ADHD (e.g., Loney et al., 1981). Yet just what facets of "aggression" are important in these predictive relationships? In other words, are aggressive/antisocial acts themselves causally linked to negative course? If so, which subtypes are casually significant? Or does the broad class of antisocial behaviors constitute a proxy for a host of underlying "third variables" that both precipitate aggressive acts and predict a negative course (R. Barkley, personal communication, September, 1991)?

For example, as we have indicated, the presence of aggression in samples of ADHD youngsters is associated with lowered socioeconomic status (Szatmari, Boyle, & Offord, 1989), with antisocial features in the family histories of biological parents (Lahey et al., 1988), with neuropsychological and motoric delays (Moffitt, 1990), and with negative family climate and discordant parent–child interactions (Cunningham & Barkley, 1979; Paternite et al., 1976). In addition to precipitating aggressive/antisocial behavior, any (or all) of these variables could itself portend a difficult prognosis. Furthermore, the likely state of causal affairs may well be reciprocal or transactional, rather than linear (see Magnusson & Ohman, 1987). A fascinating example of the complexity of the developmental, longitudinal transactions that result in aggressive, delinquent behavior is found in the sophisticated longitudinal report of Moffitt (1990), who followed members of the Dunedin (New Zealand) birth cohort from age 3 to 15.

In predicting self-reported delinquency in early adolescence, Moffitt first found that the subgroup of delinquent adolescents with a history of ADHD symptomatology in childhood had a far earlier onset of antisocial symptoms and a far worse constellation of achievement-related, neuropsychological, and familial concomitants than did non-ADHD delinquent youngsters. Thus, the ADHD-aggressive subgroup was clearly distinct from children with attentional deficits only. Furthermore, in predicting subsequent antisocial behavior, the presence of attention-disordered symptoms in early childhood showed significant statistical interactions with both family adversity and verbal intelligence. That is, discordant homes and lowered verbal skills exacerbated the risk incurred by early ADHD symptoms, whereas advantageous home environments and strong verbal skills apparently served as protective factors. These results suggest strongly that both developmental/ intellectual and familial factors may influence the risk for delinquency that is posed by ADHD, bespeaking the complexity of causal pathways (cognitive, familial, behavioral, and neuropsychological) that link attentional difficulties and aggression.

CASE ILLUSTRATIONS

In presenting two cases of boys with ADHD plus significant aggressive features we hope to illustrate the nature of such psychopathology and describe the toll it takes on such diverse areas as learning potential, self-esteem, family relations, and peer acceptance.

BE is a 12-year-old Native American boy who participated in a summer research program for youngsters with ADHD. BE has been diagnosed with both ADHD and oppositional-defiant disorder (ODD) and has been taking the stimulant medication Ritalin for several years. In addition to his inattentiveness, BE has a long history of aggressive and impulsive behaviors. He is extremely labile emotionally, shifting with extraordinary quickness from happy task involvement to rageful outbursts; his self-esteem is quite low, as indicated by his oft-spoken wishes that he were not alive; and he quite often views himself as a failure. Prior to the summer program, BE's parents went through numerous interviews and provided a detailed description of their son. The parents and BE's current teacher completed several rating scales regarding his levels of hyperactivity and aggression. On the Conners Abbreviated Symptom Questionnaire (Goyette, Conners, & Ulrich, 1978), the mother's and father's scores were 20 and 19, respectively, surpassing the usual cutoff score for hyperactivity of 15. On a checklist including the DSM-III-R symptoms for the disruptive behavior disorders, the parental scores were just below typical cutoffs for ADHD but every symptom for oppositional-defiant disorder was endorsed; on Loney's (1987) modification of the Diagnostic Interview for Children and Adolescents, the parents' responses indicated that BE met criteria for both attention problem disorder and aggressive behavior disorder. Intriguingly, his teacher (of a special day class for learning-handicapped children) described him as quite inattentive and distractable but failed to indicate any aggressive or defiant behaviors. His academic difficulties, according to the teacher, were of primary concern; these could be traced to his distractability, restlessness, and lack of concentration on his work. She did mention that he had some "devious behaviors" such as lying and acting rebelliously toward adults. BE tests as average in verbal intelligence (Wechsler Intelligence Scale for Children-Revised score of 96), yet his academic performance is below grade level (Woodcock–Johnson Psychoeducational Battery scores ranging from the 30th to 40th percentile in reading and mathematics).

BE was adopted at birth by a middle-class Caucasian couple; he has never had contact with his natural parents. Whereas there is limited information about his parents, it has been established that his mother abused alcohol. Although it is unknown whether drinking occurred during the pregnancy, it is quite plausible that this was the case. Indeed, incidence rates of varying degrees of fetal alcohol syndrome for Native Americans are alarmingly high. As discussed in the previous section on etiology, such consumption of alcohol during pregnancy could be a major factor in BE's development of hyperactivity and aggression.

According to both of his adoptive parents, BE began showing signs of hyperactivity at about age 5. He repeated kindergarten and was placed on stimulant medication at age 6. (It is noteworthy that, at one point, he was receiving over 100 mg of Ritalin per day, quite likely an extreme overdose. During the year prior to our summer program, however, he had been reduced to an ineffectively low dosage to prevent any further side effects.) Aggressive features also emerged at this time, and he was caught shoplifting in early elementary school. The presence of both physical aggression and such covert antisocial behaviors as stealing at an early age is a strong predictor of subsequent delinquency (e.g., Robins, 1979).

Key facets of BE's aggressive behavior are his low self-esteem and poor self-image. He always has been sensitive about his ethnicity and often has felt like an outcast among his peers. A dark-skinned Native American boy who lives in a predominately white, upper middle class neighborhood, BE consistently has been ostracized and shunned by his peers, with much of this exclusionary treatment consisting of racial taunts and attacks. His primary method for coping with this maltreatment has been to retaliate with physical fights; indeed, he is prone to becoming verbally and physically provocative with both peers and adults. His contentious attitude coupled with his inferior feelings about his ethnic heritage have contributed greatly to his feelings of isolation and aloneness.

BE's adoptive parents have had major difficulties in managing his behavior for years. The mother, a thin woman with often-exhibited dysphoric affect, often is afraid of his outbursts and can no longer physically contain him. The father, who has been contending with such life stressors as the loss of his job, seems alternately overinvolved in BE's life and puzzled as to which approach to take with him.

The pattern of hostile behaviors, inattentiveness, and rapidly deteriorating self-esteem escalated into more severe difficulties at age 11. BE's aggression worsened and he began manifesting conduct-disordered behaviors. He was again caught shoplifting, robbed a neighbor's home, and set a small fire in a deserted lot. Interestingly, at this same time, his mood was dysphoric and he began showing clear signs of depression. After it was decided that BE should be placed on antidepressants instead of stimulants, BE's behavior and self-esteem worsened; the remorse and guilt he felt about his current actions only heightened his self-hatred. He eventually was hospitalized at an inpatient psychiatric unit for one month. The antidepressant trial was deemed unsuccessful and he resumed taking Ritalin. He returned to the fifth grade that fall and was placed in a special day class.

Although he was no longer suffering from depression and his self-esteem was gradually improving (he also was receiving outpatient therapy), he was still defiant, impulsive, and uncontrollable. BE's reported impulsivity became instantly apparent upon his arrival during the first day of the summer research program. The first phase of the program included a family assessment in which parents and child came in together for a thorough evaluation. BE arrived with his parents, and within 2 minutes he had sneaked out a side door and sprinted down the stairs in an attempt to get out of the campus building. He was caught quickly and brought back to the clinic, devoid of any remorse or fear about his attempted escape but quite angry with staff members. That his parents were within visible distance of him did nothing to temper his brashness; in fact, he disregarded them.

During the summer program, we obtained a comprehensive picture of how BE behaves. Whereas he was oppositional and defiant with adults, he rarely acted in such fashion with peers. Indeed, he was quite popular with agemates even though he never fully associated with the "in" group. He was welcomed by the other boys, but he preferred smaller group projects and one-on-one relationships; his being on the periphery was by his own choice. Given his tumultuous past with regard to peer relations, he may have harbored some anxieties about making new friends; yet, at the same time, he seemed to realize that he was well liked and admired by the other boys.

By the middle of the program, when he became acclimated and less guarded, his impulsive acts were occurring daily. Running away and verbal outbursts were the most frequent manifestations of his impulsivity. He constantly tested the limits administered by the staff and often refused to comply or cooperate. At times he showed little fear about the subsequent consequences; at other times his mood would fluctuate to the other extreme and he expressed remorse about what he had done. Explosive rages would ensue during which he cried and claimed that nobody understood or cared for him. He was convinced that he would be forgotten quickly at the close of the summer program. Twice he verbalized the wish to be dead because, in his words, "it wouldn't matter to anyone if I died." When in the middle of a rage, BE was impossible to calm down. The escalation of these rages often resulted in physical restraint.

By the program's end, we had established that BE performed optimally on a moderate dosage of Ritalin (0.6 mg/kg, more than the dosage he had been receiving for the past year but far less than his overly high level of earlier years). The present school year has been far better than the past two, thanks in part to optimal pharmacological intervention and in part to BE's success in organized tackle football. The family is embarking on a year-long course of behaviorally oriented parent management groups coupled with group treatment of BE and five peers in a cognitive-behavioral format, as part of our research follow-up intervention. Whereas he has shown many risk factors for delinquency, depression, and a generally negative outcome over the years, there is renewed hope in the family that combining pharmacological with psychosocial intervention can change BE's course.

In contrast to the detailed description of BE, we present brief information about AL, a 10-year-old boy who participated in an earlier summer research program. This alternative presentation will give a feel for a different type of boy who is comorbidly aggressive and hyperactive. AL was, in brief, one of the most incredibly aggressive children with whom the authors have ever worked. His immediate family history was "loaded," with an alcoholic father and a depressed mother, who was besieged by his demands and physical threats. He had been a terror at home, in preschool, and in the neighborhood since preschool, having been excluded from many programs throughout his life and having dominated the home setting for years. He was rated, by parents and teachers alike, at the absolute apex of ratings for both inattention/hyperactivity and aggression; he had (not unexpectedly) no friends. His verbal intelligence was quite low—in the middle 70s— leading to the speculation that some of his aggressive tendencies resulted from an inability to employ optimal verbal mediation strategies. Somehow, through high dosages of Ritalin and active intervention by school personnel, he was continuing in regular and special education classes at a public elementary school.

During the summer research program in which he participated, behavior observation procedures revealed that his rates of noncompliant behavior on placebo medication were over 50% of all behavior he exhibited and that his rates of physical/verbal aggression were an incredible 29% of all behavior (note that the overall base rate of such aggression for the ADHD sample was around 3%). Indeed, on the first morning of the program, before medications were administered, AL somehow got into an equipment shed that was designated for staff only, found an old set of golf clubs, and began swinging them wildly around his head (narrowly missing other children) and screaming that "the Libyans are attacking!" There was a similar fervor to much of the aggressive behavior that AL exhibited, lending a feel of an almost manic quality to some of his destructive acts. His predominant interpersonal style was one of bullying and attempting to terrify peers; in addition, he was almost instantaneous in his tendencies to retaliate against even the slightest provocation. He clearly exhibited nearly all of the pertinent subtypes of aggression discussed earlier—peer-directed as well as adult-directed, physical as well as profanely verbal, proactive as well as retaliatory.

On a low dose (0.3 mg/kg) of Ritalin, AL's aggressive behavior reduced to a 3% rate; on a moderate dosage (0.6 mg/kg), the rate was 1%, which was indistinguishable from that of our nonhyperactive comparison youngsters. Yet the damage to his reputation among both staff and peers had been done during the first few days of the program, before the medication trials began; he continued to be regarded as violent and intolerable. Indeed, the effects of aggressive behavior on peer status appear quite quickly—within the first day of contact—and persist quite powerfully (Erhardt, 1991).

Despite the success of optimal dosages of stimulant medication, AL's dearth of social skills, his dismal academic performance, and his quick return to rageful aggression once medication and worn off all bode for a poor long-term course. Indeed, it is hard to believe that he will not become of the subgroup of ADHD youngsters whose subsequent life is plagued by delinquency, adult antisocial behavior, major personality disturbance, and substance abuse (Gittelman et al., 1985; Weiss & Hechtman, 1986).

SUMMARY

We have provided evidence that interpersonal aggression constitutes a major facet of the psychopathology of children with attention-deficit hyperactivity disorder. Indeed, children with ADHD who also are aggressive have family histories, academic achievement deficits, standing with peers, and long-term outcomes that are worse than those of either purely hyperactive or purely aggressive youngsters. Furthermore, although current evidence is limited and although the focus of the field to date has been on the "externalizing" aspects of the antisocial features of ADHD children, there is increasing need to examine the internalizing and even self-destructive aspects of this behavior disorder. Indeed, self-directed aggression and other-directed aggression are more intimately linked than is often acknowledged in child psychopathology; it is likely that causal agents ranging from the biological (see Brown & van Praag, 1991) to the familial (e.g., Hetherington & Martin, 1986) may predispose to destructive behavior directed both toward the self and toward others. Finally, when aggressive features are contained in a disorder (like ADHD) that is distinguished by poor impulse control, poor planning of behavior, and deficient self-regulation, the results are likely to be particularly deleterious to both the individual and those in that individual's interpersonal world.

REFERENCES

Achenbach, T. M., & Edelbrock, C. (1983). *Manual for the Child Behavior Checklist and Revised Child Behavior Profile*. Burlington, VT: Author.

American Psychiatric Association (1980). *Diagnostic and statistical manual of mental disorders*, 3rd Edition. Washington, DC: Author.

American Psychiatric Association (1987). *Diagnostic and statistical manual of mental disorders*, 3rd Edition, Revised. Washington, DC: Author.

American Psychiatric Association (1993). *DSM-IV draft criteria*. Washington, DC: Author.

August, G. J., & Stewart, M. (1983). Familial subtypes of childhood hyperactivity. *Journal of Nervous and Mental Disease, 171*, 362–368.

Barkley, R. A. (1990). *Attention deficit hyperactivity disorder: A handbook for diagnosis and treatment*. New York: Guilford Press.

Barkley, R. A., Fischer, M., Edelbrock, C. S., & Smallish, L. (1990). The adolescent outcome of hyperactive children diagnosed by research criteria: I. An 8-year prospective follow-up study. *Journal of the American Academy of Child and Adolescent Psychiatry, 29*, 546–557.

Barkley, R. A., McMurray, M. B., Edelbrock, C. S., & Robbins, K. (1989). The response of aggressive and nonaggressive ADHD children to two doses of methylphenidate. *Journal of the American Academy of Child and Adolescent Psychiatry, 28*, 873–881.

Biederman, J., Faraone, S. V., Keenan, K., & Tsuang, M. T. (1991). Evidence of familial association between attention deficit disorder and major affective disorders. *Archives of General Psychiatry, 48*, 633–642.

Brandenburg, N. A., Friedman, R. M., & Silver, S. E. (1990). The epidemiology of childhood psychiatric disorders: Prevalence findings from recent studies. *Journal of the American Academy of Child and Adolescent Psychiatry, 29*, 76–83.

Brown, R. T., Borden, K. A., Clingerman, S. R., & Jenkins, P. (1988). Depression in attention deficit-disordered and normal children and their parents. *Child Psychiatry and Human Development, 18*, 119–132.

Brown, S., & van Praag, H. M. (Eds.). (1991). *The role of serotonin in psychiatric disorders*. New York: Brunner/Mazel.

Campbell, S. B. (1990). *Behavior problems in preschool children: Clinical and developmental issues*. New York: Guilford Press.

Caspi, A., & Moffitt, T. E. (in press). The continuity of maladaptive behavior: From description to understanding in the study of antisocial behavior. In D. Cicchetti & C. Cohen (Eds.), *Manual of Developmental Psychopathology*. New York: Wiley.

Cunningham, C. E., & Barkley, R. A. (1979). The interactions of normal and hyperactive children with their mothers in free play and structured tasks. *Child Development, 50*, 217–224.

Dodge, K. A., & Coie, J. D. (1987). Social-information-processing factors in reactive and proactive aggression in children's peer groups. *Journal of Personality and Social Psychology, 53*, 1146–1158.

Douglas, V. I. (1983). Attention and cognitive problems. In M. Rutter (Ed.), *Developmental neuropsychiatry* (pp. 280–329). New York: Guilford Press.

Erhardt, D. (1991). *Behavioral and nonbehavioral predictors of initial sociometric impressions in hyperactive and comparison boys*. Unpublished doctoral dissertation, University of California, Los Angeles.

Farrington, D. P., Loeber, R., & van Kammen, W. B. (1990). Long term criminal outcomes of hyperactivity-impulsivity-attention deficit and conduct problems in childhood. In L. N. Robins & M. Rutter (Eds.), *Straight and devious pathways from childhood to adult life* (pp. 62–81). Cambridge: Cambridge University Press.

Fergusson, D. M., Horwood, L. J., & Lloyd, M. (1991). Confirmatory factor models of attention deficit and conduct disorder. *Journal of Child Psychology and Psychiatry, 32*, 257–274.

Gittelman, R., Mannuzza, S., Shenker, R., & Bonagura, N. (1985). Hyperactive boys almost grown up: I. Psychiatric status. *Archives of General Psychiatry, 42*, 937–947.

Goodman, R., & Stevenson, J. (1989a). A twin study of hyperactivity—I. An examination of hyperactivity scores and categories derived from Rutter teacher and parent questionnaires. *Journal of Child Psychology and Psychiatry, 30*, 671–689.

Goodman, R., & Stevenson, J. (1989b). A twin study of hyperactivity—II. The aetiological role of genes, family relationships and perinatal adversity. *Journal of Child Psychology and Psychiatry, 30*, 691–709.

Goyette, C. H., Conners, C. K., & Ulrich, R. F. (1978). Normative data on revised Conners Parent and Teacher Rating Scales. *Journal of Abnormal Child Psychology, 6*, 221–236.

Hetherington, E. M., & Martin, B. (1986). Family interaction patterns. In H. C. Quay & J. S. Werry (Eds.), *Psychopathological disorders of childhood* (3rd ed., pp. 349–408). New York: Wiley.

Hinshaw, S. P. (1987a). Hyperactivity, attention deficit disorders, and learning disabilities. In V. B. Van Hasselt & M. Hersen (Eds.), *Psychological evaluation of physical and behavioral disabilities* (pp. 213–260). New York: Plenum.

Hinshaw, S. P. (1987b). On the distinction between attentional deficits/hyperactivity and conduct problems/aggression in child psychopathology. *Psychological Bulletin, 101*, 443–463.

Hinshaw, S. P. (1991). Stimulant medication and the treatment of aggression in children with attentional deficits. *Journal of Clinical Child Psychology, 20*, 301–312.

Hinshaw, S. P. (1992). Externalizing behavior problems and academic underachievement in children and adolescents: Causal relationships and underlying mechanisms. *Psychological Bulletin, 111*, 127–155.

Hinshaw, S. P., & Erhardt, D. (1991). Attention-deficit hyperactivity disorder. In P. C. Kendall (Ed.), *Child and adolescent therapy: Cognitive-behavioral perspectives* (pp. 98–128). New York: Guilford Press.

Hinshaw, S. P., Lahey, B. B., & Hart, E. L. (1993). Issues of taxonomy and comorbidity in the development of conduct disorder. *Development and Psychopathology, 5*, 31–49.

Hinshaw, S. P., Heller, T., & McHale, J. P. (1992). Covert antisocial behavior in boys with attention-deficit hyperactivity disorder: External validation and effects of methylphenidate. *Journal of Consulting and Clinical Psychology, 60*, 274–281.

Hinshaw, S. P., Henker, B., Whalen, C. K., Erhardt, D., & Dunnington, R. E. (1989). Aggressive, prosocial, and nonsocial behavior in hyperactive boys: Does effects of methylphenidate in naturalistic settings. *Journal of Consulting and Clinical Psychology, 57*, 636–643.

Jacobvitz, D., & Sroufe, L. A. (1987). The early caregiver-child relationship and attention deficit disorder and hyperactivity in kindergarten: A prospective study. *Child Development, 58*, 1496–1504.

Johnston, C., & Pelham, W. E. (1986). Teacher ratings predict peer ratings of aggression at 3-year follow-up in boys with attention deficit disorder with hyperactivity. *Journal of Consulting and Clinical Psychology, 54*, 571–572.

Lahey, B. B., Placentini, J. C., McBurnett, K., Stone, P., Hartdagen, S., & Hynd, G. (1988). Psychopathology in the parents of children with conduct disorder and hyperactivity. *Journal of the American Academy of Child and Adolescent Psychiatry, 27*, 163–170.

Loeber, R., & Schmaling, K. B. (1985). Empirical evidence for overt and covert patterns of antisocial conduct problems: A metaanalysis. *Journal of Abnormal Child Psychology*, *13*, 337–352.

Loeber, R., Lahey, B. B., & Thomas, C. (1991). Diagnostic conundrum of oppositional defiant disorder and conduct disorder. *Journal of Abnormal Psychology*, *100*, 379–390.

Loney, J. (1987). Hyperactivity and aggression in the diagnosis of attention deficit disorder. In B. B. Lahey & A. E. Kazdin (Eds.), *Advances in clinical child psychology* (Vol. 10, pp. 99–135). New York: Plenum.

Loney, J., Kramer, J., & Milich, R. S. (1981). The hyperactive child grows up: Predictors of symptoms, delinquency, and achievement at follow-up. In K. D. Gadow & J. Loney (Eds.), *Psychosocial aspects of drug treatment for hyperactivity* (pp. 381–415). Boulder, CO: Westview Press.

Magnusson, D. (1987). Adult delinquency in the light of conduct and physiology at an early age: A longitudinal study. In D. Magnusson & A. Ohman (Eds.), *Psychopathology: An interactional perspective* (pp. 221–234). Orlando, FL: Academic Press.

Magnusson, D., & Ohman, A. (1987). *Psychopathology: An interactional perspective*. Orlando, FL: Academic Press.

McGee, R., & Share, D. L. (1988). Attention deficit disorder-hyperactivity and academic failure: Which comes first and what should be treated? *Journal of the American Academy of Child and Adolescent Psychiatry*, *27*, 318–325.

McGee, R., Williams, S., Bradshaw, J., Chapel, J. L., Robins, A., & Silva, P. A. (1985). The Rutter scale for completion by teachers: Factor structure and relationships with cognitive abilities and family adversity for a sample of New Zealand children. *Journal of Child Psychology and Psychiatry*, *26*, 727–739.

Moffitt, T. E. (1990). Juvenile delinquency and attention deficit disorder: Boys' developmental trajectories from age 3 to age 15. *Child Development*, *61*, 893–910.

Olweus, D. (1979). Stability of aggressive reaction patterns in males: A review. *Psychological Bulletin*, *86*, 852–875.

Parke, R. D., & Slaby, R. G. (1983). The development of aggression. In E. M. Hetherington (Series Ed.), *Handbook of child psychology* (Vol. 4, pp. 547–641). New York, Wiley.

Parker, J. G., & Asher, S. R. (1987). Peer relations and later personal adjustment: Are low-accepted children at risk? *Psychological Bulletin*, *102*, 357–389.,

Paternite, C. E., Loney, J., & Langhorne, J. E. (1976). Relationships between symptomatology and SES-related factors in hyperkinetic/MBD boys. *American Journal of Orthopsychiatry*, *46*, 291–301.

Patterson, G. R. (1982). *Coercive family process*. Eugene, OR: Castalia.

Patterson, G. R., de Baryshe, B. D., & Ramsey, E. (1989). A developmental perspective on antisocial behavior. *American Psychologist*, *44*, 329–335.

Pelham, W. E., & Bender, M. E. (1982). Peer relationships in hyperactive children: Description and treatment. In K. D. Gadow & I. Bialer (Eds.), *Advances in learning and behavioral disabilities* (Vol. 1, pp. 365–436). Greenwich, CT: JAI Press.

Pelham, W. E., & Hinshaw, S. P. (1992). Behavioral intervention for attention deficit-hyperactivity disorder. In S. M. Turner, K. S. Calhoun, & H. E. Adams (Eds.), *Handbook of clinical behavior therapy* (2nd ed., pp. 259–283). New York: Wiley.

Pelham, W. E., & Murphy, H. A. (1986). Behavioral and pharmacological treatment of attention deficit and conduct disorders. In M. Hersen (Ed.), *Pharmacological and behavioral treatment: An integrative approach* (pp. 108–148). New York: Wiley.

Price, N., & Dodge, K. A. (1989). Reactive and proactive aggression in childhood: Relations to peer status and social context dimensions. *Journal of Abnormal Child Psychology*, *17*, 455–471.

Puig-Antich, J. (1982). Major depression and conduct disorder in prepuberty. *Journal of the American Academy of Child Psychiatry*, *21*, 118–128.

Quay, H. C. (1986). Classification. In H. C. Quay & J. S. Werry (Eds.), *Psychopathological disorders of childhood* (3rd ed., pp. 1–34). New York: Wiley.

Robins, L. N. (1979). Follow-up studies. In H. C. Quay & J. S. Werry (Eds.), *Psychopathological disorders of childhood* (2nd ed., pp. 483–513). New York: Wiley.

Ross, D. M., & Ross, S. A. (1982). *Hyperactivity: Current issues, research, and theory*. New York: Wiley.

Rutter, M., Tizard, J., & Whitmore, K. (Eds.). (1970). *Health, education, and behaviour*. London: Longmans.

Satterfield, J. H., Hoppe, C. M., & Schell, A. M. (1982). A prospective study of delinquency in 110 adolescent boys with attention deficit disorder and 88 normal adolescent boys. *American Journal of Psychiatry*, *139*, 795–798.

Schachar, R. (1991). Childhood hyperactivity. *Journal of Child Psychology and Psychiatry*, *32*, 155–191.

Sergeant, J. A. (1989). In search of processing deficits of attention in ADD-H children. In L. M. Bloomingdale & J. M. Swanson (Eds.), *Attention deficit disorder* (Vol. 4, pp. 255–272). Oxford: Pergamon Press.

Shaywitz, S. E., Shaywitz, B. A., Fletcher, J. M., & Escobar, M. D. (1990). Prevalence of reading disability in boys and girls: Results of the Connecticut Longitudinal Study. *Journal of the American Medical Association, 264*, 998–1002.

Stattin, H., & Magnusson, D. (1989). The role of early aggressive behavior in the frequency, seriousness, and types of later crime. *Journal of Consulting and Clinical Psychology, 57*, 710–718.

Szatmari, P., Boyle, M., & Offord, D. (1989). ADDH and conduct disorder: Degree of diagnostic overlap and differences among correlates. *Journal of the American Academy of Child and Adolescent Psychiatry, 28*, 865–872.

Szatmari, P., Offord, D. R., & Boyle, M. H. (1989a). Correlates, associated impairments and patterns of service utilization of children with attention deficit disorder: Findings from the Ontario Child Health Study. *Journal of Child Psychology and Psychiatry, 30*, 205–217.

Szatmari, P., Offord, D. R., & Boyle, M. H. (1989b). Ontario Child Health Study: Prevalence of attention deficit disorder with hyperactivity. *Journal of Child Psychology and Psychiatry, 30*, 219–230.

Weiss, G., & Hechtman, L. T. (1986). *Hyperactive children grown up: Empirical findings and theoretical considerations*. New York: Guilford Press.

Werner, E., & Smith, P. (1982). *Vulnerable but invincible: A study of resilient children*. New York: McGraw-Hill.

Whalen, C. K. (1989). Attention deficit-hyperactivity disorder. In T. H. Ollendick & M. Hersen (Eds.), *Handbook of child psychopathology* (2nd ed., pp. 131–169). New York: Plenum.

Whalen, C. K., Henker, B., Buhrmester, D., Hinshaw, S. P., Huber, A., & Laski, K. (1989). Does stimulant medication improve the peer status of hyperactive children? *Journal of Consulting and Clinical Psychology, 57*, 545–549.

Zametkin, A. J., & Rapoport, J. L. (1987). Neurobiology of attention deficit disorder with hyperactivity: Where have we come in 50 years? *Journal of the American Academy of Child and Adolescent Psychiatry, 26*, 676–686.

CHAPTER 21

Conduct Disorder

David J. Kolko

DESCRIPTION OF THE DISORDER

Clinical Significance

Child conduct disorder (CD) is composed of a diverse array of troublesome aggressive and antisocial acts. The behaviors include fighting, stealing, lying, defiance, property destruction, temper outbursts, and other coercive or hostile acts (e.g., threats of violence, sexual aggression). Individually, these behaviors are both common and problematic in their own right. Official crime statistics indicate that more than 1.4 million juveniles in this country were arrested for nonindex crimes (e.g., vandalism, running away) and nearly 900,000 for index crimes (e.g., larceny/theft, robbery) in 1986 (Federal Bureau of Investigation, 1987). Many of these behaviors are pervasive among patient and nonpatient populations (Kazdin, 1985, 1987a). Given their prevalence, antisocial behaviors are quite costly to society. For example, the expected crime and correction costs for a repeated juvenile offender in one report were between $225,000 and $350,000 on a lifetime basis that reflected 1.5 arrests per year over a 13.3-year period of criminal activity (Greenwood, unpublished paper, cited in Shamsie & Hluchy, 1991). The other costs involved are less tangible and include the personal, family, and community impact of serious antisocial behavior.

Antisocial behaviors are of considerable durability. For example, chronicity of these behaviors is reflected in their high frequency, occurrence in multiple settings, diversity, and early onset (Loeber, 1982). Several behaviors, especially aggression and theft/stealing, are quite stable across time in children and adolescents (Loeber, 1990). Even in very young children, fighting is a stable form of disruptive behavior that tends to be associated with

This chapter was supported, in part, by grants from the National Institute of Mental Health (MH-39976) and National Center on Child Abuse and Neglect (CDP2239).

DAVID J. KOLKO • Western Psychiatric Institute and Clinic, University of Pittsburgh School of Medicine, Pittsburgh, Pennsylvania 15213.

Handbook of Aggressive and Destructive Behavior in Psychiatric Patients, edited by Michel Hersen, Robert T. Ammerman, and Lori A. Sisson. Plenum Press, New York, 1994.

heightened ratings of antisocial behavior (Tremblay et al., 1991). Moreover, serious conduct problems have shown consistency within families (Kazdin, 1987a).

Perhaps as a consequence of their stability, antisocial behaviors account for the majority of clinical referrals. In a recent study by Weisz and Weiss (1991), 14 of the 20 most "referable" problems represented individual behaviors associated with CD, with six of the top seven behaviors being vandalism, poor school work, running away from home, truancy, sexual problems, stealing outside the home, and attacking people. Interviews with parents of clinically referred boys suggest that the rates of similar behaviors, such as engaging in fistfights (45%), stealing (18%), or vandalism (17%), are of significant clinical proportions (Loeber, Green, Lahey, & Stouthamer-Loeber, 1991). Epidemiological evidence shows that CD children, specifically boys, are more likely than their non-CD peers to receive mental health/social services and special education (Offord, Boyle, & Racine, 1991). Unfortunately, these individual behaviors are quite resistive to treatment and, thus, all too often convey a poor long-term prognosis (Kazdin, 1987a). Indeed, several CD symptoms (e.g., aggression, stealing, lying, truancy) are strong predictors of delinquency (Loeber, 1990) and are often associated with subsequent problems such as school dropout, poor work histories, substance abuse, marital problems, and adult criminality (see Caspi, Elder, & Bem, 1987; Huesman, Eron, Lefkowitz, & Walder, 1984). That the adverse consequences of antisocial behavior are more frequently experienced by others (e.g., child's parents, teachers, peers) than by the CD children themselves may contribute to a lack of desire for change and, ultimately, limited therapeutic outcomes. A closer examination of the diagnostic criteria of CD may help to articulate the basis for this position.

Diagnosis

The diagnostic criteria for CD are based on the revised *Diagnostic and Statistical Manual of Mental Disorders* (DSM-III-R) (American Psychiatric Association, 1987). The diagnosis is assigned to children who exhibit chronic (i.e., for a period of at least 6 months) violations of social norms and the rights of others. The diagnostic criteria require no specific set of core symptoms for rendering the diagnosis but, rather, simply the presence of at least three individual symptoms. Repeated physical aggression directed toward peers and adults is one of the principal features of CD. Other symptoms include offenses against people (e.g., assault, rape) and property (e.g., stealing, destruction, firesetting), as well as noncriminal status offenses (e.g., lying, running away, truancy). Clearly, the antisocial acts that make up CD convey a heightened potential for physical injury and the use of coercive forms of control.

Apart from the addition of some individual symptoms, the primary difference between DSM-III-R and the prior DSM-III criteria is the absence in DSM-III-R of the aggressive–nonaggressive and socialized–unsocialized dimensions that were used in DSM-III to designate four diagnostic subtypes (see American Psychiatric Association, 1980). Instead, there are three subtypes in DSM-III-R: solitary aggressive type, group type, and undifferentiated type. The solitary aggressive type, which is similar to the undersocialized–aggressive type included in DSM-III, is characterized by persistent physical aggression exhibited by the individual alone. In contrast, the group type, which corresponds to the socialized–nonaggressive type in DSM-III, involves the display of diverse conduct problems in a group context wherein there exists some loyalty to group members. Finally, the undifferentiated type represents a category with diverse clinical features that do not easily reflect those of the two prior subtypes. Recent empirical evidence suggests greater validity to the DSM-III-R than DSM-III criteria for CD in light of their closer association with police contacts, school suspensions, and history of antisocial personality disorder in the parents (Lahey et al., 1990). In terms of differential diagnosis, CD children appear to show similar features and developmental histories to those with oppositional disorder, though they seem to be different disorders (Loeber, Lahey, & Thomas, 1991). There are several worthwhile instruments to facilitate assessment of the diagnostic characteristics associated with CD and various features associated with externalizing disorders (see McMahon & Forehand, 1988).

A few additions to and revisions of these criteria are being proposed in the DSM-IV draft criteria. CD is likely to be based on meeting 3 out of a total of 15 items, as opposed to 13 in DSM-III-R. The 2 new items being proposed reflect bullying, threatening, or intimidating others, and staying out all night despite parental prohibitions. Six of the DSM-III-R items were revised and provide more explicit descriptive or situational details for consideration (i.e., weapons use, lying or breaking promises, stealing items of nontrivial value, engaging in intentional firesetting, and running away from home over-night). The remaining 7 items are primarily unchanged from the original DSM-III-R items. DSM-IV also has proposed two new subtypes based on age of onset, namely, the childhood type (onset of at least one conduct problem before age 10) and the adolescent type (no conduct problems before age 10), and, thus, has eliminated the 3 previous categories of CD. Otherwise, the criteria for establishing the severity of the child's disorder are identical to those of DSM-III-R (i.e., mild, moderate, severe).

Even with the articulation of expanded diagnostic criteria, there is considerable diversity in the level of severity conveyed by these individual symptoms. Psychiatrically hospitalized CD children, for example, exhibit extreme forms of provocative behaviors that may have severe consequences for their "victims" and/or themselves. Not uncommonly, these children have histories of being involved with groups who commit violence or destructive acts that often result in serious physical injuries, using weapons to coerce others, making repeated homicidal threats, and perpetrating serious theft (e.g., cars), among other behaviors. The presence of extreme forms of hostility (e.g., emotional outbursts) and anger-mediated aggression (e.g., retaliation) are among several forms of antisocial behaviors found among child inpatients with CD (Kazdin & Esveldt-Dawson, 1986; Kazdin, Rodgers, Colbus, & Siegel, 1987). In many instances, the histories of antisocial behavior are extensive, despite continued intervention efforts by both the educational and mental health systems. For example, a 2-year follow-up study of hospitalized children found that CD children functioned more poorly at home and at school than non-CD children (Kazdin, 1989), even though both groups showed improvements during hospitalization.

Child Characteristics

The child correlates of CD have been described in numerous empirical studies. Because many of these characteristics have been articulated in several prior reviews (see Kazdin, 1987a; Loeber, 1990; McMahon & Forehand, 1988), an effort is made to elaborate on some of these attributes based on more recent studies.

Patterns of diagnostic comorbidity highlight the relationship of CD to other disorders. The rates of overlap between CD and attention deficit disorder with hyperactivity (ADDH) are variable, but of considerable magnitude (30–60%; e.g., August & Stewart, 1982; Shapiro & Garfinkel, 1986; Szatmari, Boyle, & Offord, 1989). Ratings of aggression and hyperactivity have also been found to be significantly related (mean $r = .56$; Hinshaw, 1987). The addition of ADDH to CD has been associated with heightened behavioral, peer, and family dysfunction (see Milich & Pelham, 1986). For example, the combination of CD/ADDH has been associated with greater antisocial behavior and peer unpopularity than CD alone (Walker, Lahey, Hynd, & Frame, 1987). Compared to heightened aggression alone, the combination of heightened aggression and hyperactivity also has been related to an increased risk for juvenile offenses, delinquency, and the continuation of antisocial behaviors into adulthood (Loeber, 1990), though the absence of differences between these groups also has been found (August & Stewart, 1982). Additional studies using factorial analyses and multiple measures from different sources are needed to document main effects of and interactions between CD and ADDH (e.g., Lahey, Piacentini, McBurnett, Stone, Hartdagen, & Hynd, 1988; Lahey, Russo, Walker, & Piacentini, 1989).

Limited evidence also suggests comorbidity with affective or anxiety disorders, especially major depressive disorder (MDD). Kovacs, Paulauskas, Gatsonis, and Richards (1988) found that 23% of MDD children later developed CD as a complication of the depression. Although comorbid CD did not influence recovery from the index depressive episode, it was associated with greater long-term impairment. Ratings of depression and conduct disorder also have been significantly related in nonreferred children ($r = .73$; Cole & Carpentier, 1990). When comparing the clinical pictures of children with different patterns of comorbidity, children described as showing "affective aggression" were more likely to have a lower I.Q., to receive neuroleptics or lithium, and to have a diagnosis of schizophrenia than those who showed "predatory aggression" (Vitiello, Behar, Hunt, Stoff, & Ricciuti, 1989). CD children with comorbid anxiety disorder exhibit less clinical impairment than those with CD alone (Walker et al., 1991).

Other subtypes of children who exhibit antisocial behavior or severe behavioral disturbances deserve mention because of their conceptual and practical implications. Loeber's (1982) initial distinction between overt or confrontive acts (e.g., fighting, noncompliance) and covert or nonconfrontive acts (e.g., stealing, lying) has been supported in several studies (see Loeber, 1985), with some evidence for "mixed" behaviors (Loeber & Schmaling, 1985a). These two types of problems have emerged in factor analytic studies of child inpatients (Kazdin & Esveldt-Dawson, 1986), and their combination has been associated with heightened family dysfunction (Forehand, Long, & Hedrick, 1987) and risk for delinquency (Loeber & Schmaling, 1985b). Subtypes of aggression based on the children's reactivity (reactive vs. hostile; Coie & Dodge, 1987) or the presence of peer rejection (Bierman, 1986) have been found to differ in severity of behavioral dysfunction.

The other individual correlates of CD are quite broad and complex, implicating problems in interpersonal, cognitive/problem-solving, academic, and self-control skills (e.g., Dishion, Loeber, Stouthamer-Loeber, & Patterson, 1984). These problems include, but are not limited to, extreme defiance, drug use, academic underachievement, depression, impulsivity, and overactivity, as well as limited frustration tolerance, empathy, or guilt (see Kazdin, 1987a; Kolko, 1989; Loeber, 1990). In terms of their peer relationships or social competence, CD children have given evidence of conversational skill deficits (Hansen, St. Lawrence, & Christoff, 1988), aggressive responses to provocation (Dodge, McClaskey, & Feldman, 1985), and deficiencies in their use of positive affect in response to peers (Panella & Henggeler, 1986). Many of these children are rejected by their peers. Peer rejection is associated with both heightened conduct problems and depression (Bierman, 1986; Cole & Carpentier, 1990). Recent evidence regarding the role peer relations failures in delinquent behavior provides an important impetus to examine more carefully the CD child's associations with delinquent peers and the nature of their general social interactions (Patterson, Capaldi, & Bank, 1991).

The relationship between the CD child's social competence and cognitive-perceptual style has been examined extensively (see Dodge, 1990). Consistent evidence has indicated that aggressive children and adolescents show a bias toward misattributing hostile intentions to others or blaming others for aggression, while also minimizing their own aggressivity (Fondacaro, & Heller, 1990; Lochman, 1987). Such misattribution may underlie the tendency to react with hostility or aggression, although, alternatively, it may reflect a consequence of the need to perceive others as coercive when one is persistently in trouble. Other evidence shows that these children may identify few prosocial solutions to interpersonal problems. For example, Lochman and Dodge (1990) reported that aggressive boys had poorer recall of social cues in ambiguous situations and tended to generate fewer assertive solutions to social conflicts than nonaggressive boys.

Children who exhibit conduct problems exhibit a preference for the use of aggression. Aggressive children, for example, acknowledge greater ease in behaving aggressively and greater difficulty in inhibiting aggressive impulses, greater self-confidence in using aggression to both produce positive outcomes and reduce aversive treatment by others (Perry, Perry, & Rasmussen, 1986), and greater value in controlling the victim, showing little concern for victim welfare or retaliation (Boldizar, Perry, & Perry, 1989). However, this style is more pronounced in older aggressive children who label their affective responses as more angry and less sad, whereas the opposite pattern has been found in younger aggressive children (Lochman & Dodge, 1990). Moreover, aggressive and nonaggressive children may actually generate a similar number of assertive or prosocial responses on their first attempt to solve a problem (Evans & Short, 1991; Rabiner, Lenhart, & Lochman, 1990), although their responses may differ on their second attempt (Evans & Short, 1991). Yet, studies are still needed that compare CD children varying in level of aggression and that use observational methods to evaluate their social problem-solving behaviors.

Evaluation of the cognitive characteristics of CD has expanded to include more global attributions for positive and negative events. Curry and Craighead (1990) compared children with a diagnosis of MDD, CD, both diagnoses, or neither diagnosis on measures of attributional style previously related to depression. MDD compared to CD children were less likely to have internal, stable, and global attributions for positive events, but did not differ on the same attributions for negative events. This latter finding is of clinical interest given the potential relationship between CD and MDD, and the possibility that some CD children may perceive themselves as being unable to control aversive events.

CD children are often described as showing limited academic and school performance, although most studies have included aggressive, rather than CD, children (e.g., Goldstein, 1987). One recent study examined the relationship between academic underachievement and both CD and ADDH (Frick et al., 1991). Although both disorders were associated with academic underachievement, logit model analyses revealed that the relationship between CD and underachievement was due to the comorbidity of CD and ADDH. In addition to the use of multivariate analyses, this study is noteworthy for its use of a formula to assess academic underachievement that determined the discrepancy between a child's predicted level of achievement and actual level of achievement, while controlling for regression and age effects.

As noted earlier, many of these correlates may be concomitants of or precursors to the progression toward more serious forms of antisocial behavior. CD may increase the likelihood that a child will experience delinquent acts, illicit drug use, school dropout, violent behavior, severe family conflict, and eventual placement out of the home (Loeber, 1990). Various child antisocial behaviors may precipitate involvement in the special education and/ or juvenile justice systems. All too often, placement in either of these systems generally appears to have an adverse impact on children's adjustment and socialization.

The temporal relationships between these antisocial behaviors are important to understand to document their progression into more serious forms. Recent reviews by Loeber (1990; Loeber and LeBlanc, 1990) describe a developmental perspective on various precursors to antisocial behavior. The earliest precursors include difficult temperament, hyperactivity, and oppositionalism. Other adjustment difficulties (e.g., cognitive biases, social and peer problems, academic failure) seem to emerge after a child has engaged in conduct problems. The relationships between these behaviors are especially linked to several parent and family characteristics.

Parent Characteristics

There is increasing documentation of the nature of parental and family dysfunction among CD children (see Patterson, 1982). Parents may experience psychiatric disorders as adults, including depression and substance abuse (Jary & Stewart, 1985). Two factorial studies examining children with CD and/or ADDH have extended these findings. CD, but not ADDH, was associated with various forms of parental psychopathology, including maternal depression, paternal substance abuse, and antisocial personality disorder (APD) in both parents (Lahey et al., 1988). Fathers of children with both CD and ADDH showed considerably more aggression and criminal behavior than those of children with just CD. CD has also been related to maternal antisocial behavior, histrionic behavior, and disturbed adjustment (Lahey et al., 1989). APD seems to be a significant correlate of the severity of conduct problems in boys (Frick, Lahey, Hartdagen, & Hynd, 1989).

Maternal depression also is associated with other impairments in functioning as well as variations in interaction patterns. In one study of young conduct problem children, depressed mothers perceived their children as more maladjusted than did their spouses or nondepressed mothers, and were more critical than nondepressed mothers (Webster-Stratton & Hammond, 1990). Interestingly, the behavior of children of depressed and nondepressed mothers showed no significant differences. Similarly, observations have shown that CD children of depressed mothers appeared more compliant and less aversive toward their mothers than their fathers, whereas the opposite pattern applied to CD children of nondepressed mothers (Dumas & Gibson, 1990). Thus, maternal depression may exacerbate parent ratings of child dysfunction and may reduce parental tolerance of the child's misbehavior. Of course, level of maternal depression also is a predictor of discontinuity in development among acting-out or withdrawn children (Egeland, Kalkoske, Gottesman, & Erickson, 1990).

Based on considerable evidence (e.g., Loeber & Stouthamer-Loeber, 1986; Patterson, 1986), parents of CD children have exhibited deficits in child management skills (e.g., few positives, many negative comments) and, to some extent, excesses in harsh or inconsistent punishment practices, as well as heightened rejection of their children. Other management skill deficits include limited monitoring and overall use of contingent discipline (Patterson, 1986; Patterson & Bank, 1986). Even among very young children, mothers of children with conduct problems have shown more behavioral inconsistency in responding to incidents involving conflict than mothers of controls (Gardner, 1989). The degree of parental inconsistency was associated with the overall level of family conflict.

In contrast to most studies documenting parent reports, one rare study has examined parental behavior from the perspective of CD children and adolescents. Rey and Plapp (1990) compared adolescents with CD, oppositional disorder, and normal adolescents on a measure of perceived parenting style. There were no differences between the ratings of the two clinical groups, although both groups rated their parents as more overprotective and less caring than the normal group. Other studies that evaluate children's perceptions of parenting skill and practices are needed to elaborate on these modest findings.

Family Characteristics

There is considerable research highlighting the role of family dysfunction in anti-social, aggressive, or CD children (see Loeber & Stouthamer-Loeber, 1986; Patterson, 1986). Among family variables, limited marital adjustment has been found to correlate significantly with child conduct problems in several studies (Jouriles, Bourg, & Farris, 1991; Jouriles, Murphy, & O'Leary, 1989) and is a common clinical problem among families with CD children. This correlation is evidently stronger in families of clinically referred (vs. nonreferred) children and low SES (vs. high SES) status (Jouriles et al., 1991). This association, however, may be mediated by the level of parental APD (Frick et al., 1989). In light of such findings, then, it may be necessary to examine other aspects of parental functioning that may help to account for the child's level of behavioral dysfunction (e.g., substance abuse).

More generally, the presence of coercion and aggression in the families of CD children is well documented (see Patterson, 1982, 1986). Families of CD children often rely upon hostile interchanges to communicate and solve problems, although they also engage infrequently in positive or supportive behaviors. As these interactions become more deviant, physical punishment and family violence may be reported (Patterson, Dishion, & Bank, 1984). The nature of parental aggression in the homes of aggressive children has been described by Lochman and Dodge (1990). In their study, parents of aggressive boys indicated that they and their spouses use more verbal and physical aggression with their children and more verbal aggression during interparental conflicts than parents of non-aggressive boys. This pattern supports prior evidence indicating that aggression is being directed toward all family members.

When parent-to-child aggression reaches extreme proportions, CD children may be at heightened risk for physical maltreatment. Higher rates of child abuse, as well as neglect, have been found among CD than non-CD children (Rogeness, Crawford, & McNamara, 1989). Approximately 55% of a delinquent group and 45% of a status offender group were found to have had a history of maltreatment. Running away was much more common among status offenders who had been sexually abused, whereas involvement in violent crimes was significantly more common among delinquents with a history of physical abuse.

EPIDEMIOLOGY

Epidemiological studies suggest that CD is one of the most prevalent categories of mental health problems of children. In this country, the prevalence of CD has been estimated at 9% for males and 2% for females, making CD the first or second most prevalent childhood disorder (Tuma, 1989). The high prevalence rates for several individual conduct problems and antisocial behaviors (e.g., suspension, fighting, lying) have been documented in clinical interviews with child outpatients and their parents and teachers (Loeber et al., 1991).

Based on a large study of Canadian youth (ages 4–16), the prevalence of CD using criteria most similar to those in DSM-III ranged from 6.5% to 10.4% for males, and 1.8% to 4.1% for females, with an overall rate of 5.5% (Offord et al., 1991). It should be noted that these findings are based on parent and teacher reports for behaviors that were rated as having occurred either "sometimes" or "very often." The most common problems included violations of social norms (e.g., school disobedience, lying/cheating) and aggressive behaviors (e.g., getting into many fights, being mean to others). This study also found the 6-month prevalence rate for one or more of the four major childhood disorders to be 18.1% (Offord et al., 1987). Variables such as large number of siblings, family dysfunction, and male sex were independently related to the presence of CD. Other problems, such as poor school performance, chronic child health problems, substance use, and suicidal behavior, were among the morbidities associated with this disorder (Offord, Boyle, Fleming, Monroe-Blum, & Rae-Grant, 1989).

ETIOLOGY

Psychosocial Perspectives

The processes that support the development and maintenance of antisocial behavior and CD have been the focus of numerous empirical studies. Patterson's (1982, 1986) seminal work provided support for a social-interactional perspective whereby child antisocial behavior is fostered by the family's interactional style. In essence, this perspective emphasizes the reinforcement of coercive family behaviors through the use of noncontingent reinforcement and punishment, along with limited monitoring and irritable exchanges. Children learn that aversive behaviors terminate undesirable family interactions and, at the same time, that positive behaviors are infrequently encouraged. The importance of inept parenting practices in the etiology of antisocial or CD children continues to receive support (see Patterson, Reid, & Dishion, 1992).

A recent extension of this approach has articulated components in the developmental progression of antisocial behavior (Patterson, DeBaryshe, & Ramsey, 1989). The model posits that poor parental discipline and monitoring result in child conduct problems in early childhood that may result in rejection by normal peers and academic failure by middle childhood. Rejection and academic failure appear to foster a child's commitment to a deviant peer group, which may then result in delinquent activities. Clearly, variations in parental practices may be associated with the emergence of different types of antisocial behaviors (Loeber & Stouthamer-Loeber, 1986; Patterson, 1982; Patterson & Bank, 1986; Patterson, Dishion, & Bank, 1984). Specifically, parents of aggressors have been observed to be more punitive, to overclassify deviant behavior, and to fail to punish coercive behavior, while parents of stealers have appeared to be more distant, tend to underclassify, and fail to punish property offenses. Because this model links different developmental periods, it may help to account for the age-related progression from trivial antisocial acts to more serious delinquent activities, and diversification toward more antisocial behaviors across both time and settings (Loeber, 1985; Patterson, 1982). Moreover, the model also suggests potential disruptors of parenting skill or family management practices, such as the presence of antisocial parents or grandparents (e.g., explosive reactivity), adverse family demographics (e.g., low income and education), and family stressors (e.g., marital conflict/divorce). The array of rigorous studies evaluating this model is impressive.

Variations in family process have figured in other etiological perspectives. A history of abuse and neglect has been associated with an earlier onset of delinquent behavior (Rivera & Widom, 1990), but not the age at first arrest for a violent offense. Among delinquent offenders, a history of abuse or family violence has been associated with adult violent crime (Lewis, Lovely, Yeager, & Femina, 1989; Rivera & Widom, 1990), whereas, in contrast to other studies, juvenile violence failed to predict adult violence (Lewis et al., 1989).

Recent evidence suggests that there are variations in the paths toward antisocial outcomes (see Loeber, 1990; Loeber & LeBlanc, 1990). Three paths have been contrasted. Children described as "versatile" generally show an earlier onset, exhibit hyperactivity and impulsivity, evince poor social skills, and exhibit multiple conduct problems. These children were most likely to have juvenile records of delinquent involvement. Property abusers were less aggressive and disturbed overall, but they had delinquent peers. Finally, the exclusive substance abuser group did not show early conduct problems. Loeber (1990) implied that evaluating children's abilities to cope with and master various developmental tasks (e.g., arrival of sibling, doing homework, passing tests, resisting peer pressure) that occur at different age periods might help to clarify the characteristics of these different paths. Such information may reveal limitations in coping that may "derail" a child's readiness to handle subsequent tasks.

An understanding of other contextual factors affecting a child (e.g., physical strength, development of personality traits, sexual maturation, opportunities for crime) may provide useful clues as to why some children progress to higher forms of deviant behavior, whereas others may desist in their conduct problems (see Loeber & LeBlanc, 1990). From a social-information perspective, hostile attributional biases are among the intrapersonal factors associated with undersocialized CD and reactive forms of aggressive behavior (Dodge, 1990; Dodge, Price, Bachorowski, & Newman, 1990). Such conditions are associated with increased involvement in violent interpersonal crimes, and are not mediated by an adolescent's level of intelligence or SES status. These factors may influence children's involvement in coercive interactions with their mothers and other adults. Indeed, some theoretical and empirical evidence has been interpreted to suggest that parental influences are reactions to, rather than precipitants of, the CD child's deviant behavior (Lytton, 1990). At the same time, sufficient evidence also indicates that parental influences, notably, insensitivity to the child's behavior, may "set the stage" for the onset of a child's misbehavior and its subsequent impact on parental reactivity (Wahler, 1990). Clearly, a cogent case can be made for the presence of reciprocal influences (child ↔ parent ↔ social system) that support an interactional perspective on the development of CD (see Dodge, 1990).

Biological Perspectives

There is emerging support for the role of biological vulnerabilities that may be associated with aggressive and antisocial behavior. Gray's (1982, 1987) two factor biobehavioral theory of antisocial behavior suggests that CD is the product of heightened activity in the behavioral activation system and limited activity in the behavioral inhibition system. Because these systems are associated with the hypothalamic–pituitary–adrenal (HPA) axis, measures of biological function related to the HPA axis have been examined in CD children. At present, there is evidence to suggest that the combination of CD and anxiety disorder is associated with greater salivary cortisol than CD alone, suggesting greater ability to inhibit behavior in the combined group (McBurnett et al., 1991). However, measures of 24-hour urinary-free cortisol did not differentiate normal, CD, and attention deficit disordered children, although urinary-free cortisol was related to long reaction times on a continuous performance task (Kruesi, Schmidt, Donnelly, Hibbs, & Hamburger, 1989).

CD children have also been found to have a lower heart rate than those with separation anxiety and to have lower blood pressures than children with major depression (Rogeness, Cepeda, Macedo, Fischer, & Harris, 1990). Reduced adrenergic function has likewise been implicated in the finding that children with CD have lower concentrations of plasma dopamine beta hydroxylase (DBH) than those with MDD (Rogeness, Javors, Maas, & Macedo, 1990). Whereas low levels of DBH have been associated with ADD, high levels were associated with a history of abuse or neglect (Rogeness, Crawford, & McNamara, 1989). Neuropsychological tests with CD adolescents have revealed greater problems on measures that are sensitive to frontal lobe (e.g., conceptual perseveration, poorly sustained attention, impaired motor tasks), but not non–frontal lobe, dysfunction (Lueger & Gill, 1990).

Recent evidence based on violent adults may facilitate our understanding of childhood CD. In terms of the serotonergic system, some evidence suggests that low cerebrospinal fluid (CSF) 5-hydroxyindoleacetic acid may be associated with a history of suicide attempts (Virkkunen, DeJong, Bartko, Goodwin, & Linnoila, 1989), parental alcoholism (Linnoila, DeJong, & Virkkunen, 9189) or a repeated violent offense (Virkkunen et al., 1989). The pattern of lower lumbar CSF serotonin metabolite (5-HIAA) concentrations in children with disruptive disorders versus obsessive compulsive disorder is in accord with these adult findings (Kruesi et al., 1990). However, it bears mentioning that these lower 5-HIAA concentrations were significantly (and inversely) associated with only a few of the measures of aggression that were collected and were not associated with either stress or social competence, as would be expected. Decreased somatostatin has also been found in disruptive behavior-disordered patients versus obsessive–compulsive children (Kruesi, Swedo, Leonard, Rubinow, & Rapoport, 1990). In terms of other hormonal measures, testosterone has been found in military veterans to be associated with heightened aggressivity (Dabbs, Frady, Carr, & Besch, 1987). Studies are now needed with children to determine the generalizability of this finding and the relationship between measures of biological functioning and child antisocial behavior. The outcomes of these investigations would no doubt encourage integrative conceptualizations by advancing a biopsychosocial approach to antisocial behavior.

AGGRESSION TOWARD SELF

Descriptions of CD children who exhibit self-directed aggression appear to be scarce. Because of their exposure to family training, history of reinforcement for coercive behavior, and general lack of introspection or the experience of "negative" affect, it is not surprising that CD children direct their aggressive behaviors outwardly. At the same time, CD has been found to be a common disorder among suicidal youth (Cairns, Peterson, & Neckerman, 1988; Pfeffer, Plutchik, & Mizruchi, 1983). In the Cairns et al. study, nearly 80% of the boys and 65% of the girls who exhibited suicidal behavior had a CD diagnosis. Many of these boys and girls had victimized their parents, parental substitutes, and peers in various ways, suggesting that suicidality was found among those youth who were severely aggressive. Assaultive psychiatric inpatients have also been found to express suicidality (Pfeffer et al., 1983). Of clinical interest was the fact that the severity of suicidality was related to the severity of parental assaultiveness. Moreover, children with some form of suicidality had been exposed to greater parental suicidality, highlighting the importance of examining parental behavior (Pfeffer et al., 1983). In general, suicidal youth have presented with a broad range of internalizing and externalizing symptoms (see Brent & Kolko, 1990). There seems to be a subgroup of adolescents who do not experience feelings of hopelessness, but who have been observed to engage in more antisocial behavior and to make impulsive suicidal acts (Brent, 1987).

AGGRESSION TOWARD OTHERS

There is a substantial literature on aggression in children and adolescents (see Dodge, 1990; Pepler & Rubin, 1991). As has been implicated with CD children, there are multiple influences on the level of aggression exhibited, such as the child's neurologic status, level of social reasoning, family support of coercion, and exposure to models in the child's peer group or the media (see Crowell, Evans, & O'Donnell, 1987).

Beyond additional descriptions of the background features of highly aggressive children, it is important to promote an understanding of the functions of aggression and ways in which aggression can be characterized. Evans and Scheuer (1987) examine various determinants of aggression and suggest ways to analyze these behaviors. They suggest that clinicians attend to specific parameters or processes that may influence its expression, as follows: (1) knowledge of one's victim, (2) role of affect (e.g., anger vs. fear), (3) self-control deficits, (4) active versus passive aggression, (5) the communicative functions of aggression, and (6) aggression as an alternative to prosocial behavior. These concepts may facilitate an appreciation for the range of aggressive responses in children's repertoires.

CLINICAL MANAGEMENT

Much has been written regarding the many significant characteristics and correlates of CD that need to be considered in selecting assessment targets for treatment (see Goldstein & Keller, 1987; Kazdin, 1987a; McMahon, 1987; McMahon & Forehand, 1988). Briefly, treatment is likely to be expedited if a comprehensive diagnostic formulation is supplemented with information from multiple sources and domains, such as an academic evaluation, the child's repertoire of both deviant and prosocial behaviors, family social/psychiatric history (e.g., developmental progress, family events, medical problems, family resources), and responses to standardized self-report instruments. By underscoring the complexity of CD, these authors have expanded the context and foci of treatment to include interdependent systems, approaches, and procedures (e.g., Horne & Sayger, 1990; Miller & Prinz, 1990; Patterson et al., 1989). Because there is an extensive literature describing and documenting the efficacy of treatment with CD and antisocial children, much of this work is not reviewed here (see Dumas, 1989; Kazdin, 1987a, 1987b; Kolko, 1989; Lochman, 1990; Miller & Prinz, 1990; Shamsie & Hluchy, 1991). Instead, special considerations and recommendations are noted to facilitate program development and application.

Selection of and Coordination between Treatment Settings

One very basic component in the delivery of services for CD children concerns the setting in which treatment is delivered. Clearly, there are several levels of care within the mental health system (see Tuma, 1989) whose applicability may be determined by the severity of the child's antisocial behavior and family dysfunction/instability, among other variables. Accordingly, inpatient settings are often needed for the more severe CD children who require constant monitoring, protection, and intensive treatment; day treatment/partial hospitalization programs generally serve CD children who may benefit from specialized academic and behavioral programming; and outpatient clinics usually serve those children and their families who can be maintained in the community with minimal involvement in treatment. The ability to use these settings according to need is important because the course of CD can be both volatile and unpredictable. In particular, specialized programs, such as day treatment or partial hospitalization, may offer intermediate levels of care that can provide intensive treatment services while the child is maintained in the community. Thus, selection of an optimal initial level of care is important to assure that the services received are the most appropriate and advantageous.

Of course, other systems involving children offer additional resources that may facilitate treatment (Tuma, 1989). CD children are commonly noted to have had prior contact with other systems, such as educational services (e.g., school psychologist), medical/health centers (e.g., emergency rooms), child welfare agencies (protective services, placement), juvenile justice (e.g., probation), and community-based programs (e.g., churches, boys clubs). To the extent that the services provided in these systems can be integrated to form a continuum of care, there may be a greater opportunity to address multiple contextual problems and improve long-term outcomes.

Irrespective of setting, efforts to treat CD children and their families have broadened to include several complementary approaches. For example, behavioral family/systems interventions generally teach parents to administer contingent consequences and to interact positively with their children. Overall, these interventions have been found to improve parental practices and child conduct problems (see Dumas, 1989; Kazdin, 1987a, 1987b). Therapeutic extensions of this approach have emphasized the need to address various cognitive-behavioral considerations in the family, such as building rapport and addressing dysfunctional parental cognitions (DiGiuseppe, 1988; Horne & Sayger, 1990).

Crisis Management/Control of Aggression

A prerequisite to initiating an intervention program is a clear policy and therapeutic approach for managing aggressive incidents. To address factors that perpetuate repeated incidents, one recent model offers a hierarchy of responses at different points in the process (e.g., ambulatory restraints, special "me-time," verbal control, seclusion) (Maier, Stava, Morrow, Van Rybroek, & Bauman, 1987). Clearly, adequate preparation of staff to handle aggressive and violent behavior is an important consideration in working with CD children. In controlled settings, seclusion and restraint are common approaches in the acute management of aggression.

Contingency Management/Response Consequences

Work with CD children often requires continuous observation of their deviant and desirable behaviors in order to apply judicious consequences accordingly. Especially pertinent to group programs, the use of prohibitions and punishing consequences for negative behavior has been found to enhance the impact of skills training efforts (Bierman, Miller, & Stabb, 1987). Routine, response feedback is necessary to help CD children learn how to inhibit their behavior and to develop prosocial repertoires. To reduce serious antisocial behavior, time-out and seclusion procedures may be needed (Gair, Bullard, & Corwin, 1984; Romoff, 1987; Soloff, 1987). More complex systems of home or clinic management using token or point systems may be needed to address multiple target behaviors, though it is sometimes difficult to identify effective consequences (see Kazdin, 1982; Kolko, 1992). For this reason, there should be a careful assessment of desired reinforcers and the availability of multiple reinforcers (e.g., a program "store" or home "reward drawer"), with similar attention being devoted to a clarification of effective punishers (e.g., items or privileges that can be removed). Surprisingly, little research has examined the application of contingent consequences with CD children in recent years.

Child Training in Cognitive-Behavioral Skills: Social, Problem Solving, and Self-Control

As mentioned earlier, CD children have difficulties inhibiting their deviant behavior and are often reinforced for aggressive, antisocial behaviors. Skills training provides opportunities to develop and then expand the CD child's prosocial repertoire since deficient interpersonal (e.g., Hansen, St. Lawrence, & Christoff, 1988) or problem-solving skills (e.g., Lochman, 1987; Rabiner et al., 1990) are common in this group. Social skills training (SST) has emphasized specific techniques (e.g., instructions, modeling, behavioral rehearsal or role playing, performance feedback, social/tangible reinforcement) designed to teach discrete social, interpersonal, and anger-control skills on an individual (Bornstein, Bellack, & Hersen, 1980) or group basis (Goldstein & Glick, 1987; Hansen, St. Lawrence, & Christoff, 1989; Kolko, Loar, & Sturnick, 1990). When adequate numbers of children are available, group training may offer some advantages by providing exposure to multiple role-plays, peers, and trainer, and the ability to use group process and social interactions as material for discussion.

Several procedural and substantive components may enhance treatment process and, possibly, outcome: (1) train skills that address idiosyncratic targets in the sample (e.g., helping, sharing, providing positive support, being empathic, showing affection) (Dubow, Huesmann, & Eron, 1987; Goldstein & Glick, 1987; Hansen et al., 1989; Kolko et al., 1990); (2) use salient audiovisual materials and specialized tasks (Bierman & Furman, 1984; Hardwick, Pounds, & Brown, 1985); (3) develop problem scenarios with increasingly more relevance to persons and conflicts in the child's natural environment (e.g., parents, teachers, peers); (4) train children using multiple partners to enhance the realism and functional significance of training (Dubow et al., 1987; Goldstein & Glick, 1987); and (5) encourage involvement in and satisfaction with peer relationships (Bierman & Furman, 1984). Overall, the results of these studies have been mixed, in that improvements in social behavior or skill may not always be associated with reduced antisocial behavior (see Dumas, 1989; Kolko, 1988).

To address limited use of cognitive-mediational strategies to regulate behavior, CD children have been taught individual problem-solving skills (e.g., problem definition, goals, waiting, generating solutions, consideration of consequences, implementation) (Camp & Ray, 1984; Kendall & Braswell, 1985; Spivack & Shure, 1982). In general, they have been taught to think constructively about personal situations and then to practice effective solutions for subsequent application on an outpatient (e.g., Pepler, King, & Byrd, 1991; Yu, Harris, Solovitz, & Franklin, 1986) or inpatient basis (Kazdin, Bass, Siegel, & Thomas, 1989; Kazdin, Esveldt-Dawson, French, & Unis, 1987a, 1987b; Kendall, Reber, McLeer, Epps, & Ronan, 1990). The use of specialized targets (e.g., empathy), materials (e.g., observing modeling videotapes), and methods (e.g., setting behavioral goals, *in vivo* practice) may expedite training (see Kazdin et al., 1989; Lochman, Burch, Curry, & Lampron, 1984; Lochman & Curry, 1986). The program described by Pepler et al. (1991) is noteworthy for its explicit training of various social and problem-solving skills (e.g., knowing feelings, responding to teasing) and its incorporation of various problem-solving steps (e.g., encoding, interpretation, response evaluation). In general, these programs have demonstrated some success in improving children's home or school behavior (Kazdin, 1987a; Kolko, 1992; Lochman, 1988, 1990). Yet, many CD or aggressive children continue to experience significant adjustment difficulties and may not show clinically significant reductions in externalizing symptoms or improved problem-solving or social skills (Kazdin et al., 1989; Pepler et al., 1991).

Attention to Parents' Repertoires and Adjustment

Parental involvement is a critical component in the treatment of CD children given their limited parenting practices and experience of significant psychiatric disturbances (Griest & Wells, 1983; Patterson, 1976, 1982). Parent training is among the most common services for CD children and may include several components: (1) training in social learning or behavior principles (Patterson, Reid, Jones, & Conger, 1975); (2) exposure to observational recording techniques; (3) discussion and supervised practice of primary management techniques (e.g., commands/warnings, attending/ignoring, positive reinforcement, time-out and response cost, play or daily review of events), among other procedures; (4) home and clinic application; and (5) development and revision of home-based contingencies. Access to *in vivo* therapist modeling of consequences and reviews of skill use at home in selected activities, such as family meetings, are some of the supplemental procedures that may promote parental skills. Empirical support for this type of intervention has been found in several studies (e.g., Fleischman, 1982; Fleischman & Szykula, 1981).

Programmatic extensions of this technology have made training more accessible and/ or applicable to the parents of CD children. The developments reflect the use of therapist-led group training (Webster-Stratton, 1984, 1985; Weinrott, Bauske, & Patterson, 1979), special audiovisual training (Webster-Stratton, Hollinsworth, & Kolpacoff, 1989) and reading materials (Barkley, 1987; Dangel & Polster, 1988; Fleischman, Horne, & Arthur, 1983), and methods to minimize resistance or increase engagement (Chamberlain & Baldwin, 1987). When offered in the context of a parent education and support program, these adjunctive services may help to enlist cooperation, reduce client expenses, and enhance the pertinence of training for each individual family.

Methods designed to enhance parental adaptation play a significant role in enhancing the clinical impact of parent training programs (see Forehand, 1986; Miller & Prinz, 1990). Treatment of concurrent parental dysfunction (e.g., maternal depression, paternal substance abuse) may be needed to enhance the parent's effectiveness and motivation (Dumas, 1989). Parallel to the application of problem-solving skills training with children, parental cognitive and affective repertoires, such as problem-solving attributions, beliefs, and distortions, as they relate to routine child-rearing situations, have been directly targeted. For example, greater attention has been paid to clinical strategies for understanding and then modifying parents' problematic constructions of and affective reactions to specific child incidents (DiGuiseppe, 1988). More globally, parents' abilities to cope with stressful circumstances are being developed by enhancing their communication skills and attentional processes, level of marital/social support, and the quality of their extrafamilial relationships (e.g., Wahler & Dumas, 1987, 1989). Potential options for accomplishing these outcomes include providing respite care, designing special family outings, or teaching parents to understand and discuss their responses to difficult situations. Finally, methods for improving generalization of parental skills to naturalistic contexts have been found to be effective, such as teaching parents how to manage child misbehavior in novel settings using planned activities (Dadds, Sanders, & James, 1987).

Targeting Family Members and Contextual Factors

Parent–child interventions recently have expanded to include interventions that target different family members or the family unit as a whole (see Miller & Prinz, 1990). Family interventions have been developed that incorporate cognitive and behavioral procedures (DiGuiseppe, 1988; Horne & Sayger, 1990; Szykula, 1987) and are consistent with the broad therapeutic context of a family-systems model (Alexander & Parson, 1982). In some applications, factors influencing individual or family functioning across broad domains have been targeted (see Henggeler & Borduin, 1990). This approach has offered clinical directions for gaining rapport with difficult clients, offering a structured plan for the use of reinforcers and punishers, conducting family problem-solving and negotiation tasks, and ascertaining children's views about their misbehavior and parental reactions.

In light of the focus upon dysfunctional interactions across domains, reciprocal influences between CD children and their parents/siblings have received much attention. One important clinical implication of this approach is the setting of priorities for treatment that will address primary problems within any given domain. Some of the more contemporary priorities that appear relevant based on clinical experience are worthy treatment targets in their own right, notably, child maltreatment, domestic and family violence, limited family income and resources, school breakdown, heightened family instability and chaos, the incarceration of family members, and neighborhood crime and violence (see Dumas, 1989; Kazdin, 1987a; Kolko, 1992; Webster-Stratton, 1990).

Results of empirical studies suggest some benefit to such an ecological approach with antisocial adolescents and their families (Henggeler et al., 1986). Henggeler et al. (1986) found that an individualized family treatment program directed toward various domains (child, parent, family) was more effective than general mental health treatment on measures of child behavior and family interaction. One recent study with delinquents provides an illustration of the potential breadth, complexity, and intensity of parent-training in the context of family intervention (Bank, Marlowe, Reid, Patterson, & Weinrott, 1991). Parents, along with their delinquent adolescents, were extensively trained to address multiple adolescent (e.g., defiance, homework, drug use) and parent targets (e.g., marital discord, external crises) using numerous monitoring and disciplinary procedures that were reviewed both in-session and on the phone. Relative to community controls, the intensive parent–child training intervention resulted in quicker control over serious delinquent behavior with less use of incarceration. This study is noteworthy for several features, specifically, its incorporation of multiple family members (parents, children), methods (contracts, work details), services (training, calls), and measures (offense reports, home observations). Moreover, such efforts lend support to the extension of treatment to various systems influencing the CD child and an expansion in both the scope and duration of treatment as family needs dictate.

Multicomponent and Multisystem "Packages"

Programs that incorporate diverse procedures may be the most likely to impact on different aspects of the child's adjustment. Some programs have taught different cognitive and behavioral skills to children (Dubow et al., 1987; Feindler, Ecton, Kingsley, & Dubey, 1986; Nardone, Tryon, & O'Connor, 1986). For example, one program provided training in social skills, imagery/self-instructions, and cue-controlled relaxation; it also reviewed homework and administered incentives to maximize outcome (Baum, Clark, McCarthy, Sandler, & Carpenter, 1986). A structured learning approach to teaching prosocial skills, anger control, and moral education also has been developed (Goldstein & Glick, 1987). Other features added to that basic program, including communication training, contracting, and contingent management (Goldstein & Keller, 1987), require further empirical evaluation to document their utility. The breadth of these comprehensive programs may be needed to develop the CD child's limited cognitive and behavioral repertoire.

Other programs have targeted two or more systems. The combination of child problem-solving skills training and parent management training (PMT) (e.g., positive reinforcement, contracting, time-out) has been used effectively with hospitalized children (Kazdin, Esveldt-Dawson, et al., 1987b), whereas child anger-coping skills training and teacher consultation have shown no relative improvements over skills training alone (Lochman, Lampron, Gemmer, Harris, & Wyckoff, 1987). The effects of PMT in reducing child conduct problems have been enhanced through the inclusion of partner-support training in marital communication, problem solving, and conflict-resolution skills (Dadds, Sanders, Behrens, & James, 1987; Dadds, Schwartz, & Sanders, 1987).

Despite their potential significance, few applications have concurrently targeted school and home settings (see Blechman, 1987; Blechman, Kotanchik, & Taylor, 1981). One early study found that academic intervention resulted in greater improvements on several desirable outcomes (less school disruption, more positive teacher attention) than social skills training (Coie & Krehbiel, 1984). A school-based program described by Hawkins and Lishner (1987) is noteworthy due to its inclusion of four components targeting different systems (family, classroom, peer, and community services). This multisystems approach was found to impact positively on the child's academic, antisocial, and peer-directed behaviors. Certainly, attention to multiple etiologic factors may be needed to produce maximum effectiveness on these and other adjustment indicators. The focus on parent training, child social skills training, and academic remediation is consistent with recent recommendations offered by Patterson et al. (1989) for prevention of antisocial behavior.

Programming for Generalization/Maintenance

Skills training has the potential to enhance generalization and maintenance. In light of the CD child's learning and motivational difficulties, skills training programs have incorporated procedures to enhance the external use of novel behaviors, such as the use of multiple partners, role-play scenarios (Goldstein & Glick, 1987; Goldstein & Keller, 1987; Hansen et al., 1989; Pepler et al., 1991), or *in vivo* monitoring and enhancement procedures during hospitalization (Kazdin et al., 1989; Kolko et al., 1990). Kazdin et al.'s (1989) study provides an excellent example of the explicit attention that can be placed upon monitoring and then reviewing children's use of problem-solving skills in difficult in vivo situations. Other studies of parent training procedures have employed generalization procedures with good results (Dadds, Sanders, et al., 1987; Dadds, Schwartz, & Sanders, 1987). Of course, teachers and other school officials, as well as community parents, could become potential change agents and/or sources that report on a child's skill use and overall adjustment in the community.

Use of Medication

The benefit of medication with CD children has been difficult to determine because so few studies have been conducted. In general, the evidence suggests moderate improvement, although mixed results have also been reported (see Stewart, Myers, Burket, & Lyles, 1990). Medications appearing to have some promise include haloperidol, lithium, and Ritalin. A few experimental studies have suggested that the aggressive features of children with ADDH have been well controlled with Ritalin (e.g., Klorman, Brumaghim, Salzman, Strauss, Borgstedt, McBride, & Loeb, 1988), which, in one case, included verbal and physical aggression, as well as more general disruptive–noncompliant behaviors (Gadow, Nolan, Sverd, Sprafkin, & Paolicelli, 1990). More recent evidence with nine aggressive CD and ADDH children is in accord with this outcome (Kaplan, Busner, Kupietz, Wasserman, & Segal, 1990). Of course, as has been found in the treatment of ADDH (Pelham, Schnedler, & Bender, 1988), the combination of pharmacological and psychosocial interventions with CD seems to be preferred to either method alone (Stewart et al., 1990). Some of the benefits to the use of medication with CD children may reflect greater control of impulsive or verbally abusive behavior, and increased attention to conversational stimuli or interpersonal situations. Increased behavioral controls may permit the CD child to be more accessible or receptive to skills-based, psychosocial interventions. Controlled studies of this nature with CD children, preadolescents, and outpatient populations, and the collection of multiple measures of dysfunction and adjustment would enhance the existing literature on this topic.

Other Clinical/Therapeutic Considerations

Because clinical work with CD children and their families is quite difficult, if not impossible at times, identification of the issues that influence the nature and outcome of treatment is a clinical prerequisite. Several of these considerations, which are frequently implicated in recent treatment studies, are listed below:

1. The impact of child and/or parent treatment on family functioning needs to be examined, especially the nature of the reciprocal influence between CD children and their families. The extent to which changes in family structure and functioning are in accord with desired therapeutic outcomes is of applied significance given the types of side effects that may occur (see Jacobson, 1985; Lytton, 1990).

2. The growing importance of family contextual or "ecological" variables noted earlier highlights the need to consider treatment with families of CD children as a constantly changing process (Mash, 1989). The process is frequently marked by alterations in the severity of child and parent functioning that often reflect the onset of sudden and serious crises (e.g., suspensions, family violence) and/or transitional events (e.g., placement, family structure changes), as well as more chronic conditions (e.g., parental criminality or drug use, marital discord). The instability caused by these family disruptions generally demands considerable therapist flexibility and, in some instances, a temporary shift in the direction that treatment has taken (see Webster-Stratton, 1991).

3. Largely because of the previous point, there is a need to forge systemic linkages

during, and usually after, treatment. A liaison with the educational or juvenile justice systems, for example, may enhance the clinical potency or urgency of mental health treatment. Of course, in some instances, these systems have already had some unsuccessful or limited involvement with the child prior to the referral process.

4. More information is needed concerning the general adjustment of the CD child and his family to common developmental tasks. Some data have identified difficulties as to how these children adjust to new peer groups or school situations (see Dodge, 1986) and how children more generally cope with stress (Compas, 1987). An understanding of the ways in which CD children and their parents interact in nondisciplinary contexts (e.g., play, personal conversations, or talk during meals) and cope with specific tasks (e.g., handling schoolwork) would identify other targets for intervention (e.g., hostile or coercive behavior, limited home activities) (see Loeber, 1990). A practical and therapeutic illustration of the clinical utility of home interactional data in routine situations is found in the work of Dadds, Sanders, et al. (1987).

5. The timing, format, and composition of intervention programs require articulation. Where we intervene and with what methods or approaches is often determined by our own conceptual and therapeutic predictions. It seems important to understand not only whether there are added benefits to using diverse interventions, but also whether the efficacy of specific interventions is maximized at a specific time (see Loeber, 1990). Moreover, continued investigation of the relative utility of combinations of intervention components is needed to determine those packages that are the most effective in addressing specific problems. Beyond the integration of parent training, child social skills instruction, and academic remediation (e.g., Patterson et al., 1989), other adjunctive components may be needed to target related problems (e.g., medication, marital treatment).

6. By addressing the aforementioned variables, treatment programs may become more individualized and, hopefully, more attentive to behavioral and systems variables that influence or mediate treatment outcome (see Buchard & Clark, 1990; Mash, 1989). This emphasis should extend to a better understanding of clients' background histories (e.g., ethnicity, cultural values) as mediators of treatment (Boyd-Franklin, 1989). Such information may be necessary to maximize the cultural sensitivity of interventions with specialized, inner-city populations (e.g., single parent, minority, low income). An exemplary program for Puerto Rican boys suggests the utility of this population-specific approach (see Malgady, Rogler, & Costantino, 1990).

LONGITUDINAL PERSPECTIVES

The antisocial behaviors of CD children are not only stable across time but they also appear to be related to clinical problems exhibited during adolescence and adulthood (see Kazdin, 1987a; Loeber, 1990). Although less than half of antisocial children become antisocial adults, the latter outcome is almost always predicted by early conduct problems. Several variables have been implicated in the continuity of child antisocial behaviors, including the severity of the child's personality disturbance and family dysfunction (Rutter & Gillmer, 1983). Similar child conduct problems have served as predictors of subsequent involvement in delinquent activities (e.g., aggression, stealing, truancy, lying; Loeber & Stouthamer-Loeber, 1986) and criminal behavior (e.g., CD symptoms, hyperactivity, poor peer relations) (Farrington, Loeber, & Van Kammen, 1990; Magnusson, 1988). Other evidence with incarcerated juvenile delinquents highlights the adverse impact of antisocial behaviors in terms of increased mortality rates, especially by violent methods (Yeager & Lewis, 1990).

Aggression and, in particular, a history of maltreatment have been found to be linked with later involvement in violent offenses (see Loeber, 1990; Rivera & Widom, 1990), as well as school dropout (Kupersmidt & Coie, 1990). In a 22-year follow-up study, initial measures of aggression were associated with subsequent measures of aggression, criminal offenses, and academic achievement, especially for males (Eron, Huesmann, Dubow, Romanoff, & Yarmel, 1987). Even hard-to-manage preschool children are at risk for developing oppositional or conduct disorder 6 years later (Campbell & Ewing, 1990).

Follow-up studies of clinic referrals provide related evidence for those variables associated with therapeutic outcome. Webster-Stratton and Hammond (1990) reported findings from a 1-year follow-up study of parent training programs directed toward young, conduct problem children. Parental reports of child adjustment problems were associated with parental depression and amount of negative life events. Interestingly, parental depression predicted more negative perceptions of the child, whereas single parenthood or marital conflict predicted more negative child behavior. A 3-year follow-up study of this program found that reductions in problem behaviors and improved social competence were reported for all treated groups, with the combination of group discussion and exposure to modeling videotapes being associated with greatest improvement (Webster-Stratton et al., 1989). At the same time, roughly half of the parents continued to express concern regarding the children's behaviors. The variables associated with limited outcome were single parenthood, maternal depression, low SES, and family history of alcoholism and drug abuse. Such findings suggest the need for early intervention and the benefit of exploring adjunctive treatments for parents and providing follow-up services to maximize long-term outcomes.

Follow-up studies of CD inpatients likewise have indicated significant improvements on standardized parent and community-teacher measures of child behavior problems at 1-year follow-up and the relationship between severity of behavioral dysfunction and poor outcome (Kazdin & Bass, 1988). In a subsequent large study, children with antisocial behavior showed poorer functioning than their nonantisocial peers, with severity of initial dysfunction, parental psychopathology, and family dysfunction serving as predictors of follow-up problems (Kazdin, 1989). Prognosis was found to be influenced by the initial level of antisocial behavior, independent of the diagnosis of CD. As has been recommended with inpatient treatment (Pfeiffer, 1989; Pfeiffer & Strzelecki, 1990), follow-up studies should give greater attention to various methodological considerations, such as the delineation of critical dimensions of treatment, definitions of follow-up success or adjustment, use of rigorous statistical methods/designs, and expansion of predictor variables (e.g., academic status, types of dysfunction, treatment regimen, family involvement).

CASE ILLUSTRATION

Background and History

B. was an 13.4-year-old, white male who lived with his mother and 12-year-old brother. He was referred by his mother because of repeated conduct problems, including aggression toward his mother and brother, defiance, temper tantrums and arguments, stealing, physical cruelty to others, lying, truancy, poor school performance (C's and D's), and school misconduct resulting in several detentions. The referral was strongly advocated by the child's school. B.'s home interactions were marked by frequently combative and hostile interchanges that often led to his being grounded and sent to his room for extended periods of time. Mother described the child as very angry, volatile, and easily annoyed by others ("irritable"). B., in turn, frequently blamed others for his own problems, especially when he lost his temper. He also had exhibited property destruction at home.

B. attended the eighth grade of a regular elementary school and had never repeated a grade, although his performance in school over the previous 3 years had been quite inconsistent. Mother was divorced 4 years prior to his referral, a stressor that was regarded as a primary precipitant of his behavior problems. She had attended college for 2 years and was working full-time as a secretary. At the time of referral, B.'s brother was beginning to exhibit similar, albeit less severe, behavior problems, but was not referred at that time.

Diagnostic and Clinical Evaluation

Psychiatric assessment revealed no symptoms of depression, suicidality, mania, anxiety, eating problems, hyperactivity (except for impulsivity), or alcohol/drug problems. A semistructured interview revealed an Axis I diagnosis of CD: solitary aggressive type, with no diagnoses on Axes II or III. This was corroborated by mother's completion of a DSM-III-R checklist which revealed involvement in nine CD symptoms, three other ODD symptoms, and one ADHD symptom. His Kiddie-GAS scores were 50 and 60 for the current time and past year, respectively. There was no history of psychotic or neurological problems, other medical illnesses, or health problems. He had never received psychotropic medication for any of these problems.

In terms of standardized measures, B. received a score of 17 on the Conners Parent Questionnaire (CPQ), and his Child Behavior Checklist (CBCL) revealed the highest T-scores on all three of the externalizing factors: delinquency (70), aggression (69), and hyperactivity (65). The CBCL scores seemed to represent underestimates of the frequency of B.'s involvement in serious antisocial behaviors based on parental interview. The T-scores for the social competence scales were within normal limits, except for the social skills scale (28). On the peer delinquency scale, B. acknowledged peer involvement in 7 of 12 antisocial behaviors, with multiple peer involvement being noted in the case of 5 of these 7 behaviors. School records indicated the need for significant improvement in 5 of 10 primary work areas in each of the past 2 years. His scores on the California Achievement Test showed a delay of approximately 2 grade levels in reading, language, and math.

Treatment

B. participated in the Children's After-School Treatment Program (CAST), an intensive partial hospitalization program serving antisocial children that was conducted on a 2-day per week basis (M-W or T-Th) and for 3 hours/per day over a 12-week period. Staffed by MA- and BA-level clinicians, the program is based on cognitive-behavioral principles and incorporates skills training procedures in three primary activities that are conducted in a group format: group treatment (e.g., social-cognitive skills training, anger control), academic remediation (e.g., homework assistance, computer instruction in the learning center), and group socialization activities (e.g., recreation, arts and crafts). B. was exposed to a comprehensive point system throughout the program in which he earned points for exhibiting various positive behaviors (e.g., saying something nice, following rules) and lost points for engaging in negative behaviors (e.g., aggression, swearing/teasing). Point earnings were exchanged once per week for tangible, activity, and/or edible reinforcers in a program store.

To facilitate cross-setting programming, a daily goal card was instituted by which B.'s completion of a criterion number of individualized target behaviors (e.g., no more than one incident of teasing, follows all learning center rules) resulted in a reinforcer delivered at home. Many of the skills trained during the program were reviewed in individual sessions with B.'s case manager/clinician, often immediately after the CAST program had ended that day. These adjunctive sessions afforded opportunities for extended role-plays, continued discussion of personal reactions to the content (e.g., angry outbursts, violence), and individualized application of problem-solving skills (e.g., how to respond to brother's provocation).

Mother participated in 12 individual parent management training (PMT) sessions with an MSW-level social worker once, and sometimes twice, per week. After many of these sessions were completed, B. and his therapist joined mother and her therapist for parent–child sessions in which they reviewed home programs. Initial training encompassed certain introductory topics (e.g., goal setting, monitoring behavior, attending/ignoring, use of commands and reinforcement), but increased behavior problems required prompt discussion of other skills (e.g., anger control, problem solving, developing and enforcing home contingencies). Most of the sessions were crisis oriented in that mother needed to be calmed down, reassured, and then coached in appropriate ways of handling both herself and her son. In a few instances, sessions lasted more than 2 hours in order to adequately process an event in the presence of B. and to develop an appropriate plan for the mother. Homework assignments were used to support the practice of these skills during difficult child interactions. Much of this information was reviewed during extended phone conversations following highly stressful family interactions. The overall duration of treatment was 6 months.

Outcomes

Pre–Post Comparisons on Standardized Scales

The course of treatment with B. and his mother revealed variable progress, marked by occasional setbacks as well as improvements. To document B.'s overall level of behavioral and emotional dysfunction and social competence, mother completed the CBCL, CPQ, and the DSM-III-R checklist both before and after treatment. The results of this assessment are shown in Table 1. On the CBCL, B. received lower posttreatment than pretreatment scores on the delinquency scale and, to a lesser extent, on the aggression and hyperactivity scales. He also received a much higher score on the social skills scale and a higher score on the activities scale. The total behavior problems score was lower after treatment. Mother also indicated that B. had fewer problems after treatment on all three disruptive behavior disorders of the DSM-III-R checklist, with a substantial reduction in the number of CD symptoms. Similarly, the CPQ ratings revealed considerably fewer problems with attention and overactivity after treatment.

Review of Process Issues/Outcomes from Session Notes

A review of progress notes from the CAST program and PMT sessions provides some clarification of the events that transpired in this case and some of the difficulties encoun-

TABLE 1.   Parent Measures Obtained before and after Treatment

Measure	Pretreatment	Posttreatment
Child Behavior Checklist		
Delinquency	70	57
Aggression	69	62
Hyperactivity	65	58
Activities	34	48
Social Skills	28	48
School performance	45	45
Conners Parent Questionnaire	17	5
DSM-III-R Symptom Checklist (#)		
Conduct disorder	9	1
Oppositional disorder	3	1
Attention-deficit hyperactivity disorder	1	0

tered during treatment. First, although she recognized this as a significant problem, mother had great difficulty "turning off" many of her statements that sounded like lecturing or threats of serious consequences that only antagonized her son. She often resorted to this type of verbal communication when B. responded with comparable hostilities that directly challenged both her authority and parental role. Her inability to exert sufficient self-control became a persistent treatment goal, one that occupied considerable therapeutic attention.

Second, B. became the most belligerent with his mother when she began to apply consistent management skills (e.g., effective commands, reinforcement, brief time-out) in an effort to uphold the contingencies she established. On one occasion early in treatment, she reported that he had punched her in the mouth and kicked his brother after an incident in which she followed through with consequences for truancy. Mother apparently grabbed him by his shirt and hit him with a large spatula before the incident evolved into a shouting match. Mother then called the police who placed the child in handcuffs, but no further action was taken because she did not want him "to be committed." On another day, he was noted to have punched his brother in the nose and caused it to bleed after his brother began to harass one of B.'s friends who was playing at their house. Despite some discussion of the use of legal consequences to address assaultive behavior, mother was unwilling to follow through with such a plan.

As treatment continued, mother was able to administer a home point system using allowance as a reinforcer before adding other consequences from a privilege menu (e.g., use of phone) to address other target behaviors (e.g., completion of school projects). She also arranged a daily chore schedule with assistance from the therapist. Fortunately, their joint participation in developing the system and some consistent application of individual consequences were followed by some improvements in B.'s home and school behavior. Since then, other problems that continued to occur (e.g., lying, unauthorized use of her credit card to purchase $90 worth of goods) were addressed promptly (e.g., restitution contract).

At the same time, B. was learning to apply some of his skills in "solving" problems he experienced at home and to use specific social skills (e.g., compliments, making requests). Mother's reports of improvements in their interactions were paralleled by B.'s own positive comments about his treatment at home ("my mother has been very fair with me."). During the next 2 weeks, mother began to discontinue some of her programming, which resulted in some deterioration in B.'s cooperative behavior. Revisions of the program were made to consolidate the targets, which then yielded favorable results. A similar pattern of generalized improvement with occasional violations of house rules was observed during the next 3 weeks, which coincided with the conclusion of the CAST program. Individual PMT and parent–child sessions were continued on a twice-monthly basis for nearly 3 months to review individual incidents, discuss problem-solving options, and revise existing procedures.

Conclusions and Clinical Implications

As is typical with any complex CD case, it is often difficult to understand, much less describe, the many critical issues and decisions that influence the course of intervention. The absence of sufficient details notwithstanding, this case illustrates some of the therapeutic considerations and issues that occur during the course of treatment with CD children and their parents. For the sake of brevity, they are simply listed below:

1. It is critical to teach parents and children how to cope directly with stressful circumstances as they happen and evolve, even if this involves a change in the direction in which treatment was headed. In some instances, novel procedures may need to be suggested and trained for this purpose, requiring considerable flexibility and availability on the part of therapists.

2. These cases often get worse before they show improvement, and such deterioration may prompt the therapist to suggest termination. And, yet, CD children and their parents may be most in need of therapeutic assistance during these critical periods. The need for continuity of care at these difficult times seems to be important in helping other systems (e.g., family, school, hospital) to "process" these highly aversive events and to prevent them from reacting adversely and, perhaps, irrationally to the child.

3. Whenever possible, it is important to establish reciprocity when developing contingency management programs, especially between parents and older CD children, by taking the time to understand each participant's observations, explanations, and requests. Participants whose interests have been only partially addressed may then perceive any established contingency as "unfair" or imbalanced. Greater attention to enhancing mutual involvement seems to elicit greater investment in the process and, ultimately, the outcome.

4. Parents, as well as their CD children, often need multiple services and may be involved in the operation of numerous contingencies and skills training programs. While of therapeutic benefit, these commitments take time and energy, which often means that they may prove burdensome or, at worst, ineffective. Programming for CD children is not only difficult to achieve, but it is also often difficult for clients to carry out consistently. Long-term outcomes may be best prompted to the extent that goal achievement is balanced by parsimony.

5. Serious physical assault is destructive to family relationships and is sometimes dangerous to family members. Both parents and therapists must be able to clearly evaluate and then respond to such incidents, whether this involves the use of in-home consequences (e.g., time-out, restraint) or other support services (e.g., police, emergency room visits). Such plans and precautions parallel those used in other psychiatric emergencies (e.g., suicide) and may enable parents to invest more heavily in an initial behavioral program because they have been prepared to "recover" from its potential failure.

6. Because of the chronicity and resistance of CD, minor improvements are sometimes the only improvements that may occur in the short term. Children and especially

their parents need to be given feedback about these improvements so that a child's recent (albeit limited) accomplishments will not be overshadowed by his or her prevailing history of troublesome behavior. In the absence of *some* hope for change, therapeutic effort by either party is unlikely.

SUMMARY

The antisocial behaviors that make up CD are chronic, compelling, and often poorly controlled. CD children evince an array of troublesome antisocial behaviors and display deficits in interpersonal, cognitive, affective, and academic functioning. These symptoms may be associated with multiple etiologies, especially those that implicate family-interactional, cognitive-attributional, and, more recently, biological influences. Based on existing evidence, treatment of CD emphasizes teaching effective management practices to parents and cognitive-behavioral skills to children to help them achieve self-control. More recently, multicomponent interventions that directly target family-systems variables, such as marital, peer, and school problems have been conducted with promising results. Indeed, certain variables, such as parental dysfunction, marital discord, and other social stressors, have been associated with poor treatment outcome. Clinical advances in the scope, duration, and systemic involvement of treatment programs are needed to address the various challenges of working with CD children and their parents. Future therapeutic directions include the development of combined psychosocial and pharmacological interventions, expansion in the contexts in which multiple treatment modalities are provided (e.g., partial hospitalization), and promotion of intensive child- and parent-directed services that establish the continuity of care over time.

ACKNOWLEDGMENTS.   I acknowledge the assistance of Brian Day, Mary Dulgeroff, Sandy Minor, Valerie Tumpa, and Dana Young in the preparation of this chapter.

REFERENCES

Alexander, J. F., & Parson, B. V. (1982). *Functional family therapy*. Monterey, CA: Brooks/Cole.

American Psychiatric Association (1980). *Diagnostic and statistical manual of mental disorders*, 3rd Edition. Washington, DC: Author.

American Psychiatric Association (1987). *Diagnostic and statistical manual of mental disorders*, 3rd Edition, Revised. Washington, DC: Author.

American Psychiatric Association (1993). *DSM-IV draft criteria*. Washington, DC: Author.

August, G. J., & Stewart, M. A. (1982). Is there a syndrome of pure hyperactivity? *British Journal of Psychiatry*, *140*, 305–311.

Bank, L., Marlowe, J. H., Reid, J. B., Patterson, G. R., & Weinrott, M. R. (1991). A comparative evaluation of parent-training interventions for families of chronic delinquents. *Journal of Abnormal Child Psychology*, *19*, 15–33.

Barkley, R. A. (1987). *Defiant children: A clinician's manual for parent training*. New York: Guilford Press.

Baum, J. G., Clark, H. B., McCarthy, W., Sandler, J., & Carpenter, R. (1986). An analysis of the acquisition and generalization of social skills in troubled youths: Combining social skills training, cognitive self-talk, and relaxation procedures. *Child and Family Behavior Therapy*, *8*, 1–27.

Bierman, K. L. (1986). Aggression and peer rejection in children and adolescents. In R. J. Prinz (Ed.), *Advances in behavioral assessment of children and families* (Vol. 2, pp. 151–178). Greenwich, CT: Jai Press.

Bierman, K. L., & Furman, W. (1984). The effects of social skills training and peer involvement on the social adjustment of preadolescents. *Child Development*, *55*, 151–162.

Bierman, K. L., Miller, C. L., & Stabb, S. D. (1987). Improving the social behavior and peer acceptance of rejected boys: Effects of social skill training with instructions and prohibitions. *Journal of Consulting and Clinical Psychology*, *55*, 194–200.

Blechman, E. A. (1987). *Solving child and behavior problems at home and at school*, Champaign, IL: Research Press.

Blechman, E. A., Kotanchik, N. L., & Taylor, C. J. (1981). Families and schools together: Early behavioral intervention with high risk children. *Behavior Therapy*, *132*, 308–319.

Boldizar, J. P., Perry, D. G., & Perry, L. C. (1989). Outcome values and aggression. *Child Development*, *60*, 571–579.

Bornstein, M., Bellack, A. S., & Hersen, M. (1980). Social skills training for highly aggressive children: Treatment in an inpatient setting. *Behavior Modification*, *4*, 173–186.

Boyd-Franklin, N. (1989). *Black families in therapy: A multisystems approach*. New York: Guilford.

Brent, D. A. (1987). Correlates of the medical lethality of suicide attempts in children and adolescents. *Journal of the American Academy of Child and Adolescent Psychiatry*, *26*, 87–89.

Brent, D. A., & Kolko, D. J. (1990). Suicide and suicidal behavior in children and adolescents. In B. D. Garfinkel, G. Carlson, & E. Weller (Eds.), *The medical basis of child and adolescent psychiatry* (pp. 372–391). Philadelphia: Saunders.

Buchard, J. D., & Clark, R. T. (1990). The role of individualized care in a service delivery system for children and adolescents with severely maladjusted behavior. *Journal of Mental Health Administration*, *17*, 48–60.

Cairns, R. B., Peterson, G., & Neckerman, H. J. (1988). Suicidal behavior in aggressive adolescents. *Journal of Clinical Child Psychology*, *17*, 298–309.

Camp, B. W., & Ray, R. S. (1984). Aggression. In A. W. Meyers & W. E. Craighead (Eds.), *Cognitive behavior therapy with children* (pp. 315–350). New York: Plenum.

Campbell, S. B., & Ewing, L. J. (1990). Follow-up of hard-to-manage preschoolers: Adjustment at age 9 and predictors of continuing symptoms. *Journal of Child Psychology and Psychiatry*, *31*, 871–889.

Caspi, A., Elder, G. H., & Bem, D. J. (1987). Moving against the world: Life course patterns of explosive children. *Developmental Psychology*, *23*, 308–313.

Chamberlain, R., & Baldwin, D. V. (1987). Client resistance to parent training: Its therapeutic management. In T. R. Kratochwill (Ed.), *Advances in school psychology* (Vol. 6). Northvale, NJ: Erlbaum.

Coie, J. D., & Dodge, K. A. (1987). Social-information processing factors in reactive and proactive aggression in children's peer groups. *Journal of Personality and Social Psychology*, *53*, 1146–1158.

Coie, J. D., & Krehbiel, G. (1984). Effects of academic tutoring on the social status of low-achieving, socially rejected children. *Child Development*, *55*, 1465–1478.

Cole, D. A., & Carpenter, S. (1990). Social status and the comorbidity of child depression and conduct disorder. *Journal of Consulting and Clinical Psychology*, *58*, 748–757.

Compas, B. E. (1987). Coping with stress during childhood and adolescence. *Psychological Bulletin*, *101*, 293–403.

Crowell, D. H., Evans, I. M., & O'Donnell, C. R. (1987). *Childhood aggression and violence*. New York: Plenum.

Curry, J. F., & Craighead, W. E. (1990). Attributional style in clinically depressed and conduct disordered adolescents. *Journal of Consulting and Clinical Psychology*, *58*, 109–115.

Dabbs, J. M., Frady, R. L., Carr, T. S., & Besch, N. G. (1987). Salivary testosterone and criminal violence in young adult prison inmates. *Psychosometric Medicine*, *49*, 174–182.

Dadds, M. R., Sanders, M. R., Behrens, B. C., & James, J. E. (1987). Marital discord and child behavior problems: A description of family interactions during treatment. *Journal of Clinical Child Psychology*, *16*, 192–203.

Dadds, M. R., Sanders, M. R., & James, J. E. (1987). The generalization of treatment effects in parent training with multidistressed parents. *Behavioural Psychotherapy*, *15*, 289–313.

Dadds, M. R., Schwartz, S., & Sanders, M. R. (1987). Marital discord and treatment outcome in behavioral treatment of child conduct disorders. *Journal of Consulting and Clinical Psychology*, *55*, 396–403.

Dangel, R. F., & Polster, R. A. (1988). *Teaching child management skills*. New York: Pergamon Press.

DiGiuseppe, R. (1988). A cognitive-behavioral approach to the treatment of conduct disorder children and adolescents. In N. Epstein, S. E. Schlesinger, & W. Dryden (Eds.), *Cognitive behavioral therapy with families* (pp. 183–214). New York: Guilford.

Dishion, T. J., Loeber, R., Stouthamer-Loeber, M., & Patterson, G. R. (1984). Skill deficits and male adolescent delinquency. *Journal of Abnormal Child Psychology*, *12*, 37–54.

Dodge, K. A. (1986). A social information processing model of social competence in children. In M. Perlmutter (Ed.), *Minnesota symposium on child psychology* (Vol. 18, 77–125). Hillsdale, NJ: Erlbaum.

Dodge, K. A. (1990). Nature versus nurture in childhood conduct disorder: It is time to ask a different question. *Developmental Psychology, 26,* 698–701.

Dodge, K. A., McClaskey, C. L., & Feldman, E. (1985). Situational approach to the assessment of social competence in children. *Journal of Consulting and Clinical Psychology, 53,* 344–355.

Dodge, K. A., Price, J. M., Bachorowski, J. A., & Newman, J. P. (1990). Hostile attributional biases in severely aggressive adolescents. *Journal of Abnormal Psychology, 99,* 385–392.

Dubow, E. F., Huesmann, L. R., & Eron, L. D. (1987). Mitigating aggression and promoting prosocial behavior in aggressive elementary school boys. *Behavioral Residential Treatment, 25,* 527–531.

Dumas, J. E. (1989). Treating antisocial behavior in children: Child and family approaches. *Clinical Psychology Review, 9,* 197–222.

Dumas, J. E., & Gibson, J. A. (1990). Behavioral correlates of maternal depressive symptomatology in conduct disorder children: II. Systemic effects involving fathers and siblings. *Journal of Consulting and Clinical Psychology, 58,* 877–881.

Egeland, B., Kalkoske, M., Gottesman, N., & Erickson, M. F. (1990). Preschool behavior problems: Stability and factors accounting for change. *Journal of Child Psychology and Psychiatry, 31,* 891–909.

Eron, L. D., Huesmann, L. R., Dubow, E., Romanoff, R., & Yarmel, R. W. (1987). Aggression and its correlates over 22 years. In D. H. Crowell, I. M. Evans, & C. R. O'Donnell (Eds.), *Childhood aggression and violence: Sources of influence, prevention, and control* (pp. 249–262). New York: Plenum.

Evans, I. M., & Scheuer, A. D. (1987). Analyzing response relationships in childhood aggression: The clinical perspective. In D. H. Crowell, I. M. Evans, & C. R. O'Donnell (Eds.), *Childhood aggression and violence: Sources of influence, prevention, and control* (pp. 75–94). New York: Plenum.

Evans, S. W., & Short, E. J. (1991). A qualitative and serial analysis of social problem solving in aggressive boys. *Journal of Abnormal Child Psychology, 19,* 331–340.

Farrington, D. P., Loeber, R., & Van Kammen, W. B. (1990). Long-term criminal outcomes in hyperactivity-impulsivity-attention-deficit and conduct problems in childhood. In L. N. Robins & M. R. Rutter (Eds.), *Straight and devious pathways from childhood to adulthood* (pp. 62–81). New York: Cambridge University Press.

Feindler, E. L., Ecton, R. B., Kingsley, D., & Dubey, D. R. (1986). Group anger-control training for institutionalized psychiatric male adolescents. *Behavior Therapy, 17,* 109–123.

Fleischman, M. J. (1982). Social learning interventions for aggressive children: From the laboratory to the real world. *The Behavior Therapist, 5,* 55–58.

Fleischman, M. J., & Szykula, S. A. (1981). A community setting replication of a social learning treatment for aggressive children. *Behavior Therapy, 12,* 115–122.

Fleischman, M. J., Horne, A. M., & Arthur, J. L. (1983). *Troubled families: A treatment program.* Champaign, IL: Research Press.

Fondacaro, M. R., & Heller, K. (1990). Attributional style in aggressive adolescent boys. *Journal of Abnormal Child Psychology, 18,* 75–89.

Forehand, R. (1986). Positive reinforcement with deviant children: Does it make a difference? *Child & Family Behavior Therapy, 8,* 19–25.

Forehand, R., Long, N., & Hedrick, M. (1987). Family characteristics of adolescents who display overt and covert behavior problems. *Journal of Behavior Therapy and Experimental Psychiatry, 18,* 325–328.

Frick, P. J., Kamphaus, R. W., Lahey, B. B., Loeber, R., Christ, M. G., Hart, E. L., & Tannenbaum, L. E. (1991). Academic underachievement and the disruptive behavior disorders. *Journal of Consulting and Clinical Psychology, 59,* 289–294.

Frick, P. J., Lahey, B. B., Hartdagen, S., & Hynd, G. W. (1989). Conduct problems in boys: Relations to maternal personality, marital satisfaction, and socioeconomic status. *Journal of Clinical Child Psychology, 18,* 114–120.

Gadow, K. D., Nolan, E. E., Sverd, J., Sprafkin, J., & Paolicelli, L. (1990). Methylphenidate in aggressive-hyperactive boys: I. Effects on peer aggression in public school settings. *Journal of the American Academy of Child and Adolescent Psychiatry, 29,* 710–718.

Gair, D. S., Bullard, D. M., & Corwin, J. M. (1984). Guidelines for children and adolescents. In K. Tardiff (Ed.), *The psychiatric uses of seclusion and restraint* (pp. 69–85). Washington, DC: American Psychiatric Press.

Gardner, F. E. M. (1989). Inconsistent parenting: Is there evidence for a link with children's conduct problems. *Journal of Abnormal Child Psychology, 17,* 223–233.

Goldstein, A. P., & Glick, B. (1987). *Aggression replacement training: A comprehensive intervention for aggressive youth.* Champaign, IL: Research Press.

Goldstein, A. P., & Keller, H. (1987). *Aggressive behavior: Assessment and intervention.* New York: Pergamon Press.

Goldstein, H. S. (1987). Cognitive development in low attentive, hyperactive, and aggressive 6- through 11-year-old children. *Journal of the American Academy of Child and Adolescent Psychiatry, 26*, 214–218.

Gray, J. A. (1982). *The neuropsychology of anxiety: An enquiry into the functions of the septo-hippocampal system.* Oxford: Oxford University Press.

Gray, J. A. (1987). *The psychology of fear and stress* (2nd ed.). Cambridge: Cambridge University Press.

Griest, D. L., & Wells, K. C. (1983). Behavioral family therapy with conduct disorders in children. *Behavior Therapy, 14*, 37–53.

Hansen, D. J., St. Lawrence, J. S., & Christoff, K. A. (1988). Conversational skills of inpatient conduct-disordered youths: Social validation of component behaviors and implications for skills training. *Behavior Modification, 12*, 424–444.

Hansen, D. J., St. Lawrence, J. S., & Christoff, K. A. (1989). Group conversational-skills training with inpatient children and adolescents: Social validation, generalization, and maintenance. *Behavior Modification, 13*, 4–31.

Hardwick, P. J., Pounds, A. B., & Brown, M. (1985). Preventive adolescent psychiatry: Practical problems in running social skills groups for the younger adolescent. *Journal of Adolescence, 8*, 357–367.

Hawkins, J. D., & Lishner, D. M. (1987). Schooling and delinquency. In E. H. Johnson (Ed.), *Handbook on crime and delinquency prevention* (pp. 179–221). New York: Greenwood Press.

Henggeler, S. W., & Borduin, C. M. (1990). *Family therapy and beyond: A multisystemic approach to treating behavior problems of children and adolescents.* Pacific Grove, CA: Brooks/Cole.

Henggeler, S. W., Rodick, J. D., Borduin, C. M., Hanson, C. L., Watson, S. M., & Urey, J. R. (1986). Multisystemic treatment of juvenile offenders: Effects on adolescent behavior and family interactions. *Developmental Psychology, 22*, 132–141.

Hinshaw, S. P. (1987). On the distinction between attentional deficits/hyperactivity and conduct problems/aggression in child psychopathology. *Psychological Bulletin, 101*, 443–463.

Horne, A. M., & Sayger, T. V. (1990). *Treating conduct and oppositional defiant disorders in children.* New York: Pergamon Press.

Huesman, L. R., Eron, L. D., Lefkowitz, M. M., & Walder, L. O. (1984). The stability of aggression over time and generations. *Developmental Psychology, 20*, 1120–1134.

Jacobson, N. S. (1985). Family therapy outcome research: Potential pitfalls and prospects. *Journal of Marital and Family Therapy, 11*, 149–158.

Jary, M. L., & Stewart, M. A. (1985). Psychiatric disorder in the parents of adopted children with aggressive conduct disorder. *Neuropsychobiology, 13*, 7–11.

Jouriles, E. N., Bourg, W. J., & Farris, A. M. (1991). Marital adjustment and child conduct problems: A comparison of the correlation across subsamples. *Journal of Consulting and Clinical Psychology, 59*, 354–357.

Jouriles, E. N., Murphy, C. M., & O'Leary, K. D. (1989). Interspousal aggression, marital discord, and child problems. *Journal of Consulting and Clinical Psychology, 57*, 453–455.

Kaplan, S. L., Busner, J., Kupietz, S., Wasserman, E., & Segal, B. (1990). Effects of methylphenidate on adolescents with aggressive conduct disorder and ADDH: A preliminary report. *Journal of the American Academy of Child and Adolescent Psychiatry, 29*, 719–723.

Kazdin, A. E. (1982). The token economy: A decade later. *Journal of Applied Behavior Analysis, 15*, 431–445.

Kazdin, A. E. (1985). *The treatment of antisocial behavior in children and adolescents.* Homewood, IL: Dorsey Press.

Kazdin, A. E. (1987a). *Conduct disorders in childhood and adolescence.* Beverly Hills, CA: Sage Publications.

Kazdin, A. E. (1987b). Treatment of antisocial behavior in children: Current status and future directions. *Psychological Bulletin, 102*, 187–203.

Kazdin, A. E. (1989). Hospitalization of antisocial children: Clinical course, follow-up status, and predictors of outcome. *Advances in Behaviour Research and Therapy, 11*, 1–67.

Kazdin, A. E., & Bass, D. (1988). Parent, teacher, and hospital staff evaluations of severely disturbed children. *American Journal of Orthopsychiatry, 58*, 512–523.

Kazdin, A. E., & Esveldt-Dawson, K. (1986). The Interview for Antisocial Behavior: Psychometric characteristics and concurrent validity with child psychiatric inpatients. *Journal of Psychopathology and Behavioral Assessment, 8*, 289–303.

Kazdin, A. E., Bass, D., Siegel, T., & Thomas, C. (1989). Cognitive-behavioral therapy and relationship therapy in the treatment of children referred for antisocial behavior. *Journal of Consulting and Clinical Psychology, 57*, 522–535.

Kazdin, A. E., Esveldt-Dawson, K., French, N. H., & Unis, A. S. (1987a). Effects of parent management training and problem-solving skills training combined in the treatment of antisocial child behavior. *Journal of the American Academy of Child and Adolescent Psychiatry, 26,* 416–424.

Kazdin, A. E., Esveldt-Dawson, K., French, N. H., & Unis, A. S. (1987b). Problem-solving skills training and relationship therapy in the treatment of antisocial child behavior. *Journal of Consulting and Clinical Psychology, 55,* 76–85.

Kazdin, A. E., Rodgers, A., Colbus, D., & Siegel, T. (1987). Children's Hostility Inventory: Measurement of aggression and hostility in psychiatric inpatient children. *Journal of Clinical Child Psychology, 16,* 320–328.

Kendall, P. C., & Braswell, L. (1985). *Cognitive-behavioral therapy for impulsive children.* New York: Guilford Press.

Kendall, P. C., Reber, M., McLeer, S., Epps, J., & Ronan, K. R. (1990). Cognitive-behavioral treatment of conduct-disordered children. *Cognitive Therapy and Research, 14,* 279–297.

Klorman, R., Brumaghim, J. T., Salzman, L. F., Strauss, J., Borgstedt, A. D., McBride, M. C., & Loeb, S. (1988). Effects of methylphenidate on attention-deficit hyperactivity disorders with and without aggressive/ noncompliant features. *Journal of Abnormal Psychology, 97,* 413–422.

Kolko, D. J. (1988). Fire setting and pyromania. In C. Last & M. Hersen (Eds.), *Handbook of child psychiatric diagnosis* (pp. 443–459). New York: John Wiley.

Kolko, D. J. (1989). Conduct disorder. In M. Hersen (Ed.), *Innovations in child behavior therapy* (pp. 324–352). New York: Springer.

Kolko, D. J. (1992). Conduct disorder. In V. B. Van Hasselt & D. J. Kolko (Eds.), *Inpatient behavior therapy for children and adolescents* (pp. 205–237). New York: Plenum.

Kolko, D. J., Loar, L. L., & Sturnick, D. (1990). Inpatient social-cognitive skills training for conduct disordered and attention deficit disordered children. *Journal of Child Psychology and Psychiatry, 31,* 737–748.

Kovacs, M., Paulauskas, S., Gatsonis, C., & Richards, C. (1988). Depressive disorders in childhood III. A longitudinal study of comorbidity with and risk for conduct disorders. *Journal of Affective Disorders, 15,* 205–217.

Kruesi, M. J. P., Rapoport, J. L., Hamburger, S., Hibbs, E., Potter, W. Z., Lenane, M., & Brown, G. L. (1990). CSF monoamine metabolites, aggression and impulsivity in disruptive behavior disorders of children and adolescents. *Archives of General Psychiatry, 47,* 419–426.

Kruesi, M. J. P., Schmidt, M. E., Donnelly, M., Hibbs, E. D., & Hamburger, S. D. (1989). Urinary free cortisol output and disruptive behavior in children. *Journal of the American Academy of Child and Adolescent Psychiatry, 28,* 441–443.

Kruesi, M. J. P., Swedo, S., Leonard, H., Rubinow, D. R., & Rapoport, J. L. (1990). CSF somatostatin in childhood psychiatric disorders: A preliminary investigation. *Psychiatric Research, 33,* 277–284.

Kupersmidt, J. B., & Coie, J. D. (1990). Preadolescent peer status, aggression, and school adjustment as predictors of externalizing problems in adolescence. *Child Development, 61,* 1350–1362.

Lahey, B. B., Loeber, R., Stouthamer-Loeber, M., Christ, M. G., Green, S., Russo, M. F., Frick, P. J., & Dulcan, M. (1990). Comparison of DSM-III and DSM-III-R diagnoses for prepubertal children: Changes in prevalence and validity. *Journal of the American Academy of Child and Adolescent Psychiatry, 29,* 620–626.

Lahey, B. B., Piacentini, J. C., McBurnett, K., Stone, P., Hartdagen, S., & Hynd, G. (1988). Psychopathology in the parents of children with conduct disorder and hyperactivity. *Journal of the American Academy of Child and Adolescent Psychiatry, 27,* 163–170.

Lahey, B. B., Russo, M. F., Walker, J. L., & Piacentini, J. C. (1989). Personality characteristics of the mothers of children with disruptive behavior disorders. *Journal of Consulting and Clinical Psychology, 57,* 512–515.

Lewis, R. O., Lovely, R., Yeager, C., & Femina, D. D. (1989). Toward a theory of the genesis of violence: A follow-up study of delinquents. *Journal of the American Academy of Child and Adolescent Psychiatry, 28,* 431–436.

Linnoila, M., De Jong, J., & Virkkunen, M. (1989). Family history of alcoholism in violent offenders and impulsive fire setters. *Archives of General Psychiatry, 46,* 613–616.

Lochman, J. E. (1987). Self- and peer perceptions and attributional biases of aggressive and nonaggressive boys in dyadic interactions. *Journal of Consulting and Clinical Psychology, 55,* 404–410.

Lochman, J. E. (August, 1988). Cognitive-behavioral intervention with aggressive boys: Three-year follow-up effects. In F. D. Armstrong (Chair), *Disruptive behavior disorders in children.* Paper session presented at the annual meeting of the American Psychological Association, Atlanta, GA.

Lochman, J. E. (1990). Modification of childhood aggression. In M. Hersen, R. M. Eisler, & P. M. Miller (Eds.), *Progress in behavior modification* (pp. 47–85). Newbury Park, CA: Sage.

Lochman, J. E., & Curry, J. F. (1986). Effects of social problem-solving training and self-instruction training with aggressive boys. *Journal of Clinical Child Psychology, 15,* 159–164.

Lochman, J. E., & Dodge, K. A. (1990, January). *Dysfunctional family and social-cognitive processes with aggressive boys*. Poster presented at the meeting of the Society for Research in Child and Adolescent Psychopathology, Costa Mesa, CA.

Lochman, J. E., Burch, P. R., Curry, J. F., & Lampron, L. B. (1984). Treatment and generalization effects of cognitive-behavioral and goal-setting interventions with aggressive boys. *Journal of Consulting and Clinical Child Psychology*, *15*, 159–164.

Lochman, J. E., Lampron, L. B., Gemmer, T. C., Harris, S. R., & Wyckoff, G. M. (1987, August). *Teacher consultation and cognitive-behavioral interventions with aggressive boys*. Paper presented at the American Psychological Association annual convention, New York.

Loeber, R. (1982). The stability of antisocial and delinquent child behavior: A review. *Child Development*, *53*, 1431–1446.

Loeber, R. (1985). Patterns and development of antisocial child behavior. *Annals of Child Development*, *2*, 77–116.

Loeber, R. (1990). Development and risk factors of juvenile antisocial behavior and delinquency. *Clinical Psychological Review*, *10*, 1–41.

Loeber, R., & LeBlanc, M. (1990). Toward a developmental criminology. In M. Tonry & N. Morris (Eds.), *Crime and justice* (Vol. 10, pp. 375–473). Chicago: University of Chicago Press.

Loeber, R., & Schmaling, K. B. (1985a). Empirical evidence for overt and covert patterns of antisocial conduct problems: A meta-analysis. *Journal of Abnormal Child Psychology*, *13*, 337–352.

Loeber, R., & Schmaling, K. B. (1985b). The utility of differentiating between mixed and pure forms of antisocial child behavior. *Journal of Abnormal Child Psychology*, *13*, 315–336.

Loeber, R., & Stouthamer-Loeber, M. (1986). Family factors as correlates and predictors of juvenile conduct problems and delinquency. In N. Morris & M. Tonry (Eds.), *Crime and justice: An annual review of research* (Vol. 7, pp. 29–149). Chicago: University of Chicago Press.

Loeber, R., Green, S. M., Lahey, B. B., & Stouthamer-Loeber, M. (1991). Differences and similarities between children, mothers, and teachers as informants on disruptive child behavior. *Journal of Abnormal Child Psychology*, *19*, 75–95.

Loeber, R., Lahey, B. B., & Thomas, C. (1991). Diagnostic conundrum of oppositional defiant disorder and conduct disorder. *Journal of Abnormal Psychology*, *100*, 379–390.

Lueger, R. J., & Gill, K. J. (1990). Frontal-lobe cognitive dysfunction in conduct disorder adolescents *Journal of Clinical Psychology*, *46*, 696–706.

Lytton, H. (1990). Child and parent effects in boys' conduct disorder: A reinterpretation. *Developmental Psychology*, *26*, 683–697.

Magnusson, D. (1988). *Individual development from an interactional perspective: A longitudinal study*. Hillsdale, NJ: Lawrence Erlbaum.

Maier, G. J., Stava, L. J., Morrow, B. R., Van Rybroek, G. J., & Bauman, K. G. (1987). A model for understanding and managing cycles of aggression among psychiatric inpatients. *Hospital and Community Psychiatry*, *38*, 520–524.

Malgady, R. G., Rogler, L. H., & Costantino, G. (1990). Culturally sensitive psychotherapy for Puerto Rican children and adolescents: A program of treatment outcome research. *Journal of Consulting and Clinical Psychology*, *58*, 704–712.

Mash, E. J. (1989). Treatment of child and family disturbance: A behavioral-systems perspective. In E. J. Mash & R. A. Barkley (Eds.), *Treatment of childhood disorders* (pp. 3–36). New York: Guilford Press.

McBurnett, K., Lahey, B. B., Frick, P., Risch, C., Loeber, R., Hart, E. L., Christ, M. G., & Hanson, K. S. (1991). Anxiety, inhibition, and conduct disorder in children: II. Relation to salivary cortisol. *Journal of the American Academy of Child and Adolescent Psychiatry*, *30*, 192–196.

McMahon, R. J. (1987). Some current issues in the behavioral assessment of conduct disordered children and their families. *Behavioral Assessment*, *9*, 235–252.

McMahon, R. J., & Forehand, R. (1988). Conduct disorders. In E. J. Mash & L. G. Terdal (Eds.), *Behavioral assessment of childhood disorders* (2nd ed., pp. 105–153). New York: Guilford.

Milich, R., & Pelham, W. E. (1986, August). Differentiating valid subgroups of hyperactive and aggressive children. In W. P. Pelham (Chair), *Subgrouping research in externalizing disorders in childhood: Toward an integration*. Symposium presented at the annual meeting of the American Psychological Association, Washington, DC.

Miller, G. E., & Prinz, R. J. (1990). Enhancement of social learning family interventions for childhood conduct disorder. *Psychological Bulletin*, *108*, 291–307.

Nardone, M. J., Tryon, W. W., & O'Connor, K. (1986). The effectiveness and generalization of a cognitive-behavioral group treatment to reduce impulsive/aggressive behavior for boys in a residential setting. *Behavioral Residential Treatment*, *1*, 93–103.

Offord, D. R., Boyle, M. C., & Racine, Y. A. (1991). The epidemiology of antisocial behavior in childhood and adolescence. In D. J. Pepler & K. H. Rubin (Eds.), *The development and treatment of childhood aggression* (pp. 31–54). Hillsdale, NJ: Lawrence Erlbaum.

Offord, D. R., Boyle, M. H., Fleming, J. E., Munroe-Blum, H., & Rae-Grant, N. I. (1989). Ontario child health study: Summary of selected results. *Canadian Journal of Psychiatry, 34*, 483–491.

Offord, D. R., Boyle, M. H., Szatmari, P., Rae-Grant, N. I., Linds, P. S., Cadman, D. T., Byles, J. A., Crawford, J. W., Munroe-Blum, H., Byrne, C., Thomas, H., & Woodward, C. A. (1987). Ontario child health study: II. Six-month prevalence of disorder and rates of service utilization. *Archives of General Psychiatry, 44*, 832–836.

Panella, D., & Henggeler, S. W. (1986). Peer interactions of conduct-disordered, anxious-withdrawn, and well-adjusted black adolescents. *Journal of Abnormal Child Psychology, 14*, 1–12.

Patterson, G. R. (1976). *Living with children: New methods for parents and teachers* (3rd ed.). Champaign, IL: Research Press.

Patterson, G. R. (1982). *Coercive family process*. Eugene, OR: Castalia.

Patterson, G. R. (1986). Performance models for antisocial boys. *American Psychologist, 41*, 432–444.

Patterson, G. R., & Bank, L. (1986). Bootstrapping your way in the nomological thicket. *Behavioral Assessment, 8*, 49–73.

Patterson, G. R., Capaldi, D., & Bank, L. (1991). An early starter model for predicting delinquency. In D. J. Pepler & K. H. Rubin (Eds.), *The development and treatment of childhood aggression* (pp. 139–168). Hillsdale, NJ: Lawrence Erlbaum.

Patterson, G. R., DeBaryshe, B. D., & Ramsey, E. (1989). A developmental perspective on antisocial behavior. *American Psychologist, 44*, 329–335.

Patterson, G. R., Dishion, T. J., & Bank, L. (1984). Family interaction: A process model of deviancy training. *Aggressive Behavior, 10*, 253–267.

Patterson, G. R., Reid, J. B., & Dishion, T. J. (1992). *Antisocial boys*. Eugene, OR: Castalia.

Patterson, G. R., Reid, J. B., Jones, R. R., & Conger, R. E. (1975). *A social learning approach to family intervention* (Vol. 1). Eugene, OR: Castalia.

Pelham, W. E., Schnedler, R. W., & Bender, M. E. (1988). The combination of behavior therapy and methylphenidate in the treatment of attention deficit disorders: A therapy outcome study. In L. Bloomingdale (Ed.), *Attention deficit disorder* (Vol. 3, pp. 29–48). New York: Pergamon.

Pepler, D. J., & Rubin, K. H. (Eds.). (1991). *The development and treatment of childhood aggression*. Hillsdale, NJ: Lawrence Erlbaum.

Pepler, D. J., King, G., & Byrd, W. (1991). A social-cognitively based social skills training program for aggressive children. In D. J. Pepler & K. H. Rubin (Eds.), *The development and treatment of childhood aggression* (pp. 361–379). Hillsdale, NJ: Erlbaum.

Perry, D. G., Perry, L. C., & Rasmussen, P. (1986). Cognitive social learning mediators of aggression. *Child Development, 57*, 700–711.

Pfeffer, C. R., Plutchik, R., & Mizruchi, M. S. (1983). Predictors of assaultiveness in latency age children. *American Journal of Psychiatry, 140*, 31–35.

Pfeiffer, S. I. (1989). Follow-up of children and adolescents treated in psychiatric facilities. *Psychiatric Hospital, 20*, 15–20.

Pfeiffer, S. I., & Strzelecki, S. C. (1990). Inpatient psychiatric treatment of children and adolescents: A review of outcome studies. *Journal of the American Academy of Child and Adolescent Psychiatry, 29*, 847–853.

Rabiner, D. L., Lenhart, L., & Lochman, J. E. (1990). Automatic versus reflective social problem solving in relation to children's sociometric status. *Developmental Psychology, 26*, 1010–1016.

Rey, J. M., & Plapp, J. M. (1990). Quality of perceived parenting in oppositional and conduct disordered adolescents. *Journal of the American Academy of Child and Adolescent Psychiatry, 29*, 382–385.

Rivera, B., & Widom, C. S. (1990). Childhood victimization and violent offending. *Violence and Victims, 5*, 19–35.

Rogeness, G. A., Cepeda, C., Macedo, C. A., Fischer, C., & Harris, W. R. (1990). Differences in hear rate and blood pressure in children with conduct disorder, major depression, and separation anxiety. *Psychiatry Research, 33*, 199–206.

Rogeness, G. A., Crawford, L., & McNamara, A. (1989). Plasma dopamine-β-hydroxylase and preschool behavior in children with conduct disorder. *Child Psychiatry and Human Development, 20*, 149–156.

Rogeness, G. A., Javors, M. A., Maas, J. W., & Macedo, C. A. (1990b). Catecholamines and diagnoses in children. *Journal of the American Academy of Child and Adolescent Psychiatry, 29*, 234–241.

Romoff, V. (1987). Management and control of violent patients at the Western Psychiatric Institute and Clinic. In L. H. Roth (Ed.), *Clinical treatment of the violent person* (pp. 235–260). New York: Guilford Press.

Rutter, M., & Gillmer, H. (1983). *Juvenile delinquent: Trends and perspectives.* New York: Guilford Press.

Shamsie, J., & Hluchy, C. (1991). Youth with conduct disorder: A challenge to be met. *Canadian Journal of Psychiatry, 36,* 405–414.

Shapiro, S. K., & Garfinkel, B. D. (1986). The occurrence of behavior disorders in children: The interdependence of attention deficit disorder and conduct disorder. *Journal of the American Academy of Child Psychiatry, 25,* 809–819.

Soloff, P. H. (1987). Physical controls: The use of seclusion and restraint in modern psychiatric practice. In L. H. Roth (Ed.), *Clinical treatment of the violent person* (pp. 119–137). New York: Guilford Press.

Spivack, G., & Shure, M. B. (1982). The cognition of social adjustment: Interpersonal cognitive problem solving thinking. In B. B. Lahey & A. E. Kazdin (Eds.), *Advances in clinical child psychology* (Vol. 5, pp. 323–372). New York: Plenum.

Stewart, J. T., Myers, W. C., Burket, R. C., & Lyles, W. B. (1990). A review of the pharmacotherapy of aggression in children and adolescents. *Journal of the American Academy of Child and Adolescent Psychiatry, 29,* 269–277.

Szatmari, P., Boyle, M., & Offord, D. L. (1989). ADDH and conduct disorder: Degree of diagnostic overlap and differences among correlates. *Journal of the American Academy of Child and Adolescent Psychiatry, 28,* 865–872.

Szykula, S. A. (1987). Child-focused strategies and behavioral therapy processes. *Psychotherapy, 24,* 202–211.

Tremblay, R. F., Loeber, R., Gagnon, C., Charlebois, P., Larivee, S., & LeBlanc, M. (1991). Disruptive boys with stable and unstable high fighting behavior patterns during junior elementary school. *Journal of Abnormal Psychology, 19,* 285–300.

Tuma, J. M. (1989). Mental health services for children: The state of the art. *American Psychologist, 44,* 188–199.

U.S. Federal Bureau of Investigation. (1987). *Crime in the United States.* Washington, D.C.: U.S. Government Printing Office.

Virkkunen, M., DeJong, J., Bartko, J., Goodwin, F. K., & Linnoila, M. (1989). Relationship of psychobiological variables to recidivism in violent offenders and impulsive firesetters. *Archives of General Psychiatry, 46,* 600–603.

Vitiello, B., Behar, D., Hunt, J., Stoff, D., & Ricciuti, A. (1989). Subtyping aggression in children and adolescents. *Journal of Neuropsychiatry & Clinical Neurosciences, 2,* 189–192.

Wahler, R. G. (1990). Who is driving the interactions? A commentary on "Child and parent effects in boys' conduct disorder." *Developmental Psychology, 26,* 702–704.

Wahler, R. G., & Dumas, J. E. (1987). Stimulus class determinants of mother-child coercive interchanges in multidistressed families: Assessment and intervention. In J. D. Burchard & S. Burchard (Eds.), *The prevention of delinquent behavior* (pp. 190–219). Beverly Hills, CA: Sage.

Wahler, R. G., & Dumas, J. E. (1989). Attentional problems in dysfunctional mother-child interactions: An interbehavioral model. *Psychological Bulletin, 105,* 116–130.

Walker, J. L., Lahey, B. B., Hynd, G. W., & Frame, C. L. (1987). Comparison of specific patterns of antisocial behavior in children with conduct disorder with or without coexisting hyperactivity. *Journal of Consulting and Clinical Psychology, 55,* 910–913.

Walker, J. L., Lahey, B. B., Russo, M. F., Frick, P. J., Christ, M. G., McBurnett, K., Loeber, R., Stouthamer-Loeber, M., & Green, S. M. (1991). Anxiety, inhibition, and conduct disorder in children: I. Relations to social impairment. *Journal of the American Academy of Child and Adolescent Psychiatry, 30,* 187–191.

Webster-Stratton, C. (1984). Randomized trial of two parent-training programs for families with conduct-disordered children. *Journal of Consulting and Clinical Psychology, 52,* 666–678.

Webster-Stratton, C. (1985). The effects of father involvement in parent training for conduct problem children. *Journal of Child Psychiatry and Psychology, 26,* 801–810.

Webster-Stratton, C. (1991). Stress: A potential disrupter of parent perceptions and family interactions. *Journal of Clinical Child Psychology, 19,* 302–312.

Webster-Stratton, C., & Hammond, M. (1990). Predictors of treatment outcome in parent training for families with conduct problem children. *Behavior Therapy, 21,* 319–337.

Webster-Stratton, C., Hollinsworth, T., & Kolpacoff, M. (1989). The long-term effectiveness and clinical significance of three cost-effective training programs for families with conduct-problem children. *Journal of Consulting and Clinical Psychology, 57,* 550–553.

Weinrott, M. R., Bauske, B. W., & Patterson, G. R. (1979). Systematic replication of a social learning approach to parent training. In P. Sjoden, S. Bates, W. S. Dockens (Eds.), *Trends in behavior therapy* (pp. 331–351). New York: Academic Press.

Weisz, J. R., & Weiss, B. (1991). Studying the "referability" of child clinical problems. *Journal of Consulting and Clinical Psychology*, *59*, 266–273.

Yeager, C. A., & Lewis, D. O. (1990). Mortality in a group of formerly incarcerated juvenile delinquents. *American Journal of Psychiatry*, *147*, 612–614.

Yu, P., Harris, G. E., Solovitz, B. L., & Franklin, J. L. (1986). A social problem-solving intervention for children at high risk for later psychopathology. *Journal of Clinical Child Psychology*, *15*, 30–40.

CHAPTER 22

Affective Disorders

Miriam S. Lerner

DESCRIPTION OF THE DISORDER

Internalizing disorders, such as affective disorders, are often thought of as distinct from externalizing disorders (i.e., those that include aggressive behaviors). Current research, however, finds that aggression can occur as part of, or in conjunction with, an affective disorder. The primary forms of aggression that are considered are (1) aggression toward self and (2) aggression toward others. Aggression toward self in the present chapter focuses primarily on suicidal behavior. Suicidal behavior is defined as serious suicidal ideation, suicide attempts, and suicide completion. Other forms of aggression toward self, such as self-mutilation, are not considered within the boundaries of this chapter because of their primary association with characterological and/or dissociative disorders, rather than with "pure" affective disorders.

Aggression toward others is generally considered diagnostically as conduct disorder and oppositional defiant disorder. Note that this author does not consider conduct problems as "masked depression," but rather as a separate diagnostic category (Cantwell, 1983). Thus, aggression toward others will be conceptualized as disorders of conduct *comorbid* with affective disorders.

EPIDEMIOLOGY

Suicidal Behavior

Among adolescents who are affectively disordered, estimates are that 37% will be seriously suicidal and that 25% will make a serious suicide attempt (Ryan et al., 1987). Suicidal behavior is more likely when the depression has an early onset, longer duration,

MIRIAM S. LERNER • Department of Child and Adolescent Psychiatry, Medical College of Pennsylvania, Pittsburgh Campus, Allegheny General Hospital, Wexford, Pennsylvania 15090.

Handbook of Aggressive and Destructive Behavior in Psychiatric Patients, edited by Michel Hersen, Robert T. Ammerman, and Lori A. Sisson. Plenum Press, New York, 1994.

and is severe (Apter, Bleich, & Tyano, 1988; Carlson & Cantwell, 1982; Kazdin, French, Unis, Esveldt-Dawson, & Sherick, 1983), although there is mixed evidence with respect to severity (Ryan et al., 1987). Presence of substance abuse or an externalizing disorder is also related to higher rates of suicidal behavior and higher degrees of suicide intent (Apter et al., 1988; Brent, 1987; Brent, Perper, Goldstein, Kolko, Allan, Allman, & Zelenak, 1988; Pfeffer, Newcorn, Kaplan, Mizruchi, & Plutchik, 1988; Robbins & Alessi, 1985; Ryan et al., 1987). Finally, when major depression is superimposed on dysthymia ("double depression") there is an increased likelihood of suicidal behavior (Ryan et al., 1987). The rate of suicidal behavior in prepubertal children is extremely low (Cantor, 1983).

Comorbidity of Affective and Conduct Disorders

There appears to be a high rate of comorbidity of affective and conduct disorders. Among children diagnosed as "antisocial," 42% were diagnosed with an affective disorder (Rutter, Tizard, & Whitmore, 1981) and 33% of a group of imprisoned youth were found to have a comorbid affective disorder (Chiles, Miller, & Cox, 1980). To the author's knowledge there are no epidemiological studies of the frequency of conduct disorder among children with a primary affective disorder diagnosis, although clinical studies have examined this population (Kovacs, Feinberg, Crouse-Novak, Paulauskas, Pollock, & Finkelstein, 1984).

ETIOLOGY

Suicidal Behavior

Family Environment

Family environment appears to be a key etiological factor in the development of suicidal behavior in children and adolescents. Children and adolescents in highly conflictual, abusive homes are more likely to have high degrees of suicide ideation and a higher level of suicide intent than those in nonabusive home environments (Brent, Kolko, Allan, & Brown, 1990; Kosky, Silburn, & Zubrick, 1986). In fact, lack of family support has been found to discriminate between suicide attempters and nonattempters among psychiatrically hospitalized children (Asarnow & Carlson, 1988). With respect to loss, suicidal children have been found to have had more stressful life events, especially pertaining to loss and separation from family, in the 12 months prior to psychiatric hospitalization than non-suicidally depressed children (Cohen-Sandler, Berman, & King, 1982). The effects of family conflict, abuse, and loss on a child are probably best described by the learned helplessness paradigm. This paradigm and supporting research suggest that when individuals are exposed to uncontrollable, aversive events, they develop feelings of helplessness and hopelessness, as well as a negative perception of themselves (Seligman, 1975; Seligman & Peterson, 1986). This paradigm describes the link between a highly conflictual, abusive home environment and childhood depression.

Cognitive Characteristics

Cognitive theorists have investigated the types of thoughts depressed and suicidal young people experience. Their findings suggest that suicidal, depressed individuals do indeed have a negative self-concept, a feeling of helplessness with respect to the social world, and a feeling of hopelessness about the future. For example, suicidality has been found to be associated with greater degrees of negative cognitions, including a higher likelihood of endorsing the following items on the Children's Depression Inventory (Kovacs, 1985): (1) "Bad things will happen to me," (2) "I feel alone," (3) "I never have any fun," and (4) "I hate myself" (Brent et al., 1990). As can be seen clearly, these cognitions are what one might expect from a child exposed to an aversive, unpredictable family environment.

Development

Cognition, however, is not the whole story. Most recently, the pendulum is swinging away from purely cognitive theories of behavior back to reexamining the role of affect. Ironically, the relationship of affect to affective disorders is in its infancy. One current trend is the examination of child's temperament and the goodness-of-fit between the child and the mother. Goodness-of-fit refers to the match between the child's temperament and the mother's adjusting responses. For example, research indicates that a "fussy baby" with an unresponsive or overstimulating mother has a higher likelihood of developing difficulties than a similar infant with a more accurately responding mother (Chess & Thomas, 1984; Thomas, Chess, & Birch, 1968). Although there is no direct evidence linking goodness-of-fit and depression or suicidality, there is indirect evidence from studies finding that depressed mothers are more likely to have depressed babies (Cytryn, McKnew, Bartko, Lamour, & Hamovitt, 1982; Kashani, Burk, & Reid, 1985). Thus, the parent–child interaction may be a crucial etiological factor for the development of childhood depression and subsequent suicidality.

Social Learning

Suicidal behavior is also thought to be "learned" to some extent. For example, exposure to a family member's suicide increases the likelihood of suicidality for an affectively disordered youngster, controlling for family history of suicide (Brent et al., 1990). Also, high school students who endorse suicidal ideation are more likely to have been exposed to suicidality (Harkavy-Friedman, Asnis, Boeck, & Diofiore, 1987; Smith & Crawford, 1986). In the last few years, an examination of the impact of peer suicide on the suicidality of other adolescents has been examined. The research indicates that rather than a peer suicide influencing all exposed adolescents, youth involved in suicide "clusters" are more likely to have an affective disorder than those who are uninvolved (Brent, Kerr, Goldstein, Bozigar, Wartella, & Allan, 1989). Thus, suicidal behavior may be "learned" or at least imitated by some affectively disordered adolescents.

Etiology of Comorbid Affective and Conduct Disorders

The etiology of conduct disorder, per se, is discussed elsewhere in this volume. This chapter addresses the etiology of depression and conduct disorder when they co-occur. One important question is whether the depression is causal or secondary to conduct problems. Rutter (1985) proposed that depression is secondary to conduct disorder because children with combinations of antisocial and emotional symptoms more closely resemble children with a conduct disorder alone with respect to sex ratios, I.Q., and associated learning deficits. One could imagine that the social impairment resulting from aggressive behavior could create depressive symptoms related to lack of social and family support. Puig-Antich (1982), on the other hand, reported evidence indicating that depression may have a causal effect on conduct disorder. He found that of 13 boys diagnosed with both disorders, 11 lost their conduct disorder when treated with a therapeutic dose of antidepressants. One could imagine that a child with a "depressive coping style" may interpret the behavior of others negatively and perceive their social world as threatening. The child might develop an aggressive style to cope (learned from the family) as a way to respond to these perceived threats. As a clinician, understanding the course of development of symptoms and the child's family and social histories may provide clues as to the primary diagnosis for a child displaying both affective and conduct problems.

AGGRESSION TOWARD SELF

An initial assessment of aggression toward self, or suicidal behavior, is part of the larger clinical interview, which includes an assessment of symptomatology, developmental history, and the family and social environment. With this information, diagnoses, treatment plans, and decisions about the child's safety can be made.

Separate interviews with children and their parents may yield the most information. Each may feel more comfortable disclosing to the clinician. Maintaining confidentiality of the child is essential, with the exception of the child's revelation that he or she may harm himself or herself or someone else. These limits of confidentiality are best expressed to both parents and children at the beginning of the interview process. Finally, it is important to inform the parent that availability of firearms increases the likelihood of suicidal behavior and to recommend that all firearms be removed from the household. A suicide assessment has a number of dimensions. Warning signs for suicidality in the clinical interview may be vague wishes to disappear, escape, or go to sleep forever. Overt statements of wishes to be dead may also occur. Hopelessness may be expressed with statements such as "It will never get better," or "Things will never change." Young children may make references to dying. Whenever statements such as these are expressed it is imperative that the clinician ask directly about suicidal ideation and intention to engage in suicidal behavior. Questions such as, "Are you feeing suicidal?" or "Do you feel like harming yourself?" are examples of ways to initiate a suicide assessment. The clinician may also begin by saying, "Some people who feel hopeless (like they want to escape, can't go on, etc.), also feel suicidal. Do you feel this way?"

Estimating the lethality of the suicidal ideation, or thought, is difficult at times. Some clues as to the individual's intent to act on the thoughts come from asking about whether the person has a plan of how to act on the suicidal thoughts, and the means with which to do so. With a specific plan and the means acquired, the likelihood of a suicidal act is higher. A greater probability of suicidal behavior may be indicated by more frequent suicidal thoughts, with longer duration. Presence or lack of deterrents to completing suicide may also influence the likelihood of suicidal behavior. Semistructured interviews that measure dimensions of suicidal ideation are the Scale for Suicidal Ideation (Beck, Kovacs, & Weissman, 1979) and the Modified Scale for Suicidal Ideation (Miller, Norman, Bishop, & Dow, 1986).

If a child or adolescent has already engaged in suicidal behavior he or she is at much higher risk to repeat the behavior and to complete suicide (Goldacre & Hawton, 1985; Motto, 1984; Otto, 1972; Shafii, Carrigan, Whittinghill, & Derrick, 1985). Assessing suicidal intent associated with lethality of the suicide attempt can be useful for estimating the likelihood of another attempt. One important question is whether the child regrets that he or she did not succeed in the attempt. If the child reports regret, this probably indicates that this child remains at-risk for suicide. Second, the suicide intent of the attempt can be assessed by evaluating the risk of suicide completion. This includes an assessment of the lethality of the means (e.g., 10 aspirin versus 100 aspirin), the child's *perception* of the lethality of the means (e.g., "How many aspirin did you think it would take to kill you?"), and the need for medical intervention. In addition, the likelihood that the child would be rescued from the attempt indicates the degree of suicide intent associated with the attempt. For example, a suicide attempt with the door closed in an empty house may indicate higher suicide intent than one in front of a family member. A semistructured interview that evaluates degree of intent associated with attempt is the Suicide Intent Scale (Beck, Schuyler, & Herman, 1974).

Lastly, identification of the precipitants of suicidal ideation or behavior can help the child begin to find ways to reduce suicidality. Precipitants are often interpersonal problems. They may be current and/or historical. For example, a current encounter with a boyfriend may trigger a memory of sexual abuse, which in turn prompts suicidal ideation. In this case there is a current and historical precipitant for the suicidal ideation. To target the suicidal behavior for clinical intervention it is helpful to identify the chain of environmental, cognitive, and affective experiences leading to suicidal thinking or behavior. For example, a fight with the mother (environmental event) may result in the child believing that he or she is "no good" or "unlovable" (cognitive event); the child may, in turn, feel extremely sad (affective experience) and may engage in a suicidal act. The chain of events for each individual is idiosyncratic and must be assessed carefully and thoroughly. Initially, a child may not be aware or be able to report cognitions and affect associated with suicidality. Part of the goal of treatment is to help the young person gain an awareness of the cognitive, affective, and environmental events leading to suicidal behavior.

AGGRESSION TOWARD OTHERS

When conduct disorders coincide with affective disorders, an assessment of the course of development of both sets of symptoms will help in the formulation of the child's difficulties. Specifically, understanding the precedence of conduct or affective symptoms will lead to the most useful treatment plan.

A developmental assessment should be conducted as part of the standard interview with children. Interviewing the parents about the child's birth through the present age, as well as about the family's development over time (e.g., birth of siblings, family crises), will provide adequate developmental information. A picture of early mother–child goodness-of-fit can be acquired by gathering information about pregnancy, birth, and infancy, such as whether the child was a "fussy" or "easy-to-calm" baby and the parental conditions at the time (e.g., depression, marital conflict, unwanted pregnancy).

School and peer relationships are additional domains from which to gather information with respect to conduct and affective disorders. These can be assessed by asking parents for teachers' comments about their child or speaking with the teachers directly. Teachers may report the child displaying high degrees of aggression or sadness, although aggression is more likely to be reported because of its disruption to the classroom. Peer relationships may also be observed in the school setting by teachers and counselors. Asking whether the child is isolative or social, aggressive or timid, will help formulate an accurate diagnosis. The comparison of the occurrence of a behavior across domains may reveal that it is generalized across domains or is domain specific. This will provide clues as to precipitants as well as direction for clinical intervention.

Lastly, the family environment is the most important to assess. For example, evaluating presence of emotional, physical, or sexual abuse in the child's environment is crucial for the treatment of aggressive behavior (self- or other-directed). The family environment may have changed in significant ways over the course of the child's life. The time sequence of family changes and psychiatric symptomatology will be informative. For example, knowledge that a child developed depressive symptoms following the parents' conflictual divorce, with aggressive symptoms observed at school, indicates that the issue of loss and separation will be important to address in treatment.

CLINICAL MANAGEMENT

Assessment for Safety

The most important part of the evaluation of clients who display aggressive behavior is to determine their safety and the safety of those around them. With respect to suicidal behavior, the *lethality* of the suicidal thoughts is one indicator of safety (or lack of safety). In addition, the child's ability to make a no-suicide contract can be used in the assessment of the risk for suicidal behavior. A no-suicide contract involves asking clients whether they will agree to keep themselves safe by (1) not engaging in suicidal behavior, (2) staying away from situations that provoke suicidal thinking (e.g., drinking alcohol), (3) telling a responsible adult if they are feeling suicidal, and (4) contacting the psychiatric emergency room if they are feeling like acting on the suicidal thoughts. Such a contract can be presented in verbal or written form. It is not considered a legally binding agreement, but rather an assessment tool of whether clients can agree to protect themselves. The contract and phone numbers for a 24-hour psychiatric emergency service are also shared with the parent. If a child cannot agree to the contract, or does so without sincerity in the clinician's opinion, psychiatric hospitalization will need to be considered to help protect the child.

A child who is aggressive toward others needs protection from hurting others. The forms of protection will vary depending on the severity of the aggressive behavior. If a child is hitting peers at school, keeping the child away from peers with a time-out may be sufficient. However, if a child is severely injuring other children, he or she may need to be removed from the classroom. Aggression toward others may be in terms of threats. For example, a child may make homicidal threats toward a parent or sibling. The lethality of these threats (i.e., the likelihood that the child will act on the thoughts) can be assessed in a similar way to suicidal thoughts. An assessment of the plan, availability of the means, and intention to act on the thoughts, as well as the ability to make a verbal agreement to avoid acting on the thoughts, are some of the ways to examine their seriousness. Parents should be informed about homicidal thoughts, and hospitalization must be considered if there is any indication that the child has intention to act, or lack of control over his or her behavior (e.g., is highly impulsive).

An assessment of the safety of the client is conducted hand-in-hand with an assessment of the safety of the client's environment. A safe environment is one that provides basic needs (food, shelter), nurturing, supervision, and protection from abuse. Many children who present with aggressive behavior come from homes that are less than optimal in terms of safety. The child may be abused at home, may be a witness to parental conflict, or may be neglected. The parent(s) may not be able to provide adequate supervision or may be part of the problem that precipitates aggressive behavior. An alternative environment may need to be considered if the parents cannot provide adequate supervision to a highly aggressive child. Other environments include respite care, psychiatric hospitalization, or out-of-home placement.

Intervention

Interventions for aggressive behavior of affectively disordered children displaying aggressive behavior vary along a number of dimensions. One immediate decision is whether inpatient or outpatient therapy is warranted. The least restrictive environment that can provide adequate safety is preferred. A second decision is whether to implement individual or family interventions. This may depend on the willingness of the family to participate, the expertise of the therapist, and the child's preference. There are no studies to date examining the relative efficacy of individual or family therapy for affectively disordered children. A third decision is whether to use medications as part of the treatment. This is best determined by a thorough psychiatric evaluation and should be considered especially for children with severe degrees of affective symptomatology. The final decision is about the length of treatment. This will vary depending on the setting, the severity of the problem, the willingness of the family and the client to participate, and the theoretical orientation of the therapist. A number of short-term and long-term interventions are discussed below.

Short-Term Interventions (3 to 6 Months)

Behavioral techniques are useful short-term interventions for aggressive behavior. Behavioral techniques for suicidal behavior include (1) contracting, (2) decreasing exposure to precipitants, (3) increasing social support, (4) increasing positive experiences, and (5) addressing interpersonal problems with structured problem-solving steps.

An example of contracting is the no-suicide contract discussed previously. Contracting can be used between the therapist and the client or between the client and his or her parent(s). This is a useful technique with adolescents engaging in risky behavior or in a home situation in which there is a never-ending cycle of conflict. For example, a contract may be used between the client and the parent, such that the child agrees to come in at the curfew set by the parent if the parent agrees to remain calm if the child is a few minutes late. Conversely, the parent may agree to stop monitoring phone calls if the adolescent introduces his or her friends to the parents.

Decreasing exposure to precipitants of suicidal thoughts or aggressive behavior may or may not be possible. If spending time alone in one's room tends to increase suicidal thinking, then spending time alone should be avoided, especially with the help of family and friends. However, ongoing parental conflict or emotional neglect from the parents may be more difficult to avoid, and other interventions may be necessary.

Increasing social support and number of positive experiences has been found to be related to reductions in depression (Lewisohn & Graf, 1973). Assessing the degree of social support and number of rewarding activities is the first step. The child may be active in extracurricular activities but not enjoying them. The child may also feel lonely among his or her present group of friends. Thus, a reevaluation of the type of activities the child might enjoy and the type of friends he or she would like to have might be even more important than assessing frequency of activities or number of friends. Also, evaluating the current and potential support within the family may reveal either lack of family support or untapped sources of support in family members. Asking a child with whom he or she can confide will reveal much about trust and support.

Interpersonal problems are often the precipitants of suicidal behavior (Clum, Patsiokas, & Luscomb, 1979). Helping individuals formulate problems and generate possible solutions can relieve some of the depression and hopelessness of suicidal individuals (Clum et al., 1979; Lerner & Clum, 1990). It is important to select problems that can realistically be dealt with and to be honest with the child about ones that are not likely to change in the near future. For example, the child probably has little control over whether his or her parent's will obtain a divorce. However, the child may decide that the problem is that he or she is "put in the middle" by the parents, with each parent talking to the child about the other. Generating alternative ways to address this problem may be a useful way to help relieve some of the feelings of helplessness and hopelessness that the child is experiencing.

Behavioral techniques for intervening with aggressive behavior toward others are discussed in detail in other chapters. Briefly, contracting, behavior modification, and social skills training have been used as short-term interventions for aggressive children. Contracting, as described for suicidal children, can be used with children who are aggressive toward others. Contracts can be formulated between the therapist and child or between the parents and the child. Behavior modification programs are useful for working with conduct-disordered children. Specifically, positive reinforcement for appropriate behavior toward others and removal of positive reinforcement or punishment for aggressive behavior may be useful to reduce aggressive behavior. It is important not to punish aggressive children with aggressive punishment because of the modeling process that occurs. Time-out procedures are a useful way to help aggressive children calm themselves and to remove positive reinforcement for the behavior. Behavior modification programs may be formalized with "star" charts, with the child receiving stars hourly or daily for positive behavior that can be traded in for a reward. This must be conducted only if the chart is understandable and meaningful to the child, and the parent is able to consistently follow through and see the potential benefit of this technique. In addition, the school may be willing to be involved in a behavioral program. Finally, social skills training can be used to teach aggressive children to express their feelings in an assertive, rather than aggressive, fashion. A psychiatric evaluation for use of medication may also be warranted if impulse control appears to be part of the problem.

Long-Term Interventions (6 Months and Longer)

A full discussion of long-term interventions is beyond the scope of this chapter. There are a large number of theoretical approaches to long-term therapy with aggressive children and adolescents. A brief overview of current thinking about cognitive-behavioral therapy is presented. There have been no comparative studies examining the relative treatment efficacy of long-term therapies with affectively disordered children and adolescents.

Cognitive-behavioral therapy has been found to be effective for treating depressed adults (Rush et al., 1977). Typically, cognitive therapy is thought to be a short-term therapy of approximately 12 to 16 sessions. Personal clinical observations, however, are that the more usual course of therapy is longer. Altering a person's cognitions that have been acquired over many years seems to require long-term intervention. Helping a suicidal person learn that he or she is indeed "lovable," after multiple experiences of being unloved, is not a 12-session endeavor.

A recent and important contribution to cognitive-behavioral therapy is the work of Leslie Greenberg and Jeremy Safran (Greenberg & Safran, 1987). They posit that significant *affective* change must occur in conjunction with cognitive change for true "healing" to result. They view affect and cognition as inextricably linked. Unlike cognitive theorists, however, they view emotion as *informational* and, at times, *adaptive* for the individual.

Affect serving an informational function is illustrated in the following scenario. In a therapy session a client begins to cry when she is asked about her mother's behavior in a given situation. The therapist may notice the crying and ask the client what is beneath the tears. The client may respond with, "Before this moment I didn't realize how hurt I was by my mother's behavior toward me." The emotion in this case is not dysfunctional, but rather has helped the client to gain a better picture of her internal reality. This scenario illustrates the informational function of affect. In response to the client's realization of feeling hurt she may become motivated to change the situation with the mother. The move toward changing the situation stimulated by the client's increased understanding of her feelings is the adaptive function of the affect.

A second departure from traditional cognitive therapy is in the response that would follow the client's statement about being "hurt." A traditional cognitive therapist may help the client explore whether her perception of the mother's behavior is real or "distorted." Within the affective-cognitive approach, the therapist is not thought to have a lease on reality. Instead, the therapist may help the client explore the aspects of the mother's behavior that felt hurtful. This approach respects the client's internal reality and helps the client gain a better understanding of her thinking and feeling.

With respect to affectively disordered children, common emotions are sadness, hurt, frustration, anger, and guilt. They may be explored through talking, or, for younger children, they may become more clear through play with puppets, stories, or drama. Emotions can be very difficult and threatening for children to admit. Sometimes talking about how other children in their situation feel or asking them to draw a picture can be helpful. Most importantly, a supportive, nonthreatening, honest therapeutic relationship will build a safe environment in which children can express themselves.

LONGITUDINAL PERSPECTIVE

There has been no longitudinal research evaluating treatment efficacy for this population. With respect to etiology, however, one elegant longitudinal study followed depressed children through adolescence, including children with comorbid conduct disorders. Kovacs and her colleagues (Kovacs et al., 1984) followed 32 boys and 33 girls, aged approximately 10 to 11 years old, for 8½ years following presentation to an outpatient clinic. These children were initially diagnosed with major depression, dysthymic disorder, or adjustment disorder with depression. Many of the children had comorbid disorders. Hence, the diagnostic control group consisted of children with disorders that were co-occurring with the depression (i.e., attention deficit disorder, conduct disorder, oppositional disorder, and anxiety disorder). Over the 8½ years, Kovacs and her colleagues found that none of the children with a diagnosis of adjustment disorder had an episode of major depression, while 5% of the control group had an episode. In contrast, 69% of the children with an initial diagnosis of dysthymic disorder and 72% of those with an initial diagnosis of major depression had an episode of major depression within the next 5 years. For those initially diagnosed with major depression, risk for a second episode was significantly increased by presence of an underlying dysthymic disorder. This study suggests that regardless of the presence of an accompanying conduct disorder (or attention-deficit, oppositional, or anxiety disorder), presence of major depression or dysthymia in childhood can be a precursor to major depression in adolescence.

Another longitudinal study examined the social development of children of affectively disordered parents (i.e., hospitalized for an affective or schizoaffective disorder) from preadolescence through early adolescence (Davis & Erlenmeyer-Kimling, 1989). These investigators found that children of affectively disordered parents had more peer aggression in preadolescence and less satisfying, poorer-quality peer networks in early adolescence compared to a control group of children whose parents did not carry a psychiatric diagnosis. Although this study does not directly examine affectively disordered children, it does suggest some link between being "at-risk" for depression and aggression toward others, which in turn leads to poorer-quality peer networks. This could presumably increase the risk of depression in adolescence. This study provides a useful prototype for examining several etiological factors over the course of development.

The longitudinal perspective on the course of adolescent depression to adulthood has not received much attention. Rutter (1985) reported findings from unpublished studies by Zeitlin that among 37 children with depressive symptoms, 31 had significant depressive symptoms in adulthood. However, very few of the children were diagnosed with depressive disorder.

A few studies have longitudinally examined suicidal behavior from adolescence to adulthood. Among adolescent psychiatric inpatients (some of whom were suicidal) 7.7% died of suicide in an 8- to 10-year follow-up (Welner, Welner, & Fishman, 1979). The risk was greatest among bipolar and schizophrenic patients. In a 10- to 15-year follow-up study of youth suicide attempters, 2.9% of females and 10% of males completed suicide (Otto, 1972). The period of greatest risk for suicide was during the first 2 years after the initial attempt. Higher rates of completed suicide were found among those who had bipolar or psychotic disorders.

CASE ILLUSTRATION

Louie is an 8-year-old boy presenting with aggressive behavior toward peers at school, disobedience at home, hitting his mother, and throwing temper tantrums. His mother brought him in for an evaluation because she had been so frustrated that she feared she could become abusive with him. She also has been contacted daily by the school because of Louie's short temper. Louie is an only child who lives at home with his natural mother and father. Louie's father is a construction worker who is employed long hours and is rarely home. Louie's mother is a housewife.

Louie's development was fairly unremarkable, with the exception of difficulties with reading because of visual-spatial skill deficits. He had been in learning disabilities classes since the first grade. He is currently in the third grade and is acquiring above-average grades. He began throwing temper tantrums when he was 2 years old, after being an easy-to-manage infant. The tantrums tapered from ages 3–4 years and began again when Louie entered kindergarten at age 5 years. This is when he became disobedient at home, began hitting his mother, and acted aggressively with peers.

The initial sessions with Louie revealed a fair-haired, gentle child who was overly compliant. When he would get angry it was mainly with himself for not perfectly completing a task he had begun. He often made negative statements about himself and was easily frustrated.

The initial sessions with the mother and father revealed concerned, but critical, parents. The mother spent long hours with her son completing homework to perfection. The father spoke openly of his own short temper and his inability to tolerate Louie's disobedience. His response over the years had been to lock Louie in his room for periods of time.

Based on the assessment, diagnoses include oppositional defiant disorder and dysthymic disorder. This youngster seemed unhappy with himself as well as aggressive toward others. Recommendations were for individual therapy and parent counseling.

Short-term interventions included (1) contracts between each of the parents and the therapist and (2) social skills training and anger-control techniques in individual therapy with Louie. The contract with the mother involved her encouraging Louie to become more independent. The rationale was that Louie needed to learn more self-control, which could be accomplished by having him learn to be more self-sufficient. Over a few months, she had Louie completing his homework by himself, as well as cleaning his own room. The contract with the father was to create a calm atmosphere for his son. The therapist explained Louie's tendency to become easily overstimulated and encouraged the father to minimize this by remaining as calm as possible. He was also informed that he could be a model for Louie with respect to anger control. The father agreed, but had difficulty following through. He also rarely attended parent counseling sessions.

Short-term interventions with Louie included role-playing situations, especially from school, in which he was provoked by other children. Over numbers of sessions, Louie began to feel more comfortable, acting assertively instead of aggressively and learning to walk away from a fight. Louie also learned several anger-control techniques. Louie learned to calm himself with deep breathing and to recognize early signs of anger. He and the therapist discovered ways he could ask for help from the teacher to reduce frustration. These techniques were practiced repeatedly, within the context of role-plays. The school reported improved self-control in the classroom and in the schoolyard following these interventions.

The long-term intervention with Louie targeted his problems gaining independence from his parents and gaining a more positive image of himself. At first Louie did not want to play in sessions or discuss any issues about his family. He would usually change the topic to sports or factual information. It was very threatening for Louie to talk about feelings. Eventually, over the course of several months of therapy Louie began to play with toys in the office, usually displaying aggressive themes or themes of building and constructing. He began to talk about how frightened he is of his father when his father gets angry. He said he is often afraid to make a mistake for fear of encountering his father's anger. He talked about feeling different at school and feeling bad when other children ridiculed him. Over this time in therapy, Louie began to understand that he is not responsible for his father's short temper, that he can feel less worried about making mistakes when he is not with his father, and that he is not "less than" other children and can stick up for himself in the school setting.

By creating a safe, calm environment Louie had the opportunity to express and explore his negative feelings about himself and his fear in the family. He learned self-control techniques and ways to assert himself with others in a constructive fashion.

SUMMARY

Children with affective disorders may engage in aggressive behavior either toward themselves or others. Identifying the lethality of the aggressive behavior and the safety of the family environment is the initial task of the clinician, so that a protective environment can be provided for the child. With respect to intervention, a thorough assessment of symptomatology, course of development, and the family environment will provide the "map" for the course of treatment. Early interventions may include behavioral contracting and behavioral modification, while later ones may include exploration of feelings and past issues triggering aggressive (or suicidal) responses. Understanding the cognitive, affective, and environmental precipitants for a child's aggressive behavior will help the clinician determine where and how to intervene. Targeting feelings, thoughts, and the family environment will provide the most opportunity for change.

REFERENCES

Apter, A., Bleich, A., & Tyano, S. (1988). Affective and psychotic psychopathology in hospitalized adolescents. *Journal of American Academy of Child and Adolescent Psychiatry, 27*, 116–120.

Asarnow, J. R., & Carlson, G. A. (1988). Suicide attempts in preadolescent psychiatric inpatients. *Suicide and Life-Threatening Behavior, 18*, 129–136.

Asarnow, J. R., Carlson, G. A., & Guthrie, D. (1987). Coping strategies, self-perceptions, hopelessness, and perceived family environments in depressed and suicidal children. *Journal of Consulting and Clinical Psychology, 55*, 361–366.

Beck, A., Kovacs, M., & Weissman, A. (1979). Assessment of suicidal ideation: The scale for suicide ideators. *Journal of Consulting and Clinical Psychology, 47*, 343–352.

Beck, A., Schuyler, R., & Herman, J. (1974). Development of suicidal intent scales. In A. Beck, H. Resnick, & D. Lettieri (Eds.), *The prediction of suicide* (pp. 45–58). Bowie, MD: Charles Press.

Brent, D. A. (1987). Correlates of the medical lethality of suicide attempts in children and adolescents. *Journal of American Academy of Child Psychiatry, 26*, 87–89.

Brent, D. A., Kerr, M. M., Goldstein, C., Bozigar, J., Wartella, M., & Allan, M. J. (1989). An outbreak of suicide and suicidal behavior in a high school. *Journal of the American Academy of Child and Adolescent Psychiatry, 28*, 918–924.

Brent, D. A., Kolko, D. J., Allan, M. J., & Brown, R. V. (1990). Suicidality in affectively disordered adolescent inpatients. *Journal of the American Academy of Child and Adolescent Psychiatry, 29*, 586–593.

Brent, D. A., Perper, J. A., Goldstein, C., Kolko, D. J., Allan, M. J., Allman, C. J., & Zelenak, J. P. (1988). Risk factors for adolescent suicide. *Archives of General Psychiatry, 45*, 581–589.

Cantor, P. (1983). Depression and suicide in children. In C. E. Walker & M. C. Roberts (Eds.), *Handbook of clinical child psychology* (453–474). New York: John Wiley.

Cantwell, D. P. (1983). Depression in childhood: Clinical picture and diagnostic criteria. In D. P. Cantwell & G. A. Carlson (Eds.), *Affective disorders in childhood and adolescence* (pp. 3–18). New York: Spectrum Publications.

Carlson, G. A., & Cantwell, D. P. (1982). Suicidal behavior and depression in children and adolescents. *Journal of the American Academy of Child Psychiatry, 21*, 361–368.

Chess, S., & Thomas, A. (1984). *Infant bonding: Mystique, origins, and evolution of behavior disorders from infancy to early adult life*. New York: Brunner/Mazel.

Chiles, J. A., Miller, M. L., & Cox, G. B. (1980). Depression in an adolescent delinquent population. *Archives of General Psychiatry, 37*, 1179–1186.

Clum, G., Patsiokas, A., & Luscomb, R. (1979). Empirically based comprehensive treatment program for parasuicide. *Journal of Consulting and Clinical Psychology, 47*, 937–945.

Cohen-Sandler, R., Berman, A. L., & King, R. A. (1982). Life stress and symptomatology: Determinants of suicidal behavior in children. *Journal of American Academy of Child Psychiatry, 21*, 178–186.

Cytryn, L., McKnew, D. H., Jr., Bartko, J. J., Lamour, M., & Hamovitt, J. (1982). Offspring of patients with affective disorders: II. *Journal of the American Academy of Child Psychiatry, 21*, 389–391.

Davis, W. R., & Erlenmeyer-Kimling, L. (1989). In B. Lerer & S. Gershon (Eds.), *New directions in affective disorders* (pp. 353–354). New York: Springer-Verlag.

Goldacre, M., & Hawton, K. (1985). Repetition of self-poisoning and subsequent death in adolescents who take overdoses. *British Journal of Psychiatry, 146*, 395–398.

Greenberg, L. S., & Safran, J. D. (1987). *Emotion in Psychotherapy: Affect, cognition and the process of change*. New York: Guilford Press.

Harkavy-Friedman, J. M., Asnis, G. M., Boeck, M., & Diofiore, J. (1987). Prevalence of specific suicidal behaviors in a high school sample. *American Journal of Psychiatry, 144*, 1203–1206.

Kashani, J., Burk, J. P., & Reid, J. C. (1985). Depressed children of depressed parents. *Canadian Journal of Psychiatry, 30*, 265–269.

Kazdin, A. E., French, N. H., Unis, A. S., Esveldt-Dawson, K., & Sherick, R. B. (1983). Hopelessness, depression, and suicidal intent among psychiatrically disturbed inpatient children. *Journal of Consulting and Clinical Psychology, 51*, 504–510.

Kosky, R., Silburn, S., & Zubrick, S. (1986). Symptomatic depression and suicidal ideation: A comparative study with 628 children. *Journal of Nervous Mental Disorders, 174*, 523–528.

Kovacs, M. (1985). The Children's Depression Inventory (CDI). *Psychopharmacology Bulletin, 21*, 995–998.

Kovacs, M., Feinberg, T. L., Crouse-Novak, M., Paulauskas, S. L., Pollock, M., & Finkelstein, R. (1984). Depressive disorders in childhood: II. A longitudinal study of the risk for a subsequent major depression. *Archives of General Psychiatry, 42, 643–649*

Lerner, M. S., & Clum, G. A. (1990). Treatment of suicide ideators: A problem-solving approach. *Behavior Therapy, 21*, 403–411.

Lewinsohn, P. M., & Graf, M. (1973). Pleasant activities and depression. *Journal of Consulting and Clinical Psychology, 41*, 261–268.

Miller, I. W., Norman, W. H., Bishop, A. B., & Dow, J. G. (1986). The modified scale for suicidal ideation: Reliability and validity. *Journal of Consulting and Clinical Psychology, 5*, 724–725.

Motto, J. A. (1984). Suicide in male adolescents. In H. S. Sudak, A. B. Ford, & N. B. Rushforth (Eds.), *Suicide in the young* (pp. 227–244). Boston: Boston Wright, PSG.

Otto, U. (1972). Suicidal acts by children and adolescents: A follow-up study. *Acta Psychiatrica Scandanavia Supplement, 233*, 5–123.

Pfeffer, C. R., Newcorn, J., Kaplan, G., Mizruchi, M. S., & Plutchik, R. (1988). Suicidal behavior in adolescent psychiatric inpatients. *Journal of the American Academy of Child and Adolescent Psychiatry, 27*, 357–361.

Puig-Antich, J. (1982). Major depression and conduct disorder in prepuberty. *Journal of the American Academy of Child Psychiatry, 21*, 118–128.

Robbins, D., & Alessi, N. (1985). Depressive symptoms and suicidal behavior in adolescents. *American Journal of Psychiatry, 142*, 588–592.

Rush, A. J., Beck, A. T., Kovacs, M., & Hollin, S. (1977). Comparative efficacy of cognitive therapy and pharmacotherapy in the treatment of depressed outpatients. *Cognitive Therapy Research, 1*, 17–37.

Rutter, M. (1985). Psychopathology and development: Links between childhood and adult life. In M. Rutter & L. Hersov (Eds.), *Child and adolescent psychiatry modern approaches* (2nd ed.) (pp. 720–739). Oxford: Blackwell Scientific.

Rutter, M., Tizard, J., & Whitmore, K. (1981). *Education, health, and behaviour*. Huntington, NY: Krieger.

Ryan, N. D., Puig-Antich, J., Ambrosini, P., Rabinovich, H., Robinson, D., Nelson, B., Iyengar, S., & Twomey, J. (1987). The clinical picture of major depression in children and adolescents. *Archives of General Psychiatry, 44*, 854–861.

Seligman, M. E. P. (1975). *Helplessness: On depression, development, and death*. San Francisco: Freeman.

Seligman, M. E. P., & Peterson, C. (1986). A learned helplessness perspective on childhood depression: Theory and research. In M. Rutter, L. E. Izard, & P. B. Read (Eds.), *Depression in young people* (pp. 223–249). New York: Guilford.

Shafii, M., Carrigan, S., Whittinghill, J. R., & Derrick, A. (1985). Psychological autopsy of completed suicide in children and adolescents. *American Journal of Psychiatry, 142*, 1061–1064.

Smith, K., & Crawford, S. (1986). Suicidal behavior among "normal" high school students. *Suicide and Life Threatening Behavior, 16*, 313–325.

Thomas, A., Chess, S., & Birch, H. G. (1968). *Temperament and behavior disorders in children*. New York: New York University Press.

Welner, A., Welner, Z., & Fishman, R. (1979). Psychiatric adolescent inpatients: Eight to ten year follow-up. *Archives of General Psychiatry, 36*, 698–700.

CHAPTER 23

Eating Disorders

David M. Garner and Lionel W. Rosen

DESCRIPTION OF THE DISORDERS

Anorexia Nervosa

The diagnostic criteria for anorexia nervosa, according to the fourth revision of the *Diagnostic and Statistical Manual of Mental Disorders* (DSM-IV) (American Psychiatric Association, 1993), are summarized as follows: (1) refusal to maintain a body weight over a minimally normal weight for age and height (e.g., weight loss leading to maintenance of a body weight less than 85% of that expected, or failure to make expected weight gain during period of growth, leading to body weight less than 85% of that expected); (2) intense fear of gaining weight or becoming fat, even though underweight; (3) disturbance in the way that body weight, size, or shape is experienced; and (4) amenorrhea in females (absence of at least 3 menstrual cycles). The new DSM-IV criteria formalize earlier overlapping conventions for subtyping anorexia nervosa into *restricting* and *binge eating/purging* types based on the presence or absence of the bingeing and/or purging (i.e., self-induced vomiting, or the misuse of laxatives, or diuretics). This is consistent with recent research favoring purging over bingeing as the marker for defining anorexia nervosa subtypes (Garner, Garner & Rosen, 1993). It is important to note that patients move between these two subtypes with chronicity leading toward aggregation in the binge eating/purging subgroup (Hsu, 1988).

Bulimia Nervosa

The diagnostic criteria for bulimia nervosa, according to the DSM-IV, are summarized as follows: (1) recurrent episodes of binge eating (binge eating is characterized by a

DAVID M. GARNER and LIONEL W. ROSEN • Department of Psychiatry, Michigan State University, East Lansing, Michigan 48824.

Handbook of Aggressive and Destructive Behavior in Psychiatric Patients, edited by Michel Hersen, Robert T. Ammerman, and Lori A. Sisson. Plenum Press, New York, 1994.

sense of lack of control over eating a large amount of food in a discrete period of time); (2) recurrent, inappropriate compensatory behavior in order to prevent weight gain (i.e., vomiting; abuse of laxatives, diuretics, or other medications; fasting or excessive exercise); (3) a minimum average of two episodes of binge eating and inappropriate compensatory behaviors per week for the past three months; (4) self-evaluation unduly influenced by body shape and weight; and (5) the disturbance does not occur exclusively during episodes of anorexia nervosa. Bulimia nervosa patients are further subdivided into *purging type* and *nonpurging type*, based on the regular use of self-induced vomiting; laxatives, diuretics or other medications; fasting or excessive exercise. Although binge eating is the key symptom of bulimia nervosa, agreement has not been achieved about the definition of this behavior. For example, the requirement that a binge consist of a "large amount of food" poses significant definitional problems and is inconsistent with research indicating that a significant proportion of binges reported by bulimic patients involve small amounts of food (cf. Garner, 1993a; Garner, Shafer, & Rosen, 1992).

Eating Disorders Not Otherwise Specified (NOS)

There are many individuals who have significant eating pathology but who fail to meet one or more of the criteria required for a formal diagnosis of anorexia nervosa or bulimia nervosa. The eating disorder NOS diagnosis is given for individuals who meet all of the criteria for anorexia nervosa except that they have regular menses or a weight that is in the normal range. The eating disorder NOS diagnosis is also assigned when all of the criteria for bulimia nervosa are met except that the binge frequency is less than an average of twice a week or for a duration of less than three months. It is also applied to patients who are at a normal body weight who regularly engage in inappropriate compensatory behavior after eating small amounts of food (i.e., in the absence of binge eating) or who repeatedly chew and spit out large amounts of food. Finally, the eating disorder NOS category is applied to patients who have what has been referred to as the "binge eating disorder," characterized by recurrent episodes of binge eating in the absence of the inappropriate compensatory behaviors evident in bulimia nervosa.

The Relationship between Different Diagnostic Subgroups

Even though distinctions between eating disorder syndromes have been emphasized, there are serious limitations to these nominal subtype designations. Eating disorder patients tend to be more alike than different (Garner, Garfinkel, & O'Shaughnessy, 1985a). There is extraordinary variability within each of these subgroups on a wide range of demographic, clinical, and psychological dimensions (Welch, Hall, & Renner, 1990), and patients have been observed to move between the two subtypes at different points in time (Russell, 1979). As indicated earlier, chronicity tends to lead to binge eating. In sum, it is important to recognize that the symptoms of bingeing, purging, and restrictive dieting occur at different body weights, the critical feature distinguishing anorexia nervosa from other eating disorders being the appearance of these symptoms at an abnormally low body weight (Garner, Garner, & Rosen, 1993). These and other diagnostic issues have been discussed in detail elsewhere (Ben-Tovin, 1988; Beumont, Al-Alami, & Touyz, 1987; Fairburn, 1987; Fairburn & Garner, 1986; Garner, 1993a; Garner, 1993b; Garner & Garfinkel, 1988; Garner, Shafer, & Rosen, 1992; Halmi, 1985; Strober, Salkin, Burroughs, & Morrell, 1982).

EPIDEMIOLOGY

Estimates of the epidemiology of aggressive and destructive behavior among eating disorder patients vary depending on the nature of the setting (clinical or community), the proportions of eating disorder subtypes seen in that setting, and the methodology used to gather data. In a review of nonclinical prevalence studies surveying the various key features of bulimia nervosa, Fairburn and Beglin (1990) found marked variation in the estimates of strict dieting, self-induced vomiting, and laxative abuse. The prevalence of strict dieting for women varied from 7% to 55% across studies, with a mean of 29%. The prevalence of current self-induced vomiting for women varied between 2% and 21% for 14 studies, with a mean of 8%. The mean prevalence for self-induced vomiting occurring with at least a weekly frequency was 2.4% for the eight studies in which this variable was examined. The prevalence of "self-destructive" behaviors among clinical samples is also of interest. Table 1 summarizes data presented by Garner, Garfinkel, and O'Shaughnessy (1985) on the frequency of certain self-destructive behaviors for a sample of patients presenting at a tertiary care center specializing in eating disorders and selected so that equal numbers of the three eating disorder diagnostic subtypes were represented (i.e., restricting anorexia nervosa, bulimic anorexia nervosa, and bulimia nervosa). The information was derived from a clinical interview at the time of initial consultation.

It is evident from Table 1 that extreme binge eating episodes (occurring once a day or more often or lasting more than an hour) characterize about one-half of the patients from

TABLE 1. Frequency of Self-Destructive Behaviors

Clinical features	Bulimia nervosa		Anorexia nervosa, bulimic subtype		Anorexia nervosa, restricting subtype	
	N	%[a]	N	%[a]	N	%[a]
Bulimic episodes[b]						
Once a day or more often	27	46	33	56	0	
More than 1 hour/day	34	57	32	54	0	
Vomiting	43	73	47	80[e]	14	24[e]
Laxative abuse	28	47	34	58	22	37
Diuretic abuse	6	10	8	14	4	7
Alcohol use more than once/month	35	60	27	45	20	34[c]
Use of street drugs	30	51	24	40[e]	11	10[e]
Stealing	17	28	15	26[c]	5	9[c]
Self-mutilation	8	14	11	19	6	10
Suicide attempts	9	16	15	25	7	12
Mood fluctuation—moderate to extreme	47	80[c]	35	60	25	43[e]
Three or more of above impulse-related behaviors	25	43	23	39[c]	11	19[d]

Note. From "The validity of the distinction between bulimia with and without anorexia nervosa" by D. M. Garner, P. E. Garfinkel, and M. Shaughnessy, 1985, *American Journal of Psychiatry*, *142*, 581–587. Adapted by permission.

[a]A superscript in this column indicates a significant difference in the planned comparison (chi-squared test) from the adjacent group on the right; a superscript to the right of a percentage for the restricting subtype group indicates a difference from the respective percentage for the normal-weight bulimic group.

[b]Statistical tests were not performed on the bulimia variables, since these were the bases on which the groups were split.

[c]$p < .05$.

[d]$p < .01$.

[e]$p < .001$.

both of the bulimic groups. Binge eating was defined as "an abnormal increase in one's desire to eat, with episodes of excessive ingestion of large quantities of food—which the patient viewed as ego-alien and beyond her control" (Garfinkel & Garner, 1982, p. 43). The majority of both bulimic groups engaged in self-induced vomiting, and this behavior is also evident in 24% of the restricting anorexia nervosa group. A history of suicide attempts was most common in the anorexic bulimic group (25%), but occurred often enough among the other groups to be a clinical concern. Table 1 also indicates that self-mutilation was more common in the bulimic groups than in the restricting group. Laxative abuse occurred in about half of the bulimic patients and also was found in more than a third of the restricting patients. Diuretic abuse occurred in a small proportion of the patients in all three eating disorder groups. Alcohol use was significantly greater in the bulimic than the restricting anorexia nervosa group, confirming the results from other studies. For example, Mitchell, Hatsukami, Eckert, and Pyle (1985) found that 23% of patients with bulimia had a history of drinking problems. Beary, Lacey, and Merry (1986) reported that 38% of their bulimia nervosa patients were "excessive drinkers" and 27% were abusing alcohol.

Hatsukami, Mitchell, Eckert, and Pyle (1986) provide a more fine-grained analysis by comparing the frequency of some of these same clinical features in patients who had bulimia nervosa alone versus those who also had a diagnosis of affective disorder or substance abuse disorder. Their results, presented in Table 2, indicate that bulimic patients who also are diagnosed with affective or substance abuse disorder are at far greater risk for most self-destructive behaviors. Obviously this is related to some degree to the fact that some of the destructive behaviors tabulated would be used to form the groups (e.g., alcohol abuse and, perhaps, suicide attempts); however, the data are interesting nevertheless. There were no suicide attempts among the group of patients with bulimia alone; however, 26.5% of those with concurrent affective disorder and 32.4% with substance abuse had attempted suicide. Bulimic patients with a history of substance abuse also report a high incidence of stealing, perhaps suggesting a more general problem with impulsivity.

If there is an association between substance abuse and eating disorders, it might be expected that there would be an overrepresentation of eating disorders among patients

**TABLE 2.   Characteristics of Bulimic Patients
with or without Concurrent Affective or Substance Abuse Disorder**

	Bulimia alone (N = 46)		Bulimia and affective disorder (N = 34)		Bulimia and substance abuse (N = 34)	
	N	%	N	%	N	%
Vomiting	43	94	24	71	33	97
Laxative abuse	24	52	17	50	24	71
Diuretic abuse	10	22	9	27	19	56
Alcohol use more than once/week	10	22	10	29	26	76
Suicide attempts	0	0	9	27	11	32
Stealing						
Since onset	20	44	11	32	23	68
Before onset	5	11	5	15	14	41

Note. From "Characteristics of patients with bulimia only, bulimia with affective disorder, and bulimia with substance abuse problems" by D. Hatsukami, J. E. Mitchell, E. D. Ekert, and R. Pyle, 1986, *Addictive Behaviors, 11,* 399–406. Adapted by permission.

presenting with alcohol or drug problems. Several studies have found such an association. Peveler and Fairburn (1990) found that, of 31 women presenting at an alcohol treatment unit, 36% reported the symptom of binge eating, 26% met diagnostic criteria for probable clinical eating disorder, and 19% had a history of probable anorexia nervosa. This confirmed earlier findings by Lacey and Moureli (1986) in a study of women referred for alcohol problems. In that investigation, 41% reported overeating and 22% had a history suggestive of anorexia nervosa. Jonas, Gold, Sweeney, and Pottash (1987) interviewed 259 consecutive callers to a National Cocaine Hotline and reported that 32% met the broad DSM-III criteria for an eating disorder.

Obviously, the ultimate self-destructive outcome in eating disorders is death. The long-term mortality risk for anorexia nervosa has been reported to be as high as 18% (Theander, 1985); however, outcome studies of a similar duration for bulimia nervosa have not been published. A review of the 45 follow-up studies published from 1953 to 1981 (Steinhausen & Glanville, 1983) and another 22 published between 1981 to 1989 (Steinhausen, Rauss-Mason, & Seidel, 1991) indicate that the mortality rate for anorexia nervosa varies widely depending on the length of follow-up, treatment setting, and age of the patient population. Data from these two reviews suggest a decline in the mortality rates in more recent studies (10% for earlier studies compared to 4.4% for those published in the 1980s). However, as Steinhausen and colleagues (1991) point out, only one study has attempted to standardize the mortality data by comparing the crude mortality rate with the expected rate for patients of comparable age. That study (Patton, 1988) reported the crude mortality rate as 3.3, and the standardized mortality rate as six times greater for anorexia nervosa patients.

ETIOLOGY

A complete understanding of aggressive or destructive behaviors for any individual patient involves a thorough analysis of the individual, family, and cultural background factors leading to the development and maintenance of the eating disorder. Clearly, the theoretical perspective or model adopted by the clinician will determine the nature of the analysis and the ultimate formulation used to account for the symptom expression. Although cognitive-behavioral, psychodynamic, family, and biological models have become increasingly refined, they are as yet unable to specify all contributing factors or to yield precise predictions regarding response to treatment. Traditionally, there has been a tension between biological and psychological models of the development of eating disorders. However, in recent years there has been a genuine integration of previously antagonistic views with an understanding that these disorders reflect a complex interplay between cultural, psychological, familial, and biological factors. In light of the popularity of psychological theory, it is important to remain circumspect regarding underlying biological vulnerabilities to eating disorders (Bakan, Birmingham, & Goldner, 1991). It has been known for years that prenatal and perinatal complications are unusually common in anorexia nervosa patients (Bakan et al., 1991; Halmi, 1974). It is also well established that the concordance rate for eating disorders among monozygotic twin pairs is significantly higher than that found among dizygotic pairs (Garfinkel & Garner, 1982; Holland, Hall, Murray, Russell, & Crisp, 1984). Thus, it is important to recognize that possible biological factors may play an as yet undetermined role in the etiology of a subset of patients who develop eating disorders and may specifically contribute to the expression of aggressive and destructive behaviors seen in these patients.

Just as biological susceptibility may play a role in the expression of eating disorders, once these disorders have developed, they can have serious biological consequences. Complications such as hypotension, hypothermia, bradycardia, and overall reduced metabolic rate are symptoms of starvation and are therefore common in anorexia nervosa (Garfinkel & Garner, 1982). Self-induced vomiting and purgative abuse may cause various symptoms or abnormalities, such as weakness, muscle cramping, edema, constipation, cardiac arrhythmias, paresthesia, and sudden death. Additionally, general fatigue, constipation, depression, various neurological abnormalities, kidney and cardiac disturbances, swollen salivary glands, electrolyte disturbances, dental deterioration, finger clubbing or swelling, edema, acute gastric dilatation and dehydration have been reported (Comerci, 1990; Mitchell, 1990; Mitchell & Boutacoff, 1986; Mitchell, Pomery, & Huber, 1988; Mitchell, Seim, Colon, & Pomeroy, 1987).

AGGRESSION TOWARD SELF

Self-destructive behaviors of eating disorder patients should be distinguished on the basis of motivation, intention, and etiology. Some behaviors, such as suicide attempts and self-mutilation, are deliberate acts of self-harm; others, such as vomiting and laxative abuse, are clearly self-destructive but this is not usually their primary intent. Sometimes aggression toward the self is directly related to the characteristic psychopathology of the eating disorder (e.g., self-punishment such as hours of exercise or fasting as atonement for violating a dietary rule), and at other times it is tied more to associated psychopathology (e.g., borderline personality disorder, affective disorder, or substance abuse disorder). For example, self-cutting may be an indirect plea for help, an act of anger toward others, a purposeful bid to end a life filled with misery and despair, or a means of modulating tension or unpleasant affect. A thorough assessment of the dangerousness and the function served by self-destructive behavior is essential when it is present with eating disorder patients.

Whether or not certain impulsive behaviors such as drug abuse, stealing, suicide attempts, or sexual promiscuity are motivated to any degree by a conscious wish to inflict self-harm varies considerably across the patient population. When suicide attempts occur in connection with a primary affective disorder, they may reflect hopelessness about recovery. On the other hand, they may be calculated attempts to punish or manipulate others. Sometimes the motivation is a mixture of these factors, and they may be experienced at varying levels of consciousness.

The motivation behind suicide attempts must be carefully evaluated with the knowledge that a significant proportion of deaths in anorexia nervosa are attributable to suicide (Theander, 1985). As mentioned earlier, suicide attempts are common, particularly among patients with the bulimic subtype of anorexia nervosa, and are much more likely in bulimia nervosa if the patient receives a concomitant diagnosis of either affective or substance abuse disorder (Hatsukami et al., 1986).

Various illicit substances, such as nonprescribed drugs or alcohol, are taken by patients, either to modulate affect, specifically reduce appetite, or induce a stupor that reduces the likelihood of eating. When questioned about why she frequently drank alcohol to the point of blackouts, one patient indicated that she had no particular desire to drink but she knew that she could not eat if she was unconscious. Patients with other medical illnesses have been reported to manipulate prescribed medications such as insulin or thyroid hormone to create or sustain weight loss (Garfinkel & Garner, 1982). Fornari, Edleman, and Katz (1990) have even suggested the manipulation of medications to change weight should constitute another diagnostic criterion for eating disorders.

Stealing is a self-destructive behavior that can be motivated by different factors. It can reflect a need for money for food or laxatives, veiled hostility toward others, or a personality disorder. In rare cases, it may be a symptom of true kleptomania. Norton, Crisp, and Bhat (1985) compared anorexia nervosa patients with a history of stealing to those not reporting this symptom. They found that the patients with a history of stealing were more likely to be bulimic, were more sexually active, and had higher levels of anxiety, depression, and hysteria than their nonstealing counterparts. These results were extended in a study of 181 consecutive referrals to an eating disorder program by Krahn, Nairn, Gosnell, and Drewnowski (1991), who compared patients with and without a history of stealing. They found that the 28.2% of the sample with a history of stealing had significantly higher levels than nonstealers of dysfunctional eating symptoms and psychological distress, including depression, interpersonal sensitivity, obsessive-compulsive symptoms, and hostility. Certainly, some of these findings may be simply related to the practical consequences of bulimic disorders that are not encountered by restricting anorexic patients. For example, the large amounts of food or laxatives used by bulimic patients may become very expensive, and this leads to stealing. On the other hand, stealing may reflect a fundamental problem with impulse control.

In evaluating patients, it is important to consider whether or not stealing occurred only after the onset of the disorder or whether it was also evident earlier, perhaps indicating a more basic behavioral pattern. Stealing sometimes can be an indirect plea for treatment. For example, one patient indicated that both she and her parents had colluded in profound denial surrounding the existence of her eating disorder. Her one rather plaintive shoplifting episode was really motivated by a desire for help with her eating disorder.

Self-cutting is relatively common among eating disorder patients. Although the etiology is most certainly multidetermined, chronic self-mutilation has been described as typically involving tension regulation. The act is described as being associated with a period of increasing tension, which culminates in cutting and is followed by relief of the tension (Pao, 1969). Patients often have difficulty communicating verbally the source of the tension, but they vividly describe the soothing and sometimes erotic experience of watching their blood flow or examining the wound without pain (Simpson, 1973). There is often an altered state of consciousness and sometimes amnesia preceding the cutting. This is similar to the type of tension reduction described by some patients following binge eating episodes (Abraham & Beumont, 1982). With bulimia nervosa patients who have borderline personality features, self-mutilation has been conceptualized as self-punishment having roots in early developmental experiences (Johnson & Connors, 1987). According to this view, feelings of worthlessness are activated in response to the perceived emotional unavailability of an earlier caretaker. Goodsitt (1985) has suggested that the painful sensations generated by some eating disorder symptoms are purposeful in that they function to mute ongoing emotional turmoil. Although he has conceptualized the process in psychological terms, it may be that starvation, bingeing, vomiting, and even self-inflicted pain may modulate mood or stress by altering endogenous beta-endorphins or other neuropeptides (cf. Yates, 1991). Cases of repeated self-mutilation are often associated with a general clinical picture of impulsivity and can lead to repeated and turbulent hospitalizations. Simpson (1973) described a case in which a women with an eating disorder engaged in repeated episodes of self-mutilation, including wrist, breast, and vaginal cutting. Numerous hospitalizations were precipitated by self-cutting, fainting, hyperventilation, and complaints of abdominal pain. While in hospital, she swallowed metal objects, engaged in various forms of self-mutilation, and smashed windows. With the suggestion of discharge, she tried to strangle herself. She described a sustained preoccupation with self-mutilation and admitted to planning most incidents carefully. She reported no experience of pain when cutting and also described a fascination in watching herself bleed. Although this type of severe and sustained self-mutilation is rare in eating disorders, when it occurs, there is usually extreme ambivalence about treatment, illustrated by alternating demands for care and withdrawal or active interference with those offering help.

Although usually it has less perilous consequences, "compulsive exercise" among eating disorder patients may serve a similar function to self-mutilation. Yates (1991) suggests that "obligatory exercise" can serve various intrapsychic functions such as self-regulation, self-definition, a defense against receptive pleasure, separation and maintenance, and self-hurt. The function of the pain generated from exercise is considered to function to distract from emotional discomfort.

Lacey and Evans (1986) have underscored the common themes in the literature on impulsivity in substance abuse disorders, eating disorders, self-harm, classical impulse control disorders (i.e., gambling, kleptomania, pyromania, explosive disorders), and personality disorders. They suggest there is a distinct group of patients who display "multiple impulsive personality disorder," who have a poor prognosis, and who require specialized treatment.

AGGRESSION TOWARD OTHERS

Some psychodynamically oriented clinicians have identified aggressive themes and fantasies of death as common in eating disorders (Jackson, Davidson, Russell, & Vandereycken, 1990; Sours, 1980); however, overtly aggressive or violent behaviors are not typical of these patients. Nevertheless, there are times when eating disorder patients will express intense rage and overt aggression toward others. This may be in response to perceived coercion by others, who are seen as forcing patients to eat or gain weight. Clinicians experienced in treating eating disorder patients can usually recall at least one case in which a threat of enforced weight gain has transformed a demure, frail, emaciated young woman into a ferocious adversary capable of demolishing an entire ward. These violent outbursts are rare, particularly when clinical staff are well trained and there is adequate attention devoted early on to enlisting the patient's cooperation as a collaborator in treatment. Less extreme expressions of anger are common when patients feel caught in the conflict between the demands of others for symptom control and their own internal imperatives to control weight or avoid eating feared foods.

Masked aggression is probably a more common motif accounting for a range of different symptoms seen in eating disorder patients. A rather obvious example is illustrated by one 14-year-old bulimic patient who persisted in placing bowls of vomitus in strategic locations around her home. Although she initially denied that this was related to feeling anger toward anyone in her family, she admitted later that her behavior was motivated by outrage at her parents for their inability to resolve marital conflicts (cf. Garner, Garfinkel, & Bemis, 1982). Once the interpersonal conflicts were articulated, and the patient was helped with the guilt that she felt about expressing her feelings of anger toward her parents, she was able to adopt more direct means by expressing her concerns. Similarly, many anorexia nervosa patients initially deny any aggressive intent behind refusal to eat; however, insight into their motivation leads some to acknowledge that their symptoms are, at least in part, related to anger toward a family member who is perceived to be intrusive, controlling, or insincere. This passive–aggressive interpersonal style is often viewed as manipulative or deceitful by others and can elicit intense negative emotional reactions or even maltreatment of eating disorder patients (Garner, 1985; Shisslak, Gray, & Crago, 1989). Understanding the fears and sense of helplessness that underlie these feeble attempts at assertion can greatly attenuate negative reactions toward these patients (Hamburg & Herzog, 1990).

CLINICAL MANAGEMENT

Warmth, genuineness, empathy, honesty, acceptance, and an ability to set limits are qualities that should be part of the repertoire of all skilled therapists. These qualities are essential in the treatment of those with eating disorders, since patients may begin the therapeutic process with the conviction that the goal of the clinician is to deprive them of certain ego-syntonic symptoms (e.g., thinness, dieting, and weight control) that patients view as vital to well-being (Andersen, 1985; Bruch, 1973; Casper, 1987; Crisp, 1980; Garner et al., 1982; Garner & Bemis, 1982; Stern, 1986; Vandereycken, Kog, & Vanderlinden, 1989). Success in managing aggressive and destructive behaviors clearly depends on the strength of the therapeutic relationship.

Assessment is the first step in managing self-destructive symptoms displayed by those with eating disorders. Complete psychiatric assessment of personality functioning, psychological state, depression, anxiety, family functioning, history of sexual abuse, self-esteem, social and vocational adaptation, and impulse-related features is important in confirming Axis II diagnoses and in treatment planning.

Specific questioning should be directed toward weight-controlling behaviors such as vomiting, laxative and diuretic abuse, taking diet pills or other drugs to control appetite, use of emetics, prolonged fasting, and vigorous exercise for the explicit purpose of controlling body weight. Details regarding specific probe questions for assessment of these areas have been provided elsewhere (Fairburn, 1987; Foreyt & McGavin, 1988; Garner, 1991; Garner & Parker, 1993). Information should be gathered regarding the frequency, amount, and pattern of drug and alcohol use. It is vital to determine whether substance abuse began before or after the onset of the eating disorder. As indicated earlier, if these symptoms began after the onset of the eating disorder, then this may indicate that the initial motivation for use was related to appetite control or mood modulation. If the substance abuse predated the eating disorder, then it may reflect a more fundamental personality disturbance that may be a more ominous prognostic sign. In some cases, the abused substance initially serves one role but later acquires a different function. For example, a patient may begin using diet pills for weight loss, but eventually come to rely on them primarily to regulate her mood. One patient described initially using laxatives for weight control but later they were taken either to punish herself for deviating from her strict dietary regimen or to displace her distress following a perceived social blunder. She was very specific in describing "the pain" as providing "penitence" for unacceptable behavior. If she was prohibited from taking laxatives, she described a uncontrollable urge to hurt herself in some other way before she could resume her normal daily routine.

It is important to be aware of the fact that patients may become dependent upon laxatives to maintain regular lower bowel function or to try to reduce fluid retention. This becomes a self-perpetuating cycle since discontinuing the laxatives causes constipation and "rebound" edema. Although laxative withdrawal is difficult for most patients, we recommend the guidelines established by Mitchell (1990), including: (1) abrupt withdrawal (since it has not been established that gradual tapering will benefit the patient), (2) maintenance of an adequate fluid intake, (3) helping the patient expect and tolerate a period of constipation, which may be treated with natural fiber and addition of bran to the diet, and (4) regular exercise to facilitate bowel functioning (as long as excessive exercise is not a target symptom in the therapy).

Attention to detail should also be taken in assessing suicide attempts and acts of self-mutilation. Whether these behaviors preceded or followed the onset of the eating disorder may provide important clues regarding initial management. Also, it is crucial to explore the current meaning these behaviors have to the patient, the historical base for their function, and the potency of the maintaining factors. Probing must be done gradually with special sensitivity to the possibility that questioning might elicit feelings of humiliation (because the behavior is viewed on one level as bizarre), hostility (because the questions are perceived as intrusive, derisive, or attacking), or depression (because focusing on the behavior stimulates feelings of hopelessness). It may be helpful to convey the message that behavior that may initially look grotesque or bizarre to others is almost always understandable once there is a clear awareness of its function.

Reassessment during the course of treatment is desirable since it may not be initially apparent whether psychological distress, cognitive impairment, and behavioral symptoms signal fundamental emotional disturbance or are secondary elaborations resulting from weight loss and chaotic dietary patterns (Fairburn, Cooper, Kirk, & O'Connor, 1985; Garner, Olmsted, Davis, Rockert, Goldbloom, & Eagle, 1990). In this sense, treatment (i.e., brief, educationally oriented therapy) is an important aspect of assessment since some patients show rapid improvement with more consistent eating patterns and weight restoration (Olmsted, Davis, Garner, Rockert, Irvine, & Eagle, 1991).

The major focus of treatment is on individual, familial, and sociocultural background factors that contribute in various ways to the development and maintenance of the eating disorder. These background factors have formed the basis for different theoretical approaches to eating disorders that have resulted in treatment orientations characterized as primarily behavioral, cognitive-behavioral, educational, psychodynamic, and family systems in focus. Full discussion of these psychological approaches to eating disorders is far beyond the scope of the current chapter, and they have been reviewed elsewhere (Garner & Garfinkel, 1985; Humphrey, 1989; Johnson & Connors, 1987; Minuchin, Rosman, & Baker, 1978; Strober & Humphrey, 1987; Vandereycken et al., 1989). While certain core features may be common to many eating disorder patients, individual differences in premorbid personality and levels of psychological functioning contribute to major differences in the manifestation of key symptoms (Tobin, Johnson, Steinberg, Staats & Dennis, 1991). While a significant minority of patients respond favorably to educational or short-term cognitive-behavioral treatment (CBT) methods (described in detail elsewhere, e.g., Edgette & Prout, 1989; Fairburn, 1985; Garner & Bemis, 1982, 1985; Garner, Rockert, Olmsted, Johnson, & Coscina, 1985; Garner & Rosen, 1990), many of the patients who have an established pattern of engaging in self-destructive behavior within the context of a personality disorder probably require much more than education or brief therapy, regardless of the orientation. While CBT for bulimia nervosa is the standard treatment, other approaches are proving effective.

In a carefully controlled study, Fairburn, Jones, Peveler, Carr, Solomon, O'Connor, Burton, and Hope (1991) compared CBT to behavioral psychotherapy and interpersonal psychotherapy (IT), neither of which includes procedures specific to CBT. Findings at the end of treatment indicated that, while all three treatments resulted in improvement on measures of binge eating and general psychopathology, CBT was more effective than the other treatments in modifying extreme dieting, self-induced vomiting, and disturbed attitudes toward shape and body weight. However, IT also led to significant improvements in binge eating for many patients without focusing on restrictive dieting at all. This is consistent with results of a study by our group, in which CBT and supportive-expressive psychotherapy were compared (Garner, Rockert, Garner, Davis, & Olmsted, 1993). Similarly, unpublished data described by Agras (1991) indicate that IT is as effective as CBT in the treatment of obese binge eaters who do not purge.

Drug treatment may play a valuable role in treating some patients with bulimia nervosa (Mitchell, 1988). A recent study by Agras, Rossiter, Arnow, Schneider, Telch, Raeburn, Bruce, Perl, and Koran (1992) compared desipramine, CBT, and a combination of the two (with the drug withdrawn at either 16 or 24 weeks). It was found that the combined drug and CBT treatment was superior to the other conditions as long as the medication was continued for at least 24 weeks. While this study supports earlier research indicating that medication alone is not the most effective treatment for bulimia nervosa (Mitchell, Pyle, Eckert, Hatsukami, Pomeroy, & Zimmerman, 1990), it provides new data suggesting that antidepressant therapy may add significantly to the effects of CBT.

With all of the treatment options available and the apparent effectiveness of a number of them, how should the clinician choose an approach? In the treatment of eating disorders, it has been argued that a sequence of treatments should be followed, where the least intrusive approach is applied first, followed by potentially more disruptive interventions if initial efforts fail (Garner, Garfinkel, & Irvine, 1986). There are general guidelines for determining the likely initial treatment of choice. Unless there are compelling contraindications, family therapy should be considered the optimal modality for treatment if the patient is young or living at home. It may be worthwhile to blend individual therapy with family therapy if a major goal of treatment is facilitating autonomy in either the patient or the family. If the disorder is long-standing, or if the self-destructive symptoms pose serious medical risks, an inpatient setting should be considered as an initial step; however, without adequate outpatient follow-up, relapse is very likely. In an inpatient setting, structured group treatment, aimed at specific problem areas, may be a valuable adjunct to individual therapy and medical management. Drug treatment may be considered as an adjunct to psychotherapy for bulimia nervosa patients who fail to respond to psychosocial interventions alone. Tricyclics or bicyclic formulations are generally recommended to precede the use of MAOIs (which may be useful in a minority of cases). There is more latitude in the psychotherapeutic orientation of the therapist, particularly if the issue of dietary management is integrated into therapy.

In cases where the self-destructive or aggressive behaviors are of immediate danger to the patient, hospitalization must be considered (cf. Andersen, 1985; Garfinkel & Garner, 1982; Garner & Sackeyfio, 1993; Lucas, Duncan, & Piens, 1976). The decision to implement hospitalization can involve the delicate philosophical balance between free will and determinism (Crisp, 1980; Goldner, 1989). On the one hand, the eating disorder patient may be seen as free to choose an alternative way of life (i.e., anorexia nervosa), even if it is self-destructive; on the other hand, the patient may be seen as unable to exercise free choice because of supervalent psychological determinants that cloud judgment regarding medical risks. Both points of view have merit, and there appears to be no consensus regarding the solution to the dilemma. However, Goldner (1989) has provided a summary of recommendations designed to minimize treatment refusal, and they may be paraphrased as follows: seek a voluntary alliance, identify the reasons for treatment refusal, carefully explain reasons for treatment recommendations, remain flexible, show respect for the patient's belief in the importance of thinness, minimize intrusive interventions, weigh the risks and benefits of active treatment, avoid punitive interventions, involve the family where possible, and consider involuntary treatment only when nonintervention constitutes an immediate or serious danger. The primary aim of hospitalization is to provide a safe, protective environment in which structure may be helpful to patients who are learning to tolerate the guilt experienced with the inhibition of their symptomatic eating behavior.

The mortality risk and self-initiated nature of some of the symptoms in eating disorders can initiate feelings of fear, anger, frustration and helplessness among treatment staff (Brotman, Stern, & Herzog, 1984; Garner, 1985). The volitional nature of many of the self-destructive symptoms displayed by eating disorder patients may cause them to be perceived as manipulative, uncooperative, deceitful, and less deserving of treatment than patients with other psychiatric problems. We believe these portrayals are unjustified since most patients are not generally deceitful. They behave as would be predicted given their terror about giving up symptoms that could result in weight gain when their weight or shape is the sole or predominant criterion for inferring self-worth.

There is a subgroup of very difficult eating disorder patients who exhibit unremitting self-destructive behaviors such as persistent self-mutilation, substance abuse (with laxatives, emetics, illicit drugs, or alcohol), or suicide threats (or attempts). Many of these patients have a long history of affective instability with periods of intense dysphoria, irritability, anxiety, and elation (Johnson, Tobin, & Enright, 1989; Levin & Hyler, 1986). They usually meet criteria for either borderline or histrionic personality disorders. Their vacillation between helplessness or compliant behavior, on the one hand, and threatening, demanding, and argumentative behavior, on the other, can make treatment a frustrating and arduous process. Some of these patients seem to profit from a treatment that emphasizes building on a strong therapeutic alliance, in which consistency, reality testing, and limit-setting are the recurrent themes. For some eating disorder patients, the self-mutilation and other destructive behaviors can be best conceptualized in social learning terms. Here, the treatment focuses on changing the social contingencies that appear to maintain self destruction. In these cases, the paradigm proposed by Wooley, Blackwell, and Wingate (1978) for the management of "chronic illness behavior" is particularly instructive. According to this model, a wide range of chronic illness behaviors (presenting as headaches, factitious illness, cardiac symptoms, pain of unknown origin, and eating symptoms) are elicited and then maintained by their interpersonal consequences, loosely defined as "caretaking." For some eating disorder patients, who show a remarkable lack of social competency, their self-cutting, escalating suicide gestures, and myriad of other symptoms have been shaped by a social environment that may at first unwittingly dispense interpersonal contact and concern in response to patients' symptoms. Later, concern or medical intervention is extracted by the social and medical reality of patients' potentially dangerous symptoms. There is a gradual evolution of a "lifestyle" in which these symptoms become crystallized and the patient's identity comes to revolve around an "illness role" (e.g., Garner, 1988).

Understanding the social contingencies that maintain the symptoms can lead to strategies that make care-giving contingent on self-initiated behaviors and independence seeking. At the most basic level, this begins with explicitly linking appointment frequency and length to the inhibition of self-destructive behaviors or the implementation of coping behaviors. This is usually very different from the reinforcement schedule that has naturally evolved during the course of the disorder. Clearly, a primary concern must be the safety of the patient; thus, self-destructive behaviors, regardless of their function or intention, should be met with appropriate medical care. However, it is important to distinguish between an intervention designed to address acute medical complication and psychotherapy. After establishing a therapeutic alliance and identifying self-destructive behaviors that are maintained by interpersonal contingencies, the clinician can gradually take steps to increase care-giving in the therapeutic context but make this dependent on the cessation of serious self-destructive acts.

In summary, social learning principles can be adapted to different therapeutic orientations to address such serious symptoms as self-mutilation by (1) identifying and eliminating social reinforcers for the symptoms that have been unwittingly provided by family, friends, and health care workers; (2) structuring treatment to identify skills, self-awareness, and coping behavior that is then immediately reinforced by the therapist and others in the patient's social system; (3) reducing avoidance behavior by reducing fears related to food, weight, and interpersonal rejection and by increasing skill levels and improving self-esteem; and (4) providing models for successful achievement of social competence (Garner et al., 1982; Wooley et al., 1978).

LONGITUDINAL PERSPECTIVES

Theander (1985) has provided the most extended evaluation of the suicide potential in anorexia nervosa in a long-term follow up of 94 patients first seen in the early 1960s (after a mean observation time of 15 years since the onset of the disorder) and again seen in 1984 (after a mean observation time of 33 years). Table 3 presents outcome status for the sample 5, 15, and 33 years after the onset of the disorder, and indicates an aggregation over time of patients into the recovered and deceased categories. The data in Table 3 dramatically illustrate the self-destructive potential for anorexia nervosa as well as the fact that the appraisal of outcome depends on when the assessment is performed. It is evident that after many years of illness, patients tend either to improve or to die. Of the patients who died,

TABLE 3. Long-Term Outcome
for 94 Anorexia Nervosa Patients

Outcome status	Years after onset		
	5	15	33
Recovered (%)	55	63	76
Intermediate (%)	19	17	1
Poor (%)	18	7	6
Deceased (%)	8	13	18

Note. From "Outcome and prognosis in anorexia nervosa and bulimia: Some results of previous investigations, compared with those of a Swedish long-term study" by S. Theander, 1985, *Journal of Psychiatric Research, 19,* 493–508. Adapted by permission.

approximately one-third committed suicide and two-thirds died of complications from their disorder.

While outpatient treatment can benefit most patients with eating disorders, hospitalization is occasionally required, with a long period of subsequent outpatient care. For some patients, their eating disorder and associated self-destructive behaviors have a chronic course. However, past treatment failures do not always predict future failure. Even for those patients who have had multiple hospitalizations, some recover after multiple relapses once motivation changes or once changes in their interpersonal lives make recovery possible. It is important to be cognizant of the range of reasons for patients' initial refusal of treatment as well as principles that can assist patients in the choice of treatment when it is appropriate (Goldner, 1989). Finally, it is important to recognize that there is a subgroup of chronic patients who often are neglected because the prospects for recovery seem so dismal. These patients may do quite well in a "chronic patient group," where the goals are not recovery but rather close monitoring of their physical condition with brief admissions when their situations deteriorate. Occasionally, these groups break through the denial where other methods have failed, and patients will do well because they can no longer disavow in themselves the bleak future that they now see in others.

Some patients can be considered to be fully recovered at follow-up, while others who recover in terms of weight and eating remain disturbed in other areas of functioning. Casper (1990) reported that about 25% of patients classified as having a good outcome in an 8- or 10-year follow-up were still weight preoccupied and depressed. In a study of 60 anorexia nervosa patients followed 5 to 14 years after presenting for treatment, Toner, Garfinkel, and Garner (1986) found that 38% were asymptomatic, 27% improved, 27% remained unchanged, and 8% were deceased. While a significant proportion of the sample met DSM-III criteria for affective (34%) or anxiety disorders (47%) in the year prior to follow-up, those in the asymptomatic group had scores equivalent to non–eating disorder controls on most measures of psychosocial functioning.

Thus, it may be concluded that the length of follow-up greatly influences the interpretation of outcome for anorexia nervosa. Moreover, while there are some patients who remain symptomatic for many years or who do not recover, there are others who fully recover from their disorder.

CASE ILLUSTRATION

The patient NK is a 26-year-old single woman referred to the eating disorder outpatient unit with a 7-year history of self-induced vomiting, food restriction, and laxatives abuse. When initially seen, NK weighed 137 pounds and was 5'4" tall. She had an extensive psychiatric history dating back to age 14, when, after a disagreement with her boyfriend, she inflicted several superficial cuts on her wrist. She was treated and discharged by a local emergency room. A year later, she was treated and discharged from a local emergency room following the ingestion of 14 over-the-counter diet pills for reasons that were never clarified. Two months later, she was hospitalized following threats that she was planning to shoot herself following the breakup of a relationship with a boyfriend. She was diagnosed as suffering from depression and was treated with antidepressants. Following discharge, she received dynamically oriented psychotherapy. At age 16, after reporting that "voices" told her to cut herself, she was hospitalized and treated with antipsychotic medication. Two years later, she was diagnosed as suffering from an atypical depression and received treatment at a local community mental health center with a combination of psychotherapy and a MAO inhibitor medication. Later that same year, after being apprehended for shoplifting, NK was rehospitalized because of another self-cutting event. She was diagnosed as suffering from a bipolar disorder, with a secondary diagnosis of borderline personality, and treated with a combination of a phenothiazine drug, lithium carbonate, and a tricyclic antidepressant.

At age 19, NK was hospitalized for the first time on an eating disorder unit for 4 weeks. This resulted from her admission to her therapist that she was inducing vomiting after eating to lose weight. She told the therapist that she learned about vomiting behavior after she saw a movie in which the main character was bulimic. At that time NK weighed 127 pounds. She was rehospitalized at age 20 on an eating disorder unit for 2 weeks and was subsequently discharged with a diagnosis of bulimia nervosa and a borderline personality disorder.

NK was involved in weekly psychotherapy until, at age 22, she was hospitalized again on an eating disorder unit for 3 weeks and then was transferred to the general psychiatric unit after cutting herself during an art therapy session. At age 23, she was hospitalized in a general psychiatric unit after revealing to her therapist that, for the past month, she was routinely burning various parts of her thorax and abdomen with various implements including a curling iron.

Between the ages of 23 and 26, NK continued to restrict and purge, resulting in several more rehospitalizations, once on an emergency basis after it was discovered that her potassium level reached 2.5 meq/L. At age 25 she was arrested for shoplifting, and while being held in the local jail she refused to eat and vomited on the floor. She was quickly transferred from jail to an inpatient eating disorder unit. She was discharged with little psychological improvement and referred to our outpatient program. After an extensive reassessment, it was clear that NK met diagnostic criteria for both borderline personality disorder and antisocial personality. Although it had never been the focus of treatment, we learned that NK had regularly used alcohol and occasionally illicit drugs as early as 12 years of age. More recently, she had been arrested several times for driving under the influence of alcohol. It was clear that her reports of hallucinatory experiences, depression, alcohol abuse, and drug abuse predated her eating disorder and were likely manifestations of her Axis II diagnosis. Her treatment differed markedly from the sequencing of treatment mentioned earlier as appropriate for most eating disorder patients (Garner et al., 1986). Rather than beginning with education and a therapy that focused on the eating disorder (Garner & Rosen, 1990), the characterological symptoms and their interpersonal implications were the predominant focal points of NK's treatment from the very beginning.

The treatment approach was based on cognitive-behavioral and social learning principles. It was assumed that the "caretaking" role assumed by professionals and others had contributed to the initiation and escalation of the symptom picture. This was certainly the case with her eating disorder, which initially developed and then was maintained by NK's perception that individuals suffering from eating disorders were both attractive and especially deserving of attention. She described a pattern of seeking precisely the same type of support from the psychiatric community as she felt was depicted in the portrayal of the film character who was bulimic. It was also evident that her self-induced vomiting was not clandestine nor associated with any perception of shame. In fact, she often failed to remove evidence of her purging, which was more likely to bring this behavior to the attention of those around her. Family members and other individuals who knew her agreed that all of her troublesome behaviors were performed in a manner to maximize the attention and involvement of as many people and organizations as possible (i.e., family, friends, mental health centers, crisis centers, police, support groups).

The treatment strategies instituted were all designed to minimize the response to her troublesome behavior and to maximize interpersonal support related to improved (asymptomatic) functioning. The rationale for this treatment approach was explained to NK. Great care was taken to avoid dismissing her symptoms as simply "attention seeking" or deceitful behaviors. At the same time, her need for interpersonal support was described as genuine and quite legitimate. Her means for attaining interpersonal support were clearly self-defeating, and while they had the benefit of providing "attention" on demand (i.e., control), these behaviors almost always resulted in interpersonal loss. A plan was developed in which she would be briefly hospitalized and medically stabilized on a medical unit if she developed life-threatening sequelae to her purging. There would be no psychiatric intervention while hospitalized. Meetings were conducted with members of the correction system and it was agreed that if she committed a crime, she would not be removed from jail because of her vomiting but, instead, would have medical surveillance and, if necessary, be quickly stabilized and maintained in jail.

Her self-cutting and self-burning behavior was treated using a version of the technique described by Rosen and Thomas (1984), using a nondamaging, pain-inducing exercise to replace the injurious behavior. Finally, she received two psychotherapy sessions of 20 minutes duration each week that could be expanded up to an hour, each contingent upon her ability to prevent self-destructive acts. Her family was involved in the treatment, and they had to be encouraged repeatedly to maintain the "new" contingency system. In therapy, NK was rewarded for signs of competence and independence seeking. This approach was met by her repeated testing of the contingencies, but there was a gradual decline in her self-destructive symptoms over the course of the 1 year in therapy.

SUMMARY

Three eating disorder syndromes have been described, including anorexia nervosa, bulimia nervosa, and binge eating disorder. However, it should be recognized that these subtypes are by no means distinct. Eating disorder patients tend to be more alike than different across demographic, clinical, and psychological dimensions, and they may move between subtypes at different points in time. Almost by definition, patients with eating disorders are self-destructive, exhibiting self-induced vomiting as well as diuretic, laxative, and diet pill abuse. In addition, it is not unusual to find that these individuals abuse other illicit drugs and alcohol. Finally, patients with eating disorders frequently are involved in self-mutilation and/or attempt or complete suicide. Violence toward others is much less frequent, and may be seen when clinicians strictly enforce weight gain. More typical is a passive–aggressive interpersonal style.

Treatment for this group of patients must begin with a complete psychiatric assessment of a wide variety of potentially relevant aspects, including personality functioning, psychological state, family relationships, and adaptive behaviors. In particular, questioning should address weight-controlling behaviors, such as vomiting; fasting; use of laxatives, diuretics, diet pills, or other drugs; and vigorous exercise. With this information, an Axis II diagnosis can be established, and treatment planning can begin. A major focus in most therapy approaches is on individual, familial, and sociocultural background factors that contribute in various ways to the development and maintenance of the eating disorder.

Although brief treatments designed to educate the patient about eating disorders have sometimes proven effective, many patients who have an established pattern of engaging in self-destructive behavior within the context of a personality disorder probably require more than brief approaches. In addition, although outpatient therapy is the intervention of choice, it is clear that severe self-destructive behavioral components require hospitalization to reduce medical risks. One intervention highlighted in this chapter can best be described as focusing on social learning principles, that is, eliminating social reinforcers for symptoms, establishing reinforcers for coping behaviors and independence skills, building skills, and providing models of social competence.

REFERENCES

Abraham, S. F., & Beumont, P. J. V. (1982). How patients describe bulimia or binge eating. *Psychological Medicine, 12*, 625–635.

Agras, W. S. (1991). Nonpharmacologic treatments of bulimia nervosa. *Journal of Clinical Psychiatry, 52*, 29–33.

Agras, W. S., Rossiter, E. M., Arnow, B., Schneider, J. A., Telch, C. F., Raeburn, S. D., Bruce, B., Perl, M., & Koran, L. M. (1992). Pharmacologic and cognitive-behavioral treatment for bulimia nervosa: A controlled comparison. *American Journal of Psychiatry, 149*, 82–87.

American Psychiatric Association (1987). *Diagnostic and statistical manual of mental disorders*, 3rd Edition, Revised. Washington, DC: Author.

American Psychiatric Association (1991). *DSM-IV options book: Work in progress*. Washington, DC: Author.

American Psychiatric Association (1993). *DSM-IV draft criteria*. Washington, DC: Author.

Anderson, A. E. (1985). *Practical comprehensive treatment of anorexia nervosa and bulimia*. Baltimore: Johns Hopkins Press.

Bakan, R., Birmingham, C. L., & Goldner, E. M. (1991). Chronicity in anorexia nervosa: Pregnancy and birth complications as risk factors. *International Journal of Eating Disorders, 10*, 631–645.

Beary, M. D., Lacey, J. H., & Merry, J. (1986). Alcoholism and eating disorders in women of fertile age. *British Journal of Addiction, 81*, 685–689.

Ben-Tovin, D. I. (1988). DSM-III, draft DSM-III-R, and the diagnosis and prevalence of bulimia in Australia. *American Journal of Psychiatry, 145*, 1000–1002.

Beumont, P. J. V., Al-Alami, M. S., & Touyz, S. W. (1987). The evolution of the concept of anorexia nervosa. In P. J. V. Beumont, G. D. Burrow, & R. C. Casper (Eds.), *Handbook of eating disorders* (pp. 105–116). New York: Elsevier.

Brotman, A. W., Stern, T. A., & Herzog, D. B. (1984). Emotional reactions of house officers to patients with anorexia nervosa, diabetes, and obesity. *International Journal of Eating Disorders, 3*, 71–77.

Bruch, H. (1973). *Eating disorders: Obesity, anorexia nervosa and the person within*. New York: Basic Books.

Casper, R. C. (1987). The psychopathology of anorexia nervosa: The pathological psychodynamic processes. In P. J. V. Beumont, G. D. Burrow, & R. C. Casper (Eds.), *Handbook of eating disorders* (pp. 117–127). New York: Elsevier.

Casper, R. C. (1990). Personality features of women with good outcome from restricting anorexia nervosa. *Psychosomatic Medicine, 52*, 156–170.

Comerci, G. D. (1990). Medical complications of anorexia nervosa and bulimia nervosa. *Medical Clinics of North America, 74*, 1293–1310.

Crisp, A. H. (1980). *Anorexia nervosa*. New York: Grune and Stratton.

Edgette, J. S., & Prout, M. F. (1989). Cognitive and behavioral approaches to the treatment of anorexia nervosa. In A. Freeman, K. M. Simon, L. E. Beutler, & H. Arkowitz (Eds.), *Comprehensive handbook of cognitive therapy* (pp. 367–384). New York: Plenum.

Fairburn, D. G. (1985). Cognitive-behavioral treatment for bulimia. In D. M. Garner & P. E. Garfinkel (Eds.), *Handbook of psychotherapy for anorexia nervosa and bulimia* (pp. 160–192). New York: Guilford Press.

Fairburn, D. G. (1987). The definition of bulimia nervosa: Guidelines for clinicians and research workers. *Annals of Behavioral Medicine, 9*, 3–7.

Fairburn, D. G., & Beglin, S. J. (1990). The studies of the epidemiology of bulimia nervosa. *American Journal of Psychiatry, 147*, 401–408.

Fairburn, C. G., & Garner, D. M. (1986). The diagnosis of bulimia nervosa. *International Journal of Eating Disorders, 5*, 403–419.

Fairburn, C. G., Cooper, P. J., Kirk, J., & O'Connor, M. (1985). The significance of the neurotic symptoms of bulimia nervosa. *Journal of Psychiatric Research, 19*, 135–140.

Fairburn, D. G., Jones, R., Peveler, R. C., Carr, S. J., Solomon, R. A., O'Connor, M. E., Burton, J., & Hope, R. A. (1991). Three psychological treatments for bulimia nervosa: A comparative trial. *Archives of General Psychiatry, 48*, 463–469.

Foreyt, J. P., & McGavin, J. K. (1988). Anorexia nervosa and bulimia. In E. J. Mash & L. G. Turdal (Eds.), *Behavioral Assessment of childhood disorders* (pp. 776–805). New York: Guilford Press.

Fornari, V., Edleman, R., & Katz, J. L. (1990). Medication manipulation in bulimia nervosa: An additional diagnostic criterion? *International Journal of Eating Disorders, 9*, 585–588.

Garfinkel, P. E., & Garner, D. M. (1982). *Anorexia nervosa: A multidimensional perspective*. New York: Brunner/Mazel.

Garner, D. M. (1985). Iatrogenesis in anorexia nervosa and bulimia nervosa. *International Journal of Eating Disorders, 4*, 701–726.

Garner, D. M. (1988). Anorexia nervosa. In M. Hersen & C. G. Last (Eds.), *Child behavior therapy casebook* (pp. 263–276). New York: Plenum.

Garner, D. M. (1991). *Eating disorder inventory-2: Professional manual*. Odessa, FL: Psychological Assessment Resources.

Garner, D. M. (1993a). Binge eating in anorexia nervosa. In C. G. Fairburn & G. T. Wilson (Eds.), *Binge eating: Nature, assessment, and treatment* (pp. 50–76). New York: Guilford Press.

Garner, D. M. (1993b). Pathogenesis of anorexia nervosa. *Lancet, 341*, 1631–1635.

Garner, D. M., & Bemis, K. M. (1982). A cognitive-behavioral approach to anorexia nervosa. *Cognitive Therapy and Research, 6*, 123–150.

Garner, D. M., & Bemis, K. M. (1985). Cognitive therapy for anorexia nervosa. In D. M. Garner & P. E. Garfinkel (Eds.), *Handbook of psychotherapy for anorexia nervosa and bulimia* (pp. 107–146). New York: Guilford Press.

Garner, D. M., & Garfinkel, P. E. (1985). *Handbook of psychotherapy for anorexia nervosa and bulimia*. New York: Guilford Press.

Garner, D. M., & Garfinkel, P. E. (1988). *Diagnostic issues in anorexia nervosa and bulimia nervosa*. New York: Brunner/Mazel.

Garner, D. M., & Parker, P. (1992). Eating disorders. In T. H. Ollendick, & M. Hersen (Eds.), *Handbook of child and adolescent assessment* (pp. 384–399). New York: Pergamon Press.

Garner, D. M., & Rosen, L. W. (1990). Anorexia nervosa and bulimia nervosa. In A. S. Bellack, M. Hersen, & A. E. Kazdin (Eds.), *International handbook of behavior modification and therapy* (pp. 805–817). New York: Plenum.

Garner, D. M., & Sackeyfio, A. H. (1993). Eating disorders. In A. S. Bellack & M. Hersen (Eds.), *Handbook of behavior therapy in the psychiatric setting* (pp. 477–497). New York: Plenum.

Garner, D. M., Garfinkel, P. E., & Bemis, K. M. (1982). A multidimensional psychotherapy for anorexia nervosa. *International Journal of Eating Disorders, 1*, 3–46.

Garner, D. M., Garfinkel, P. E., & Irvine, M. J. (1986). Integration and sequencing of treatment approaches for eating disorders. *Psychotherapy and Psychosomatics, 46*, 67–75.

Garner, D. M., Garfinkel, P. E., & O'Shaughnessy, M. (1985). The validity of the distinction between bulimia with and without anorexia nervosa. *American Journal of Psychiatry, 142*, 581–587.

Garner, D. M., Olmsted, M. P., Davis, R., Rockert, W., Goldbloom, D., & Eagle, M. (1990). The association between bulimic symptoms and reported psychopathology. *International Journal of Eating Disorders, 9*, 1–15.

Garner, D. M., Rockert, W., Olmsted, M. P., Johnson, C. L., & Coscina, D. V. (1985). Psychoeducational principles in the treatment of bulimia and anorexia nervosa. In D. M. Garner, & P. E. Garfinkel (Eds.), *Handbook for psychotherapy for anorexia nervosa and bulimia* (pp. 513–572). New York: Guilford Press.

Garner, D. M., Shafer, C. L., & Rosen, L. W. (1992). Critical appraisal of the DSM-III-R diagnostic criteria for eating disorders. In S. R. Hooper, G. W. Hynd, & R. E. Mattison (Eds.), *Child psychopathology, diagnostic criteria and clinical assessment* (pp. 261–303). Hillsdale, NJ: Lawrence Erlbaum Associates.

Garner, D. M., Garner, M. V., & Rosen, L. W. (1993). Anorexia nervosa restricters who purge: Implications for subtyping anorexia nervosa. *International Journal of Eating Disorders, 13*, 171–185.

Garner, D. M., Rockert, W., Garner, M. V., Davis, R., & Olmsted, M. P. (1993). Comparison between cognitive-behavioral and short-term psychodynamic therapy for bulimia nervosa. *American Journal of Psychiatry, 150*, 37–46.

Goldner, E. (1989). Treatment refusal in anorexia nervosa. *International Journal of Eating Disorders*, *8*, 297–306.

Goodsitt, A. (1985). Self psychology and the treatment of anorexia nervosa. In D. M. Garner & P. E. Garfinkel (Eds.), *Handbook for psychotherapy for anorexia nervosa and bulimia* (pp. 55–84). New York: Guilford Press.

Halmi, K. A. (1974). Anorexia nervosa: Demographic and clinical features in 94 cases. *Psychosomatic Medicine*, *36*, 18–25.

Halmi, K. A. (1985). Classification of the eating disorders. *Journal of Psychiatric Research*, *19*, 113–119.

Hamburg, P., & Herzog, D. (1990). Supervising the therapy of patients with eating disorders. *American Journal of Psychotherapy*, *XLIV*, 369–380.

Hatsukami, D., Mitchell, J. E., Eckert, E. D., & Pyle, R. (1986). Characteristics of patients with bulimia only, bulimia with affective disorder, and bulimia with substance abuse problems. *Addictive Behaviors*, *11*, 399–406.

Holland, A. J., Hall, A., Murray, R. R., Russell, G. F. M., & Crisp, A. H. (1984). Anorexia nervosa: A study of 34 twin pairs. *British Journal of Psychiatry*, *145*, 414–419.

Humphrey, L. L. (1989). Is there a casual link between disturbed family processes and eating disorders? In W. G. Johnson (Ed.), *Bulimia nervosa: Perspectives on clinical research and therapy*. New York: JAI Press.

Hsu, L. K. G. (1988). The outcome of anorexia nervosa: A reappraisal. *Psychological Medicine*, *18*, 807–812.

Jackson, C., Davidson, G., Russell, J., & Vandereycken, W. (1990). Ellen West revisited: The theme of death in eating disorders. *International Journal of Eating Disorders*, *9*, 529–536.

Johnson, C., & Connors, M. E. (1987). *The etiology and treatment of bulimia nervosa; A biopsychosocial perspective*. New York: Basic Books.

Johnson, C. L., Tobin, D., & Enright, A. (1989). Prevalence and clinical characteristics of borderline patients in an eating disorder population. *Journal of Clinical Psychiatry*, *50*, 9–15.

Jonas, J. M., Gold, M. S., Sweeney, D., & Pottash, A. L. C. (1987). Eating disorders and cocaine abuse: A survey of 259 cocaine abusers. *Journal of Clinical Psychiatry*, *49*, 47–50.

Krahn, D. D., Nairn, K., Gosnell, B. A., & Drewnowski, A. (1991). Stealing in eating disordered patients. *Journal of Clinical Psychiatry*, *52*, 112–115.

Lacey, J. H., & Evans, C. D. H. (1986). The impulsivist; A multi-impulsive personality disorder. *British Journal of Addiction*, *81*, 641–649.

Lacey, J. H., & Moureli, E. (1986). Bulimic alcoholics: Some features of a clinical subgroup. *British Journal of Addiction*, *81*, 389–393.

Levin, A. P., & Hyler, S. E. (1986). DSM-III personality diagnosis in bulimia. *Comprehensive Psychiatry*, *27*, 47–53.

Lucas, A. R., Duncan, J. W., & Piens, V. (1976). The treatment of anorexia nervosa. *American Journal of Psychiatry*, *133*, 1034–1038.

Marcus, M. D., & Wing, R. R. (1987). Binge eating among the obese. *Annals of Behavioral Medicine*, *9*, 23–27.

Minuchin, S., Rosman, B. L., & Baker, L. (1978). *Psychosomatic families; Anorexia nervosa in context*. Cambridge, MA: Harvard University Press.

Mitchell, J. E. (1990). *Bulimia nervosa*. Minneapolis: University of Minnesota Press.

Mitchell, J. E., & Boutacoff, L. I. (1986). Laxative abuse complicating bulimia: Medical and treatment implications. *International Journal of Eating Disorders*, *5*, 325–334.

Mitchell, J. E., Hatsukami, D., Eckert, E. D., & Pyle, R. L. (1985). Characteristics of 275 patients with bulimia. *American Journal of Psychiatry*, *142*, 482–485.

Mitchell, J. E., Pomery, C., & Huber, M. (1988). A clinician's guide to the eating disorders medicine cabinet. *International Journal of Eating Disorders*, *2*, 211–223.

Mitchell, J. E., Pyle, R. L., Eckert, E. D., Hatsukami, D., Pomeroy, C., & Zimmerman, R. (1990). A comparison study of antidepressants and structured intensive group psychotherapy in the treatment of bulimia nervosa. *Archives of General Psychiatry*, *47*, 149–157.

Mitchell, J. E., Seim, H., Colon, E., & Pomeroy, C. (1987). Medical complication and medical management of bulimia nervosa. *Annals of Internal Medicine*, *107*, 71–77.

Mitchell, P. B. (1988). The pharmacological management of bulimia nervosa: A critical review. *International Journal of Eating Disorders*, *7*, 29–41.

Norton, K. R. W., Crisp, A. H., & Bhat, A. V. (1985). Why so dome anorexics steal? Personal, social and illness factors. *Journal of Psychiatric Research*, *19*, 385–390.

Olmsted, M. P., Davis, R., Garner, D. M., Rockert, W., Irvine, M., & Eagle, M. (1991). Efficacy of a brief group psychoeducational intervention for bulimia nervosa. *Behavior Research and Therapy*, *29*, 71–83.

Pao, P. N. (1969). The syndrome of delicate self-cutting. *Journal of Medical Psychology*, *42*, 195–206.

Patton, G. C. (1988). Mortality in eating disorders. *Psychological Medicine, 18*, 947–951.

Peveler, R., & Fairburn, C. (1990). Eating disorders in women who abuse alcohol. *British Journal of Addiction, 85*, 1633–1638.

Rosen, L. W., & Thomas, M. A. (1984). Treatment technique for chronic wrist cutters. *Journal of Behavior Therapy and Experimental Psychiatry, 15*, 33–36.

Russell, G. (1979). Bulimia nervosa: An ominous variant of anorexia nervosa. *Psychological Medicine, 9*, 429–448.

Shisslak, C. M., Gray, N., & Crago, M. (1989). Health care professionals' reactions to working with eating disorder patients. *International Journal of Eating Disorders, 8*, 689–694.

Simpson, M. A. (1973). Female genital self-mutilation. *Archives of General Psychiatry, 29*, 808–810.

Sours, J. A. (1980). *Starving to death in a sea of objects*. New York: Jason Aronson.

Spitzer, R. L., Devlin, M., Walsh, B. T., Hasin, D., Wing, R., Marcus, M., Stunkard, A., Wadden, T., Yanovski, S., Agras, S., Mitchell, J., & Nonas, C. (1991). Binge eating disorder: To be or not to be in DSM-IV. *International Journal of Eating Disorders, 10*, 627–629.

Steinhausen, H. C., & Glanville, K. (1983). Follow-up studies of anorexia nervosa—A review of research findings. *Psychological Medicine, 13*, 239–249.

Steinhausen, H. C., Rauss-Mason, C., & Seidel, R. (1991). Follow-up studies of anorexia nervosa; A review of four decades of outcome research. *Psychological Medicine, 21*, 447–454.

Stern, S. (1986). The dynamics of clinical management in the treatment of anorexia nervosa and bulimia: An organizing theory. *International Journal of Eating Disorders, 5*, 233–254.

Strober, M., & Humphrey, L. L. (1987). Familial conditions to the etiology and course of anorexia nervosa and bulimia. *Journal of Consulting and Clinical Psychology, 55*, 654–659.

Strober, M., Salkin, B., Burroughs, J., & Morrell, W. (1982). Validity of the bulimia-restrictor distinction in anorexia nervosa: Parental personality characteristics and family psychiatric morbidity. *The Journal of Nervous and Mental Disease, 170*, 345–351.

Theander, S. (1985). Outcome and prognosis in anorexia nervosa and bulimia: Some results of previous investigation, compared with those of a Swedish long-term study. *Journal of Psychiatric Research, 19*, 493–508.

Tobin, D. L., Johnson, C., Steinberg, S., Staats, M., & Dennis, A. B. (1991). Multifactorial assessment of bulimia nervosa. *Journal of Abnormal Psychology, 100*, 14–21.

Toner, B. B., Garfinkel, P. E., & Garner, D. M. (1986). Long-term follow-up of anorexia nervosa. *Psychosomatic Medicine, 48*, 403–419.

Vandereycken, W., Kog, E., & Vanderlinden, J. (1989). *The family approach to eating disorders*. New York: PMA Publishing.

Welch, G. W., Hall, A., & Renner, R. (1990). Patient subgrouping in anorexia nervosa using psychologically-based classification. *International Journal of Eating Disorders, 9*, 311–322.

Wooley, S. C., Blackwell, B., & Winget, C. (1978). A learning theory model of chronic illness behavior: Theory, treatment, and research. *Psychosomatic Medicine, 40*, 379–401.

Yates, A. (1991). *Compulsive exercise*. New York: Brunner/Mazel.

CHAPTER 24

Tic Disorders

LORI A. HEAD AND FLOYD R. SALLEE

DESCRIPTION OF THE DISORDER

Tics are involuntary movements or sounds that are rapid, sudden, repetitive, and stereotyped. Tics are highly distinct from other movement disorders of childhood and are rarely confused with choreoathetoid movement dysfunctions. Tic disorders are classified by age of onset, duration of symptoms, and the presence or absence of vocal or phonic tics along with the usual motor tics. Key clinical features are their occurrence at random intervals and their apparent voluntary suppression for varying periods of time. The norm is for tics to occur without apparent cause, but they are sometimes triggered by environmental stimuli and are exacerbated by stress, fatigue, or underlying medical illness. Some patients frequently describe a premonitory sensory urge for which tics are voluntarily performed to relieve the urge. A waxing and waning course in severity as well as a change in anatomical location from time to time are also common features. Motor tics are subdivided into simple or complex types. Simple motor tics are fast, darting, meaningful muscular movements that occur in isolated muscle groups or in one anatomical location. They can be embarrassing and sometimes physically painful, such as jaw snapping or blepharospasm. Frequently, self-abusive acts that are the consequence of an unchecked simple motor tic (e.g., arm flailing) can be the cause of considerable distress to patients and families. Complex motor tics are often slower and more purposeful in appearance. These include hopping, clapping, or tensing of multiple muscle groups, touching objects or people, making obscene gestures, or engaging in socially inappropriate acts. Complex motor tics frequently are difficult to separate from compulsions when the activity is organized and ritualistic in character. Self-destructive behaviors such as head banging, eye poking, or biting are complex tics that require immediate intervention. Aggressive behavior toward others can be the result of complex tics, but the context for the patient is usually embarrassment and anxiety about restraining these untoward impulses.

LORI A. HEAD and FLOYD R. SALLEE • Department of Psychiatry, Medical University of South Carolina, Charleston, South Carolina, 29425.

Handbook of Aggressive and Destructive Behavior in Psychiatric Patients, edited by Michel Hersen, Robert T. Ammerman, and Lori A. Sisson. Plenum Press, New York, 1994.

Simple vocal tics are sounds and noises such as hissing, coughing, barking, or spitting. The tics of the sniffing and throat-clearing variety precipitate investigations for allergy, upper respiratory infections or sinusitis, and other ear, nose, and throat abnormalities. Complex vocal tics involve meaningful words or phrases (e.g., "Oh boy," "That's right") and are not particularly hostile or aggressive. Dysfluencies of speech that resemble stammering or undue word emphasis and/or alterations in speech volume and phrasing can also be complex vocal tics. Frequently, speech blocking during speech initiation or at transition phrases is quite common. The most dramatic and distressing complex vocal symptom is coprolalia. This is an explosive occurrence of foul or "dirty" words. Coprolalia is present in only a minority of Tourette's patients, but is by far the most dramatic symptom. It is not necessary to have coprolalia for a diagnosis of Tourette's, and linguistic context frequently determines presence or absence of coprolalia. Presence of coprolalia is frequently outside the social context of verbal aggression, once again causing the patient much embarrassment. The words and phrases themselves usually express hostility and are frequently sexualized. Other bizarre and unusual symptoms present in Tourette's patients include tendency to imitate what they have seen (echopraxia), or have heard (echolalia), or have said (palilalia). These more unusual symptoms are present in a series of patients with very low frequency (less than 20%).

Associated Features

Associated clinical features of tic disorders include related psychiatric and cognitive dysfunctions. As tics are socially disabling, the presence of severe tics for long time periods can precipitate psychiatric disorder (e.g., social phobia). Some psychiatric disorders are frequently comorbid with tic disorders, such as attention deficit and hyperactivity disorder (ADHD) and obsessive-compulsive disorder (OCD). ADHD, however, occurs independently of tic disorder, and severity of tic disorder does not predict presence or absence of ADHD. However, patients with tic disorders are 78 times more likely than the general population to have ADHD. Obsessive-compulsive disorder, however, is genetically linked to tic disorders, with a 51–74% incidence of comorbidity in patients with Tourette disorder (TD) (Frankel, Cummings, Robertson, Trimble, Hill, & Benson, 1986; Stefl, 1983). Other personality traits, such as aggression, hostility, and depression, have been found in samples of TD patients in addition to OCD and ADHD (Stefl, 1983), but a full-scale study of comorbidity has not yet been accomplished. Lately, due to its potential seriousness, much attention is being directed to self-injurious behavior in patients with TD. Robertson, Trimble, and Lees (1989) reported that 30 of 90 patients with TD exhibited self-injurious behavior and aggression, including one fatality. In our own experience, aggressivity in the TD population (7–17 years of age), when compared to children with ADHD alone, reveals that TD patients have significantly less aggressivity, self-destructive behavior, and even social withdrawal (Sallee, Rock, & Kunins, 1991), as assessed by the Child Behavior Checklist Teacher Report (Achenbach & Edelbrock, 1983). Therefore, the reader should consider that severe self-injurious behavior and assaultive behaviors occur rarely within the TD population as a whole.

EPIDEMIOLOGY

Tics are the most common movement disorder of childhood, occurring in 5–18% of children between the ages of 6 and 16. Transient tics account for the majority of cases. Stress is counted as the major factor in tic onset for transient tic disorders of childhood. TD, once thought to be uncommon, occurs in 1 person in every 2,500 in its complete form and approximately 3 times that number in partial expressions that include chronic motor tics (Brunn, 1984, 1988). From a large epidemiological study by Caine, Mcbride, and Chiverton, (1988), the point prevalence of TD in children under the age of 17 is approximately 3 per 10,000. As the incidence of transient tics is quite common in the population, the task of the clinician is to determine when tics are likely to be a more progressive and debilitating syndrome leading to TD. No pathophysiological factors have yet been identified in the etiology of tic, although genetic factors play a significant role in a subset of patients (Pauls & Leckman, 1986). At present there is no definitive diagnostic test other than careful clinical evaluation. Diagnosis is based solely on observable signs and symptoms. Secondary tics, however, can be the result of postencephalitic or traumatic injury and can sometimes be drug induced (e.g., stimulants, levodopa neuroleptics, carbamazepine, phenytoin, and phenobarbital; carbon monoxide poisoning or chorea resulting from traumatic insult can also lead to ticlike clinical features). Most tic disorders are idiopathic, and a genetic basis can be found only in approximately 50% of all cases.

ETIOLOGY

The most supported theory concerning the origin of tics involves an overactivity of central dopaminergic systems. Dopamine is the primary negative feedback control of an inhibitory loop of the caudate putamen to globus pallidus involving the basal ganglia GABAminergic system. An overactivity of dopamine in this negative feedback loop allows the escape of these areas, resulting in uncoordinated rapid motoric outbursts recognized as tics. The evidence for central dopamine overactivity comes from three sources: (1) biochemical, (2) pharmacological, and (3) clinical observation. Biochemical evidence comes by examination of a cerebrospinal fluid breakdown product of dopamine—homovanillic acid (HVA). HVA is consistently decreased in Tourette's disorder patients (Singer, Butler, Tune, Zuczek, & Coyle, 1982), indicating decreased central turnover of dopamine perhaps mediated by supersensitive dopamine receptors. Pharmacological evidence comes from administration of dopamine agonists such as L-dopa, which can exacerbate tics or precipitate a toxic Tourette syndrome. Inhibitors of dopamine synthesis (a-methyl-p-tyrosine) decrease tics as well. Clinical evidence of a role for dopamine in tic pathophysiology consists of the tremendous clinical efficacy of dopamine-blocking drugs such as the neuroleptics.

Only recently have attempts been made to understand the involvement of noradrenergic or cholinergic neurochemical systems. Specifically, much attention has been directed to researching the efficacy of clonidine, an alpha-2-adrenergic agonist. Cohen, Young, and Nathanson (1979) were the first to report beneficial effects of clonidine in the treatment of TD. The mechanism of action of clonidine has not been firmly established yet. Researchers speculate that the effectiveness of clonidine in treating TD may be due to the ability of the alpha-2-adrenergic receptor agonist to reduce the firing rate and the release of catecholamines from central noradrenergic and dopaminergic neurons (Cohen et al., 1979).

A variety of biochemical mechanisms for self-injurious behavior in TD have been suggested. Several studies have implicated dopaminergic system involvement in this patient population as well (Corbett & Campbell, 1980; Gorea & Lombard, 1984; Jones & Barraclough, 1978). More recently, neuropeptides are receiving much attention in the self-injurious behavior literature. Corbett and Campbell (1980) note a possible link between endorphins, which have probable central analgesic action, and the clinical observations in persistent self-injurious behavior. This suggests a possible release of endogenous opiates in response to these stereotyped behaviors. Endogenous opiates are opiode peptides that are similar in structure to morphine and bind to the same receptors in the CNS as morphine and heroin. Clinical proof of this neuromodulation theory comes from mainly two sources: (1) case reports of noloxone efficacy in self-injurious behavior, and (2) neurobiologic evidence of increased plasma metenkephalia levels associated with self injury, and blunted response to dopaminergic challenge in self-injurious patients. When given naloxone, a narcotic/opiode antagonist, patients with self-injurious behavior no longer experience the endogenous opiate and are able to feel the self-inflicted pain, causing them to cease the self-injury. Sandyk and Bamford (1987) reported blunted gonadotrophin levels in response to dopamine agonist challenge, indicating heightened hypothalamic dopaminergic activity. Coid, Allolio, and Rees (1983) found significantly raised mean plasma metenkephalin concentrations in patients with self-injurious behavior compared to healthy controls.

AGGRESSION TOWARD SELF

Self-aggression is encountered in many clinical syndromes, including Tourette's disorder. With regard to TD, self-aggression or self-injurious behavior (SIB) is underrecognized (33% incidence) (Robertson et al., 1989) and a potentially fatal sequelae. Self-injurious behavior is defined as repetitive, self-inflicted, nonaccidental injurious behavior. These self-injuries are most commonly characterized by excessive picking at skin, scalp, and sores, head banging, eye poking, biting of the tongue, cheeks, lips, and extremities, and self-hitting. All of these symptoms can range in severity from mild biting, to vision impairment from self-inflicted eye injury, to fatal subdural hematoma as a result of head banging. The types of SIB reported in patients with TD are generally not typical of those encountered in other syndromes such as Lesch-Nyhan, choraacanthocytosis, schizophrenia, depression, or personality disorders, but are nonspecific and not related to cognitive function. Self-injurious behavior can be further subdivided into self-injurious behavior as a manifestation of self-destructive obsessions and compulsions or self-injurious behavior that is more stereotypical in nature and related to complex tics.

Self-injurious behavior secondary to obsessions and compulsions is by far the most dangerous and most difficult to treat. Self-injurious behavior and obsessive-compulsive disorder share some striking characteristics. Using standardized rating scales (e.g., obsessionality section of the Tavistock Inventory) self-mutilators differed from controls by their higher score on the obsessionality scale (Bennun, 1983; Gardner & Gardner, 1975; Primeau, & Fontaine, 1987; Robertson et al., 1989). Also, the most frequently reported driving force behind self-injurious behavior is relief of tension. Rituals in OCD fulfill the same function. Some reported examples of self-injurious behavior secondary to obsessions and compulsions include feeling compelled to place one's hand on a hot stove, pulling hair, blinding oneself, repeated self-cutting, and holding one's breath for a long period of time.

Self-injurious behavior that has been related to complex tics includes eye poking and head banging. Many clinicians feel these stereotypes are within the context of a complex tic and should not be deemed self-injurious behavior, a possible explanation for the underreporting of self-aggression in TD. Although the movement may relieve tension, it is not done in response to a continuous thought or theme. Eye poking in a stereotypical fashion is different from poking one's eye to cause blindness in an attempt to erase a traumatic, recurring scene.

Psychopathology in patients who injure themselves has also been assessed. Using standardized rating scales (CCEI, EPI, obsessionality section of the Tavistock Inventory, HDHQ), researchers have found significantly higher scores on hostility, and general psychopathology (Bennun, 1983; Gardner & Gardner, 1975; Robertson et al., 1989). These findings correlate with the known comorbidity of the tic disorders. Furthermore, a 41% incidence of physical and/or sexual abuse before the age of 2 in patients who injure themselves has been reported (van der Kolk, 1989). This presents a possible link between early trauma and self-mutilation.

AGGRESSION TOWARD OTHERS

Physical injury toward others in patients with tic disorder is uncommon if aggression is defined as purposefully inflicting harm to others. In TD, harm to others is usually in the context of a stereotypy or compulsion (e.g., pinching others, unprovoked hitting of others, etc.). Patients who are redirected around these behaviors often respond by saying "I know it is wrong to pinch my mother, but I just can't stop. I just have to do it." Malicious intent is usually not an issue in TD patients. In more serious cases of harm to others, the aggression may stem from extreme hostility. It is known that many TD patients have a lower threshold for stress, lower frustration tolerance, or a higher incidence of impulsivity than patients without TD and may lash out with little provocation. Such lashing out may initially be in the form of verbal aggression. This verbal language is, many times, out of social context, is viewed as inappropriate by others, and may lead to a physical confrontation. The aggression is usually not directed at others but to objects. For example, a patient may take a sledge hammer to his car if he is unable to start it. The aggression toward objects or others is not premeditated. The biochemical basis for the intermittent lack of control in the patient population has not been established. It is thought by many to be linked to the comorbid ADHD prevalent in so many patients with TD. In support of this, in a matched controlled study of classroom behavior of children with TD, results indicate that aggression is only slightly increased in children with TD when compared to their "normal peers." However, when compared to children diagnosed with TD and comorbid ADHD and children with ADHD alone, TD children did not demonstrate as much physical or verbal aggression as the other two groups (Sallee et al., 1991).

CLINICAL MANAGEMENT

Treatment of Tourette's syndrome and other tic disorders has been problematic and in many cases disappointing. There is no one highly accepted treatment regimen, and strategies must be decided on a case-by-case basis, reflecting the heterogeneity of tic symptoms and/or their behavioral sequelae. In patients with more severe forms of behavioral complications, such as self-injurious behavior, management is even more of a challenge. In patients with tic disorders and self-injurious behavior, one thought is to treat the severe symptomatology and psychopathology of the tic disorder and the self-injurious behavior will resolve or reduce in severity and/or risk (Robertson et al., 1989). Behavior therapy, pharmacotherapy (principally with neuroleptics and/or clonidine for the tic disorder and some adjunctive treatments involving medications), family work, school, or work consultation, and psychotherapy should all be considered. Treatment success depends on a multimodal approach that considers quality-of-life issues, not simply tic suppression alone or elimination of self-injury and aggression alone.

Behavior Therapy

Since 1958, a variety of behavioral techniques have been employed in the treatment of tic disorders and self-injurious behavior (Ollendick, 1981). For tic symptom reduction, the most effective techniques include self-monitoring and habit-reversal procedures. In several case studies (Maletzky, 1974; Ollendick, 1981; Thomas, Abrams, & Johnson, 1971), the combination of self-monitoring and habit reversal was reported to decrease tics and was associated with long-lasting remission of symptoms. Self-monitoring is usually carried out by asking the patient to keep a log of tic symptomatology. By keeping an inventory, the patient is more aware of the tics; increased awareness is thought to lead to more control. Habit reversal is carried out by employing a competing response upon awareness of the onset of the tic. For example, the patient may tense a muscle group antagonistic of the tic (Ollendick, 1981). At this time, no controlled studies of these practices have been performed; therefore, it is difficult to assess the reliability of behavior therapy in children. It is felt that behavior therapy alone may be an effective treatment in only mild cases of tic disorders. In the more severe cases, behavior therapy in combination with medications is thought to have the best chance for success. The evaluation of treatment progress in behavior therapy should consider the waxing and waning course of the illness.

In TD patients with SIB, behavior techniques employed are more along the lines of functional analyses. Functional analysis is designed to elicit the consequent effects of the self-injury. Self-injurious behavior is thought to be attention-seeking, demand-related, or to involve sensorimotor stimulation. If attention-seeking or demand related, behavior therapies can be employed.

Pharmacotherapy

Pharmacotherapy is the mainstay of treatment for most tic disorders, with or without comorbidity. We are now able to decrease tic symptomatology by up to 95% in most cases by use of neuroleptic drugs with dopamine receptor blocking activities. By blocking the dopamine receptors, dopaminergic overactivity is temporarily corrected, but not without significant neurological side effects. The neuroleptics most effective in treating tic disorders are those known to have a high affinity to D2 receptors, such as haloperidol and pimozide. Sulpiride, an exclusive D2 blocking agent has also been quite successful. Unfortunately, no sulpiride-like drug is available for use in the United States (Robertson, Schnieden, & Lee, 1990). In the clinical setting, neuroleptics are also the drug most often used to treat self-injury. However, in a well-designed placebo-controlled, double-blind study done by Singh and Aman (1981), thioridazine had no effect in self-injury. The sedating effects of the neuroleptics may explain the minimal benefits reported in earlier studies.

Haloperidol, a selective D2 blocker, is the drug of first choice to treat patients with Tourette's disorder and related tic disorder since its successful use in 1961 (Shapiro et al., 1989). Haloperidol is effective in 90% of cases, with tic symptom reduction in the range of 60–80% (Bruun, 1984; Shapiro, Shapiro, & Eisenkraft, 1983; Shapiro, Shapiro, & Wayne,

1973). In addition to sedative effects, haloperidol is difficult to use because of a narrow therapeutic window. In 60% of the patients treated with haloperidol, significant side effects outweigh the therapeutic benefits, and the patients must be removed from the medication. Side effects affect motor (extrapyramidal), cognitive (attention, learning, memory), and affective (lethargy, phobia, depression) functions. The extent to which haloperidol impairs learning is controversial and variable as quality studies are few (Comings & Comings, 1987; Mikkelsen, Detlor, & Cohen, 1981; Shapiro et al., 1989). In a more recent study by Shapiro et al. (1989), 20% of the patients treated with a mean daily dose of haloperidol of 4.5 ± 2.7 mg reported moderate or marked loss of motivation, depression, and/or cognitive dulling. However, Bornstein and Yang (1991) compared Tourette's disorder patients who were taking neuroleptics to Tourette's disorder patients who were not taking medication and found that they did not perform differently in terms of educational, intellectual, and neuropsychological tests. Although these results are encouraging, haloperidol has definite side effect limitations that should be strongly considered before initiating treatment. Despite these limitations, haloperidol is still considered the single most successful treatment for TD.

At this time, no precise dosage range for the use of haloperidol for the treatment of tic disorders with or without self-injurious behavior has been established. A common goal of clinicians is to aim for a 75% reduction in tics, a range designed to maximize benefit and minimize side effects. The dosage required for the treatment of patients with tics is considerably less than that used to treat psychoses. Studies on blood levels done by Erenberg (1988) corroborate that the levels necessary are only one-seventh of those needed to treat other psychiatric disorders. There is, however, no definitive relationship between blood level and decrease in psychotic symptoms, tic symptom reduction, or side effects. Because the attainment of CNS steady state plasma levels takes approximately 4 days, medication changes should not be made any more often than this, in order to completely evaluate the impact of the most recent change. The medication can be given in a single daily dose, but, if side effects arise, twice- or thrice-daily regimen may be better tolerated.

The initiation of a neuroleptic medication can be associated with acute extrapyramidal side effects, which can be avoided by starting the medication at a very low dose and increasing by slow, steady increments; if indicated, a prophylactic anticholinergic medication can be given. If an acute reaction is suspected, immediate treatment with an intramuscular or oral anticholinergic medication will reverse the reaction quickly and safely. Although many exceptions exist, most frequently the pediatric patient receives a 0.05 mg/kg per day (Erenberg, 1988). In light of the fact that haloperidol is effective but carries with it many deleterious side effects, a principal goal of clinical research in TD is to find a therapeutic agent with the same or greater efficacy at tic symptom reduction as haloperidol, but with fewer side effects and greater acceptability among patients.

The drug of second choice is pimozide, a diphenylbutylpiperidine (Shapiro et al., 1983; Shapiro, Shapiro, & Fulop, 1987). Like haloperidol, pimozide preferentially binds the D2 receptor, but is thought to have few akinetic and sedative side effects (Regeur, Pakkenberg, Fog, & Pakkenberg, 1986). In a study done by Shapiro et al. (1989), haloperidol, pimozide, and placebo were compared for efficacy and side effects in a double-blind, crossover design in patients with TD. The results of this controlled study ($n = 57$) suggested that both haloperidol and pimozide were more effective than placebo, but that haloperidol was slightly more effective than pimozide, with no statistical differences in the side effects of haloperidol versus pimozide, including akinesia and sedation. Furthermore, ECG results were compared and revealed statistically significant prolongation of the QTc for pimozide versus haloperidol. The clinical significance of this QTc abnormality is thought to be minimal. Thus, results of this study, which is the only double-blind, placebo-controlled study of haloperidol versus pimozide to date, continue to support haloperidol as the treatment of first choice for TD. However, in patients who do not respond adequately to haloperidol, a therapeutic trial of pimozide may be indicated. Use of pimozide to treat self-injurious behavior or aggression has not been reported in the literature.

In terms of dosage and administration, pimozide is similar to haloperidol with approximately half the potency (1 mg haloperidol is equivalent in action to 2–2.5 mg pimozide) (Erenberg, 1988). When adverse reactions occur, they are exactly the same as other neuroleptics, requiring the same management. Treatment is started with 1 mg of pimozide daily at bedtime. The dosage is increased by 1 mg daily on a weekly basis until clinical efficacy is achieved or until intolerable side effects occur. The current recommendation is that children not exceed a maximum of 10 mg/day or 0.2 mg/kg/day of pimozide. Adolescents and adults may receive a maximum of 20 mg/day. The manufacturer recommends routine follow-up ECGs. Sallee, Pollock, Stiller, Stull, Everett, and Perel (1987) conducted a study to characterize the pharmacokinetics of pimozide in adults and children with Tourette's disorder. The results indicate extreme intersubject variability and a trend for the biological half-life of pimozide to be shorter in children than in adults; however, more study is warranted.

Clonidine is the drug of first choice when dealing with mild and transient tic disorders. Clonidine is also indicted alone or in conjunction with a neuroleptic when attentional problems or ADHD-like syndrome is part of the clinical presentation. Although clonidine has not been used extensively to treat self-injurious behavior, it is used with good results to decrease impulsivity in ADHD. Thus, clonidine may be useful in decreasing uncontrolled outbursts and aggression toward others or objects that characterizes some patients with TD. This effect seems to be independent of its effect on motor tic behaviors (Leckman et al., 1991). The opinion that clonidine has a place in the treatment of tic disorders is widespread, but it is not yet conclusive. Some studies have concluded that up to 62% of the patients have responded favorably (Leckman et al., 1985), while one author found clonidine to be no better than placebo (Goetz et al., 1987) in tic symptom reduction. The potential for improving comorbid behavioral problems and decreasing tic activity is appealing. In general, the neuroleptic agents do not improve behavior. The side effects of clonidine are mild and include dizziness, nausea, and orthostatic hypotension. Clonidine does not cause extrapyramidal side effects.

In general, treatment with clonidine is started at 0.05 mg twice daily. The response to clonidine is delayed, even up to several weeks, which is a concern in patients who need more immediate relief of tic symptoms. If the initial dose is tolerated, it can be increased by 0.1 mg twice daily. After 4 weeks, the dosage can again be increased to a maximum of 1.2 mg or until sedation or dizziness is reported. The usual daily dose is 5.5 μg/kg/day (Erenberg, 1988). If compliance is an issue, a clonidine transdermal patch is available. If clonidine is to be discontinued for any reason, it must be tapered off slowly, over a minimum of 1 week, to avoid a rapid increase in blood pressure and possible cardiac arrhythmias.

Alternative Treatments

The search for alternative treatments for tic disorders with and without self-injurious behavior and aggression continues. Many other dopamine receptor blocking agents have been tried (fluphenazine, sulpiride, and piquindone, a selective D1 receptor agonist). To date, fluphenazine and sulpiride appear to be the most promising. Fluphenazine, a piperazine phenothiazine, is thought to be an alternative treatment for patients with multiple tics who cannot tolerate haloperidol. Side effects often diminish without loss of tic control (Goetz, Tanner, & Klawans, 1984). Fluphenazine has been used in three patients with self-injurious behavior. Fluphenazine did not decrease the self-injury, but when it was discontinued, self-injury increased, suggestive of a supersensitivity phenomenon (Goldstein, Anderson, Reuben, & Dancis, 1985; Jones et al., 1991). Sulpiride, a substituted benzamide, with selective D2 receptor blocking effects, has been reported to have a lower incidence of extrapyramidal side effects than traditional neuroleptics. In a retrospective study done by Robertson et al. (1990), sulpiride proved useful in the control of motor and vocal tics. Its effects on self-injurious behavior and aggression have not been reported in the literature. Sulpiride, which is currently used widely in Europe, is said to have less deleterious effects on memory and learning than haloperidol (Robertson et al., 1990). Double-blind, placebo-controlled, long-term prospective studies need to be done to more clearly establish the role of fluphenazine and sulpiride in the treatment of this patient population.

Unfortunately, in the treatment of Tourette's disorder and related tic disorders, there is no "miracle cure." The neuroleptic agents now available are the most effective for tic symptom reduction; however, they are ineffective in treating all the major behavioral sequelae, and the possibility of significant side effects is quite high. Successful treatment of this disorder takes not only skilled clinicians to manage the pharmacotherapy, but also hard work and understanding on the part of the patient and the patient's family or support system.

Adjunctive Treatment

Recently, the association between tic disorders and obsessions and compulsions has attracted much interest. Although the proposed etiologies of tic disorders and OCD are quite similar, their pharmacotherapies are quite different. To date, there are only case reports in the literature supporting the use of anti-OCD drugs, such as fluoxetine and clomipramine, in combination with neuroleptics in the treatment of tic disorders (Ratzoni, Hermesh, Brandt, Lauffer, & Munitz, 1990). In a case report involving the use of clomipramine, OCD and tic symptomatology abated. In three case reports of fluoxetine, the obsessive-compulsive symptoms were markedly improved in all patients; tics improved in one patient, worsened in one, and were unchanged in the other (Riddle, Hardin, King, Scahill, & Woodston, 1990). Self-injurious behavior appeared or intensified during fluoxetine treatment of OCD in six patients (ages 10 to 17 years old) who were among 42 young patients receiving that drug. The authors hypothesize that emergence or exacerbation of this behavior could be due to drug-induced activation or a specific serotonergic-mediated effect on the regulation of aggression (King, Riddle, Chappell, Hardin, Anderson, Lombroso, & Scahill, 1991). In patients with TD and self-injurious behavior, use of fluoxetine is probably not warranted and should be used with caution.

Attention deficit and hyperactivity disorder is also more prevalent in patients with tic disorders than in the general population. If ADHD is severe enough to raise the issue of pharmacological treatment, a trial of clonidine alone or in combination with a neuroleptic is appropriate. Administration of psychostimulant drugs to a child with a tic disorder is indicated in only very rare cases (Golden, 1990). Psychostimulants offer no benefit and may worsen self-injurious behavior (Jones et al., 1991).

In the management of tic disorders and concurrent self-injurious behavior and/or aggression toward others and objects, resources are limited. Naloxone and naltrexone offer the most promising pharmacological treatment of self-injury. Several researchers have reported a positive outcome when using these opiate antagonists in mentally retarded patients with self-injurious behavior (Barrett, Feinstein, & Hale, 1989; Davidson, Keene, Carroll, & Rockowitz, 1983; Sandyk, 1985; Szymanski, Kedesdy, Sulkes, & Cutler, 1987). Naloxone, which is only available parenterally, and naltrexone, given orally, are relatively safe drugs. Dose-related hepatotoxicity and depressive symptoms in 10% of the population have been reported (Jones et al., 1991). Although promising, these studies all have several limitations and/or drawbacks, and interpretation of the results warrants much scrutiny.

As discussed earlier, neuroleptics offer little or no relief in self-aggression. Clonidine may decrease the impulsivity in this patient population and thereby decrease self-destructiveness or aggression toward others or objects. There is limited research on the use of benzodiazepines, although they are widely used. In a double-blind trial using an experimental benzodiazepine, 3 of 23 patients responded favorably (Elie, Albert, Cooper, Clermont, & Langlois, 1977). The particulars of these three patients are unknown. It must be cautioned that benzodiazepines can cause antegrade memory loss and impair cognitive functioning, which may greatly influence the benefit versus risk ratio for this group of patients. Lithium may be used in self-aggression. In a methodologically flawed study ($n = 8$), self-injurious behavior ceased in six patients, decreased in one subject, and did not change in one subject. These patients were also on other medications, including anticonvulsants and neuroleptics (Micev & Lynch, 1974). To date, no controlled studies using antidepressants, carbamazepine, or beta-blockers in self-injurious behavior have been reported. Tricyclic antidepressants, especially imipramine, and carbamazepine have been used with varying results to treat impulsivity in ADHD and might offer some benefit to patients with aggression and TD.

In cases of severe self-injurious behavior, protective measures must be taken. These precautions often take the form of padded helmets and mittens, knee guards, and at times restraints. Such precautions are designed to prevent fatal self-injuries, but can also be a therapeutic tool.

Psychotherapy and stress management are also very valuable adjunctive tools to medication management, and in many cases imperative to a positive outcome. In moderate to severe cases of tic syndromes, with or without severe behavioral symptomatology, psychotherapy alone or medication alone is responded to less favorably than the combination of these therapies. It is also known that during periods of stress, tic symptomatology as well as the coexisting behavioral problems are exacerbated. In fact, even when the tic disorder has been in remission for years, stressful times can cause recurrence of the hyperkinesis and, if applicable, aggression, both to self and others. Stressful situations cannot always be avoided; therefore, to prevent unnecessary relapse, it is important that the patient have advanced stress management techniques.

LONGITUDINAL PERSPECTIVES

It is impossible to predict the future of the tic disorders. Each patient diagnosed with a tic disorder carries a different short- and long-term prognosis. This interpatient variability is due not only to the characteristic waxing and waning of the tic disorder itself, but also to the many different complicated behavioral sequelae. Furthermore, even when tic symptoms and behavioral difficulties are well controlled, the psychological damage of tic disorders can be devastating. In each case, the patient's chance for a good prognosis increases when treatment is maximized and individualized and outside obstacles are minimized. These goals are best obtained by early diagnosis, compliance with all aspects of treatment, a supportive environment, and active patient participation.

Treatment Individualization

Although there is no evidence to support that early pharmacological treatment of tic disorders will alter the course of the illness, early nonpharmacological intervention is necessary for a positive outcome. The patient and the patient's family must begin immediately to understand the nature of the tic disorders and what to expect. Early diagnosis also allows the clinician to obtain baseline tic symptom and behavioral rating scales to guide future therapy decisions and monitor progression or regression of the disorder.

As discussed, comorbid behavioral and/or attentional disturbances such as ADHD, OCD, self-injurious behavior, and aggression are quite common among the tic disorders and must be addressed early as well. In fact, the behavioral problems are often the presenting symptom and more problematic than the underlying tic disorder. The tic disorder may not need pharmacological intervention, even though the behavioral deficits warrant medication management. Behavioral problems should be treated in such a way as to maximize concentration, learning, cognitive, and if applicable, school functioning as early as possible and minimize tic exacerbation. For example, if a patient presents with ADHD and also has a mild chronic motor tic, a psychostimulant would most likely exacerbate the tic, jeopardizing the desired improvement in the ADHD. On the other hand, clonidine has been shown to alleviate symptoms of both disorders and should be the drug first chosen. In the case of TD and self-injurious behavior, no proven effective treatments have been elucidated. The opiate antagonists naloxone and naltrexone offer benefit to some patients who self-injure and do not exacerbate tic symptoms and could therefore be of therapeutic value. The latter two scenarios are excellent examples of situations in which early pharmacological intervention is appropriate and how treatment must be individualized.

Another important step to individualizing treatment is knowing when to treat. When tics become increased from baseline and are disruptive to the point of causing psychosocial impairment, pharmacological intervention for the tic disorder should begin. Since tolerance of tic behavior, ego structure, and coping skills vary from patient to patient, patients must be involved in any and all decisions regarding treatment. A certain chronic motor tic may be only slightly noticed by one patient, but considered intolerable in another, leading to social withdrawal. The latter patient may need medication sooner than the former. Input from the family is also necessary because tics are often more bothersome to parents and family members than the patient.

In making specific medication choices many issues must be considered. The most widely used approach is to initiate treatment with clonidine in those patients who have tics of mild to moderate severity. Although the success rate with clonidine is below that of the neuroleptics, the side effects are minimal. A trial of clonidine often leads to long-term benefits and reduces the need for neuroleptics. There also is the potential for behavioral improvements, including decreasing aggression, if this is an issue. The threshold for use of neuroleptics should be quite high, given their potential for side effects. However, if tics are severe or causing significant impairment, they should not be withheld. When a neuroleptic drug is indicated, haloperidol or pimozide are the drugs of choice, with similar efficacy and side effect profile. Some investigators feel that pimozide is associated with less sedation and akinesia. In some refractory cases, combinations of clonidine, pimozide, or haloperidol can be used. In patients with comorbid aggression and/or self-injurious behavior, the neuroleptics are now thought to have no net effect.

Compliance

Besides the available treatments being less than optimal, there are many other problems in carrying out pharmacological as well as nonpharmacological interventions. The biggest obstacle is that of compliance. Noncompliance can take many forms. The most common form is refusal to medicate, even when strongly indicated. This is thought to be partly due to the stigma of taking "psychiatric drugs." Also, if initial side effects are experienced, the patient may discontinue medication and refuse to take it in the future. Patients may also discontinue medication in periods of remission, the feeling being it is no longer needed. In the cases of comorbid behavioral syndromes, medication may be discontinued to sabotage treatment. Noncompliance can also take the form of overuse or abuse of medication. Since the medicines most commonly used to treat tic disorders have a low abuse potential, overuse of medications is most commonly seen when parents overmedicate their child to stop the tics for their own solace.

Compliance with other aspects of treatment is also a problem. Many patients and family members will refuse psychotherapy, even when strongly urged. In patients with concurrent self-injurious behavior and/or aggression, precautions to avoid self-harm and harm to others must be taken. These include protective clothing and at times restraints. Patients and families often fight this, but safety must always come first.

Support

A child with a tic disorder needs a great deal of support for normal psychosocial development and to prevent unnecessary comorbid behavioral problems or regression in level of functioning. The child already faces many hurdles in peer groups and greatly needs stability. Support can come from many different sources. In most cases, the major support system usually comes from the family. However, not all patients with tic disorders have this resource. A second avenue for support is from the physician. Most clinicians who are treating tic disorders are quite invested in the care of their patients and are willing to lend support whenever necessary. In addition, there are many support groups around the country that provide counseling. This also gives patients and family members a chance to learn that they are not alone and share experiences.

Patient Participation

Even in the worse-case scenario, when a patient is invested in treatment, the prognosis is brighter. The best avenue to patient participation is through early education. Patients, including children, must be kept informed and involved in the decisions regarding all aspects of the illness. The patient must learn how to monitor symptoms and side effects of medications. The patient must also learn behavioral strategies to hopefully decrease hyperkinesis. Parents and family members must also be involved in medication and therapy decisions. In most cases, the patient is a child and the parents are the primary caregivers, and they must be able to titrate medication if necessary. Patient and family must also know what to do in the event of acute side effects. Parents and family members must also learn coping skills in dealing with this syndrome. It is never easy to see a loved one in distress.

The child's teachers, pastor, coaches, friends, and others all must be educated about the disorder and given some practical tools for dealing with some of the bizarre behaviors they will witness. Knowledge is palliative for all involved.

CASE ILLUSTRATION

Tim is a 9-year-old male who was brought to the Youth Division Neuropsychiatric Assessment Center by his mother with complaints of school failure and "habits." Tim was an only child of his working-class parents, who had placed him in outpatient psychotherapy at the local mental health center for the year prior to seeking a comprehensive assessment. Presenting complaints were talking to himself, "I'm doing a million things wrong per minute," and ruminating thoughts. An overlay of depressive affect was present as well, and the parents stated that Tim's only outlet was playing school. He would drill and redrill himself with math problems and berate himself when he made an error. On presentation he was grunting and making gestures with his hands, and making faces at the examiner. If attention were brought to his behavior he would hide his face. He had poor peer relations, and the rest of the students on his bus made fun of his "faces," which were dystonic tics. His "faces," hand gestures, and grunting occurred about once per 5-minute period and were a cause of deep embarrassment to Tim, who wanted desperately to stop. He became angry and hostile to others when teased; he became so frustrated with being unable to complete work that he would lash out at his mother in anger. He evidently was failing school, not because he could not handle the material but because he could not produce homework or complete a test. He would sit at his desk erasing and redoing his answers so that no progress was made. He was viewed by school personnel as extremely obsessional, and despite all efforts to accommodate him through a reduced work load, he was still failing. He had a brief treatment trial with imipramine (3 mg/kg) at the mental health center, with some reduction in obsessions but worsening of tics and gestures.

Mental status examination revealed a very obsessional child with poor self-esteem and inwardly directed anger. He stated that he was "so stupid" because he could not finish his work. He would talk about playing school alone with himself and play both the part of the teacher and the pupil. He would scream at himself and make the "pupil" redo the work. He was not delusional or psychotic. His affect could be described as sad and angry. He stated that he had experienced an intense desire to place his hand on the open burner of a stove. Even though he knew this would produce severe injury he felt compelled to do this. He ruminated about the hot burner and could not get this thought out of his mind. His preoccupation was intense and prevented him from sleeping or doing homework. He had every indication that his judgment was intact and that he did not mean necessarily to harm himself but he felt he could no longer keep himself from performing the act.

Neurological examination was unremarkable except for presence of vocal and motor tics at about 30-minute intervals. The motor tics were of the complex type and included making "faces" at all times of the day both in and out of a social context. He also made hand gestures of a semipurposeful nature, which seemed to attract a considerable amount of attention to himself. Gross and fine motor coordination were age appropriate. A formal rating of tics using the Tourette Syndrome Global Scale (Harcherik et al., 1984) indicated a severe level of tics primarily of the complex type and a considerable contribution of obsessive-compulsive behavior to the determination of severity.

Diagnoses of Tourette disorder and obsessive-compulsive disorder were made based on persistent (> 1-year duration) vocal and motor tics complicated by severe obsessive thinking. Tim was successfully treated with a combination of clomipramine (Anafranil) (150 mg) and haloperidol (0.5 mg/day) over the course of 6 weeks. Initially, significant reduction of complex tics were noted to the level that children on the bus stopped making fun of him. His inward frustrations decreased as clomipramine dosage was gradually raised. Persistent thoughts to put his hand on the stove decreased in intensity but were still present. Anger and hostility in this case came from a persistent expectation of high functioning on his part with punitive reaction to his self-assessed failure. As his obsessive thinking decreased he became able to concentrate more and accomplish seatwork tasks. Interestingly, as his competence in the classroom grew, he became less interested in "playing school" both at home and during psychotherapy sessions. Self-directed anger stemming from frustration around his school performance could be one reason for the persistent obsession of placing his hand on the stove burner. In addition to psychopharmacological management, considerable effort went into school consultation with regard to in-school management of his obsessional thinking. Nonthreatening redirection was used with considerable success to decrease performance stress. The family entered family therapy around how to manage the patient's anger and hostility, which frequently occurred during homework. Presence of a supportive environment, collaboration of school personnel, and effective combination pharmacotherapy resulted in a positive outcome.

SUMMARY

Tic disorders, which are the most common movement disorders of children and adolescents, continue to pose quite a challenge to the patient, the patient's family, the community, and the clinician. Tic disorders frequently carry comorbid behavioral difficulties, which in general worsen the prognosis. Although progress has been made over the last several years in the assessment, diagnosis, and treatment of tic disorders and the behavioral sequelae, much more research is necessary to effectively manage this difficult patient population.

The advances in the treatment of tic disorders that have been made are, unfortunately, only palliative, and to date no ideal treatment regimen is available. Only a few medications (e.g., haloperidol, pimozide, clonidine) have been found to be useful in tic symptom reduction. Although usually effective, these medications can have some deleterious side effects and provide only symptomatic relief.

More recent advances have been made in treating associated psychiatric symptoms such as ADHD, OCD, self-injurious behavior, and aggression. These treatments include use of fluoxetine and clomipramine for OCD, clonidine for ADHD and possibly aggression, and a trial of naltrexone for self-injurious behavior. Depending on the clinical presentation, often the combination of haloperidol or pimozide with clomipramine and/or clonidine is an effective regimen for improving associated behavioral difficulties and suppression of tic activity. It must be stressed that no one treatment or combination of treatments is effective for everyone. The most important feature to a positive outcome is individualizing the therapy. Furthermore, due to the psychological sequelae of tic disorders, adjunctive therapies such as psychotherapy, family therapy, school counseling, and stress management are quite relevant to a positive course.

Even with the best clinical management, approximately one-third of patients with significant tic disorders will not benefit from the currently available treatment approaches (Erenberg, 1988). When significant behavioral problems are present, treatment failures increase. This has motivated researchers all over the world. Hopefully, in the near future, a larger number of safe and effective treatments will be available.

REFERENCES

Achenbach, T. M., & Edelbrock, C. S. (1983). *Manual for the Revised Child Behavior Checklist and Profile*. Burlington, VT: University Associates in Psychiatry.

Barrett, R. P., Feinstein, C., & Hale, W. (1989). Effects of naloxone and naltrexone on self-injury: A double-blind, placebo controlled analysis. *American Journal of Mental Deficiency*, *93*, 644–651.

Bennun, I. (1983). Depression and hostility in self-mutilation. *Suicide and Life-Threatening Behavior*, *13*, 71–84.

Bornstein, R. A., & Yang, V. (1991). Neuropsychological performance in medicated and unmedicated patients with Tourette's disorder. *American Journal of Psychiatry*, *148*, 468–471.

Bruun, R. D. (1984). Gilles de la Tourette's syndrome: An overview of clinical experience. *Journal of the American Academy of Child Psychiatry*, *23*, 126–133.

Bruun, R. D. (1988). The natural history of Tourette's syndrome. In D. J. Cohen, R. D. Bruun, & J. F. Leckman (Eds.), *Tourette's syndrome and tic disorders: Clinical understanding and treatment* (pp. 22–39). New York: Wiley & Sons.

Caine, E. D., McBride, M. C., & Chiverton, P. (1988). Tourette's syndrome in Monroe County school children. *Neurology*, *38*, 472.

Cohen, D. J., Young, J. G., & Nathanson, J. A. (1979). Clonidine in Tourette's syndrome. *Lancet*, *2*, 551–553.

Coid, J. M., Allolio, B., & Rees, L. H. (1983). Raised plasma metenkephalin in patients who habitually mutilate themselves. *Lancet*, *ii*, 545–546.

Comings, D. E., & Comings, B. G. (1985). Tourette syndrome: Clinical and psychological aspects of 250 cases. *American Journal of Human Genetics*, *37*, 435–450.

Comings, D. E., & Comings, B. G. (1987). A controlled study of Tourette syndrome. I. Attention-deficit disorder, learning disorders, and school problems. *American Journal of Human Genetics*, *41*, 701–741.

Corbett, J. A., & Campbell, H. J. (1980). Causes of severe self-injurious behavior. In P. Mittler & J. M. Dejong (Eds.), *Mental retardation new horizons: Vol. II Biomedical aspects* (pp. 285–292). University Park Press: Baltimore.

Davidson, P. W., Keene, B. M., Carroll, M., & Rockowitz, R. J. (1983). Effects of naloxone on self-injurious behavior: A case study. *Applied Research in Mental Retardation*, *4*, 1–4.

Elie, R., Albert, J., Cooper, S. F., Clermont, A., & Langlois, Y. (1977). Efficacy of SCH-12679 in the management of aggressive mental retardates. *Current Therapeutic Research*, *21*, 786–795.

Erenberg, G. (1988). Pharmacologic therapy of tics in childhood. *Pediatric Annals*, *17*, 395–404.

Frankel, M., Cummings, J. L., Robertson, M. M., Trimble, M. R., Hill, M. A., & Benson, D. F. (1986). Obsessions and compulsions in Gilles de la Tourette's syndrome. *Neurology*, *36*, 378–382.

Gardner, A. R., & Gardner, A. J. (1975). Self mutilation, obsessionality and narcissism. *British Journal of Psychiatry*, *127*, 127–132.

Goetz, C. G., Tanner, C. M., & Klawans, H. L. (1984). Fluphenazine and multifocal tic disorders. *Archives of Neurology*, *41*, 271–272.

Goetz, C. G., Tanner, C. M., Wilson, R. S., Carroll, V. S., Como, P. G., & Shannon, K. M. (1987). Clonidine and Gilles de la Tourette's syndrome: Double-blind study using objective rating methods. *Annals of Neurology*, *21*, 307–310.

Golden, G. S. (1990). Tourette syndrome: Recent advances. *Neurology Clinics*, *8*, 705–714.

Goldstein, M., Anderson, L. T., Reuben, R., & Dancis, J. (1985). Self-mutilation in Lesch-Nyhan disease caused by dopaminergic denervation. *Lancet*, *9*, 338–339.

Gorea, E., & Lombard, M. C. (1984). The possible participation of a dopaminergic system in mutilating behavior in rats with forelimb deafferentation. *Neuroscience Letters*, *48*, 75–80.

Harcherick, D. F., Leckman, J. F., Detlor, J., & Cohen, D. J. (1984). A new instrument for clinical studies of Tourette's syndrome. *Journal of the American Academy of Child Psychiatry*, *23*, 153–160.

Jones, I. H., & Barraclough, B. M. (1978). Auto-mutilation in animals and its relevance to self-injury in man. *Acta Psychiatrica Scandinavica*, *58*, 40–47.

Jones, C. C., Vallano, G., Ryan, E., Helsel, W. J., & Rancurello, M. D. (1991). Self-injurious behavior: Strategies for assessment and management. *Psychiatric Annals*, *21*, 310–318.

King, R. A., Riddle, M. A., Chappell, P. B., Hardin, M. T., Anderson, G. M., Lombroso, P., & Scahill, L. (1991). Emergency of self-destructive phenomenon in children and adolescents during fluoxetine treatment. *Journal of the American Academy of Child and Adolescent Psychiatry*, *30*, 179–186

Leckman, J. F., Detlor, J., Harcherik, D. F., Ort, S., Shaywitz, B. A., & Cohen, D. J. (1985). Short- and long-term treatment of Tourette's syndrome with clonidine: A clinical perspective. *Neurology, 35,* 343–351.

Leckman, J. F., Hardin, M. T., Riddle, M. A., Stevenson, J., Ort, S., & Cohen, D. J. (1991). Clonidine treatment of Gilles de la Tourette's syndrome. *Archives of General Psychiatry, 48,* 324–328.

Maletzky, B. M. (1974). Behavior recording as treatment: A brief note. *Behavior Therapy, 5,* 107–111.

Micev, V., & Lynch, D. M. (1974). Effect of lithium on disturbed severely mentally retarded patients. *British Journal of Psychiatry, 125,* 110.

Mikkelsen, E. J., Detlor, J., & Cohen, D. J. (1981). School avoidance and social phobia triggered by haloperidol in patients with Tourette's disorder. *American Journal of Psychiatry, 138,* 1572–1576.

Ollendick, T. H. (1981). Self-monitoring and self-administered overcorrection: The modification of nervous tics in children. *Behavior Modification, 5,* 75–84.

Pauls, D. L., & Leckman, J. F. (1986). The inheritance of Gilles de la Tourette's syndrome and associated behaviors: Evidence for an autosomal dominant transmission. *New England Journal of Medicine, 315,* 993–997.

Primeau, F., & Fontaine, R. (1987). Obsessive disorder with self-mutilation: A subgroup of responsive to pharmacotherapy. *Canadian Journal of Psychiatry, 32,* 699–701.

Ratzoni, G., Hermesh, H., Brandt, N., Lauffer, M., & Munitz, H. (1990). Clomipramine efficacy for tics, obsessions, and compulsions in Tourette's syndrome and obsessive-compulsive disorder: A case study. *Biological Psychiatry, 27,* 95–98.

Regeur, L., Pakkenberg, B., Fog, R., & Pakkenberg, H. (1986). Clinical features and long-term treatment with pimozide in 65 patients with Gilles de la Tourette's syndrome. *Journal of Neurology, Neurosurgery, & Psychiatry, 49,* 791–795.

Riddle, M. A., Hardin, M. T., King, R., Scahill, L., & Woolston, J. L. (1990). Fluoxetine treatment in children and adolescents with Tourette's and obsessive compulsive disorder: Preliminary clinical experience. *Journal of the American Academy of Child and Adolescent Psychiatry, 29,* 45–48.

Robertson, M. M., Schnieden, V., & Lees, A. J. (1990). Management of Gilles de la Tourette syndrome using sulpiride. *Clinical Neuropharmacology, 13,* 229–235.

Robertson, M. M., Trimble, M. R., & Lees, A. J. (1989). Self-injurious behavior and the Gilles de la Tourette syndrome: A clinical study and review of the literature. *Psychological Medicine, 19,* 611–625.

Sallee, F. R., Pollock, B. G., Stiller, R. L., Stull, S., Everett, G., & Perel, J. M. (1987). Pharmacokinetics of pimozide in adults and children with Tourette's syndrome. *Journal of Clinical Pharmacology, 27,* 776–781.

Sallee, F. R., Rock, C., & Kunins, N. (1991). [Unpublished raw data.]

Sandyk, R. (1985). Naloxone abolishes self-injuring in a mentally retarded child. *Annals of Neurology, 17,* 520.

Sandyk, R., & Baithford, C. A. (1987). Deregulation of hypothalamic dopamine and opiode activity and the pathophysiology of self-mutilatory behavior in Tourette's syndrome. *Journal of Clinical Psychopharmacology, 7,* 367.

Shapiro, A. K., Shapiro, E., & Eisenkraft, M. A. (1983). Treatment of Gilles de la Tourette syndrome with pimozide. *American Journal of Psychiatry, 140,* 1183–1186.

Shapiro, A. K., Shapiro, E., & Fulop, G. (1987). Pimozide treatment of tic and Tourette disorders. *Pediatrics, 79,* 1032–1039.

Shapiro, A. K., Shapiro, E., & Wayne, H. (1973). Treatment of Tourette syndrome with haloperidol, review of 34 cases. *Archives of General Psychiatry, 28,* 92–97.

Shapiro, E., Shapiro, A. K., Fulop, G., Hubbard, M., Mandeli, J., Nordlie, J., & Phillips, R. A. (1989). Controlled study of haloperidol, pimozide, and placebo for the treatment of Gilles de la Tourette's syndrome. *Archives of General Psychiatry, 46,* 722–730.

Singer, H. S., Tune, L. E., Butler, I. J., Seifert, W. E., & Coyle, J. T. (1982). Dopaminergic dysfunction in Tourette syndrome. *Annals of Neurology, 12,* 361–366.

Singh, N. N., & Aman, M. G. (1981). Effects of thioridazine dosage on the behavior of severely mentally retarded persons. *American Journal of Mental Deficiency, 85,* 580–587.

Stefl, M. E. (1983). *The Ohio Tourette study.* School of Planning, University of Cincinnati.

Szymanski, L., Kedesdy, J., Sulkes, S., & Cutler, A. (1987). Naltrexone in treatment of self-injurious behavior: A clinical study. *Research Developmental Disabilities, 8,* 179–190.

Thomas, E. J., Abrams, K. S., & Johnson, J. B. (1971). Self-monitoring and reciprocal inhibition in the modification of multiple tics of Gilles de la Tourette's syndrome. *Journal of Behavior Therapy & Experimental Psychiatry, 2,* 159–171.

van der Kolk, B. A. (1989). The compulsion to repeat the trauma. Re-enactment, revictimization, and masochism. *Psychiatric Clinics of North America, 12,* 389–411.

CHAPTER 25

Substance Abuse

Oscar G. Bukstein

Substance abuse and aggressive or self-destructive behavior have a long association. From the psychodynamic concept of suicide as aggression or anger turned inward (Freud, 1917) and Menninger's (1938) description of "focal or partial suicide" in describing the self-destructive behavior of alcoholics, we have come to a polythetic understanding of the relationship of substance abuse and destructive behaviors throughout the life cycle. Although several reviews have critically examined the relationship between destructive behaviors and substance abuse in adults (Flavin, Franklin, & Francis, 1990; Galanter & Castaneda, 1985), these relationships appear to apply to adolescents as well. In this chapter, the literature on adolescent substance abuse and its relationship to destructive behaviors is reviewed. Based on information from the literature, evaluation and treatment issues are examined and a relevant case study is presented.

DESCRIPTION OF THE DISORDER

Despite a public consensus of an adolescent substance abuse epidemic (Johnston, 1991), there appears to be little agreement as to what actually defines pathological use of alcohol and/or other drugs among adolescents. Generic and popular definitions abound, although many clinicians use the DSM-III-R psychoactive substance use disorders (American Psychiatric Association, 1987) as a guide to making formal categorical diagnoses. DSM-III-R psychoactive substance use diagnoses represent a broadening of the definition of dependence to include clinically significant behaviors, cognitions, and symptoms indicating a substantial degree of involvement with a psychoactive substance (Rounsaville, Spitzer, & Williams, 1986). In contrast to DSM-III (APA, 1980), with its concept of dependence that could rarely be applied to adolescents due to the relative infrequence of physical symptoms or sequelae of substance use, more adolescents likely meet DSM-III-R

OSCAR G. BUKSTEIN • Department of Psychiatry, Western Psychiatric Institute and Clinic, Pittsburgh, Pennsylvania 15213.

Handbook of Aggressive and Destructive Behavior in Psychiatric Patients, edited by Michel Hersen, Robert T. Ammerman, and Lori A. Sisson. Plenum Press, New York, 1994.

psychoactive substance dependence criteria. Implicit in the concept of dependence in DSM-III-R is impaired control over use. Past research has given little or no attention to this phenomenon in adolescents. The diagnosis of psychoactive substance abuse may be useful in identifying mild problems and relies on impairment in functioning or negative consequences as basic criteria. This assumes that impairment and negative consequences are the result of abuse and not due to preexisting or concurrent factors, such as another psychiatric disorder or family dysfunction.

The release of the final draft criteria for substance-related disorders in DSM-IV (APA, 1993) shows a subtle but significant change in the criteria for dependence and more significant changes in the criteria for abuse. The changes in dependence criteria for DSM-IV consist of elimination of the DSM-III-R criteria for frequent intoxication or withdrawal symptoms when expected to fulfill major role obligations, addition of subtyping according to the presence or absence of physiological signs of dependence (tolerance or withdrawal), and elimination of duration criteria. While the preservation of behavioral and cognitive criteria in a diagnosis of dependence in a subtype without physiological dependence allows for substantial numbers of youth to meet dependence criteria, the elimination of the criteria for inability to fulfill role obligations due to substance use may reduce the number of adolescents meeting DSM-IV substance dependence criteria.

The DSM-IV criteria for substance abuse represent a more substantial change from DSM-III-R. DSM-IV expands criteria of maladaptive pattern of substance use to require clinically significant impairment or distress and provides two additional examples of a maladaptive pattern of use which include recurrent use resulting in a failure to fulfill major role obligations (omitted from DSM-IV dependence criteria) and recurrent substance-related legal problems. As with the diagnosis of dependence, DSM-IV no longer includes duration criteria to establish a substance abuse diagnosis.

Perhaps the most significant change in DSM-IV is the addition of a requirement that the maladaptive pattern of substance use lead to clinically significant impairment or distress. In the past, the presence of a maladaptive pattern of use, by whatever subjective criteria, was sufficient to meet diagnostic criteria. The requirement of impairment or distress may present a difficult problem of whether to attribute the impairment or distress to substance use rather than to the variety of problem behaviors, psychopathology, or adverse environmental circumstances which are often seen in adolescents who use psychoactive substances. Failure to meet even a minimal level of impairment or distress despite a perceived maladaptive pattern of use may reduce the number of adolescents who meet criteria for a DSM-IV diagnosis of substance abuse. For the DSM-IV diagnosis of substance dependence, elimination of the criteria for frequent intoxication or withdrawal symptoms when expected to fulfill major role obligations at work, home or school may reduce the number of adolescents receiving a dependence diagnosis. The essential change in DSM-IV is away from the behavior(s) of substance use toward evidence of psychosocial dysfunction. This change may be more significant in the diagnosis of adolescents as use and related behaviors may be much more prevalent and obvious than dysfunction directly attributable to substance use. Although research is needed to establish the relevance and validity of adult DSM-IV diagnoses in adolescents, the use of criteria-based or symptomatic behaviors in DSM-III-R/DSM-IV psychoactive substance dependence is a reasonable starting point. The DSM-IV category of psychoactive substance abuse may also be useful in identifying a set of less affected adolescents who manifest recurrent problems related to their substance use.

Patterns of psychoactive substance dependence among adolescents can be distinguished from dependence in adults in that overt, severe symptoms of tolerance and withdrawal are rarely seen in adolescents (Vingilis & Smart, 1981). Adolescents have different role obligations than adults. Since many of today's adolescents appear occupied in few constructive activities, the reduction in such activities due to substance use may hardly be noticed. Generally, because less is expected of adolescents than adults, increasing involvement with drugs and alcohol and related activities may not be evident. Despite almost universal application of these same criteria to adolescents, many differences exist between adolescents and adults in a variety of substance use characteristics, including use patterns and consequences (Blane, 1979; Weschler, 1979). Consideration of adult and adolescent substance abuse as fundamentally the same disorder is called into question by evidence of discontinuity in problem-drinker status between adolescence and young adulthood (Jessor, 1984). Frequent heavy drinking in adolescents and the problems resulting from drinking appear to be self-limiting and are not highly predictive of alcoholism in adults (Blane, 1979). Similarly, patterns of involvement with marijuana and other illicit drugs peak in late adolescence (Kandel & Logan, 1984). However, the clinical picture of psychoactive substance dependence in adolescents and adults is similar, particularly in adolescents' increasing preoccupation with drug and alcohol use as the central activity of their lives.

Psychoactive substance abuse may be more problematic to distinguish from normal adolescent experimentation with drugs and alcohol, and the common occurrence of concurrent behavioral and emotional problems unrelated or not directly related to substance use. However, the existence of recurrent social, occupational, and psychological problems directly related to or exacerbated by use suffices to identify an abusive pattern of substance use in adolescents.

Aggression and self-destructive behaviors in adolescents can be used as fulfilling diagnostic criteria when they are the direct result of intoxication or use. Illustrative is the adolescent who gets into repeated fights or suffers from suicidal ideation secondary to the disinhibitory or depressant effects of alcohol.

EPIDEMIOLOGY

Two national surveys, the University of Michigan Monitoring the Future (Johnston, 1991) and the National Household Survey on Drug Abuse (ADAMHA, 1991), serve as the primary data sources of patterns of substance use among adolescents. Monitoring the Future annually surveys high school senior students for types and frequency of drug, alcohol, and tobacco use. The National Household Survey on Drug Abuse (NHSDA) includes information on the use of various drugs in the past year, the past month, and any lifetime use for the 12- to 17-year-old age group as well as for several adult age groups.

According to the 1990 Monitoring the Future study (Johnston, 1991), trends show a continuing decline in the proportion of students actively using any illicit drug as well as a decline in the proportion using marijuana, cocaine, crack, stimulants, and sedatives. Declines in the use of sedatives and marijuana represent a continuation of long-term declines from the 1970s. Cocaine did not begin to decline until 1986. Nevertheless, a considerable proportion of youth exhibit drug involvement. In 1990, a third of all high school seniors reported using at least one illicit drug during the past year, 27% report marijuana use in the past year, while 5.3% report using cocaine some time in the past year. Daily use of marijuana is reported by 2.2% of students, with other drugs (except alcohol) each having being used daily by less than 0.1% of students. Almost 20% of students report daily cigarette use, with 11.4% smoking a half pack or more per day. The use of alcohol remains high among adolescents, with a monthly prevalence of 57% (down from a peak of 72% in 1980). Thirty-two percent of high school seniors claim to have had at least one episode of heavy drinking (five or more drinks in a row) in the prior 2 weeks. Daily use of alcohol is reported by 3.7% of students. Although Johnston and associates found that high school seniors reported an increase in perceived availability of such drugs as cocaine and marijuana, these adolescents also reported an increase in the perceived risk of drug use during the period of decline in the prevalence of use of these drugs. As the Monitoring the Future study surveys only current high school students, the figures above may underestimate substance use in the population of adolescents who have dropped out of high school. These adolescents may represent a higher risk population in terms of higher substance use and severity of pathology, including aggressive behavior.

The NHSDA data show an 8.1% monthly prevalence of use of any illicit drug among youth aged 12–17 years. Approximately 5% of this age group reports use of alcohol once a week or more. While these surveys demonstrate substantial substance use among adolescents, unfortunately, no studies have examined the prevalence of substance use among community samples of youth. Attempts to operationalize a definition of adolescent problem drinking involving frequency of drunkenness and/or negative consequences related to alcohol use have led to estimates of adolescent "problem drinking" ranging from 19% of 14- to 17-year-olds (Rachel et al., 1980) to 28% of males in a high school sample.

Given the limited accessibility to most potentially abusive substances, limited exposure, and a smaller range for possible addiction pathology in adolescents, it appears likely that the lifetime prevalence of alcohol and other drug abuse disorders is less than that found for adults, which is estimated at 13.5% for alcohol disorders, 6.1% for other drug disorders, and 16.7% for any substance use disorder [as determined by the Epidemiologic Catchment Area (ECA) study] (Regier et al., 1990).

ETIOLOGY

Risk Factors and Stages of Use

Identifying risk factors or antecedent factors correlated with increased adolescent use and abuse is important in not only describing the range of pathological substance use, but also designing a comprehensive assessment of the adolescent. Environmental antecedents are among the most robust predictors of adolescent substance use, with parental attitudes and behavior the most significant among these factors (Kandel, 1982). In addition to parental role modeling, the quality and consistency of family communication and parental behavior management are also strong predictors of adolescent use (Kandel et al., 1978; Donovan & Jessor, 1978).

Among peer-related factors predicting adolescent use are peer drug-use behaviors and attitudes (Kandel et al., 1978), and perceived use of substances by peers (Jessor & Jessor, 1978). Reported peer drinking has the strongest relationship with adolescent drinking. Individual adolescent drinking behavior resembles that of peers. The greater the peer use, the more likely an adolescent will initiate and progress to heavier levels of use (Donovan & Jessor, 1978; White, 1987).

Individual factors, including beliefs, attitudes, substance use expectancies, and preexisting psychopathology, are further implicated as antecedents of adolescent use and abuse. Preexisting and current beliefs about alcohol are associated with current drinking patterns (Christiansen et al., 1982), and favorable attitudes about drug use preceding initiation appear to facilitate initiation into drug use (Kandel et al., 1978). Substance use-related expectancies—the effects attributed to a substance that the individual adolescent anticipates when using that substance—are related to future substance use (Brown, 1985) as well as current use patterns (Christiansen et al., 1985).

Preexisting as well as concurrent psychopathology in the adolescent is often associated with use. Antisocial behavior often predicts adolescent substance use (Johnston et al., 1978; Kandel et al., 1978), with delinquency occurring prior to substance use. Other studies suggest that depression (Christie et al., 1988; Deykin et al., 1987) and attention deficit disorder (Gittleman et al., 1985) may precede substance use or abuse. Tarter and associates (1985) have suggested that vulnerability to substance use could be explained in terms of temperamental traits, such as quality or lability of prevailing mood. Specific temperament traits may be the basis for a common diathesis for substance abuse and antisocial behavior and/or other psychiatric disorders.

A number of researchers have used the above risk factors to construct theories explaining adolescent substance use and progression to abuse. Kandel (1982) proposed four developmental stages of use: (1) beer and wine, (2) cigarettes and/or hard liquor, (3) marijuana, and (4) other illicit drugs. Participation in each stage is a necessary but not sufficient condition for progression to a later stage. There are stage-specific predictors of initiation into various legal and illegal drugs. For involvement in alcohol, both peer and especially parental influences, such as modeling, are critical. Peer influences are more important in predicting marijuana use. Use of illicit drugs other than marijuana is influenced by parental use, poor family relationships, and psychological distress.

AGGRESSION TOWARD SELF

There is a significant relationship between the use of alcohol and other psychoactive substances in adults and increased risk for suicide and other forms of self-destructive behavior (Flavin, Franklin, & Francis, 1990). Only recently has a similar relationship been recognized and investigated in youth. Suicide is currently the second leading cause of death among youth (Centers for Disease Control, 1985). Given the rise in suicidal behavior and the increasing importance of evaluation of suicidality in an emergency setting, examination of substance use and abuse as a possible contributing factor is critical.

Despite the obvious limitations in determining substance use or abuse in studies of suicide completers, the literature supports psychoactive substance abuse as a risk factor for suicidal behavior, including ideation, attempted, and completed suicide (Crumley, 1990). In a study of completed suicides in Allegheny County, Pennsylvania, from 1960 to 1983, Brent and associates (1987) found a marked increase in the suicide rate among youth, particularly among white males aged 15 to 19 years old. The proportion of suicide victims having detectable alcohol levels rose 3.6-fold to 46% in 1978 to 1983. Suicide victims who used firearms were 4.9 times more likely to have been drinking than those using less lethal methods of suicide. Both the increased use of alcohol and the availability of firearms may have significantly contributed to the increased rate of suicide among adolescents. In a study of completed suicides in San Diego, 53% of 133 consecutive young suicides (less than 40 years old) had a principal diagnosis of substance abuse (Rich, Young, & Fowler, 1986).

Sixty-six percent of young suicides in the same study group were substance abusers (Rich et al., 1986). Eleven percent of the substance-abusing group committed suicide before age 20.

In other studies of adolescent suicide completers, significant percentages of victims were substance abusers. Shaffer and colleagues (Shaffer, Garland, Gould, Fisher, & Trautman, 1988) found substance abuse to be associated with 37% of male and 5% of female suicides. A similar male predominance in suicide completions is noted in Hoberman and Garfinkel's (1988) retrospective study of 229 adolescent completers. Twenty-two percent of the victims were determined to be substance abusers. Other studies show ranges of substance abuse in suicide completers from 27.6% (Poteet, 1987) to 70% (Shaffi et al., 1985). The increased risk of completed suicide among adolescent substance abusers is further supported by Benson and Holmberg (1984) in a 10-year follow-up of two groups of adolescents. When compared with a group from the general population, adolescents with a prior history of substance abuse had a two to eight times greater death rate, with one-half of the deaths due to suicide.

It is not clear whether substance use or abuse is more common in suicide completers than attempters. Brent and associates (1988) found that the diagnosis of substance abuse was not significantly different between groups of adolescent completers versus attempters and ideators with a lethal plan. A number of studies show high rates of substance abuse among adolescent suicide attempters. Studies of hospitalized adolescent attempters reported substance abuse rates from 23% (Stevenson et al., 1972) to 50% (Crumley, 1979; Pfeffer et al., 1986). In a study of 340 outpatient adolescent substance abusers, suicide attempts were three times more likely among substance-abusing youth than a group of normal matched controls (Schwartz & Berman, 1990). Adolescent suicide attempters with a diagnosis of substance abuse may have more serious or potentially lethal attempts (Brent et al., 1986; Pfeffer et al., 1983). Substance abuse in depressed adolescents appears to increase both the risk of multiple attempts and the medical seriousness of the attempts (Robbins & Alessi, 1985).

Substance abuse may distinguish attempters from ideators (Kosky et al, 1990), although substance abuse has been identified as a risk factor for suicidal ideation among college students (Levy & Deykin, 1989). Like completers, a male predominance among adolescent substance abusers with suicidal attempts and ideation is noted (Kotila & Lonnggvist, 1988; Levy & Deykin, 1989).

In attempting to answer the question of why adolescent substance abusers have a high risk for suicidal behavior, one can examine several possible mechanisms, including acute and chronic effects of substance use or abuse. Adolescent suicide victims are frequently using alcohol or other drugs at the time of suicide (Brent et al., 1987; Friedman, 1985). The acute use of substances may produce a transient but intense dysphoric state, disinhibition, impaired judgments, and increased levels of impulsivity. The acute use of alcohol or other drugs may exacerbate preexisting psychopathology, including depression and anxiety (Schuckit, 1986). Adolescents often have less tolerance for extreme mood states and limited judgment and behavioral controls when compared with adults. Therefore, the acute effects of substances on behavior may have more potentially severe effects on adolescents. In fact, drugs are often the method for the suicidal act (Garfinkel et al., 1982).

Chronic effects of substance abuse include pharmacological effects such as depression (Mayfield, 1968) or serotonergic depletion (Ballanger et al., 1979), or social effects including disruption of peer and family relationships. Youth experiencing an acute stressor involving a social loss or a blow to self-esteem are at greater risk for suicidal behavior

(Hoberman & Garfinkel, 1988). As noted in studies of adult populations, alcoholics with hopelessness and interpersonal losses are at increased risk for suicide (Beck et al., 1976; Murphy et al., 1979). Since many adolescent substance abusers have dysfunctional families with parents who also abuse substances (Kandel, 1974), environmental stress may be further increased. In a report of 58 consecutive suicides by adolescents and young adults, Runeson (1990) reported that exposure to parental substance abuse, early parental divorce, and suicide attempts in the family were most frequent in the 47% of the sample diagnosed with substance abuse.

The association of adolescent substance abuse with other forms of psychopathology may also mediate both the acute and chronic effects noted above in suicidal behavior in this population. Substance abuse in adolescents is often evident concurrently with a number of other psychiatric disorders, including mood disorders, anxiety disorders, bulimia nervosa, schizophrenia, and conduct disorder (Bukstein et al., 1989; Greenbaum et al., 1991). Each of these disorders confers an increased risk of suicidal behavior in adolescents (Brent & Kolko, 1990) as well as an increased risk of substance abuse (Bukstein et al., 1989). However, comorbidity, especially mood disorders with other nonmood disorders including substance abuse, is one of several putative risk factors for completed suicide (Brent et al., 1988). Depression and substance abuse often appear together in a variety of additional psychiatric disorders. Borderline personality disorder, particularly when comorbid with mood disorders, often leads to suicidal behavior, including completions (Runeson, 1990) and attempts (Crumley, 1979; McManus et al., 1984). Similarly, schizophrenia has high rates of suicidal behavior and comorbid mood disorders (Runeson, 1990).

Conduct disorder is observed, more often than not, as being comorbid with substance abuse (Milan et al., 1991). A diagnosis of conduct disorder is often noted in adolescents with suicidal behavior (Shaffer, 1974; Shaffi et al., 1985). Although conduct disorder is also commonly comorbid with mood disorders (Ryan et al., 1987), many adolescents with substance abuse and conduct disorder manifest suicidal behavior without the presence of mood disorder (Apter et al., 1988). Aggression and impulsivity, both common in conduct disorders, may be important factors in the risk for suicidal behavior in substance-abusing adolescents (Apter et al., 1988).

The study of impulsivity and aggression as risk factors for suicidality may reflect underlying cognitive problem-solving styles or underlying neurobiology rather than discrete diagnosis as the true risk factors. Adolescents with high rates of the aggressive type of conduct disorder and attention-deficit hyperactivity disorder (ADHD) are more likely to engage in substance abuse than youth with ADHD alone or nonaggressive conduct disorder (Milan et al., 1991). Youths displaying explosive, aggressive outbursts appear to be at greatest risk for repetitive suicidal behavior (Pfeffer et al., 1988). Also, research linking low serotonergic states with suicidal and aggressive behavior in substance-abusing adults (Roy & Linnoila, 1986) is now being applied to adolescents. Impulsivity and aggression may be as important as depression in the etiology of suicidal behavior as evidenced by adolescents with conduct disorder having higher suicidality scores than adolescents with major depression (Apter et al., 1988).

In summary, substance-abusing adolescents appear to be at increased risk for suicidal behavior across the continuum from ideation to completion. This increased risk is mediated by both the acute and chronic effects of substance abuse. Adding to the risk of suicidal behavior are comorbid psychiatric disorders, or personality characteristics such as depression and impulsivity, which are commonly noted in suicidal or substance-abusing adolescents.

AGGRESSION TOWARD OTHERS

Aggressive behaviors are present in a large number of adolescents who abuse substances (Milan et al., 1991). The pharmacological effects of various substances of abuse can explain some of the violent behavior found in substance-abusing youth. Consumption of certain substances such as alcohol, amphetamines, and phencyclidine increase the likelihood of subsequent aggressive behavior (Tuchfeld, Clayton, & Logan, 1982). Such direct pharmacological effects resulting in aggression may be further exacerbated by the relative inexperience of adolescents with some agents, the use of multiple agents simultaneously, and the presence of preexisting psychopathology such as bipolar disorder or neurological disorders such as temporal lobe epilepsy.

Acute pharmacological effects do not explain the entire relationship between substance abuse and aggression. When viewed from a developmental perspective, chronic aggressive behavior among adolescents is associated with other concurrent antisocial behaviors in an aggressive form of conduct disorder (Loeber, 1991). Conduct disorder or delinquency almost always precedes substance use (Loeber, 1990). Such aggressive behavior patterns can be noted early in males, with aggressiveness in grade one being predictive of substance use 10 years later (Kellam et al., 1983). Youth who display a high frequency or early onset of aggressive behavior are more likely to persist in being aggressive in later years. Early aggressive behavior predicts subsequent substance abuse (Kandel et al., 1978; Robins, 1966). Likewise, the more serious the interpersonal aggressive behavior before drug use, the more serious the subsequent involvement with drugs (Johnston, O'Malley, & Eveland, 1978). While nonaggressive antisocial behavior appears to be more predictive of later substance use or abuse, aggressive antisocial behavior is more predictive of polydrug abuse, especially in males (Loeber, 1990). Adolescents committing violent crimes and behavior are noted to have characteristic drug abuse histories (i.e., heavy use of several types of "hard" illicit drugs during adolescence, Chaiken & Chaiken, 1984). Generally, the more serious the substance use, the higher the likelihood of more serious forms of delinquency (Bohman et al., 1982; Dishion & Loeber, 1985). Early fighting is predictive of later drug use, except for marijuana (Simcha-Fagen, Gersten, & Langner, 1986).

Among all substance abusers, adolescents and young adults may be more prone to violent behavior. Data from the Epidemiologic Catchment Area (ECA) study indicate that those reporting violent behavior within the preceding year tended to be young, male, from lower socioeconomic classes, and to have engaged in alcohol or drug abuse (Swanson et al., 1990). Early onset of alcoholism (less than 20 years old) appears to differentiate groups of alcoholics. The early-onset group has more parental alcoholism, violent criminal behavior, depression, and four times more suicide attempts than the older-onset group (Buydens-Branchey et al., 1989). Other studies have reported similar results in addition to the younger onset group having more bipolar and panic disorder (Roy et al., 1991).

In attempting to explain early aggressive behavior among youth who abuse substances, one finds increased rates of comorbid psychiatric disorders such as attention-deficit hyperactivity disorder (ADHD), learning disabilities, or mood disorders among this population (Bukstein et al., 1989). In ADHD, the frequent occurrence of comorbid conduct disorder is the critical variable in that aggressivity, and not ADHD alone, appears to predict later substance use (Augusta, Stewart, & Holmes, 1983; Halikas et al., 1990).

On a biochemical level, a variety of neurotransmitters including the noradrenergic, serotonin, and GABA/benzodiazepine systems have been implicated in the neurochemistry of aggressive behavior (Eichelman, 1987). Each of these neurotransmitter systems appears to have a role in the pathogenesis of several psychiatric disorders, which can also be characterized by relatively high aggressive or violent behaviors. Several studies have identified serotonin metabolism as having a possible role in both aggressive and suicidal behavior (Asberg et al., 1976; Branchey et al., 1984). Linnoila and colleagues (1989) found a 97% rate of alcohol abuse among a population of adult violent offenders and impulsive firesetters. Among the 60% of this group with alcohol fathers, lower CSF 5-HIAA and higher impulsivity scores were found. Similarly, in a group of children and adolescents, externalizing, hostility, and aggressive behavior scores were inversely correlated with low central serotonergic activity (Birmacher et al., 1990).

The association between suicidal and aggressive behaviors was originally described in the psychodynamic formulation of suicide as hostility, aggression, or anger turned against the self (Freud, 1917). Individuals manifesting aggressive and suicidal behaviors often share similar personality characteristics such as impulsivity and aggressivity (Flavin, Franklin, & Frances, 1990). Aggressive and suicidal individuals also appear to share certain biological correlates such as serotonin deficiency (Brown & Goodwin, 1986). Recent aggressive behavior is strongly associated with suicide attempts among female psychiatric patients (Pfeffer et al., 1988) and with suicidal ideation among adolescents in a community sample (Moscicki, 1989).

CLINICAL MANAGEMENT

Evaluation

Given the multiple risk factors and frequent comorbidity present in adolescents with substance abuse, the evaluation of self-destructive and aggressive behaviors in this population requires a comprehensive assessment of many areas of possible psychopathology and psychosocial functioning. In view of the frequent presence of both aggression and suicidal behavior in substance-abusing adolescents, a thorough evaluation of each type of destructive behavior should occur regardless of the presenting problem. Assessment of lethality is the cornerstone of emergency management and, indeed, every comprehensive mental health evaluation should consider the presence and/or history of lethal or dangerous behavior. In addition to providing immediate information for appropriate emergency management, a clinically relevant and valid assessment provides the target symptoms and behaviors for treatment.

In approaching the adolescent substance abuser, or suspected abuser, the clinician must realize that such youth rarely present voluntarily for evaluation and treatment. As adolescents are often "on guard" in such situations, beginning with a less confrontational approach often serves to engage the adolescent while providing useful data as well. A suggested approach is inquiring about the adolescent's current life circumstances (e.g., where they live, their school, current academic progress, home composition, and relationships, friends, and preferred activities). Very often, such seemingly innocent questions provide a natural opening for inquiry into the deviant behavior (including substance use) of peers and self, family problems, and substance use. Inquiry into the adolescent's life circumstances should serve as a survey for risk factors or correlates of adolescent substance abuse. By identifying such correlates, the clinician raises an increased suspicion of substance abuse despite the adolescent's actual report and also identifies areas for possible intervention.

For the detailed assessment of substance abuse and related behaviors, questions should include onset of use of each substance, onset of abusive patterns of substance use, and age of regular or frequent use. The clinician should obtain data regarding past and current frequency and quantities of the substances used, context of use, direct and perceived negative and positive consequences of use, expectancies of use, and the adolescent's explicit reasons for use. Context of use constitutes the time and place of use, with whom the use occurs, peer use levels, who acquires the substance(s), and the adolescent's mood and attitude both prior to and subsequent to use. This is essentially a functional analysis of the substance use.

Further inquiry should follow DSM-III-R criteria. Does the adolescent view his or her substance use as a problem? Has the adolescent attempted to stop use? Does the adolescent spend more time than planned obtaining and using alcohol and/or other drugs? Does the adolescent feel compelled to use or does he or she "lose control" of the amounts used once an episode of use has begun? Despite the lower prevalence of physical sequelae of substance use and the presence of withdrawal symptoms in adolescents, questions about these features are essential and, if answered in the affirmative, indicate a severe level of substance dependency for an adolescent.

Questions should be substance specific. If use of a particular substance is endorsed, the clinician should proceed with more detailed inquiry about the context and consequences of use of that substance. Despite the need to be appropriately skeptical about an adolescent's self-report of substance use, self-reports of adolescent use appear to be reliable (Barnea et al., 1987) and temporally consistent (Winters et al., 1991).

Because adolescent substance abuse is usually identified by psychosocial dysfunction in one or more areas or domains of function, evaluation of each area is critical in completing a comprehensive evaluation (see Table 1). Tarter (1990) describes a multilevel evaluation procedure for adolescents with suspected substance abuse. Following the identification of areas of dysfunction through the use of a comprehensive screening instrument, each area or domain is then more thoroughly assessed by use of a variety of standardized instruments that are designed to assess that specific domain.

The use of standardized instruments to measure adolescent substance abuse and associated problems is not far advanced. A number of investigators have developed questionnaires for use in epidemiological studies of adolescent substance use (Singh, Kandel, & Johnson, 1975), and in measuring quantity–frequency and context of substance use (Jessor, 1976). The Adolescent Alcohol Involvement Scale (AAIS), developed by Mayer and Filstead (1979), represents an attempt to develop an adolescent-specific screening instrument to measure adolescent problem drinking. Tarter (1990) proposed a comprehensive screening instrument, the Drug Use Screening Inventory (DUSI), to systematically screen and identify areas or domains of disturbance that are frequently noted in substance-

TABLE 1. Domains for Assessment

1. Substance use behavior
2. Psychiatric and behavioral problems
3. School and/or vocational functioning
4. Family functioning
5. Social competency and peer relations
6. Leisure and recreation

abusing youth. The Personal Experience Inventory (PEI, Henley & Winters, 1988) is among several instruments that comprehensively assess several domains. The PEI measures quantity, frequency, and history of substance use and evaluates environmental circumstances and personality characteristics of the adolescent.

The Adolescent Problem Severity Index (APSI) (Metzger, Kushner, & McLellan, 1991), the Adolescent Drug Abuse Diagnosis (ADAD) Instrument (Friedman & Utada, 1989), and the Teen Addiction Severity Index (Kaminer et al., 1991) are interview instruments in the multiple domain format. These instruments are modeled after the Addiction Severity Index (McLellan et al., 1980).

Structured and semistructured diagnostic interviews such as the Kiddie-SADS (Orvashal et al., 1981) and the Diagnostic Interview for Children and Adolescents (Herjanic & Reich, 1982) contain substance abuse sections, although little is known about the validity and reliability of these sections.

While many of these instruments measuring adolescent substance abuse and related areas are currently establishing appropriate psychometric properties, each instrument has its limitations and is best used in a specific setting and with a specific goal in mind (e.g., screening for abuse or comprehensive assessment of a given domain). In other words, clinicians should not rely on any single instrument to obtain a comprehensive evaluation in a clinical setting.

Additional evaluation concerns for treatment include testing for human immunodeficiency virus (HIV) and screening urine or blood for substance use. Although there are many adolescents with high-risk behaviors for acquired immunodeficiency syndrome (AIDS) and HIV infection, not all adolescent substance abusers are at high risk. The clinician should review potential high-risk behaviors for HIV infection during evaluation and use appropriate informed consent and confidentiality procedures if HIV testing is warranted. Toxicology screens of blood and/or urine samples for the detection of substance use requires knowledge of laboratory methods of analysis, indications for testing, and ability to understand and interpret the results (Gold & Dackis, 1986). While the use of toxicological screens can be useful as part of a comprehensive assessment and as follow-up compliance with aftercare treatment, clinicians should not overemphasize their value.

In view of the significant comorbidity of adolescent substance abuse with other behavioral and emotional disorders, assessment of psychopathology is essential. In every substance-abusing adolescent, specific questions about depression, suicidal ideation and behavior, and aggressive ideation and behavior are mandatory. During the specific assessment of both self-destructive and aggressive behavior, inquiry should be made into the presence of such behavior both when intoxicated or using substances and when not using them. The presence of either suicidal or aggressive behavior either only when "sober" or when both sober and using alcohol and/or other drugs may indicate concurrent psychopathology such as a mood disorder. The presence of suicidal and aggressive behavior only when using substances may be more an indication of the pharmacological effects of the substance used, although not less potentially lethal or dangerous. The clinician may follow a risk factor model in assessment of potential lethality. Following an overt demonstration of suicidal or aggressive behavior or revelation of ideation or plan(s), the clinician must make decisions based on an assessment of risk for lethal behavior. Table 2 lists risk factors for suicide. The presence of current and especially severe drug and alcohol abuse raises the risk for all other factors for suicide. A conservative and cautious approach is necessary due to the impairment in judgment and increased disinhibition and impulsivity produced by many substances of abuse.

**TABLE 2. Suicidal Risk Factors
for Substance-Abusing Adolescents**

1. Characteristics of suicidal behavior
   Suicidal ideation with plan and intent
   Lethal suicide attempt
       Planning and prepatory actions
       High intent
       Violent or lethal means
       Precautions against discovery
   Previous attempts
2. Psychiatric status
   Mood disorders
       Bipolar disorder
       Severe depression
   Psychosis
   Conduct disorder
   History of significant aggression and impulsivity
3. Environment
   Parental psychiatric history
       Mood disorders
       Suicidal behaviors
       Substance abuse
   Lack of parental support or supervision
   Presence of physical or sexual abuse
   Recent loss, disappointment, or severe embarrassment

Emergency Management

The clinician is often asked to make decisions based on immediate risk of repeated, short-term lethality or dangerousness. For evaluation of the suicidal adolescent, the presence of significant risk factors necessitates inpatient psychiatric hospitalization. The potential for lethality is increased with the presence of multiple risk factors, especially poorly controlled substance use. While the availability of a structured, well-monitored, and protective environment outside the hospital may influence the clinician's decision, the clinician should be very familiar with the adolescent's environment and its ability to keep the adolescent safe. The "no-suicide" contract is often a useful clinical tool and measure of therapeutic alliance in uncertain or equivocal cases (Brent & Kolko, 1990; Drye et al., 1973). The no-suicide contract is an agreement between therapist and patient that the patient will not attempt suicide and that if the patient does feel suicidal, he or she will contact either the clinician or an identified significant other. Unfortunately, in the case of an adolescent with a history of significant and impulsive suicidal ideation or behavior while using substances, the reassurance of a no-suicide contract may appear minimal when the adolescent is cognitively impaired by substances. If necessary, when the potentially lethal adolescent does not agree to a no-suicide contract or will not voluntarily agree to inpatient hospitalization, the use of involuntary commitment may be necessary. In addition to protecting the safety of the adolescent with potentially lethal behaviors, inpatient hospitalization serves to limit access to drugs, prevent running away, and provide a more intensive treatment experience.

The emergency assessment and management of the aggressive substance-abusing adolescent is similar to the management of suicidal youth. In fact, the additional presence of impulsivity and aggression in a potentially suicidal adolescent may increase the risk of subsequent suicide significantly. If suicidal behavior is not a concern, the potential for immediate dangerousness should nevertheless be assessed. The risk factors for future violence (Table 3) are very similar to those for suicide. If the current environment is unstructured or in some manner provoking to the adolescent, serious consideration should be given for temporary removal—to either an inpatient psychiatric setting, shelter, or juvenile detention facility. If crisis management is successful in modifying the previously noxious environment, return may be considered. If placement in a nonpsychiatric facility is considered, assessment of suicide potential again needs to be considered. Although others may be protected from the adolescent, the adolescent may be a danger to himself or herself. The clinician should always inquire about the availability of firearms and request that the weapons be removed prior to the adolescent's return home.

Treatment

In approaching the treatment of the adolescent substance abuser with suicidal or aggressive behavior, two basic but ultimately interdependent management concerns are apparent: (1) treatment of the substance use behaviors and (2) treatment of the suicidal or aggressive behavior and coexisting disorders. Although traditional models of substance abuse treatment have emphasized an almost exclusive focus on the substance abuse and associated behaviors, a more realistic and possibly efficacious approach is concurrent treatment directed toward each salient problem—substance abuse and coexisting behavioral and emotional problems (Bukstein et al., 1989).

Although treatment programs for adolescent substance abusers include a variety of different modalities (such as individual, group, and family oriented treatments), in a variety of different settings (such as outpatient, inpatient, residential, day treatment, and aftercare), many if not most treatment programs are based on the Minnesota Model (Wheeler & Malmquist, 1987). The Minnesota Model, also forming the basis of most adult substance abuse treatment, uses group therapy in an inpatient setting where patients work the 12-steps of Alcoholics Anonymous (AA) (Alcoholics Anonymous, 1976). Other characteristics of Minnesota Model treatment include use of recovered addicts as counselors, provision of aftercare, and recommendation of intensive ongoing attendance at self-support group (AA, Narcotics Anonymous, NA) meetings. Although initial inpatient evaluation and treatment is common, a similar step-work and self-support group focus can be delivered in day treatment and outpatient settings. Despite the popularity of the Minnesota Model, few studies describe the efficacy of inpatient treatment with adolescent substance abusers. Alford, Koehler, and Leonard (1991) compared treatment completers and noncompleters in an inpatient adolescent treatment program utilizing AA/NA principles. Although both

TABLE 3.   Risk Factors
for Aggressive Behavior

1. Past violence
2. Drug and alcohol abuse
3. Family history of aggressive behavior
4. Aggressive peers
5. Availability of weapons

groups demonstrated less substance use after treatment than before, at 6 months post-discharge, treatment completers had much higher rates of abstinence. However, abstinence rates for males in both groups declined sharply at 1- and 2-year follow-ups, with no difference between groups at the latter follow-up. Despite return to substance use at 2-year follow-up, 17% of treatment completers appeared to be successful in social-civil behavioral functioning.

Several salient differences exist between treatment for adolescent substance abusers and that for adults. Adolescents appear to have a higher incidence of family disorganization, have a history of earlier psychological treatment, respond to external pressures to stay in treatment, and require a larger role for educational needs and family support (DeLeon & Deitch, 1984).

Several treatment studies describe the effects of a treatment modality without the use of a control or comparison group. Day treatment, community-based education, inpatient (Williams & Baron, 1982), and community-based multimodality interventions (Barrett, Simpson, & Lehman, 1988; Feldman, 1983) all have shown reductions in substance use and associated problem behaviors. A variety of behavioral modalities including contingency contracting (Frederickson et al., 1976) and covert sensitization (Duehn, 1978) have also produced positive changes.

Two large studies of adolescents in substance abuse treatment show no significant differences between the studied treatments (Hubbard et al., 1985; Sells & Simpson, 1979). In these studies, despite increases in productive behavior and success in reducing drug use other than marijuana and alcohol, adolescents' use of alcohol and marijuana were at pretreatment levels at follow-up (Beschner & Friedman, 1985). Grenier (1985) compared an AA-based residential treatment program and a waiting-list control. The treatment group demonstrated greater abstinence than the control group. Hawkins and associates (Hawkins, Catalano, & Well, 1986) compared social skills training to a standard institutional program for juvenile offenders. The social skills group demonstrated higher scores in drug avoidance, problem solving, and self-control.

Family treatments, including both conjoint and individual family therapy, are effective in improving family functioning and decreasing drug use (Szapocznik et al., 1983). Additional family treatment modalities include psychoeducation, family support groups, parent management training, and multiple family groups (Stanton, 1979). Although comparison of functional family therapy with parent groups shows no significant differences in outcome (i.e., substance use), the family therapy method produced increased family communication and decreased negative role-taking behavior by the client within the family (Friedman, 1990).

Catalano, Hawkins, Wells, and Miller (1990–91) summarized the available studies and data by stating that some treatment is better than no treatment, but no superiority of specific treatments or modalities has been established. In view of the absence of a treatment of choice for adolescent substance abusers, the clinician should use one or more modalities that are matched with identified problems or deficits such as social skills or family conflict. Although the use of strategies directed specifically at substance use and achievement of abstinence should be a primary goal, additional interventions should be carried out addressing problems in multiple domains of the adolescent's life. Type of treatment setting may also be important. In their study of 30 adolescent treatment programs, Friedman and Glickman (1986) found several program characteristics that predict outcome. These characteristics include (1) treatment of large numbers of adolescents, (2) having special schools for dropouts and special services for vocational counseling, (3) having relatively large budgets and counselors with more than 2 years experience, and (4) having a variety of treatment methods including crisis intervention and group confrontation. Friedman and Glickman (1986) found that time in treatment was significantly related to treatment success in outpatient treatment programs. In a group of 94 adolescent substance abusers, successful prognosis was associated with female gender, fewer legal difficulties, less pathological MMPI scores, and higher verbal I.Q. (Knapp et al., 1991). Therefore, research indicates that the best treatment centers are those that offer comprehensive services and longer-term follow-up.

The frequent presence of comorbid psychiatric disorders and suicidal and aggressive behavior in adolescent substance abusers necessitates concurrent attention to these problems. Patient characteristics have significant effects on outcome. For example, McLellan et al. (1983) found that adult substance abusers with severe psychiatric problems show less improvement than those with less severe problems. Feigelman (1987) reported that moderately or seriously depressed adolescents in a day care program were less likely to complete treatment. However, Friedman and Glickman (1987) found that adolescents with more psychiatric symptoms and interpersonal problems showed a tendency for more treatment improvement. In view of possible differential treatment effects for adolescents with comorbid psychopathology, a number of authors have suggested matching types of patients with types/or levels of intervention or treatment (Hester & Miller, 1988; McLellan et al., 1983; Rounsaville, Kosten, et al., 1986). For adolescents with suicidal behavior, specialized treatment on an inpatient psychiatric unit may be indicated. Significant aggressive behavior also may require the structure and intensity of an inpatient program. Comorbid mood disorders may suggest the need for medication treatments (e.g., antidepressants, lithium) and/or psychosocial treatments such as cognitive therapy, despite the lack of specific research establishing the efficacy of these treatments in comorbid adolescent populations. The recent development of "dual-diagnosis' programs provides a more comprehensive treatment approach with ongoing evaluation and treatment of psychiatric problems as well as substance abuse treatments based on the Minnesota Model.

Treatment of comorbid psychiatric disorders may directly or indirectly affect substance abuse behaviors, and, likewise, substance abuse treatment may have beneficial effects on psychopathology. In a large study of adolescent substance abuse treatment efficacy, Hubbard, Cavanaugh, Craddock, and Rachal (1985) found that outpatient and residential treatment clients reported reduced suicide thoughts or attempts.

A number of treatments, such as social skills training and cognitive-behavioral treatments, have demonstrated efficacy in both adolescent substance abusers (Hawkins et al., 1986) and depressed adolescents (Lewinsohn et al., 1990). Use of social skills, cognitive therapy, and problem-solving skills training should be considered in adolescents with suicidal behavior and/or problems with aggression (Brent & Kolko, 1990).

Pharmacological treatment is often a useful adjunct to psychosocial treatments for suicidal and aggressive behavior in substance-abusing youth. Agents must target specific symptoms, behaviors, or disorders rather than aim at the general heterogenous substance-abusing or suicidal adolescents. Bipolar disorder has a specific suggested treatment in the form of lithium and/or carbamazepine. However, research has not established the efficacy of antidepressant medication in adolescents with unipolar depression (Campbell & Spencer, 1988). For aggressive behavior, a number of agents including neuroleptics, lithium, carbamazepine, and propranolol are potentially useful (Stewart et al., 1990). Psychostimulants, in the case of comorbid ADHD, and benzodiazepines should be avoided given their abuse potential.

Brent and Kolko (1990) suggest that both pharmacological and psychosocial approaches are likely to be effective in reducing the risk of suicidal behavior in depressed, impulsive, and/or suicidal youth. The same guidelines apply to substance-abusing youth with problems of suicidal or aggressive behavior. Medical and psychosocial approaches must target specific behaviors; symptoms, or disorders that are identified by a comprehensive evaluation of substance abuse related behaviors, cognitive, social, and problem-solving skills; anger control and affect regulation; and family functioning. Multiple interventions should be aimed at each risk domain for substance abuse, and suicidal and aggressive behaviors.

LONGITUDINAL PERSPECTIVES

Substance abuse and suicidal and aggressive behavior in adolescents are not random phenomena. The distribution of risk factors among the population points to specific populations of children and adolescents being "at risk" for the subsequent development of substance abuse, destructive behaviors, or both. Early onset of deviant behaviors (e.g., stealing, truancy, vandalism, aggression) and the variety and number of such behaviors predict substance abuse in the form of problem drinking (Donovan, Jessor, & Jessor, 1983; Loeber, 1990). Early onset of drinking and drug use may further identify deviant adolescents with high levels of aggressive behavior, antisocial behavior, as well as mood instability and increased suicidality in adulthood (Buydens-Branchey et al., 1989; Roy et al., 1991). On the other hand, a later onset of substance use or abuse in adolescence, particularly with minimal or no concurrent deviant behaviors, decreases the risk of later illicit drug use (Kandel & Logan, 1984). This late-onset group appears to have a significantly decreased risk of developing problems with aggressive or suicidal behavior in adulthood (Roy et al., 1991).

The relationship between depression, a risk factor for suicidal behavior, and subsequent alcohol and/or drug problem underscores the at-risk relationship. Data from the ECA show an increased risk for the subsequent development of alcohol and/or drug abuse in adolescents with a history of depression or anxiety disorder (Christie et al., 1988). Deykin and associates (1987) reported a similar relationship between the early onset of depression and later substance abuse. Identification of multiple comorbid disorders may be easier in adolescence than in adulthood when more persistent and severe substance use and resulting cognitive deterioration may further confuse clinical presentation.

Focusing on at-risk populations, especially in childhood, and relevant risk variables for intervention, offers the best opportunity for decreasing rates of adolescent substance abuse and concurrent problems with suicidal and aggressive behavior. The following are two basic at-risk areas with possible targets for prevention intervention.

1. *Family*. Given the vulnerability of children with family histories of substance abuse and suicidal behavior, these children should be identified so as to provide appropriate follow-up and early treatment for problems with conduct, mood, or impulsivity. Intervention with family discord and violence may also be indicated.
2. *Child-Centered*. Given noted deficiencies in social and problem-solving skills in substance-abusing adolescents (Van Hasselt et al., 1978), aggressive adolescents (Patterson, 1974), and suicidal adolescents (Hawton et al., 1982), such behavioral skills training appears appropriate with the potential for multiple preventative

benefits in several potential problem areas. The presence of hostility, irritability and other dysphoric affects prior to substance use, and suicidal or aggressive behavior, are common features. Possible interventions include anger control, relaxation training, cognitive therapy, and medication treatment.

CASE ILLUSTRATION

Jim is a 17-year-old white male admitted to a dual-diagnosis program based in a large academically oriented psychiatric hospital. On the day prior to admission, after having drunk one-half gallon of wine, Jim jumped into a nearby river in a suicide attempt. Only a friend's valiant effort saved Jim, who could not swim. At the time of admission, Jim reported having always felt depressed with additional depressive symptoms of anhedonia, apathy, social withdrawal, decreased ability to sleep, decreased appetite, hopelessness, and pervasive negative thoughts about himself, his future, and the world. Over the preceding 2 years, Jim had often made suicidal threats and admitted to frequent suicidal ideation, which increased during periods of intoxication. Jim also acknowledged almost daily use of alcohol, marijuana, and less extensive but frequent use of other illicit drugs including hallucinogens, cocaine, solvents, and oral opiates. He denied intravenous drug use.

Jim had a long history of problem behaviors. At age 9, his grades began to deteriorate. Oppositional, defiant behaviors and poor peer relations became evident at age 12, with the rapid, subsequent onset of a variety of deviant behaviors including nonaggressive and aggressive stealing, truancy, vandalism, gang activity, and frequent fighting resulting in several injuries to himself and others. By the sixth grade, Jim had already begun regular alcohol and marijuana use. Previous legal history included violation of curfew, trespassing, and possession of drugs. Medical history indicated the presence of a familial neuromuscular disorder. At the time of admission, Jim lived with a maternal aunt. Jim's mother, stepfather, and numerous maternal family members were described as alcoholic. Jim had no knowledge of or previous contact with his biological father.

Following admission, Jim initially appeared resistant to treatment and angry at being saved from the suicide attempt. He endorsed frequent craving and preoccupation with drug use. Control of his anger was tenuous with frequent threats toward staff and peers. He would "hold in" his anger and suddenly explode, using verbal threats of physical aggression and punching walls. A semistructured diagnostic interview indicated DSM-III-R diagnoses of (1) conduct disorder, solitary, aggressive type; (2) major depressive disorder, recurrent; (3) alcohol dependence; and (4) marijuana dependence. His score on the Beck Depression Inventory indicated depressive symptoms in the severe range.

In the inpatient dual diagnosis treatment program, Jim received multiple interventions involving (1) achieving and maintaining abstinence through a 12-step program, psychoeducation about substance abuse, and self-support group meetings; (2) anger control and improved interpersonal communication through social skills, problem solving, relaxation, and anger-control skills training; and (3) control of depressive symptoms through cognitive interventions.

Three weeks after admission, Jim continued to have significant depressive symptoms. A program psychiatrist prescribed the tricyclic antidepressant nortriptyline, which was increased to therapeutic levels. Jim reported improved mood and similar improvement in associated depressive symptoms. Staff noted overall improvement in interpersonal skills, anger control, and self-esteem, despite his occasional expressions of doubt about his future.

Jim was discharged after approximately 6 weeks. Follow-up included treatment at a local outpatient drug treatment center and medication checks at the local mental health center.

Approximately 6 months later, Jim was briefly readmitted with complaints of depression and suicidal ideation. He reported good progress for 2 to 3 months following discharge, although he had discontinued the antidepressant after 8 weeks. Two months prior to readmission, he had resumed occasional alcohol and marijuana use. He was subsequently noncompliant with outpatient treatment due to fear of being detected through the treatment center's random urine drug testing. Three days after readmission, Jim signed out of the inpatient program against medical advice. His family was not involved in his treatment.

Jim's case illustrates a common presentation of an adolescent substance abuser into inpatient treatment. The relatively early onset of school failure, deviant behaviors, and substance use led to severe dysfunction in multiple areas of Jim's life by midadolescence. Poor anger control and aggressive behaviors punctuated poor interpersonal relations. The addition of a severe, persistent mood disorder increased Jim's risk for suicidal behavior. Ultimately, intoxication produced the circumstances for a very serious and near fatal suicide attempt.

Prototypical inpatient treatment is also described. Multiple modalities directed at specific target symptoms and behaviors included substance abuse-oriented treatment to achieve abstinence, cognitive therapy and medication to relieve depression, and behavioral skills oriented treatment to improve anger control and interpersonal relations.

Unfortunately, the intermediate-term poor outcome described for Jim is also very common. The lack of comprehensive, intensive outpatient services directed at both substance abuse and comorbid psychopathology, lack of family involvement and structure, and lack of social supports ultimately produced deterioration in Jim's original treatment gains.

SUMMARY

The evaluation and management of adolescent substance abusers represents a difficult challenge. With the addition of destructive behaviors such as suicide and aggression, the challenge becomes one of always utilizing a comprehensive approach in considering risk factors for destructive behaviors such as suicide and aggression in every adolescent who acknowledges substance use and in considering multiple deficits as areas for possible treatment intervention.

Early identification of childhood aggressive behaviors, family histories of suicide, mood disorders and comorbid mood disorders in a child or adolescent, or early onset of substance use provide points for prevention or early intervention in youth. We still have much to learn about the biology of destructive behaviors, the effects of social stressors and deprivation on aggression and suicidality in adolescents, and the efficacy of medication and psychosocial treatments in this population.

REFERENCES

Alcohol Drug Abuse and Mental Health Administration (ADAMHA) (1991). *National household survey on drug abuse: Population estimates 1990*. Washington, DC: U.S. Government Printing Office.
Alcoholics Anonymous (1976). New York: Alcoholics Anonymous, World Services Inc.

Alford, G. S., Koehler, R. A., & Leonard, J. (1991). Alcoholics Anonymous-Narcotics Anonymous model inpatient treatment of chemically dependent adolescents: A 2-year outcome study. *Journal of Studies on Alcohol, 52,* 118–126.

American Psychiatric Association (1980). *Diagnostic and statistical manual of mental disorders* 3rd Edition. Washington, DC: Author.

American Psychiatric Association (1987). *Diagnostic and statistical manual of mental disorders,* 3rd Edition, Revised. Washington, DC: Author.

American Psychiatric Association (1993). *DSM-IV draft criteria.* Washington, DC: Author.

Apter, A., Bleich, A., Plutchik, R., Mendelsohn, S., & Tyano, S. (1988). Suicidal behavior, depression, and conduct disorder in hospitalized adolescents. *Journal of the American Academy of Child and Adolescent Psychiatry, 27,* 696–699.

Asberg, M., Traskman, L., & Thoren, P. (1976). 5-HIAA in the cerebrospinal fluid: A biochemical suicide predictor? *Archives of General Psychiatry, 33,* 1193–1197.

Augusta, G. J., Stewart, M. A., & Holmes, C. S. (1983). A four-year follow-up of hyperactive boys with and without conduct disorder. *British Journal of Psychiatry, 143,* 192–198.

Ballenger, J. C., Goodwin, F. K., Major, L. F., & Brown, G. C. (1979). Alcohol and central serotonin metabolism in man. *Archives of General Psychiatry, 36,* 224–227.

Barnea, Z., Rahav, G., & Teichman, M. (1987). The reliability and consistency of self-reports on substance use in a longitudinal study. *British Journal of Addiction, 82,* 891–898.

Barrett, M. E., Simpson, D. D., & Lehman, W. E. K. (1988). Behavioral changes of adolescents in drug abuse intervention programs. *Journal of Clinical Psychology, 44,* 461–473.

Beck, A. T., Weissman, A., & Kovacs, M. (1976). Alcoholism, hopelessness and suicidal behavior. *Journal of Studies on Alcohol, 37,* 66–77.

Benson, G., & Holmberg, M. D. (1984). Drug related criminality among young people. *Acta Psychiatrica Scandanavica, 70,* 481–502.

Beschner, G. M., & Friedman, A. S. (1985). Treatment of adolescent drug abusers. *International Journal of the Addictions, 20,* 271–293.

Birmacher, B., Stanley, M., Greenhill, L., Twomey, J., Gavrilescu, A., & Rabinovich, H. (1990). Platelet imipramine binding in children and adolescents with impulsive behavior. *Journal of the American Academy of Child and Adolescent Psychiatry, 29,* 914–918.

Blane, H. (1979). Middle-aged alcoholics and young drinkers. In H. Blane & M. Chafetz (Eds.), *Youth, alcohol and social policy* (pp. 5–38). New York: Plenum.

Bohman, M., Cloninge, R., Sigvardisson, S., & von Korring, A. L. (1982). Predisposition to petty criminality in Swedish adoptees. *Archives of General Psychiatry, 39,* 1233–1241.

Branchey, L., Branchey, M., Shaw, S., & Lieber, C. S. (1984). Depression, suicide and aggression in alcoholics and their relationship to plasma amino acids. *Psychiatric Research, 12,* 219–226.

Brent, D. A., & Kolko, D. J. (1990). The assessment and treatment of children and adolescents at risk for suicide. In S. J. Blumenthal & D. J. Kupfer (Eds.), *Suicide over the life cycle* (pp. 253–302). Washington DC: American Psychiatric Press.

Brent, D. A., Kalas, R., Edelbrock, C., Costello, A. J., Dulcan, M. K., & Conover, N. (1986). Psychopathology and its relationship to suicidal ideation in childhood and adolescence. *Journal of the American Academy of Child Psychiatry, 25,* 666–673.

Brent, D. A., Perper, J. A., Allman, C. (1987). Alcohol, firearms and suicide among youth: Temporal trends in Allegheny County, Pennsylvania, 1960 to 1983. *Journal of the American Medical Association, 257,* 3369–3372.

Brent, D. A., Perper, J. A., Goldstein, C. E., Kolko, D. J., Allan, M. J., Allman, C. J., & Zelenak, J. P. (1988). Risk factors for adolescent suicide: A comparison of adolescent suicide victims with suicidal inpatients. *Archives of General Psychiatry, 45,* 581–588.

Brown, G. L., & Goodwin, F. K. (1986). Human aggression and suicide. *Suicide and Life-Threatening Behavior, 16,* 1441–161.

Brown, S. A. (1985). Reinforcement expectancies and alcoholism outcome after a one year follow-up. *Journal of Studies on Alcohol, 46,* 305–308.

Bukstein, O. G., Brent, D. A., & Kaminer, Y. (1989). Comorbidity of substance abuse and other psychiatric disorders in adolescents. *American Journal of Psychiatry, 146,* 1131–1141.

Buydens-Branchey, L., Branchey, M., Noumair, D., & Lieber, C. S. (1989). Age of alcoholism onset, II relationship to susceptibility to serotonin precursor availability. *Archives of General Psychiatry, 46,* 231–236.

Campbell, M., & Spencer, E. K. (1988). Psychopharmacology in child and adolescent psychiatry: A review of the past five years. *Journal of the American Academy of Child and Adolescent Psychiatry, 27,* 269–279.

Catalano, R. F., Hawkins, J. D., Wells, E. A., & Miller, J. (1990–91). Evaluation of the effectiveness of adolescent drug treatment, assessment of risks for relapse, and promising approaches for relapse prevention. *International Journal of the Addictions*, *25*, 1085–1140.

Centers for Disease Control. (1985). *Suicide surveillance 1970–1980*. Atlanta, GA: U.S. Department of Health and Human Services, Public Health Service, Violent Epidemiology Branch, Center for Health Promotion and Education.

Chaiken, M. R., & Chaiken, J. M. (1984). Offender types and public policy. *Crime and Delinquency*, *30*, 195–226.

Christiansen, B. A., Goldman, M. S., & Brown, S. A. (1985). The differential development of adolescent alcohol expectancies may predict adult alcoholism. *Journal of Addictive Behaviors*, *10*, 299–306.

Christiansen, B. A., Goldman, M. S., & Inn, A. (1982). Development of alcohol-related expectancies in adolescents: Separating pharmacological from social learning influences. *Journal of Consulting and Clinical Psychology*, *50*, 336–344.

Christie, K. A., Burke, J. D., Regier, D. A., Rae, D. S., Boyd, J. H., & Locke, B. Z. (1988). Epidemiologic evidence for early onset of mental disorders and higher risk of drug abuse in young adults. *American Journal of Psychiatry*, *145*, 971–975.

Crumley, F. E. (1979). Adolescent suicide attempts. *Journal of the American Medical Association*, *241*, 2404–2407.

Crumley, F. E. (1990). Substance abuse and adolescent suicidal behavior. *Journal of the American Medical Association*, *263*, 3051–3056.

DeLeon, G., & Deitch, D. (1984). Treatment of the adolescent abusers in a therapeutic community. In A. S. Friedman & G. M. Beschner (Eds.), *Treatment services for adolescent drug abusers*. Rockville, MD: National Institute on Drug Abuse.

Deykin, E. Y., Levy, J. C., & Wells, V. (1987). Adolescent depression, alcohol and drug abuse. *American Journal of Public Health*, *77*, 178–182.

Dishion, T. J., & Loeber, R. (1985). Adolescent marijuana and alcohol use: The role of parents and peers revisited. *American Journal of Drug and Alcohol Abuse*, *11*, 11–25.

Donovan, J. E., & Jessor, R. (1978). Adolescent problem drinking—psychosocial correlates in a national sample study. *Journal of Studies on Alcohol*, *39*, 1506–1524.

Donovan, J. E., Jessor, R., & Jessor, L. (1983). Problem drinking in adolescence and young adulthood: A follow-up study. *Journal of Studies on Alcohol*, *44*, 109–137.

Drye, R. C., Goulding, R. L., & Goulding, M. E. (1973). No-suicide decisions: Patient monitoring of suicidal risk. *American Journal of Psychiatry*, *130*, 171–174.

Duehn, W. D. (1978). Covert sensitization in group treatment of adolescent drug abusers. *International Journal of Addictions*, *13*, 485–491.

Eichelman, B. (1987). Neurochemical and psychopharmacologic aspects of aggressive behavior. In H. Y. Meltzer (Ed.), *Psychopharmacology: The third generation of progress* (pp. 697–704). New York: Raven Press.

Feigelman, W. (1987). Daycare treatment for multiple drug abusing adolescents: Social factors linked with completing treatment. *Journal of Psychoactive Drugs*, *19*, 335–344.

Feldman, H. W. (1983). *A summary of the youth environment study final reports*. Sacramento, CA: State of California, Department of Alcohol and Drug Programs.

Flavin, D. K., Franklin, J. E., & Francis, R. J. (1990). Substance abuse and suicidal behavior. In S. J. Blumenthal & D. J. Kupfer (Eds.), *Suicide over the life cycle* (pp. 177–204). Washington, DC: APA Press.

Fredericksen, L. W., Jenkins, J. O., & Carr, C. R. (1976). Indirect modification of adolescent drug abuse using contingency contracting. *Journal of Behavior Therapy and Experimental Psychiatry*, *7*, 377–378.

Freud, S. (1917). Mourning and melancholia. In S. L. London (Ed.), *The standard edition of the complete psychological works of Sigmund Freud, Vol. 14* (pp. 237–260). London: Hogarth Press.

Friedman, A. S. (1990). Family therapy versus parent groups: Effects on adolescent drug abusers. In A. S. Friedman & S. Granick (Eds.), *Family therapy for adolescent drug abuse* (pp. 201–215). Lexington, MA: Lexington Books.

Friedman, A. S., & Glickman, N. W. (1986). Program characteristics for successful treatment of adolescent drug abuse. *Journal of Nervous and Mental Diseases*, *174*, 669–679.

Friedman, A. S., & Glickman, N. W. (1987). Effects of psychiatric symptomatology on treatment outcome for adolescent male drug abusers. *Journal of Nervous and Mental Diseases*, *175*, 425–430.

Friedman, A. S., & Utada, A. (1989). A method for diagnosing and planning treatment of adolescent drug abusers. *Journal of Drug Education*, *19*, 285–319.

Friedman, I. M. (1985). Alcohol and unnatural deaths in San Francisco youths. *Pediatrics*, *76*, 191–193.

Galanter, M., & Castaneda, R. (1985). Self-destructive behavior in the substance abuser. *Psychiatric Clinics of North America, 8*, 251–261.

Garfinkel, B., Froese, A., & Hood, J. (1982). Suicide attempts in children and adolescents. *American Journal of Psychiatry, 139*, 1257–1261.

Gittleman, R., Mannuzza, S., Shenker, R., & Bonagura, N. (1985). Hyperactive boys almost grownup: I. Psychiatric status. *Archives of General Psychiatry, 42*, 937–947.

Gold, M. S., & Dackis, G. A. (1986). The role of the laboratory in the evaluation of suspected drug abuse. *Journal of Clinical Psychiatry, 47*, 17–23.

Greenbaum, P. E., Prange, M. E., Friedman, R. M., & Silver, S. E. (1991). Substance abuse prevalence and comorbidity with other psychiatric disorders among adolescents with severe emotional disturbances. *Journal of the American Academy of Child and Adolescent Psychiatry, 30*, 575–583.

Grenier, C. (1985). Treatment effectiveness in an adolescent chemical dependency treatment program: A quasi-experimental design. *International Journal of the Addictions, 20*, 381–391.

Halikas, J. A., Melle, J., Morese, C., & Lyttle, M. D. (1990). Predicting substance abuse in juvenile offenders: Attention deficit disorder versus aggressivity. *Child Psychiatry and Human Development, 21*, 49–55.

Hawkins, J. O., Catalano, R. F., & Well, E. A. (1986). Measuring effects of a skill training intervention for drug abusers. *Journal of Consulting and Clinical Psychology, 54*, 661–664.

Hawton, K., O'Grady, J., Osborn, M., & Cole, D. (1982). Adolescents who take overdoses: Their characteristics, problems and contacts with helping agencies. *British Journal of Psychiatry, 140*, 118–223.

Henly, G. A., & Winters, K. C. (1988). Development of problem severity scales for the assessment of adolescent alcohol and drug abuse. *International Journal of the Addictions, 23*, 65–85.

Herjanic, B., & Reich, W. (1982). Development of a structured interview for children: Agreement between child and parent on individual symptoms. *Journal of Abnormal Child Psychology, 10*, 307–324.

Hester, R. K., & Miller, W. R. (1988). Empirical guidelines for optimal client–treatment matching. In E. R. Rahdert & J. Grabowski (Eds.), *Adolescent drug abuse: Analyses of treatment research* (pp. 27–39). National Institute of Drug Abuse Research Monograph 77. Rockville, MD.

Hoberman, H. M., & Garfinkel, B. D. (1988). Completed suicide in children and adolescents. *Journal of the American Academy of Child and Adolescent Psychiatry, 27*, 689–695.

Hubbard, R. L., Cavanaugh, E. R., Craddock, S. G., & Rachal, J. V. (1985). Characteristic behaviors and outcomes for youth in the tops. *Treatment services for alcohol and substance abusers*. Rockville, MD: National Institute on Drug Abuse.

Jessor, R. (1976). Predicting time and onset of marijuana use: A developmental study of high school youth. *Journal of Consulting and Clinical Psychology, 44*, 125–134.

Jessor, R. (1984). Adolescent problem drinking: Psychosocial aspects and developmental outcomes. In L. H. Towle (Ed.), *Proceedings: NIAAA-WHO Collaborating Center Designation Meeting and Alcohol Research Seminar*. Washington, DC: Public Health Service.

Jessor, R., & Jessor, S. L. (1978). Theory testing on longitudinal research. In D. B. Kandel (Ed.), *Longitudinal research on drug use: Empirical findings and methodological issues* (pp. 41–71). Washington, DC: Hemisphere (Halstead-Wiley).

Johnston, L. D. (1991). 1990 Monitoring the Future Survey. Ann Arbor, MI: University of Michigan Institute for Social Research.

Johnston, L. D., O'Malley, P., & Eveland, L. (1978). Drugs and delinquency: A search for causal connections. In D. B. Kandel (Ed.), *Longitudinal research on drug use: Empirical findings and methodological issues* (pp. 137–156). Washington, DC: Hemisphere-Wiley.

Kaminer, Y., Bukstein, O., & Tarter, R. E. (1991). The Teen Addiction Severity Index: Rationale and reliability. *International Journal of the Addictions, 26*, 219–226.

Kandel, D. B. (1974). Inter- and intragenerational influences in adolescent marijuana use. *Journal of Social Issues, 30*, 107–135.

Kandel, D. B. (1982). Epidemiological and psychosocial perspectives on adolescent drug use. *Journal of the American Academy of Child Psychiatry, 21*, 328–347.

Kandel, D. B., & Logan, J. A. (1984). Pattern of drug use from adolescence to young adulthood: I. Periods of risk for initiation, continued use and discontinuation. *American Journal of Public Health, 74*, 660–666.

Kandel, D. B., Kessler, R. C., & Margulies, R. Z. (1978). Antecedents of adolescent initiation into stages of drug use: A developmental analysis. In D. B. Kandel (Ed.), *Longitudinal research on drug use: Empirical findings and methodological issues* (pp. 73–99). Washington, DC: Hemisphere-Wiley.

Kellam, S. G., Brown, C. H., Rubin, B. R., & Emsminger, M. E. (1983). Paths leading to teenage psychiatric symptoms and substance use: Development epidemiological studies in Woodlawn. In S. B. Guze, F. J. Earls, & J. E. Barrett (Eds.), *Childhood psychopathology and development*. New York: Norton.

Knapp, J. E., Templer, D. I., Cannon, W. G., & Dobson, S. (1991). Variables associated with success in an adolescent drug treatment program. *Adolescence, 26*, 305–317.

Kosky, R., Siburn, S., & Zubrik, S. R. (1990). Are children and adolescents who have suicidal thoughts different from those who attempted suicide. *Journal of Nervous and Mental Disease, 178*, 38–43.

Kotila, L., & Lonnggvist, J. (1988). Adolescent suicide attempts: Sex differences predicting suicide. *Acta Psychiatrica Scandanavica, 77*, 264–270.

Levy, J. C., & Deykin, E. Y. (1989). Suicidality, depression and substance abuse in adolescence. *American Journal of Psychiatry, 146*, 1462–1467.

Lewinsohn, P. M., Clarke, G. N., Hops, H., & Andrews, J. (1990). Cognitive-behavioral treatment for depressed adolescents. *Behavior Therapy, 21*, 385–401.

Linnoila, M., DeJong, J., & Virkkunen, M. (1989). Family history of alcoholism in violent offenders and impulsive fire setters. *Archives of General Psychiatry, 46*, 613–616.

Loeber, R. (1990). Development and risk factors of juvenile antisocial behavior and delinquency. *Clinical Psychology Review, 10*, 1–41.

Loeber, R. (1991). Antisocial behavior: More enduring than changeable? *Journal of the American Academy of Child and Adolescent Psychiatry, 30*, 393–397.

Mayer, J. E., & Filstead, W. J. (1979). Empirical procedure for defining adolescent alcohol abuse. *Journal of Studies on Alcohol, 40*, 291–300.

Mayfield, D. G. (1968). Psychopharmacology of alcohol: Affective change with intoxication, drinking behavior and affective state. *Journal of Nervous and Mental Diseases, 146*, 314–321.

McLellan, A. T., Luborsky, L., Woody, G., & O'Brien, C. (1980). An improved diagnostic evaluation instrument for substance abuse patients: The addiction severity scale index. *Journal of Nervous and Mental Diseases, 168*, 26–33.

McLellan, A. T., Luborsky, L., Woody, G., O'Brien, C. P., & Druley, K. A. (1983). Predicting response to alcohol and drug abuse treatments: Role of psychiatric severity. *Archives of General Psychiatry, 40*, 620–625.

McManus, M., Lerner, H., Robbins, D., & Barbour, C. (1984). Assessment of borderline symptomatology in hospitalized adolescents. *Journal of the American Academy of Child Psychiatry, 23*, 685–694.

Menninger, K. (1938). *Man against himself*. New York: Harcourt, Brace.

Metzger, D. S., Kushner, H., & McLellan, A. T. (1991). *Adolescent Problem Severity Index (APSI)*. Philadelphia, PA: Biomedical Computer Research Institute.

Milan, R., Halikas, J. A., Meller, J. E., & Morse, C. (1991). Psychopathology among substance abusing juvenile offenders. *Journal of the American Academy of Child and Adolescent Psychiatry, 30*, 569–574.

Moscicki, E. (1989). Epidemiologic surveys as tools for studying suicidal behavior: A review. *Suicide and Life-Threatening Behaviors, 112*, 814–820.

Murphy, G. E., Armstrong, J. W., Hermele, S. L., Fischer, U. R., & Clendenin, W. W. (1979). Suicide and alcoholism: Interpersonal loss confirmed as predictor. *Archives of General Psychiatry, 36*, 65–69.

Orvaschal, H. M., Weissman, N., Padian, N., & Lowe, T. L. (1981). Assessing psychopathology in children in psychiatrically disturbed parents: A pilot study. *Journal of the American Academy of Child Psychiatry, 20*, 112–122.

Patterson, G. (1974). Intervention for boys with conduct problems: Multiple settings, treatment and criteria. *Journal of Consulting and Clinical Psychology, 42*, 471–481.

Pfeffer, C.R., Plutchik, R., & Mizruchi, M. S. (1983). Suicidal and assaultive behavior in children, classification, measurement and interrelation. *American Journal of Psychiatry, 140*, 154–157.

Pfeffer, C. R., Plutchik, R., Mizruchi, M. S., & Lipkens, R. (1986). Suicidal behavior in child psychiatric inpatients and outpatients and in nonpatients. *American Journal of Psychiatry, 143*, 733–738.

Pfeffer, C. R., Newcorn, J., Kaplan, G., Mizruchi, M. S., & Plutchik, R. (1988). Suicidal behavior in adolescent psychiatric inpatients. *Journal of the American Academy of Child and Adolescent Psychiatry, 27*, 357–361.

Poteet, D. J. (1987). Adolescent suicide: A review of 87 cases of completed suicide in Shelby County, Tennessee. *American Journal Forensic Medicine and Pathology, 8*, 12–17.

Rachel, J. V., Guess, L. L., Hubbard, R. L., Maisto, S. A., Cavanaugh, E. R., Waddler, R., & Bearud, C. H. (1980). *Adolescent drinking behavior research*. Triangle Park, NC: Research Triangle Institute.

Regier, D. A., Farmer, M. E., Rae, D. S., Locke, B. Z., Keith, S. J., Judd, L. L., & Goodwin, F. R. (1990). Comorbidity of mental disorders with alcohol and other drug abuse. *Journal of the American Medical Association, 264*, 2511–2518.

Rich, C. L., Young, D., & Fowler, R. C. (1986a). San Diego suicide study: I. Young vs. old subjects. *Archives of General Psychiatry, 43*, 577–582.

Rich, C. L., Young, D., & Fowler, R. C. (1986b). San Diego suicide study: II. Substance abuse in young cases. *Archives of General Psychiatry*, *43*, 962–965.

Robbins, D. R., & Alessi, N. E. (1985). Depressive symptoms and suicidal behavior in adolescents. *American Journal of Psychiatry*, *142*, 588–592.

Robins, L. (1966). Deviant children grown up. Baltimore: Williams & Wilkins.

Rounsaville, B. J., Kosten, T. R., Weissman, M. M., & Kleber, H. D. (1986). Prognostic significance of psychiatric disorders in treated opiate addicts. *Archives of General Psychiatry*, *43*, 739–745.

Rounsaville, B. J., Spitzer, R. L., & Williams, J. B. W. (1986). Proposed changes in DSM-III substance use disorders: Description and rationale. *American Journal of Psychiatry*, *143*, 463–468.

Roy, A., & Linnoila, M. (1986). Alcoholism and suicide. *Suicide and Life-Threatening Behaviors*, *16*, 244–273.

Roy, A., DeJong, J., Lamparski, D., Adinoff, B., George, T., Moore, V., Garnett, D., Kerich, M., & Linnoila, M. (1991). Mental disorders among alcoholics. *Archives of General Psychiatry*, *48*, 423–427.

Runeson, B. (1990). Psychoactive substance use disorder in youth suicide. *Alcohol and Alcoholism*, *25*, 561–568.

Ryan, N. D., Puig-Antich, J., Ambrosim, R., Rabinovich, H., Robinson, D., Nelson, B., Iyengars, S., & Twomay, J. (1987). The clinical picture of major depression in children and adolescents. *Archives of General Psychiatry*, *44*, 854–861.

Schuckit, M. A. (1986). Genetic and clinical implications of alcoholism and affective disorder. *American Journal of Psychiatry*, *143*, 140–147.

Schwartz, R. H., & Berman, A. (1990). Suicide attempts among adolescent drug users. *American Journal of Diseases in Children*, *144*, 310–314.

Sells, S. B., & Simpson, D. D. (1979). Evaluation of treatment outcome for youths in the drug abuse reporting program (DARP). A follow-up study. In G. M. Bescher (Ed.), *Youth drug abuse: Problems, issues, and treatments* (pp. 571–628). Lexington, MA: Lexington Books.

Shaffer, D. (1974). Suicide in childhood and early adolescence. *Journal of Child Psychology and Psychiatry*, *15*, 275–291.

Shaffer, D., Garland, A., Gould, M., Fisher, P., & Trautman, P. (1988). Preventing teenage suicide: A critical review. *Journal of the American Academy of Child and Adolescent Psychiatry*, *27*, 675–687.

Shaffi, D., Carrigan, S., Whittinghill, J. R., & Derrick, A. (1985). Psychological autopsy of completed suicide in children and adolescents. *American Journal of Psychiatry*, *42*, 1061–1064.

Simcha-Fagan, O., Gersten, J. C., & Langner, T. S. (1986). Early precursors and concurrent correlations of patterns of illicit drug use in adolescence. *Journal of Drug Issues*, *16*, 7–28.

Singh, E., Kandel, D., & Johnson, B. (1975). The internal validity and reliability of drug use responses in a large scale survey. *Journal of Drug Issues*, *5*, 426–443.

Stanton, M. D. (1979). Family treatment approaches to drug abuse problems: A review. *Family Procedures*, *18*, 251–280.

Stevenson, E. K., Hudgens, R. W., Held, C. P., Meredith, C. H., Hendrix, M. E., & Carr, D. L. (1972). Suicidal communication by adolescents: Study of two matched groups of 60 teenagers. *Diseases Nervous System*, *33*, 112–122.

Stewart, J. J., Myers, W. C., Burket, R. C., & Lyles, W. B. (1990). A review of the pharmacotherapy of aggression in children and adolescents. *Journal of the American Academy of Child and Adolescent Psychiatry*, *29*, 269–277.

Swanson, J. W., Holzer, C. E., Ganju, V. K., & Tsutomu Jono, R. (1990). Violence and psychiatric disorder in the community: Evidence from the epidemiologic catchment area surveys. *Hospital and Community Psychiatry*, *41*, 761–770.

Szapocznik, J., Kurtines, W., Foote, F., Perez-Vidal, A., & Hervis, O. (1983). Conjoint versus one-person family therapy: Some evidence for the effectiveness of conducting family therapy: Some evidence for the effectiveness of conducting family therapy through one person. *Journal of Consulting and Clinical Psychology*, *51*, 889–899.

Tarter, R. (1990). Evaluation and treatment of adolescent substance abuse: A decision tree method. *American Journal of Drug and Alcohol Abuse*, *16*, 1046.

Tarter, R. E., Alterman, A. I., & Edwards, K. L. (1985). Vulnerability to alcoholism in men: A behavior-genetic perspective. *Journal of Studies on Alcohol*, *6*, 329–356.

Tuchfeld, B. S., Clayton, R. R., & Logan, J. A. (1982). Alcohol, drug use and delinquent and criminal behaviors among male adolescents and young adults. *Journal of Drug Issues*, *2*, 185–198.

Van Hasselt, V. B., Hersen, M., & Milliones, J. (1978). Social skills training for alcoholics and drug addicts: A review. *Addictive Behaviors*, *3*, 221–233.

Vingilis, E., & Smart, R. G. (1981). Physical dependence on alcohol in youth. In Y. Israel, F. B. Gleser, & H. Kalant, et al. (Eds.), Research advances in alcohol and drug problems, Vol. 6. New York: Plenum.

Wechsler, H. (1979). Patterns of alcohol consumption among the young: High school, college and general population studies. In H. Blane & M. Chafetz (Eds.), *Youth, alcohol and social policy* (pp. 39–58). New York: Plenum.

Wheeler, K., & Malmquist, J. (1987). Treatment approaches in adolescent chemical dependency. *Pediatric Clinics of North America*, *34*, 437–447.

White, H. R. (1987). Longitudinal stability and dimensional structure of problem drinking in adolescence. *Journal of Studies on Alcohol*, *48*, 541–550.

Williams, S. G., & Baron, J. (1982). Effects of short-term intensive hospital psychotherapy on youthful drug abusers: I. Preliminary MMPI data. *Psychological Reports*, *50*, 79–82.

Winters, K. C., Stinchfield, R. D., Henly, G. A., & Schwartz, R. H. (1991). Validity of adolescent self-report of alcohol and other drug involvement. *International Journal of the Addictions*, *25*, 1379–1395.

PART V

SPECIAL ISSUES

CHAPTER 26

Family Violence—Adult

WILLIAM J. WARNKEN AND ALAN ROSENBAUM

DESCRIPTION OF THE DISORDER

Over the past 20 years family violence* has been identified as one of the nation's largest health problems. Child, spouse, and elder abuse have become the concern of police, judges, legislators, psychiatrists, psychologists, and social workers. Although legislators have responded to the public's concern about some forms of domestic violence with mandated reporting laws and by imposing stiffer consequences for perpetrators, social service and mental health systems (i.e., hospitals, clinics, and private practices) have shouldered much of the burden of dealing with this problem. Consequently, it is important that clinicians become familiar with the psychiatric characteristics of those individuals involved, and with the interventions used to treat this problem.

This chapter reviews the literature pertaining to the etiology and treatment of family violence, focusing specifically on the psychiatric disorders most often associated with this phenomena. Since other chapters examine the psychological factors related to child abuse, we will concentrate on the aggression that occurs between adult family members.[1] The focus of this chapter is the etiology and treatment of husband to wife, wife to husband, and adult child to parent aggression.

Neither marital aggression nor elder abuse can be understood by examining a single precipitating factor or event. Rather, they appear to be multidetermined phenomena resulting from a complex interaction of several psychological, social, and organic variables (Rosenbaum, Cohen & Forsstrom-Cohen, 1991). There is some disagreement as to the role of psychiatric disorder in the etiology of domestic aggression, and there is some

---

*The terms *abuse*, *violence*, and *aggression* will be used interchangeably in this chapter, as is typical of the family violence literature. Similarly, the term *marital* will subsume all intimate heterosexual relationships, including couples who date frequently or cohabitate (Rosenbaum, 1988).

WILLIAM J. WARNKEN AND ALAN ROSENBAUM • Department of Psychiatry, University of Massachusetts Medical Center, Worcester, Massachusetts 01655.

Handbook of Aggressive and Destructive Behavior in Psychiatric Patients, edited by Michel Hersen, Robert T. Ammerman, and Lori A. Sisson. Plenum Press, New York, 1994.

concern that viewing this problem from a psychiatric perspective will somehow absolve perpetrators of accountability for their abusive behavior. As we examine those factors that have been demonstrated by empirical research to be associated with domestic violence, we hope the reader will gain an appreciation of the contributions of the psychiatric perspective, both to our understanding of the problem and the potential contributions to its treatment.

EPIDEMIOLOGY

Estimates as to the rate of domestic violence vary; however, it is generally believed that approximately 1.6 million women are abused annually by their mates in the United States (Straus & Gelles, 1986). It has further been suggested that one in three marriages may experience marital violence, and that nearly half of all dating and marital relationships include some form of interpartner aggression (O'Leary et al., 1989). Prevalence of this behavior has caused spouse abuse to be called the most common cause of injury to women (Browne, 1987; Stark & Flitcraft, 1988). Each year, more than one million abused women will seek medical attention for their injuries in the United States alone (Brown, 1987). Frequently these injuries result in disfigurement, disability, or death. Statistics indicate that 30% of all women who are murdered are killed by a husband or boyfriend during a domestic dispute (Federal Bureau of Investigation, 1982).

Male to female aggression has been considered to be a more common occurrence than female to male. This, however, is not supported by available empirical data. Straus, Gelles, and Steinmetz (1980) reported that women used aggressive behavior in their interactions with their partners more frequently than did males. Numerous empirical studies (O'Leary, Barling, Arias, Rosenbaum, Malone, & Tyree, 1989; Steinmetz, 1977; Straus & Gelles, 1986) have reported that women assault men more often then vice versa. Studies of dating couples report comparable results (Elliot, Huizinga & Morse, 1986; O'Leary et al., 1989).

The nature and meaning of female–male aggression is the subject of some debate. Historically, there has been agreement among researchers that male to female aggression is more serious than female to male abuse, in that it is more physically and emotionally damaging to the victim (Browne, 1987). As a result, research has focused primarily on the etiology and treatment of male to female spouse aggression. According to Steinmetz and Lucca (1988), this position ignores the empirical data that suggest that female to male abuse is a significant problem in its own right: one that impacts physically and emotionally on the victim and his children. By downplaying female to male violence, as well as situations where both partners are aggressive, there is an implicit message that this form of domestic violence is inconsequential—an attitude which only a decade ago prevailed about male to female violence. This attitude may also help to obscure etiologically important dynamics.

The incidence rates of elder abuse show a great deal of variance. Gioglio and Blakemore (1983), using a random sample of New Jersey elderly, reported an incidence rate of less than 1% for abuse and neglect, and suggested that only one in five of those individuals reported the occurrence of physical violence. A retrospective study of records from public agencies and interviews with the elderly and human service personnel produced a 4% rate of elder abuse, with 38% of those individuals experiencing physical abuse (Block & Sinnott, 1979). Pillemer and Suiter (1988) extrapolated from these figures and concluded that nearly one million elders have experienced abuse and/or neglect. The House Select Committee on Aging (1985) reported that up to 10% of the elderly experience abuse, significantly raising the estimated number of abused elders in this country. These figures, coupled with reports that elder abuse, like spouse abuse, is not typically an isolated occurrence but a recurring event (Pepper, 1986), establish elder abuse as a major national health concern. Further, the fact that all forms of domestic aggression stigmatize both victim and perpetrator, increasing the likelihood of underreporting, suggests that these problems may be even more frequent.

In addition to identifying the incidence of abuse, there is a growing body of research examining the characteristics of perpetrators and victims of marital and elder abuse. We turn now to a review of these characteristics and their etiological significance.

ETIOLOGY

As the magnitude of the various forms of domestic aggression has become common knowledge, initial efforts to expose the problem have given way to research aimed at understanding the etiology. There is a substantial body of literature examing the characteristics of batterers, their victims, and the dynamics of their interpersonal relationships.

The inquiry into the etiology of marital aggression and elder abuse has focused on three broadly defined domains: (1) the intrapersonal—background and personality characteristics, including pathology and organic dysfunction; (2) the interpersonal and systemic—marital and family dynamics; and (3) the sociocultural—environmental stressors, racial and status differences, and societal attitudes. As mentioned earlier, it is important to recognize that intrafamily aggression most likely results from interactions of these factors.

Much of the empirical literature has been devoted to identification of the characteristics that distinguish abusers and their victims from their nonviolent and nonvictimized counterparts. These studies have examined the background variables, including exposure to aggression in the family of origin, personality traits, substance use and abuse, and psychiatric disorders in both perpetrators and victims.

While a number of these studies suffer from design flaws, raising questions about their reliability and validity (Hotaling & Sugarman, 1986; Rosenbaum, 1988), they have produced useful information about abusers and their victims. For example, age is a variable in both marital and elder abuse. Marital violence, whether it be husband—wife or wife—husband, is likely to occur in couples under the age of 30 and less likely in those couples over the age of 65 (Straus & Gelles, 1986). Elders over the age of 65 are therefore less likely to be abusive to each other than are younger couples. They are, however, most likely to be abused by other family members.

Several studies indicate that the elderly who are most frequently abused, emotionally and physically, are women over the age of 65 (Block & Sinnott, 1979; Boydston & McNairn, 1981; Lau & Kosberg, 1979). The most likely perpetrators of this abuse are family members (Lau & Kosberg, 1979), primarily daughters (Block & Sinnott, 1979) and sons (Boydston & McNairn, 1981) who either live with or are dependent upon the victim (McLaughlin, Nickell, & Gill, 1980). However, in a more recent study, Pillemer and Finklehor (1989) indicated that spousal aggression may occur at rates equal to, or greater than, the abusive incidences perpetrated on them by their children, making elderly males as likely to abuse their wives as are their children. Unlike marital violence, several studies have also reported that the victim of elder abuse may suffer from either a mental or physical disability (Sengstock & Liang, 1982; Wolf & Pillemer, 1989).

Male spouse abusers have been demonstrated to have low self-esteem and poor self-concepts (Goldstein & Rosenbaum, 1985; Walker, 1979). They exhibit traditional values and views regarding sex roles (Rosenbaum & O'Leary, 1981; Telch & Lindquist, 1984). Some abusers exhibit poor impulse control (Gondolf, 1991). They are more likely to come from violent families (Hotaling & Sugarman, 1986; Kalmuss, 1984; Rosenbaum & O'Leary, 1981) and are more likely than nonbatterers to have experienced child abuse (Kalmuss, 1984; Telch & Lindquist, 1984). One of the strongest findings is that spouse-abusive men are likely to have witnessed intraparental violence in their families of origin (Caesar, 1988; Hotaling & Sugarman, 1986).

Most studies of abused women have failed to identify intrapersonal characteristics or pathology that differentiated them from nonabused comparison groups, with the possible exception of witnessing intraparental violence in their families of origin. Although several studies implicated low self-esteem (Hartik, 1979; Hofeller, 1980) as a characteristic of battered women, Telch and Lindquist (1984) did not find them to have any lower self-esteem than their nonabused counterparts. Stark and Flitcraft (1988) noted that some battered women may exhibit aggressive, independent, and hostile behavior toward their abusers. Rosenbaum and O'Leary (1981) were unable to differentiate abused from nonabused women on measures of assertion and sex role attitudes.

Witnessing intrapersonal violence may also be characteristic of victims. Hotaling and Sugarman (1986) summarized risk markers for abused women and reported that witnessing intraparental violence was the only factor that emerged sufficiently often to be considered a risk marker. Other studies, however, have not corroborated this finding (Rosenbaum & O'Leary, 1981; Telch & Lindquist, 1984). It has been suggested that sampling differences may account for this discrepancy. All of the studies reporting this factor as a positive finding employed nonagency samples. Studies utilizing agency samples have not supported the finding.

Another element frequently mentioned as a dynamic in family violence, either marital or elder abuse, is the role of psychoactive substance abuse. Although it is not clear how alcohol precipitates generalized aggressive behavior, there are several theories, including disinhibition, that explain the interaction between alcohol use and violence. Consequently, there are significant data to support the claim that alcohol use may be a factor in aggressive behavior (Taylor & Leonard, 1983). Kantor and Straus (1986) examined alcohol use in a sample of men involved in marital violence. They reported that male spouse abusers were frequently alcoholic and that heavy drinkers were more likely than moderate drinkers to become aggressive toward their wives. However, they also noted that the majority of alcoholics are not wife beaters and that even among abusers who used alcohol, a significant number of abusive incidents were not associated with alcohol use.

Substance abuse is also prevalent among the victims of spouse abuse. In fact, Stark and Flitcraft (1988) called battering the "single most important context" for understanding female alcoholism. They reported that the rate of alcoholism was significantly greater among battered than nonbattered women (Stark & Flitcraft, 1988).

In a survey of health care providers who rank ordered reported causes of elder abuse, substance abuse was identified as the second most important causal factor (Douglas, Hickey, & Noel, 1980). Further, when Pillemer (1986) compared a population of elder abusers with a comparison group, he found that the abusers were likely to be identified as alcoholic. Nevertheless, Wolf and Pillemer (1989) argue that case-control studies are needed in order to establish the causal role of alcohol and substance abuse among the elder-abusing population.

Biological factors have only recently been studied in relation to family violence. Elliot

(1982), in his study of the "episodic dyscontrol syndrome," found that 102 out of the 286 individuals he interviewed exhibited recurrent acts of rage and aggression following a brain insult or the onset of brain disease. He later noted that the remaining 184 individuals had demonstrated explosive and violent behavior since childhood, also the result of minimal brain damage (Elliot, 1987). He concluded that brain damage and the episodic dyscontrol syndrome may be contributing factors to domestic violence (Elliot, 1988).

Lewis et al. (1986, 1988), in studies of adult and adolescent death row inmates, reported that a significant portion of those inmates sentenced to death for committing violent crimes suffered from neurological deficits due to brain damage, suggesting the value of examing neurological factors in maritally aggressive populations. Rosenbaum and Hoge (1989) examined the incidence of head injury among batterers who had been referred to a treatment group at the University of Massachusetts Medical Center and found that 61% of those interviewed had a history if significant head injury. Rosenbaum (1991), reporting the preliminary results from a follow-up study that utilized control groups, standardized measures, and a blind design, found that batterers were significantly more likely to have sustained a significant head injury prior to their abusive behavior than were men in the nonviolent (discordant or happily married) couples. Additionally, neuropsychological batteries administered to these men suggested dysfunction in the frontal and temporal lobes. These are the areas of the brain responsible for self-regulation and impulse control. Damage to these areas has been linked to aggressive behavior (Lezak, 1983).

In other studies of marital violence, male abusers, when compared to both unhappily married nonviolent males and happily married nonviolent males, have demonstrated an inability to be properly assertive with their spouses (Rosenbaum & O'Leary, 1981). Others have suggested that batterers also have deficits in their ability to express their emotions (LaViolette, Barnett, & Miller, 1984). Such inability may impact on the batterer's interpersonal relationships. Indeed, there is evidence linking deficits in communications between spouses with an increased risk of marital violence (Maiuro, Cahn, & Vitaliano, 1986; Neidig & Freidman, 1984). Also, in their attempts to communicate, batterers tend to display increased affectual arousal and demonstrate negative behaviors during their communications with their spouses (Margolin, John, & Gleberman, 1988).

Coupled with the findings that maritally violent couples argue over recurring themes and tend to strive for resolution more than do nonviolent couples (Lloyd, 1990), we get a picture of how some of these interindividual factors interact to produce aggressive responses. This problem is further exacerbated by the fact that perceived seriousness of the topic being discussed may also act as a predicator for marital violence (Golash & Rosenbaum). The integration of these dynamics supports Lloyd's conclusions that maritally violent men strive for problem resolution and get frustrated when no resolution is obtained. The lack of productive communication skills, coupled with high affectual arousal, facilitates use of less productive problem-solving methods, including intimidation and verbal and physical abuse.

Dependency, whether physical, financial, or emotional, is an interpersonal factor that may contributed to elder abuse. Initially, it was believed that elder abuse was the result of the elderly parent's dependency on their children (Davidson, 1979). Steinmetz (1983) referred to this as "generational inversion," a situation in which roles are reversed and the parent becomes physically and/or emotionally dependent on his or her children. This supposedly produced increased stress in caregivers, promoting the perception that they were in a one-way giving relationship—one in which they were being taken advantage of, increasing the potential for abuse.

There are data, however, that contradict the "generational inversion" model. In fact, there is evidence to suggest it may be the child or caregiver dependency on the elder that precipitates violence. Wolf et al. (1982) and Hwalek et al. (1984) reported that the financial dependency of the abuser on the victim was a factor in elder abuse. Pillemer (1985) found that 64% of the abusers he examined were financially dependent on their victims and that 55% of them needed housing from their victim. Abusers, therefore, may be more likely to be dependent upon their victim than vice versa.

Social isolation has been associated with all forms of domestic violence. Gelles (1972) reported that male batterers socially isolate themselves. Abusive males also have difficulty establishing and maintaining support networks (Rosenbaum, Cohen, & Forrstrom-Cohen, 1991). They may also coerce their partners into distancing themselves from family and friends, destroying any external support network (Browne, 1987). In case-control studies of elderly abusive families, Phillips (1983) found that abused elders were also frequently socially isolated. Isolation from other nonabusing family members and friends keeps abuse from being disclosed, prevents interventions by legal and social service agencies, and allows abuse and exploitation to continue.

Status differences and power differentials, perceived or real, may contribute to the occurrence of domestic aggression. Hotaling and Sugarman (1986) reported that ideological and racial differences (Wasileski, Callahan-Chaffee, & Chaffee, 1982) among partners was a factor in domestic violence. One such ideological difference that may precipitate interspouse aggression is the pairing of traditional husbands with nontraditional wives. Such pairing has been shown to produce lower marital satisfaction (Bowen & Orthner, 1983) and has been associated with couple violence (Walker, 1984). Additionally, differences in social status between husband and wife, whether because the woman earns more money or has obtained a higher level of education, increase the likelihood that marital aggression will occur (Hornung, McCullough & Sugimoto, 1981). Rosenbaum et al. (1991) conclude that disparities in education, income, and social status are factors that exacerbate the abusive male's poor self-esteem.

A final factor is the role of external stress in domestic violence. Straus, Gelles, and Steinmetz (1980) reported that abusive males have higher levels of life stressors, including being dissatisfied with their vocation. They conclude that the higher the overall subjective level stress of the abuser, the greater the possibility that he or she may become violent. Although Sengstock and Liang (1982) provide some evidence that this may be true of elder abuse as well, Pillemer and Suiter (1988) warn that to date, no "systematic exploration has been conducted of the relationship between stress and elder abuse" (p. 257).

Psychiatric Interfaces

A brief review of the functioning levels of elder and spouse abusers reveal several consistent findings. Abusers are likely to habitually abuse psychoactive substances. Maritally violent men are more likely to behave aggressively with people other than their wives (Walker, 1984). They become quickly frustrated and angry during disagreements with their victims and may react impulsively with violence. Substance abuse, impulsivity, and poor interpersonal skills contribute to vocational difficulties, resulting in feelings of failure and inadequacy and higher levels of subjective stress. Since these behavioral patterns are chronic, batterers are often diagnosed with personality disorders.

Although no singular battering personality profile has emerged from the studies of perpetrators, marital and elder abuse research data indicate that abusers display a range of personality disorders. Hamberger and Hastings (1986) used the Million Clinical Multiaxial Inventory (MCMI) to assess male spouse abusers and identified three personality types associated with battering. Even though the MCMI scores were within normal ranges, they reported that batterers possessed asocial/borderline, narcissistic/antisocial, and dependent/compulsive features. Margolin et al. (1988) summarized the results of other studies, in which abusers had been described as sadistic, passive–aggressive, addiction prone, jealous, and dependent.

Walker (1984) contends that many abusers do not limit aggression to their wives, noting that they can also be violent toward their children, parents, animals, and objects. She states that they are also more likely than nonviolent males to have been arrested and convicted of criminal offenses. Batterers exhibiting this type of problem, often coupled with the frequently accompanying substance abuse problems, may meet the diagnostic criteria for antisocial personality disorder, as defined by the *Diagnostic and Statistical Manual of Mental Disorders* (DSM-III-R) (American Psychiatric Association, 1987).

In this regard, Offutt (1989), in examing the battering population utilizing the MCMI, also reported that batterers possessed a variety of antisocial characteristics. He found them to exhibit increased overall aggressiveness, alcohol and substance abuse problems, impulsivity, and manipulative behaviors.

Studies of elder abusers show similar results. Chen et al. (1981) stated that personality disorders and substance abuse problems were common characteristics of elder abusers. Wolf and Pillemer (1989) reported individual pathology on the part of the abuser as highly correlated with violence against the elderly. In this study, Wolf and Pillemer quantitatively compared abused and nonabused elders and discovered that the elder abusers, as identified by their elderly victims, were more prone to mental and emotional problems than were their nonabusive counterparts. The abusers were significantly more likely to have been hospitalized for a psychiatric problem and much more likely to be alcohol and substance abusive. In the same study, a qualitative analysis of the data revealed that many of the elders blamed their abuse on the "psychosis, alcoholism, or other psychological problems" of the abuser (Wolf & Pillemer, 1989, p. 70). Not surprisingly, over half of the respondents viewed the personality traits of their abusers as a primary catalyst for their abuse.

Batterers can exhibit a broad range of symptoms that can lead to various and multiple Axis I and II disorders. Bland and Orn (1986) suggest that when combinations of disorders are present the individual may be more volatile. They suggest, for example, that a combination of substance abuse and antisocial personality or depression combined with substance abuse is particularly volatile.

Women who have been chronically abused also present with a diversity of psychiatric diagnoses. Women who witnessed their mothers being abused by their fathers may have learned that men can treat women in a violent manner, without expecting consequences. They might have witnessed their mothers making excuses for their fathers, including blaming herself for his violent behavior (Browne, 1987). They have probably learned how difficult it is to leave an abusive partner—fearing being physically abused again, or worrying that he may hurt someone else or himself (Browne, 1987). If this child, as an adult, enters into a relationship with an abusive partner, not only will she experience the violence first hand, but the information she gathered in her family of origin about the futility of resistance can lead to fear, anxiety, trepidation, and fatigue—a constellation of symptoms that Walker (1984) identifies as learned helplessness. This is often manifest as dysthymia or depression. In fact, 37% of battered women being treated by mental health professionals "carry a diagnosis of depression or another situational disorder" (Stark &

Flitcraft, 1988, p. 303), while nearly 50% of the battered women who are treated in emergency rooms are diagnosed with depression (Gondolf, 1991).

One in ten battered women may also experience psychosis after onset of abuse (Stark & Flitcraft, 1988). Often such psychosis is in the form of a delayed response to the chronic abuse incurred that can emerge several months to years after the violence has ceased. In these cases, battered women are frequently diagnosed with posttraumatic stress disorder (Douglas, 1979).

Clinicians should also be aware of the proposed changes from the DSM-III-R to the DSM-IV (American Psychiatric Association, 1987, 1993) regarding domestic aggression. One of the changes from the DSM-III-R to the DSM-IV is that there will be specific diagnoses that identify domestic aggression as the focus of clinical treatment. In the DSM-III-R there was a diagnosis for marital problems. This category in the DSM-III-R was used when the "focus of attention or treatment is a marital problem that is not apparently due to a mental disorder" (p. 360). The use of this diagnosis did not necessarily include the presence of marital aggression. In the DSM-IV, however, there are several proposed diagnostic codes that are specific to different forms of domestic violence. The DSM-IV offers a diagnosis for physical abuse of a child, sexual abuse of a child, neglect of a child, sexual abuse of an adult, and physical abuse of an adult. The diagnosis of physical abuse of adults can be used "when the focus of clinical attention is physical abuse of an adult (e.g., spouse beating, abuse of an elderly parent)" (p. U:5). While the DSM-III-R did not specifically address the issue of domestic violence, the DSM-IV offers specific diagnostic codes for identifying the problem of elder, spouse, and child abuse.

AGGRESSION TOWARD SELF

Because the disorders associated with those individuals involved in family violence include substance abuse and character and depressive disorders, clinicians should be aware that perpetrators and victims alike may threaten to use aggression toward themselves and may attempt suicide. Stark and Flitcraft (1988, p. 304) called battering the "single most important context" yet identified for female suicide attempts, noting that abused women are at five times the risk for suicide than nonbattered women. Meanwhile, Walker (1984) reports that one-half of all batterers threaten suicide during their interactions with their wives. Estimates regarding the percentage of battered women who consider or attempt suicide range from 10% (Stark & Flitcraft, 1988) to 33% (Walker, 1984).

To date there are no reliable statistics that measure the attempt and completion rates for male spouse abusers. There is, however, no reason to assume that the impulsivity, depression, and aggression exhibited by these men toward women would be entirely outwardly directed. Indeed, Gondolf (1991) cites a case example where these attributes were associated with the batterer's suicidal ideation. Whether the threats are idle and manipulative or real, clinicians must be aware that batterers are at risk for committing suicide and must be assessed in this regard.

In their three-region study of elder abusers, Wolf et al. (1984) reported that 3.2% to 6% of abusers had actually tried to harm themselves. O'Malley et al. (1979), reporting on a sample of 183 batterers, stated that only 2% of these perpetrators had attempted suicide. While we know of no study that examines abuse as a catalyst for elder suicide, there is information to suggest that battered elders should be evaluated for self-destructive behavior. In her book on suicide and the elderly, Osgood (1985) lists a number of "high-risk markers" for suicide attempts. She identifies the elder who is isolated, has recently moved, possesses low self-esteem or concept, is lonely, feels rejected or uninvolved with others, and has a history of poor interpersonal relationships as an individual most at risk for suicide. These symptoms are similar to the traits of the elder victim, as identified earlier in this chapter. Coupled with the fact that elders over 60 have an extremely high rate of suicide completion (Quinn & Tomita, 1986), these factors suggest that clinicians should be cognizant of the risk for suicide among abused elderly.

AGGRESSION TOWARD OTHERS

While this chapter focuses specifically on intrafamily violence, it should be noted that those individuals who are aggressive toward their wives, husbands, and parents may not limit their aggression solely to family members. Of 300 psychiatric patients in Binder and McNeil's (1986) study who had committed assaults 2 weeks prior to admission, 15% were almost as likely to aggress against nonintimates (46%) as against family members (54%).

More recently, Gondolf (1991) reported that 66% of the psychiatric patients examined in an emergency room setting indicated that they has been aggressive toward other people at one time or another. Among the group of patients who had been assaultive within the 3 months prior to evaluation, 41% had been aggressive toward a family member, 14% toward nonfamily members, and 44% had been aggressive toward both family and nonfamily members. Those patients who have been assaultive within 2 weeks of their evaluation showed a modest increase in non-family-related violence; 44% had been aggressive toward family members, 56% had been violent toward nonfamily members, and 3% had been aggressive toward both groups.

In a study that compared a variety of characteristics of male spouse abusers to both unhappily married and happily married nonviolent men, Warnken and Rosenbaum (1991) found that the batterers were over twice as likely to have been aggressive toward others; 64% of the batterers had been aggressive toward nonfamily members, as compared to 25% of the discordant and 20% of the happily married men.

These findings suggest that not only do those psychiatric patients who are assaultive victimize family members, they may also be aggressive toward nonrelated individuals as well.

CLINICAL MANAGEMENT

The complex interaction of the etiological factors associated with family violence necessitates an integrative approach to treatment. The etiological variables must be identified, their interrelationship explored, and a client-specific treatment plan formulated. Because of the high physical and emotional consequences of domestic aggression to the victim and perpetrator, the treatment of intrafamily violence warrants maximum impact therapies—therapies that utilize those interventions most likely to promote the immediate cessation of family abuse.

The treatment process begins during the initial evaluation. Unfortunately, while physicians, psychologists, and social workers find themselves in the position to identify and assess marital and family aggression, they frequently do not. Although intake protocols generally require assessment of child abuse, histories of marital and adult child–parent abuse are often ignored. Client discomfort about revealing such intimate family secrets such as violence (Goldberg & Tomlanovich, 1984), coupled with clinician's inattention to, or discomfort with, this problem, often results in professional inaction. Mental health professionals must be trained to assess domestic violence information in the same manner they would any other interpersonal dysfunction.

Whether the client is perceived as victim or perpetrator, during the history-taking portion of the initial evaluation, clinicians should ask aggression-related questions. Because intake protocols usually evaluate presenting problems, relevant history, family background, use of psychoactive substances, academic and vocational histories, criminal record, medical history, and mental status, the apparatus is in place to access pertinent information regarding family violence. While gathering the client's personal history, the clinician should be encouraged to ask direct questions about intrafamily aggression. Opportunity to speak privately with the potential victim should be built into the evaluation process. It must be remembered that victims are often afraid to disclose information about their victimization, especially in the presence of the perpetrator.

Since those who are involved in family violence can represent a spectrum of psychiatric disorders, during the mental status exam it is important to determine the etiology of the patient's anxiety, depression, and suicidality. As Gondolf (1991) notes, these symptoms, rather than intrafamilial aggression, are often identified as presenting problems.

At the onset of the evaluation, clinicians must inform their patient's family of the limits of confidentiality. Mandated reporting laws stipulate that child or elder abuse must be reported to appropriate state agencies, and patients should be informed of this obligation. Clinicians are also obliged to inform patients that should they state intent to harm another individual or themselves, appropriate measures to protect threatened individuals or themselves will be taken. This may involve notifying the police, warning the intended victim, or commitment to a psychiatric facility. In essence, when the lives of the patient or others are at risk, confidentiality must be breached.

Following the initial evaluation, a client-specific treatment plan should be formulated. Included in the formulation of the treatment plan are the following considerations.

Treatment of Victims

Although victims may be reluctant to further antagonize their abuser or disrupt the family by seeking legal intervention, it has been shown, at least in spouse abuse cases, that arresting men after the first abusive incident reduced the likelihood of violence recurring (Sherman & Berk, 1984). Not only does this action send a message to the perpetrator that violence will not be tolerated, but it facilitates the contact of the legal system and human service agencies with those individuals who are most isolated and without support networks. In some jurisdictions, judges have the authority to mandate the perpetrators into treatment programs. Treaters' of course, should be aware of the regulations in their state.

The literature on elder abuse (Block & Sinnott, 1979; O'Malley, Segars, Perez, Mitchell & Kneupfel, 1979) suggests that removal of the victim from the abusive situation may be the most common intervention to protect her safety. In spousal abuse situations, leaving the violent spouse may also be the victim's best option.

Many victims of family violence feel unable to leave the abusive relationship. Concerns about care of children and pressures from family (his and hers), social pressures, and financial dependency often make leaving the abusive relationship difficult (Stevens & Rosenbaum, 1991). In those cases, therapy focuses on decreasing the psychological dependency on the abuser, improving self-esteem, relieving the victim of the responsibility for the spouse's violent behavior, developing an intolerance for such aggression, and establishing a sense of power, control, and self-advocacy (Sedlak, 1988). Therapy then promotes the notion that the woman is not a helpless victim of violence, but a person who has power over her life. Most larger cities and many smaller ones have shelters and other agencies specializing in treatment of victims of family violence. Referral to such agencies is often the most useful intervention. Since elder abuse victims share similar feelings of depression and helplessness (Pillemer & Prescott, 1989), these issues are also relevant to the therapy of abused elders.

Whether victims choose to remain in the relationship or leave, all should be informed about the resources available to them. They should be made aware of legal advocacy programs, informed of the procedures for implementing restraining orders, and introduced to the diverse services offered by women's shelters. The more women are aware of their options, the less "trapped" they will feel in their relationships.

Treatment of Perpetrators

There are a variety of modalities utilized in the treatment of male spouse abusers, some of which may also be relevant for elder abusers. While these treatment approaches emerge from different program ideologies, most programs have as their primary goal cessation of aggression. They also share similar therapeutic strategies. Rosenbaum and Maiuro (1990) identify the following as five strategies in the treatment of spouse abusers: (1) educating batterers about their ownership, responsibility, and accountability for their violent behavior; (2) enhancing batterers' ability to identify, articulate, and manage the negative feelings and emotions that contribute to their violence; (3) increasing social contact; (4) providing a therapeutic environment that encourages social interaction and use of support networks; and (5) developing alternative nonviolent, productive methods of interacting with spouses. In addition, it is important to focus on abuse as a form of coercion and control, the importance of sharing power in a relationship, and empathy with the victim. Different programs vary with respect to the importance they attribute to each of these strategies.

While there are multiple modalities that are used in the treatment of batterers, group therapy is particularly well suited to this population. Group therapy provides a forum in which the men can be both confronted and supported. Since social isolation (Hotaling & Sugarman, 1986) and communication deficits (Maiuro, Cahn, & Vitaliano, 1986) have been identified as risk factors for domestic violence, group treatment also strives to establish a therapeutic environment that promotes development of a support network for the batterer, while providing a place where violent men can openly discuss their problems (Lion, Christopher, & Madden, 1977).

Use of male and female coleaders in group therapy also contributes to the therapeutic process. Through the interactions of coleaders, group members observe an egalitarian relationship between a man and woman (Geffner & Rosenbaum, 1990) and view interchanges that challenge their established pattern of male–female interactions and stereotypes. From observing the therapists' behaviors, abusers learn alternative methods of interacting with women, including productive, nonadversarial problem solving and communication.

Because perpetrators appear to escalate during conflict (Margolin, John, & Gleberman, 1988) and/or have high levels of impulsivity (Gondolf, 1991), time-out techniques are often incorporated into the batterer's treatment regimen. The purpose of this intervention is to de-escalate the volatile situation by interrupting the interaction prior to expression of aggression. This procedure is readily learned by the men and allows them time to think about the consequences of their actions.

Batterers are taught to be cognizant of their negative affective arousal by monitoring physiological cues (i.e., stomach discomfort, increased respiratory and heart rates, clenching of fists, raising of voice, etc.). If, after this "check in," they believe that they are at risk for becoming violent, they are encouraged to call a time-out or leave the situation. This technique has also proven to be successful in the treatment of impulsive behavior exhibited by a head-injured population (Frazen & Lovell, 1987), some of whom may be batterers. It is, of course, helpful if they receive cooperation from their wives in facilitating time-outs. However, if their wives do not cooperate and the men fear that violence will erupt, they are encouraged to leave in a nonviolent manner regardless. Battering men are instructed to be cognizant of alternative "escape" routes, so that direct physical confrontation is avoided. A woman cannot be battered if the violent partner leaves the situation.

As part of the time-out technique, perpetrators are instructed in various relaxation and arousal reduction methods (Rosenbaum & Maiuro, 1990). Relaxation techniques, including breathing and guided imagery, decrease the physiological arousal that accompanies assaultive behavior. One of the chief complaints of batterers in discussing their inability to control aggression is that the situations happen too fast to control. By decreasing their physiological arousal they have taken time to slow down, thus the likelihood of violence decreases.

Since marital violence usually involves discord, conjoint marital therapy may be incorporated into the batterer's treatment plan. Geffner and Rosenbaum (1990) suggest that in addition to addressing the batterer's violence, marital therapy can also address anger management, "improve self-esteem, reduce stress, increase assertiveness and improve communication" (p. 138). Marital therapy can also be used to support such treatment interventions as time-outs. The woman can be taught to allow the man to take a time-out or learn to call it herself if she senses an escalation.

Given the communication problems that exist in battering relationships, one of the benefits of marital therapy is the ability to enhance the couple's communication skills through role playing and modeling. Without adequate communication skills, perpetrators and victims will be unable to express their needs, resulting in increased frustration and the potential for violence. However, as Bogrod (1984) and Dell (1989) caution, the therapist must be careful not to "blame the victim" for the violence in the marriage. Too often the shared responsibility in improving communication skills implies shared responsibility for the violence. Therapists should clearly delineate the differences between these two responsibilities, making the perpetrator alone responsible for his or her violent behavior.

Counseling of couples also creates a potentially dangerous situation (i.e., the batterer and the spouse are in the same room and are discussing difficult marital issues). This form of counseling should only be considered if the victim has freely decided to remain in the relationship and the victim's safety can be assured. If the couple is not living together, the session may afford an opportunity for a violent interaction. If the victim is living in an undisclosed location, that may be jeopardized. Strategies for dealing with these problems include having the couples come in separate cars and allowing the wife a "head start" before the husband leaves the clinic, calling for a police escort for the wife, and requiring nonviolence contracts. Providing these safety issues are properly dealt with, couple counseling can apparently be an effective strategy for dealing with marital aggression. (The reader is referred to Mantooth et al. (1987) for an excellent description of a couples counseling approach.)

There is a final consideration in the treatment of batterers. Because batterers, as well as their victims, often use alcohol or drugs, it is a problem that must be addressed conjointly or prior to treatment for battering. Since batterers often present as depressed, anxious, and impulsive (Gondolf, 1991), the disinhibiting effects of alcohol or substance abuse pose a serious threat to the success of treatment. If alcohol use is a factor in domestic violence, the perpetrator should be referred to AA, outpatient treatment, detoxification, or long-term rehabilitation programs prior to or in conjunction with the treatment for battering. Violent men are likely to fail at their attempts to manage their aggression if their judgment is impaired by alcohol or substance abuse.

Whether or not we believe that batterers suffer from a psychiatric disorder that accounts for their abusive behavior, we can agree that they are often in need of psychiatric intervention. This may involve treatment of depression, personality disorder, or providing an avenue for discussion of childhood abuses, as well as current stressors. Psychiatric hospitalization is often necessary as a holding strategy for either suicidal or homicidal behavior. Tarasoff-like situations may be satisfied by hospitalization of a batterer threatening to harm his spouse. Antiseizure medication, such as Tegretol, and beta-blockers, such as Inderal, have shown some promise in the treatment of violent individuals and may eventually prove to be useful adjuncts to psychotherapy in the treatment of batterers (Brizer, 1988).

While a number of the interventions employed in the treatment of marital violence may be useful in the treatment of elder abusers (i.e., legal intervention, time-outs, substance abuse counseling, group, and family counseling), there are etiologic factors specific to elder abuse that must also be addressed. If the generation inversion model is correct and aggression toward the elderly is the result of overburdened caretakers, these caretakers need to establish relationships with those social service agencies that can help shoulder the burden of caring for their dependent elders. Wolf (1990) notes that treatment of elder abusers "most often consists of bringing help to the family in the form of skilled nursing care, homemaker assistance, personal care, meals-on-wheels, chore services, respite care, or adult day care" (p. 318). She concludes that the purpose of this intervention is to relieve caretaker stress by providing support services, while improving the caretaker's coping and caretaking skills.

In situations where the abuser is dependent upon the elderly parent, efforts should be made to help him or her become more autonomous (Pillemer & Suiter, 1988; Wolf, 1990). Service providers should help the dependent perpetrator have access to vocational training, housing assistance, and appropriate counseling services. The goal of this intervention is clearly to help the abuser become less dependent upon his or her victim, thus improving feelings of self-worth and competence.

LONGITUDINAL PERSPECTIVES

Family violence cannot be viewed as a phenomenon that affects only one generation of a family; rather, intrafamily aggression can be passed on from generation to generation. Bowen (1978) argues that families teach interactional patterns to children by having them witness the interaction of adult and sibling members. Similarly, Bandura's (1973, 1977) social learning model describes aggression as behaviors that are learned through our violent interactions with society, including family and friends. O'Leary (1988) noted that, "modeling or observational learning has been used as a mechanism to explain why certain individuals acquire physical aggression as an appropriate response to a spouse" (p. 41). Intergenerational transmission of abuse also remains a popular explanation for child maltreatment (Starr, 1988).

Studies that have examined wife and elder abuse from a multigenerational transmission perspective have yielded conflicting results. As mentioned earlier, studies of marital violence identify exposure to violence in the family of origin as a risk marker for male batterers and possibly for their victims as well. Studies have demonstrated that batterers are likely to have been abused (Kalmuss, 1984; Telch & Lindquist, 1984) and/or to have witnessed intraparental aggression in their family of origin (Hotaling & Sugarman, 1986). Additionally, Hotaling and Sugarman (1986) also identify witnessing intraparental violence as a background factor of battered wives. These findings support the multigenerational model.

Pillemer and Suiter (1988) stated that "no evidence exists at present to determine whether elder abusers have experienced violent upbringings" (p. 255). While they postulate that there may be differences between spouse abuse and elder abuse, they concede that an association between parent–child aggression and elder abuse seems likely. This assumption, however, is based on findings in other areas of domestic violence. They suggest two possible patterns that may be relevant to the study of elder abuse. First, they suggest that the elder abuser may become aggressive toward the parent because he or she was abused by that person as a child. The second possibility is that the elder abuser becomes aggressive toward his or her parent because he or she had witnessed that parent being abusive to his or her own elderly parents. These models await empirical validation.

Because family violence is apparently passed on from one generation to the next, it is critical that the cycle of violence be disrupted. If it is not, future generations will continue to employ aggressive and violent behaviors in their interactions with family members.

CASE ILLUSTRATIONS

Adam

Adam is a 33-year-old Caucasian male who was referred to the male batterer's workshop by his probation officer following conviction for assault and battery on his wife, Eve. This is not Adam's first arrest for this charge. He has two prior arrests and convictions for assault and battery, one on a former girlfriend. He is currently separated from his wife, who has a restraining order in place against him.

His most recent arrest, like the others, stemmed from an argument with his wife around his drinking. He has been drinking daily since he was laid off from his job. Past girlfriends and his wife, however, had complained about use of alcohol prior to the loss of his most recent job. He stated that his wife does not understand the pressure he is under and "nags" him to find a job. He stated that she does not listen to his explanations as to why he remains unemployed, and whenever the topic is raised, the couple start to yell at each other.

In March of 1991, Adam, after meeting some friends at a bar, became intoxicated. Upon arriving home, Eve complained that he had once again been out drinking instead of looking for a job. Disinhibited by the effects of alcohol, the argument quickly escalated from verbal threats to his "slamming her against the cabinet in their kitchen." The impact of the push required Eve to have six stitches to the back of her head, and she suffered a mild concussion.

Although Adam regrets his use of force and states that it would not have occurred had he not been drinking, he stated that she was as much to blame for her injuries as was he.

She should not have verbally abused him about his joblessness, especially after he had been drinking. After all, it is a "woman's place" to support her husband, not criticize him. He would not tolerate a woman confronting him and telling him what to do. He had learned from his father that if a woman "gets out of hand," it is a male's prerogative to use force.

Eve had married Adam to escape her chaotic home life. Her father was alcoholic and violent toward her mother and the children. When she first met Adam she was aware that his alcohol use was excessive, but that he did not drink as much as her father. Early in their relationship, she found him to be carefree and loving. She noted that he became increasingly hostile and angry about being forced to take "menial" jobs to support his family. In retrospect, however, she never remembered him being able to hold a job. The longer she knew Adam, the more she was convinced that he had no confidence in himself and that he was not the "strong" person she thought she married.

She noted that he was first abusive to her while they were dating, but that he never really hurt her. The frequency of the abuse had increased the longer they had been together, to the point where he would get drunk and be abusive approximately once a month. For several years she had tried to help him stop drinking, but her efforts had failed. She had thought about leaving on several occasions, but had no place to go and insufficient money to leave. She felt trapped, frustrated, angry, and depressed. It was not until he was arrested the last time that she gathered the courage to go to a woman's shelter with her children.

Harriet

Harriet, 70, has just decided to move to a retirement home. She reached this decision when it became apparent that her son no longer wished to assist her. In fact, her son, Ivan, had begun to resent having to take care of her, stating "Yeah, I need a place to stay and money to spend, but this is not worth the aggravation." Lately, after he had been drinking, he had been "a little rough" when putting her to bed. She also noticed that he was becoming increasingly agitated at her attempts to monitor her money, on which they both existed. On one occasion, when she refused to give him money to go out "gambling and drinking," with his friends, he knocked her to the floor and watched her struggle to get on her feet again. He said that if she did not give him free access to "their" money, she would "spend a lot more time on the floor."

She had always felt that Ivan was a "troubled" man, unable to hold a job due to his excessive drinking and gambling, but still, he was all she had. All her friends and relatives had died, and although Ivan often abused her, she could not abandon him, regardless of his behavior.

This position quickly changed in January of 1991, when Ivan came home intoxicated and demanded $1,000 to pay off a "bookie." When she informed him that it was 1:00 a.m. and that she did not have that amount of cash available, he began screaming and yelling at her.

Eventually, he struck with enough force to knock her to the floor, alerting the people who lived below them that there was a problem. The police were called, and Ivan was arrested. Since the state had a mandated reporting law, when Harriet was taken to the emergency room for evaluation, a state social worker was contacted. After a brief discussion with the social worker, Harriet realized that she could no longer live in fear of her son. She could also not change him. She decided to enter an elderly community residence. It was the only way she would have the support to set limits on her son and protect herself.

SUMMARY

Domestic violence remains one of the nation's largest health concerns. The cost, physically, emotionally, and financially to those individuals involved, and society in general, is significant. Because psychiatrists, psychologists, and social workers are often in a position to identify and intervene in the domestically violent family, it is essential that practitioners understand the etiology and treatment of this problem from a psychiatric perspective. Clinicians need to be aware that perpetrators and victims of family violence represent a broad range of psychiatric disorders, including personality, affective and mood, organic, impulse control, and adjustment disorders.

REFERENCES

American Psychiatric Association (1987). *The diagnostic and statistical manual of mental disorders*, 3rd Edition, Revised. Washington, DC: Author.

American Psychiatric Association (1993). *DSM-IV draft criteria*. Washington, DC: Author.

Bandura, A. (1973). *Aggression: A social learning analysis*. New Jersey: Prentice-Hall.

Bandura, A. (1977). *Social learning theory*. New York: The General Learning Press.

Binder, R. L., & McNeil, D. E. (1986). Victims and families of violent psychiatric patients. *Bulletin of American Academy of Psychiatry Law*, *14*, 131–139.

Bland, R., & Orn, H. O. (1986). Family violence and psychiatric disorder. *Canadian Journal of Psychiatry*, *31*, 129–137.

Block, M. R., & Sinnott, J. D. (Eds.). (1979). *The battered elderly syndrome: An exploratory study*. College Park: University of Maryland, Center on Aging.

Bogrod, M. (1984). Family systems approaches to wife battering: A feminist critique. *American Journal of Orthopsychiatry*, *54*, 558–568.

Bowen, G. L., & Orther, D. K. (1983). Sex-role congruency and marital quality. *Journal of Marriage and the Family*, *45*, 223–230.

Bowen, M. (1978). *Family therapy in clinical practice*. New York: Aronson.

Boydston, L. S., & McNairn, J. A. (1981). Elder abuse by adult caretakers: An exploratory study. In *Physical and Financial Abuse of the Elderly* (Pub. No. 07-297). San Francisco, CA: U.S. House of Representatives, Select Committee on Aging.

Brizer, D. A. (1988). Psychopharmacology and management of the violent patient. *Psychiatric Clinics of North America*, *11*, 551–568.

Browne, A. (1987). *When battered women kill*. New York: The Free Press.

Caesar, P. L. (1988). Exposure to violence in the families-of-origin among wife abusers and maritally non-violent men. *Violence and Victims*, *3*, 49–63.

Chen, P. N., Bell, S. L., Dolinsky, D. L., Doyle, J., & Dunn, M. (1981). Elder abuse in domestic settings: A pilot study. *Journal of Gerontological Social Work*, *4*, 3–17.

Davidson, J. (1979). Elder abuse. In M. R. Black and J. D. Sinnott (Eds.), *The battered elderly syndrome: An exploratory study*. College Park, MD: Center on Aging.

Dell, P. F. (1989). Violence and the systemic view: The problem of power. *Family Process*, *28*, 1–14.

Douglas, M. A. (1979). Post-Traumatic Stress Disorder and battered women. In N. Porter (Chair), *Post-Traumatic Stress Disorder in women: Normal reaction to abnormal events*. Symposium Conducted at the Annual Convention of the American Psychological Association, New Orleans, Louisiana.

Douglas, R. L., Hickey, T., & Noel, C. (1980). *A study of maltreatment of the elderly*. Ann Arbour, MI: University of Michigan.

Elliot, F. A. (1982). Neurological findings in adult minimal brain dysfunction and dyscontrol syndrome. *Journal of Nervous and Mental Disease*, *170*, 680–687.

Elliot, F. A. (1987). Neuroanatomy of aggression *Psychiatric Annals*, *17*, 385–388.

Elliot, F. A. (1988). Neurological factors. In V. B. Van Hesselt, R. L. Morrison, A. S. Belleck, & M. Hersen (Eds.), *Handbook of family violence* (pp. 359–382). New York: Plenum.

Elliott, D. S., Huizinga, D., & Morse, B. J. (1986). Self-reported violent offending: A descriptive analysis of juvenile violent offenders and their offending careers. *Journal of Interpersonal Violence*, *4*, 472–514.

Federal Bureau of Investigation. (1982). *Uniform crime reports*. Washington, DC: U.S. Department of Justice.

Franzen, M. D., & Lovell, M. R. (1987). Behavioral treatments of aggressive sequelae of brain injury. *Psychiatric Annals, 17*, 389–396.

Geffner, R., & Rosenbaum, A. (1990). Characteristics and treatment of batterers. *Behavioral Sciences and the Law, 8*, 131–140.

Gelles, R. J. (1972). *The violent home: A study of physical aggression between husbands and wives*. Beverly Hills, CA: Sage.

Gioglio, G. R., & Blakemore, P. (1983). *Elder abuse in New Jersey: The knowledge and experiences of abuse among the old New Jerseyans*. Trenton: New Jersey Department of Human Services.

Golash, L. R., & Rosenbaum, A. *Cognition and aggression in beginning marriages*. Unpublished manuscript, University of Massachusetts Medical School, Worcester, MA.

Goldberg, W. G., & Tomlanovich, M. C. (1984). Domestic violence victims in the emergency department: New findings. *Journal of American Medical Association, 251*, 3259–3264.

Goldstein, D., & Rosenbaum, A. (1985). An evaluation of the self-esteem of maritally violent men. *Family Relations, 34*, 425–428.

Gondolf, E. W. (1991). *Psychiatric response to family violence*. Lexington, MA: D.C. Heath.

Hamberger, L. E., & Hastings, J. E. (1986). Personality correlates of men who abuse their partners: A cross-validation study. *Journal of Family Violence, 1*, 323–341.

Hartik, L. M (1979). Identification of personality characteristics and self-concept factors of battered women. *Dissertation Abstracts International, 40*, 893B.

Hofeller, K. H. (1980). Social, psychological and situational factors in spouse abuse. *Dissertation Abstracts International, 41*, 408B.

Hornung, C. A., McCullough, B. C., & Sugimoto, T. (1981). Status relationships in marriage: Risk factors in spouse abuse. *Journal of Marriage and the Family, 43*, 675–692.

Hotaling, G. T., & Sugarman, D. B. (1986). An analysis of risk markers in husband to wife abuse: The current state of knowledge. *Violence and Victims, 1*, 101–124.

House Select Committee on Aging. (1985, May). *Elder abuse: A national disgrace* (Executive Summary). Washington, DC: Government Printing Office.

Hwalek, M., Sengstock, M., & Lawrence, R (1984). *Assessing the probability of abuse of the elderly*. Paper presented at the Annual Meeting of the Gerontological Society of America, San Antonio, Texas.

Kalmuss, D. (1984). The intergenerational transmission of marital aggression. *Journal of Marriage and the Family, 46*, 11–19.

Kantor, G. K., & Straus, M. A. (1986, April). *The drunken bum theory of wife beating*. Paper presented at the National Alcoholism Forum Conference on Alcohol and the Family, San Francisco, CA.

Lau, E., & Kosberg, J. I. (1979, September/October). Abuse of elderly by informal providers. *Aging*, pp. 11–15.

LaViolette, A. D., Barnett, O. W., & Miller, C. L. (1984, July). *A classification of wife abusers in the BEM sex-role inventory*. Paper presented at the Second National Conference of Research on Domestic Violence, Durham, New Hampshire.

Lewis, D. O., Pincus, J. H., Fledman, M., Jackson, L., & Bard, B. (1986). Psychiatric neurological, and psychoeducational characteristics of 15 death row inmates in the United States. *American Journal of Psychiatry, 143*, 838–845.

Lewis, D. O., Pincus, J. H., Bard, B., Richardson, E., Prichep, L. S., Feldman, M., & Yeager, C. (1988). Neuropsychiatric, psychoeducational, and family characteristics of 14 juveniles condemned to death in the United States. *American Journal of Psychiatry, 145*, 584–589.

Lezak, M. (1983). *Neuropsychological assessment* (2nd ed.). New York: Oxford University Press.

Lion, J. R., Christopher, R. L., & Madden, D. J. (1977). A group approach with violent outpatients. *International Journal of Group Psychotherapy 27*, 67–74.

Lloyd, S. A. (1990). Conflict types and strategies in violent marriages. *Journal of Family Violence, 5*, 269–289.

Maiuro, J. M., Cahn, T. S., & Vitaliano, P. P. (1986). Assertive deficits and hostility in domestically violent men. *Violence and Victims, 1*, 279–289.

Mantooth, C. M., Geffner, R., Franks, D., & Patrick, J. (1987). *Family preservation: A treatment manual for reducing couple violence*. Tyler, TX: East Texas Crisis Center.

Margolin, G., John, R. S., & Gleberman, L. (1988). Affective responses to conflictual discussions in violent and nonviolent couples. *Journal of Consulting and Clinical Psychology, 56*, 24–33.

McLaughlin, J. S., Nickell, J. P., & Gill, L. (1980). An epidemiological investigation of elderly abuse in southern Maine and New Hampshire. In *Elder Abuse* (Pub. No. 68-463). U.S. House of Representatives, Select Committee on Aging.

Neidig, P. H., & Freidman, D. H. (1984). *Spouse abuse: A treatment approach for couples*. Champaign, IL: Research Press.

Offutt, R. (1989). *Domestic violence: Psychological characteristics of men who batter*. Unpublished doctoral dissertation, Antioch University/New England, Keene, New Hampshire.

O'Leary, K. D. (1988). Physical aggression between spouses. In V. B. Van Hasselt, R. L. Morrison, A. S. Bellack, & M. Hersen (Eds.), *Handbook of family violence* (pp. 31–55). New York: Plenum.

O'Leary, K. D., Barling, J., Arias, I., Rosenbaum, A., Malone, J., & Tyree, A. (1989). Prevalence and stability of physical aggression between spouses: A longitudinal analysis. *Journal of Consulting and Clinical Psychology, 57*, 263–268.

O'Malley, H., Segars, H., Perez, R., Mitchell, V., & Kbuepfel, G. (1979). *Elder abuse in Massachusetts: A survey of professionals and paraprofessionals*. Unpublished manuscript, Legal Research and Services for the Elderly, Boston.

Osgood, N. J. (1985). *Suicide in the elderly: A practitioners guide to diagnosis and mental health interventions*. Rockville, MD: Aspen Publications.

Pepper, C. (1986, January). *Elder abuse: A national disgrace*. National Association of Home Care, Washington, DC.

Phillips, L. (1983). Abuse and neglect of the frail elderly at home: An exploration of theoretical relationships. *Journal of Advanced Nursing, 8*, 379–392.

Pillemer, K. A. (1985). The dangers of dependency: New findings on domestic violence against the elderly. *Social Problems, 33*, 146–158.

Pillemer, K. A. (1986). Risk factors in elder abuse: Results from a case control study. In K. A. Pillemer & R. S. Wolf (Eds.), *Elder abuse: Conflict in the family*. Dover, MA: Auburn House.

Pillemer, K. A., & Finklehor, D. (1989). Causes of elder abuse: Caregiver stress versus problem relatives. *American Journal of Orthopsychiatry, 59*, 179–182.

Pillemer, K. A., & Prescot., D. (1989). Psychological effects of elder abuse. *Journal of Elder Abuse and Neglect, 1*, 65–73.

Pillemer, K. A., & Suiter, J. J. (1988). Elder abuse. In V. B. Van Hasselt, R. L. Morrison, A. S. Bellack, & M. Hersen (Eds.), *Handbood of family violence* (pp. 247–270). New York: Plenum.

Quinn, M. J., & Tomita, S. K. (1986). *Elder abuse and neglect: Causes, diagnosis, and intervention strategies*. New York: Singer Publishing.

Rosenbaum, A. (1988). Methodological issues in marital violence research. *Journal of Family Violence, 3*, 91–104.

Rosenbaum, A., (1991). *Neurological factors in marital aggression: A preliminary report* (Grant #44814). Rockville, MD: National Institute of Mental Health.

Rosenbaum, A., Cohen, C., & Forsstrom-Cohen, B. (1991). The ecology of domestic aggression toward adult victims. In M. Hersen & R. T. Ammerman (Eds.), *Case studies in family violence* (p. 39–56). New York: Plenum.

Rosenbaum, A., & Hoge, S. K. (1989). Head injury and marital aggression. *American Journal of Psychiatry, 146*, 1048–1051.

Rosenbaum, A., & O'Leary, K. D. (1981). Marital Violence: Characteristics of abusive couples. *Journal of Consulting and Clinical Psychology, 49*, 69–71.

Rosenbaum, A., & Maiuro, J. M. (1990). Perpetrators of spouse abuse. In R. Ammerman & M. Hersen (Eds.), *Treatment of family violence: A sourcebook* (pp. 280–309). New York: John Wiley & Sons.

Sedlack, A. J. (1988). Prevention of wife abuse. In V. B. Van Hasselt, R. L. Morrison, A. S. Bellack, & M. Hersen (Eds.), *Handbood of family violence* (pp. 319–358). New York: Plenum.

Sengstock, M., & Liang, J. (1982). *Identifying and characterizing elder abuse*. Unpublished manuscript, Wayne State University, Institute of Gerontology, Detroit, MI.

Sherman, L. W., & Berk, R. A. (1984). The specific deterrent effects of arrest for domestic assault. *American Sociological Review, 49*, 261–271.

Stark, E., & Flitcraft, A. (1988). Violence among intimates. In V. B. Van Hasselt, R. L. Morrison, A. S. Bellack, & M. Hersen (Eds.), *Handbook of family violence* (pp. 293–317). New York: Plenum.

Starr, R. H., Jr . (1988). Physical abuse of children. In V. B. Van Hasselt, R. L. Morrison, A. S. Bellack, & M. Hersen (Eds.), *Handbook of family violence* (pp. 119–155). New York: Plenum.

Steinmetz, S. K. (1977). Secondary analysis of data from "The use of force for resolving family conflict: The training ground for abuse." *Family Coordinator, 33*, 19–26.

Steinmetz, S. K. (1983). Dependency, stress, and violence between middle-aged caregivers and their elderly parents. In J. I. Kosberg (Ed.), *Abuse and maltreatment of the elderly* (pp. 134–139). Littleton, MA: John Wright PSG.

Steinmetz, S. K., & Lucca, J. S. (1988). Husband battering. In V. B. Van Hasselt, R. L. Morrison, A. S. Bellack, & M. Hersen (Eds.), *Handbood of family violence* (pp. 233–246). New York: Plenum.

Stevens, L., & Rosenbaum, A. (1992). Domestic violence. In H. May (Ed.), *Emergency medicine* (pp. 1666–1671). Boston: Little, Brown.

Straus, M. A., & Gelles, R. J. (1986). Societal change and change in family violence from 1975 to 1985 as revealed by two national surveys. *Journal of Marriage and the Family, 48,* 465–479.

Straus, M. A., Gelles, R. J., & Steinmetz, S. (1980). *Behind closed doors: Violence in the American Family.* New York: Doubleday.

Taylor, S. P., & Leonard, K. E. (1983). Alcohol and human physical aggression. In R. G. Green and E. I. Donnerson (Eds.), *Aggression: theoretical and empirical reviews* (pp. 77–99). New York: Academic Press.

Telch, C. F., & Lindquist, C. V. (1984). Violent versus nonviolent couples: A comparison of patterns. *Psychotherapy, 21,* 242–248.

Walker, L. D. (1979). *The battered woman.* New York: Harper and Row.

Walker, L. D. (1984). *The battered woman syndrome.* New York: Springer.

Warnken, W., & Rosenbaum, A. (1991). *Extramarital aggression by male batterers.* Unpublished manuscript, University of Massachusetts Medical School, Worcester, MA.

Wasileski, M., Callahan-Chaffee, M. E., & Chaffee, R. B. (1982). Spousal violence in military homes. *Military Medicine, 147,* 762–765.

Wolf, R. A. (1990). Perpetrators of elder abuse. In R. T. Ammerman & M. Hersen (Eds.), *Treatment of family violence* (pp. 310–327). New York: Wiley Interscience Publications.

Wolf, R. S., Godkin, M. A., & Pillemer, K. A. (1984). *Elder abuse and neglect: A final report from three model projects.* Worcester, MA: University of Massachusetts, Center on Aging.

Wolf, R. S., & Pillemer, K. A. (1989). *Helping the elderly: The reality of elder abuse.* New York: Columbia University Press.

Wolf, R. S., Strugnell, C., & Grodkin, M. (1982). *Preliminary findings from three model projects on elderly abuse.* Worcester, MA: University of Massachusetts Medical School.

CHAPTER 27

Family Violence—Child

HONORE M. HUGHES AND JOHN W. FANTUZZO

INTRODUCTION

Aggressive and destructive behaviors are daily realities in our global community and on our city streets. We spend massive amounts of revenue on national defense, local law enforcement, and personal security to cope with these threats. Nevertheless, the most ruinous outbreak of violence is violence in the home. Outbreaks of violence in families weaken the very structure of our society by disrupting the stability of the family and undermining the well-being of our children.

For the past three decades professionals from a variety of disciplines (e.g., medicine, law, social work, and psychology) have been trying through clinical and scientific inquiry to gain a better understanding of how family violence affects children (Ammerman & Hersen, 1990). These investigations have focused on questions like: (1) What is family violence and how do we know that it has occurred? (2) How do we determine the effect that this violence has on direct (child physical abuse) and indirect (witnessing intrafamilial physical violence) child victims? (3) What should be done immediately to protect children and what actions can be taken to reduce the likelihood of subsequent traumatic events? and (4) What actions can be taken to prevent these traumatic events from ever occurring in a family?

Unfortunately, these questions have proven to be very difficult to answer. Research investigations to date have made us aware of the complexities and intricacies in this field of study and how urgently we need more precise assessment and treatment technologies. For example, although a definition of abusive events is basic to any study of violence, researchers have found it nearly impossible to obtain operational definitions of private family violence episodes. Thus, at present, we are compelled to conduct our "scientific inquiry" based on the self-report of traumatized victims or the confessions of interrogated perpetrators.

HONORE M. HUGHES • Department of Psychology, St. Louis University, St. Louis, Missouri 63103. **JOHN W. FANTUZZO** • Graduate School of Education, University of Pennsylvania, Philadelphia, Pennsylvania 19104.

Handbook of Aggressive and Destructive Behavior in Psychiatric Patients, edited by Michel Hersen, Robert T. Ammerman, and Lori A. Sisson. Plenum Press, New York, 1994.

Advanced formulations and concepts drawn from the contemporary family violence and child victimization literature emphasize the importance of a more complex, multivariate model of understanding the relationships between psychological problems evidenced by child victims, their developmental capacities, familial dysfunction, and a broader sociocultural context (Cicchetti & Carlson, 1989). This literature calls for a perspective that extends beyond a simplistic linear model, which seeks to relate *a* traumatic event to *an* observed adjustment problem of a child victim, to a recognition that these traumatic events are disruptions of the very process of family life and child development that have far-reaching consequences.

The purpose of this chapter is to review the status of our scientific study of child physical abuse and children's exposure to interparental physical aggression. This includes an examination of the (1) incidence and prevalence of these two categories of family violence, (2) theoretical models proposed to account for these types of traumatic events, (3) empirical studies documenting the psychological maladjustment associated with physical abuse and exposure to interparental violence, and (4) clinical management issues.

EPIDEMIOLOGY

Epidemiology is the study of the occurrence of a physical or mental disorder in a given population. Of particular interest is the prevalence of the disorder in the population at any given time and the rate of new occurrences during a fixed time period (e.g., annually). Epidemiological study in medicine requires precise definitions for both the pathogenic or disease process and the resulting syndrome or characteristic pattern of symptoms. In the study of the incidence and prevalence of children being victimized by physical abuse or by witnessing interparental aggression, we are doubly handicapped—we have *no* precise definitions of the manifold forms of these types of violence, and we have *no* clearly identifiable childhood syndrome (Cicchetti & Carlson, 1989). Nonetheless, at this stage of inquiry, we do have some direct and indirect tallies that provide more general indications of the number of children in the United States who are victims of family violence.

The American Association for Protecting Children, a division of the American Humane Association, has provided a nationwide annual examination of official child protective service reports of child maltreatment for over a decade. Despite some of the methodological weaknesses inherent in these reports (e.g., differential reporting criteria across the U.S., lack of reliability data), they provide a national profile of the child victims of physical abuse. The most recent data indicate that physical injury accounted for 27.6% of the over 2.1 million reports of maltreatment in 1986 (American Association for Protecting Children, 1988). The reports reveal an overrepresentation of younger child victims. This is particularly true for the most severe forms of physical maltreatment. Even though the average age of all child victims was 7.27 years in 1986, the average age for fatalities and victims of major physical injury was 2.8 and 5.54 years, respectively.

The National Center on Child Abuse and Neglect has also sponsored two national incidence surveys (NCCAN, 1981, 1988). The most recent survey indicated that over 1.5 million children were abused or neglected in the United States in 1986, with an incidence rate of 25.2 children per 1,000. The incidence rate for physically abused children was approximately 5.7 per 1,000. A comparison of surveys revealed that the rate of physical abuse increased by 58% from 1980 to 1986. According to the more recent survey (NCCAN, 1988), family data showed that children living in poverty (income less than $15,000) were significantly more likely to be physically abused than children from higher-income families. Lower-income children "suffered 3 times the fatalities, nearly 7 times the serious injuries, and more than 5.5 times the moderate injuries, and 6 times the probable injuries compared to the higher income children" (pp. 5–31).

Unfortunately, there are many children also being victimized by their exposure to widespread interparental violence. It is estimated that between three and four million children witness this type of violence each year (Jaffe, Wolfe, & Wilson, 1990). In the absence of direct tallies, data from major national surveys of spousal abuse provide the only reasonable estimates of the scope of this problem. Major national surveys indicate that about 12% of female respondents report incidents of spousal violence in the home (Strauss, Gelles, & Steinmetz, 1980). Moreover, physical violence between partners has been found to be inversely related to income and age (Strauss et al., 1980), such that young, low-income couples—those most likely to have small children—report the highest levels of physical aggression. These findings are supported by a longitudinal study of couples (O'Leary, Barling, Arias, Rosenbaum, Malone, & Tyree, 1989) showing high rates of interspousal physical aggression that were most intense during the early stages of the couples' relationships.

Although we lack precision in studying the incidence and prevalence of child victimization, these estimates indicate that an alarming number of children are direct and indirect victims of violence in the home.

ETIOLOGY

Due to the lack of precise definitions and clear syndromes associated with family violence, a straightforward discussion of etiology in the classic sense is not possible. Therefore, rather than etiology per se, several theoretical models that have been proposed to assist in understanding the different phenomena of child maltreatment are briefly discussed.

Within the last 10 years, some agreement has emerged among researchers that the conceptual formulation for the etiology of child maltreatment needs to be based on a model that is integrated and interactive, taking into account a number of dimensions, including (1) characteristics of the individual parents, (2) characteristics of the individual children, (3) family interaction patterns, (4) family "climate" (e.g., economic level, situational factors, other stresses), and (5) the social/community/cultural context (e.g., Belsky, 1980; Geffner, Rosenbaum, & Hughes, 1988; Wolfe, 1985, 1987).

In terms of an interactive model, researchers concerned with both groups of children—those who have been physically abused and those who have observed abuse—make the point that parent characteristics and family interactions plus family climate are the primary contributors to understanding the etiology of maltreatment, with child factors being secondary, though still important (e.g., Ammerman, 1990; Hansen, Conaway, & Christopher, 1990; Jaffe, Wolfe, & Wilson, 1990; Schilling, 1990).

Child Physical Abuse

While there are no specific factors by which parents who engage in different types of maltreatment can be distinguished reliably from nonmaltreating parents, some characteristics that place parents at high risk have been identified. Those variables that have been associated most strongly with physically abusive parents include very problematic child-rearing patterns and attitudes, low self-esteem, social isolation, distorted self-appraisals and attributional cognitions, skill deficits in the areas of anger and stress management, and difficulties with social problem solving (e.g., Ammerman, 1990; Kelly, 1990; Rosenberg & Repucci, 1984; Schilling, 1990).

Characteristics of children that seem to place them at higher risk for being physically abused are low birth weight or prematurity, having special needs (e.g., disability, gifted), and being of "difficult" or "intense" temperament (e.g., Ammerman, 1990). However, Ammerman (1990) stresses that little research evidence is available for the above characteristics playing a primary role, and suggests that their contribution may be manifest by exacerbating stresses for an already at-risk parent. In addition, Hansen et al. (1990) mention that there are numerous child characteristics correlated with child abuse that are assumed to be consequences of maltreatment, though they may also play a role in its occurrence (e.g., developmental delays or aggressiveness).

Two models have been proposed to explain the occurrence of physical child abuse, the "social-interactional" (Parke & Collmer, 1975; Patterson, DeBaryshe, & Ramsey, 1989) and "transitional" (Wolfe, 1987) models. In both paradigms, the interactions among a number of factors are considered to be important to their explanatory framework. With the social-interactional model, the parent–child relationship is the focus; characteristics of the parent and child, along with situational factors, contribute to explanations for the incident of child abuse. For example, parents who are deficient in good parenting skills, in combination with a defiant child, may be at high risk for abuse.

In examining the social-interactive model more closely, several specific family variables have been hypothesized to play a primary role in the development and maintenance of physical abuse; they are relevant to child aggressiveness as well. These factors include coercive family interactions (see Ammerman, 1990; Wolfe & St. Pierre, 1989) and marital discord (e.g., Jouriles, Barling, & O'Leary, 1987; Reid & Crisafulli, 1990).

Regarding coercive family interactions, one important area of skill deficit is child management abilities and disciplinary practices. It is interesting to note that the types of parenting practices used both by parents who are physically abusive (Ammerman, 1990) and by parents of boys with antisocial behavior (Patterson et al., 1989) have many similarities. Thus, it is likely that these coercive interactions are relevant not only for understanding the development of physical abusiveness on the part of the parent, but the development of children's aggressiveness as well.

According to Patterson et al. (1989), families of children who are aggressive and considered antisocial are characterized by poor monitoring and supervision of children's activities, little positive parental involvement, and harsh and inconsistent discipline. Adherents of the social-interactional perspective take the view that family members directly train children to engage in antisocial behavior. Inept parenting practices permit many coercive interactions to occur daily, with the end result that the family exists in a highly aversive social system. Children and other family members gradually escalate the intensity of coercive behavior, which often leads to hitting and physical attacks.

Similarly, Ammerman (1990) described the research on coercive interactions that have been found in physically abusive families, in which there is a strong association between the rates of children's noncompliance/oppositional behavior and parental threats or physical punishment. More punitive parenting and more anger and conflict has also been reported in abusive families. For example, Trickett and Kuczynski (1986) found that physically abusive parents used more punishment (verbal or physical) than nonabusive parents, and they used punishment as the primary type of discipline, regardless of the type of misbehavior. In addition, Youngblood and Belsky (1990) discussed the coercion model and the relationship dysfunction associated with such a pattern of interaction. One of the conclusions they drew in their review was that, among physically abusive families, there is more aversive coercive behavior among family members than in nonabusive families or in families where parents were experiencing difficulty with child management.

In terms of "family climate" variables, there are a number of factors that interact with parent–child relationships. Marital discord has been implicated as contributing to stress in the family and interfering with parenting (Vondra, 1990). Patterson et al. (1989) also point out that stressors such as unemployment, family violence, marital discord, and divorce can disrupt parenting. They emphasize the importance of considering family climate factors as well as the parent–child relationship, since in their work they have found that there is strong support for interactions among factors, with associations consistently found between stress, disrupted discipline, and antisocial behavior.

In the second prototype, the transitional model, Wolfe (1987) also includes parent and child characteristics, family interaction patterns, and family climate variables. He proposed both destabilizing (e.g., weak preparation for parenting, conditioned emotional arousal) and compensatory (e.g., improvement in child's behavior, socioeconomic stability) factors, with the presence of those two types of variables in a family's life contributing to the occurrence of abuse. His conceptualization of the relationships between the complex myriad of factors is that they are dynamic and interactive, and he views abuse as the outcome of a gradual escalation in power assertive parenting practices. Ammerman (1990) points out that while the primary mechanism for abuse in this model is also a gradual escalation in coercive parenting practices, an important aspect of the transitional model is the interaction of both protective and high-risk variables in the development of abuse.

Child Observers

Compared with child physical abuse, less is known about the etiology for child observers of spouse abuse, partially due to the fact that these victims of family violence have come to the attention of researchers and clinicians only recently. Models per se have not been proposed, though there are some hypotheses related to the mechanisms by which spouse abuse has an impact on children. Again, it seems clear that the primary causes are parental and family factors; some researchers have called child observers "unintentional" victims.

A combination of factors provides the best explanation for spouse abuse, with those variables seen as functioning interactionally. According to Geffner and Pagelow (1990), personality characteristics, marital relationships, and family interactions all play a role in the occurrence of spouse abuse, as well as cultural and social factors. These latter variables, more specifically, include gender-role stereotyping and a patriarchal value system. The authors identified the following particular risk factors for spouse abuse: (1) witnessing parental violence as a child, (2) social isolation, (3) status differences between partners, and (4) alcohol use. In addition, Rosenbaum and Maiuro (1990) add verbal skills deficits and cognitive mediators (e.g., particular types of self-talk) to the list of risk factors.

On the surface, the impact on children of observing spouse abuse seems much less apparent than the impact of being physically abused, and people do not usually think about this indirect violence as exerting a negative influence. One way to encourage a better understanding of the impact on children of observing parental violence is to conceptualize it as psychological or emotional abuse. Hart and Brassard (1990) define psychological maltreatment as "acts of omission and commission . . . which damage immediately or ultimately the behavioral, cognitive, affective, or physical functioning of the child" (p. 78). In their research, the following categories of emotionally abusive behaviors have received some preliminary research support: spurning, isolating, corrupting/exploiting, denying emotional responsiveness, and terrorizing (Hart & Brassard, 1986). Observing spouse abuse would be a specific example of the latter type of emotional abuse.

Many professionals who work with children of battered women find that another heuristic conceptualization of the family is that the children are in a situation that frequently leads to posttraumatic stress disorder (PTSD) (e.g., Jaffe, Wolfe, & Wilson, 1990). While this type of formulation is not as relevant for understanding aggressiveness, it is helpful in understanding the anxiety symptoms displayed by many observers of spouse battering.

IMPACT OF DIRECT AND INDIRECT VIOLENCE

Consequences for Children

Generally, empirical investigations of the impact of different types of child maltreatment indicate that children show a variety of responses to the abuse, including aggressiveness toward others. In keeping with the focus of this book, we examine the relationship between family violence and patterns of antisocial and aggressive behavior evidenced by child victims.

Children who have been physically abused are reported to exhibit a variety of symptoms, including problems with cognitive impairment, school adjustment and academic performance, self-esteem, and attachment behavior, as well as difficulties in social skills and social competence (see Ammerman, Cassisi, Hersen, & Van Hasselt, 1986; Conaway & Hansen, 1989; Lamphear, 1985). While mixed evidence for difficulties in the foregoing areas has been provided, the most substantial empirical support has been obtained for problems with aggression (e.g., Conaway & Hansen, 1989). Amounts of aggression that are beyond those of age peers have been found across childhood in a number of studies (Youngblood & Belsky, 1990). For example, maltreated toddlers were found to be more aggressive than peers (Main & George, 1985), and physically abused school-age children were also more aggressive than their age-mates (Kaufman & Cicchetti, 1989).

Observing parental violence has also been found to be detrimental to the adjustment of children. An increased number of descriptions of the behaviors and adjustment of child observers of spouse abuse have become available recently, and overall, children of battered women seem to exhibit high levels of both internalizing and externalizing behaviors (Fantuzzo & Lindquist, 1989; Fantuzzo, DePaola, Lambert, Martino, Anderson, & Sutton, 1991; Hughes, Parkinson, & Vargo, 1989). Consistent differences between observers and comparison children in anxious or depressed behaviors have been found, with some, though less consistent, differences seen in aggressive/disobedient behaviors (Hughes et al., 1989).

Findings regarding externalizing behaviors are equivocal, with Brown, Pelcovitz, and Kaplan (1983) and Hershorn and Rosenbaum (1985) noting differences between their observer and comparison children, while Kraft, Sullivan-Hanson, Christopoulos, Cohn, and Emery (1984) and Wolfe, Zak, Wilson, and Jaffe (1986) found no differences. One reason for the inconsistency in results is that the latter finding of no significant differences between child observers and comparison children seemed to be the result of the low-income comparison children also receiving elevated externalizing scores, rather than observers having low scores.

One indication of the "extent" of impact of spouse abuse on children is the proportion of children out of the entire sample of child observers who receive behavior problem scores that are above a level indicating a need for clinical services. In the studies in which extent has been examined, the percentage of children above that clinical cutoff ranges from 28% to 65%, depending on the age and gender of the children (Christopoulos et al., 1987; Hughes, Vargo, Ito, & Skinner, 1991; Wolfe, Jaffe, Wilson, & Zak, 1985). While all of these results need to be viewed with caution since they could be influenced in some way by the distress of the mother who provided the ratings, they do indicate that a substantial number of child observers are negatively affected by being exposed to spouse abuse.

More specifically related to aggressiveness, several researchers have provided evidence for an association between observing parental violence and engaging in aggressive behaviors against others. For example, Moore, Peplar, Weinberg, Hammond, Waddell, and Weiser (1990) found that mothers in violent, spouse abusive homes reported more extreme forms of physical aggression between siblings than mothers from nonviolent homes. For boys, more prolonged exposure to parental violence was associated with higher levels of intersibling aggression. Moreover, Carlson (1990) studied adolescent observers of marital violence and reported similar results. Over half of the observer females in her sample had hit their mothers, while 20% of the boys had done so. Boys who observed violence were more than twice as likely to have hit their mothers than nonobservers. As for hitting fathers, 40% of boys and 25% of girls who had been exposed to spouse abuse reported this. For both boys and girls, observers were twice as likely to have hit their fathers than nonobservers.

Since the co-occurrence of different types of family violence is high, observers are also at risk for physical abuse. The overlap among types of violence, especially between spouse abuse and child physical abuse, is about 40% to 60% (Forsttrom-Cohen & Rosenbaum, 1985; Rosenbaum & O'Leary, 1981; Straus, Gelles, & Steinmetz, 1980). Research suggests that while the behavioral/emotional impact on children of observing violence is very similar to that of experiencing physical abuse, there are indications that the impact of both observing spouse abuse and experiencing physical abuse is even greater (Hughes et al. 1989, 1991).

In one study in which both types of family violence were investigated, Jaffe, Wolfe, Wilson, and Zak (1986) compared three groups of boys (those who had observed parental violence, those who had been physically abused, and a comparison group) in order to examine the repercussions of exposure to the two types of violence. For externalizing behaviors, they found that the two groups who had been exposed to violence received significantly higher scores than the comparison group; in addition, the abused boys received significantly higher scores than the observer group. However, these findings are difficult to interpret, since the authors acknowledged that in the two violence-exposure groups, there was a strong possibility that some of the abused boys had observed spouse abuse, and some of the observer boys may have been physically abused as well.

To investigate more closely the impact of different types of family violence, Hughes and her colleagues examined the "double-whammy" hypothesis, whereby children who are exposed to more than one type of violence (i.e., both spouse abuse and physical maltreatment) show greater levels of behavioral difficulty. In the first study (Hughes, 1988), the Eyberg Child Behavior Inventory (ECBI) was used. Using this measure of conduct-disorder type problems, Hughes found that the abused/observer children did indeed receive significantly higher problem scores than comparison or observer youngsters. In addition, age played a role in the pattern of results, with the youngest (3–5 years) and middle (6–8 years) abused/observer children receiving the highest scores.

Hughes et al. (1989) also investigated the double-whammy notion, using the Child Behavior Checklist as the measure of problems. They found that on Total Behavior Problems, the abused/observer children were significantly different from the other two groups, and the observer children's scores were also significantly higher than the comparison group's. In addition, on externalizing-type problems, the abused/observer children were significantly different from the comparison group, with the observer children in the middle. While the proportion of children above the clinical cutoff was not investigated in that study, one indication of the extent of the behavioral difficulties is the level of the mean scores. On both the total behavior problem and the externalizing scores, the average score was right at the cutoff indicating clinically problematic difficulties (t score $m = 63$, $SD = 9.5$; $M = 65$, $SD = 10$, for Total Behavior Problems and Externalizing scales, respectively).

VARIABLES MEDIATING THE IMPACT ON CHILDREN

Child Physical Abuse

A number of variables that might influence the impact of abuse upon the child have been proposed, and can be grouped generally into child factors and situational/contextual variables. In terms of the former, as previously stated, low birth weight or prematurity, having special needs (e.g., disability, gifted), and being of difficult or intense temperament (e.g., Ammerman, 1990) have been identified as important factors. In addition, Ammerman and Hersen (1990) stressed that the biopsychological status of the child, including genetic factors, learning history, and ecological influences, must also be considered.

In terms of situational/contextual variables, characteristics of the abuse plus other mediating variables play a role in the impact on children that is seen. Ammerman and Hersen (1990) emphasized that the characteristics of the actual physical abuse—type of assault, severity, frequency, age at onset, length of maltreatment—influence the adjustment of the child. Mediating variables that play an influential role include the amount of stress the child and family experience in addition to the abuse, as well as factors relating to family climate. These latter variables include the quality of parent–child relationships and the parents' disciplinary practices. These mediating factors need to be examined in a way that allows for the interaction between the child and situational variables.

Child Observers of Spouse Abuse

Mediating variables for child observers can also be separated into child factors and situational/contextual variables. In terms of the former, temperament, self-esteem, cognitive abilities, gender, attributional style, coping abilities, and age all are child factors that play a role in the impact on the child (e.g., Grych & Fincham, 1990; Moore et al., 1990). Grych and Fincham discuss age with regard to the developmental implications for children's understanding of conflict between parents, and develop a framework for understanding the impact of marital conflict on children. In terms of the situational/contextual variables, the authors subdivide them further into (1) distal and proximal variables (i.e., more stable and less stable) related to the child, and (2) marital conflict factors. Included in the distal category are such factors as past experience with conflict and the perceived emotional climate of the family. Marital conflict variables involve factors such as frequency, intensity, content, resolution, whether overt or covert, age of child at onset, and length of time the violence has been occurring.

Mechanisms by Which Marital Conflict Impacts Children

Grych and Fincham (1990) also proposed a conceptual model for mechanisms by which the conflict produces consequences for children, including those that are direct and indirect. Direct sources of influence consist of modeling and stress, while indirect influences include changes in the parent–child relationship and parental disciplinary practices. As a direct source of influence, the modeling hypothesis is especially relevant for the development of aggressive behavior. Not only do children learn to be aggressive by watching others act in that fashion, but there is a "disinhibitory" impact, too, in that watching someone else be aggressive gives one permission also to be aggressive. Since children are more likely to imitate a model they view as powerful and successful in achieving goals (Bandura, 1973; Pagelow, 1984), modeling in the case of spouse abuse can be especially salient.

Related to stress as a direct source of influence, physically violent marital conflict definitely functions as a major stressor. It needs to be conceptualized as emotional abuse, with the understanding that the conflict can produce difficulties of various types, including symptoms of posttraumatic stress disorder. Marital conflict is very disruptive to children's lives, in terms of it being very unpredictable in occurrence and in its effect on their mothers. In addition, in some cases, the disruption in youngsters' lives is even greater when mothers decide to seek refuge with family members, friends, or a shelter for battered women, since their lives change totally and unpredictably.

In terms of the proposed indirect mechanisms by which marital conflict influences children's functioning, both relate to the quality of the parenting present in the particular family, including (1) characteristics of parent–child interactions and/or changes in the relationship, and (2) the form of disciplinary practices. Depending on the parameters of spouse abuse and the mental health of the parents, they may or may not be able to function effectively in their parental role. Some mothers may be able to continue nurturing their children even if they are abused. However, many battered women are depressed (e.g., Hughes & Rau, 1984), and research indicates that children of depressed women are at risk for adjustment difficulties (Jaenicke, Hammen, Zupan, Hiroto, Gordon, Adrian, & Burge, 1987; Lee & Gotlieb, 1989).

For child observers, mediating variables have been examined empirically in only a very preliminary way, and most relate to the child victims' age and gender. In terms of age, evidence is equivocal, since rarely are children divided by developmental level when results are analyzed. Hughes (1988) found that the youngest group of children (preschool age) were functioning the most poorly, while Hughes et al. (1989), using a different behavioral problem measure, found the middle group of children (ages 6–8) to be having the most difficulty, according to their mothers.

Evidence for differences by gender is mixed. Some researchers find no differences between boys and girls, while others do, with results that depend on the ways data are analyzed and the comparison samples used. When the mean behavior problem scores of children of battered women are investigated, boys and girls both in and out of shelters receive scores that are high (at least 1 SD above the mean), with no differences seen between them (Christopoulos et al., 1987; Hughes et al., 1989, 1991; Jaffe et al., 1986; Jouriles, Barling, & O'Leary, 1987; Wolfe et al., 1986).

However, it is interesting that when adjustment is examined in terms of the percentage of children who receive ratings that are at or above a certain score indicating need for clinical intervention (upper 2–10% of the standardization sample), differences are noted. Wolfe et al. (1985) found on total behavior problem scores that when a cutoff score of $t > 70$ is used, 34% of boys and 20% of girls have scores above that level (16% of boys and 23% of girls in the comparison group were above the cutoff). However, Christopoulos et al. (1987) reported that more girls received scores above the cutoff, with 36% of girls and 28% of boys above that level on externalizing behaviors. Several other researchers have also found more girls to be above the cutoffs, with Moore and Peplar (1989) reporting three times as many girls as boys within the clinical range on internalizing and externalizing problems.

Hughes et al. (1989, 1991) also found that more girls were above the clinical level, using a cutoff of t score > 65. In addition, they examined the impact of physical abuse on the child, and found that there was a cumulative impact as children were exposed to more types of violence, although the influence interacted with gender. In a study investigating the proportion of observer and abused/observer children who were considered to be within the clinically problematic range of behavioral difficulties, for Externalizing, 29% and 57% of the observer and abused/observer boys, respectively, were above the cutoff, while 35% of the girls in both groups were above the cutoff. On Total Problems, a greater proportion of girls were found to have difficulties within the clinical range (45% and 65% of girls vs. 30% and 43% of boys, observer and abused/observer, respectively).

In terms of the proposed indirect mechanisms by which spouse abuse can influence children's adjustment, neither parent–child interactions nor disciplinary practices have been examined directly. However, Wolfe, Jaffe, Wilson, and Zak (1985) investigated the extent to which shelter mothers' physical and mental health influenced children's adjustment. They found that maternal stress variables predicted child adjustment better than physical violence between parents, and suggested that the impact on the child of observing spouse abuse may be partially a function of the mother's impairment following specific events, such as being beaten, as well as the accompanying disruption and uncertainty in the family. A mother's impairment could likely include depression, which, if severe enough, may lead to changes in a mother's interactions with her children and in her disciplinary practices.

Fantuzzo et al. (1991) found that temporary shelter residence was associated with a more serious set of emotional and social disturbances for child observers. A comparison between children living at home and children in temporary shelter residence who were exposed to the same levels of interparental violence indicated that shelter residence was associated with significantly higher levels of emotional problems and lower levels of social functioning and perceived maternal acceptance. These findings support a cumulative stress hypothesis (Rutter, 1980) that "more stressors lead to greater child distress" and that these stressors affect the social competencies of preschool children.

CLINICAL MANAGEMENT

In assessment and intervention with any type of family violence, it is essential that clinicians always ask about other types of violence when one kind of family violence is encountered, since, as stated above, the co-occurrence of different types of family violence is quite common. It has become clear recently that family violence is more prevalent than anyone had imagined, and it is very likely that clinicians will come into contact with violent families, even if violence is not mentioned initially as part of the presenting problem.

Problems abound in the empirical research in this area, with a real paucity of research available related to the most effective types of treatment for the two types of child-related family violence. While some sparse evidence exists for the efficacy of intervention for the perpetrators of child physical abuse, this discussion is limited to intervention directly related to the child (see Kelly, 1990, Schilling, 1990, and Walker et al., 1988, for reviews of interventions with perpetrators). Generally, to guide their interventions, clinicians have focused on the "impact issues" (i.e., consequences) for children of each type of maltreatment.

For child physical abuse, the consequences have been enumerated in the foregoing section, and include problems with cognitive impairment, school adjustment and academic performance, self-esteem, and attachment behavior, as well as difficulties in social skills and social competence. A major difficulty for abused children, as well as a primary concern clinically, is the heightened level of aggressiveness often seen. For intervention with aggressiveness, empirical support has been obtained for the efficacy of training older children and adolescents on an individual basis in problem-solving skills (e.g., Kazdin, Esveldt-Dawson, French, & Unis, 1987) and anger control (Feindler & Ecton, 1986). While these have been shown to reduce aggressiveness among youngsters in a number of different populations, thus far those techniques have not been evaluated specifically in abused children (Hansen et al., 1990; Mannarino & Cohen, 1990). However, given the similarities among the children involved, extrapolating from the studies in which effectiveness has been demonstrated seems to be quite reasonable.

Fantuzzo and his associates have demonstrated the effectiveness of an intervention strategy aimed at increasing the positive play interactions of preschool child victims of abuse (Fantuzzo, 1990). This strategy was designed to be implemented in regular preschool settings and to harness the therapeutic benefit of playing with resilient peers—children who come from the same environment as child victims but who display high levels of positive play with children and adults. This research has indicated that resilient preschool children can, with training, become useful friends to and models for nonresilient, abused preschool children, resulting in significant improvements in prosocial behavior (Fantuzzo & Holland, 1992).

Regarding child observers, no systematic investigations of the effectiveness of various treatment approaches for these children are available, though two studies present some information regarding efficacy. Jaffe, Wolfe, and Wilson (1990) and Grusznski, Brink, and Edleson (1988) both conducted evaluations of their group interventions with children in shelters. Their results were encouraging, though no comparison groups were included.

While aggressive behavior has most specifically been associated with physically abused children, as previously discussed, research indicates that youngsters who experience indirect maltreatment through observing violence also occasionally exhibit aggressiveness. Kazdin (1987, 1991) offers guidelines for treating aggressive and/or antisocial children.

To briefly summarize those resources, Kazdin (1991) points out that treatment methods depend on the age of the child and severity of aggressive behavior, with the most evidence for success achieved with treatment of younger children with oppositional or noncompliant behaviors. Options for intervention include parent management training (especially for younger children), and, for older children, anger management and the development of prosocial skills, such as social perspective-taking or empathy training. Functional family therapy (Alexander & Parsons, 1982) is also recommended for work with the entire family.

Regarding interventions for child observers, focusing on the impact issues would include addressing both externalizing and internalizing behavior, as well as social competence and social problem solving. Rosenberg and Rossman (1990) discuss the pros and cons of individual and family treatment for child observers, and basically recommend either individual or group interventions for these children. They also include helpful guidance for addressing issues related to parent–child relationships and parenting practices. (For readers who are interested in more detail than it is possible to include here, see Jaffe et al., 1990, and Rosenberg and Rossman, 1990, for more information about assessment and intervention issues.)

CASE ILLUSTRATION

To assist readers with understanding the impact of family violence upon children and seeing the above-mentioned factors operating together, a detailed case example follows. The names and identifying information have been changed to protect the confidentiality of family members. Keep in mind the direct mechanisms of modeling and stress, plus the indirect mechanisms of parent–child interactions and disciplinary practices, when considering the negative impact for the child in this case.

One theoretical formulation related to the direct factor of stress that helps guide the assessment and intervention with families in these circumstances is Rutter's (1978, 1980) notion of "cumulative stressors." Rutter reported a dramatic increase in the probability of children developing behavioral disorders as a function of the number of serious family stressors that they encountered. He identified six significant family stressors: (1) father having unskilled/semi-skilled job, (2) overcrowding or large family size, (3) mother experiencing depression or a neurotic disorder, (4) child ever having been "in care of the local Authority" (i.e., been reported for physical abuse), (5) conviction of father for any criminal offense, and (6) marital discord. Rutter (1978) found that any one of these family stressors occurring in isolation will not substantially increase the likelihood that a child will have adjustment problems, but when two or more of these stressors interact, the chances are two to four times as great that a child will develop emotional/behavioral difficulties.

J. is a 14-year-old white male who was brought to the clinic by his mother, C., with the presenting problems of having been expelled from school several times for behavior problems, including aggressiveness; recently he was in minor trouble with the law, being with a group of boys who had been caught stealing. His mother also felt that J. might be depressed, and was seeking treatment for him.

There were eight people in the family, J., his mother, C., age 32, his father, D., age 35, and five siblings, one older (an 18-year-old sister, who has a 1-year-old child and who no longer lives with the family) and four younger siblings, aged 8, 7, 4, and 1. The father makes about $20,000 a year, and C. was not employed outside the home at the time of the assessment. The family situation was a chaotic one, with frequent moves and other family difficulties. In order to deal with J.'s behavioral difficulties in school, the family had moved five times in the last 4 years. However, J. continued to experience problems in all of the schools, and was expelled from each.

C. reported that her husband occasionally physically abused her in front of the children; in addition, he also used to physically abuse the children. She "put a stop to that" when she moved out for 3 months with the children. He has not physically abused any family member since she returned to the home, although he continues to be verbally and emotionally abusive. Currently, C.'s husband is home every other weekend, and when he is there, he yells at the children frequently, expecting to be "waited on hand and foot." During the time the father is away from home due to his employment, the children receive little discipline from their mother. For example, when J. does not feel like attending school, C. does nothing to see that he goes to school, and disciplines him by talking with him if he has verbal fights with his younger siblings.

C. seemed to be quite stressed, and an independent evaluation was recommended for her, to which she agreed. The results of the assessment indicated that she was feeling depressed and overwhelmed, as well as confused and socially isolated. She appeared to be very ambivalent regarding treatment for herself, stating that she had previously consulted a physician for her difficulties. However, when the clinician wanted to recommend an antidepressant, she refused to take it. C. missed and rescheduled appointments repeatedly, and it took the clinician who conducted the assessment approximately 2 months to finally meet with C. to provide feedback from the evaluation. At that time C. stated that she had obtained employment, and would not be returning for services.

C. seemed to be better able to bring J. in for his evaluation appointments, and they were regular in their attendance. J. was a very quiet adolescent, with whom the clinician felt it was difficult to establish rapport. Results of the evaluation indicated that he was experiencing a substantial amount of stress, and was also feeling quite depressed and isolated. His aggressive outbursts at school seemed to be related to a buildup of feelings of frustration on the part of J. that he was not getting his emotional needs met, and a little incident could be the trigger for an outburst.

Between the time of feedback from the assessment at the end of December, and the attempts in January to begin treatment, J. had been suspended from school, and was in danger of being expelled. A number of attempts were made to set up appointments, but each time the family called to cancel. In March, the clinician spoke with J. about whether he wanted to attend therapy, and he said he did, even though his mother said he did not. The plan to work on anger control was explained to J., who seemed reasonably enthusiastic about it. However, four appointments in a row were canceled due to several family crises or illnesses. When C. obtained a job, it was even more difficult to schedule appointments due to her work schedule, and the family ultimately did not follow through on the recommendation for treatment.

The above case illustrates many of the typical factors involved in dealing with children of battered women in a mental health setting, and reflects the difficulties with intervening in a traditional sense in a crisis-oriented, multiproblem family. From this description one is able to see in operation the direct mechanisms of modeling of aggression and of cumulative stressors, plus the indirect processes of negative parent–child interactions and ineffective disciplinary practices.

SUMMARY

Little debate exists among professionals that the trauma of severe family violence is associated with disturbed social functioning in child victims. However, much more research is needed to delineate specific pathogenic processes and to identify innovative and practical ways to respond to this troublesome set of social problems. Given the empirical knowledge base to date, the design, implementation, and evaluation of a strategic assessment and treatment plan for child victims should be guided by three important considerations. First, clinicians should attend carefully to developmental factors and place a high priority on improving the social effectiveness of both parents and young victims, that is, providing parents and children with skills that will allow them to access resources from peers in their community. Second, clinicians should recognize the multiple problems and minimal resources of these troubled families and consider the need for more *practical* and *acceptable* service delivery systems. It would be a significant manifestation of professional neglect to recommend strategies for parents and child victims without adequate consideration of their total family needs and environmental realities. Specific treatment programs should be developed in the context of culturally relevant, community-based outreach to engage socially isolated families and keep them in a therapeutic process. Third, clinicians should include a careful assessment of parent and child *strengths*. An exclusive emphasis on family deficits disempowers the family and alienates them from service providers. Family strengths and indigenous community resources are an tremendous source of untapped potential for families suffering from family violence.

Determining the nature and extent of how family violence harmfully affects the psychological functioning of children and trying to treat and prevent these consequences is a critical need and an enormously perplexing task. The purpose of this chapter was to provide a brief overview for clinicians and researchers interested in this challenging area. We have focused on a number of aspects of this problem area to acquaint the reader with the numerous clinical and research issues related to child victimization.

REFERENCES

Alexander, J., & Parsons, B. V. (1982). *Functional family therapy*. Monterey, CA: Brooks/Cole.

American Association for Protecting Children (1988). *Highlights of official child neglect and abuse reporting 1986*. Denver: American Humane Association.

Ammerman, R. T. (1990). Predisposing child factors. In R. T. Ammerman & M. Hersen (Eds.), *Children at risk: An evaluation of factors contributing to child abuse and neglect* (pp. 199–224). New York: Plenum.

Ammerman, R. T., & Hersen, M. (1990). Research in child abuse and neglect: Current status and an agenda for the future. In R. T. Ammerman & M. Hersen (Eds.), *Children at risk: An evaluation of factors contributing to child abuse and neglect* (pp. 3–19). New York: Plenum.

Ammerman, R. T., Cassisi, J. E., Hersen, M., & Van Hasselt, V. B. (1986). Consequences of physical abuse and neglect in children. *Clinical Psychology Review, 6*, 291–310.

Bandura, A. (1973). *Aggression: A social learning analysis*. Englewood Cliffs, NJ: Prentice-Hall.

Belsky, J. (1980). Child maltreatment: An ecological integration. *American Psychologist, 35*, 320–335.

Brown, A. J., Pelcovitz, D., & Kaplan, S. (1983, August). *Child witnesses of family violence: A study of psychological correlates*. Paper presented at the annual meeting of the American Psychological Association, Anaheim, CA.

Carlson, B. E. (1990). Adolescent observers of marital violence. *Journal of Family Violence, 5*, 285–299.

Christopoulos, C., Cohn, D. A., Shaw, D. S., Joyce, S., Sullivan-Hanson, J., Kraft, S. P., & Emery, R. E. (1987). Children of abused women: I. Adjustment at time of shelter residence. *Journal of Marriage and the Family, 49*, 611–619.

Cicchetti, D., & Carlson, V. (Eds.). (1989). *Child maltreatment: Theory and research on the causes and consequences of child abuse and neglect*. New York: Cambridge University Press.

Conaway, L. P., & Hansen, D. J. (1989). Social behavior of physically abused and neglected children: A critical review with implications for research and intervention. *Clinical Psychology Review, 9*, 627–652.

Fantuzzo, J. W. (1990). Behavioral treatment of victims of child abuse and neglect. *Behavior Modification*, *14*, 316–340.

Fantuzzo, J. W., & Holland, A. (1992). Resilient peer training: Systematic investigation of treatment to improve the social effectiveness of child victims of maltreatment. In A. W. Burgess (Ed.), *Child abuse research handbook* (pp. 275–292). New York: Garland.

Fantuzzo, J. W., & Lindquist, C. U. (1989). The effects of observing conjugal violence on children: A review and analysis of research methodology. *Journal of Family Violence*, *4*, 77–94.

Fantuzzo, J. W., DePaola, L. M., Lambert, L., Martino, T., Anderson, G., & Sutton, S. (1991). Effects of interpersonal violence on the psychological adjustment and competencies of young children. *Journal of Consulting and Clinical Psychology*, *59*, 258–265.

Feindler, E. L., & Ecton, R. B. (1986). *Adolescent anger control: Cognitive behavioral techniques*. Elmsford, NJ: Pergamon.

Forsttrom-Cohen, B., & Rosenbaum, A. (1985). The effects of parental marital violence on young adults: An exploratory investigation. *Journal of Marriage and the Family*, *47*, 467–472.

Geffner, R., & Pagelow, M. D. (1990). Victims of spouse abuse. In R. T. Ammerman & M. Hersen (Eds.), *Treatment of family violence* (pp. 113–135). New York: Wiley.

Geffner, R., Rosenbaum, A., & Hughes, H. M. (1988). Research issues concerning family violence. In V. B. Van Hasselt, R. L. Morrison, A. S. Bellack, & M. Hersen (Eds.), *Handbook of family violence* (pp. 457–481). New York: Plenum.

Grusznski, R. J., Brink J. C., & Edelson, J. L. (1988). Support and education groups for children of battered women. *Child Welfare*, *67*, 431–444.

Grych, J. H., & Fincham, F. D. (1990). Marital conflict and children's adjustment: A cognitive-contextual framework *Psychological Bulletin*, *108*, 267–290.

Hansen, D. J., Conaway, L. P., & Christopher, J. S. (1990). Victims of child physical abuse. In R. T. Ammerman & M. Hersen (Eds.), *Treatment of family violence* (pp. 17–49). New York: Wiley.

Hart, S. N., & Brassard, M. R. (1987). Psychological maltreatment: Integration and summary. In M. R. Brassard, R. Germain, & S. N. Hart (Eds.), *Psychological maltreatment of children and youth* (pp. 254–266). New York: Pergamon.

Hart, S. N., & Brassard, M. R. (1990). Psychological maltreatment of children. In R. T. Ammerman & M. Hersen (Eds.), *Treatment of family violence* (pp. 22–112). New York: Wiley.

Hershorn, M., & Rosenbaum, A. (1985). Children of marital violence: A closer look at the unintended victims. *American Journal of Orthopsychiatry*, *55*, 260–266.

Hughes, H. M. (1988). Psychological and behavioral correlates of family violence in child witnesses and victims. *American Journal of Orthopsychiatry*, *58*, 77–90.

Hughes, H. M., & Rau, T. J. (1984, August). *Psychological adjustment of battered women in shelters*. Paper presented at the annual meeting of the American Psychological Association, Toronto.

Hughes, H. M., Parkinson, D. L., & Vargo, M. C. (1989). Witnessing spouse abuse and experiencing physical abuse: A "double whammy"? *Journal of Family Violence*, *4*, 197–209.

Hughes, H. M., Vargo, M. C., Ito, E. S., & Skinner, S. K. (1991). Psychological adjustment of children of battered women: Influences of gender. *Family Violence Bulletin*, *7*, 15–17.

Jaenicke, C., Hammen, C., Zupan, B., Hiroto, Gordon, D., Adrian, C, & Burge, D. (1987). Cognitive vulnerability in children at risk for depression. *Journal of Abnormal Child Psychology*, *15*, 559–572.

Jaffe, P. G., Wolfe, D. A., & Wilson, S. K. (1990). *Children of battered women*. Newbury Park, CA: Sage.

Jaffe, P. G., Wolfe, D. A., Wilson, S. K., & Zak, L. (1986). Family violence and child adjustment: A comparative analysis of girls' and boys' symptoms. *American Journal of Psychiatry*, *143*, 74–77.

Jouriles, E. N., Barling, J., & O'Leary, K. D. (1987). Predicting child behavior problems in maritally violent families. *Journal of Abnormal Child Psychology*, *15*, 165–173.

Kaufman, J., & Cicchetti, D. (1989). The effects of maltreatment on school-aged children's socioemotional development: A study in a day camp setting. *Developmental Psychology*, *25*, 516–524.

Kazdin, A. E. (1987). *Conduct disorders in children and adolescents*. Newbury Park, CA: Sage.

Kazdin, A. E. (1991). Aggressive behavior and conduct disorder. In T. R. Kratochwill & R. J. Morrison (Eds.), *The practice of child psychotherapy* (pp. 174–221). Elmsford, NJ: Pergamon.

Kazdin, A. E., Esveldt-Dawson, K., French, N. H., & Unis, A. S. (1987). Problem-solving skills and relationship therapy in the treatment of antisocial child behavior. *Journal of Consulting and Clinical Psychology*, *55*, 76–85.

Kelly, J. A. (1990). Treating the child abuser. In R. T. Ammerman & M. Hersen (Eds.), *Children at risk: An evaluation of factors contributing to child abuse and neglect* (pp. 269–287). New York: Plenum.

Kraft, S. P., Sullivan-Hanson, J., Christopoulos, C., Cohn, D. A., & Emery, R. E. (1984, August). *Spouse abuse: Its impact on children's psychological adjustment*. Paper presented at the annual meeting of the American Psychological Association, Toronto.

Lamphear, V. S. (1985). The impact of maltreatment on children's psychosocial adjustment: A review of the research. *Child Abuse & Neglect, 9,* 251–263.

Lee, C. M., & Gotlieb, I. H. (1989). Maternal depression and child adjustment: A longitudinal analysis. *Journal of Abnormal Psychology, 98,* 78–85.

Main, M., & George, C. (1985). Responses of abused and disadvantaged toddlers to distress of age-mates: A study in a day care setting. *Developmental Psychology, 21,* 407–412.

Mannarino, A. R., & Cohen, J. A. (1990). Treating the abused child. In R. T. Ammerman & M. Hersen (Eds.), *Children at risk: An evaluation of factors contributing to child abuse and neglect* (pp. 249–268). New York: Plenum.

Moore, T., & Peplar, D. (1989, August). *The impact of domestic violence on children's adjustment: Exploring the linkage*. Paper presented at the annual meeting of the American Psychological Association, New Orleans.

Moore, T., Pepler, D., Weinberg, B., Hammond, L., Waddell, J., & Weiser, L. (1990). Research on children from violent families. *Canada's Mental Health Journal, 38,* 19–23.

National Center on Child Abuse and Neglect. (1981). *Study findings: National study of the incidence and severity of child abuse and neglect* (DHHS Publication No. OHDS 81-30325). Washington, DC: U.S. Government Printing Office.

National Center on Child Abuse and Neglect. (1988). *Study findings: Study of national incidence and prevalence of child abuse and neglect: 1988* (DHHS Publication No. OHDS 20-01099). Washington, DC: Author.

O'Leary, K. D., Barling, J., Arias, I., Rosenbaum, A., Malone, J., & Tyree, A. (1989). Prevalence and stability of physical aggression between spouses: A longitudinal analysis. *Journal of Consulting and Clinical Psychology, 57,* 263–268.

Pagelow, M. D. (1984). *Family violence*. New York: Praeger.

Parke, R., & Colmer, C. (1975). Child abuse: An interdisciplinary review. In E. M. Hetherington (Ed.), *Review of child development research* (Vol. 5, pp. 509–590). Chicago: University of Chicago Press.

Patterson, G. R., De Baryshe, B. D., & Ramsey, E. (1989). A developmental perspective on antisocial behavior. *American Psychologist, 44,* 329–335.

Reid, W. J., & Crisifelli, A. (1990). Marital discord and child behavior problems: A meta-analysis. *Journal of Abnormal Child Psychology, 18,* 105–118.

Rosenbaum, A., & Mauiro, R. D. (1990). Perpetrators of spouse abuse. In R. T. Ammerman & M. Hersen (Eds.), *Treatment of family violence* (pp. 280–309). NY: Wiley.

Rosenbaum, A., & O'Leary, K. D. (1981). Children: The unintended victims of marital violence. *American Journal of Orthopsychiatry, 51,* 692–699.

Rosenberg, M. S., & Repucci, N. D. (1984). Abusive mothers: Perceptions of their own and their children's behavior. *Journal of Consulting and Clinical Psychology, 51,* 674–682.

Rosenberg, M. S., & Rossman, B. B. R. (1990). The child witness to marital violence. In R. T. Ammerman & M. Hersen (Eds.), *Treatment of family violence* (pp. 183–210). New York: Wiley.

Rutter, M. (1978). Family, area, and school influences in the genesis of conduct disorders. In L. A. Hersov & D. Schaffer (Eds.), *Aggression and antisocial behavior in childhood and adolescence* (pp. 95–114). Oxford: Pergamon.

Rutter, M. (1980). Protective factors in children's responses to stress and disadvantage. In M. W. Kent & J. E. Rolf (Eds.), *Primary prevention of psychopathology: Vol. 3. Promoting social competence and coping in children* (pp. 49–74). Hanover, NH: University Press of New England.

Schilling, R. F. (1990). Perpetrators of child physical abuse. In R. T. Ammerman & M. Hersen (Eds.), *Treatment of family violence* (pp. 243–265). NY: Wiley.

Straus, M. A., Gelles, R. J., & Steinmetz, S. K. (1980). *Behind closed doors: Violence in the American family*. New York: Doubleday.

Trickett, P. K., & Kuczynski, L. (1986). Children's misbehaviors and parental discipline strategies in abusive and nonabusive families. *Developmental Psychology, 22,* 115–123.

Vondra, J. T. (1990). Sociological and ecological factors. In R. T. Ammerman & M. Hersen (Eds.), *Children at risk: An evaluation of factors contributing to child abuse and neglect* (pp. 149–170). New York: Plenum.

Walker, C. E., Bonner, B. L., & Kaufman, K. L. (1988). *The physically and sexually abused child*. New York: Pergamon.

Wolfe, D. A. (1985). Child abusive parents: An empirical review and analysis. *Psychological Bulletin, 97,* 462–482.

Wolfe, D. A. (1987). *Child abuse: Implications for child development and psychopathology*. Newbury Park, CA: Sage.

Wolfe, D. A., Zak, L., Wilson, S., & Jaffe, P. (1986). Child witnesses to violence between parents: Critical issues in behavioral and social adjustment. *Journal of Abnormal Child Psychology, 14*, 95–104.

Wolfe, D. A., Jaffe, P., Wilson, S., & Zak, L. (1985). Children of battered women: The relationship of child behavior to family violence and maternal stress. *Journal of Consulting and Clinical Psychology, 53*, 657–665.

CHAPTER 28

Serial Murder

ANN W. BURGESS, ROBERT A. PRENTKY, ALLEN G. BURGESS,
JOHN E. DOUGLAS, AND ROBERT K. RESSLER

DESCRIPTION OF THE DISORDER

Murder is the unlawful taking of human life. It is a behavioral act that terminates life in the context of power, personal gain, brutality, and sometimes sexuality. Murder is a sub-category of homicide, which also includes lawful taking of human life (e.g., manslaughter, deaths resulting from criminal and noncriminal negligence, and unpremeditated vehicular deaths; Megargee, 1982). Although we note that a distinction is made in the literature between homicide and murder, for the purpose of this chapter, the terms are used interchangeably.

This chapter surveys the literature on clinical and empirical attempts to reduce the heterogeneity of murderers through the creation of taxonomic systems. We also present the findings of an FBI study of 36 sexual murderers, the majority of whom were serial killers, and a case from the study.

EVOLUTION OF SYSTEMS FOR CLASSIFICATION OF MURDER

There are three principal conceptual and theoretical approaches to the classification of murder: (1) psychiatric and psychoanalytic, (2) sociocriminological, and (3) law enforcement/investigative.

ANN W. BURGESS • University of Pennsylvania School of Nursing, Philadelphia, Pennsylvania 19104.
ROBERT A. PRENTKY • Joseph J. Peters Institute, Philadelphia, Pennsylvania 19101.   ALLEN G.
BURGESS • College of Business Administration, Northeastern University, Boston, Massachusetts 02115.
JOHN E. DOUGLAS • Investigative Support Unit, Federal Bureau of Investigation Academy, Quantico,
Virginia 22135.   ROBERT K. RESSLER • Forensic Behavioral Sciences, Spotsylvania, Virginia 22553.

Handbook of Aggressive and Destructive Behavior in Psychiatric Patients, edited by Michel Hersen, Robert T.
Ammerman, and Lori A. Sisson. Plenum Press, New York, 1994.

Psychiatric/Psychoanalytic

The psychiatric/psychoanalytic approach clearly has the longest pedigree, extending back at least three decades to the classification systems of Abrahamsen (1960), Guttmacher (1960), Bromberg (1961), and others. These early systems were characterized either by simple distinctions between the presence or absence of classifiable psychiatric disorders (Abrahamsen, 1960; Bromberg, 1961) or, as Megargee (1982) aptly puts it, "a kaleidoscopic variety of explanatory constructs . . . with no central organizing principle" (p. 94).

These early systems were, for the most part, not theory driven and, most certainly, not empirically corroborated. The interest in bootstrapping mainstream nosological systems designed for psychiatric disorders for use in homicide classification has, nevertheless, persisted. Unfortunately, this approach to developing a viable classification system for homicide has failed in its primary mission, namely, to reduce heterogeneity through the creation of cohesive, theoretically meaningful, homogeneous subgroups.

In a recent report, for instance, Yarvis (1990) noted his "disquiet"when considering that the findings in the extant literature on homicide "are discordant and contradictory" (p. 250). Yarvis noted that the rates of psychosis in perpetrators of homicide range from 4% to 83%, substance abuse from 3% to 40%, antisocial personality disorder (APD) from 8% to 28%, dissociative reactions from less than 1% to almost 70%, and no psychiatric disorder from 0 to almost 90%. In his own examination of 100 murderers referred for psychiatric evaluation, Yarvis (1990) found that, on Axis I of the *Diagnostic and Statistical Manual of Mental Disorders*, Third Edition, Revised (DSM-III-R) (American Psychiatric Association, 1987), 35% of his sample were classified as substance abusers, 29% were classified as psychotic, 13% received other Axis I diagnoses, and 14% received no Axis I diagnosis. On Axis II, 38% were classified as APD, 18% as borderline personality, 18% as other personality disorders, and 26% received no Axis II diagnosis.

Yarvis (1990) also looked at "homicide pattern" with respect to diagnosis. He partitioned his sample according to whether the homicide was the only offense, whether the homicide was committed in conjunction with armed robbery, and whether the homicide was committed in conjunction with rape. The two "double-offense" groups resulting from this simple categorization evidenced somewhat greater diagnostic homogeneity. The homicide–robbery group, for instance, was characterized by substance abuse on Axis I (81.8%) and APD on Axis II (90%). The homicide–rape group was characterized by substance abuse (40%), all other diagnoses (40%), and no diagnosis (20%) on Axis I, and APD (90%) on Axis II. These findings are based, however, on very small subgroups ($N = 11$ and 10, respectively). The homicide-only group ($N = 79$) was as manifestly heterogeneous as the combined sample.

It is noteworthy that when Yarvis (1990) examined diagnosis relative to the presence or absence of prior criminal convictions, he found that 59% of those with prior convictions ($N = 56$) were diagnosed as APD, compared with only 11.4% of those with no prior convictions. Such a finding is predictable, and underscores the role of lifestyle impulsivity as a correlate of criminal behavior as well as a key feature of APD.

The relation between homicide and major mental illness is highly equivocal and, it would appear, at least partly a function of sample selection. Lanzkron (1964) examined the records of 150 consecutive admissions to a New York state hospital that involved a charge or an indictment for murder. Of the 150 cases, 137 (91%) were diagnosed, in one manner or another, as psychotic. In a more recent study, Benezech, Yesavage, Addad, Bourgeois, and Mills (1984) examined commitments for homicide to a French state hospital for the criminally insane. Out of 109 individuals committed to the hospital as not guilty by reason of insanity (NGRI), 64 (59%) met DSM-III criteria for schizophrenia and 37 (34%) met DSM-III criteria for paranoia. Gillies (1976), on the other hand, examined 400 persons accused of murder in western Scotland and found a "high percentage of psychiatrically normal persons." Indeed, of those examined between 1965 and 1974, "no material psychiatric abnormality was seen in 90% of the males" (p. 105).

Failure to identify any consistent pattern of findings using standard psychiatric nomenclature led investigators to adopt models that appeared, *a priori*, to have face validity for homicide. Perhaps the earliest systematic attempt to adapt and test such a model for homicide was Megargee's (1966) now well-known typology. Megargee proposed that the "chronically overcontrolled assaultive" individual is overly inhibited in the expression of anger. This individual internalizes feelings until the buildup culminates in what appears to be an isolated, explosive act. As offenders, these men are hypothesized to have relatively few, albeit very violent, crimes. The "undercontrolled assaultive" individual, by contrast, has few inhibitions against acting out, and typically presents with a long track record of less violent crime. The utility of this bipartite classification for homicide was tested by Blackburn (1971), who examined 56 males admitted to Broadmoor for homicide. Using the psychometric data that he collected, Blackburn found that the majority of offenders could be assigned to one of four groups. Group 1, the "overcontrolled repressors," tended to be older, married, and of higher intelligence. Relatively few of them had prior criminal convictions, and their victims were, for the most part, known to them. About one-third of this group was diagnosed as schizophrenic. This group is most directly comparable to Megargee's overcontrolled type. Group 2 is the "depressed-inhibited" category. Although very similar to Group 1, Group 2 is distinguished from Group 1 by being predominantly schizophrenic and unmarried. Group 2 members were similar to Group 1 in having a low incidence of prior criminal offenses. Group 3 consists almost exclusively of psychopaths. Those assigned to this group tended to be younger and most had criminal records. None were diagnosed as schizophrenic. This group corresponds most closely to Megargee's undercontrolled type. Group 4, the "paranoid-aggressives," tended to be the youngest, unmarried, and have criminal records. Although Group 4 is similar in some respects to Group 3, Group 4 members were more likely to have a major mental illness. Over half of this group was diagnosed as schizophrenic. In addition, these offenders tended to be the least intelligent, and were more likely to victimize strangers or casual acquaintances. Interestingly, of the seven homicides in Blackburn's sample that included an "overt sexual component," four were assigned to this group.

We may reasonably conclude at this point that taxonomic systems, such as the DSM-IV (APA, 1993), that were designed to embrace putatively homogeneous psychiatric disorders, fail to differentiate among heterogeneous samples of murderers. This conclusion is not surprising given that the DSM-III-R was never intended to discriminate among those who murder. Like any manifestly heterogeneous group of behaviors, the task of taxonomic differentiation for homicide requires the identification and examination of theoretically plausible constructs or dimensions that have presumptive importance for the domain of behaviors under scrutiny.

Sociocriminological Contributions

Researchers have stressed the importance of sociological studies of murder, not only to gain a better understanding of the forces that give rise to murder, but also to understand society's complex interrelationships. In a study of several sensational murders that took place during the Victorian era, for instance, Attick (1970) focused on the social fabric revealed through these cases. Statistics quoted by Attick suggest that while the characteristics of individual murderers may change from one historical period to another, patterns of murder do not. For example, during the period 1837–1901, Attack found that most murders were domestic in nature, while the next largest group was homicides committed during the commission of a felony. A comparison of these statistics with the 1984 Department of Justice Uniform Crime Report data shows the pattern is much the same today as it was a century ago.

In contrast to classification systems based on individuals, criminological studies have conceptualized homicide as a social phenomenon. Included in this category are sociological studies that examine violent crime within the context of the society in which it occurs. These studies consider social and cultural factors that might contribute to aggressive behavior. Like sociologists, historians have also studied murder, with the belief that an analysis of the patterns of violence within a given society at a given time provides a unique glimpse at other facets of social structure (Buchanan, 1977).

One such approach to studying violent crime is exemplified by Wolfgang and Ferracutti (1982). These researchers suggest that the sociological approach, with its emphasis on cultural influences, and the psychological approach, with its emphasis on individual differences, should be integrated. Although understanding the social forces that impinge on the perpetrator is as important as understanding the psychological makeup of the perpetrator, the valuable information gleaned from sociological research is not readily available for practical application by the homicide investigator.

With this need for integration as their starting point, Wolfgang and Ferracutti studied murders that resulted from passion or from an intent to harm but not to kill. They theorized that within many societies there is a subculture of violence, and that these presumptively homogeneous subcultures are responsible for the highest homicide rates. A subculture of violence is characterized by a set of values that is fundamentally discordant with the values of society at large. One such value is the accepted use of extreme force as a solution to problem solving. Although the idea that values translate into motives for specific behaviors, such as the expression of interpersonal violence, may well be an oversimplification, there is ample evidence to suggest that in at least one domain of criminal violence— sexual aggression—cognitions or attitudes are importantly related to behavior (e.g., Murphy, 1990; Segal & Stermac, 1990). That is, for some types of sexual offenders, their distorted attitudes about sexuality in general and their victims in particular serve to justify and sustain the assaults.

Law Enforcement/Investigative Efforts

The law enforcement perspective focuses on the investigation (i.e., suspect identification, suspect apprehension). Unlike other disciplines concerned with interpersonal violence, law enforcement does not, as a primary objective, seek to explain the actions of a murderer. Instead, the task is to ascertain the identity of the offender based on what is known about the crime. Described by one author as an emitter of signals during commission of a crime (Willmer, 1970), the criminal must be identified through "clues" that suggest a "profile" of personal and behavioral characteristics. Although studies explaining why certain individuals commit violent crimes may aid them in their search, law enforcement investigators must adapt study findings to suit their own particular (i.e., investigative) needs.

Classification systems devised for law enforcement purposes include the Uniform Crime Report (URC), National Crime Information Center (NCIC), classification by type and style, investigative profiling, and, most recently, the Crime Classification Manual (CCM), which represents the first taxonomy of homicide based upon hypothetical motivational constructs.

Uniform Crime Report

The oldest system for classification of homicide is the Uniform Crime Report (UCR). The UCR, prepared by the FBI in conjunction with the U.S. Department of Justice, presents statistics for crimes committed in the United States within a given year. A survey of the figures reported in the UCR for all murders committed in the period between 1976 and 1989 shows that the number of murders in the United States has fluctuated from 16,605 in 1976 to a peak of 21,860 in 1980, dropping to 20,613 in 1986 and up to 21,500 in 1989 (U.S. Department of Justice, Uniform Crime Report, 1977, 1981, 1987, 1989). The UCR also cites information about age, race, and sex of victims and offenders, types of weapons used, and situations in which killings took place.

The current UCR classifies murders as follows:

1. Felony murder (occurs during commission of a felony).
2. Suspected felony murder (elements of felony are present).
3. Argument-motivated murder (noncriminally motivated).
4. Other motives or circumstances (any *known* motivation not included in previous categories).
5. Unknown motives (motive fits into none of the above categories).

Percentages for all categories of murders, except the "unknown" category, have remained relatively stable over the past decade. For example, felony-connected murders represented 17.7% of all murders in 1976, 17.2% in 1981, 18% in 1984, and 19.4% in 1986. The percentages for those murders placed in the "other" category are as follows: 1976, 18.6%; 1981, 17.1%; 1984, 17.6%; and 1986, 18.6% (U.S. Department of Justice, Uniform Crime Reports, 1977, 1982, 1985, 1987).

The number of murders classified in the "unknown motive" category, however, has risen dramatically. These murders represented 8.5% of all murders in 1976, 17.8% in 1981, 22.1% in 1984, and 22.5% in 1986. This trend is particularly noteworthy in that it suggests both the heterogeneity of motives that give rise to murder and the clear inadequacy of a system that partitions murder essentially into three categories: felony, noncriminal, and "other." The "other" and "unknown" categories represent, of course, wastebasket classifications. A classification system that fails to capture 40–50% of the cases (other and unknown) clearly is suboptimal in its ability to explain the "universe of behavior."

National Crime Information Center

The National Crime Information Center (NCIC) publishes an expanded list of UCR offenses. There is an NCIC code number for each offense. Unlike the UCR, which categorizes according to two dimensions—the presence or absence of a discernible motive and the co-occurrence of a felony—the NCIC categorizes according to three dimensions—the crime, victim, and weapon.

The NCIC code for homicide (0900; see Megargee, 1982) incudes 12 categories. The three primary distinctions for assigning a case to one of these categories involve whether (1) the killing was "willful" or negligent (i.e., manslaughter); (2) the victim was a family member, a nonfamily member, a public official, or a police officer; and (3) a gun or some other weapon was used. The NCIC code, like the UCR, derives from uncertain theoretical ancestry and has never been empirically corroborated.

Homicide Classification by Victims, Type, and Style

The FBI Academy's Behavioral Science Unit at Quantico, Virginia, began contributing to the literature on the classification of homicide with the Hazelwood and Douglas (1980) publication on typing lust murderers. The classifying of homicides by number of victims, type, and style, was published by Douglas and colleagues in 1986. A single homicide is defined as one victim and one homicidal event. A double homicide is defined as two victims that are killed at one time in one location. A triple homicide is defined as three victims that are killed at one time in one location. Any single event, single location homicide involving four or more victims is classified as *mass* murder (see Table 1).

There are two subcategories of mass murder: classic and family. A classic mass murder involves one person operating in one location at one period of time. The time period could be minutes or hours, or even days. The prototype of a classic mass murderer is a mentally disordered individual whose problems have increased to the point that he acts out against groups of people who are unrelated to him or his problems, unleashing his hostility through shootings and stabbings. One classic mass murderer was Charles Whitman, who in 1966 armed himself with boxes of ammunition, weapons, ropes, a radio, and food, barricaded himself in a tower at the University of Texas-Austin, and opened fire for 90 minutes, killing 16 people and wounding more than 30 others. He was stopped only when he was killed during an assault on the tower (Ressler, Burgess, & Douglas, 1988).

The second type of mass murder is family-member murder. If four or more family members are killed and the perpetrator takes his own life, it is classified as a mass murder/suicide. Without the suicide and with four or more victims, the murder is classified as mass-family. Examples include John List, an insurance salesman who killed his entire family in 1972. List disappeared after the crime and his car was found at an airport parking lot. He was located 17 years later following a television program describing the murders.

A *spree* murder is defined as a single event with two or more locations and no emotional cooling-off period between murders (see Table 1). The single event in a spree murder can be of short or long duration. On September 6, 1949, spree murderer Howard Unruh of Camden, New Jersey, took a loaded German lugar with extra ammunition and randomly fired the handgun while walking through his neighborhood, killing 13 people and wounding 3 in about 20 minutes. Even though Unruh's killing took a short length of time, it was not classified as a mass murder because he moved to different locations (Ressler et al., 1988).

Serial murder is defined as three or more separate events in three or more separate locations with an emotional cooling-off period between homicides (see Table 2). The serial murder is hypothesized to be premeditated, involving offense-related fantasy and detailed planning. When the time is right for him and he has cooled off from his last homicide, the serial killer selects his next victim and proceeds with his plan. The cooling-off period can

TABLE 1. Classification by Type and Style:
Mass and Spree

Mass murder	Spree murder
1. 1 subject	1. 1 or more subjects
2. 4 or more victims	2. 2+ victims
3. 1 event	3. 1 event (long or short)
4. 1 location	4. 2+ locations
5. No cool-off period	5. No cool-off period
6. Victims can be family	

last for days, weeks, or months, and is the key feature that distinguishes the serial killer from other multiple killers. Ted Bundy is an example of a serial murderer. Bundy killed 30 or more times over a period of many years in at least five different states (Ressler et al., 1988).

There are other differences that are hypothesized to distinguish the mass, spree, and serial murderers. In addition to the number of events and locations and the presence or absence of a cooling-off period, the classic mass murderer and the spree murderer are not concerned with who their victims are; they will kill anyone who comes in contact with them. In contrast, the serial murderer usually selects a type of victim. He thinks he will never be caught, and sometimes he is right. A serial murderer carefully monitors his behaviors to avoid detection, whereas a spree murderer, who oftentimes has been identified and is being closely pursued by law enforcement, is usually unable to control the course of events. The serial killer, by contrast, will plan, pick, and choose victim and location, sometimes stopping the act of murder if it is not "meeting the requirements." With a sexually motivated murderer, the offense may be classified as any of the aforementioned types.

An overview of homicide classification by style and type is presented in Table 3.

Investigative Profiling

Investigative profiling is best viewed as a strategy enabling law enforcement to narrow the field of options and generate "educated guesses" about the perpetrator. It has been described as a collection of leads (Rossi, 1982), as an informed attempt to provide detailed information about a certain type of criminal (Geberth, 1981), and as a biographical sketch of behavioral patterns, trends, and tendencies (Vorpagel, 1982). Geberth (1981) has noted that investigative profiling is particularly useful when the criminal has demonstrated some clearly identifiable form of psychopathology. In such a case the crime scene is presumed to reflect the murderer's behavior and personality in much the same way as furnishings reveal the homeowner's character.

TABLE 2. Classification by Type
and Style: Serial Murder

1. 1 subject	5. Cooling-off period evident
2. 3+ victims	6. Premeditation
3. 3+ events	7. Planning
4. 3+ locations	8. Fantasy

TABLE 3. Overview of Homicide Classification by Style and Type

	Single	Double	Triple	Mass	Spree	Serial
No. of victims	1	2	3	4+	2+	3+
No. of events	1	1	1	1	1	3+
No. of locations	1	1	1	1	2+	3+
Cool-off period	N/A	N/A	N/A	N/A	No	Yes

Profiling is, in fact, a form of "retroclassification," or classification that works backwards. Typically, we classify a "known" entity into a discrete category based upon presenting characteristics that translate into criteria for assignment to that category. In the case of homicide investigation, we have neither the entity (e.g., the offender) nor the victim. It is thus necessary to rely upon the only source of information that typically is available—the crime scene. This information is used to "profile" or classify an individual. In essence, we are forced to bootstrap, using crime scene related data, to make our classifications. This bootstrapping process is referred to as profiling. At present, there have been no systematic efforts to validate these profile-derived classifications.

Crime Classification Manual: A Motivational Model for Classification of Homicide

The first published FBI Behavioral Science Unit system for typing lust murder (Hazelwood & Douglas, 1980), which Megargee (1982) properly described as a syndrome rather than a typology, delineated two categories, the "organized nonsocial" and the "disorganized asocial," that were not intended to embrace all cases of sexual homicides. This early work on lust murder evolved into a programmatic effort to devise a classification system for serial sexual murder (Ressler, Burgess, & Douglas, 1988). Approximately 2 years ago, the agents from the Investigative Support Unit at the FBI Academy joined with the Behavioral Science Unit to begin working on a crime classification manual (CCM), using the DSM-III-R as a guide. Work groups were assigned to the major crime categories of murder, arson, and sexual assault. An advisory committee representing federal and private associations was formed. The purpose of the CCM is to (1) standardize terminology within the criminal justice field, (2) facilitate communication with the criminal justice field and between criminal justice and mental health, (3) educate the criminal justice system and the public at large to the types of crimes being committed, and (4) develop a data base for investigative research (Douglas, Burgess, Burgess, & Ressler, 1992).

Although many of the conceptual and theoretical underpinnings of this model derive from earlier writings on the subject, this is the first attempt, as far as we are aware, to operationalize a decision-making process based upon a well-defined set of criteria. We want to emphasize at the outset that this rationally derived system has not been implemented or tested. Although we are in the most rudimentary stage of model development, we have at least progressed to the stage of advancing a testable system. Presentation of the system at this point (cf. Douglas et al., 1992) should provide the reader with a general overview of the presumptively important dimensions that have been incorporated into this hypothetical model. Classification of homicide by motive is presented in Table 4.

TABLE 4. A Motivational Model for Classification of Homicide

I. Criminal Enterprise
  a. Contract killing (third party)
  b. Gang-motivated murder
  c. Criminal competition
  d. Kidnap murder
  e. Product tampering
  f. Drug murder
  g. Insurance/inheritance-related death
    i. Individual profit
    ii. Commercial profit
  h. Felony murder
    i. Indiscriminate
    ii. Situational
II. Personal Cause
  a. Erotomania motivated killing
  b. Domestic
    i. Spontaneous
    ii. Staged
  c. Argument/conflict murder
    i. Argument
    ii. Conflict
  d. Authority killing

  d. Authority killing
  e. Revenge
  f. Nonspecific motive killing
  g. Extremist homicides
    i. Political
    ii. Religious
    iii. Socioeconomic
  h. Mercy/hero homicides
    i. "Mercy"
    ii. "Hero"
  i. Hostage murder
III. Sexual Homicide
  a. Organized
  b. Disorganized
  c. Mixed
  d. Sadistic murder
IV. Group Cause
  a. Cult
  b. Extremists: Political/religious/socioeconomic
    i. Paramilitary
    ii. Hostage murder
  c. Group excitement

ETIOLOGICAL CONSIDERATIONS

The Repetitive Offender

One of the most disturbing patterns that is notable in the study of homicide is that of the serial or repetitive offender. It has been surmised by criminologists that a small percentage of criminals may be responsible for a large number of crimes. This core group of habitual offenders has come to be referred to as the "career" criminal. This phenomenon was first documented with juvenile delinquents (Wolfgang, Figlio, & Sellin, 1972), and subsequent studies have reported similar results (Figlio & Tracy, 1983; Hamparian et al., 1978; Shannon, 1978), with estimates suggesting that 6% to 8% of delinquents comprise the core of the delinquency problem.

To address this problem, law enforcement investigators have concentrated their efforts on developing techniques to aid in apprehending these highly repetitive offenders. These techniques require an in-depth knowledge of the "criminal personality," an area that, until recently, was researched primarily by psychiatrists or psychologists (e.g., Yochelson & Samenow, 1977), who examined criminals from a psychological framework, or by sociologists and criminologists, who studied the demographics and social stratification of crime. Missing from these areas of inquiry were critical aspects of offender apprehension important to the law enforcement community. Thus, researchers with a law enforcement perspective began to shift the focus to the investigative process of crime scene inquiry and victimology.

Within this area falls our research: the first study of crime scene patterns in sexual homicide was published in 1985 (Ressler & Burgess, 1985). This study included an initial appraisal of a profiling process, and lengthy, structured interviews of incarcerated murderers conducted by FBI special agents. The interview booklets were filled out by the agents using information derived from the interview as well as detailed record information derived from the institutional file. A subsample of 36 sexual murderers was selected for preliminary analysis of profiling characteristics. This sample was selected for its repetitiveness, accounting for a total of 109 known murders, or an average of three victims per offender. In this section, we present what we learned about these 36 men. It is important to recognize that we are making general statements about these 36 offenders. Not all statements are true for *all* offenders, although they may be true for *most* of the 36 men or for most of the offenders from whom we obtained data. Responses were not available from all offenders for all questions.

Background Characteristics

Although their birth years ranged from 1904 to 1958, most of the 36 offenders (all male) grew up in the 1940s and 1950s. They were almost all white, and were usually eldest sons (first or second born).

Most of these men, as adults, had pleasant general appearances, suggesting that as boys they were physically attractive. Their heights and weights were within the normal range, and few had distinguishing handicaps or physical defects to set them apart in a group of boys or men. The majority performed in the average range or above on intelligence tests, with one-third having superior to very superior intelligence.

The majority initially began life in a two-parent home. Half of the mothers were homemakers and did not work outside of the home. Although the majority of fathers worked at unskilled jobs, they were steadily employed. Only five men reported that their family lived at or below marginal economic levels. Thus, poverty appears not to have been a significant factor in the families of these men. In general, the mothers were in the home, the fathers were earning stable incomes, and the subjects were intelligent, white, eldest sons.

Family Background

It is often argued that the structure and quality of a family interaction is an important factor in the development of a child, especially in the way the child perceives family members and their interaction with him and with each other. For children growing up, the quality of their attachments to parents and other members of the family is critical to how these children relate to and value other members of society. From developmental and social learning perspectives, these early life attachments evolve into detailed architectural plans for how the child will interact with his or her world. A study of 81 sexual offenders (54 rapists and 27 child molesters) incarcerated at the Massachusetts Treatment Center (Prentky, Knight, Sims-Knight, Straus, Rokous, & Cerce, 1989), reported the following three noteworthy findings. First, sexual and nonsexual aggression in adulthood each were related to distinct aspects of developmental history. Caregiver inconstancy and sexual deviation in the family were associated with amount of sexual aggression, whereas childhood and juvenile institutional history and physical abuse/neglect were associated with amount of *non*sexual aggression. Second, contrary to previous studies of other criminal populations, the *amount* of aggression rather than frequency of crimes was predicted by developmental history. Third, the presence of caregiver inconstancy *and* family sexual deviation accounted for 87.5% of all cases of extreme sexual aggression in adulthood. The presence of institutional history and physical abuse/neglect accounted for

81.2% of all cases of extreme nonsexual aggression in adulthood. The results of this study suggest that the quality of early interpersonal attachments and the experience of sexual abuse as a child may be important to understanding sexual aggression in adulthood. Given these rather compelling findings, we were especially interested in looking at factors that best addressed the level of interpersonal attachment of the subjects in our sample of serial murderers.

The family histories of these men revealed multiple problems. Half of the offenders' families had members with criminal histories, and over half of the families had members with psychiatric problems, suggesting, at the very least, inconsistent contact between some family members and the offender as a child. In addition, however, there was evidence of irresponsible and maladaptive parenting in a large number of cases. Nearly 70% of the families had histories of alcohol abuse, and one-third had histories of drug abuse. Sexual deviance among family members was present or suspected in almost half of the cases. Thus, the likelihood that these offenders experienced a high quality of family life as children is remote.

When examining the child-rearing patterns described by the murderers, one is most impressed by the high degree of family instability and by the poor quality of attachment among family members. Only one-third of the men reported growing up in one location. The majority (17) said they experienced occasional instability, and 6 reported chronic instability or frequent moving. Over 40% lived outside the family (e.g., in foster homes, state homes, detention centers, mental hospitals) before age 18. Twenty-five of the men for whom data were available had histories of early psychiatric difficulties. In general, these families were bereft not only of internal or nuclear attachments but external or community attachments as well. Thus, it stands to reason that the children of these families had few opportunities to develop stable, healthy attachments within the community, thus reducing the child's opportunities to develop positive, stable relationships outside the family, relationships that might otherwise have compensated for family instability.

As we stated earlier, one or both parents were absent in about 40% of cases, with father absent in 10 cases, mother absent in 3 cases, and both parents absent in 2 cases. It is noteworthy, however, that in 17 cases the biological father left home before the boy reached 12 years old. This absence was due to a variety of reasons, including separation and divorce. Thus, it is not surprising that for 21 subjects, the dominant parent during the rearing phase of their life was the mother. Only nine offenders said that the father was the dominant parent, and two said both parents shared parenting roles. In general, most offenders said that their relationship with their father was unsatisfactory and that their relationship with their mother was highly ambivalent. Sixteen of the men reported cold or uncaring relationships with their mothers, and 26 reported similar relationships with their fathers. In addition, they frequently reported discipline as unfair, hostile, inconsistent, and abusive. These men felt they were not dealt with fairly by adults throughout their formative years.

Twenty of the men had no older brothers and 17 had no older sisters. Thus, in terms of having a strong role model during their formative years, these men lacked an older sibling to fill in for parental deficiencies. Rather, they had to compete with their younger siblings in an emotionally deprived environment.

These data suggest that most of the 36 murderers, as children, had little or no attachment to family members. They felt a high degree of uninvolvement with their fathers, ambivalence toward their mothers, and little attachment to siblings. The parents were preoccupied with their own problems of substance abuse, psychiatric disturbance, and criminality. They tended to engage in aberrant sexual behavior and often argued and fought with each other. Although the parents offered little constructive guidance, it appears that they did offer ample role modeling of deviant behavior.

Individual Development

Two additional factors are noteworthy: a dominant fantasy life and a history of personal abuse. Many of the murderers described the central role of fantasy in their early development, expressed in part through a variety of paraphilias. When asked to rank their sexual interests, the highest-ranking activity was pornography (81%), followed by compulsive masturbation (79%), fetishism (72%), and voyeurism (71%). These fantasies were often violent and sadistic in nature. Twenty offenders had rape fantasies prior to the age of 18, and seven of these men acted out these fantasies within a year of being consciously aware of them. There was evidence of physical and sexual abuse in close to half of the killers, and an even higher percentage of emotional neglect. In general, it is interesting to note the isolated pattern of these deviant sexual expressions. The men seemed to engage either in paraphilias that were solitary in practice or in sexually violent activities, neither of which reflected any degree of interpersonal contact.

In addition, when questioned about the murders themselves and their preparations for the murders, the men identified the importance of fantasy to the crimes. After the first murder, the men found themselves deeply preoccupied and sometimes stimulated by the memories of the act, all of which contributed to and nurtured fantasies about subsequent murders.

One begins to see how an early pattern used to cope with a markedly deficient and abusive family life might turn a child away from that reality and into his own private world of violence where he can not only exert control but exact retribution for the physical and emotional injuries inflicted upon him. The control evidenced in these fantasies appears to be crucial not only to the child but later to the adult. Importantly, these are not fantasies of escape to a better life, as one often sees in children recovering from sexual assaults and abusive treatment. These men did not compensate by retreating to a fantasy world in which love reigned and abuse did not occur. Rather, their fantasies were fueled by feelings of aggression and mastery over those who were abusing them, suggesting a projected repetition of their own abuse and identification with the aggressor. As one murderer put it, "Nobody bothered to find out what my problem was and nobody knew about the fantasy world."

Performance

Examination of performance behavior of these murderers reveals another paradox. Despite reasonably high intelligence and potential in many areas, performance in school, employment, social relationships, and military service was often poor. In all of these areas, performance fell far short of potential.

Although these men had the native intelligence to perform well in school, academic failure was the norm. The majority had to repeat elementary grades and did not finish high school. In addition, school failure was frequently mentioned by the men as an early fortifier of their sense of inadequacy. The men also had the ability to perform skilled jobs. In reality, however, most offenders had poor work histories in unskilled jobs, and only 20% had ever held steady jobs. About half of the offenders entered the military. Only 4 of the 14 who were in military service received honorable discharges, and one of the four had a criminal history in the service. Two men received general discharges, three were dishonorably discharged, three had undesirable discharges, and two received medical discharges. Finally, the sexual performance of the offenders generally was limited to self-stimulation or autoeroticism. Although 20 men were able to state an age of first consenting sex to orgasm, they did not report an extensive, peer-related sexual history. The ages of first consenting sexual experience ranged from 11 to 25. Of the 16 who did not report an age, it was clear to the interviewers that many never experienced consenting "normal" sex. There was a clear preference for autoerotic (i.e., noninterpersonal) activity.

The interviews with the offenders revealed many expressions of low self-esteem prior to and during their criminal careers. Many offenders felt an acute sense of failure and inadequacy beginning at a young age. Again, we can speculate, in this regard, on the important role of fantasy. It appears that what compensates for chronic failure may be a fantasy in which success and mastery can be controlled and assured.

The Presumptive Role of Fantasy as a Drive Mechanism

Based on the study of 36 murderers, a fantasy-based motivational model for sexual homicide was reported by Burgess and her colleagues (Burgess, Hartman, Ressler, Douglas, & McCormack, 1986). The model has five interactive components: impaired development of attachments in early life; formative traumatic events; patterned responses that serve to generate fantasies; a private internal world that is consumed with violent thoughts and that leaves the person isolated and self-preoccupied; and a feedback filter that sustains repetitive thinking patterns. Using the same sample, Ressler et al. (1986) examined the role of the organized/disorganized dichotomy, which has proven to be a relatively powerful discriminator in two important areas (crime scene investigation and life history variables) (see Ressler et al., 1986). Classification as organized or disorganized is made with the use of data present at the scene of a murder, and is based upon the notion that highly repetitive, planned, well thought-out offenses will be distinguishable from spontaneous, random, sloppy offenses. According to prediction, the former organized case should be more characterized by a fantasy life that drives the offenses than the latter disorganized case. Ressler et al. (1986) found support for numerous differences between organized and disorganized offenders with respect to acts committed during the offense.

Prentky, Burgess, et al. (1989), using a sample of 42 murderers, examined the presumptive role of fantasy as a drive mechanism for repetitive sexual murder. The term fantasy was based on an information-processing model that interprets thoughts as derivations of incoming stimuli that have been processed and organized (Gardner, 1985). A fantasy was defined as an elaborated set of cognitions (or thoughts) characterized by preoccupation (or rehearsal), anchored in emotion, and having origins in daydreams. Daydreaming was defined as any cognitive activity representing a shift of attention away from a task (Singer, 1966). A fantasy is generally experienced as a collection of thoughts, although the individual may be aware of images, feelings, and internal dialogue. A crime fantasy was positively coded for the study if interview or archival data indicated daydreaming content that included intentional infliction of harm in a sadistic or otherwise sexually violent way.

The preliminary findings provided tentative support for the hypothesis that fantasy life may be importantly related to repeated acts of sexual violence. Recent evidence from both clinical (e.g., MacCulloch et al., 1983) and empirical (e.g., Ressler et al., 1986) studies has underscored the importance of fantasy as a presumptive drive mechanism for sexual sadism and sexual homicide. Prentky, Burgess, et al.'s (1989) findings provided support for that general conclusion as well as evidence for greater specificity in the role of fantasy. That is, fantasy was present in 86% of the serial murderers and only 23% of the solo murderers, suggesting a possible functional relationship between fantasy and repetitive assaultive behavior. Although the precise function of consummated fantasy is speculation, we concur with MacCulloch et al. (1983) that once restraints inhibiting the acting out of fantasy are no longer present, the individual is likely to engage in a series of progressively more accurate "trial runs" in an attempt to "stage" the fantasy as it is imagined. Since the trial runs can never precisely match the fantasy, the need to restage the fantasy with a new victim is established. As MacCulloch et al. suggest, the shaping of the fantasy and the motivation to consummate it can be understood in terms of classical conditioning. The more that the fantasy is rehearsed *in vivo*, the more power it acquires and the stronger the association between the conditioned stimulus (fantasy content) and the conditioned response (sexual arousal). We may also speculate that the evolution of fantasy-driven crimes is, in part, a function of habituation. That is, when fantasy content is repeatedly rehearsed, it ceases to elicit arousal with the same intensity, hence the fantasy must be modified.

Since it is commonly accepted that "normal" people often have sexually deviant fantasies (Crepault & Couture, 1980), merely having a sadistic and/or homicidal fantasy does not mean that the fantasy will be acted out (Schlesinger & Revitch, 1983). In fact, fantasy may function as a substitute for behavior. Kaplan (1979) has argued, for instance, that sadistic fantasies in "normals" may serve the purpose of discharging anger. According to Kaplan (1979), sex and aggression are incompatible affects. The fantasy temporarily discharges the anger, thereby permitting the expression of sexual feelings. A critical question with regard to the role of fantasy concerns the disinhibitory factors that encourage the translation of symbolic activity (e.g., the paraphilias) or cognitive activity (e.g., fantasies) into reality.

We also found that serial murderers evidenced a higher frequency of paraphilias than solo murderers (Prentky, Burgess, et al., 1989). This is entirely consistent with the greater role of fantasy in serial murderers. Not only does "paraphilia" suggest a preference for fantasy, but the paraphiliac may be seen as something of a fantasy-stimulus collector who seeks out secret experiences to add to his private, internal world of fantasy. Thus, acts such as peeping or exhibitionism serve to cultivate new secret experiences, which not only activate fantasy but provide the incentive (or motive) for translating fantasy into reality. As Money (1980) commented, "the paraphiliac's ideal is to be able to stage his/her erotic fantasy so as to perceive it as an actual experience" (p. 76).

It is interesting to note that of the five paraphilias examined in the Prentky, Burgess et al. (1989) study, the two with the largest group differences—fetishism and cross-dressing—are also the ones that represent the enactment of some aspect of fantasy life. There is, in fact, some evidence that these two paraphilias (fetishism and transvestism) are more often associated with sexual aggression than other paraphilias. Wilson and Gosselin (1980) studied a large number of fetishists, sadomasochists, transvestite/transsexuals, and normal controls, finding that 88% of the fetishists also engaged in either sadomasochism or transvestism. More precisely to the point is the study by Langevin, Paitich, and Russon (1985). These investigators found that not only is transvestism multifaceted (i.e., it is associated with other paraphilias) but it may go "hand in hand with violent sexuality" (Steiner, Sanders, & Langevin, 1985, p. 272). Langevin et al. (1985) concluded that sadomasochistic fantasies in conjunction with the degree of force used may be premonitory signs of extreme dangerousness, including a predisposition to sexual murder.

When the "paraphilia" is sexual homicide, the experience of the act—obtaining the victim, performing ritualistic acts, engaging the victim sexually either before or after death, killing the victim, disposing of the body, eluding detection, and following the police investigation in the media—provides a compelling motive for repetition (Burgess et al., 1986). To the extent to which these "components" of the crime are contemplated and thought through beforehand, some element of fantasy is likely to be involved. Indeed, evidence of forethought in the planning and/or execution of the crime is highly associated with degree of organization (Ressler & Burgess, 1985). Indeed, the serial sample had almost three times the percentage of organized murders as the solo sample (Prentky, Burgess et al., 1989), suggesting a relation between fantasy, planning, repetition, and crime scene organization.

CLINICAL MANAGEMENT

The following principles, based on our clinical experience, are offered for the inpatient management of murderers.

1. *Honest disclosure*. Offenders need an environment in which they can honestly disclose and admit what they have done and what they are preoccupied with doing to others. They may be limited in their capacity and awareness to do this because they do not believe in the value of social and personal control, they are ignorant of the rules of social and personal control, or they have extensive impairments in understanding the antecedents and consequences of behavioral acts. All of these areas become critical points for assessment and clinical management in any kind of residential program.

The counterpoint to this is the prosecution of the case. The legal defense can interfere with honest recall and integration of the facts. Clinicians need to know what lawyers are advising their client to say or not to say. Psychotherapy cannot, in any meaningful sense, be conducted if the offender cannot discuss his crime.

2. *Classify the murder using the CCM* (see Table 4). Homicide classification may suggest that management strategies will be different in the initial stages of clinical management of the offender. Clinicians will probably see more Personal Cause offenders in hospital settings than Criminal Enterprise types, with the latter more likely to be seen in prison settings.

3. *Assess for current dangerousness*. An individual who has committed an index crime such as murder has made a statement that he is "dangerous." It is important to assess the individual's self-control as well as his current dangerousness. This assessment requires familiarization with the nature and type of murder that has occurred and all available forensic information (e.g., autopsy and investigative reports, police reports, crime scene photographs, as well as the offender's history of aggression).

4. *Assess deviant sexual fantasies and diagnose paraphilias*. A careful history of the onset and content of sexual, deviant, and sadistic fantasies needs to be taken. Prior criminal history will provide some information and the degree of honest disclosure by the offender.

5. *Family assessment*. The literature suggests that the extended family (i.e., all important caregivers) plays a critical role in the developmental history of offenders. Family members may provide important insights for understanding the offender.

6. *Substance use assessment*. The high percentage of offenders using drugs underscores the need for careful assessment of substance use. Drugs may be used for a variety of reasons, such as blocking feelings (e.g., heroin) or heightening feelings (amphetamines,

LSD, PCP), or for their differential effect (cocaine). Thus, it is important to understand the nature of the drug use and the role it plays in the life of the offender.

7. *Suicide risk*. Suicidal potential needs to be assessed in all situations, but especially in situations in which the murder is classified as impulsive and in which the offender expresses remorse after the realization that the victim has been killed. If the anger that was expressed in the context of the offense is internalized, the offender may be at risk to hurt himself.

8. *Staff's countertransference response*. Murderous acts are sometimes held in awe by the general public, staff included. Thus, a management principle is not to treat the murderer as "special." Murderers should be treated neither as celebrities nor as pariahs. Staff should not aggrandize the murder or make the murder event so singularly important and distinctive that it creates a secondary gain for the offender. Also, clinicians should not allow their own abhorrence to interfere with their responsibilities to the offender. In essence, service providers must come to terms with their own emotions and reactions to the criminal behavior and not respond with anger or cruelty. Staff need to be alert to the offender conning them. Much of this is avoided by reviewing official records and reports of the crime and being able to deal in a factual way with the offender about all aspects of the criminal behavior.

CASE ILLUSTRATION

The Murder

On Tuesday, July 31, 1973, Martha Z. failed to report for work. A telephone call was placed to her house, which brought much concern when there was no answer. Ms. Z.'s employer drove to her home, but found the door secure. He located the landlord, and with the aid of a pass key both men entered the residence. Martha Z. was found lying lifeless and nude on the dining room floor, suffering from what appeared to be multiple stab wounds. She was in a partially seated position, with the back of the head and shoulders supported by the staircase.

The residence was a two-story brick row house in a middle-class area of the city, directly behind a military barracks facility. The interior portion of the house was found to be neat and moderately furnished. The crime scene itself was limited to the dining room portion of the house.

Recovered from the dining room floor, alongside the victim, was a pair of women's yellow panties and a blue-and-white-flowered dress. Numerous other articles were collected as evidence: a handwritten note, articles such as pieces of jewelry, pieces of broken furniture, and a piece of flesh, which was subsequently identified as the right breast nipple of the victim. Numerous strands of hair were also collected from the dining room rug.

Victimology

Martha Z. was an attractive, white female, 25 years old, 5'2" tall, 110 pounds, with long brown hair. She lived alone in her townhouse. She came to the Washington, D.C., area from Pennsylvania and was one of two children. Her first job was with the Federal Bureau of Investigation as a stenographer. She then worked as a legal secretary with a law firm. Her final job was as an office manager with a national health care agency.

She was described as quiet but friendly and liked by everyone. She was an active member of an organization which, among other functions, raised money for charity. Her co-workers in the organization described her as one who loved life and people, one who never asked anything of anybody.

Investigation

The medical examiners report noted that a massive bruise covered the left forehead, left upper and lower eyelids, and left cheek; on the right cheek an incised cutting wound of 3½″ long and ¼″ in depth was found. A 6″-long laceration was located in the front portion of the neck, severing the jugular vein on both the left and right sides. The chest exhibited four stab wounds, three of which were located on the left breast area, the fourth located in the lower left chest. Numerous cutting wounds were also found on the chest area.

The abdominal area exhibited a 15″-long incised cutting wound measuring ½″ to ¾″ deep. Several other gaping-type wounds were found on all four extremities. No injury was noted to the vagina or rectum. Semen was found in the vagina. There was also exhibited multiple rib fractures and contusion of the small bowel, an indication of a severe blunt force injury. Death was due to stab wounds to the chest. It was estimated she was dead for approximately 12 hours when discovered.

Investigators noted that the victim's window faced the military barracks. They learned that Martha had been receiving obscene notes. These notes were first placed under the windshield of her automobile and then under the door to her townhouse. The notes were written on a pretense of asking for a date; however, they became derogatory and obscene. The writer said he enjoyed watching her at night and it made his heart beat fast. He indicated he was going to come and visit her and told her what he was going to do to her (i.e., how he wanted to undress and fondle her).

Suspect Apprehension

Investigators learned who wrote the notes and who watched the victim at night through careful interviewing of the victim's neighbors. On August 2, 1973, CRH was invited to the homicide office for an interview. He agreed to accompany investigators and was friendly and polite. He talked about general subjects on the way to the office. He was advised of his rights.

After several hours, the conversation developed to the point that suspicion fell on him as a suspect. He was again advised of his rights and this time charged in connection with the murder.

After being charged the interview continued, and the victim was freely discussed by CRH. He said he had been watching the victim for 5 months. He related how he had gone to her apartment on the evening of July 30, 1973, after drinking five or six beers for courage. He had a funny feeling in his stomach when he knocked on her door. He often claimed periods of blackouts. He could not account for several hours on the night in question.

He stated that he wanted to see if she would talk to him. While he was in her house he stated that he played with her cat and talked about her legs and how she kept moving them toward him. She was dressed in a light-weight short robe, which he mentioned several times. He said he then left and went home, but couldn't sleep soundly that night or the next two nights; however, he did not know why. He never admitted killing her, but said he could be responsible. He told investigators he was capable of being violent when panicked, and he knew he needed professional help.

He felt his blackouts were caused by minor reasons, such as hard times, pressures from others, strain, and restless days and nights.

He completed his statement by saying that now that he knows she is dead, he should not have waited so long to tell someone he might be responsible, but he wanted to wait awhile to see what would develop.

The note found in the victim's house was identified as being written by CRH. A search warrant was executed at CRH's apartment, at which time a pair of pants, undershorts, pocket knife, and shoes, all with blood on them, were recovered. The victim's blood was group A and CRH's blood was O+. The blood on the items found in CRH's room belonged to Group A.

Psychiatric Evaluation

All of the clinicians who examined CRH had access to the background material as well as the results of many tests. One psychologist found him to be an obsessive-compulsive personality of no more than moderate degree. Furthermore, the examiner noted that the diagnosis would not meet criteria of mental disease or defect that would substantially affect his mental and emotional processes or impair his behavioral controls. She concluded her diagnosis by saying the offense, if committed by him, was not a product of a mental disorder.

Prosecution witnesses included military associates who testified they had never seen CRH exhibit any sort of bizarre behavior. An important witness was a young woman CRH had wanted to marry. She testified that following her refusal, he had appeared at her house one night, slashed open the screen door on the veranda with a knife, and begged her to let him in so they could talk. She let him in. He sat in silence for about an hour and then as he was about to leave suddenly had turned and knocked her unconscious. She said that when she had regained consciousness, he had undressed her and demanded that she have sexual relations with him. She said that she had stalled his advances by promising to marry him and finally managed to talk him into leaving. She said that he had seemed aware of everything he was doing and not in a trance.

Psychiatrists for the defense felt CRH had been suffering from a severe and long-standing mental disorder. They found his personality one of mixed type (with hysterical, dissociative, and passive-aggressive features). This would substantially impair his behavioral controls, and the offense, if committed by him, was the product of this mental disorder.

After 3 hours of deliberation, the jury found CRH not guilty by reason of insanity (NGRI) on second-degree murder and armed assault with intent to commit rape. He was found guilty of burglary while armed. Under this unusual split verdict, CRH was liable for a prison sentence as well as confinement to a mental hospital until he was no longer considered dangerous. He was sentenced to 15 years to life for burglary, the prison term to run concurrently with the hospital confinement, which would take priority.

Family History

CRH was a white, single male, age 21. His father died before he was 6 years old and his stepmother adopted him. She remarried when he was 7. He had an older stepsister.

Paraphilia History.   When CRH was 13 years old he showed sadistic traits when he placed needles in the carpet in order to hurt his older sister, who would step on them. He also slashed pictures of nude women with a pocket knife.

On numerous occasions he would call his best friend and threaten him with bodily injury. While sitting in front of the television for long periods of time, he would be seemingly unaware of his surroundings and would cut, lacerate, and destroy the furniture. When he was referred to a psychiatrist, who saw him on four occasions, the doctor focused totally on his family environment rather than CRH's thoughts.

Dangerousness History.   When CRH was a high school student, he physically assaulted a friend's sister and on another occasion he physically assaulted another girl. Neither time could CRH give an explanation. No charges were placed on either occasion as a result of a conference with the local sheriff.

Family Relationships.   In August, 1969, he physically assaulted his sister by choking her. No formal charges were placed against him. After a consultation with his family physician it was suggested that CRH go for a series of psychological tests. After the assault on his sister, their relationship became very strained. He had no correspondence with her until August, 1973, when he sent her a birthday card with 30 dollars. The envelope was postmarked two days after he killed Martha Z.

On Christmas Eve of 1971, while at his aunt's house, he approached his niece and demanded she take her clothes off, at which time he physically assaulted her.

Psychiatric History.   CRH had no memory of what occurred and could give no explanation for any of the assaults. He saw psychiatrists on five occasions but, because he would not cooperate, it produced no useful record.

School and Work History.   Although CRH completed high school and won a partial golf scholarship at a local junior college, he completed only 1 year with poor grades. In the second year of college he quit after a confrontation with the golf coach, which resulted after he finished a poor game of golf. He took a golf club and bent it over his knees and cursed the coach.

He had two jobs before enlisting in the military. He did not have any girlfriends while he was enlisted. He was quite and shy and never dated.

Discussion

What can we glean from this discussion of murderers in terms of the case illustration? First, the typing of the murder from the Crime Classification Manual is Sexual Homicide, Disorganized. That is, the motivation was rape and murder, and both crimes were committed. CRH's claim of memory loss could be an important area for challenge and inquiry especially in light of having access to investigative and autopsy reports. His intent to con staff in order to be released would have to be assessed.

Second, data suggest a possible underlying sexually deviant fantasy. CRH was guarded in his disclosure of personal history, so we can only observe aspects of his behavior. A key point is the missing information on his mother and his developmental history up to age 7. Father's death and the substitution of a stepfather needs to be explored. Part of his reluctance to discuss his thoughts and feelings may be due to his need to control the memories.

We can speculate that child/adolescent energies were channelled into fantasies, rather than into goal-directed learning behavior. Sadistic behavior was noted as well as visual preferences for isolated sexual experiences (such as voyeurism and obscene note writing). These behaviors relate to his fantasy world.

Important information was gained from interviews with his sister. Also, trial testimony of a former female friend provided data on his ongoing level of dangerousness. School and work history suggests his difficulty with male authority and would be an important clinical consideration in terms of transference reactions.

SUMMARY

What, then, can we speculate from this discussion of serial murders in terms of clinical application? Study findings stress that any speculations are general in nature and will not apply to every sexual killer. Nevertheless, from the FBI sample, it appears that child/adolescent energies were funnelled into fantasies, rather than into goal-directed learning behavior. Excessive involvement in solo sex, noted through the high level of masturbation, and the visual preferences for isolated sexual experiences (such as fetishes and voyeurism), may have a link with the offender's dominant fantasy world. The high interest in pornography detracts from engaging in reality and relationships and further reinforces the fantasy. Excitement is within, not with other people.

The generic roots for the murderer's actions appear to arise from his background characteristics. The triangle of variables of low social attachment, physical and/or sexual abuse, and a dominance of violent, sexualized fantasy life sets into motion the attitudes and beliefs that trigger the deviant behaviors of rape, mutilation, torture, and murder. One of the major relationship deficiencies for these murderers is their interactions with men, perhaps stemming from an absent, cold, and unavailable father. This longing for a male authority is documented in their postcrime behavior, where they interject themselves into the police investigation.

Understanding some of the dynamics behind sexually deviant behaviors is important to clinicians because it tells something about patients' behavior they are trying to assess. For the skilled clinician working on a forensic psychiatric unit, these insights will assist in the diagnostic and evaluation process regarding repetition of dangerous behaviors.

REFERENCES

Abrahamsen, D. (1960). *The psychology of crime*. New York: John Wiley.
American Psychiatric Association (1987). *Diagnostic and statistical manual of mental disorders*, 3rd Edition, Revised. Washington, DC: Author.
American Psychiatric Association (1993). *DSM-IV draft criteria*. Washington, DC: Author.
Attick, R. D. (1970). *Victorian studies in scarlet*. New York: Norton.
Benezech, M., Yesavage, J. A., Addad, M., Bourgeois, M., & Mills, M. (1984). Homicide by psychotics in France: A five year study. *Journal of Clinical Psychiatry*, *45*, 85–86.
Blackburn, R. (1971). Personality types among abnormal homicides. *British Journal of Criminology*, *11*, 14–31.
Bromberg, W. (1961). *The mold of murder*. New York: Grune & Stratton.
Buchanan, J. (1977). *Society and homicide in the 13th century England*. Stanford, CA: Stanford University Press.
Burgess, A. W., Hartman, C. R., Ressler, R. K., Douglas, J. E., & McCormack, A. (1986). Sexual homicide: A motivational model. *Journal of Interpersonal Violence*, *1*, 251–272.
Crepault, C., & Couture, M. (1980). Men's erotic fantasies. *Archives of Sexual Behavior*, *9*, 565–581.

Douglas, J. E., Ressler, R. K., Burgess, A. W., & Hartman, C. R. (1986). Criminal profiling from crime scene analysis. *Behavioral Sciences and the Law*, *4*, 401–21.

Douglas, J. E., Burgess, A. W., Burgess, A. G., & Ressler, R. K. (1992). *Crime classification manual*. New York: The Free Press.

Figlio, R. M., & Tracy, P. E. (1983). *Chronic recidivism in the 1968 birth cohort*. Unpublished manuscript, Washington, DC, NIJJDP.

Gardner, H. (1985). *The mind's new science*. New York: Basic Books.

Geberth, V. (1981). Psychological Profiling. *Law and Order*, *1*, 46–49.

Gillies, H. (1976). Homicide in the west of Scotland. *British Journal of Psychiatry*, *128*, 105–127.

Guttmacher, M. A. (1960). *The mind of a murderer*. New York: Farrar.

Hamparian, D. M., Schuster, R., Dinitz, S., & Conrad, J. P. (1978). *The violent few*. New York: Lexington/Macmillan.

Hazelwood, R. R., & Douglas, J. E. (1980). The lust murderer. *FBI Law Enforcement Bulletin*, 18–22.

Kaplan, H. S. (1979). *Disorders of sexual desire*. New York: Simon and Schuster.

Langevin, R., Ben-Aron, M. H., Wright, P., Marchese, V., & Handy, L. (1988). The sex killer. *Annals of Sex Research*, *1*, 263–301.

Langevin, R., Paitich, D., & Russon, A. E. (1985). Are rapists sexually anomalous, aggressive or both? In R. Langevin (Ed.), *Erotic preferences, gender identity, and aggression in men: New research findings* (pp. 17–38). Hillsdale, NJ: Lawrence Erlbaum.

Lanzkron, J. (1964). Psychopathology of the homicidal patient. *Corrective Psychiatry and Journal of Social Therapy*, *10*, 142–155.

MacCulloch, M. J., Snowden, P. R., Wood, P. J. W., & Mills, H. E. (1983). Sadistic fantasy, sadistic behavior and offending. *British Journal of Psychiatry*, *143*, 20–29.

Megargee, E. I. (1966). Undercontrolled and overcontrolled personality types in extreme antisocial aggression. *Psychological Monographs*, *80* (3, Whole No. 611).

Megargee, E. I. (1982). Psychological determinants and correlates of criminal violence. In M. E. Wolfgang & N. A. Weiner (Eds.), *Criminal violence* (pp. 81–170). Beverly Hills, CA: Sage.

Money, J. (1980). *Love and love sickness*. Baltimore: The Johns Hopkins University Press.

Murphy, W. D. (1990). Assessment and modification of cognitive distortions in sex offenders. In W. L. Marshall, D. R. Laws, & H. E. Barbaree (Eds.), *Handbook of sexual assault: Issues, theories and treatment of the offender* (pp. 331–342). New York: Plenum.

Prentky, R. A., Burgess, A. W., Rokous, F., Lee, A., Hartman, C. R., Ressler, R. K., & Douglas, J. E. (1989). The presumptive role of fantasy in serial sexual homicide. *American Journal of Psychiatry*, *146*, 887–891.

Prentky, R. A., Knight, R. A., Straus, H., Rokous, F., Cerce, D., & Sims-Knight, J. E. (1989). Developmental antecedents of sexual aggression. *Development & Psychopathology*, *1*, 153–169.

Ressler, R. K., & Burgess, A. W. (Eds.). (1985). Violent crimes. *FBI Law Enforcement Bulletin*, *54*, 1–31.

Ressler, R. K., Burgess, A. W., & Douglas, J. E. (1988). *Sexual homicide: Patterns and motives*. New York: Lexington/Macmillan.

Ressler, R. K., Burgess, A. W., Douglas, J. E., Hartman, C. R., & D'Agostino, R. (1986). Sexual killers and their victims: Identifying patterns through crime scene analysis. *Journal of Interpersonal Violence*, *1*, 288–308.

Rossi, D. (1982). Crime scene behavioral analysis: Another tool for the law enforcement investigator. *The Police Chief*, *2*, 152–155.

Schlesinger, L. B, & Revitch, E. (1983). *Sexual dynamics of anti-social behavior*. Springfield, IL: C. C. Thomas.

Segal, Z. V., & Stermac, L. E. (1990). The role of cognition in sexual assault. In W. L. Marshall, D. R. Laws, & H. E. Barbaree (Eds.), *Handbook of sexual assault: Issues, theories, and treatment of the offender* (pp. 161–174). New York: Plenum.

Shannon, L. W. (1978). A longitudinal study of delinquency and crime. In C. Wellford (Ed.), *Quantitative studies in criminology* (pp. 28–30). Beverly Hills, CA: Sage Publications.

Singer, J. L. (1966). *Daydreaming*. New York: Random House.

Steiner, B. W., Sanders, R. M., & Langevin, R. (1985). Crossdressing, erotic preference, and aggression: A comparison of male transvestites and transsexuals. In R. Langevin (Ed.), *Erotic preference, gender identity, and aggression in men: New research studies*. Hillsdale, NJ: Lawrence Erlbaum Associates.

U.S. Department of Justice, Uniform Crime Reports. (1976–1989). *Crime in the United States*, Washington, DC: U.S. Government Printing Office.

Vorpagel, R. E. (1982). Painting psychological profiles: Charlatanism, charisma, or a new science? *The Police Chief*, *2*, 156–159.

Willmer, M. (1970). *Crime and information theory*. Edinburgh: University of Edinburgh.

Wilson, D., & Gosselin, C. (1980). Personality characteristics of fetishists, transvestites, and sadomasochists. *Personality and Individual Differences*, *1(12)*, 289–295.

Wolfgang, M. E., & Ferracuti, F. (1982). *The subculture of violence*. London: Tavistock.

Wolfgang, M. E., Figlio, R. M., & Sellin, T. (1972). *Delinquency in a birth cohort*. Chicago: The University of Chicago Press.

Yarvis, R. M. (1990). Axis I and Axis II diagnostic parameters of homicide. *Bulletin of the American Academy of Psychiatry and the Law*, *18*, 249–269.

Yochelson, S., & Samenow, S. S. (1977). *The criminal personality*. New York: Jason Aronson.

Index